The More We Are Together

Peter Gamble outside Anglo-American College,
photographed at the time of the BBC documentary, 1971.
Photograph by Clive Barda

'THE MORE WE ARE TOGETHER'
Memoirs of a Wayward Life

by

PETER GAMBLE

PAUL WATKINS
STAMFORD

Typeset and published by
PAUL WATKINS *Publishing*
18, Adelaide Street,
Stamford, Lincolnshire, PE9 2EN.

ISBN
1 871615 52 6

Printed on long-life paper

Printed and bound by Woolnoughs of Irthlingborough

CONTENTS

ACKNOWLEDGMENTS

I begin by paying my grateful thanks to two people. First to Adrian Room, who encouraged me to publish this account, transferred my many pages of typescript to computer disk, supervised the results at its many stages, and pursued a tireless quest for a sympathetic publisher until he had found one. Second to Shaun Tyas, of Paul Watkins Publishing, who became that publisher, and who has shown constant enthusiasm for, and interest in, the narrative that is contained in the handsome volume he has now produced.

I also owe thanks to the following for help in locating photographs: Mrs Maria de Botello, John Roland Dove, David Lockwood, Harry Guest, Roger Mills, John Ryder, the Headmaster of Milton Abbey School, the Headmaster and Barry Hobson of Millfield School, the Headmaster and Jim Golland and Roy Murray of Harrow School.

And of course, my thanks for everything to all my dear family and all my dear friends.

This is a true record, but the names of some persons and places have, for obvious reasons, been changed.

P.G.

FOREWORD

As the subtitle of the following narrative suggests, this is no ordinary autobiography. It is the account of one man's personal quest: not only that from the heart, for justice, honesty, and truth, but that from the soul, for love, beauty and innocence, and in particular for the love, beauty and innocence of youth.

The story is remarkable even when taken at face value. It tells the tale of a life that began in the 1920s in a suburban London family and that ranged through a whole host of disparate experiences in various places: as a conscientious objector in Exeter prison, as a coalminer in Derbyshire, as a parish priest in Birmingham, as an embassy chaplain on the Continent, and as a college principal in Oxfordshire.

The title thus refers to relationships formed during these periods, and in particular to the close but fragile bond that existed between the author and his large family, to his lifelong search for perfect unity and happiness in that family.

Further, it refers to the homosexual drive which, as Peter Gamble frankly admits, has been the mainspring of much of his personal life. In recent times the potentially loving and honest relationship that can develop between two people of the same sex has been grievously sullied by media coverage, especially when, as here, one partner is adult and the other adolescent. There are, indeed, those who have turned to selfish and damaging advantage the life-enhancing rapport that can develop between two such persons. The reader will soon see, however, that the affection shown by Peter Gamble for the boys he has encountered in his life was not of the latter type.

The publication of this readable and moving account of personal gain and loss is therefore highly appropriate for the social and moral climate of today, when on the one hand homosexuals are readily 'coming out' and when, on the other, an affectionate relationship between an adult and a younger person (of either sex) is often popularly regarded with suspicion. It is equally timely in that it expresses the philosophy of a man who, as a priest, held unorthodox and rationalistic views which frequently involved him in controversy and protest.

Peter Gamble has spent most of his professional life in education, whether as a dedicated teacher or as the head of a college of further education. (The vivid account of the pioneering foundation and calamitous collapse of his brainchild forms one of the most absorbing sections of his narrative.) Hence the aptness of the attractive picture that adorns the front cover of this book. It represents the frontispiece of an old school story called *Three Years at Wolverton*, 'by an Old Boy,' alluded to in the text as a favourite of the author when a child. Today, almost a century on, the reader may like to regard its rays of sunlight not as heavenly shafts piercing the soul of the pious Victorian schoolboy, as was doubtless the original intention, but as the genuine radiance of love and affection that can emanate from one human being to another in a healthy and happy relationship.

Adrian Room
March, 1993

PART ONE: FIRST STEPS

1

'Christmas can't be far off: Uncle Len's catskin's out to air.'

That's as good a start as any I can find, for it marks my first awareness of the passage of time, the slow march of the festivals. Uncle Len played Dick Whittington's cat at the Empress, or anywhere else that would have him. I don't think he played anything except the cat, so out of the pantomime season Auntie Doris was the regular breadwinner. Mostly he kept his house, except for occasional forays beside Auntie Doris, his plump and panting wife, to whose back was strapped a great bass drum, the improbable instrument she played in a theatre orchestra 'up west' (as London's West End was generally referred to). Uncle Len was too diminutive to carry the drum. He simply trod beside her: silent, morose, and ineluctably feline.

This was on Streatham Hill, where I was born not long after the First World War and spent my first eight years. I was the fourth child and my mother cherished me because my predecessor had died aged three of meningitis. The image of this sister I never knew faded very slowly from the family. There was a photo of her on the drawing room mantelpiece: a beautiful child whose large, sad eyes seemed to me haunted and haunting. This picture always made me feel both guilty for being alive and fearful of being dead like her. Her name, Angela, was disturbing, too. I was glad to be told my eyes were very different. Wicked eyes, my mother would say indulgently, and would tell me again what the doctor who delivered me had said: 'Look at those eyes. Darting everywhere. He's not going to miss much.'

Streatham Hill (which merged into Brixton Hill) then was an intriguing compound of the shabby genteel and the vaguely Bohemian. Its great, partitioned houses lay far back from the main road behind extensive unkempt gardens and sweeping gravel drives once busy with carriages. Because of its all-night tram service between the Embankment and Croydon, it had also become a centre for those who insecurely trod the boards as well as for any whose professions (including, apparently, the oldest) entailed late and uncertain hours.

If Uncle Len and Auntie Doris had ever possessed real nephews and nieces they were long gone into oblivion. Nor could this glum couple have retained their titles because of anything benignly avuncular about them. On the contrary, they were fish out of water in that little ocean of swarming bonhomie. But he played his part. Dour as John the Baptist, and clad like him in animal skin, he proclaimed for us in each bleak midwinter the coming of the Messiah.

1

I have no memory of my own birthdays in those early years. Only of His, about which so much more fuss was made. In any case mine was a midsummer birth and I could never really believe I'd been upgraded until the number of the year changed after His birthday.

I knew Christmas was His birthday because Mary-and-Jean were rather unctuously insistent on it. They were the children of a neighbouring Irish family of devout Roman Catholics. Both parents were on the stage: he a light comedian, she a fading soubrette. They were rigorously training their two daughters for the profession. But as jugglers, which only now strikes me as rather odd. Father was a daunting figure, a cruel and irascible taskmaster with a raucous voice. The children's instructor was Uncle Alec, who would have been kindlier but for the light comedian who paid his fees. Each midday instruction, each evening's practice, was accompanied by shouts from father, wails from the children, sometimes tearful protests from mother, all punctuated by the thuds of dropped balls and slaps on bare flesh. Never a word from the intimidated Uncle Alec.

Mary, the older girl, never made it, but Jean was to become an international cabaret star, with a penthouse in Los Angeles and a chaotic pad in the Fulham Road.

The other member of their household was a warmhearted young Irishwoman of uncertain status and terrifying fabulosity. She taught me how to know a cluricaune by his hands and how to interpret the horror of a banshee's wail. Her considerable word-hoard was unlocked on our slightest encouragement. My favourite, which I frequently invoked and shivered at, was a stark personal anecdote. She'd once been companion to a beautiful young actress killed in a train disaster, and she had known her mistress would die that day. 'How, Jenny?' I'd breathe. 'How did you know?' She shrugged almost defiantly. 'Sure and wasn't it when I made her bed that morning it *smelt of earth*.' And I'd sit numb and think it all out again. I very much wanted to ask my mother if Angela's bed had smelt of earth. But I knew I mustn't.

My function in this rather hysterical set-up was to fulfil the vigorous potential mother the two little girls displayed as soon as they were let off the leash. Almost every morning they collected me and lugged me off somewhere or other. In early days I was in my pram; later, I went alternately on foot and in their straining arms. I suffered it without question. It was part of the world as He'd made it. Every few yards they would stop to comb my hair or straighten my leggings or scrub my face with a licked handkerchief. All a bore to me and a joy to them. As were the interminable commands, reproofs, wheedlings and denunciations these two little parrots indulged in.

Occasionally our promenades would be transfigured for me by a fourth party. Sometimes it was their dog Scottie, an inexhaustible bundle of mongrel madness and affection. I adored him, not only for himself but for the joy I took in his boundless indiscipline. He loved me, too, his little yokefellow. I didn't mind when he knocked me over or covered my face with a dozen rasping licks or seized the lollipop I was raising to my mouth. I didn't mind because it was all part of his total defiance of authority, on his own behalf and mine.

And I was heartbroken when he was chained up in disgrace, whimpering piteously. Sometimes I would creep to my bedroom window in the evening and call his name over the garden walls. Instantly, in his tethered solitude, he'd raise a barking and howling that set the whole canine neighbourhood ablaze. When he paused from exhaustion I'd urge him on with shriller calls, until authority put a stop to it, with yelps from him and wails from me.

He figured largely in my world, as did Nigger, one of our three cats (he who, I am told, had almost asphyxiated me by curling up on my face as I lay sunning in my pram), and Bess, 'my' horse. Bess was the magnificent mare who drew the baker's cart. I would accompany her from door to door the whole length of our road. Our house was at the foot of a rather steep incline and I'd wait at our gate for her to appear at the top of the hill. As soon as I saw her I'd begin the breathless ascent, my spindly legs flailing, my hot fists full of the sugar cubes she loved. And before I'd gone a yard she had started to neigh her greeting, ears erect and great iron feet impatiently pawing the road. When I reached her, panting and triumphant, she'd lower her head for me to kiss her beautiful velvet-soft nose. I was as fearless with her as she was gentle with me. Once the baker put me on her back and she turned her head, stared at me and burst out laughing. Nobody else ever believed in that laugh but I'm as sure of it now as I was then.

But occasionally, and all too rarely, my walks with Mary-and-Jean were irradiated by another presence: a boy of about fourteen, a cousin of theirs called Jonah (because his name was Jones). He was darkly beautiful, lithe, sullen. I imagine he'd been ordered to take the air with this obviously despised trio. He seldom spoke and did his best to walk apart from us, head lowered, hands in pockets, feet spurning the pebbles. Once or twice I'd tried to take his hand but he'd shaken me off roughly. So I trotted along beside him until my breath gave out, gazing up into his unforgotten face: my powerful young pagan god, the first human deity I can recall.

All my deities were pagan: the roistering, amorous Scottie, the disdainful Nigger, the grave and splendid Bess, and Jonah, my dark and dangerous faun. There was no domestic suggestion of any other deities. My older brothers and I were all unbaptized. No hint of Christian belief and practice seems to have touched my mother's family, and my father was in decisive retreat from a boyhood surfeit of them. But Mary-and-Jean began to worry about the state of my soul and asked permission to take me to mass each Sunday. My parents felt no antagonism to the church, viewing it with the detached indulgence of grown-ups for children's games. And I was usually ready enough for a safe new experience. So off I trotted one Sunday morning and found it all quite diverting, if rather long-drawn-out. I liked the dressing up, the music and movement, and soon became intrigued by a golden box or cupboard on or above the altar. It was very ornate and the priest seemed to be afraid of it. What was in it? I asked Mary-and-Jean, who promptly told me God was in it. I was rather sceptical, chiefly on account of the size of the cupboard. I asked my father how big God was. He laughed and said: 'Very big, I imagine.' That was what I thought because it was Mary-and-Jean's own mother who'd told me that thunder was God speaking to the wicked people. Such lungs, I reasoned, required a considerable body.

I made up my mind to see into this cupboard, which Mary-and-Jean smugly said was called 'the holy of holies,' words which to me suggested only what you dug in the garden or darned in socks. The puzzling words whetted my appetite and I set out to get myself a ringside seat. Sunday by Sunday I pestered to leave home ever earlier, impressing the Irish family with my zeal and mildly amusing my own ménage. I finally succeeded in gaining a place in the front row, rather to one side, and kept my eyes riveted on the cupboard, even climbing on my chair when the priest inserted his little golden key in it. It struck me that he was doing his best to obscure my view, and everyone else's, too. My suspicions increased as I caught a glimpse of silver and much fumbling before the door was resolutely relocked.

I told Mary-and-Jean I didn't believe God was in the box at all. They were suitably shocked by this blasphemy, so I repeated it, adding, for safety's sake, that if He was, it was cruel to keep Him locked up all the time. My parents had once told me it was cruel to keep Scottie chained up in his kennel so much. If these people could do that to so lovable a creature as Scottie ('whom I had seen'), they'd obviously think nothing of imprisoning such a thing as God ('whom I had not seen'). I soon refused to attend further masses. Mary appealed tearfully to my mother, who said: 'Well, I suppose he's got over it, dear.' This equation of mass with measles seemed to me eminently sensible, and I didn't re-enter a parish church for about twenty years.

While on this subject, I jump ahead two or three years to a time when my mother must have felt I was ripe for a little cultural exposure. We toiled round London: the Tower, Westminster Abbey, St Paul's and the South Kensington museums. It was in St Paul's that I became fascinated by an elderly man who knelt alone amid the sea of chairs in the nave, his head with its wild shock of white hair devoutly bowed in silent prayer. For ages he knelt there, only occasionally raising closed lids to the roof, lips soundlessly moving the while. I asked my mother what was wrong with him. 'A religious maniac,' she replied crisply.

4

Now this was *really* intriguing. Better as a spectacle than the old God-in-a-box. I'd never heard of a religious maniac before, but I knew what a maniac was because my brothers derisively called me that when I lost my temper under their teasings.

A maniac. And at large, unguarded. I could scarcely tear myself away from him, wanting yet dreading the moment when he'd leap to his feet and begin to smash the place up.

And that, I'm afraid, is how I was conditioned to regard even a moderate churchgoer. As deranged, or at best as a simpleton. Even now I must resist the temptation to explain a really devout person in terms of arrested development.

2

I think I was, even for a child, rather excessively committed to the familiar, the known and loved. At least so far as the senses and emotions were concerned. (The imagination was another matter: thither, gazing at nothing or head on pillow, I would see the horrors flock from their confines, not entirely unbidden.)

I loved my family and was in seventh heaven when, at weekends, we were all there together, and when I was still too young to chart the undercurrents or smell the smouldering fires. Despite my brothers' baitings, despite my tears and blind rages, despite even the more terrible hints of parental conflict, this was my own place and these were my own people, imperfect but predictable, noisy and restless and eternally coming and going, yet all in reality dancers round that one matriarchal maypole.

I liked neighbours and visitors, too, but in moderation. I was very curious about people, but wary. In one's family one could *bask*; with others you had to be on your guard.

Nevertheless there were one or two neighbours I was so fond of that I almost gave them family status.

Mrs Johnson was fat and pretty, overdressed and over-rouged. She had a glass cabinet full of bric-à-brac which she'd let me play with: little china dogs and models of the Eiffel Tower and the Coronation Chair, and souvenirs from all over the place. She was recklessly generous and would give me more or less anything that caught my fancy, but 'only if you come and love me a bit.' This meant sitting on her lap and being kissed and tickled, both of which operations after a while verged on the naughty. I knew quite well they were naughty, and knew equally well that they were harmless and I enjoyed them. They'd invariably conclude with a heavy sigh from Mrs Johnson (echoed by me) and the words: 'Oh you are a poppet. I could eat you all up.'

There was only one thing faintly disturbing about Mrs Johnson, and that was her precise identity. She was Mrs Johnson or Mrs Albertini or Mrs

Edwards, and she answered quite happily to any of these names. It was puzzling but seemed somehow in character, all a part of her cowlike opulence. She lived with a Mr Edwards, whom she described as her nephew and a chemist. He was always very affable with me and I think he first roused in me a love of books. I mean the sheer pleasure of seeing and handling and smelling them, for this was before I could read. He had a handsome motorbike and sidecar, a real arm-gaunt steed, from and into which he was frequently transporting piles of multicoloured volumes. I'd sometimes help him unload, and occasionally he'd say of some garish book: 'No, not that one. I'll take that.' Then we'd arrange them in dark cupboards in the hall, to be locked up out of sight. This seemed rather a pity, but he explained that they were valuable and the sunlight would spoil them. I admired such loving care.

I asked him once if any of them had pictures. He chuckled and said: 'Only the very best ones.' And I remember Mrs Johnson told him to be quiet. All such puzzles were fleeting. One accepted that grown-ups were odd, and if the oddities posed no threat one forgot them at once.

It was some years later that I learned his pharmacy was of the most dubious kind and that his main income came from trading in pornography. My brother Brian told me this when I was twelve and he a worldly-wise seventeen. He also claimed that Mrs Johnson had in earlier years been a real courtesan of some repute. She and Mr Edwards were apparently quite happy together. (Why she felt obliged to call him her nephew I never discovered.) If Brian's solemn assurances about Mrs Johnson's past had any basis in fact, then I was for a couple of very tender years her sole remaining client: a poppet she could eat up. I remember her as the embodiment of lovingkindness.

My other favourite was Mrs Mackenzie. I loved her Scottish accent and her shining cleanliness. In an immaculate starched white apron she always smelt of soap. Mrs Johnson was all ashes of roses; Mrs Mackenzie all coal tar. No canine pet could have been more appreciative of their respective smells than I was. She too solicited my kisses, but hers were always chaste. My day invariably began with boisterous calls on these two ladies, who always made me feel, as I rattled impatiently on their letter boxes, that I was the eagerly-awaited harbinger of their day.

But melancholy surrounds Mrs Mackenzie in my memory. She had once had a little boy, an only child too much adored, who had died of diphtheria before I was born. (Even in the twenties infant mortality was a common enough grief.) He was very real to me as another poor little ghost, for she would show me photos of him and tell me, weeping, what a lovely and lovable child he'd been. I would add my own ever-ready tears to hers and this seemed to do her good. Once she took me into his little bedroom and from under his bed pulled a tray full of toys. I was enthralled by the train set but she gently caught my itching fingers: 'No, you mustn't touch them, dear. They're Stewart's, you see.'

The aura of loss and sadness which pervaded her home affected me strongly, even unhealthily. I responded with too eager a sympathy. Loss and longing were emotions I knew, knew *then*. I am not imposing adult reactions on the child. At no time of my life have I been without this conviction, that there was once a state of perfect fulfilment secure from all chance and change. There, in the perfect family, I had dwelt with the perfect friend. And I had a curious little self-indulgence no one ever knew about, not even Mrs Mackenzie, whose drawing room was its only setting. In one corner of this room was a small, upright piano and beside it hung a painting of wild Highland scenery in whose foreground two young boys leaped and laughed together, while nearby their grown-ups sprawled indolently over a picnic, gazing affectionately at one another as they ate and drank. I thought it was a beautiful, timeless picture, and a very sad one. The intimation was lost immortality. It was all there: the united family, the little friends at play, the everlasting hills and lakes and trees. And beneath it in Gothic script was its title, which Mrs Mackenzie read me (and I still hear) in her sweetly modulated Scots: 'The More We Are Together.'

But this was only half my catharsis. Tinkering with the piano, I found one particular note whose plaintive tone seemed to evoke in sound all that the picture gave to my eye. And, marrying the two senses, I would gaze deep and long into the painting as I softly pressed the key, *my* key, over and over again. I surrendered myself to the waves of sadness that washed over me. I was looking, I knew, on an Eden I had lost and must forever seek, and the piano intoned my lament. When at length Mrs Mackenzie called out: 'Oh, that's enough, dear,' I would force hand and eye away like a guilty thing surprised.

Mr Mackenzie was an even greater ogre in my life than the light comedian with the heavy hand. I avoided him if I could, but sometimes he would corner me when his wife wasn't there and in assumed Tod Slaughter tones say: 'I'm going to boil your mother alive. I've a great pot heating now.' This would send me running home to guard her. I don't know why he did it. Perhaps some sort of revenge for the loss of his own child.

He seemed to deal in silverware. At times he had quantities of it spread over the floor of a spare room. Then it would disappear and when I asked Mrs Mackenzie where it had gone she would say indulgently: 'He's sold it, dear. But he'll be getting some more.' It was, of course, a later revelation from Brian, that man of the world: 'He was a fence, y'know. A receiver of stolen property.' All these revelations may have been Brian's fantasies, but mother laughingly told me in after years: 'If you asked Mrs Mackenzie what her husband did for a living, she would tell you proudly, "He lives by his wits".' Dear, innocent Mrs Mackenzie thought that was a compliment.

My days then were delightfully enlivened by tradesmen's visits. I knew them all, and the hours at which most were due. Bert the milkman came first. He had a small two-wheeled chariot filled with churns out of which he ladled the rich, creamy milk. I liked to see all the little bubbles it formed in the jug. A miniature horse drew this chariot, which tilted alarmingly when Bert stood on its back step. Like all milkmen then he could yodel his wares.

Then mid-morning saw the arrival of Bess the Magnificent and her baker's cart. Mr Fox the baker had a cart worthy of his steed. It was very big, with dozens of wooden trays slotted into racks, and its interior smelt refreshingly sweet with dough and yeast, pastry and fruits. Loaves of all sizes and shapes were on the tray Mr Fox brought to the door for our inspection, together with a fine array of colourful cakes over which my darting eyes would play in greedy expectation. Choosing these eccles and banburies, cheesecakes and madeleines, was a serious business.

There was another baker called Stevens who came round just before teatime. He had a very small cart drawn by a real Shetland pony who on hot summer days wore a great straw bonnet with his ears sticking through it. I thought it one of the funniest sights ever. But he was a vicious little creature, permanently muzzled, who frequently lashed out at his cart with those delicate hooves. He knew he was born for better things. Stevens' cakes were dearer than Mr Fox's but loyalty to Bess would never let me admit their superiority.

The last of the regulars was Bowman the greengrocer, Mr and Mrs and their young son, James-Arthur. Their arrival was quite unpredictable, anywhere between lunch and dinner, because all three were compulsive talkers with no sense of time or place. First Mr and Mrs would call with the display basket (a capacious work of art) and try to engage mother in some lengthy discussion about anything but the fruits of the earth. Then they would depart with the order and some time later James-Arthur would return with the goods and a further instalment of his life story. Mother was too polite to stem the flow, so she often sent me or our daily to deal with it. Not that I did any better. Indeed, I positively encouraged James-Arthur, who was a picture of good health: brown as a berry, with light blue eyes and strong white teeth. He would put twin cherries round my ears or produce magic grapes from my hair. Surprisingly, this child of wind and weather played the violin. 'James-Arthur's hartistic,' said his mother emphatically, as though it were a complaint with which one must come to terms. 'He loves his fiddle and wants to go to music school.' Then she'd pull out this photo of a fiddle-brandishing boy in a tight blue suit and gaze at it dubiously, as if anticipating conflicts between bow and bananas.

3

My circle was expanding. I was becoming more aware of things and of people. Outside the French windows was a fairly large concreted area beyond which the earth and grass and flowers began. In sunny weather I was placed on this area while still at the crawling stage. I remember it as a world of which I was the cartographer. There were splits and cracks in the concrete with which I had an intimate rapport, tracing them with my fingers, poking and stroking and generally approving them. Finding them there, immutable, each morning was an assurance that all was right with the world. When toddling supervened, I became a connoisseur of earth and its insects: ants and woodlice and centipedes and those aristocratic caterpillars we called Brighton walkers.

Less comforting things were clothes. From an early age I reacted quite violently to some garments. I couldn't stand wool next to my skin or any even remotely rough material. I hated any tight garment. I would sob: 'It's diggery, it's diggery,' and do my best to tear the offending article from my body. No one really understood this hyperaesthesia, though I kicked up such a fuss they had to indulge it.

One crisp winter's evening a business friend of my father came to dinner. He was 'Mr Day' and he suddenly asked me if I had seen the stars. When I said I hadn't he insisted on showing them to me. So I was well wrapped up for this novel trip into a Stygian garden in his arms. He pointed them all out to me and no doubt named them, though none of the names registered with me. I never forgot this. For years after, when my father mentioned a colleague or acquaintance, I would ask eagerly: 'Is that Mr-Day-who-showed-me-the-stars?' I don't think I ever saw him again, but I heard one anecdote about him which seemed in character. To amuse his little boy he ran the child's clockwork train over his own head, where it became so horribly entangled that he had to go to hospital to have most of his hair cut off and his wounded scalp dressed.

In these early years I needed much prodding out of the family nest if invited to some playmate's birthday or Christmas party. Tony Packard's party is an abiding, if clouded, memory. It was a rather grand affair in big rooms festooned with Christmas decorations. After the feast we children were all seated in a semicircle on the floor. We knew something special and nice was about to happen, but the reality surpassed all expectation. For into the room, propelled by Tony's father, came a gorgeous replica of the Lord Mayor's coach, fastened to a fine rocking horse. I think Tony's father must have spent the whole year making this coach. It was quite large (someone was seated in it) and had been fashioned and painted with loving skill. It stopped amid us goggle-eyed guests, Mr Packard opened the door, and with a low bow handed out a little vision even lovelier than the gilt coach. It was an exquisite Prince Charming. Tony was a pretty child in any guise but now, in satin suit and silk stockings, powdered wig and tricorn hat, he was quite ravishing. I couldn't take my eyes off him. From inside the coach he produced a brightly wrapped present for each of us, but I was reluctant to transfer my gaze from him to the packet. Seeing this, his mother knelt beside me and, as she helped me untie the string, whispered in my ear: 'Next Christmas, Peter, we'll make *you* the Prince Charming in the coach.' For a whole year I kept this prospect bright within me, but somehow Tony and I saw less and less of each other and when Christmas came I wasn't even invited to his party. This betrayal was to rankle with me during much of my childhood. It is a terrible thing for an adult to forget a commitment to a small child.

Sometimes I was taken to visit mother's or aunt's friends. These were rather boring occasions for me, with the grown-ups chattering incomprehensibles and only occasionally pausing to regard me, sometimes admiringly, more often with reproof. I was required to call these alien ladies 'auntie.' I knew they weren't and had a vague idea I was being duped but couldn't imagine why. Auntie Muriel was a chiropodist. I was, surprisingly, allowed to play with her surgical chair, which went up and down and round in circles. And I liked the smell of ether pervading her house. I can't put a face to Auntie Muriel but I remember her as small and birdlike. Likewise my remaining impression of Auntie Phoebe is of someone comfortable and expansive. But her flat in Putney remains vivid for its abundance of coloured cushions and matching curtains. And for a shelf of brightly jacketed books which I was urged to note because 'Auntie Phoebe has written every one of them.' She was a once popular and prolific novelist called Hebe Elsna whose books I sometimes find on old bookstalls. I'm afraid I've never read one, but when I see her name on a book I am easily back amid a sea of cosy chintz and those pink and white iced cakes commonly known as 'fancies.'

When I was five two events of cataclysmic importance shook my world, and both were noised abroad long before they arrived: I had a sister and I started school.

My mother took to her bed and a nurse joined the household. I didn't like this. It upset routine and posed a threat. The table beside my mother's bed was covered with strange foods and medicines in which I took a great interest. 'What's that?' I asked, covetously eyeing an attractive jar. 'That's calves'-foot jelly,' she replied, 'and it's not for you.' I collected bright new words and phrases like a jackdaw seizing tinsel. I stood mouthing it silently: 'Calves' foot-jelly, calves' foot-jelly.' I didn't know what calves were so I naturally misplaced the hyphen. My mother was in bed because there was something wrong with her feet. Well, that wasn't too bad. The jelly application would work the trick and she'd soon be up and about again.

Our daily was called Mrs Clackett. A Dickensian name, and she came from a Dickensian slum neighbourhood we children were forbidden to approach. But once my brothers, swearing me to secrecy, walked me all the way there.

I expected to be frightened and I was. I met, without knowing them, the roots of despair and aggression: rickety limbs and consumptive faces and that instinctive hatred nursed by the deprived against the nourished and shod. From one dark hovel emerged an old man wearing what looked like sacks. The skeletonic horse and cart outside were his and only too well I knew them both. There was no mistaking him: the rag and bone man who rang his bell and howled his needs in our road once a week. For four clean jam jars he would give a child a little celluloid windmill on a stick. But never to me, for I was too terrified of his unearthly cries and clothes to have any truck with him. Seeing him thus on his home ground was somehow worse. When a group of menacing urchins muttered battle cries to one another we fled for our lives. All the way home, with never a backward glance.

It seemed an unlikely place for our jolly and long-suffering Mrs Clackett to spring from. She reminded me of Bess in her bulk and patience, and perhaps also because she spent most of her time at our house on all fours. I'd climb on her back as she moved slowly round, scrubbing, polishing and talking all the while to anyone or no one. It was she who told me: 'Oh, your nose'll be out of joint soon. 'Cos a new baby's comin'.' 'When, Mrs Clackett? When's a new baby coming? What'll happen to my nose?' 'Any old day now. And you won't be little Lord Muck then, you won't. Never no more.'

Well, she was right about the baby, which arrived very soon after this conversation. On an exceptional day when Mary-and-Jean had taken me for interminable walks and then back to their house for tea. All unusual. I knew something was happening. When I was finally taken home it was to be shown the baby in its pretty cot and told: 'That's your baby. Your little sister.' I adored it on sight. Mine. I never doubted it was a present for me personally and my jealous care of it became a standing joke. I didn't mind, for the whole thing had proved a triumph of good management. My mother's feet were mended, my nose flourished intact, and the baby (a happy girl, to efface Angela) got fatter and prettier every day. All very satisfactory.

The prospect of school both fascinated and appalled. My brothers enjoyed painting me lurid pictures of it. On my very first day they led me into the echoing building, pushed me through some velvet curtains, and abandoned me. We must have been late, for what I saw when I parted the heavy curtains was an enormous room filled with desks at which some

11

twenty little boys and girls sat in prim silence, arms folded and feet neatly neighboured. Miles away, on a dais, sat a tall lady. She began to call out names and each child in turn piped 'Present, Miss.' No one noticed me. I wasn't going to get a present. I fought to find the opening in the curtains and flee. But they resisted me as I panted inward the strange, intimidating smell of the place.

Then she saw me and with an exclamation advanced swiftly. She was taller than anyone I had ever seen, and her severe dress, reaching almost to her ankles, accentuated her height.

'Now, who are you, dear? I think you must be... Yes, I can see a likeness. You must be... '.

I whispered my name.

'Of *course* you are.' She caught me suddenly in her arms and raised me. I was only five, a mere wisp in her strong embrace. Up and up I went until my face was close to hers. Then she kissed me. 'Yes, you're Peter. And those naughty brothers of yours didn't introduce you. Oh, you wait till I see them.' Only then I ventured to look at her. She wasn't angry. She was smiling, smiling out of the kindest face you could imagine. Kinder even than Mrs Johnson's or Mrs Bruin's in *Tiger Tim's Weekly*. And at once the sun burst forth and all the birds sang to me. She loved me. And I loved her. It was the beginning of a love affair I've never forgotten.

She put me down, took my hand and led me up the room between the rows of desks. 'This is Peter,' she was saying. 'We've all been waiting to meet Peter, haven't we, children?' 'Yes, Miss,' they cried in perfect unison.

'Now this is your desk, Peter. Your very own, special desk. And you're going to be very happy here, aren't you?'

'Yes, Miss,' I whispered, and I meant it.

'I'm Miss Tierney,' she went on, 'and all your lessons are with me. This lesson is our talking lesson. We tell one another all our news. But you don't have to if you don't want to.'

I was an adept pupil and I came to know it. I set out to become the star pupil, and I became it. All for Miss Tierney. I learned to read with a celerity that occasioned some small wonder. And there seemed to be no limit to the number of poems that I could learn by heart. My first ever reading book was a simplified version of *The Water Babies*. It was illustrated in pen and ink and Tom was very beautiful. I bled for his sufferings. Grimes was, of course, Mr Mackenzie, and nice Mrs Doasyouwouldbedoneby was Miss Tierney to a T. And the indignant, incredulous mystery was how Grimes could be so blind to Tom's charms as to cover them in soot.

Once, during the war, I sat in a train opposite a young naval cadet of a beauty very similar to Tom's. His complexion was flawless, so delicate that one could trace the blue veins beneath the porcelain skin. But his hands were grubby with much travelling and at one terrible moment he raised one of them to an irritation on his face. With his dirty and rather bitten fingers he rubbed and scrubbed his cheek quite brutally. There escaped from me a little, involuntary cry of protest, which I had quickly to turn to a cough. The buried image of Tom had surfaced embarrassingly.

4

My school, Surrey College, was really a relict of the dames' schools of an earlier age and self-consciously opposed to the 'council schools.' From the first I was made aware of this social divide, for part of the route to my own school was shared by the local roughs at the other place. They were big and noisy and crude. They had weird, yodelling cries and many of them, little older than I, had voices made hoarse as an old man's by their ceaseless screaming and shouting. And a few walked barefoot. I knew I must avoid them and knew, too, how secretly I coveted them. They were 'common' boys, 'council school kids,' but many were pure and handsome Saxons with very blue eyes and with hair the colour of sun-bleached flax. Augustine and Walt Whitman had loved the type before me and Blake had hymned their barefoot joy. But it wasn't innocence I saw in them, even if I had known what innocence was. Nor was my longing for them innocent, as like lovely and dangerous animals they swore and fought and spat, and once, before my very eyes, pee'd casually against a wall.

Surrey College took girls to any age and boys to the age of about twelve. This was to avoid the moral dangers of coeducation in a climate still unaware of Freud, but all it did was to ensure the puzzled seduction of the weaker sex by the stronger, of pretty little boys by puberulous girls. I soon fell a victim to the old, hated adoption by groups of senior girls, who insisted I play the exploited offspring in games of 'mothers and fathers.'

Whenever possible I would at breaktime quickly involve myself with groups of boys, our favourite game being 'chariots.' This entailed tying lengths of string to the arms of a chosen boy, holding the ends as reins, and galloping around at furious speed with a stick as one's whip. I was never so happy as when I had a steed I approved of, and almost as content with the masochistic role if my master were sufficiently eye-catching. But sooner or later I'd fall over and reopen one of the many scabby wounds on my knees. Then some adolescent harpy would swoop and bear me off to the washroom. (That same washroom where I was once made to wash out my mouth with carbolic soap because I had said 'Damn.')

Much of our learning was accomplished through marching, chanting and hand-clapping. In no time, it seemed, we learned all our tables up to twelve times simply by rhythmic stamping, clapping and yelling. These good ladies – there were four of them, plus a godlike and barking Mr Elliott who taught the top forms – were, I am sure, quite untrained. No foreign theories had been planted in their heads, no textbook nonsenses had to be slavishly followed. Their aim was not to entertain us, amuse us, indulge us with copious supplies of 'play material.' It was to teach us the three Rs in the secure knowledge that we liked learning as much as they liked teaching. And indeed they were the best teachers I ever had. Love, discipline and unerring instinct made them so.

In my second year I left Miss Tierney with sobs to enter the domain of Miss Plumbridge, who was short and fat and quite unacceptable because she was not and never could be Miss Tierney. I recall the utter misery of my first entry to Miss Plumbridge's classroom, of sitting sullen and unbiddable before her. And I recall with wonder the splendid psychology of her opening words, which as by magic dispelled all my fears and resentment: 'Now, boys and girls, lots of you have come from Miss Tierney's class and you are very sad to leave her because she's so nice and kind and you've been very happy with her.' I waited, breathless; she had read my mind, knew just how I felt. 'But,' and here she laughed a fat and jolly laugh, 'but I'm nice, too, and you're going to be happy with me. And I'll tell you a secret: Miss Tierney will come once a week to teach you your Bible stories.' And it was all quite true. If I never loved her as I did Miss Tierney, I came to enjoy her and all her lessons. 'La plume, the...?' and we'd all yell 'pen!' as she held it aloft. 'La table, the...?' And we'd all bellow 'table!' before she had time to thump it. 'A noun is the...?' We'd all jump up and down in our seats to be the first to gabble 'name-of-a-person-place-or-thing!'.

Then there were pothooks and hangers and great flourishing copybooks in which we laboriously copied meaningless words like 'Charity begins at home.' Sometimes there hadn't been room in the book to complete a proverb, but this hadn't bothered the compiler and it didn't bother us. 'A rolling stone gathers no' we would scratch, tongues out and brows puckered. Four times to a page.

Otherwise our work was done with slate pencils on screeching slates. Modelling in plasticine was the one weekly play material treat. But not for me. I wasn't dexterous and soon tired of my unsuccessful attempts to make the lumps of stuff resemble something.

If a child had a cold, its handkerchief (and it was a punishable offence not to have one) was liberally sprinkled with eucalyptus oil from the bottle kept in each classroom. This and the plasticine produced the strange smell that had assailed me on my first morning. The school was quite hooked on eucalyptus oil.

Mrs Hall was the headmistress. She was as tall and angular as Miss Tierney, whose sister she was said to be (but I never believed it). The school had been founded by Mr Hall, whose portrait hung in the assembly room. It was a very large blow-up of a rather poor photograph. Mr Hall had an abnormally long neck encased in a high, stand-up collar, and the likeness to the giraffe in that much thumbed animal book of mine was accentuated by the brown speckles of age all over headmaster Hall and his portrait.

And Mr Hall, like Queen Alexandra and Dr Barnardo, had a 'Day.' Once a year, on 'Mr Hall's Day,' we were solemnly paraded before his picture and treated to a little eulogy. Mr Hall had been very clever and successful, Mr Hall had been good and kind and had loved little children. The implication, intended or not, was that Mr Hall was one up on Jesus, and when the proceedings concluded with the hymn 'There's a friend for little children, Up above the bright blue sky' the identification was complete. For we knew that the maculate Mr Hall, too, both was and wasn't dead.

Miss Plumbridge's class was divided into an upper and a lower and we spent a year in each part. Beyond this lay once more the feared unknown. Her name was Miss Bevan and my brothers fed me incessantly with tales of her cruelty and caprice. She taught, they said, with a cane which emphasized her words with sudden lashings at desk or knuckle or knee. And her pride and joy was the museum in her classroom. I once crept in to glimpse it and it was for me the final horror: long rows of glass cases filled with rocks and stones. Clearly nothing precious about these. I knew they were merely ammunition, to be hurled when the cane was no longer sufficient for her fury.

The First World War was only seven or eight years past and we children heard much of its thrills and terrors. Maimed and blinded beggars were common sights and they filled me with guilt, especially a legless man on a trolley who sold boxes of matches. He wore medals and had a small notice round his neck. I insisted on having this read to me until I had the puzzling words by heart: 'I gave my legs at Mons for my country.'

We had a lurid history of the Great War. In weekly parts at sixpence each, it abounded in drawings of fiendish enemies and noble friends and terror-stricken horses with great distended nostrils. When I could read I learned the villains were called 'Hun' or 'Boche' or, more contemptuously, 'Fritz.' The ones who especially peopled my nightmares were the Uhlans with their terrible spiked helmets. I thought the Kaiser looked rather handsome but his son, 'little Willie,' mean and stupid. In my gallery of visual horrors, this history vied with a huge book I often pored over in Mary-and-Jean's house: it was a Doré, but whether his Bible or his Dante I don't know.

Small boys played soldiers more than other games and 'You've got to be a German' was the fate of the unpopular ones. In those days I wasn't. In spite of my growing wilfulness which was to make other boys tread rather warily with me, I was actually something of a ringleader.

THE MORE WE ARE TOGETHER

Armistice Day was an outstanding annual event for me, more so than the Boat Race or the Lord Mayor's Show. Once my mother took me up to the Cenotaph in Whitehall. I remember the dense crowds and being perched rather frighteningly atop a high wall. Then the awful silence, which seemed to go on and on as if the world could never rewaken. Until, somewhere quite near me, it was broken by a low, intense sobbing. Then came the crunch-crunch of the maroons in Hyde Park and the infinitely sad and moving reveille. A general sigh escaped the crowd and hats were replaced and feet began to shuffle.

Once I was in Streatham High Road for the silence. All the traffic stopped dead and every pedestrian froze, hat in hand. Even the nodding horses seemed to acquiesce in mourning their slaughtered brothers. But, to my intense indignation, one man kept on walking with covered head. Not for long, though. A burly workman took one swipe and the man's trilby went flying into the road. The man just stood stupidly still in astonishment, while I gazed with admiration at his assailant. I had a great sense of protocol.

Smells and sweets and weather all played large parts in my child's world. Long hot summer days of course abounded, with the delicious scent of newly tarred roads and the vision of men with monstrous tongs delivering equally monstrous blocks of ice to the fishmonger's. Days when the end of the road would seem to dance in the heat haze and from far away a dog would bark or a cock crow with a kind of infinite ennui. Once a dragonfly landed on a gatepost and a small crowd gathered to admire its exotic beauty.

Winter had its lesser delights. There was the coalman with his strange headgear: a wide-brimmed hat that ended in a leather flap reaching halfway down his back. His sacks smelt lovely. There were days so cold that I would be imprisoned in the drawing room, bored and restless, scraping eyeholes in the frosted panes and cooking grapes on a shovel in the fire, or painting faces on my breakfast eggshell. In the afternoon I would sit on my mother's lap as we took it in turns to read from *Rainbow* or *Tiger Tim's Weekly*. Idyllic hours, all too soon broken by my brothers' noisy return from school.

The Great Silver Thaw was something not to be forgotten. The snow had melted and the temperature suddenly dropped again, leaving the streets covered with a thin, treacherous sheeting of ice. Nothing could remain upright. Poor Bess sat down so often that she had to be taken from her shafts and tethered in a garden. And the milk in Bert the milkman's churn had a half-inch of ice on top. I tried to take the jug out to him as usual but I went head over heels and the jug smashed to smithereens. Nor could I get to my feet for all my efforts. It was terrifying, a world gone mad overnight. Bert picked me up and took me home, explaining proudly how he alone in all this anarchy could remain on his feet: 'I've got a thick pair of socks over me boots, see. That's how it's done.'

There were November fogs, in one of which I was (oddly) taken on to the Hill to see the King drive by. He had been ill and was going to the seaside to get better. But before he appeared a long funeral procession wound slowly along the Hill to Streatham cemetery. For years I thought a hearse was indispensable to a royal progress. And what a funeral, such a one as no child could ever forget. The ornate hearse with its purple pall and piles of wreaths, the driver seated on high with his whip and his top hat fluttering with black streamers, the sad black horses with gigantic black plumes nodding on their heads. All in swirling fog. To cap it all I learned that Streatham cemetery was in a district officially known as 'Lonesome.'

When at last the King appeared he struck me as a decided anticlimax. Just a fleeting glimpse of a small, bearded man wearily lifting a hand to thin cheers. Not half such a good show as the funeral.

The General Strike was more rewarding as a spectacle, with my aunt going off to business on a lorry and a soldier or a policeman perched beside each bus driver. I think I was a little surprised no one clapped politely as they did at the Lord Mayor's Show.

5

Buses and trams figured largely in my life. Trams were thrilling because you could watch the driver at work. One big brass handle and one small black one, and a warning bell he stamped on with his foot. Sometimes he would release the big brass handle with a flourish and it would whizz round on its own. At certain interesting halts which I came to know he would alight to pull a lever beside the track, or to fish something from beneath the vehicle with a long pole.

But there was a serious drawback to a tram. It was confined to the centre of the road, so that when you alighted you had to risk the traffic that sped heedlessly between you and the safety of the pavement. This was a terror to me because, despite the conductor's flapping arm, the cars and lorries and horses just *would* not stop, or if they did, you had to thread your way through monsters who at any second might leap back into life.

I don't recall being looked after in these and similar perils, only myself doing all the looking after. I considered my mother's attitude to the traffic to be quite irresponsible, and my hated role was that of a sheepdog amid impossible hazards. I herded home mother and aunt and, above all, little sister Pam, whose hand I gripped in a desperate vice on such outings. Mother would laugh at my fears and precautions, never knowing how real my agonies were. I was obsessed by a sense of external threat to this family of mine, so dear, so ill equipped for the terrors of existence.

Buses were safer, but only if you got the right kind. 'Generals' and 'Thomas Tillings' were usually all right, a homely red and fairly sane. But there were buses known as 'Pirates,' black and brutal, restrained by no timetables, sheer cutthroats who scarcely halted at all for passengers to get on or off. Waiting at the stop, I would feel my heart fall within me if a 'Pirate' hove into view. Even the friendlier 'Generals' could be impatient, and if the inside was full the journey to the upper deck (open to the skies) could be fearsome, for the stairs curved out over rushing seas of manure and macadam into which I felt one lurch of the vehicle could fling you. Just by these stairs hung the bellpull: a length of black, greasy leather you tugged once for 'Stop' and twice for 'Go.' My greatest ambition then was to pull it. I brooded and brooded over the possibility. It became a temptation so compelling I just knew one day I'd yield to it.

I did. A particularly irritable and impatient conductor had been yelling: 'Hurry along, please. Outside only. Hurry *along*.' Gulping in a deep breath which my hammering heart seemed to be denying me, and quick as lightning, I gave the cord two glorious jerks on my way upstairs. Gears crashed, the bus lurched forward, and a chorus of screams and curses filled the air. All caused by me, with a couple of tugs no one had witnessed. The conductor then began pulling the cord feverishly and the bus stopped with such abruptness that those standing inside or on the platform almost all lost their balance.

When we were seated upstairs and things had sorted themselves out, the conductor began a bellowing enquiry first down and then up.

'Who did it? Who pulled the bloody bell? *I* didn't. We're not going on till I find out. Now who was it?'

'Me,' I said shyly, in the same way I answered when Miss Plumbridge asked who had top marks in a test. The conductor seized and shook me.

'You? You little devil, you could have caused a nasty accident, you could.' My mother pushed the conductor away, apologized to him, and at the same time boxed my ears (sort of). The conductor kept repeating: 'Some kid I didn't see did it. I didn't pull the bell. Might have caused a nasty accident, it might.' I had already noticed that 'common people' always said things two or three times, and in an extraordinarily detached fashion I was waiting for the conductor once more to begin the same verbal round.

'Oh, do be quiet,' mother said to him. 'It's only a child, after all.'

'Old enough to know better,' shouted the conductor (quite rightly). He then went downstairs and rang the bus off. With careful attention I heard him recounting the whole thing over and over again to the lower deck. My own reaction to all this was quite surprising, even to me. I didn't cry or even look ashamed. All quite out of character. I think I just felt satisfied. An ambition achieved. A revenge taken.

Ordinary sweets were twopence a quarter, the superior ones fourpence. We children seldom bought either. It was more fun to buy an assortment of farthing and halfpenny lines: tubular packets of brown coconut tobacco, gobstoppers that lasted a whole morning, licorice pipes and licorice bootlaces, aniseed balls with a tiny leaf embedded in their concentric colours, cupid's kisses whose mottoes you sucked into oblivion, triangular packets of sherbet containing a stick lollipop you licked and jabbed into the powder, and paper packs of sweet cigarettes with red tips and real cigarette cards.

I soon learned that Mr Shuttleworth and Mr Needler (as compared with Messrs Cadbury, Fry, Rowntree and Terry) made chocolate bars within my price range. I had to wait until Christmas or a birthday or even the turning of adult backs to taste the supreme joys: petits fours or chocolate liqueurs or philippine biscuits, or the bliss of Nestlé's milk frantically sucked from a twice-punctured tin. It may be thought that I was a greedy child. 'Now, don't be greedy' was an injunction often given me by the grown-ups and more often jeeringly mimicked by my brothers. But never by my father, who earned my gratitude on these occasions by saying: 'He's *not* greedy. He just likes a lot.'

I took this very seriously and once at a party, accepting yet another cake, solemnly assured my hostess: 'I'm not greedy, you know. I just like a lot.'

I certainly had a sweet tooth. With savoury things I was far more fastidious, and in a curious way mother encouraged me in this. She would never have any kind of 'offal' in the house, even liver or kidney. I am still astonished to discover that there are people who eat hearts and sweetbreads and oxtails. And I was told as a child not to ask for water or bread with my dinner as in friends' houses, because only the poor had to eke out good food with such staples. Many of these early taboos persist with me, to the extent of real disrelish for any animal product insufficiently disguised on my plate.

When I was old enough to be sent on occasional shopping errands it was impressed on me that the word 'best' must figure in all orders ('best fresh butter' and 'best short back'), and in any choice one must always choose the more expensive.

It seems to me in retrospect that I took an inordinately long time to come to terms with any vegetable other than the potato. Most children dislike things like cabbage and spinach, but I extended the embargo to almost everything a greengrocer sold. Again, I was encouraged to dismiss all root vegetables except the ubiquitous (and delectable) spud as 'cattle food.' This I consider quite just. Not even in days of wartime scarcity did we ever stomach a turnip or swede or parsnip, and I don't think I have ever tasted them. And carrots I eat only if trapped as a guest. I remember vividly my 'first veg' (runner beans) and how surprised I was to find them so inoffensively nice. Peas soon joined them in my favour, but cabbage and spring greens waited many a year for endorsement.

I would drift around the nearby roads consuming my candy delicacies with a serious attention to detail. They had to be eaten in a manner that left the best to the last. Once I lost a whole new sherbet packet in circumstances that left a sour taste of injustice. In a road parallel to ours stood a row of old cottages whose long gardens were filled with flowers so large that they seemed to belong to another planet. Great sunflowers and hollyhocks nodded far above a child's head. It was as though Marzipan, my favourite magician in *Rainbow*, had waved his magnifying wand there.

In one of these cottages lived Henry Irving and his wife Mrs Stephens. They were not popular, for they considered themselves superior to the other theatricals in the neighbourhood as being legitimate theatre. He wore the requisite large-brimmed black hat and his rather odd wife affected a cloak. ''Enery Irvin',' the common boys would sometimes chant after him. 'Mister 'Enery Irvin'!' But I knew I must call him Mr Stephens.

The memory of our first meeting is sharply etched. I was running past his cottage as he tended his triffids. Hurtling past, I should say, for I seemed to launch myself with no sense of speed, balance or gravity, and so was always falling over. On this occasion I fell just outside his gate and opened up old wounds on my knee. He picked me up, and just as I prepared to bawl he rapped out in surprisingly peremptory tones: 'Now remember this and never forget it: "Old soldiers never die and young soldiers never cry".' I was so surprised I quite forgot the wails and tears. I stared at him open-mouthed as he added: 'Now please repeat that after me: "Old soldiers never die and young soldiers never cry".'

I did so, word perfect. 'Well done,' he said, but without smiling. 'Always remember that.'

That was our first encounter. Our last was even more memorable. I was idling round his gate, trying to tear open my sherbet packet, when I became aware that his wife was staring at me in a strange fashion. She looked wilder even than usual. Suddenly she said: 'Would you like to see poor Mr Stephens?' I didn't really want to but I knew the polite answer was 'Yes, please.'

I followed her through the long jungle into the cottage, which the jungle seemed to have invaded for it was filled with potted plants, some of ceiling height. She opened an inner door and disclosed Mr Stephens lying on a bed in his pyjamas. I particularly noticed that he had his socks on and through one protruded a big toe. His eyes were closed.

'Hullo, Mr Stephens,' I said. 'Aren't you well today?'

Suddenly she rounded on me. 'Oh you stupid boy,' she cried. 'Go *home!*'

This frightened me so much that I dropped my sherbet packet and ran all the way home. I told my mother: 'I've seen Mr Stephens and he's in bed and Mrs Stephens was nasty to me.'

My mother was incredulous at first, and then rather angry. 'What a stupid woman that is,' she said. 'Poor Mr Stephens died last night.' I repeated the last words to myself: 'Died last night, died last night.' It took a long time to sink in. I'd seen a dead cat once and I knew what a funeral was. I knew Angela had gone to Heaven, and Stewart Mackenzie, too. Now I'd actually seen a dead body, and I felt cheated because I hadn't known it was a dead body. I begged my mother to take me back for a harder look, but she wouldn't hear of it, wouldn't even go on her own to retrieve my bag of sherbet. In vain I explained that Mrs Stephens *wanted* people to go in and look. I felt Mrs Stephens knew she had something worth exhibiting and, although I didn't like her, I felt vaguely she was being generous. But no pleas would move my mother. All part of the unaccountable grown-up world. The only indisputable fact I could lay hold of was that Mr Stephens certainly hadn't been an old soldier.

6

Very soon after I had learned to read I discovered a rival attraction to books. The cinema engulfed me. At our local palace of delights, called 'The Golden Domes,' the seats were priced at fourpence, sixpence and eightpence. If I went with grown-ups, it was in the eightpennies, if to a matinée with my brothers, the sixpennies were good enough. Never did we descend to the fourpennies, for they were 'common' and it was even rumoured you could 'catch things' in them.

I'd been to the live theatre only once, to a Christmas pantomime. I don't know what it was, but it wasn't *Dick Whittington* for I would certainly have remembered Uncle Len's 'Cat.' My one firm recollection is of being puzzled and not at all entertained or amused. There was no story I could grasp and no real characterization. It was all rhyme and no reason. It disturbed me, just as later my first encounter with *Alice in Wonderland* was to disturb me. What upset me most, I think, was the one really catchy song because it was called 'The More We Are Together,' the very title of Mrs Mackenzie's painting and my secret world, which I felt had been invaded and somehow spoiled. Thus I found the celluloid world of the cinema more acceptable, more soul-satisfying and more *real*, than the flesh and blood world of the stage.

I encountered the cinema in the last heyday of the silent screen. One usually had to queue, even for the matinées. I would pray that the commissionaire's dreaded arm would not fall just in front of us, perhaps delaying entrance beyond the bounds of economic good sense.

When I went in the afternoon I liked us to get there early and take our seats before the lights went down. Then one could savour all the exquisite preludes. My happiness, as I sat there entranced and expectant, was something unique in my life at that time. It was hard to believe such happiness was real. I would try to analyse it for flaws. I suppose it was the peculiar joy of imminent aesthetic experience. I knew that soon I would be caught up into a magic world, and without my lifting a finger. All I had to do was sit there and be marvellously spellbound. All the security of the womb but with all the senses atingle and the imagination raught to capacity.

Oh, that wonderful, artful build-up to delight! First, the arrival of the musicians, the trio who colluded with the film to prey on our emotions. Their tunings-up evoked in me frissons of delicious excitement. How strangely their crazy scrapings and tinklings and boomings affected me. Even now, to hear instrumentalists tuning is in an instant to be transported back to tip-up seats and usherettes' torches and a low hum of talk and nostrils full of close and cheaply scented air. The lights at last would lower. The curtains would swish back. Tunings would become melody and the silver screen would flicker to life. And I would be lost to the waking world.

Audience reactions were often touchingly innocent. I remember when the splendid Rin Tin Tin was being ill treated by some black-eyed villain a man in front of me called out: 'Stop it, you brute, stop it!' On some similarly harrowing occasion I remember a man hurrying out with the words: 'I can't take it. I just can't take it.' When the lights went up many a man or woman was mopping at eyes, and once or twice the St John Ambulance man who was always in attendance was called to someone slumped in a faint across his seat. We liked our withers wrung in those days, and none, I suspect, more so than I. Of course, I yelled a bit at the comics, but they weren't my favourites. Indeed I preferred their adventures in tabloid form, in *Comic Cuts* and *Film Fun*. No, here in their true home I wanted stronger meat.

My greatest thrill was *Michael Strogoff*: Tourjansky's version, with Mosjoukine as Michael. I went, all alone, to see it one afternoon. I was seven or eight at the time and I must, surely, have gone without permission. I sat there, insulated from the world in a cocoon of wonder. I remember now only the scene that shattered me, haunted me for months. In this Michael, blind, is staggering through snowdrifts towards a precipice when he (or someone) prays for his sight to be restored if only for a moment. Angels appear in a radiant sky, the finger of God reaches down and Michael sees. I thought this so wonderful that I had to see it again. And again. In fact I was well into the third showing when torches were flashed along row after row until I was found and dragged back into the light of common day. Or rather, of night, for it was nine o'clock and Mrs Johnson and a policeman were waiting for me in the foyer.

I have never seen this film since, nor have I read Jules Verne's novel. Maybe my memory of it all is faulty. But it was, for me, the first towering aesthetic peak I scaled in the cinema.

22

Ben Hur and Beau Geste were other highlights. And the sufferings of the Messiah in De Mille's King of Kings had me in persistent tears. The Jesus was H.B. Warner, whose lean, ravaged features were forever sanctified in my eyes. I wept for him on Calvary, but I wept even more when he repeated his Jesus role in modern dress a year later, as Captain Sorrell in Warwick Deeping's jeremiad, Sorrell and Son. The tears I shed over that gallant Captain's crucifixion, both in 1927 and in the 1934 remake!

For these projected figures were very real people to us early cinema addicts. Real and near and often dear. I don't recall any female attachments. The nearest perhaps was Hepburn's boyish Jo in Little Women, but I was decidedly eclectic over the male stars. The faces of Charles Ray and Charles Farrell pleased me then, and poor Ramon Navarro's limbs and Richard Cromwell's barefoot charm in Tol'able David. Lew Ayres in the great All Quiet on the Western Front was a stricken bloom I cherished for years.

My dearer possessions were certain boy actors whose appeal was disturbingly exploited, and fairly early on I learned to be rather secretive about them. Who now but me remembers Phillipe de Lacy or William Janney or Frankie Darro or Frankie Thomas? But my standards were high, and remained so. I couldn't weave private romances about the Coopers or Bartholomews or Breens or Kilburns. Tommy Kelly and Dickie Moore, yes, and a ready acceptance of the Mauch twins and Roddy McDowell and Dean Stockwell and Antony Wager, and not forgetting William (who became James) Fox. And that sad, lost company: Jeremy Spenser and John Charlesworth, Ray Jackson and the older Brandon de Wilde. Then, as the Swinging Sixties closed, that dearest of Romeos and most immemorial of Tadzios, Leonard Whiting and Bjorn Andresen. I make no apology for saluting them all, just as Ben and Will saluted their boy actors long, long ago.

In 1929, after months of ballyhoo, came the first talkies. Our first was In Old Arizona. As I sat in the cinema with my mother before the lights went down, the atmosphere was electric. There was a curious, charged hush as we all awaited the new miracle. No little orchestra now, and even the usherettes spoke in whispers. I remember I was surprised to find my palms sweating with excitement. Then, at last, it began: strident music from a soundtrack, interminable credits on the screen. My pounding heart didn't want music but words, words actually issuing from those long dumb, celluloid lips. We weren't in the picture house but before the Oracle at Delphi.

And there was Warner Baxter about to speak to Lupe Velez (or perhaps it was Dolores del Rio). And speak he did. And she replied. A moment of stunned silence from the whole auditorium, then a ripple of laughter which spread until waves of guffaws drowned the film. For the language was alien, almost incomprehensible. No one in that cinema had heard American English before.

After all those years of waiting for the miracle to dawn the joke was on us. We had to serve quite an apprenticeship before we mastered this new accent and idiom.

7

Another and, to me, less intriguing joke in those days was radio. A joke called 'wireless': 'I can make a wireless set with only two wires.' 'How?' 'Take one away and that's a wire less, isn't it, stupid?' My brothers, who were practical, made cat's whisker sets and we would take it in turns to don the earphones and obligingly strain our imaginations. Sometimes, patiently tickling crystal with whisker, one would cull from limbo half a phrase of speech or music and my brothers would be puffed out with pride. But the thing rarely spoke even that much to me. I preferred the gramophone.

I wasn't practical. Unlike most boys in those days I had no desire to probe the secrets of the internal combustion engine. Nevertheless, my first car was ecstasy. It belonged to Uncle Frank, my father's youngest brother and something of a flighty bachelor. He came to stay with us one summer, driving all the way from Yorkshire in this splendid chariot. I don't know its make but it was high off the ground, stood open to the sky, had generous running boards and an arrogant klaxon hooter. For me it was above all a smell, the smell elicited by sunshine from real leather upholstery, the smell of pure romance. I pestered to be taken out in it, and as we bowled along dusty Surrey lanes I was in every sense transported, hoped the golden day would never end, the royal odyssey reach beyond the sunset.

But my parents didn't seem to approve of Uncle Frank. I once overheard them refer to him as 'Uncle Swank,' and they hinted darkly at his 'cruising along, picking up girls.' I was shocked by their attitude. It seemed to me unjust, not to say treacherous, for when they were together it was all affectionate banter and noisy good cheer. To me, Uncle Frank was a happy man and a kind one. Playing tennis and driving his car seemed his only pursuits, and I couldn't see anything wrong with that. Or with giving rides to girls. (Not quite my taste, of course, but I was prepared to be tolerant.)

I was similarly shocked when I heard my father refer to Mrs Johnson as 'a waggonload of monkeys.' I didn't quite understand this stricture, but a stricture I knew it was. And on my Mrs Johnson whose character I considered nothing less than angelic. I recall wondering, seriously and sadly, if my parents could be rather unkind people. The images I had of such folk as made up my world derived solely from their attitude to me. Too young to look further, I saw them simply as they liked to see themselves. Only much later had I the black art to see the truths about them which they hid from themselves, and I don't know that the world was happier or I the wiser for seeing that Uncle Frank *was* rather a bigmouth and Mrs Johnson something of a sponger.

Around this time my father took me for a week's holiday to his parents in Yorkshire. I looked forward to it with intense excitement, for I had been told that they lived in the country next door to a farm. We went by train and my grandfather's car met us at the station. He was a successful builder who had already retired, a JP and a lay reader, and I didn't like him at all. This was partly because he had a beard and looked like George V, partly because he said nothing and did nothing but sit in an armchair and continually replenish his glass from a stone flagon by his feet. 'Grandpa's medicine,' my grandmother explained to me. So I associated him with sickliness and silence, just like George V, who was himself associated in my mind with funerals. Also, by some process below consciousness, I was aware that my father didn't like him and he didn't like my father. My grandmother looked severe but was really very kind. She seemed to live in a perpetual unease, shielding her husband from annoyance and apologizing for any misconceptions that might arise.

But my first acute disappointment had come before we even reached the house. I couldn't understand why we had to get in this gloomy limousine with its gloomy chauffeur, and inside I fidgeted abominably, asking my father over and over: 'When do we get out? When?' He told me sharply to be quiet and sit still, and when I didn't he slapped my leg, which was unlike him and set me snivelling. 'Whatever's the matter with you?' he asked in exasperation. He didn't understand; how could he? And I lacked the words to explain. All I could mutter between tearful spasms was: 'But they've got roads.'

It was that picture book of mine again. As a suburban child I relied on it for my ideas of the country. On the picture book and on Mrs Mackenzie's bitter-sweet painting. Both told me that in the country there should be rolling hills and valleys, streams and lakes, copses and cows and cottages, but never, never a single road. One wandered, preferably barefoot, over endless grassland, and only trees interrupted the sweeping skyline. *That* was the country. And this wasn't it.

I remember very little domestically about that holiday. Just an enormous silver-covered dish which I assumed would contain food piled commensurably high. I secretly thought it rather funny when the dish was shown to contain a few slices of something in a thin sauce. But meals were generally very tasty and agreeably abundant. Sometimes, though, they were intimidating, so that I dare not mop up my breakfast egg and bacon with speared bread, as I did at home. And sometimes they were odd, in that we had the Yorkshire pudding on its own before the roast beef and veg.

Father had two brothers and four sisters, and one of each still lived at home, namely the cheerful Uncle Frank and a very nice Aunt Grace who twice took me with her as she played golf. The golf course atoned for much in its resemblance to real countryside.

Grandma and Aunt Grace made quite a fuss of me. That was nice, of course, but I felt it could be a mixed blessing when I overheard them saying: 'A nice-looking little boy, but he needs building up. Cod liver oil and malt, that's what he needs. I'll tell John.' I hoped they wouldn't, or that he'd forget if they did, for I disliked fish and at home liver was rather a dirty word gastronomically.

The threats lurking in this big and dark and quiet house were not always verbal. One rather cold night Grandma said my bed needed warming before I disappeared into it. At home this meant a nice, cuddly hot-water bottle. But not here. I watched in consternation as the maid slid a large warming pan between the sheets. The beastly thing monopolized the small bed, and seldom had I seen anything less cuddlesome, less inviting as a bedfellow. What a relief when the girl eventually carried it off elsewhere. I suffered several such first encounters in that house, and they were unsettling. I didn't know I was in for a much nastier shock.

The day of my eagerly awaited visit to the nearby farm seemed a long time in coming, but at last the farmer's teenage son arrived to collect me. I had very definite ideas about farms and they were as vulnerable as my ideas about the countryside. I knew farmers had hundreds of animals, and I assumed they had them because they loved them as I loved Nigger and Scottie and Bess. True, when driving past the farm I had looked in vain to see someone romping with a pig or cuddling a hen, but I accepted that in daytime hours these people were too busy for such indulgences. My kindly young guide took me round, explaining all in tones of proud possession. Finally we came within sight of a long, low building from which animal screams emerged and into which pigs and sheep, already close to panic, were being ferociously driven by a couple of ageing farm hands. The farmer's son painstakingly outlined to me the nature and purpose of an abattoir. It was a recent acquisition and he couldn't help sounding rather boastful about it. He was clearly mystified by my incredulity, mounting horror and eventual tears. It so upset me that I couldn't wait to leave this cruel, alien land. I pestered father to take me home. I think the unsuccessful holiday was in fact cut short by a day. I loved every belch and snort of the great steam engine that succoured me. An inverted Cathy Earnshaw, I jumped out of that phoney Yorkshire heaven to awake sobbing for joy on the cultivated plains of suburbia.

I never went back to my grandparents' house, and father returned only once, for Grandpa's funeral. Father told me one day that his forebears had left Scotland for Yorkshire after the massacre of Glencoe and had changed their name from Campbell to Gamble, so it seemed only natural to me that they should end up next to an abattoir.

All this left a sour taste in my mouth, and I looked now with a jaundiced eye on the classroom painting of Jesus, the Good Shepherd, nursing a pretty little lamb. You couldn't fool me any more.

8

After three years, academically the brightest of my life, I left Surrey College and the home and the neighbourhood which had been my whole wondrous, nascent world. Left Mary-and-Jean, and Scottie and Jonah, left Mrs Johnson and Mrs Mackenzie and Mrs Clackett, left Miss Tierney and Miss Plumbridge and all my gay little charioteers, left the ragged, barefoot boys and the stately iron-shod Bess. And all without one tear.

For none of it, mercifully, registered as a parting. Rather it was the breathless opening of a new book of delights. We were moving house. Four enormous shire horses drew the pantechnicon into which, to everyone's surprise, all our furniture was eventually crammed. My mother and I had a last look round the empty rooms. There was no sense of valediction in my capering excitement, for neither eye nor ear now knew this as a home. 'Goodbye' I shouted in each room, but only for the fun of an echo-answer they'd never vouchsafed before. It was a very cold day and I was astonished to see clouds of steam rising from the great, sweating hides of the removal horses.

My father was apparently prospering. He was a quantity surveyor and it was becoming known that almost any estimate he tendered secured the contract. I would watch him costing all the ingredients of some huge building-to-be, all out of his head, his pencil covering the foolscap sheets with figures, very few of which he would need to erase and rewrite, then casting up the columns of pounds, shillings and pence at unbelievable speed.

We moved to Streatham (as distinct from Streatham Hill), to a spacious, three-storeyed house, two or three of whose rooms my parents furnished entirely from the Ideal Home Exhibition of the previous year. We now had a billiard room and a maid and a new car and the very latest in big cabinet gramophones.

My father was a handsome man and, in those days, something of a dandy. I remember his spats and his shammy leather gloves and his beautifully rolled umbrella. He carried himself well and insisted his sons did the same. Indoors, he stressed, 'Sit with a straight back,' and out-of-doors, as I trotted the pavement holding his hand, he would repeatedly remind me: 'Always fix your eyes on the top of the next lamppost.' I found that quite difficult in days when my stature was so much less than his. I was to find it

27

even more difficult, in fact impossible, to emulate his pencils. He sharpened them with his little silver smoker's knife and they were almost works of art, elegant and tapering as Dürer hands.

He was fond of me in those early years, and I of him. He would often bring me home a little gift: a bar of chocolate, a story book, some crayons. In bed, I would try to stay awake for his homecoming, but his hours were extremely erratic. Sometimes I would wake up and call to him from the stairhead: 'Daddy, are you coming up to see me?'

'Yes,' he'd call back.

'When?'

'In two shakes of a dead lamb's tail.'

This would silence me for a moment as once more I pondered the image the words evoked and tried to make sense of it.

'Have you brought me a present?'

Even if he hadn't, he would reply: 'Yes.'

'What is it? What have you brought me?'

'I've brought you the best Daddy in all the world.'

This was a stock response and I soon learned that it meant no present that night. It irritated me. Strangely, it seemed to irritate my mother, who greeted it with what is usually called a 'snort of contemptuous disbelief.'

Gradually, I came to recognize that I had two fathers: the one who left the house cheerfully in the morning and was an affectionate presence for most of Sunday, and the other a quite different being of uncertain temper whom I saw in the evenings and on Saturday afternoons. This change I soon came to recognize in his features, which became in a curious way relaxed, as if he couldn't quite fix his regard or control the set of his mouth. Very soon, too, it was communicated to me from my mother that this latter person was far from acceptable. A person who swayed on his feet and found fault with everything and everybody in a series of sarcasms that bit for all their slurred delivery. A person who wanted trouble and who had a mania for switching off lights, something that infuriated my mother, who liked to have them all merrily blazing. I acquired a new role, that of a sick, inerrant little barometer always seeking to avert the storms it predicted. Storms mostly verbal, but once or twice almost horrifyingly physical.

I could never understand why my mother always rose to his taunts. 'Don't answer him, Mummy,' I'd plead in tears, 'don't answer him.' But she was constitutionally incapable of ignoring his ripostes. On and on the battle of cruel words would go until, defeated, he would slink to bed.

She always won.

9

I changed my school. Montrose College was a fairly large, independent school in Streatham which was just beginning to lose some of its local prestige under a new headmaster. Its name-board had once carried the arrogant definition: 'For the Sons of Gentlefolk Only.' That had long since become 'For the Professional Classes Only,' and even that was now rather loosely interpreted. In vain to be reminded that a former mayor, a successful draper subsequently knighted, had failed, because he was 'in trade,' to secure entry for his son. That had been under Dr Bray, much lamented, and it was whispered that his successor, Mr Stewart, undoubtedly a clever man, and almost as surely a gentleman, worshipped Mammon rather than Minerva, and didn't much care who knew it. The school was a business from which he intended to retire in as much affluence and in as short a time as possible. Thus, rubbing shoulders with the progeny of doctors and clergy and solicitors, we now had an influx of 'showbiz kids': Lotingas and Lupinos and Flanagans and others who have since become household names on television.

However, academic results were still good, and we were thoroughly ground through the Latin machine. Manners hadn't really slipped. Ceaseless vigilance attended our vowels, our donning and doffing of caps, our sittings and risings and bowings and scrapings. And there were odd relics of grander days. Our expensive caps and blazers boasted the most opulent gold braid, our books were likewise embossed with the school crest in gold, and once a year we took over London's County Athletics Ground for our Parents' Day. It was then one of the finest stadia in the country and we lived up to it. Our flag fluttered proudly above an Ascot of suburban finery, the Metropolitan Police band serenaded us throughout the afternoon, the pavilion teas were lavish enough for the biggest Bunter, and the presentations table sagged beneath an array of prizes donated by parents vying to create a memorable splash.

I started there well enough after my excellent grounding at Surrey College. One of my delights was community singing on a Friday afternoon. Not that I myself could sing, or even wanted to. It was the words, and the pictures behind them, that stirred me. It surprised me that none of the other boys seemed as affected by them as I was. I liked the sad songs best: 'Clementine' and 'Old Black Joe' and 'Loch Lomond.' They had something of that loss and longing in them that drew me to Mrs Mackenzie's painting. The only real rivals to these elegiac ditties were the 'boy songs,' as I called them: 'The Skye Boat Song' and 'Charlie is My Darling' and Tom Moore's wonderful 'Minstrel Boy.' And best of all was a certain bonny boy I made my own on account of his name, his legs and his hair:

Bobby Shaftoe's gone to sea,
Silver buckles on his knee,
He'll come back and marry me,
Bonny Bobby Shaftoe.
Bobby Shaftoe's bright and fair,
Combing down his yellow hair,
He's my ain for ever mair,
Bonny Bobby Shaftoe.

Clearly I saw the gold of his wind-blown locks and the buckles at his shapely calves, and in my odd mind we had many an adventure together on the rolling main, uninterrupted by any image of a henpecked domestic life ashore.

I often filled out the bare bones of such songs with my own romantic urges. Christmas gave the best scope for this, for we didn't have the printed words of some carols and what I misheard and misunderstood enriched the fantasies.

Good King Wenslus last looked out
On the feast of Stephen.

I knew Stephen was an English king and now these garbled words told me he was a usurper. He had grabbed the throne from that nice King Wenslus and driven him out into the snow, while he himself and the turncoat barons held a great, roistering feast in the purloined palace. Out in the cold, poor Wenslus could only gaze in at the window on all that had once been his: the hall, the furniture, the crockery, the delicious food, and all those treacherous, fawning nobles. I revelled in this vivid historical reconstruction. I saw Wenslus at length turn heavily away from the window and begin his terrible *winterreise*. Then, and this was the story's brilliant, redemptive climax, out of the palace's back door came running that lovely, loving, loyal pageboy. Without a word he took his master's hand and trudged beside him into immortality. I was torn between the two roles in my ensuing fantasies. Sometimes I was the gallant page, faithful unto death just like the Minstrel Boy, sometimes I was Wenslus, sheltering the boy within my scanty robes. I didn't know I was inventing the whole thing. The page image was supplied by the boy Prince of Wales as clad for his investiture at Caernarvon Castle in 1911, a picture of which was in my school history primer.

I rather collected adolescent royalty at that time. Michael of Rumania was distinctly attractive and so, incredible as it may seem in the light of what he became, was the boy Farouk of Egypt. But the most haunting of all such figures was the tragic little Russian Tsarevich.

After a couple of years or so at Montrose it would have been clear to anyone interested that my early academic promise was disappearing rapidly. I don't think anyone *was* really interested. The family found me difficult to counsel, and they weren't, in any case, natural mentors. And my form master, Mr Hector, disliked me and didn't make much effort to conceal the fact. I was undoubtedly slipping as much personally as academically. I was becoming a loner where once I'd been a leader, a prig where once I'd been a reasonably nice, unaffected little boy. I was an unappetizing blend of inferiority and superiority. Inferior at maths and sciences and all games, superior in languages and any form of verbal self-expression. This was a most unfortunate juxtaposition, for I naturally used the latter to make up for the former. I knew I was more literate than the other boys. It wasn't too difficult to score off them, or even off Mr Hector, and I soon became noted for an uncertain temper and a nasty tongue.

Mr Hector was as keen on games as his pupils were, and I had long before demonstrated my hopelessness at them. Jack Hobbs, a parent or uncle, had come one day to give us a little coaching at the nets. My turn came to stand at the wicket. Perhaps I exaggerated my stance of incompetence and my expression of disdain. Without bowling me one ball the great man said: 'Right, next,' and I came out to general derisive laughter.

I played one game of soccer as a full back, and I kicked the ball behind me into my own goal. This was not intentional, although Mr Hector and my team all thought it was. I really had no idea what was going on and I was in any case wearing my brother Brian's too-big football boots, my parents having wisely refused to buy me boots of my own. After this I raised such hell at home and school that I was unofficially but unequivocally 'off all games.' Instead, I was a soccer linesman and a cricket scorer. I actually became a competent, even conscientious, cricket scorer, but without ever being interested in the game. And not even to myself would I admit my envy of those many boys blessed with physical coordination and an eye for a ball.

After any match, Mr Hector would spend the first morning period discussing the finer points of the previous day's play, while I made my disapproval apparent with extravagant fidgetings and sighs, until at length he was driven to exclaim: 'But I see we're boring Gamble, who is anxious to get down to work.' This, as intended, enlisted the resentment of the whole form against me, and I was well aware of the dirty trick. But I was also aware of certain aces I held. Our fees were not paid for such invasions of the academic timetable, and also I was good at Mr Hector's subjects, for he taught us English and Latin.

His dislike of me became actual detestation after one incident I now blush with shame to recall. I had spoiled another of his football or cricket post mortems and as usual he had said: 'Gamble is bored, poor boy.' He then added, amid the usual sotto voce boos: 'He urges us to have resource to a little Latin.' And I murmured loudly enough for him to hear: 'Recourse.' He gave me a venomous look but said nothing.

We then got down to some Latin. Next to me sat a boy of whom I was extremely jealous, for he was an excellent games player and something of a teacher's pet. Worse, he was quite attractive and hated me. He always tried to keep a games discussion going, often because, as on this occasion, he hadn't done his prep. He now showed his resentment by slyly pushing my books and pencils and ruler off the desk at half-minute intervals. I thumped him as hard as I could on the arm, not failing to admire how hard it was with muscle and exercise.

'Right,' snapped Mr Hector. 'Out in front, Gamble. Out behind the board.' I opened my mouth to protest, but Mr Hector was still smarting from the wound I'd inflicted. He rose and yelled: 'Not a word. Don't dare utter a word. Out, out before I come and fling you out.'

He was tall and I was still a child. As slowly as I dared, I walked smouldering to the corner behind the blackboard. The lesson proceeded. I glanced round at my deskmate, who contorted his face in a silent grin of triumph and then very slowly pushed my pen off the desk.

I was beside myself. Not all the Hectors in creation should prevent me from executing instant justice. I ran back to my desk, seized the villain by the throat and hammered his head on the wall until he howled for mercy. Mr Hector had to pull me off him.

'He,' I panted, '*he*'s to blame. *He* should have gone behind the board, not me.'

The bell went for the end of the lesson and Mr Hector, to my surprise, let the whole thing slide into oblivion. I think he realized the injustice of his action and I think the strength of my fury took even him aback.

I didn't really dislike Mr Hector, just disliked his disliking me. There were times, indeed, when I enjoyed his lessons. But it's hard even for an adult to proffer liking to dislike. For a child it's impossible. Only in later years did I realize how much I owed him. Not for his teaching but for his Saturday fives. For on that last period of the week he read to us, and most of the books he read were by Rider Haggard. First *King Solomon's Mines*, then the meatier *Allan Quatermain* and then some of the great Zulu sagas, *Marie* and *Child of Storm*. Haggard was often a slipshod stylist and his Zulus perhaps owed more to East Anglia than to South Africa, but at his best he was magnificent and I hero-worshipped his literary persona, Allan Quatermain. Haggard was my first great literary love, the books and the man behind the books. Mr Hector had fashioned an addict, who soon exhausted Streatham library's stocks and had to cast his net further, to the twopenny lending libraries which were springing up at that time. Haggard fed in me tastes already developing and magically awoke others: for the savage and primitive, for the historical, for the epic, for the supernatural, and, in Allan Quatermain, for the shrewd, humorous goodness of an English country gentleman with whom I so readily and so oddly identified.

All this was a gift from Mr Hector. If only he had just once spoken nicely to me in private, appealed to my better nature, hinted, however difficult it may have been, that he wanted me to make it possible for him to like me. For there *was* a better nature, a longing for his approval, a deep need too proud to show itself. And I was such a little romantic that I would have gone to any lengths to justify an appeal made in friendship's name.

But he didn't, and so we remained at odds to the very last. His relief must have been as real as mine when eventually I left him for the upper school.

He died tragically of a brain tumour while I was still at the school. He was only thirty-three, and as we all lined up outside the school for his sad, slow cortège to pass, no tear could have been bitterer than mine, for mine sprang as much from guilt as from sorrow.

10

I should have liked history but it seemed to be taught with little sense of its poetry and romance. Geography old-style was a bore, and when a new master arrived to teach the subject enthusiastically as a kind of science I was even more alienated and soon dropped it altogether with a confused mental residue of meteorology, geology and economics. But my most deplorable showing was in maths and science. These were taught by the headmaster himself, who was excellent with any boy naturally inclined that way but quite hopeless with creatures like me, to whom the subjects had to be sold. Only with algebra did I make any headway, simply because I found letters friendlier than figures. Arithmetic in those days must have been deeply involved with the world of commerce and finance, for I remember long and losing struggles with compound interest and stocks and shares. But the total mystery was geometry. I never saw one glimmer of light there. I think it would have been otherwise if someone had gently suggested it was logic, for I rather prided myself on being logical, and I was good at Latin. I just learned theorems by heart and was thrown completely if Mr Stewart stuck up on the board a figure labelled with different letters. Like many others I saw that cheating was inevitable for survival. I would copy the beastly stuff from the book on my knee under the desk, but, astonishingly, Mr Stewart would often despise even a proof thus copied verbatim. He would glance at what I'd written and fling my book back at me with one or other of two comments: either 'too quick' or 'too slow.' It was the incomprehensibility of these judgments that convinced me both Euclid and Mr Stewart were mildly insane and removed any initial qualms I may have had about cheating. I longed to say: 'But, Sir, I've just copied it word for word from Hall and Stevens.' Only

THE MORE WE ARE TOGETHER

now does it occur to me that perhaps Mr Stewart knew that perfectly well and was tickled by my bafflement.

Science was compartmentalized into other mysteries such as 'Electricity and Magnetism' and 'Heat, Light and Sound,' and I soon parted company with them, too. Our academic aim was London Matric, which required you, on one and the same occasion, to pass in five subjects. Fail to measure up in just one of the five and you had nothing to show for a dozen years of schooling. Arithmetic, algebra and geometry were one compulsory subject, as were English language and English literature. It was decided my other three would be French, Latin and history. Montrose dominies knew their subjects but very few could teach. They couldn't understand, let alone anticipate, the almost limitless capacity for confusion possessed by some boys in some subjects. Never in imagination could they project themselves from master's dais to pupil's desk. And in other ways the gulf between these two was disastrous, for it was unthinkable in such a situation to confess to confusion or request further enlightenment.

But I sound like a bad workman blaming his tools, when indeed much of the blame for these early failures is undeniably mine. Mr Stewart had a pronounced Scottish accent and certain eccentricities of behaviour no bored boy could overlook. I was very bored, unusually observant, and soon learned I was a fair mimic.

In the midst of an exposition Mr Stewart would suddenly go far away, gazing out of the window with vacant eye and hanging jaw. Then after a minute or two he would redirect his gaze upon us, but as if our nature and presence were inexplicable to him. He also had a habit of suddenly clapping his hands together, loudly exclaiming 'Further' (which he rhymed with 'mother'), and walking silently from one end of the room to the other, absorbed in measuring his long and elegant shoes against the floorboards. He had, or at any rate evinced, no shred of a sense of humour, except for one joke which he produced over and over again, and always with much apologetic blushing and humming and head-wagging. This joke seemed to us entirely irrelevant and quite extraordinarily unfunny, but its warning signals set up in some of us that silent shaking which can herald hysterics.

The joke was likely to occur when we trotted out, verbally or on paper, some such parrot phrase as 'by hypothesis' or 'by substitution' or 'reductio ad absurdum.' Then he would ask: 'Have you heard - ah - of the old lady who - um - visited Mesopotamia? Have you heard of her, Gamble?' I was already incapable of speech, so I lyingly shook my head. 'All she could ever say when she got back home was - ah - "Mesopotamia, Mesopotamia, Mesopotamia".'

At last one could let go. The relief was indescribably sweet as we sobbed and roared our appreciation. It never seemed to surprise Mr Stewart, who merely looked rather ashamed of having revealed to his charges a human trait.

In time, my Stewart imitations actually became rather sought after. So I studied the poor man with a horrible earnestness. No intonation, grimace or gesture escaped me. He, no doubt, saw me as a slow but conscientious pupil hanging touchingly on his every word. Actually, as time went on, I heard less and less of what he said. Sometimes my cronies and I would be so devastated by his antics that I had to stuff an entire handkerchief in my mouth and pray: 'Oh, please God shut him up before I burst.'

As I grew older I came to have little twinges of conscience about him, for I suspected that his moments of silent abstraction were grieving remembrances of his only son, killed in the war. A large photo of this son, clad in a captain's khaki and looking almost uncannily like our Mr Stewart, hung on the wall in one of his three studies. (He had one for interviewing parents, one for caning boys, and one for relaxing between periods. This last had a communicating door with a classroom and one could peep through the keyhole and witness the son's portrait and the father's chain-smoking and drinking.) With my innate taste for the lugubrious, I reconstructed all the parental hopes and dreams that were shattered by a bullet in Flanders and accounted for the dim, flitting figure of Mrs Stewart and the heavily nicotined fingers of her husband. Only years later did I discover that they had never had any children, and that the portrait was of Mr Stewart himself, who was probably around forty when I knew him. But when you're ten, forty is Methuselah.

11

Such was the school front. And on the home front there was little enough to recall me to my senses. My father was regularly presented with hampers of delicacies and cases of spirits by firms grateful for his services. The new home was for a while a place of light and laughter. There were frequent parties at which quantities of food and drink were downed by old friends from old scenes and by newer people I didn't know. I remember noisy games and charades, which I liked to watch because it was good to see everybody so happy and loving. But I didn't want to be involved and sometimes even had to resist physically some well-meant assaults on my independence. No doubt the visitors privately decided I was a spoiled little brat when I refused to join in 'postman's knock.' But I just didn't want to go out of the room and kiss girls. I'd been caught once with the 12-year-old daughter of a neighbour and I hadn't enjoyed it at all, so when the same situation arose, with possibly the same child, I absolutely refused to budge. Through gritted teeth the company said: 'Oh, it's a shame to make him. He's shy.' On this occasion Mrs Johnson's daughter Phyllis was present with her fiancé, an extraordinarily handsome young man called Michael. I had been his secret admirer for a long time and all I wanted was to be left alone to look at him and listen to him. Suddenly he called out: 'Perhaps he'd like to come outside with *me*? How about it, Peter?'

I can't imagine what made him say it. Perhaps he was a little tipsy. Or perhaps he'd noticed me staring at him. It wasn't said unkindly. There was nothing sarcastic or disapproving in his tone. He laughed as he spoke.

There was a moment's silence, then some uncertain laughter, then the whole thing was drowned in chatter and movement. But I was appalled. I felt I'd been stripped in public, my deepest thoughts plumbed and broadcast. Crimson faced, I escaped and hid. I was about eleven.

I had one or two intimate friends at school, of course, but they were seldom the community's pin-ups, for I'd decided that the good-looking boys were usually not my type, by which I meant not very nice. They tended to be spoilt, athletic, extrovert and humourless, so I just loitered appreciatively among them like the poet in the Grecian gallery. No, my few real friends were chosen for one reason only, for their readiness to laugh at what I laughed at, enjoy what I enjoyed. With them I led a largely fantasy life, peopled initially with adults we knew and with characters I invented. With one particular friend, Robbie, I concocted a Brotherhood of Burners, dedicated pyromaniacs whose delights, I remember, included the firing of little girls' plaits and the propulsion of ignited clergy through their own stained glass windows. At Christmas, they would sell to children perfect working models of the Calvary crucifixion and do-it-yourself kits labelled 'de haeretico comburendo.' These characters were sharply differentiated, bearing such intimidating names as Silas, Jasper, Ebenezer and Olga. Material for their antics was gleaned also from literature and, of course, the pervasive silver screen. Their eventual star performer was a beautiful woman surgeon who performed unspeakably hideous operations on the men who succumbed to her. It was all, I suppose, a release of tension and a protest against the bourgeois conventions. Robbie, who was to make a name for himself as a rather exotic architect and a non-gay Lothario, was a talented draughtsman who would from our combined unsavoury imaginations produce drawings *à la* Bosch and Peake.

There was a gentle, somewhat myopic boy called Billy whose friendship was more like hero worship, inexplicable but flattering. At school his doglike attendance could be embarrassing, for he was something of a butt. In the holidays, however, his readiness to fall in with any proposal I made appealed to the rather bossy little egoist in me. I was vaguely aware and ashamed of this, so I sometimes made myself consult his wishes for a change. But it seemed he had none, other than those of pleasing me. He had an elderly father and a much younger, frustrated mother who in my memory is always floating extravagantly round the room in tune with the gramophone. Billy's health was parlous. He was anaemic and had regularly to consume raw liver, something that made him almost vomit to chew. His compensating dream was to become a tough professional soldier 'when I'm a man.' To which his pirouetting mother once responded gaily: 'If, Billy, you live to be a man.' I never forgot that remark: it has lingered with me, the prime example of The Thought You Never Utter.

Billy and I spent many a happy holiday at the Crystal Palace where everything was rather frighteningly gigantic: the great glass galleries, the statues of huge upreared horses it was a small terror to stand under, and the marvellous, lifesize prehistoric monsters wrought on an island in the grounds. Billy liked to watch the motorcycle dirt track races, but I didn't because the fears here were fact, not fantasy, when a rider crashed or some spectators scattered in alarm.

Another delight was the shilling all-day ticket you could get on the trams. With this we explored London, day after day of the holidays, the *pièce de résistance* being the fairly new 33 route through the Kingsway subway. Its surfacing at Southampton Row was a terror that never lost its force and fascination. When the tram halted at the peak of its incredibly steep rise, I could never believe it would make it. Upstairs in the front we would hold our breath and hear the hammering of our hearts. For what brake could possibly restrain this 45-degree juggernaut? How could its iron wheels grip iron rails? What power could launch it from a standstill over that last terrible hump? I would gaze back down our precipitous ascent and freeze myself with a picture of that backward plunge to oblivion, with a rehearsal of the agonized screams, the shattering glass, the sickening crunch of mangled metal and bones. With overwhelming relief we would reach horizontal safety, and I'd lead Billy off to the British Museum, whose Egyptian galleries, thanks to Rider Haggard, were my especial delight at that time. (I had rather fallen for the boy-king Tutankhamun.)

Our other great day out was at the London Zoo, where I became fiercely addicted to the study of certain marvellous bipeds for which the Zoological Society could claim no credit. For one day, weary after making several tours of our favourite creatures, I espied an obviously rapt crowd on a bridge over the canal. Drawing closer, I saw mothers dragging away reluctant little girls, and ladies passing quickly on after the first curious glance. When, with all a small boy's ruthlessness, I had elbowed my way to the front of the now all-male throng, and climbed the balustrade with a ferocious disregard for safety, oh, what a reward for my goggling eyes! There on the bank they stood shivering, some half dozen of those flaxen-polled London urchins I adored, of all ages and sizes from ten to sixteen. And all stark naked. There they stood with chattering teeth, one or two of the older ones making a half-hearted show of covering their private parts with their hands, and one and all gazing up at us like hungry puppies. Then I discovered why, as a man near me threw a penny into the water. At once all the boys dived in, surfaced, and dived again and again with flashing buttocks and waving feet. I soon learned the ropes, *my* ropes, at any rate. I would let them stand on the bank as I feasted my eyes frontally, then, when I desired other perspectives, I would throw in one of my precious pennies and consider that surely was a pleasure never cheaper bought. The intoxicating spectacle ended only when a portly policeman hove into sight at the end of the towpath. The divers grabbed their clothes and fled with shrieks of simulated terror.

After this, poor Billy was dragged to the Zoo again and again. And once inside I would make a dash for my stolen waters. Sometimes I was lucky. Sometimes the canal bank was empty and Billy had to bear the brunt of my unaccountable sulks. And for the first time there must have entered my unconscious mind some realization that the uniformed law rigidly opposed my dearest pleasures.

Friendships such as those with Robbie and Billy were neither erotic nor romantic. Sometimes in bored moments they might take a fleeting physical turn, but only for an uncommitted giggle. My fantasy life of romantic friendship was something far removed from this, and a source of idealism and pain, the pain of contrasting my dream world with that around me. If I had at that time known Sir Philip Sidney's claim that the gods deliver us a brazen world but the poet gives us a golden one, then I might have diagnosed my pain as a poet's. Luckily, I didn't.

At school, I had the reputation of being pure and noble, for I never joined in their smutty talk, never used bad language, never grabbed at fly buttons or made indecent gestures. This was because I wanted to be worthy of my dream world, which was becoming more and more like some story of beautiful endeavour which had cast me as its hero. This, together with my discovery at age twelve of the auto-erotic pleasures, was producing in me a reserve that removed me even further from my healthy, uncomplicated fellows. And with all this grew a horrible conviction of my own utter hypocrisy, for I knew that if the boys were attractive, I had an eye and an ear eager enough for their silly antics. Alas, my public image was all too credible and they soon learned not to take their innocent animal pleasures before my corrupter gaze.

My father, as his nicely engraved visiting cards told me, was now managing director of a builders' combine in Knightsbridge, and his Jekyll and Hyde manifestations became more frequent and more marked. The distance between him and my mother also increased sadly. Rather I should say between him and all the rest of us, for instinctively we ranged ourselves solidly behind her. We had little choice, for she faultlessly supported the fabric of our world, against which our father's growing threats were as yet fearful but unavailing.

One member of the family was the chief cause of the friction. This was my mother's sister Nora, one of nature's saints with a gift for creating martyrs. She had been with us all my life and I couldn't imagine the family circle without her. Her marriage to a journalist had ended with his death as a war correspondent before I was born. He had left her some rather seedy property in north London from whose rents she derived a small income, and she had returned to her premarital job as a ledger clerk in the City. It was a romantic place I loved to visit. She and another sister, Aunt Madge, worked there in almost Dickensian surroundings: in a counting house designed for Bob Cratchit, perched on high stools at gargantuan desks the like of which I have seen only in *Zéro de conduite*. The little old empire she slaved so happily in had its London headquarters in Upper Thames Street, right on the river bank, where barges delivered great bales of paper straight into its warehouses. Enormous dray horses dragged their loads along the narrow cobbled streets and the smell of hops and yeast from the adjacent brewery flavoured the whole neighbourhood. A neighbourhood which scurried with cheerful life: in and out of the offices and warehouses, the still gaslit pubs and the countless little cafés which fed you in their crowded, crazily staircased rooms, or sold you sandwiches, bread pudding and mouth-watering ham rolls over the counter.

The place swarmed with other life, too. Rats, both terrene and aquatic, abounded, and unending war was waged upon them. But they had a fearless champion in my Aunt Nora. Possessing the innocent's affinity with the animal kingdom, she fed them, sprang their traps, warned them of imminent danger, and wept when one of them fell to the human predator. Near the floor by her desk was a hole though which one could glimpse dirty shingle and restless Thames. Through this, trained to it over the years, would poke one wicked whiskered face after another and feed from her hand. I saw it all, crouching down beside her, quite rapt, when the other clerks had disappeared for lunch.

Nora was small and thin, Aunt Madge small and plump, my mother taller and in between sizes. Nora had inexhaustible energy. She rose long before the sun in winter and with it in summer. She did some initial housework and, in termtime, gave us our breakfasts before she hurtled off to work.

This was after our first maid, Florrie, disappeared. She deserves a word here. She was always in one of two extreme moods: either giggling wildly or weeping bitterly. She was inordinately sensitive and must have been a bit simple. And very religious. She made me feel distinctly uneasy with the large poster she had stuck up in her room: 'Jesus is the unseen guest in this house, the sharer of every meal, the listener to every word,' or something like that. And the first time Florrie brought in the tea tray it contained one additional cup, saucer and plate. I of course assumed this was for Jesus. But no, it was for Florrie. We never dared challenge this for fear of weepings and wailings. So she had tea with us every day except Thursday, which was her day off and the only one on which we could invite anybody of our own. Florrie fortunately married after a few months with us. Just once she invited herself, husband and baby to tea, then vanished forever. Husband and baby were surprisingly presentable. Florrie, I think, went far. She deserved to.

To return to Aunt Nora. Home from her office at about six in the evening, she would regale us with breathless anecdotes from her Thames-side world. All its characters lived for me, all its fun and feuds, all its little victories and tragedies. The occasional grim episode took lasting root in my imagination: the slow decline of Mr Banks' little boy, who did fretwork till his fingers became too locked in dystrophy, and the dreadful death of Jerry, the mischievous office boy, who one foggy night stepped out of his train into the path of another. The radio and television soap operas of today seem tame stuff by comparison with Nora's spirited, artless serial.

Aunt Madge was married to Uncle John who was entirely *non grata* to my parents, for whom he was a sly rogue living off the wife he'd somehow tricked into matrimony. But Aunt Madge presented him to us in quite a different light, as the stern and parsimonious breadwinner beneath whose ideals of childhood excellence we all fell far short. Aunt Madge was, like all my mother's family, almost absurdly generous. She was an habitual dispenser of money and chocolate to us children. But never in front of the breadwinner, and always with the urgent, whispered injunction: 'Don't let your Uncle John know.' They both went out to business, John first and Madge second. She would close her front door, push it, cross the road, and stand and wave farewell to the blank windows of her empty house. Always she did this. Mystified, I once asked her why. 'Burglars,' she said darkly, leaving me more puzzled than ever.

When I knew Uncle John better in after years I found him the most inoffensive and long-suffering of men, who had philosophically weathered a life sentence of his wife's uncertain temper and internecine feuds. They were always moving house, for Aunt Madge specialized in campaigns against neighbours.

Terry, my eldest brother, was Aunt Madge's favourite, and Brian, two years younger than Terry and five years ahead of me, was Nora's. Neither childless aunt had much time for me. I was just there to be tolerated. I didn't mind. I think I somewhere knew I was my mother's favourite, although she never showed any maternal preferences.

12

I had one more aunt on my mother's side and it is fitting she should make her entry last, for she was self-consciously and determinedly top o' the bill. In her earlier years she had been one of those Edwardian beauties who figured on picture postcards, brightly coloured, and spangled with tiny beads of glass to represent tiaras and necklaces. On the strength of this profitable public exposure she had married a famous *maître de ballet* and gone to live with him in South America. Perhaps he died, or they were divorced, for when I saw her she was the wife of a megalithic ship's captain one saw very rarely and then reluctantly. I have always felt that Carlyle's description fitted Uncle Charles much better than William Wordsworth: 'a cold, hard, silent, practical man, of an immense head and great jaws like a crocodile's.'

This Aunt Barbie was distinctly snooty and had brought up her two sons and her daughter to be the same. The two boys boarded at a minor public school where Aunt Barbie's *grande dame* act was so convincing that one year she was invited to present the prizes on speech day. My mother, who herself had none, found these pretensions rather amusingly silly. Unless they went too far, when she was quite capable of giving her elder sister a good dressing down. I saw this on one occasion and was astonished not only by my mother's daring but by the rapidity of my aunt's deflation. It was when we met her outside some place we were to lunch in. I timorously raised my cap, but Aunt Barbie promptly snatched it from my head with the words: 'You take your cap *off* to me.' Mother then told her to stop her play-acting which was impressing nobody.

She would come over to lunch with daughter Valerie, who was aged between Pam and me and whom I once described to her face as 'exactly like Elizabeth Bott in the William books.' Sometimes she would be spiteful with Pam, and then I hit her. Aunt Barbie said witheringly: 'Fancy a boy hitting a girl, and one younger than himself.' To which, quite unabashed, I replied: 'She asked for it.'

They never came over to us by public transport. Often a neighbour of theirs, a dimly conventional figure with furs and nasty poodle, would drive them over and, after eating a lunch I resented as greedier than mine, fight a losing fireside battle over sleep. And if this comatose lady couldn't bring her, Aunt Barbie hired a chauffeur-driven car. This was an extravagance against which the ship's captain raged whenever he docked, this, and her drinks bill. She always brought a bottle of wine with her and, since mother and Nora didn't touch it, and the tranter took only a few genteel sips, she downed most of the bottle. Sometimes, when I was rather older, I would say sweetly: 'May I have a drop please, Aunt Barbie?' I didn't like it, but I did enjoy her attempt to conceal her venom as she grudgingly poured me a little.

She was never one hundred per cent English, in word or deed. She called coffee 'cawfee' and depot 'deep-oh.' She pronounced 'clerk' as it was written and always referred to knickerbockers by the even absurder name of 'bombatchers.' An india rubber was a 'bungie.' She would elaborately greet one by seizing one's face between her hands and then planting ritual Gallic kisses on both cheeks. I also owe to her one anecdote as imperishable in my mind as Jenny's tale of the bed of earth. It concerned her native servant in Manaos who was chopping wood when a tarantula leapt out and bit his hand. Without a second's hesitation he chopped off his hand at the wrist 'and so saved his life.'

Poor Aunt Barbie. As an adult I grew quite fond of her. I, and Pam even more, found her determined efforts to live and tipple lavishly somehow gallant and touching. The last time she came to lunch with me, I noticed her preoccupation with a tall, round tin in which I kept old paintbrushes. I commented on this and she said, with a kind of wistful honesty, as though it didn't matter any more: 'I was just thinking: what a marvellous place to hide a bottle.'

13

I think we children enjoyed my mother's anecdotes best of all. At teatime, or over long breakfasts in the school holidays. She was a great dreamer. Nobody was more alert or dominant in waking hours, but in bed at night, or occasionally during an afternoon nap, she would plumb the most entertaining depths. We would wait for it to come: 'I had *such* a funny dream last night.' Then she'd launch into a farrago that had us alternately shivering with mock fear or shouting with laughter. None of it was invented and the seeds of much of it she could herself identify in events of the preceding day. We all got quite skilled in such hermeneutics. Once she dreamt, well in advance, a winning outsider in the Derby. And once the death of a very fit young actor who succumbed to a heart attack.

Sometimes we'd have to prompt her. 'Didn't you have any dreams last night?' 'No,' she'd say. 'No, I don't think I did.' So we had to get her talking about her childhood and the beaux she'd had before my father came on the scene and captured her heart. About her parents and about her dear old Uncle William, who was a naturalist and lived in a wonderful old house called Lord Mayor's Cottage, where once Oliver Cromwell or Charles I had successfully taken refuge. She had spent many a childhood summer there and I knew from her loving descriptions that it had been 'the real thing,' pure, unenclosed, unroaded countryside. Her father had been a clerk at the Royal Courts of Justice, a humorous old man with many a grisly yarn about poisoners and gibbets. Her mother was German. She came from Leipzig and was a Wagner and actually a distant cousin of the great Richard, or so we were told. But all this was recounted in hushed tones, for in the war they'd had to play an elaborate and successful game of deception to prevent her internment. Nan, as we called her, had also lived in Paris, where the beauty of her hands and feet made her a successful artist's model. I thought of her later when I read *Trilby*. I have one sharp memory of her. She lay on a couch, dying. I stood before her, aged four or five, and eyed the bunch of luscious grapes on her table. 'May I have one, Nan?' I asked. 'Yes,' she replied slowly, 'but only one, my little piglet.' And she smiled from a face already beautiful with death. The face, the setting, above all the words with their unenglish intonation, remained with me always.

In the happy, far-off days of her childhood, mother told us, their big house was never still. There were four girls and a boy, and always strings of German guests. There was Plaut, quite a clown, and Stüdemann ('he was very handsome and wanted to marry me, but I wouldn't go and live in Germany'), and the intimidating Fräulein Tisch, who had a deep voice and big feet and disappeared in May 1914: 'Oh, it was a man dressed up, you know. A spy. No doubt about that.' Then we'd all laugh long and loud at the thought of the Fräulein's difficulty in sustaining her role.

'Didn't she have to shave?' we asked.

'Supposing you were out somewhere and she wanted to go to the lavatory?'

'Didn't any men try to chat her up?'

'Oh, she was far too unattractive for that.'

Then, as the laughter subsided, mother would conclude the session with her usual disconcerting sigh: 'Well, I don't know what we've got to laugh about, I'm sure.'

Sometimes, skating on thin ice, we'd ask her how she'd met our father. A faraway look came into her eyes. 'Well, I think my father brought him to the house one day. I don't know how or where they'd met. He was so good-looking and so well dressed.' Then, in a darker strain, and more to herself than to us: 'He told me once, before we were married, that if he once started to drink, he'd never be able to leave it alone. Weak, you see.'

I have photos of them both from those years. Their good looks are very different: his, mild, amiable, a little insipid; hers, purposeful, with more than a hint of intransigence. I stare at them and try to grasp the mystery that, blended, these two made me.

Mother made of her sister Nora and of her children a wall through which my father could seldom penetrate. Aunt Nora was his principal bane. Once, when spitefully drunk, he spoke to me of her as 'your mother's bloody Siamese twin.' That was his punishment. Whether this exclusion was the cause or the result of his drinking I never could decide. Probably even they could not remember whether his plastered, ten o'clock homecomings began before or after the hostile phalanx formed.

But there it certainly was. We'd be happily chatting round the fire in the drawing room when we'd hear his key fumbling in the lock. Silence would fall. We waited, ears strained, and I'd silently pray: 'Please God, don't let him come in here, make him go straight to bed.'

Sometimes he would, switching off all the lights and cursing audibly. Sometimes he would go into the dining room and mess about with his dinner, all congealed on the hotplate.

Occasionally, he would open the drawing room door and stand swaying on the threshold, meeting our hatred with his own. 'My family,' he'd sneer, 'my wonderful family.' Nora would gaze into the fire, plucking her handkerchief to pieces, her eyes big with fear. I'd look ashamed, Brian defiant, Terry just irritable. Pam was still too young to fear an ogre and had to be restrained on mother's lap.

Then my prayers would be all for mother. 'Please God, make her ignore him. Don't let her say anything and then he'll go.' But I despaired of that prayer even as she was saying with cold contempt: 'Get out of here. You're a disgrace.' Then the vile slanging match would commence. Perhaps he'd say something I didn't understand which was hurtful enough to make her cry. That was the ultimate agony for me, worse even than the times when I'd pushed myself between them.

Every night I hated him with a smouldering, hopeless hatred, and every morning my heart would break with pity for him, and I don't know which was worse. I would go to absurd lengths to spare him the embarrassment of meeting me in the morning, even hiding in rooms and round corners to avoid him. But inevitably we met and, without a vestige of the pride and guilt I thought must be consuming him, he would say cheerfully: 'Hullo, lad, how's the bike going now?' or 'Did you get all your homework done, Peter?'

I never could fathom it out. Was this nice morning Jekyll really unaware of Hyde's nocturnal shame? And therefore not responsible for it? Or was it all bluff? I felt so sorry for him, but couldn't bear to admit it to myself. I couldn't forget the old days when we'd been fond of each other. So when he ruffled my hair and gave me sixpence I could scarcely whisper: 'Thank you, daddy.'

Sundays were especially difficult. He would drift about the house all morning, singing, and asking my mother questions like: 'Can I help with the lunch, dear?' or 'Shall I set the table, darling?' For a while she'd ignore him altogether and I had to pretend I too hadn't heard his question. But after a time she would make a brief reply and I'd know the ice was melting.

After tea I'd sometimes entertain them to a gramophone recital. I was a sort of archetypal disc jockey, saying a few words about each composer as gleaned from our old encyclopaedia. Apart from the usual show pieces I would play records by those great artists, Layton and Johnstone, and these would contribute peculiar tensions to the recital, for so many of their songs seemed painfully appropriate to my parents' conflicts. I couldn't believe I was the only one to see this. I would watch my father secretly for signs of discomfiture as they sang 'Some day you'll be sorry that you grieved me' and 'Forgive me, I didn't mean to make you cry' and 'What can I say, dear, after I've said I'm sorry?', all words that seemed to distil the whole week's marital clashes, but which apparently were water off a duck's back so far as the others were concerned. It puzzled me that the embarrassment should be mine alone, but I couldn't talk to anyone about it.

On the whole, these Sundays were happy little oases. For hours at a time I could almost believe we were the united, affectionate family I dreamed of. In the evening, father and I would prepare coffee and sandwiches and cheese and celery and load them on the trolley with the sausage rolls and jam tarts that mother had spent half the day making. Father put me off blue cheeses for life by assuring me their coloured veins were made by maggots. I think he coveted the gorgonzola for himself alone.

I would often read to Pam, who was so abnormally tender-hearted that she began weeping long before the protagonist in the story suffered, especially if he were four-footed. I could never get past the first stanza of Tennyson's *Queen of the May* before her tears flowed and I was told to stop teasing her.

On these Sunday interludes Nora would keep a low profile over her book and father would politely press sandwiches on her. Mother would read, one after another, all the Sunday papers. She had an omnivorous appetite for newspapers and would share gobbets from them with anyone who would listen. Brian and Terry might play cards or discuss in undertones certain local schoolgirls they favoured. Father would smoke his pipe and read his book. He got through scores of books in a year, and every single one was a detective story.

14

I was growing apace. Down was evident on my upper lip, voice control was becoming uncertain, hands and feet even more refractory. And I didn't like it. I didn't want to lose so soon what I cherished in others. Even my current idol, who was almost sixteen, was still stirringly smooth of cheek and light of voice. His name was Carter and I considered him by far the handsomest boy in the school. Handsome in a curiously 'cad' fashion, which added to his charms. I had made up my mind to inspect him in the pavilion showers on Parents' Day.

Now that I no more fouled a football pitch or picked a long stop's desperate daisies, I had graciously consented to become a steward on Parents' Day, the only boy elevated to this office, that of an official greeter of visitors and seller of programmes. I knew why I had been chosen for this honour: because my appearance was acceptable and my manners couldn't be faulted. It was a lucrative job, for most of the visitors felt committed to a lordly 'Oh, keep the change.' So into one pocket of my blazer went the programme dues and into the other the tips, and it was in keeping with my new, self-conscious idealism that I never once cheated. Indeed, when I occasionally refused payment from someone who looked rather poor or very attractive, I punctiliously transferred a shilling from tips pocket to dues pocket.

Once the proceedings were well under way, I stationed myself near the changing rooms and kept my eyes skinned for Carter, who was, of course, a successful athlete. Several times he entered and emerged, but at last the length of his stay and the point we had reached in the agenda assured me that he was having his shower.

So he was indeed, and no one else in there, because only Carter would be so selfish as to cut the events he wasn't displaying himself in. I lurked behind pegs of clothes till he emerged and then I stood, incautiously lost in wonder, as he dried himself slowly and sensually. A Greek god, a perfection of adolescence, and there was something about the way in which he caressed his body with the towel that suggested even he himself was not blind to the marvel that he was.

Then he saw me and, in the manner of cads, curled his lip. 'Having a good eyeful, Gamble?' he asked. There was a world of scorn in his voice.

'Yes,' I said simply. It was all I could think to say. A lie would have been so fatuous. And how would he have taken the truth: 'I am admiring you because you are so beautiful'?

All he did was to turn his back and say over his shoulder: 'You know what you are, Gamble? You're a bloody mess, that's what you are.'

I didn't care. Nor did I go, because, contrary to expectation, the rear view was almost as pleasing as the front one.

I think that was the only conversation cad Carter and I ever had. He became a prosperous businessman, a silent Tory MP, and died in his early fifties. He never knew that for the whole of my thirteenth year he was all the world to me.

15

Montrose, being mostly a day school, was depressingly 'normal' in its boy relationships. Romantic friendships seemed unknown to all but me. More and more I was coming to see that I inhabited a world not designed for the likes of me; a world so perverse that my fellows were actually fascinated by the local girls' high school when here on their doorstep was the possibility of love 'passing the love of women.' Even so, for one whole summer term, I had an almost idyllic relationship with a slightly younger boy called Gerald White. He was attractive and rather shy and perpetually astonished by my overtures. 'Really, Gamble,' he'd say with a yielding giggle, 'I didn't know *you* were like this.' He was responsive, even gave hints of affection, so that this affair came nearer than any so far to real romantic love on my part. But in September it was as vanished as if it had not been. We never referred to it again, though even then I suspected I'd never forget it.

Perhaps, I thought, people like me were a sort of sideline for boy-god Eros, a mischievous hobby he was careful to conceal from his orthodox mamma. For he certainly wasn't going to let me off the hook. After the delightful fulfilment of Gerald White he sent me a tantalizing vision of the unattainable. He was Master Graham Payn, a 14-year-old boy soprano who had twice granted me an epiphany on the stage of the Streatham Astoria.

We were entering the great age of the supercinemas, and both Brixton and Streatham could now vie with Xanadu in their stately pleasure domes. The Brixton Astoria's motif was the universe, no less, beginning with a rosy sun suffusing auroral clouds and ending with a great night sky atwinkle with stars. The Streatham Astoria was dressed as a palace from ancient Egypt, adorned with all the treasures a thousand near-mummified bourgeoisie could desire.

I spent occasional Saturday afternoons, with mother, aunt and little sister, in one or other of these dream worlds. You got two major films and a quite spectacular stage show for ninepence: never before or since did we have it so good. Not that I can claim to have appreciated it. So many of the films were westerns or musicals and I was allergic to both. The stage shows, too, were either boring or embarrassing. Comedians weren't funny, jugglers juggled and tap-dancers tapped in vain, while troupes of dancing girls almost sent me to sleep. So when the infrequent highlights came (Clive Brook in *Cavalcade* and Laughton in *The Barretts of Wimpole Street*, for example) they were dazzling indeed.

Then, one afternoon, before my incredulous and enraptured eyes, I was rewarded for all my hours of boredom by the descent of this angel upon the stage. Master Graham made his studiously modest bow, opened his pretty lips and wafted me on high with 'Hear my prayer' and 'Oh, for the wings of a dove.' I thought him lovely to look at, eye-moistening to listen to, and, to add to the pain of my longing, he was dressed in an Eton collar and bumfreezer. The artful amalgam of purity and greasepaint, of soulfulness and spotlights, reduced me to sternly concealed adoration. It was an experience of the numinous, and sandwiched between the O'Gorman Brothers and Terry's Juveniles.

Master Graham was later to shine in Coward revue and to become the Master's devoted and lifelong friend. But I can't believe he ever shone as unforgettably for anyone as he did at fourteen for me.

I have said that his stage uniform added to my pain. This was because the inhabitants of my secret Eden wore just such clothes. One exciting day, in the loft of our new Streatham home, I had found three large, tattered volumes of *The Boy's Own Paper*, bound-up issues of the 1890s. Their intrinsic fascination for me was intensified by the fact that all of them 'spoke of something that was gone,' gave 'thoughts that lie too deep for tears.' It was the old burden of nostalgia, it was Mrs Mackenzie's painting brought a little nearer the knuckle. For many of the splendidly written stories were set in such great public schools as Arnold had dreamed up: Christian in their fears, stoic in their struggles, platonic in their loves. The *BOP* correspondence columns enjoined cold baths and threatened hellfire, while their fictional characters skated deliciously on the thinnest of comradely ice. It was all fare just made for me. The stories, the excellent illustrations, the mere evocative titles, conjured for me worlds of high romance. I found titles especially haunting when, in the fashion of those days, they were accompanied by alternatives that seemed to extend the magic vistas: 'Burton and Son OR Found on the Shore,' 'Heroes of the Fourth OR Friends for Life,' 'Allan Adair OR Here and There in Many Lands.' My favourite was so rich in suggestion that it neither had nor needed an alternative. It was 'The Russian Prince and the Cabin-Boy,' and it was maddeningly cut short at the end of the third volume, so I never discovered what they got up to.

I had for some years been pouncing upon and devouring almost any book that fell before me. Most were presents or prizes given to my parents and aunts. I read *The Wide, Wide World* because, like Everest, 'it was there,' and in the same way I romped through Rhoda Broughton and Marie Corelli. I distinctly remember being disturbed by the reactions of the characters in these novels. Nuances and subtleties were at that time lost on me, so that what these people said and did seemed rather frighteningly crazy: Elinor Glyn read like Kafka.

But there were no such troubles with school stories. Those *BOP* volumes gave me my first taste for the genre, those and a dog-eared tome called *Three Years at Wolverton, by An Old Boy*, which I grew very fond of for its sad old text and sad old pictures. Soon I began to seek out school stories: Thomas Hughes, H. A. Vachell, Tom Bevan, Gordon Stables, Talbot Baines Reed, all became favourite authors. And, of course, those two marvellous boys' weeklies, *The Magnet* and *The Gem*, in which the redoubtable Frank Richards had created an immutable boy-world for people like me. In his famous essay, 'Boys' Weeklies,' Orwell analysed their appeal in terms of snobbery, chauvinism, wealth-fantasy and political nostalgia. All very true, but he oddly missed what was surely one element in their success: their paedophilic appeal. When many years later, I met Frank Richards, I wondered which aspects of his astonishing output had satisfied *him* most.

So the lost Eden of my imagination became the traditional public boarding school: that exclusive, all male hothouse which was already changing even as I appropriated it. Of course, I adapted and refined the materials I used: my dream schoolboys were more intelligent and more sensitive than those I found in print. *My* boy-Eden was, in defiance of Genesis and theology, both pre-Eve and post-lapsarian. *My* boys had never heard of girls and, though essentially moral, knew no silly piety, had no silly hang-ups about private sex. 'Essentially moral'? Yes, indeed, for I insisted their moral beauty matched their physical beauty, in that they would never stoop to smut, deceit, lies, dishonesty or, above all, disloyalty. They lived for their friendships and would unhesitatingly have died for them.

I wasn't bemused by this Eden I had fashioned. If one foot was planted firmly in it, the other was no less surely set in the no-less-loved world of common, daily fact. Mercifully so, for that was how I kept my balance, remained sane in the stormy adolescent years. I knew, for example, that it would be quite disastrous for me to become a pupil in such a school. While I liked my Tom Browns and David Blaizes and John Verneys and Harry Whartons to suffer in such institutions (for that enabled me to empathize with them, cast myself as their champion), I was perfectly well aware that I wouldn't myself last more than a few weeks there. If I didn't walk out, I'd be thrown out.

However, despite this, I knew twinges of temptation when, in my thirteenth year, it was mooted that I should go to Dulwich College, which still projected the classic public school image. Its boys looked, I thought, so very nice in the little caps perched on the backs of their heads, and quite ravishing in their summer term boaters. Surely amongst them I might find that ideal friend who eluded me at Montrose?

So I read and weighed every word of the literature Dulwich had sent to my father. And knew it was assuredly not for me. Of course, it all looked far worse in cold print than it could be in fact, but I wasn't to know that. I read with mounting horror of all the rules and regulations, of compulsory games and PT and medicals and OTC. I foresaw nothing but regimentation and exploitation, and I wisely, but sadly, decided to continue my almost-reign in my almost-Hell.

Yet I did more. I wrote quite a passionate letter of protest to the chairman of the Dulwich governors, a Major General Lord Loch. I have his reply before me now:

Sir,
Have you ever stopped to consider how impossible life would be if everyone
were as self-centred as you seem to be?
                              Yours faithfully,
                                   Loch.

God knows what I had written to the poor man, but it was, I suppose, decent
of him to reply even in those chilling terms.

I was indeed becoming painfully self-conscious. And developing certain
compulsion neuroses without anyone to reassure me that they were quite
common in adolescence. One such was Dr Johnson's own: the need to touch
a certain number of railings or gateposts in the course of a walk, OR ELSE...
My own 'OR ELSE' was, typically, the fear that I'd get home to a family
disaster: the death of my mother or an accident to my little sister.

I didn't know who I was or what I wanted. Soul and body were playing
me up. In one mood I coveted a deprived urchin to educate and refine. In
another, I dreamed of seducing some fair and noble youth. Locked in to
myself, I sometimes thought I must be some kind of a freak. But somebody
helped me keep a sense of proportion, preserved the clarity of my eye, made
sure the founts of laughter were kept bubbling. And that was Charles
Dickens.

When I was ten or eleven I spent some wretched weeks in bed with a
mastoid. A neighbour lent me *The Old Curiosity Shop* and it proved the
perfect anodyne. It is the only time in my life that a book has made me forget
real physical pain. I didn't cry again until I'd finished it, and those tears
sprang from the pain of parting. Thus began my Dickens craze, which has
never really ended, although now I can laugh at the havoc he played with my
developing social consciousness. He gave me a sharp sense of human
caricature, convinced me wealth was a sure corruption and all poverty was
ennobling. He made me both very knowing and very sentimental, and he
confirmed for me forever the Jesus-eye perspective on mankind.

16

Then when I was thirteen I had my accident and as a result met a novel so
perfectly attuned to me that it set the seal on what I was and in large measure
shaped what I was to be.

I was a reckless cyclist, with an unfortunate habit of attending more to
what was following than to what lay in front. Brian and Terry had a
succession of rather glamorous bikes with romantic carbide lamps and bells
that whirred implacably. Mine was a humble second-hand machine with a
back-pedal brake I never fully adapted to.

I had cycled to Streatham High Road to get some cakes for tea. I was to
get a shilling's worth and, since they were advertised as 'seven for sixpence,' I

expected fourteen of them. But a rather unpleasant woman in the shop insisted they were thirteen for a shilling, and so I set out to prove to her how illogical this was. We both became rather heated.

'Don't come in here with your airs and try to teach me my job,' she snapped.

'Well, someone ought to,' I countered, and added that I would buy seven for sixpence, leave the shop and return immediately for a further seven for sixpence.

'I wouldn't serve you,' she cried angrily, so I told her I'd take my custom elsewhere.

I expect my indignation made me an even less competent cyclist. I was speeding along the busy High Road, continually glancing over my shoulder to make sure nothing would run me down from the rear. Suddenly there was an explosive impact followed by oblivion. I wasn't unconscious for more than a couple of minutes. When I came to, I found myself lying in the road, my face covered with blood which was flowing on to my shirt and blazer. I was surrounded by people more curious than helpful. My eyes fixed on two teeth lying in the road beside me: big teeth complete with their roots. I thought this was odd but didn't really register they were my teeth. Then I saw my bike. It was under a lorry and looked quite undamaged. I got up, fell down, and got up again. I began to pull my bike clear, helped now by a nice young labourer from some nearby roadworks. The handlebars were out of true but he soon straightened them by putting the front wheel between his strong legs. Then he said I ought to sit down and wait for an ambulance. He said someone had gone to find a policeman and the policeman would call an ambulance.

Muzzy though I was, I worked out what had happened. The lorry was stationary and facing the right way. I had simply gone full tilt into it from the rear and, because its tailboard was fairly high, taken the full force of the collision on my face. Then I realized an ambulance would be speeding me to hospital if I didn't act fast. The labourer, protesting but out of his depth, guided me and my bike to a horse trough just round the corner and there he washed my face. I clearly remember thinking how absurd it was to be washing in a horse trough but also how nice it was to be washed by him. Then, thanking him humbly, I rode slowly and shakily home.

Of course, the doctor was called and of course he sent me to hospital for an X-ray. Nothing much seemed to be wrong and I wasn't detained, but for a couple of months I was a weekly outpatient at Guy's hospital. How I loathed the indignity of it all, the lack of privacy, the bored and clinical eyes inspecting me, the new and nasty sense of being a Thing. The young intern once called in the consultant for an opinion. Embarrassed and resentful, I endured the expert's appraisal then heard him say: 'Um-m-m, typical.' To this day I have no idea what he meant. Had it been years later, and had his been the psychiatrist's ear rather than the physician's eye, his comment might have made more sense. All I really discovered was that I'd slightly damaged one eye, and even this, after a few months behind what I secretly considered a rather fetching eyeshade, righted itself and left no ill effects.

But Guy's outdid Gilead in another balm it supplied. This came via a kindly Sister who took rather a fancy to me and liked to discuss books. 'Have you,' she asked, 'ever read a book called *Tell England*?' I shook my head. 'Well, you must. I know you'll like it.' And she wrote it down for me: '*Tell England*, by Ernest Raymond.'

I asked father to give me a copy for Christmas. And how right that dear Sister was. I still wonder how much rare perspicacity lay behind her recommendation. For had he written it to my own specification Mr Raymond could not have served me better. In every sense it was just what the doctor ordered.

Tell England is an innocent book, full of touching acceptance, unspoiled ideals and unselfconscious love. I recognized at once that the author was himself in love with his dazzling boy protagonists, and that as never before by any book that love had been re-created in me. The first half of *Tell England* is a school story of a vintage so rare that it seemed to unroll before me the whole panoply of my secret Eden: a brew I think even its author found heady enough to betray him into an incautious comment by a character on the beauty of the boy Rupert Ray. He would, says the school doctor, have won first prize in a boy show. There is, of course, no such thing as a Boy Show, except in the humorous fantasy some of us sometimes permit ourselves.

The second half of the book is a war story, set in the wicked waste of Gallipoli, where Raymond himself had served. Astonishingly, neither half of the book implies condemnation: either of the repressive, conveyor-belt public school system, or of the massacre of the innocents by feuding nations. I could not read *Tell England* now, but then it seemed to me the most beautiful book in the world. I wept buckets over it, just as its author intended. I also reacted in ways he would not have wished. I questioned the public school's right to constrict the individual and I bitterly denied the state's right to annihilate him.

Yes, the book shattered me. The loss of Rupert Ray and Edgar Gray Doe was felt as a personal bereavement, and one that could be assuaged only by my vow to be worthy of them. I told myself that for their sakes I must strive for higher ideals than those I commonly saw around me. For their sakes I would dedicate my life to friendships nothing could betray. Too easy now to smile at what was, after all, testimony to the ethical value of an intense aesthetic experience.

I dearly wished to share this experience, but there wasn't anybody to share it with. This was an old problem: the adolescent's thwarted need to describe his love. And the fear of casting a dear pearl before an unsuspected swine.

Finally I got my brother Brian to read *Tell England*. He liked it but he wasn't devastated by it. Intuitively, I knew it didn't go with his world of cars and girls. And he had a cruel eye for the ridiculous. No romantic little sentimentalist like me, he could fasten on Mr Raymond's less successful traits, inflate them, and stick his pin in them. I would try in vain to maintain disapproval as he elaborated his parody:

'Doe stood at the wicket, his pretty girlish lips parted to reveal a mouthful of black, rotting teeth'; '"Marvellous arse that Doe's got," said Dr Chapman approvingly, as Housemaster Radley's jaw set in jealous rage.'

And one afternoon, he invented a film version of *Tell England* with Wee Georgie Wood as Doe, Mickey Rooney as Ray, Jackie Searle as Pennybet, and a gallery of American bit-part actors (on whom we were by now authorities) outrageously miscast all along the line: De Witt Jennings as Radley, J. Farrell Macdonald as Dr Chappy, Franklin Pangborn as Padre Monty. Up he piled the horrors until, ashamed of my perfidy, I was impelled to join in.

But the hunger to share my joy in the book at length produced a solution so obvious that I couldn't imagine why it had taken so long to find. Who better to talk to about it than its creator? So I poured out my grateful heart to Mr Raymond (c/o Cassell and Company) in terms I suspect were more off-putting than flattering. However, he wrote me a charming reply. I sent him my nice, leather-bound edition for his autograph. He wrote in it a personal message, a quotation from one of his other novels, suggesting that only joy in living could justify life. I wrote again. (The young seldom know when to stop, and I certainly didn't.) He then recommended me to read his *We, the Accused*: 'a much better book.' I did so, and admired it greatly, but loyally reasserted my greater love for *Tell England*.

Then he invited me to have tea with him at his house in Haywards Heath. I went, but it was a mistake. Not that he failed me in any way. He was kindness itself, even took me for a long ride in his car so that he could point out the Sussex settings of his later novels. But I was too shy, too filled with silent veneration, to create anything but the most insipid impression. And miserably I knew it.

We corresponded spasmodically for several years. I sent him books I admired and reviews I wrote. And in my last letter I told him how, for better or for worse, he had in large part shaped me. I hope it didn't sound like a rebuke.

For *Tell England* was to make me a pacifist, and *We, the Accused* (his finest achievement, based on the Crippen case) made me a dedicated campaigner against the death penalty. And Doe and Ray continued to lead me, like Housman's 'Merry Guide,' through much mud and tares but also fresh fields and pastures old as time.

17

Now nearing fourteen, I was beginning to realize not simply how different I was from my fellows but also perhaps why. One day I asked Brian (for whose knowledge of life I had great respect): 'What's a homosexual?' It wasn't really an innocent question because I'd been secretly reading all I could find about Oscar Wilde, but I was quite unprepared for Brian's casual answer:

'Oh, that's what you are.'

Blushing was a wretched affliction at that time and for many years after. Deep, scarlet blushes that suffused face and neck and lingered abominably as I stooped to pick up unreal objects or jumped from the table to fetch needless cutlery.

On this occasion I instantly became a tomato which I tried to hide in a handkerchief. 'Why?' I asked, in poorly feigned amusement. 'Why do you think I'm one?'

'Well,' said Brian, who was enjoying my discomfort, 'you're not interested in girls, are you?'

'I don't really know any,' was my feeble response. (Was my life's secret so horribly easy to lay bare?)

'Exactly.' Brian was pleased with his cleverness. 'That's just what I mean.'

Actually, I did know a couple of girls and knew one of them was very keen on me. Not girls of my finding, of course, but somewhat older friends of Pam, my sister, who was now attending a rather snooty girls' school in Dulwich. These two girls were always in and out of our house, one in pursuit of horses (she and Pam went to a nearby riding school), and the other in pursuit of me. This latter was Joan, a thoroughly nice girl with strong views on everything, especially marriage, for she had a father, a retired naval commander turned cinema manager, who was (she hinted darkly) a philanderer husband and an indifferent parent. Joan was a hundred-per-cent female in both appearance and character, which could not recommend her in my eyes. But I quite liked her as a person and especially enjoyed arguing with her, heatedly and at length, until she scared me off with some such remark as: 'I don't know how such a sweet person can hold such dreadful views.' Poor Joan could not go for long without offering an endearment, signalling an appeal for affection, and that was my warning light. I escaped if I could. If not, I displayed a deafness, an obtuseness, that must have caused a sad conflict between her need and her almost perfect propriety. I've had to play the same silly game often enough since.

With the alliterative Hyacinth Hazel O'Higgins it was quite different. She was strikingly pretty with distinctly boyish good looks. In fact I'd seen her as a boy in one of their school plays and was torn between a fantasist's desire and a realist's frustration. She was also still in the tomboy stage, with no more desire to evince breasts than I had to behold them. So we got on well. I recall grooming myself with care to take her out one evening a few years later. It's a vivid memory because unique in my life. I remember at the time wondering rather confusedly why I was doing it.

She was an attractive personality who, as Hy Hazell, was to become one of Britain's leading musical comedy stars and no mean actress. I saw her occasionally in after years and we enjoyed reminiscing. She died tragically young.

Now in the upper school at Montrose, I was forming new relationships with masters. Mr Bullock was small, dapper, and insufferably pompous, but after one or two brushes with him I decided he was all right, mainly because he was keen on English as creative writing, and so was I. The closest I came to something like popularity at school was when he read out some imaginative essay of mine and the form applauded.

The most conventional of men, he nevertheless gave us literary advice which made a lasting impression on me.

'Get out of the rut,' he yapped. 'Don't be a ten-a-penny. Original, always original, that's what you must be if you're going to get anywhere.' It was bad advice, especially for me, leading me into bizarre emulations and absurd posturings that I hoped all would see as very original indeed.

But he was generous and encouraging. He lent me, whenever I asked, his portable typewriter, which must have been a rarely prized possession for he was pretty poor. For it, I gladly endured, and even defended, his pomposity, his rather impossible idea of discipline.

I once asked him, with an acute shyness of which he was quite unaware, if he had ever read a book called *Tell England*.

'*Teddington*, sir, *Teddington*? Never heard of it,' he barked back. I gave up and never again tried to give him my heart. But we remained friends. After Mr Stewart retired, his pile made, Mr Bullock inherited the school, moved it to Devonshire, and tried to give it the air of Greyfriars. One of his pupils there was John Osborne, the playwright. I imagine he was goaded beyond endurance by the little martinet, for he once smacked poor Mr Bullock's face. I hope he came to regret it, if only because soon after that Mr Bullock, loyally cheering his boys from the touchline despite a heavy cold, succumbed to pneumonia and died. His reign was brief but I'm glad he had it. He had always demanded rather than earned respect, but to those who gave it he was a good friend.

Mr Vyvyan was a very different kettle of fish. He was a friend and patron of Mr Hector, whom he had taught as a boy, and I knew quite well that Mr Hector had warned him against me as an odious little prig. So Mr Vyvyan was quite prepared to dislike me, and I him. But Mr Vyvyan had an immemorial feud with Mr Bullock, who once gave me four detentions in one go for not marching in step. I duly reported these to Mr Vyvyan as my form master.

'I have to report four detentions from Mr Bullock, sir,' I said with ineffable contempt (for this was before the days of the typewriter loan). Then I added:

'For some reason best known to himself.'

'Now, now, dearie,' said Mr Vyvyan reprovingly, but clearly relishing my disdain. Mr Vyvyan called every boy 'dearie,' after, I think, Mrs Gamp, where Mr Bullock always called us 'sir.'

This, I saw, rather melted the ice between Mr Vyvyan and me. And it was to be quite dissolved by my unfeigned delight in Mr Vyvyan's cynicism and verbal eccentricities. He had a remarkable knowledge of the Bible, which he used solely as a fount of ridicule. If one of us grumbled about excessive prep, he would stare at the plaintiff with infuriating smugness and say: 'Joseph is not, and Simeon is not, and all these are against me.' Or it might be: 'And last of all the woman died also.' After dishing out some punishments, he would regard the victims triumphantly and conclude with the words: 'So we boiled my son and did eat him.'

He would insist on the deeply spiritual import of the quotation: 'Northward four a day, southward four a day; at Parbar westward, four at the causeway and two at Parbar.' This was frequently offered to us as consolation or guidance, or even as a punitive exercise to be written out fifty times and learned.

For some reason, all this tickled me greatly, as did his risqué comments on the aims and ideals of Montrose. I sometimes had to wipe the tears from my eyes. Like all comedians, Mr Vyvyan loved a good audience, and I think I must have been one of the best he'd had.

Then one day, in a history lesson, he said: 'I don't suppose any of you have read Haggard's *The World's Desire*?' And he added quickly, rather wearily: 'No, of course not. What a silly question.'

My heart leapt. 'I have, sir. He wrote it with Andrew Lang,' I murmured.

We then had a long discussion about it, while the rest of the class fidgeted. The tables turned indeed. And for me a new, a delightful, experience as I came face to face and tongue to tongue with a fellow enthusiast.

Mr Vyvyan had a private income and a good library, of gramophone records as well as of books. Opera was his great love and Eva Turner (whom he knew) his great idol.

Each summer he took a party of carefully selected boys to a large house he owned near Bognor. But not me. My virtuous image again deprived me of pleasures just made for me in a brotherhood we all somehow knew to be masonic in its secrecy.

But he lent me books as fast as I could read them. And, later, gramophone records. Quite often, when I'd returned some book I'd enjoyed, he would say: 'Oh, you can keep it. I don't want it any more.' The most wonderful such gift was Rider Haggard's autobiography, *The Days of My Life*. I hugged the two large volumes greedily all the way home and had read them two or three times within the year.

Mr Vyvyan performed his kindnesses, his great generosities, with an offhand indifference that quickly cut short any threatened burst of gratitude. I think he never quite knew how to take me. In the very midst of his largesse he remained oddly self-protective, wary. I sensed this but could not formulate it.

Otherwise school continued to be rather a bore, I myself an indifferent pupil, and my secret quest ever more of an obsession. Uniforms were now my daily torment. There was a lovely lad (I see him so clearly a lifetime later when he is old, diseased, dead) in a peaked cap tilted on one ear, a boy who delivered our grocery orders. I would hang around his shop for a glimpse of him, and in my fantasy he would deliver one day when I was alone in the house. Together we'd check the invoice, heads almost touching. With galloping heart I'd touch his cheek, drink in his melting eyes.

And telegraph boys in their belted tunics and pillbox hats made a mere casual stroll a medieval pageant of eternal damnation. I would even gaze enviously at the saddles of their red-painted bikes and wonder if in all the world there was a creature more depraved than I.

18

But as the dreams grew more garish life got distinctly greyer. The early thirties were taking their toll of the vulnerable classes in general and of my father in particular. His bright future was becoming a thing of the past. He had a succession of jobs, each a little dingier than the one before, partly because of the economic climate, partly because of his growing subservience to the bottle. Miraculously, his skills could still get him jobs, but his addiction just as surely lost them.

Bills began to pile up, but he never so much as opened a letter that suggested payment. They went straight into the fire or into his pocket for disposal off the premises. There was rent to pay, and rates and school fees, but food and clothing and lighting and heating consumed more than the unpredictable amount he gave my mother each week. He would lie to her that bills were paid until tradesmen beat insolently on the door and county court summonses arrived mid-morning by registered post.

The billiard table was sold, then most of the festive glass and cutlery, now long disused. The spring on the gramophone broke and we couldn't afford to have it mended. I missed that and used to play the records by propelling them with a licked finger on the labels. A compensation was that you could now play records backwards, achieving quite futuristic music.

Then came a severe blow. My aunts' firm had to axe staff and of course chose the longest-serving first. After forty years' service apiece they were stood off without pension or handshake. And all I ever heard them express was sympathy for the firm to which they'd given the better parts of their lives. People were like that then.

The restless Brian had gone first to Canada and then to Spain in search of that crock whose gold was tinsel anyway. Still, he seemed to live comfortably enough as a hotel receptionist in the one country and as a salesman in the other. He rather liked uncertainties and surprises and driftings. There was more than a little of my father in Brian. He had some of his charm and some of his blarney. Now he was back in England and making a distinctly erratic living selling encyclopaedias. If he liked a family who were poor but gullible he'd tell them not to sign up for the books.

Terry was most certainly not like father. He was 'in the city,' in insurance, and following that demi-profession ever more assiduously and loathing it ever more fiercely. He had a job and he had a dream like thousands of young clerks who scuttled daily to Cheapside and back. He had graduated now from Boswell's Johnson, his first literary hero, to Tolstoy and Havelock Ellis and Gerald Heard. Then Richard Jefferies and Thoreau and W. H. Hudson began rather uncertainly to call forth at week-ends sandals and nut cutlets as viable alternatives to bowler and brolly and steak and kidney pie. Yes, Terry was at that time in half a ferment and one that left me not untouched.

We had become friends during Brian's absence. He was more serious, more moody, than Brian, but he had his own rather acid humour.

I would wait for him to come home in the evening so that after dinner we could go for some marathon walk and talk, its goal being coffee in a distant café which we knew to keep late hours.

When he arrived home from his office he would invariably give me a quick warning: 'Don't talk to me yet. I'm foul.' And I'd have to wait as patiently as I could for the iron of the rat race to melt from his soul.

On these walks, far-ranging topics would be seasoned with homelier advice. He would urge me to work harder at school and get my matric. 'You're the brightest of us,' he'd say, 'but you're lazy, undisciplined.'

He would even suggest a university might not be impossible. But I knew it was. There was no money to pay for one, of course, and a scholarship was mere fantasy, more wild than my usual fantasies. I doubted if I would even pass my matric, my maths were so hopeless.

Terry's sense of responsibility was as great as his sense of dignity. Brian and I could find in our way of life a certain detergent Bohemianism, a puckishness we could see in no other families we knew and which was not altogether unpleasing. But Terry reacted to it all with distaste and irritation. 'Dreadful family,' he would say waspishly. 'Your father's entirely irresponsible. A menace to us all.' (I thought it odd that he always said 'your father' as if disclaiming personal propinquity.) He always insisted, too, that he himself was an irrevocable failure and I must see in him The Terrible Warning. He was scarcely out of his teens at the time.

We had no car now, of course, and no maid. Even the daily came only twice a week. And a kind of Dick Swiveller evasiveness entered my life. One would lurk, breath bated, in a back room when the type of knocking on the front door suggested a creditor. My mother coped miraculously with the basics, but all her triumphs there would be nullified by the unlooked-for swoop of a dunner from nowhere, perhaps some moneylender into whose hands my foolish father had fallen. He was a Micawber in whose exploits we were beginning to find less fun than threat. Nor had he, poor man, a Mrs Micawber to help keep him afloat.

Once I came home from school to find a strange giant of a man seated impassively in the hall. Some sort of a tipstaff. On and on he sat as it grew darker and darker and I wondered if we were supposed to feed him. When my father made his unsteady, belated appearance, the official clapped papers in his hand and then merged quite silently with the night. It was more than fiscal, it was positively eery.

Another time I was greeted by the sight of a great removal van outside the house. They had come to 'distrain our goods,' which meant they were going to take away our furniture (I was now *au fait* with the sordid jargon). But mother was equal to this as to most occasions. Somehow she got through on the phone to someone called the High Sheriff of London and told him how unthinkable such conduct was. He in turn spoke to the head bailiff and in a few minutes the men departed with their empty van. How she did it we never knew. 'Such a charming man,' was all she said.

The new poverty then hit my schooling. My father was somehow inveigled into calling on Mr Stewart, who cracked a bottle of Scotch with him and over it said: 'You're my worst creditor but I don't know a pleasanter parent.' It was agreed between them that my father should pay the fees weekly, a weird arrangement he would once have found insulting. Each Monday morning I was supposed to present Mr Stewart with a cheque, but, of course, as often as not I didn't. Father would say to me as he hurried out of the house: 'Can't stop now, Peter. Tomorrow.' And tomorrow he'd say: 'I'll send him double next week.' And Mr Stewart would call me out as we filed into school and say anxiously: 'Has your father sent me anything, Gamble?' It was humiliating for me to disappoint him, but not, apparently, for him to solicit.

Sometimes my father would send a letter courteously signalling the cheque he'd forgotten to enclose. Once he was even cleverer. There to my astonishment was the cheque, and he hadn't forgotten to date it, had simply fallen back in a reverie to some happier year of his history. Sometimes I thought I detected in Mr Stewart's eye more relish than annoyance.

But in the ensuing holidays Mr Stewart wrote to my mother to say that I could not return next term unless all arrears and a term in advance were duly paid. And of course they weren't.

I missed that entire term's schooling. Someone called a school enforcement officer called and my mother managed to convince him my absence was due to ill health. Somehow she got our doctor to support her.

But it couldn't, of course, be worked again. Equally indisputable was my dismissal of a council school. Mother wrote to my grandmother, who said she was sorry but she could do no more. She had, it seemed, bailed us out on more occasions than anyone except my father had known. From her own money and without my silent grandfather's knowledge. Things looked black indeed as the new term loomed nearer. So I myself wrote an impassioned letter to my grandmother, which caused her to send Mr Stewart all his arrears and a whole year in advance. Whether it did me good I'll never know, but at least I've always blessed her name for it.

About this time Terry decided to take wing. The stern taskmaster at Cheapside had induced in him a nervous dyspepsia that even the funny stuff called slippery elm food couldn't alleviate. One evening, swearing me to secrecy, Terry said he was off at the next crack of dawn. To join a community called 'The Cotswold Bruderhof.' He had been in secret communication with them for some time and all was now fixed. Just after sunrise he was on his way, his bike oiled and polished. He left a letter of regrets for my mother. It was quite dramatic, almost like a suicide note in tone.

'He'll be back soon,' was all mother said. Then she added characteristically: 'I'll miss his money though.'

She was quite right. Within a month he was back, and a week later he had re-entered the tough world of insurance. He didn't talk about the pantisocrats he'd abandoned. Just once he told me: 'Impossible people. Quite irresponsible.'

Then the inevitable happened and my father, thrown out of one job, couldn't find another. For a whole year he was at home. Poor Nora sold her property for a song and handed over the lot. My grandparents sent a monthly hamper. Even some of the friends once royally entertained paid us visits which were really excuses for little lifelines. But what affected me most was the extraordinary peace and goodwill that reigned in the household. My father never drank during those twelve months, never went out on his own, never uttered a cruel word to anyone. A model husband, a paragon of a parent. It was the happiest family year of my life, and, I do not doubt, of his also.

Then at last his good or bad angel came up trumps once more. A trial tender he submitted to Bovis's was so impressive that they took him on at a handsome salary plus a car. And slowly, inexorably, the old, unhappy routine began to re-establish itself.

At school I more or less made up my term's losses in subjects other than maths. That already puny infant sickened almost to death from twelve weeks' lack of nourishment.

19

Norman Perez was a school friend of Brian, a half-Spanish boy whose dark good looks and lissom body had disturbed me increasingly during the past two years at Montrose. He was Brian's age, five years older than I, who had, of course, been beneath his contempt at school and no better regarded by him since. He was working now for his father and, with a sports car and apparently unlimited cash, seemed something of a playboy. On a Saturday he and my brothers would drive down to Brighton, savour its mysterious sins, and return in the small hours of Sunday. I had no idea what they got up to in Brighton and so my unschooled imagination had free rein. All I sensed for sure was that their sins would not be my sins.

One Saturday I plucked up courage to ask, in a small and unhopeful voice, if I could go with them. 'Oh, we don't want the bloody kid with us,' said Norman with his usual brutality. But Brian, who was capable of compassion, said: 'Oh, let him come. He won't be any trouble.'

So, in seventh heaven I went, jammed in a dickey seat whence I could admire the crisp black hair curling round Norman's shapely ears.

The wicked, fleshly exploits proved to be very tame: to me, very boring. One drove along the front looking for girls to pick up. It might have been a fairly civilized operation in Uncle Frank's generous roadster. Here, it was hideously uncomfortable. Or so I thought, as some fat, giggling and offensively sweaty Proserpina was dumped on top of me and whirled off to Dis. That is to say, to the backward reaches of Rottingdean, where we'd stop for some mild petting. No one got out of the car. The two girls would be passed to and fro between the driving bench and the dickey seats, like sandwiches I'd have relished so much more. What shocked me was the attitude of these two trollops to my own handsome heart-throb. I had assumed my brothers, though certainly personable, wouldn't get a look-in with Norman around. But the girls didn't seem to care for him. Perhaps he was too overtly carnal. It was exasperating for me to overhear his vain entreaties, all wrong to find a god begging a favour of a slave. And what, I thought scornfully, what blind slaves they were.

The girls would eventually be driven to their respective homes and part with kisses and promises no one present believed for a moment. It was all so harmless. The least innocent member of the party was I, passing off my aloofness as youth and modesty and virtue.

A year later, in the summer of 1934, we took a house for a month in Skegness, a quiet and roomy resort in days devoid of holiday camps. The house was big enough for all of us plus friends, and Norman Perez joined us for two weeks. This pleased me, although I expected the same old set-up: me looking and dreaming, Norman seemingly unaware I even existed. 'He's a selfish bastard,' Brian confided to me after some tiff between them, and I silently agreed.

One noonday Norman and I were left alone on the beach, the rest having drifted back to the house for lunch. He was in swimming trunks, rather outré in those times of full costumes. He lay face down among the gorse-crowned sand dunes, and I sat beside him with a book. I secretly surveyed his dusky limbs, his tousled head turned away to sea. I glanced at my book with distaste and threw it aside. I stood up, and realized suddenly how enclosed we were with dunes, how unpeopled was the beach, how private this place was. It had been selected as a natural suntrap, but (and my heart began to pound) it was ideal for other, less innocent, pleasures.

I sat down again. How to start? How to ensure that the overtures, if savagely repulsed, might be passed off as a harmless game? Would he lash out at me? Would he blab his indignation to my brothers? Would he even depart for London, hinting to my parents the shock he'd received?

I was too far gone to care. The hungry are less prudent than inventive. I began to scoop and pat the damp sand all round his feet and ankles.

'What are you doing?' he asked irritably.

'I'm forming an outline impression of you on the sand.' It was difficult to get my words out naturally. 'You must keep still. It'll be very artistic.'

He made no reply. Nor did he stir as I shaped the sand firmly along the outside of his body: along his legs, his thighs, his ribs, and up to his armpits. Then I applied my trembling hands to the inside of his legs: his calves, his knees, his crotch. I paused there, concentrating my skills in forming a firm arch of sand between his legs, compressing the tendons in his graceful limbs, rubbing the youthful skin whose hairs were in places more down than bristle. His lips gave no protest. His body hinted assent.

Then I took the plunge, inserting one hand within his trunks, caressing his buttocks, moving down over his thighs. The day swam in sunlight.

At last he spoke, and in a tone I'd never heard from him before, languorous, strangely submissive. 'I can get a girl to do that, Peter,' he breathed with a little, unsteady laugh. The words were meaningless. I was in control. He was floundering.

'Even,' I asked, triumphant, 'even *this*?'

With a long, shuddering sigh he whispered: 'Especially that.'

I said no more. I worked. I was masterful, almost brutal. I might have been an unerring sculptor, an inspired artisan. Yet also somewhere was a knowledge that I must gather every rosebud that might never come my way again.

And I smiled proudly, for he had called me Peter. Humbly, gratefully, he had for the first time called me Peter.

How long the minutes lasted. Then he thrust away my hand and scrambled to his feet. I watched him, aloft on a sand dune for a moment. Incredibly tall and upright he seemed now. Then, clutching his towel before him, he stumbled away. Without a word, without a glance.

I lay for a long while staring at my hand and all the unbelievable evidence of conquest and surrender.

I wondered what would now be the public face Norman presented to me. I was amused that he who had never noticed my regard was now rather carefully avoiding it. I just bided my time. I hungrily wanted him.

Several nights later he arrived home very late. I was still reading in bed, my head filled with him. The rest of the house slept. I waited an age for him to come upstairs to his room. At last I crept down, pyjamaed and barefoot. I found him in the kitchen, lying back in a chair, gazing foolishly at the ceiling.

'Are you all right?' I whispered.

'Of course I am,' he said almost impatiently. 'Just had rather a night of it, that's all.'

'Shall I carry you up to bed?' I asked. (From what depths did I dredge thoughts and words like these?)

'I'd like to see you try,' he dared humourlessly.

'All right, I will.' But instead I deliberately closed the door and drew the curtains over the windows. Then I stood over him. He looked up at me like an expectant dog. He was beginning to breathe heavily.

I put my hands under him, lifted him carefully and dumped him on the floor. I then proceeded to strip him slowly, this prostrate idol still worthy of all my care. He asked me to put out the light. I refused.

I gave him fierce, whispered instructions: 'Kneel. Lie down. Turn over.' Once he grumbled and I hissed: 'Do as you're told or I'll thump you.' Then I buried my face beside his and we both giggled long to think what a crazy, handy-dandy world we'd fashioned between us. I felt tender towards him but somewhere hazily knew he could never feel like that for me. Or for anyone.

His fortnight with us neared its end and I was determined to spend the night with him before he left. When all the lights were out and all the house was still I crept into his room and bed. I wanted to nurse him all night. But for him the night's work was business, and, the business done, one must shut up shop and go home to bed.

He slept late on that, his final night, breakfasted late and gave me never a glance as he drove off.

But I was grateful to him for he had given me my first, confident, guilt-free fulfilment. He had shown me I was acceptable, taught me that love (or some version of it) can always find a way. And I perhaps had taught him something: to be less of a selfish bastard. He was nineteen and a womanizer. I was fourteen and a fish out of water.

It was in every sense a seminal experience in my life. 'My Norman conquest,' I said to myself. And felt sad there was no human soul with whom I could share it all.

20

We still called it the billiard room though now I had taken it over as a 'study,' furnishing it with bits and pieces I scrounged and with crazy bookcases Brian knocked together out of floorboards secretly vandalized from the loft. One of these bookcases was so top-heavy it had to be lashed to the wall with a rope, and its shelves were so narrow books scarcely perched on them. We called it Jacob's Ladder and I hated it. Brian pretended to admire it. 'It's baroque,' he decided, and added: 'Well, if you get any more damned books you can hang them round the walls in carrier bags.'

For I had quite a collection now. Elliott's, the local secondhand bookshop, had a great many bargains at less than a shilling, and most of my weekly pocket money was swallowed up there. I always found out something somewhere about any author I had acquired and by this means came to know my way about 'Eng Lit' from a fairly early age. Odder was the knowledge I picked up of publishers, their lists, bindings, formats, even typefaces. Some imprints were in themselves a recommendation while others spelt popular stuff.

Mr Elliott had only one eye. We always knew him as Twala, the one-eyed chief in *King Solomon's Mines*. Unlike Twala, he was a gentle soul. Brian would make him an offer for some book I wanted (I never had the courage for it), and usually he would accept it in a rather sad, dispirited fashion. And when we were hard up we would sell the books back to him, and sometimes even at a profit. But his small wife was shrewd and undupable. She recognized her old stock, and she would assess any book in a physically brutal way, bending boards and straining spines before sneering: 'A poor copy. Threepence, that's all.' We learned when she was likely to be absent and Brian could bully Twala in safety.

I was always dusting and rearranging my books and standing back to admire their finery. I would classify them and catalogue them and put brown paper covers round the more delicate ones. And sometimes on cold winter days we would light a fire in the billiard room, making a merry blaze with more floorboards, and Brian would settle himself before Mr Bullock's portable and I'd walk up and down excitedly dictating some story to him.

But the end was always the same. After a page was finished I'd ask him to read it back to me. He'd start giggling almost at once: some typing error or some words misheard would set him off. Then he would begin to analyse a character's motives in a scurrilous fashion. I'd try to be indignant but it was no good. Very soon I'd join in some surrealist exercise beneath which my nice story was smothered forever. Often, holding our stomachs and writhing, we'd beg each other to stop. It wasn't the best treatment for an aspiring little writer without a shred of confidence in himself, but it certainly stopped me taking myself too seriously.

Ridicule and denigration were our modi operandi in living. Cynicism was the face we almost dutifully wore. Although in fact the most united of families (father set aside), we despised any display of affection. No terms of endearment were used by parents or children to one another, only by my father to my mother when (we said) he wanted to get round her. I was astonished when I heard friends call their mothers 'dear' and quite embarrassed when my friend Robbie at sixteen kissed his mother before leaving the house. I don't think I ever after the toddler stage kissed my mother or was kissed by her. Nor did she 'dear' or 'darling' any of us. We didn't need such things. Our ranks were so loyally closed at all times, against my father, against creditors, against all outsiders, that any overt display of that solidarity would have been considered rather vulgar, excessive.

Brian was the worst of the debunkers. I caught it from him and in time surpassed him. Pam was catching it fast. Even my mother would condone it, at first by sharing the laughter, later by contributing caustic comments of her own. As for Terry, almost his every word was splashed with acid. The family was a magic circle into which certain outsiders were welcomed, but at their peril. We were, of course, extremely hospitable. People would sometimes comment cattily on the ceaseless comings and goings of our friends, the brewings of coffee and making of sandwiches. But when the doors had closed behind them, they were analysed, at length, with no holds barred. Oh, we would concede their good points, but somehow virtues were dull, foibles endlessly entertaining.

In time, I came to wish that a few friends I cared for might be spared, but it was a forlorn hope. Terry was especially unpredictable. I had noticed him in company showing every sign of enjoyable camaraderies, and when we were alone at last I'd say eagerly: 'Weren't they nice? It was a jolly good evening, wasn't it?' Terry would ponder for a moment then say darkly: 'Good enough. But didn't you detect the undercurrent?'

He was a great one for these undercurrents, and I felt I must be extremely obtuse to register so few of them. Eventually it became a joke with Brian and me. After meeting some entirely charming and uncomplicated person, I'd raise my eyebrows and say: 'Yes, but didn't you...?' And Brian would nod with narrowed eyes and add: 'The undercurrent? Oh yes. Yes indeed. Really quite vicious.'

21

Was my family in its way as odd and unacceptable as I was? I thought about this quite earnestly as I leaned out of the billiard room window surveying the panorama. The house was on a hill and the room was at the top of the house so I commanded quite a wide prospect. It was a hot Sunday morning and I was bored.

In separate roads I could see the rival milkmen diving in and out of the side entrances, whistling and clattering to the sun. The bells of St Michael's were making their usual First-day din. The vicar was a handsome, conceited man to whom I always raised my cap. I had recently decided to do this to all the local clergy, and they seemed to like it. It didn't occur to me that they would have liked it better if even occasionally I'd darkened their doors.

Some people were church bound, as they wanted you to know from their sombre clothes, grave expressions and clutched prayer books. Mr Gray opposite set off for his tabernacle with his whole entourage. He was Plymouth Brethren: 'open not closed,' he always added breathlessly as if terrified that you'd misplace him. I had no idea what it meant. He was something of a joke with us because he was always clipping his hedge, which was the stalking horse behind which he mentally undressed each girl that passed. I was often a counterspy, observing from my window his darting, lascivious eyes wreathed in privet.

Further down the road Maurice Black was oiling his bike with loving care. He looked very nice in his shorts, and I was again sorry we couldn't be friends. I'd once been to tea with him but he'd been engrossed in the workings of some ridiculous machine which could sometimes be coaxed to hiss out steam. I went home, suddenly and ungraciously, without waiting for tea.

But nice he did look. He'd be meeting his lucky pals outside Streatham station and together they'd conquer the long and dusty highways to Whyteleafe. He'd be back in the evening, bronzed, exhausted and triumphant, his bike laden with his spoils: scores of drooping bluebells for his mother.

Mr Henpecked Haycraft was strolling home with his Sunday papers. They were not delivered because fetching them in a slow, extended detour was Mr Haycraft's Great Escape. He averted his eyes guiltily as he passed the sabbatical Gray ménage. To their obvious satisfaction.

The flighty daughters of number 32 were hanging out their finery in the garden, glancing up hopefully at the sun which had to dry it all in time for the weekly exposure in the park.

In all the houses people would be preparing their Sunday roasts, tradition making no concession to the mounting heat. Terry affected to despise such fare as he tackled the omelette I knew he hated.

Some roads away a Salvation Army band performed earnestly; lively, brassbound hymns were peppered with hoarse and inarticulate preachings. A strange dog hurried purposefully down the road. Laden bees made slower progress round the garden. A blackbird gave itself a vigorous dust bath.

Behind me, in our house, the hubbub never ceased: Brian shouting 'Has anyone seen my blue silk shirt?', Nora wrestling with the Hoover, almost as big as she was and much more intractable, my father calling: 'Shall I get you some mint from the garden, dear?', Pam impressing on the cats they had a gastronomic treat in store and must behave themselves.

And mother seated at her dressing table, combing, powdering, appraising herself, as she answered all the queries, settled all the problems, directed the whole Sunday ritual. The Captain on her bridge.

And I? I was the lookout boy, aloft in the crow's nest.

But looking out for what? That was the depressing question. I yearned, but in a sort of vacuum. I thought of Norman Perez. A whole year ago, that feast. I'd seen him often since then, of course, but he pretended no shadow of memory clouded his mind. To me it excited still and I knew it would never die. (Not that he had been that Ideal Friend I dreamed of.)

I remembered the man who'd followed me all the way to Streatham library, stopping when I stopped, taking absurd detours that I took, and just smiling at me when at last I turned and faced him. I'd told a policeman, but when we both looked the man had vanished.

I was, I suppose, what that man had been seeking. It all seemed such an unnecessary muddle, and the odds against two seekers finding fulfilment in each other must be millions to one. Mr Vyvyan had once said that Plato called friendship 'one soul in two bodies.' I liked that so much that I told it to Brian, who said Mr Vyvyan's own definition was actually 'two bodies in one bed.' Typical Brian.

Yet in a way I was glad to defer an encounter with this ideal of mine. I felt I wasn't ready for him yet, I hadn't sufficiently spring-cleaned myself for him. I was becoming more and more discontented, with myself and with the whole suburban octopus. And discontented with my discontent, for it seemed so like a betrayal.

Moodily I sat down and thumbed once more through Rider Haggard's autobiography. He had died before I had even learned to read, a lasting regret because I would have liked to tell him how grateful I was. Then I suddenly decided I would write to his widow. I knew from Debrett that she was still alive.

I wrote there and then, pages of it. And posted it before lunch.

It wasn't the real quest but it was, surely, allied to it. It wasn't that longed-for gift from the gods but it was a self-injection that might add a little colour to my days.

How long she took to reply: almost a week. But Friday was certainly worth waiting for. It brought not a letter but a large packet. I knew it was from her before I'd seen the postmark for it was addressed in an old lady's hand just like my grandmother's.

She told me she valued my letter for it showed her Sir Rider's memory lived on in boys' hearts just as he would have wished. And she enclosed a photograph of him which I might like to have. It was a studio portrait, nicely mounted. But I felt the tiniest twinge of disappointment amid my gratitude. Haggard was a very handsome man but you wouldn't know it from this. He was older here, and perhaps not in good health. The face was clouded, even a little petulant.

Still, I was elated with it and showed it proudly to Brian. He gazed at it in a way I knew only too well. 'You realize, of course,' he said, 'that he's a rotter? Written all over him.'

'Now don't you dare,' I replied, ashamed of the hint of a giggle in my voice.

Somewhere I knew poor Rider's fate was sealed from that moment. Brian invented for him a querulous rustic accent that seemed uncannily right for the expression on the portrait's face, and in a few weeks there had formed a rounded character in a clear-cut setting: mean and shabby, a loafer without grace, a sponger without charm, the despair of his family and scourge of his friends. On one occasion Brian went so far as to post me a crude begging letter signed 'Yours hopefully, Rider.' It seemed no god of mine was ever to keep his fair pedestal.

As with Ernest Raymond, I prolonged the correspondence and eventually Lady Haggard was moved to suggest that I visit Ditchingham House in Norfolk to see Sir Rider's study where he wrote his books and kept the trophies he'd gathered in a long and active life.

This was the greatest adventure yet, the furthest I had been from home on my own. The chrysalis was splitting. I was on the way to imago.

Terry took charge of the arrangements, plotting my itinerary and doubtless providing some of the cash. He also said it was out of the question for me to embark without a hat, a trilby. It must, moreover, be a Lincoln Bennett. He bought me one, which I dutifully carried to Ditchingham and back. For Terry's life was largely compounded of a protocol he apparently despised but would in no jot offend. 'Nobody goes without a hat,' was one of his rules. But it was all very puzzling, for I'd had lunch with him in the City more than once when we had left his office on a distinctly cold day with a keen wind and, once, even swirling snowflakes. 'Aren't you going to put a hat and coat on?' I'd asked in astonishment.

'Nobody,' he'd snapped in scorn, 'nobody in the City puts on hat or coat to go out to lunch.'

22

I don't remember my journey at all, which is surprising, for London to Norfolk and back in a day must have been quite a feat, especially as Ditchingham itself was off the beaten track.

I entered an entirely feminine domain. Lady Haggard was rather frail and clearly to be protected from social chores. She welcomed me with a few perfunctory questions and then, even as I still stood before her in all my stickiness and shyness, desperately casting about for some words I could myself contribute, her eyes showed she had utterly dismissed me, ceased to be aware I had ever existed. It disconcerted me. I began to feel like Pip before Miss Havisham.

But her daughter Lilias was no Estella. She took me over and did her duty graciously. She was herself a skilled writer whose *I Walked By Night*, the memoirs of an old Norfolk poacher, was to become something of a classic. She took me on a tour of Rider's study, showed me his manuscripts and photograph albums, his assegais and tollas and oxhide shields, his amulets and figurines and scarabs. And she was amused to find I had acquired from her father's books quite a smattering of Zulu.

Lunch was, to my surprise, rather poor. I had a more than healthy appetite and I'd been accustomed to eating well. I remember quite clearly that we had no first course, stuffed marrow as a main dish, and rice pudding and pears to finish off. And my second surprise was that as soon as any plate was cleared it was put on the floor at our feet to be licked clean by two or three dogs. I wondered if the plates would be washed.

After lunch Lady Haggard's plump and jolly nurse took me and the dogs for a long tramp round the grounds. I was glad of the interlude yet I suspected rather miserably that the family wanted to get rid of me for a while. I knew that strangers to whom I'd written were surprised to find their garrulous correspondent so wearingly tongue-tied.

Then we went in to tea, where I found a new arrival: a small, elderly intelligent-looking lady who was introduced as 'Mrs Gladwyn Jebb.' I don't know if they'd told her I was something of a handful to entertain, but she at once patted the sofa beside her and said: 'I'd like you to come and talk to me, Mr Gamble.'

She was so nice and I was so intrigued that I lost my shyness, found my tongue, and soon began to question her eagerly. 'Are you,' I asked her (and the veneration in my tone must have been flattering), 'are you the Mrs Gladwyn Jebb I have read about in Sir Rider's autobiography?'

'The very same,' she smiled. 'And I hope he said nice things about me. It is a long time since I read it.'

'Oh yes,' I said warmly. 'And how brave, how... how intrepid, you and Mr Gladwyn Jebb were as explorers. In South America. Looking for El Dorado.'

'Yes,' she said rather wistfully, 'it *was* wonderful. Now it is as much as I can do to get to Norfolk.' She laughed. 'Well, nearly.'

The time passed quickly now and I had to be reminded of my train. I blushed as I realized I must have outstayed my welcome some time before. But Mrs Jebb ('Forget the Gladwyn. Such a mouthful') must have seen this for as I stammered out my thanks 'for a wonderful day' she said: 'You live in London, Mr Gamble. So do I. I wonder if you'd like to come to tea with me one Sunday?'

'Oh yes,' I replied, and so fervently she looked really pleased.

'Then I can get the address from Lady Haggard, and I'll write to you later in the year.'

I almost danced down the drive and into the freedom of the leafy lanes. What an ordeal it had been. How glad I was to escape. But even more glad to have weathered such an experience.

And in due course Mrs Jebb wrote to me and I began the ritual that was to last four or five years: tea in Kensington on the first Sunday of each month. She became, as she intended, not only a valued friend but also a powerful influence, one that I had in the end, with real sorrow, to repudiate.

Many years later I wrote an article on Haggard in a literary weekly and sent a copy to Lilias Rider Haggard. She wrote me a charming reply, saying she remembered my boyhood visit to Ditchingham very well. I wondered if my gaucherie had been really so memorable.

23

About this time I read a pleasantly sentimental story by L. P. Jacks, called *The Magic Formula*, about a captivating schoolboy who irradiates the features of even the crustiest old gentlemen with a dazzling 'Please sir, can you tell me the time?' So successful is the formula that he tries it on Gladstone, the Pope and (quite logically) God.

I liked the story so much that I of course became a pen friend of its author. When, many years later, I met his son, I wanted to tell him of this but somehow never found the right moment for it.

However it did seem to hint at a respectable, even commendable, motive for my epistles to the eminent. For this was to become something of a practice of mine. I must add, however, in fairness to myself, that I never wrote to anybody unless I was really involved in appreciation or, sometimes, commiseration.

I wrote to Leopold, king of the Belgians, when his beautiful young queen was killed in a motoring accident. He replied with a warmth and sincerity I had myself found in writing.

And in *The Illustrated London News* I saw a picture of the ex-Kaiser chopping up logs in his exile at Doorn. I hoped my letter might be a kind of magic formula to cheer him up. But his reply when it came seemed only to add to his pathos. It was a rather cheap postcard of him in his heyday, all waxed moustachios and jackboots, and on it he had written simply: 'Danke - Wilhelm' and the date.

I was even more touched by the vulnerability of Lord Alfred Douglas. From Twala I had acquired for sixpence a copy of Douglas's *Selected Poems* which I genuinely admired. Some of the paedophilic ones struck me as quite beautiful. I wrote to thank him for them. By return he wrote very warmly to commend my good taste and to complain of the conspiracy of neglect to which he had been subjected, and to enclose a batch of eulogistic press cuttings about his work. That correspondence, too, continued, and in due course (and without any prompting this time) he sent me a charmingly inscribed copy of his latest book on Wilde. He struck me as eccentric but I couldn't detect that strain of inherited madness at which some writers hinted in their hagiographies of poor Oscar.

It was thus inevitable that I should write to Hitler. It was a priggish letter. I told him that, while I did not support all the retributive measures of the Versailles treaty, I was sure that he could never want war between 'our two great countries' and that he realized there were better ways to assert the greatness of Germany than by armaments. I also shared with him my new-found adoration of Wagner, for Mr Vyvyan had lent me his recordings of *Tristan* and *The Ring*, to which my response had been as immediate and ecstatic as Ludwig's own.

Victor Lutze, head of the SS, wrote me a graceful reply. He told me how much the Fuehrer had appreciated my words and how he had agreed with most of my sentiments. Perhaps the Fuehrer really had read what I had written, for even a tempered tribute from an English schoolboy must have been something of a novelty in 1935, when the Fuehrer would indeed have been hoping for an alliance with Britain.

There was an embarrassing, even dangerous, sequel to this. Each month until the outbreak of war I received unsolicited Nazi propaganda, most of it lavishly produced in English. But it had quite the opposite effect from that intended. Dr Goebbels hadn't realized what this verbal bombardment would do to a cussed schoolboy determined to resist all external conditioning.

When I was about sixteen I wrote a short story (carefully concealed from Brian) which had something to do with a youthful friendship offered and repulsed. It was heavily symbolic and, of course, ended tragically. I sent it to Godfrey Winn for his opinion. Not such an odd choice as it may seem, for he was at that time the most successful and influential columnist in Britain. I also, I admit, suspected it might be his cup of tea, for I was losing my innocence.

He said he liked it very much. It showed real talent. It reminded him of a story he himself had written at my age 'and two years later I had my first novel published so that ought to encourage you!' He also asked me if I'd like to call on him at his flat in Ebury Street.

When I got there, at 6 pm sharp, he quite disconcerted me by being in a mad whirl of preparation. He was going to be late, and he hated that, he explained in a loud monotone from his bedroom. The phone rang and he came in trouserless to answer it. It was his mother, to whom he spoke in the most extravagant terms as 'darling' and 'sweetheart' and 'precious.'

Ready at last, he said he'd drop me off at Victoria station en route for his engagement. For the first time he paused. He looked at me, as I stood there waiting for him to open the door. Then he came up to me, put his arms round my waist and said: 'You're a lovely big boy, aren't you?'

It was such a shock that I recoiled, quickly and decisively, which caused him to do the same. 'Come on, then,' he said briskly. 'I can just make it if we hurry.' I followed him in something of a daze.

In the car he told me the enormous sums he was making and how frustrating it was to have reached the top of the tree so comparatively young. At the station he dropped me with a hand-squeeze and a funny little laugh.

It took me quite a time to realize I'd behaved pretty badly. I'd misled him and then insulted him, and it was small consolation to think that I hadn't intended either.

I sat my London matric and, as I confidently expected, failed the maths. In other words, I had failed the whole exam, failed to matriculate. There was no question of my remaining at Montrose to resit the thing. Even if I'd wanted to. Finding the fees was a problem, and I felt it was time I contributed to the family coffers. In any case, I had exhausted all the place had to offer.

24

So there I was, sixteen and a half, with no qualifications, no contacts, and nothing in my head but the vague idea of journalism, and no idea (fortunately) how to set about that. All I knew was to scan the vacancies columns of the *Daily Telegraph* under 'J' for 'Junior Clerk.' And there I saw that a magazine called *The Review* needed a 'capable junior,' which I felt sure I was. I carefully ignored the nasty sentence 'Some ability with figures required.' I applied. I was granted an interview.

It was in Fetter Lane, off Fleet Street, and I was interviewed by the editor, Mr Winch. He was an elderly man with a shock of white hair and a green eyeshade right across his brow. He told me the magazine was devoted to the affairs of the insurance world and most of the work would be of a statistical nature. Did I think I could do it? I swallowed hard and said I thought I could, but wasn't there any actual literary work? He explained there were occasional reviews, of books 'with an insurance flavour.' I must have looked rather blank for he added, a little wearily: 'Oh, memoirs of retired insurance magnates. That sort of thing.' We ended by staring at each other in some perplexity. I sensed that he wanted to turn me down but didn't know how to do it without hurting my feelings.

Suddenly he pointed to the book I was clutching. It was an old friend I'd been rereading on the tram.

'What's your book?'

'Oh, it's *Father and Son*. Edmund Gosse,' I mumbled. I always became shy if anyone spoke about a book dear to me.

'Let's see it,' he ordered as if he didn't believe me.

He thumbed through it. 'Like it?' he quizzed.

'It's a wonderful book,' I replied.

'It's a lucky one,' was his rejoinder. 'It's got you a job. Start on Monday. Nine o'clock sharp. Twenty-five shillings a week.'

I walked out on air. Mr Winch, like Norman Perez, hadn't rejected me. And I'd be in Fleet Street, and 'I'm on *The Review*, you know' would sound rather good. And, best of all, I could at last give my mother some money each week.

I enjoyed everything about *The Review* except the job I was paid to do and couldn't. It was at the top of a hundred wooden stairs in a crazy old building and the whole neighbourhood was teeming and colourful. It was also very much of a boy world. In those days junior clerks and office boys and messenger lads and merry printers' devils seemed to support the whole fabric. The only trouble was that they were always in such a hurry.

I worked in a large room with a portly Scandinavian gentleman and a rather odious boy of my own age. He was what Brian would have called a 'fifty-penciller,' that is, the sort of schoolboy who was both mean and clever, who shielded his exercise book from your pathetic gaze and wouldn't lend you one of his many pencils no matter how great your need. This youth understood statistics and clearly enjoyed my sorry ignorance of them.

There was a little, spiteful machine that time has in no way dimmed for me. It looked like a miniature cash register and it had umpteen levers you set in accordance with some dark designs you had. You then twirled a handle (the number of twirls being apparently a matter of whim) and read off an answer at the foot of the contraption. I survived nine months of these twirls without ever knowing what I was doing. The kindly Dane explained it again and again but in the end had to do it himself while the fifty-penciller sniggered audibly.

The only bright moments came when Mr Winch dumped some book on my desk and asked for about five hundred words by Friday. In these little reviews I artfully flattered the author and his dreary insurance background.

After nine months Mr Winch called me into his office and said without looking at me: 'The time has come to determine your appointment here.'

'Oh yes,' I said brightly, quite misunderstanding his old-fashioned use of 'determine' to mean 'terminate.' I was half expecting a rise.

He went on to say the reviews I had written were excellent, but unfortunately this was only a minor part of the work I had to do. Then it dawned on me, and really I wasn't too sorry. I didn't mind being slave to a typewriter, but not to that little twirling dervish.

We parted almost affectionately. Mr Winch wrote me a glowing testimonial, the kindly Dane apologized (I suppose on behalf of the machine), and even the fifty-penciller looked suitably shamefaced.

25

So here I was again: seventeen and back on the market after two decided failures. To boost my morale I read up and took the Royal Society of Arts advanced certificate in English language and literature. I had discovered that a first class pass (which I got) qualified you to teach English in London evening institutes. After a series of interviews I was put on the LCC panel, though I never taught in any institute.

I also engaged a very kind, highly qualified but distinctly pixillated old lady to teach me typing and shorthand. My typing became quite good but my shorthand was always more mine than Sir Isaac's. Terry paid her fees: two shillings an hour.

Just before I'd left *The Review* I had joined Reader's Union, a new book club with some literary standards, which also published a small but lively magazine called *Reader's News*. The second of their monthly 'choices' had been an uninhibited Italian novel called *The Wheel Turns*, by Gian Dauli. I was ripe for such fare, equating shockingness with power and frankness with truth. And it was in any case a book of some merit. I was thus irritated when the next issue of the magazine contained howls of protest from members, many of whom resigned from the club in disgust. I thought all this was British bourgeois hypocrisy at its nastiest. So I wrote a long defence of the book and sent it to the editor of *Reader's News*.

This piece of rather special pleading duly appeared *in toto*, set out not as a letter but as an article and introduced by an appreciative editorial comment. My mother was by nature and by necessity a pragmatist. She was also the most unimpressionable woman in the world. Visits to Lady Haggard and letters from Hitler she took as matters of course. Even when I'd had tea with a real live duchess she had to be reminded to question me about it. (That was the Duchess of Hamilton of the Animal Defence League, whom I'd congratulated on wearing artificial ermine on her robes at the George V anniversary in 1935. What a horribly precocious boy I must have been.)

But she read my comments on *The Wheel Turns* because she'd read the book and thoroughly enjoyed being scandalized by it. In fact it became one of the chief books of her later years. I remember her rereading it with failing eyes and renewed chuckles in her eighties.

So in her most businesslike manner she said: 'Now you must write to this editor man and tell him how old you are and that you're looking for a job.'

I demurred, saying it seemed like taking advantage. But she insisted. 'Nothing venture, nothing win,' she stated with finality.

So I wrote to John Baker, who was not only the editor of the magazine but also managing director of the whole enterprise. He replied promptly, asking me to call on him.

'JB,' as everyone called him, was an interesting man. His origins and ideals were proletarian, his socialism romantic rather than political, his roots in Morris and Ruskin, his branches in Shaw and Wells. He believed in the dignity of labour, in art by the people and for the people. His faith was in the ability of the craftsman to perceive beauty and his vocation was the production of good and handsome books. A sort of Tolstoy of Charing Cross Road.

I always felt his business flair, all his bright ideas for marketing and selling, were a tiny bit unconvincing as not having first call on his heart. But he was backed by one of Britain's venerable publishing houses and he had to keep them happy.

His reactions during my interview with him seemed to me distinctly odd, for he was a type quite new to me. A frown clouded his face as soon as I opened my mouth and I felt it was not because of what I was saying. The frown deepened when I mentioned Montrose College, although he brightened when I said I'd failed my matric. He wasn't interested when I mentioned my diploma, but he seemed to approve my two-shillings-an-hour lessons in typing and shorthand, and he actually smiled to hear of my pocket money gleanings in Twala's dusty fields.

Though I didn't realize it then he was very much in two minds about me. He liked to gather round him young protégés of modest backgrounds and no means and I didn't seem to fit the picture. His role as patron was not likely to be very rewarding in my case. But in the end he said I could join him on a month's trial. At two pounds a week. Starting on Monday at 9 am.

It all began disastrously. In fact, exactly as he expected. Reader's Union (or RU as they all called it) had a rather handsome showroom just off the Strand which was also a well-stocked bookshop. Two young men of undoubtedly proletarian origin and most impressively *au fait* with the publishing scene ran this bookshop between them. I entered it in good time on Monday and asked for Mr Baker. They were as deferential as I thought they should be and told me apologetically that Mr Baker didn't come in until 9.30 or 10. Had I an appointment? My explanation that I'd come to work there produced a marked change of attitude. One of them gave me a duster and asked me to dust the stock. I swallowed hard but told myself the advent of Mr Baker would soon change all this. Just before ten he entered and passed me without any sign of recognition. I concluded he hadn't seen me, but when frequent passages failed to elicit a greeting I began to smoulder. On the second day I was told to deliver some very heavy tomes to an address in Hampstead so I took a taxi all the way and presented the flabbergasted showroom buffs with the bill. On the third day I decided I'd had enough. I entered JB's office with a carefully prepared speech. I placed the duster firmly on his desk and said with what I hoped was acid irony: 'There seems to have been some mistake, Mr Baker. I didn't know you were requiring a housemaid.'

I was not only prepared for the sack but wanted it. I hated the whole place. In the seconds before JB replied I reviewed my entire future and found it a wasteland. For a moment JB looked at me with angry red spots forming on his cheeks. Then he seemed to find my hauteur irresistibly funny. He burst out laughing and immediately I found my face creasing with a grin.

'You snooty little devil,' he said. 'So it's all taxis and no dusters, is it?' Seeing me try not to laugh, he produced words which seemed to surprise him as much as me. 'I suppose I'll have to find something more acceptable. Go off to lunch and I'll see what I can bring out of my hat for you this afternoon.'

As I left the room he threw the duster at my head with the words: 'Keep it. Keep it as a reminder of either a bloody silly or a bloody clever day's work.'

Then I laughed and thanked him, for I guessed he liked me in spite of himself. And that was how it began, the love-hate relationship that was to last years.

When I got back after lunch the company secretary called me in and gave me the money I'd spent on the taxi to Hampstead. He also gave me a little lecture. He said: 'You didn't ought to do such things, Gamble, you really didn't ought.' And I thought: 'Even the company secretary's working class.' That was how my little mind worked in those days.

That afternoon JB took me up to a vast, open-plan office filled with desks and hubbub and activity. In one corner was a desk with a typewriter on it and a bookcase beside it. 'This is your base, Gamble,' he said, 'and here's your challenge.' He handed me a box file crammed with unanswered letters. 'These are from members and they need answering personally and quickly. Mr Burgess'll give you the stationery. Do as many as you can and bring them down to me for signing at five o'clock.'

I was enthralled by the letters. Some sought information, some were abusive, some grateful. Some were rather sad literary exercises for appraisal, some just the outpourings of little, lonely lives. I answered them all with individually tailored care. I was informative or appreciative, defensive or aggressive, serious or light-hearted, and when it was needed I was even compassionate. I'd never enjoyed myself so much. The hours sped by. And when I took them down to JB for signing he didn't conceal his pleasure in them. 'Well, you've taken to that like a duck to water. Keep it up.'

I kept it up for two years. Not one of the members (now thirty thousand strong) who wrote in editorially failed to receive from me a courteous and considered reply. Many wrote regularly each month, even if they had nothing but greetings to pen. The task took on pastoral overtones. Regular correspondents hinted at secret ambitions, at little crosses they had to carry. I was Auntie Vera or Nurse Sarah. All over Britain, it seemed, were these nice humble people, kind people, brave people, who found solace in books, and, in RU, a new-found sense of belonging. Some even called at the office and apologetically took me out to tea.

JB was tickled by the agony aunt element I'd introduced into all this, and, moreover, sharply aware of its commercial value, although neither he nor I would have expressed it in those terms. After a while JB said: 'Sign them yourself in future. Call yourself 'Manager, Editorial Department.' Just let me see any unusually interesting ones.'

And my list of duties lengthened. I had to scan the reputable weeklies for any likely additions to RU's list. I became deputy editor of *Reader's News* and was expected to contribute one or two articles each month. I was also one of JB's secretaries. He would call me in for his more literary correspondence, knowing he didn't have to dictate punctuation. My shorthand, under pressure, became even more idiosyncratic. But nobody guessed.

I was lucky, and I hope I knew it. The morning postbag was a thrill that never palled, and when JB deposited on my desk for approval a pile of mint-fresh books I would caress them almost sensually, smell them, too, as I did the musty old volumes in Streatham library. These piles of books had to be assessed quickly, so I acquired the dubious skill of extracting the heart from a book in a series of predatory hops and swoops. At least, I hoped I did. Few of the books so read became dear to me. But one day JB dropped on me a novel called *Peter Waring* by Forrest Reid. I knew nothing of the book or its author, but after very few pages I knew not only that it was a distinguished piece of work but also that it was to become a cherished part of my life.

Peter is sixteen and I fell in love with him because I knew that his creator loved him too. It is a love story, the eternal triangle, but with a difference, oh such a difference. Peter falls in love with Katherine, because she is attractive and rather more sophisticated than he is himself. And Katherine's slightly older brother, the intelligent and gifted Gerald, falls in love with Peter. Katherine is essentially indifferent to Peter, while Peter seems blind to Gerald's love. The pain, the hopelessness, of it is set out with delicacy and assurance. To offset the haunting lyricism of this love world is Peter's cousin George, a boy of his own age who is coarse, insensitive and over-sexed. He is not bad, though, and certainly not unauthentic. The author's intelligence and humour save a plot that could be too contrived. Even the priggish Owen, who involved Peter in studying Tolstoy (and in writing to him, and in getting a reply), is entirely convincing as an adolescent type.

The novel had gained rave reviews, and it immediately enslaved me. I read it all the afternoon that JB dropped it on my desk. I read it going home on the tube. I read it to the end in bed that night. And so determined was I to miss no subtlety, no nuance, that I started it again over breakfast the next morning. I was reading it as I walked to my bus. On this first walk of the day I was often passed by a Dulwich schoolboy on his bike. He was a very handsome boy of about fifteen, dark, thoughtful, sensitive-looking. I had been in love with him since my first sight of him. Of course I never spoke to him, but he remains very clear and very alive in my mind. And because he passed me as I read *Peter Waring* that morning, he has always been Peter to me.

I as good as insisted RU should make the book one of their monthly choices, and they did. I filled *Reader's News* with eulogies of it, and impatiently I awaited the appreciative letters from members. Not one did we ever receive, but quite a few nasty ones were dropped on my desk. Most were quite indifferent to it. Those who troubled to condemn it scarcely understood it. The experience took some of the gilt off my gingerbread job. Our members seemed to wax lyrical only over travel books and biographies. They couldn't have enough of them.

I set about discovering all I could about Forrest Reid. I found he'd written many novels, that E. M. Forster and Walter de la Mare were his great friends and champions. And, how could it be otherwise, I wrote to him. Like Tolstoy in *Peter Waring* he replied, carefully, kindly, wisely. In pencil, on several sheets of thick, cream-laid writing paper. Like many of my cherished letters, but none more regretfully, this perished in the blitz. But I remember one passage: 'You are clearly an intelligent person. You know the difference between right and wrong. You must thus work out your salvation for yourself. No one else can do it for you.' I had written to him frankly about my love for boys, and I took his words as much to heart as a rather arrogant 18-year-old can. I didn't ever write to him again, but I read all of his I could get my hands on. And, through my fascination with Forrest Reid's work, I was to make contacts, richly rewarding, mutual contacts, in the strange years ahead.

26

In spite of all my new responsibilities, in spite of acquiring my own secretary (a torpid giggler of a girl who was always bleating: 'Don't use such big words'), my sense of inferiority grew alarmingly. I felt horribly ignorant of life, but I was more bothered about my ignorance of literature. My many years of voracious reading had been so haphazard, I now realized, so very undisciplined. I didn't stop to think it had also been very enjoyable. In the early years I read anything lying around in the house, then anything that caught my fancy on Twala's shelves, then Dickens, Wilkie Collins, Thackeray, the Brontës. But, I moaned to myself, why wasn't I in my early teens reading James and Joyce and Huxley and Lawrence and Virginia Woolf and the rest of the brood so dear to the literati I now worshipped?

I confided in Stan, one of the two showroom experts and a nice person. He knew just what was being read and by just what sort of people. He put me on to Frank Swinnerton's *Georgian Literary Scene*, which was certainly informative, but rather too prosaic for the aspiring literary snob. Then, one fatal day, he said to me: 'Go to Queenie. She'll put you right.' 'Queenie?' 'Queenie Leavis. *Fiction and the Reading Public*. We've got some in stock.'

So to Queenie, a real bargain at any price (and I got a third off), I duly went. I don't know how much of the blame for what followed is due to Queenie and how much to my eager misappropriation of her, but, like her husband Frank later, she fed my already keen appetite for the snide and the snooty. Spurred on by her and by a horrible insincerity of my own, I was soon pretending to admire what bored me and to sneer at what I'd once loved. Reading had always been a joy, sheer self-indulgence. Now it was becoming a duty. There were such great gaps to fill, so little time to fill them. I made many onslaughts on Joyce (both traditional and advanced) and made out I admired him greatly. Actually, his verbal dexterity might well have captivated me, if only his subject matter wasn't so yawningly uncongenial. Heterosexuality in the novel was becoming a real stumbling block to me, if, that is, its outlines were too glaringly sharp, its edges unsoftened by the symbolic and the eternal. Heathcliff and Cathy never put a foot wrong. Nor did Chaucer's bawdy or Shakespeare's wit or Donne's cynicism or Dickens' sentimentality or Virginia Woolf's two-edged probings. But D.H. Lawrence... How could I ever have convinced myself that I was a Lawrence fan? I think because *Sons and Lovers* did have a splendour in parts. Also because I had several times started *The Boy in the Bush*, misled by its title and by its first paragraph, and was always hoping it would take off into my world. Many years later I grappled as justly as I knew how with *Women in Love*, which so shouted its profundity from every page that far wiser heads than mine were intimidated. Finally I knew I must be honest and, however insensitive, pronounce *Women in Love* as plain ridiculous and poor Lawrence a most terrible bore.

I was under the impression that Conrad wrote sea stories, which I didn't like. So he did, but not quite in the manner of W. W. Jacobs. In any case, he was so very hard to get into. Therefore the greatness of books like *Nostromo* did not illuminate my teens, I am sorry to say. On the other hand Huxley's novels did, or I thought they did. I liked the intelligence and ignored the fact there wasn't much more. With Henry James I got no further than *The Turn of the Screw* and *The Princess Casamassima*, but they proved gold indeed.

Virginia Woolf's *To the Lighthouse* I found hard work, but worth it, though of course I then had to lie about my admiration for *The Waves*, and for *The Years*, which had just come out and I couldn't make head or tail of. But what a relief Forster was. Indeed, I wondered how anyone so delightfully readable could enjoy Queenie's imprimatur, though I had a sneaking suspicion that I was liking the right person for the wrong reason. In fact Queenie disturbingly suggested just that. Oddly, I didn't read any Hardy at that time, though later he was to become one of my deities. Perhaps he was suffering some post-demise depression at that time. He'd slipped away just ten years earlier.

Isherwood I found for myself: a triumph, for he was not only hard to put down but also a darling of that avant-garde I sedulously courted. By what quirk was he coupled with Auden, whose general incomprehensibility proved to my bemused head he was A Great Poet?

For it was the same old hypocrisy with poetry. I liked de la Mare, but so many of the people I knew smiled rather condescendingly when I mentioned him. 'Ah yes,' said one, 'I expect you like Max Beerbohm's jolly old crowd of pinafores.' I bit my lip and hurried off to find out what he was talking about. When I did, I made the silly quip my own.

Housman I met through Vaughan Williams' *On Wenlock Edge*. As soon as I'd saved up enough I bought Housman's *Collected Poems*, just issued, and read them over and over until I had many by heart. I read Housman with the tribute he himself prized: the constricted throat and blurred eyes, the hair rising on the scalp, the *frisson* of the spine. But even as I read him I suspected he'd be unacceptable in the smart new world I'd entered. He was wry, passionate and comprehensible, so I knew they'd sneer at him and they did. He became another skeleton in my now bulging book cupboard. Of course, the names of Rider Haggard and Ernest Raymond I now never so much as breathed to a soul. I never admitted, scarcely even to myself, that I enjoyed the novels of Bennett and Wells, that *Kim* was a joy, and that in bed at night (and almost under the blankets, as it were) I lapped up Henry Williamson's *The Flax of Dream* sequence and Mackenzie's *Sinister Street* and, oh, shame, even Hugh Walpole's *Jeremy* books. After reading Virginia Woolf's *Mr Bennett and Mrs Brown*, I even kept quiet about my passion for Dickens, the only real giant among a pretty inflated brood. And when, at Christmas, JB gave me a copy of Bennett's *Literary Taste* I put it aside, with a superior smile, unread.

The same turn of character that led to the worship of Housman led me via *On Wenlock Edge* to lieder. The generous Mr Vyvyan, who was already feeding my keen appetite for Wagner, now lent me his recording of *Die*

Schöne Müllerin, and that was another instant rapport. Convinced of Schubert's at least bisexual tastes, I saw the poor boy who sacrificed himself to the abominable maid of the mill as a lad unaware of his true bent, just like Forrest Reid's Peter Waring. Only slowly, as I groped my way out of my teens, did I lose my appetite for schmaltz.

Crude, muddled and horribly insincere as it all was, it could also be very exciting. When I wasn't going to get-togethers of other affected 'intellectuals' in dark and remote cellars (I remember L. A. G. Strong reading Joyce and Enid Starkie on Rimbaud, with whom I was in love for his looks and his crimes), I was hurrying to recherché little theatres to see Russian and Irish gems and Strindberg and Pirandello and Auden-cum-Isherwood. I seldom knew what was going on and the only real thrills I had were from Ibsen, who struck me as truly great. Perhaps my chief joy in those days was dashing off to Sadler's Wells after office hours and queueing for the gallery. Ninepence bought a metal ticket you surrendered at the top of hundreds of stone steps, and then three hours of glory: *Tannhäuser* and *Die Walküre* and *Aïda* and, once, the quite unexpected battery of *The Wreckers*, with Dame Ethel Smyth herself stomping on stage for an ovation.

There was the old Queen's Hall next door to the BBC and long hours of cheerful sentinel duty in the prom, and weird, sometimes hysterical, visits to the Forum cinema in Villiers Street, where nobody cared that the quite incomprehensible Russian soundtrack was drowned by the thunder of trains overhead.

27

Far-off days, bitterly sweet with the ghost of the youth who imbibed them. Not a very nice youth, I think. I had no social accomplishments, couldn't dance or play any games or offer any small talk, and always the great gulf fixed between me and every normal, beer-swilling, girl-chasing youth under the sun. Yet not really a tragic chasm because, even in my most lugubrious mood, laughter, often helpless, paralytic laughter, with Pam or Brian or Robbie was near at hand. In less affectionate, more challenging company I felt I could hold my own only with my tongue, which was becoming more cruelly barbed. Very often I didn't mean my words to be hurtful, but I became punch-drunk with verbal duelling, and quite lost sight of the wounds I was inflicting. I delighted in my spiteful vocabulary, soon almost forgetting that nothing impresses like courtesy and kindness, honesty and naturalness. Yet I longed in new company to make a good impression.

The devils really were at me in those days. After Queenie I sold my soul to a band of Teutonic goblins: Hirschfeld and Freud and Wilhelm Stekel and Krafft-Ebing and company. I had convinced myself that if only I could master the *psychopathia sexualis* I should achieve a knowledge of human nature so profound that I could unmask innocence itself, for even innocence hid behind disguises. It did not occur to me (perhaps had not occurred to Freud) that a philosophy grounded on clinical confessions was scarcely equipment for the sage, still less for the humanitarian. Now in nearly all my social intercourse I hunted the hidden motive, never doubting that everyone was a self-deceiver and every motive shabby. Only the unworthy was real and only the practised cynic could expose it.

There is, of course, a kind of vanity which delights in deploring what one *was*. Perhaps I exaggerate my unattractiveness of those days. Certainly I then formed friendships with good people, intelligent people, and some of those friendships endure today.

Our large, open-plan office was grouped roughly into departments. I was Editorial. In the opposite corner was Production and Layout. Between us lay Membership and Despatch. The rest of the space was variously strewn with certain bookselling specialists: Medical and Technical, Educational, Overseas, Reference. In a fairly solid phalanx at the far end of the great room was Accounts. They seemed to perpetuate a real distinction, almost a sense of caste, wearing suits where we arty ones flaunted corduroys and sports jackets and bow ties. All their comings and goings were silent and punctual, but we laughed and chattered and despised the clock. In the midst of it all, on a dais encased in glass, sat the company secretary, drilling his financial zombies and looking with suspicion on us, the outposts of culture.

I went in some awe of Production and Layout. Not being over-gifted visually, and instinctively shying away from anything that seemed technical, I was most impressed by their familiarity with typefaces and design. I picked up some of the typographical jargon and sometimes parodied it, marking my copy with crazy instructions, but I did learn to appreciate a page of well-designed type and display, a little training in aesthetics for which I remain grateful. Johnny Ryder was the doyen in this department. He was not much older than I, who came to envy his array of recondite interests, which included anatomy and ballistics, as well as informed opinions about Joyce and Dali and Stravinsky. He represented for me the avant-garde *par excellence*, and with his puckish humour and warmth of heart he is a valued friend to this day.

Not so Ronald Clark, who wrote copy furiously all day and was obsessed with the Great Outdoors. In the office he showed little desire to fraternize, a lonely and discouraging figure with thick glasses. Out of the office he apparently cycled or potholed or climbed mountains with the same fanatical application and absence of all overt enjoyment. But his industry and dedication were later to be rewarded, as they rightly deserved, by several publishing triumphs.

My work load grew as the RU membership grew, which was rapidly. One day JB asked me: 'Have you heard of a poet called Clifford Dyment?' I had to admit I hadn't. I even wondered if he was contemporary or Victorian, or possibly a Metaphysical. JB enjoyed enlightening ignorant youths and I sensed he was especially glad to do this in my case, for my nasty guard seldom slipped. 'Well,' he went on, 'he's well regarded. More and more so. Dent's publish him. He's in need of a job. I thought he could help you with RU.'

Someone else to go in awe of, really badly in awe. But there never was a man who wanted it less. I had some trouble identifying him, as time passed and we became deeper friends, with the up-and-coming poet I often read about. Not that I ever took him for granted, ever ceased to remember his reputation. I couldn't bring myself to give him orders. JB, I think, guessed this and once when Clifford was late with some assignment I was reprimanded for not chivvying him. I lamely told JB that he was too distinguished for me to chase up. 'Distinguished be damned,' JB snapped. 'He's your assistant and paid for it.'

In and out of the office Clifford and I chatted together like fishwives. More than once I've known us talk all round the universe from 9 am to 1 pm and then go to lunch, which was usually no let-up in our gabble as we ate our sandwiches walking round and round St James's Park.

Clifford was a gentle creature of rare sensibility. Perhaps a little too serious for me, but I think he liked that. He told me I was the only person who could always make him laugh, no matter how bad the worries. His poetry means more to me now that he's gone, alas, than it did then.

James Turner and Tom Glover were also poets. They, like Clifford, were some years older than I. This didn't matter at all then but does now, for they make their exits earlier. I reviewed a novel by James called *The Mass of Death* which was so pretentious that I kidded myself I much admired it. We corresponded long before we met. He sent me the manuscript of his second book of poems, which I criticized at length, venturing to suggest a little more care with syntax and punctuation would make the reader's task so much easier. I had started to be a little resentful of needless obscurity. Complexity of thought was one thing, blithe disregard of the interpreter quite another.

I eventually went to dinner with James and his wife, Catherine, in their flat above a wine merchant's in the King's Road. I was awed again: by James, of course, by Catherine, whose father I discovered was a general, by their flat, which was not only in Chelsea but also devoid of any electricity. Candles in saucers seemed so chic, even after they'd explained that the supply had been disconnected because they couldn't pay the bill. Which I thought so splendidly Bohemian after poor old Streatham. How lightly James took it all, and after Lancing and Oxford and great country houses with teas on the lawn. I silenced the little voice within me that questioned the inability of these in-laws to pay the electric light bill. I regarded as vulgar my own childhood dependence on well-heeled relatives.

James always struck me as a rather penumbral person who could easily converse with departed spirits and would attract psychic phenomena. I had my first, and distinctly unpleasant, experience of the 'supernatural' when staying with them in an ancient Essex rectory. But neither of them had sensed anything wrong with the house, and when, some years later, they lived in Borley Rectory, they remained similarly impervious to anything remotely like a haunting. In fact James wrote an amusing book about his life at Borley.

A sensitive and intelligent-looking young man arrived one day to work at invoices on the edge of RU's accounts department. His work put me off him, as did his weekend participation in Beckenham Rugby Club. Yet this Tom Glover, I discovered, was well-read (much better than I) and a tireless writer of both verse and prose. It took me ages to fathom Tom, if I ever did. Of all the people I have known, Tom was the most devoted to literary creation. We were friends for forty years and I remember him with great respect. He published and broadcast a good deal of poetry, and a novel and some good school text books. But he never got anywhere in worldly terms. Poor health, lack of money, family worries, personal anguish, and a growing pile of rejection slips never daunted or silenced him. And he never wrote a poem in all those struggling years without sending me a carbon copy of it.

What a rich diversity these friends brought me in my uncertain teens: Clifford's uncomplaining years as skivvy in a bicycle shop, Johnny's keen adventures with microscope and scalpel, Tom's puzzling transitions from muddied oaf to Muse's darling. And not least James, insisting he would deny himself no experience, intellectual or sexual or social, that would enrich life's store. (A point of view that rather shocked me, for I was nothing if not eclectic in my lifestyle.)

My busy life at RU was well-nigh all-absorbing. Only Sunday was free, for unlike all the publishers, we worked on Saturdays. I don't remember the ghost of a complaint from anybody about working hours or wages, even though the one was long and the other short. We all seemed rather innocent and obstinately happy, although I knew spasms of self-pity like any teenager. Sometimes, as I fell in love and could do nothing about it, I asked the age-old 'Why me?' My mid-European sages had never doubted that homosexuality was a sort of sickness, though they certainly doubted their ability to cure it. Havelock Ellis and Edward Carpenter wrote with understanding if not with much hope. Lowes Dickinson's *The Greek View of Life* came as something of a revelation. Yet what help to the misfit to know that he is also an anachronism? What solace for me to locate my lost Eden in fifth-century Athens?

The plain truth was that I just didn't want to be cured. How could one conceive, let alone desire, the annihilation of the only psyche one had ever known? Moreover, I had to admit to myself that it was a psyche whose innate superiority I never for one moment doubted. I wasn't kidding myself: I took secret pleasure in a sexual orientation not duplicated anywhere in my lengthening list of acquaintances. When I saw every youth around me not only responding to the same old biological urges but also, more needlessly, prodded into early marriage by social conditioning and family pressure, well, I felt both very grateful and really rather special. I didn't blame the womenfolk, whose natural arachnidism I only too well understood, whose general sensitivity I wished the coarser male could share. I came to see myself as a paradox, as a member of a persecuted but most fortunate élite.

There was also the pleasure to be found in the role of an enigma. It wasn't just the need for unremitting caution. I had come to know all about that. No, I really enjoyed foxing people. No bland assumptions could be made about *me*. I was not to be docketed and pigeon-holed. I was not one of the pipes the world could play on. A whispered 'Hasn't he got a girlfriend?' gave way in time to a blunt 'Aren't you the marrying kind?' Before both such assaults I maintained the impassive and irritating silence of a sphinx. Of course, I could play a part when necessary. When Jack Jones gave me two tickets for his play, *Land of My Fathers*, with the strict injunction that I was to bring my girlfriend, I quite happily took Joan, who of course played the part to the life and even earned some admiring comments from RU colleagues.

Luckily, I was not in the least effeminate in appearance or manner, and I certainly wasn't attracted to those who were. I didn't have any homosexual friends and didn't want any. I just liked boys, youths, and I assumed that was very rare. It was also necessary to keep it quiet as death. Even in the street I had learned to ration strictly the admiring glances I had in more innocent days cast around so freely. (The temptation, if not the need to resist it, was surely known to that Stratford poet who described 'as fair a youth as ever made eye swerve.')

My sexuality may have been unorthodox but it certainly wasn't feeble. I knew there must be other Norman Perezes around: 'normal' but also more than game. Instinctively I mastered the language of the eye, of challenging scrutiny and wholly ambiguous gesture. And many, many times I found a ready response. I was enthralled by working-class youths who were in those days often shy, inexperienced and repressed, and I, it seemed, was not unacceptable to them. In cafés and cinemas, in trains and on buses, even fleetingly holding a glance under a streetlamp, I would achieve these Cavafy-like encounters. I was astonished by the number of them. But sad, too, for always I wanted so much more than they could give: the sexual pleasure, of course, but beyond it real friendship, affection, loyalty. But they seemed to know only clumsy hunger and fast-ensuing guilt. Even as I planned the books and the music I'd introduce them to, the dinners and the outings I'd treat them to, they were preparing to run off into their remorseful night. Strange to think that in the minds of so many working-class men now retired I am, perhaps, the indelible, guilty memory.

Nevertheless, I would not wish to be eighteen today. Where is the danger, the thrill, the excitement or the sadness for today's young adolescent, so boringly free of the closet?

28

I mustn't forget suburbia, of which I was the product and for which I had much contempt and more affection. Streatham as well as the Strand could extend horizons. For there had recently moved into a house immediately opposite ours a family of formidable and intimidating females. Five of them, a mother and four daughters. Vast quantities of solid, old-fashioned furniture were disgorged from pantechnicons, followed by a parrot with a resounding sneer and an Irish setter with its tail between its legs.

From the windows of their drawing room there issued a daily babble of voices in conflict and frequent bursts of wild, hooting laughter. They intrigued me but I was too shy to make any move towards acquaintance.

Not they, however. I was coming home from the office one summer's eve and being, as often, deep in a book, walked right past our house, until something between a bellow and a hoot from opposite recalled me. I glanced across and there were all five mocking faces at their windows. I blushed and grinned and right-about-turned to hurry indoors. This led to 'Good mornings' and 'Good evenings' when I passed them pottering among the blooms of their unkempt front garden, as they seemed now in the habit of doing.

James-Arthur, our young greengrocer, told me that the mother had asked him about 'those handsome boys across the road.' I was wary. This, I decided, was not Miss Alcott's Marmee but Miss Austen's Mrs Bennett, complete with brood to match. I learned that the eldest daughter, Amy, who must have been nearing forty, was the housekeeper for them all, that the two middle ones worked in a City bank, and that the youngest was still at school. I sensed that they had rather come down in the world and ends didn't easily meet.

Incredibly, Amy asked me if my brothers and I would care to take tea with them one Sunday. I was rather panicked into acceptance and more or less forced Brian and Terry into accompanying me.

So we went.

THE MORE WE ARE TOGETHER

The mother sat in a corner of the room in a high-backed wing chair with a footstool. Yet not a chair but a throne. On her right was the parrot's stand, on her left the dog cringed in its basket. All around her were grouped the daughters: on stools, on pouffes, on the floor. A carefully set tableau. The dog stirred uneasily, Mrs Fraser boomed: 'Still, Bruce', the parrot sneered, and all the daughters gushed forth words and hoots and coughs and ringing laughter. When they subsided somewhat, we visitors were able to enjoy some conversation, though they were all so bursting with energy that lines were frequently crossed. I gathered that Commander Roderick Fraser, RN, was quite recently deceased. This was told me in an urgent undertone during an outburst of hoots, for Mrs Fraser must not be reminded of anything that could distress her. Otherwise they were enormously amusing and encouraged us to be so. We found we had a somewhat similar sense of humour, especially when the topic was our road and its often cranky residents. Amy had made a large and toothsome fruit cake and mother dispensed tea from an urn they insisted was a samovar.

The daughters had crazy names for each other and we had to learn them in order to keep abreast of what was happening. One was 'Mrs Blenkinsop', another was 'Hooper' (without a handle), and another was 'BD'. Only on a later visit did I learn that 'BD' stood for 'Bottom Drawer' because Meg, its owner, had a most plebeian taste for cockles and mussels acquired on a maritime expedition with father. They had many such private jokes which time elucidated. And they wrote long, chatty letters to one another, filled with scandalous gossip about fictitious characters they took with great seriousness.

They stand, in my memory, somewhere between the Brontës and the Mitfords. They possessed sheer gusto in greater measure than I have ever met elsewhere. As they fought with one another (but never mother) for conversational mastery, they would bounce in their seats, hoot deafeningly and emphasize their words by driving clenched fists floorward. The home was a shrine, its deity the commander, his relict the Sibyl. Most of the votaries she had herself created, but now and again she would deliver an oracle in a voice of thunder: 'Hoo, the commander never could abide marzipan,' or 'The commander *dwarfed* any sword he wore,' or 'The commander said all Germans should colonize the floor of the Atlantic.' Remarks like the last did not go down well with Terry (who soon refused further invitations), or with Brian (who thought them infantile), or with me (who deplored them as the only jarring notes in these choruses of fun). The Sibyl delighted in anecdotes that glorified the commander's virility, her reiterated favourite being his treatment of an insolent rating. The triumphant bellow of its final sentence is something Brian and I never forgot: 'The commander took him by the scruff of the neck *and flung him to the lower deck.*'

The Sibyl was actually quite small in stature (only once did I see her off her throne, and then by an oversight) but her immense head and overriding lung power conveyed the prodigious. And we soon learned that there never was less of a Mrs Bennett in any mother. Mrs Fraser, as the commander's Sibyl, had imposed on the daughters their roles in life as vestal virgins. We discovered there were two more children: Anne, whom we never saw, who had actually deserted the shrine to marry 'some engineer fellah,' and Clarence, who had also married, and turned up one Sunday in a sports car. His wife remained in the car and Clarence remained on the doorstep, denied access by a tearful Amy. I was in the drawing room at the time. In the deathly silence mother swelled and purpled, the Sibyl became Medusa.

Once, and rather maliciously, I enquired after Anne. In the terrible hush that supervened, mother suddenly cried: 'Hoo, we don't mention her in this house.'

So what on earth were we three doing there? I honestly believe our function was to test the rigid allegiance of the daughters to their vocation. Brian, I'm afraid, quite fell for the youngest, 16-year-old Hil. Brian once waylaid her coming home from school, and Hil told the Sibyl all about it. She, in an unforgettable interview, verbally flung poor Brian to the lowest of decks. So he, too, was banished. Only I was left, and because I really did like the daughters, and enjoyed my Sunday teas with them, I would not break the magic spell the Sibyl wove around me. And did she, in some unacknowledged far recess of her mind, divine that I was safe? That I could never rescue any maiden to make her mine?

29

Then the wonderful world where I earned my living cast up something so marvellous that the home front was all but obliterated.

The premises of our parent company adjoined ours and sometimes I had to visit the secretaries of their directors with lists of book club suggestions: up to the roof in the lift and across a caged bridge into a more sedate world. And on one such visit I almost collided with a vision of such loveliness that I literally gasped and staggered. One hesitates to say of any particular individual that he was the most beautiful boy one has ever seen, for there are so many kinds of beauty and one has been so many times enslaved. But I think that even at this remove I must pay that tribute to young Jimmy Armstrong. He was sixteen and fairly tall and moved like a gazelle. His limbs were exquisitely moulded and he bore himself with an unknown pride that betokened some real d'Urbervilles ancestry. But the wonder, of course, was the face. Set in an unblemished complexion were delicate nose and chiselled lips and long-lashed eyes that simply and unselfconsciously shone. It was a face any girl of taste would have coveted. Yet there was nothing effeminate about its essentially Greek and essentially male perfection. Socrates would have swooned to see it and so almost did I, especially when a very faint blush responded to my stare.

As swing doors swung and typewriters clattered and busy people brushed by, I fought in our silence for some word to detain him. At last I murmured:

'Do you work here? I mean, I've not seen you before.'

'Yes. I'm the office boy. I've been here a year now. I expect you've seen me before.'

Emboldened by his friendliness and his apparent reluctance to move on, I said with deliberate emphasis: 'Oh no, I certainly wouldn't have forgotten if I'd seen you before.'

I was rewarded by the merest deepening of the pink in his cheeks. He spoke a careful Cockney. Every word was a shade over-articulated, every 'h' a little over-aspirated, in a manner that was infinitely attractive.

'I work for Reader's Union, in the other building,' I said, never removing my eyes from his face.

He brightened. 'That's funny. I'm coming to work there. In the accounts department. Next month. I've been transferred.'

This, I felt, must be a dream. Out of it I heard my voice faintly: 'What a bit of luck. Perhaps you'll be near me. I'm in the editorial department. The accounts share our office.'

'Oh, do they?' I couldn't tell whether he was pleased or not. Then he braced himself and said: 'Must be getting on. Lots to do.'

'Tell me your name before you go.' I felt like Jacob wrestling with the sublime.

'Armstrong.'

'What's your first name?'

'James.'

'Jim? Or Jamie? Jimmy?' I so wanted to get it right.

'Well, Jimmy if you like.' Now he seemed pleased.

'So long, Jimmy. Looking forward to seeing you at RU.'

And it was all true. And his desk was very near mine. Oh, never again would I doubt a divinity shaping my ends.

I embarked on a courtship which was inevitably beset with difficulties. Most adolescent boys are aware when they are being wooed and enjoy playing with the fire. With great care, and without ever exciting notice or comment, I contrived meetings in all sorts of places: in less frequented passages, in an agreeably poky stationery room, sometimes in the street at lunchtime. When I saw him heading for the washroom with his soap and towel, I'd hurry out of the office in the other direction, circumnavigate the building and enter the washroom by the back stairs. In such corners and by such means, I would pursue my verbal wooings. As time went by our conversation became more outrageous. Delightfully, he was always ready for my sallies.

I'd open with some such words as: 'And how's my beautiful boy today?'

He'd grin and say: 'Very well, thank you. And how's yourself?'

'Very happy now that I can gaze at you. You know, of course, that I'm hopelessly head-over-heels in love with you?'

He laughed. 'And you know you're barmy?'

'Not barmy. Just madly in love.'

'You want to get yourself a girl, you do. That's your trouble.'

'No, I don't want a girl. I want you. You're far more beautiful than any girl could ever be.'

He pretended to look serious and shook his head. 'Very sad case, doctor. Quite young, too. Well, you're not going to have me, see?'

'Not just one kiss from those honied lips?'

'Nope, not one. Anyway, I wouldn't kiss you with that old stuff over your face.' For, in pursuit of the badge of intellectualism, I was trying to grow a beard.

'Ah, that means you would kiss me if I shaved it off?'

'I bet you wouldn't.'

'I bet I would. You just wait and see.'

And I did. But I still didn't get the kiss.

Sometimes I'd say: 'Let's spend the day together on Sunday. What do you do on Sundays?'

'Well now, let me see. I get up late, then I have my bath, then I go and play football in the park.'

I lifted my eyes to heaven. 'Oh, visions, visions!'

He looked puzzled. 'Visions?'

'Yes, pure vision of beauty: you in your football shorts. Even sublimer, you in the bath.'

He tutted. 'He's off again. Past cure, I'm afraid, doctor.'

Very occasionally, when the coast was especially clear, I'd tickle him: doubled up, falling to the floor, wildly giggling, he'd be tickled all over. He loved it. Once he said admiringly: 'Coo, you're strong. You scored a bullseye that time. Got the whole lot in your hands, you did.'

I chuckled evilly and twirled my imaginary moustache. 'And again, my fine filly?' As I advanced he backed against the wall and covered himself. 'No, not again,' he laughed. 'It's all private property. I've got a notice there saying trespassers will be prosecuted.'

'Oh, but I'm not a trespasser. I'm your adoring lover. A lover's never a trespasser.'

I often wondered, and wonder still, why he should have enjoyed this banter so much. I don't think it had anything to do with vanity. I once asked him how he could be unaware of his beauty. Did he never gaze in a glass and perceive it? Apparently not. I like to think he enjoyed the real affection behind the banter. After all, there was only a couple of years between us.

At last I persuaded him to have an evening out with me. I told him I'd take him to an opera at Sadler's Wells. He got his parents' permission and we arranged to leave the office separately and meet in the waiting room on Charing Cross station. I was delighted by the readiness with which he entered into this collusion and couldn't resist asking him why. His reply was disappointing yet oddly touching. 'Well, I'm only the office boy,' he said simply.

We had some supper in a café. He wanted to pay for himself but I was determined the whole evening should be my treat. Over our supper I told him the story of *Aïda*. I asked him if I could hold his hand during the performance. 'No,' he said. 'Someone might see. It'd look daft.' I told him no one could see under my raincoat and he made no further protest. And hold his hand I did, for most of three wonderful hours.

As we parted at the Angel Underground station, I said to him: 'Do you believe, Jimmy, can you believe, that I really do love you?' It was the only time I saw him look solemn, even sad. 'I believe you *like* me,' he said very deliberately after a pause. Then he brightened and added: 'And I like you. A lot.' Before I could say more he ran for his train.

Those words and the handholding were the only rewards I ever obtained, and I wouldn't now wish for any others.

After the war I tried to find him again. No enquiries at RU could yield a living address. His old Hackney address was now a sea of rubble. Old stagers who'd been at RU with us couldn't remember the face or the name. Tom de Quincey never sought his Ann more diligently than I sought Jimmy Armstrong. Perhaps he was killed in the war. He was just the kind of eager, willing kid who was destined for cannon fodder.

30

Of course I couldn't get through my teens without brushing against religion and politics, which were now becoming intertwined. In my home circle the older generation continued to regard any religious concern with mildly amused indifference, while the younger reacted with a more positive contempt. If I had, as a child, been pressed to an answer, and could have formulated it, I should have said I couldn't conceive of man without God or life without a heavenly goal. A fairly independent-minded child reared in an irreligious environment will show some interest in the phenomenon. But it wasn't with me just cussedness. If pressed further I might have conceded I couldn't think of God without a conviction that he was distinctly fond of me. I don't know whether this was a child's simple faith or an uglier manifestation of my egotism. Always, seeping through from Miss Tierney's Bible stories, was this image of Jesus as the disturbing friend you both did and did not want.

When I was about twelve I had joined the Crusaders, an evangelical body with a ministry to 'public and private schoolboys only.' In its literature the 'only' was printed in heavy type, presumably to reassure bourgeois parents that it was well aware of the distinction between religious conditioning and social contamination. I joined it because the rather attractive boy opposite (the son of Mr Gray the Plymouth Rock) used to patronize the Crusaders on Sunday afternoons. I wasn't at all sure that I wanted to know him, coming from such a family, but I felt there was no harm in having a closer look. In any case, the 'leaders' were nice, earnest men of some local standing who collected and delivered us boys in sleek limousines I rather approved of. So, doubtless for reasons no worthier than those of our medieval namesakes, I became a Crusader.

The Sunday meetings were quite enjoyable, with catchy 'choruses' and holy pep talks from both of which I remained rather surprisingly aloof. I didn't get to know young Jonathan Gray either. I was convinced his parents had told him not to be friends with a godless boy, something I certainly invented. Much better than the Sunday classes were the weekend camps in the green belt. I went on one. There were campfire singsongs and tasty barbecues and organized games no one forced you to play. In the dormitory after lights out there were other games wild horses couldn't have kept me from playing. So, at least, it was with me and my immediate neighbour, a merry little extrovert with as much sense of sin as Falstaff. As if to redress the balance, a very pleasant, studious boy of about seventeen, who was at Dulwich and heading for Oxford, took an entirely chaste fancy to me. We would go for long walks and talks through the fields, which some earnest leader or other would invariably interrupt. I thought this was because they wanted me to attend a prayer meeting or join in a healthy game, but now I'm not so sure.

It all made quite an impression on me, and some of the moral dousings surely cleaned me up a bit. They never affected my amorous tastes, though, because I refused to believe that these were wicked.

After a few years I gave up the Crusaders, suddenly and decisively. I think there was some talk of my being 'saved,' of 'making a commitment,' and I neither liked lying nor intended to renounce what seemed to me harmless pleasures but to them cardinal sins. So I saved myself, from graduation as fledgling prig to feathered Pharisee.

Partly from a genuine interest, and partly no doubt from feelings of guilt about my defection, I went on dutifully reading my New Testament, that is, the Gospels, where I skipped or ignored all that was uncongenial to me. By such time-honoured means I fashioned my own Jesus out of the many Jesuses the evangelists provided. Mine was a charismatic rebel poet with a tart tongue and the brilliant weapon of a proffered cheek. I might as easily have fashioned an irascible and intolerant meddler who didn't always practise what he preached, but I didn't because that wasn't what I needed. We had had divinity lessons at Montrose, of course, but they were taken by Mr Stewart, which would in any case have been the kiss of death. Moreover, Mr Stewart was obsessed with Paul's missionary journeys and I don't remember ever doing anything but *Acts* with him. I think he saw in Paul an archetypal Scot who left home to exploit the Sassenachs of Asia Minor.

One of the favourite hymns among the Crusaders had been the lively old 'I will make you fishers of men,' and as I journeyed on through my teens it certainly seemed I was being made such a fisher. Or, more accurately, a fisher of youths. Now less of a search for the ideal playmate, more of a sexual quest. Yet that innocent little Eden of Mrs Mackenzie's painting was never far removed from my yearnings, even at their most carnal. The sons of neighbours, the younger brothers of Brian's and Terry's friends, boyfriends of Pam, even distant cousins known only by hearsay, were all grist to my imaginary mills.

For example, Jimbo, Francis and Eric, the sons of father's sister, Winifred, and her husband, Uncle Will. I had never set eyes on any of them, but I heard a great deal about the three boys because my brothers had several times in my childhood spent holidays with them. They lived near Burton-on-Trent, where Uncle Will was accountant to one or more of the great Burton breweries, and all three boys went to Repton. Brian and Terry came home filled with stories about Aunt Winnie and Uncle Will, but most of all, of course, about their wild and adventurous offspring. That's what they seemed to me, I think mostly because they were always taking Brian and Terry sculling. Sculling on the Trent seemed to be the consuming passion of the whole family. A passion they seemed determined to transmit to their rather overurbanized cousins. The very first time I heard talk of sculling I entirely misunderstood its nature, associating it with head-hunting. And even though I was soon put right, with vehemence, scorn and ridicule, it never lost a rather grim aura in my mind. Nor did Francis and Eric. Not Jimbo though, because I had from the first appropriated him for myself. I liked his name, I liked his being, like me, the youngest boy, and I treasured up some offhand remark of my mother's to the effect that he was 'the best-looking of the bunch.'

So when, one crazy Sunday in 1938, Brian and Terry hired a car for the day and decided to go hell-for-leather for Staffordshire to visit the mad scullers, I eagerly went with them. My brothers shared the driving, and I shudder now to think of it. But I suppose there was less on the roads in those days, and perhaps they were less harum-scarum than I now believe.

At last I fished up these young men, and their boyhood images were finally laid to rest. For the twins, Francis and Eric, were *not* attractive. To my horror, they were ginger-haired, which was my idea of the untouchable. Jimbo was more presentable, but still far from my romantic visions. They lived in a big house with several servants, and they greeted us very hospitably, which was pretty good since we were entirely unexpected. I remember a stone-walled dining room with a long refectory table at which we were given a hearty lunch with flagons of ale (from their father's brewery, I imagine). I didn't drink the ale, and I didn't see Aunt Winifred or Uncle Will because they were away. I didn't ever see them. Or the three boys again. The war scattered them, and how many of them survived it, I don't know. We Gambles were southerners, Londoners, and my father's family were never quite admissible, being 'come-ups' or Midlanders.

But that trip survives in my mind as something rather sad, rather wistful: a sort of deliberate leave-taking of that prewar world, of my boyhood, of peace, a madcap last fling before Armageddon.

31

Our Streatham neighbours were odd. Or perhaps we had too sharp an eye for oddities in anybody. Quite apart from the hooting Frasers, who were enlivening my Sunday afternoons, there were our immediate neighbours on the left: Mr Henpecked Haycraft, his Tory-campaigning wife, and his frightfully patriotic daughter Kathleen, who was the age of Brian and Terry and had recently become an MP's secretary. Mrs Haycraft had bridge parties and political teas, into neither of which did mother and Nora fit. But they often had tête-à-tête tea parties with Mrs Haycraft, who, I think, was secretly relieved to let her hair down on these occasions when no sense of duty marred the dainty sandwiches and home-made sponges and even homelier gossip. Mr Haycraft sometimes worked at home, at his big draughtsman's table in one of the attics. No one who visited the house ever found him anywhere but in the attic, his bolt hole. He was surprisingly kind. He gave my brother Brian £20 (a lot of money in those days) when the lad set off for Canada as a purser's assistant. I think poor Mr Haycraft found a vicarious thrill in this teenager's voyage to the New World.

Our neighbours on the other side were as different from the Haycrafts as our bourgeois minds could imagine. They were professional musicians and Quakers and socialists. They were also aggressive, warring with us and their other neighbours about fences and hedges and bones given to their dog. I think this dispirited animal was compelled to be, like his owners, a strict vegetarian. They were also fresh-air fiends. We sometimes wondered if their house was furnished, since they spent all daylight hours, even in chilly weather, on benches in the garden. Father was an opera singer, who employed his lungs not only on arias but also on tradesmen. If they were obsequious he fiercely preached to them the brotherhood of man. If they showed any sign of expecting a tip he fumed about the dignity of labour before slamming the door. He did this most memorably one Christmas to a wretched dustman who'd called for a Christmas box. Skulking behind curtains and nearly exploding with laughter, we treated ourselves to the whole libretto, then meanly rejoiced in the dustman's flight without any contribution from us. Almost as good an entertainment to spy on was a string quartet they once had playing on their lawn. Again my family of Philistines giggled behind curtains at the antics of these inspired Davids. I blush now to recall how barbarian we were. Many years later, when they'd moved off elsewhere, and I was a bit maturer, I met this family at a lieder recital and found them not only very pleasant but also most amusing.

I was trying to fashion myself into something I considered rather more sophisticated. At least once a week I deserted Clifford and the Green Park ducks we shared our sandwiches with for the bliss of a leisurely lunch in the Strand brasserie. I loved the food there, but even more I loved the attentions of a waiter. After the lunch, over a long coffee, I'd pretend to read my paper, which was *The Morning Post*, bought for its classy image and never its boring articles. I made an even more spectacular revolution in my travelling arrangements. I'd noticed, at the foot of St Martin's Lane, a firm called The Railway Season Ticket Instalment Company. I discovered I could there buy a three-monthly first-class season ticket for so much per week. It was a marvellous new life: to and from work in style, enjoying not least the secret disappointment of the jumpers who were quite sure they'd landed a catch in this adolescent youth ensconced amid all the plutocratic city gents. With never a glance upward from my *Morning Post*, I'd hold up my virgin white, first-class season, my passport to a better world. Streatham Hill to London Bridge then right across the station for further plush travel from London Bridge to Charing Cross. No more buses and tubes, no more straphanging and sardinery. I refused to feel embarrassed about it, even when I sometimes met one of the Fraser daughters on Streatham Hill station. 'Please excuse me now,' I said as our train came in. 'I have to go first class because I have so much stuff to read for the office.' ('Oh well,' I said to my sometimes uneasy conscience, 'if I've had the enterprise to discover how to do it, all credit to me.')

I had become aware in 1937 that some were beginning to see in Hitler a threat to world peace, while others saw in him the hoped-for bastion against Marxism. To yet others, a minority, but a powerful and growing one, he was the architect of a state Britain should emulate. Mosley and his British Union of Fascists were increasingly active, and, less ostentatious and therefore perhaps more dangerous, so were organizations like the Anglo-German Bund and Admiral Sir Barry Domvile's The Link, of which I came to hear more than I wished. But these people would have approved of young men like Brian and Terry who, with motives purely amorous and a political naivety characteristic of the bourgeoisie, were seeking liaisons with German pen friends. Girls, of course. (My own desperate dreams were of their leather-knickerbockered young brothers in the Hitler Youth. But all my devious hints to Brian never produced a line from any of them.)

Both Brian and Terry worked hard at the Linguaphone German course and finally netted a young fräulein called Edith who came to stay with us. She was a serious-minded girl, quite pretty in a rather heavy way, and with impeccable manners. Whenever she encountered my father, she would drop half a curtsey, and he (whose manners were also impeccable) would give half a bow. It amused us greatly. We'd await almost with bated breath this little minuet of Mandarin courtesy. All I really remember about the fair Edith is the tone of hushed adoration in which she described Hitler's ride through her native town in her father's very own automobile and by her father's very side. Even then, before any political stances had hardened within me, I found the whole anecdote, and the way she told it, rather sickening.

I wasn't ever by nature a political animal, but it was impossible in those thirties to ignore Japan in China or Mussolini in Ethiopia or Hitler ranting in almost every cinema newsreel or jackbooted Nazis goose-stepping all over Europe. I loathed and despised the lot of them. Any militarism, regimentation, mass hysteria, quite horrified me, and the sight of any uniform other than a telegraph boy's made my lip curl. I didn't really know it then but I loved my country dearly; the way of life, the national character, the urban sprawls and the Surrey hills, were what I had been nourished on and coveted. But taint any of that with jingoism and even the concept of patriotism was horribly suspect. Whatever else in my character might be posturing and affectation, this at least was sincere. I feared anything that threatened to annihilate the individual. The only group I'd ever really identified with was the family, which meant everything to me, yet even there I had of necessity become a member with a secret life. Elsewhere I tended to be a loner, the sick little bull rejected by the herd he needed and feared. My reactions were largely emotional, but I liked to kid myself they were intellectual; I was no different from any teenager in being a sprouting muddle.

32

The atmosphere at RU was at first, through JB, rather that of an old-fashioned guild socialism. But already in 1938 the influence of the leftist camp at RU was militant, given to commitment and protest. The young poets and idealists of the day had made Spain first a literary cause and then a violent crusade. This astonished me, that young men of superior education and great talent should pin their hopes of a better world on bullets and bayonets. We knew nothing in those days of the horrors to be fully uncovered when Germany was defeated. Nothing of concentration camps and gas chambers and genocide. To me, Hitler was just one more patriotic leader fighting to restore his country's status, fighting crudely, stupidly, truculently, but then they nearly all did the same when the dice were loaded against them. The British in Ireland, the British in India, the British in South Africa: there didn't seem much to choose between any of the cocky, flag-waving nations of Europe. Hitler, Mussolini, Franco were bubbles that would burst as soon as they got too big.

So I'd no time for any of the ranting masses, left or right. Just down the road from RU was Victor Gollancz and his Left Book Club. I often had to go in there, and I'd see the rather frantic mills of the LBC turning, and Victor himself, an intimidating figure in a seedy office, and I'd feel the inevitable resistance building up inside me. I came to admire the more mature Victor of the *Letters to Timothy* and the stand against postwar revenges, but in those late thirties he seemed just a part of the international bomb-behind-the-back brigade.

An addition to RU's despatch department at this time was a six-foot-four Cockney who'd been wounded in the International Brigade and was only too ready to recount his adventures. Others hung on his words, and in the eyes of some I saw the same adoration I'd seen in Fräulein Edith's eyes, and it gave me the same creeps. There was a hatred in his tones, at times even a blood lust, the innate sickness of the mercenary.

I went to a great LBC rally at Olympia in which speaker after speaker condemned the fascist hordes of Europe, and I could applaud that. But not their admiration for the growing might of Europe's enigma, the USSR. When the enthusiastic audience sang 'The Red Flag' and passed the hat round for Spanish Republican arms I felt unable to respond with tongue or hand.

There was a more restrained meeting at the Queen's Hall, billed as 'Writers Declare Against Fascism.' There was an impressive platform: everyone from Spender to de Madariaga, from Wells to Walpole. Each speaker seemed more passionate than his predecessor in demanding the swift rearmament of Britain. Except, that is, for poor old Hugh Walpole whose cry I remember still: 'All I ask is to be left alone, just left alone to get on with my work.' They were words that went down ill with that militant audience, but they certainly had an echo in my tepid breast. I could picture my stubborn old boyhood Jesus sadly shaking his head. At the end of the proceedings there was a call from the platform for all who supported armed resistance to fascism, if necessary, to rise promptly to their feet. With a pounding heart I alone kept my seat. I gazed unhappily at the floor sooner than meet the contemptuous glances I must be incurring. I wanted to tell everyone I wasn't a fascist. I was... I was... (and it was the first time I found a label for myself) a *Christian pacifist*. Yes, if I had to have some placard round my neck, that was the only one that would do.

But it wasn't just Jesus in whose name I sat. It was in Aldous Huxley's. I'd just read his *Ends and Means* and the impact had been great. I wasn't too sure about his nonattachment, being myself much more of a humanist than a mystic, an E. M. Forster man who believed in 'personal relationships for ever and ever.' But Huxley finally convinced me that the pacifist message alone made sense, both spiritually and politically. And convinced me if war came I'd have to be a conscientious objector. I knew quite well there could be unworthy motives in this decision: sentimentality, cowardice, pride, sheer rebelliousness. But I couldn't elsewhere find a place to lay that confused head which had for some time now been bombarded from both right and left. The attack from the left was confined to RU and many of my friends there, and it was incidental, fragmentary, aimed around me rather than at me. The attack from the right had for the past two years been more concentrated. There were Hitler's monthly postal blandishments, too cheap and crude to have any effect. And there were the more formidable assaults over tea in Kensington on the first Sunday in each month, from the Mrs Gladwyn Jebb I had met at Lady Haggard's.

I greatly enjoyed and valued those Sunday tea parties. I artlessly pumped Mrs Jebb about past literary figures she'd known: Rider Haggard, of course, and Kipling and Belloc and Barrie. She'd known many such celebrities, but she tired rather quickly of talking about them. She was much more forthcoming about the politicians: Gladstone, Joseph Chamberlain, Balfour, Asquith, Baldwin. She was severe on them all. For all, it seemed, had been in varying degrees blind, and Lloyd George the blindest bat of all. It frankly bored me, and I became less bored than refractory when she began to promote Oswald Mosley as the only hope for Britain.

So I switched when I could to her memories of a bygone age. She told me her husband, Joshua Gladwyn Jebb, had been considerably older than she and had played some part in quelling the Indian Mutiny, but there surely either her memory or mine must be at fault. She said she must have been one of the first young women to smoke. I suppose she meant one of the first in her social bracket. She painted amusing pictures of her subterfuges: on all fours in her bedroom, exhaling up the chimney.

It was an odd communion. On one side of the tea and muffins sat a boy in love with the past. On the other sat this elderly woman whose great concern was for the future of Europe. More and more the conversation veered to politics. Small, vivacious, birdlike, she must have been an attractive girl, for she combined with her good looks a sharp mind and tongue. What could be her interest in me, I wondered? She told me once she had been brought up to see that wealth and rank entailed responsibility: good works and patronage were a duty. I wondered uncomfortably if she was patronizing *me*. I also sensed that I was proving a disappointment to her. I was lacking in the right ideals, which were, to her, enmeshed in patriotism and militarism. She sat in silent disapproval as I spoke my views more boldly. We did better, I felt, on paper. I have sheaves of letters from her, tenderly preserved like so many others across all the years. I regularly sent her reviews I wrote and her replies were always encouraging. She sent me little anecdotes: encounters in Harrods, discoveries in an old bureau, a conversation with a retired general who found solace in directing his many regiments of toy soldiers. This was, if I remember aright, a Sir George MacMunn, who wrote a most charming article about his hobby in *The Times*. I wrote to congratulate him on it, but regretted he should feel so much nostalgia about a life of violence and death. He replied warmly. That is to say, he ticked me off with some heat for my lack of pride in my country's achievements. I have never forgotten the last sentence of his letter: 'I can only give you good advice I heard when I was young: "keep your mouth shut and your bowels open".' I thought this too indelicate to show to Mrs Jebb. A pity; she would have relished it.

There was almost a rift between us when she lent me a book about a young climber killed on Everest. I think he was a relative of hers. I thought his early death was a deplorable waste. Again, Mrs Jebb found in me not the expected admiration, only a rather bitter condemnation of this sorry world in which the old so often encouraged the young, the brave, the beautiful, to throw away their lives for nothing.

As time passed and the war clouds grew thicker over Europe, Mrs Jebb seemed to try harder to redeem me. She was, of course, delighted to hear of my correspondence with Hitler. She hoped I had studied carefully the literature he had sent me. My reply again produced in her a tight-lipped disdain. I often expressed to her some views I had encountered at RU, and at RU I took a malicious pleasure in propagating her wholesale condemnation of the USSR. I really felt I couldn't trust either side. In Orwell's later words, I 'looked from pig to man, and from man to pig, and from pig to man again, but already it was impossible to say which was which.'

She urged me to contact the local agent of the British Union of Fascists, Mosley's party machine. I resisted for a long time, but she said this was the only fair-minded course for me to take. It was unthinkable that an intelligent young man should not at least examine Mosley's political diagnoses. Such flattery and bullying finally prodded me into a kind of action. The BUF promptly sent round a man I can't now visualize. He called several times and as he left he would pause at the garden gate to give me the fascist salute. Needless to say, I never returned it. Indeed, I think it was that rather than any of his stupid words that finally convinced me. I wrote to him to say that I found the party's aims incompatible with all I believed in and, for priggish good measure, all that Christianity taught. He wrote me a rather sad and silly reply to the effect that he couldn't see anything unchristian in love of one's country. Poor young man, I'm sure he eventually became an obedient conscript, perhaps even a gallant one. Mrs Jebb agreed with his words and trounced my pacifism as at best irrelevant and at worst craven-spirited.

My visits became fewer. Yet I missed them and was sorry to have forfeited her respect. I had hoped to find in her a wise and affectionate counsellor, an extender of horizons. In me she had hoped for a protégé she could in some measure fashion. I last saw her for tea in the Army and Navy Stores soon after war broke out. She felt that if they'd listened to Mosley there wouldn't have been a war. I felt, but forbore to say, that her patriotism must now be under a severe strain.

33

At a desk near mine in RU's main office sat a nice girl called Katie Legge. Intelligent, and quite lacking in female wiles, she was the only girl there whose company I could enjoy without suspicion or embarrassment. She always called me by my surname, and I almost forgot her gender. We sometimes had lunch together at the brasserie. She of course paid for herself. It was that kind of relationship.

One day she was sniffing and crying as she typed. I asked her what was wrong but she just shook her head. She was one of JB's secretaries and at five o'clock she took her letters down to him for signing. When she returned she handed me one of them with the words: 'I'm terribly sorry, Gamble.'

It was from JB and very much to the point: 'I can only see your letter in this week's *Times Literary Supplement* as a direct attack on me and all that RU stands for, and so I find no alternative to giving you a week's notice.'

I was flabbergasted. True, I had contributed to a debate on current trends in fiction, never imagining they would print my silly letter, still less that JB's eyes would fall on it. I had penned an attack on the proletarian novel, with which I was growing heartily fed up. I went down to see JB, his letter in my hand. I felt pretty tearful but hoped I was showing nothing but indignation.

'Well,' I began, 'I haven't come to apologize.'

'No, I knew you wouldn't, you little bugger,' he snapped.

We looked at each other and I said, still angrily, but with an honest enough desire to set the situation to rights before I decamped: 'I wasn't attacking you at all. Or RU.' That was almost quite true. I'd thought I was gallantly defending Virginia Woolf.

He suddenly reached out his hand. 'Show me that letter,' he ordered.

I handed it to him, wondering. He tore it into pieces and threw them into his wastepaper basket.

'Oh forget it,' he said. Then, in a kind of exasperation, added: 'The trouble with you is that you were born with a silver spoon in your mouth and you've no idea how to toe the bloody line.'

The injustice of this unlocked my tongue and I poured it all out. I told him about the hard times: father's unemployment, the unpaid bills, the summonses, the vans calling for our furniture, the humiliations of my schooling. I spoke in a torrent, without pride or reservation, with no aim but to rid him of this false image of me as a youth who'd never had to face reality.

He said simply: 'I'm sorry. I never guessed. You're due for a rise. I'll arrange for another pound a week.'

I didn't feel embarrassed, didn't protest my words had had no such aim. I just felt there was a bond between us which moved me strangely and made me want to escape. I blurted out my thanks and ran. After a few minutes in the washroom I told Katie the happy outcome. 'Oh, Gamble, I'm so glad,' she said, and held out her hand. It was the sober, heartfelt conclusion to a day of battle. I felt that in some odd way I'd never be quite the same. I'd cast off my lendings.

In 1938 I found for myself a tutor in maths. Some sense of the insecurity of things urged me to try again for my matric. He was an interesting young man with a lively mind. Unhappily, he was also a consumptive who had been unable to follow a profession since leaving Cambridge a few years before. I found it difficult to keep our noses to this very uncongenial grindstone when there were so many fascinating topics to discuss. Nor could he have found any pleasure in trying to teach someone so devoid of aptitude for his subject. Somehow I memorized crude lines of attack that yielded answers occasionally correct. I learned by heart the essential formulae without ever knowing what they meant. The other subjects I mugged up for myself, and in the summer I rather despondently faced this wretched hurdle again at the Imperial Institute in South Kensington. The instant I reached my desk in the examination hall I grabbed a piece of paper and jotted down all the formulae I'd still been silently mouthing as we queued on the stairs.

To my astonishment it worked. I even passed with distinction. It was my first piece of real self-discipline. And of cynicism about academic attainments.

I also about this time made a preposterous attempt to become a pianist. I think the matric success swelled my head. My mother had been a competent pianist, but the demands of a family and the lack of a piano had put an end to her playing. I felt I should see what the next generation could do. Of course, there must be no half measures. I obtained a very large and very handsome grand piano on the never-never, and a tutor of equal distinction at five shillings per weekly lesson. He was a concert pianist who gave public recitals and frequently broadcast. He was so good that I felt sure he would prove a magician. Nothing short of a magician could have made a pianist of me. I was soon able to play with both hands a simple little piece, reading the music correctly but for one thing: I could never understand how you discovered what the timing was. After my tutor had played the piece to me I could reproduce it correctly by ear, but how to make the notes a tune I never fathomed. So I got discouraged and the piano went back to the shop and the tutor went back to the concert platform.

War loomed, then seemed to retreat decisively. One day, seeing a crowd outside number 10 Downing Street as I was on my way home, I joined it for a moment. They were waiting to cheer Chamberlain as he returned from Munich with his bit of paper. The dominant mood of all those good people was relief, and although many of the staff at BU were disgusted by the ditching of Czechoslovakia I shared the common emotion for once. Very clearly I see a little man who stood near me in Downing Street and muttered something about a sellout, and a bruiser in a homburg wagged a podgy finger under his nose and asked him truculently: 'You one of these bloody communists?' The little man backed in alarm. 'No, mate, no, not me,' he protested, and quickly lost himself in the crowd.

1939 came, our great watershed year. Hitler ranted defiantly on. Clouds and rumblings once more made themselves known. Air-raid shelters were being dug in parks and commons. My Sunday teas with the Frasers became more and more uneasy. Their wholesale condemnation of everybody and everything German grew more stupid, to my mind more childish. I had to protest, even, in the end, to declare my pacifist allegiance. The Sibyl purpled and roared: 'The Commander ranked pacifists lower than socialists.' I said: 'I think I'd better be going home now.' One of the daughters ventured: 'Oh, mother, please don't let him go like that,' but became stone before the Medusa look. I left the room to the final and terrible execration: 'Yes, go home, go home and wash your brains out, *coward*!'

And that was the end of the Frasers. A few months later they moved away. Only a few roads away, but far enough to prevent contamination. I missed them. Like Mrs Jebb, they presented me with what was to become a deepening mystery, namely, how people who attracted me with their humour, intelligence, kindliness could in this one area prove incredibly stupid, blind, cruel. The years have never lessened the disturbing load of surprise: I suddenly find an ugly wart in a person I have taken to. I don't like warts in my friends, and there are certain warts I have never come to terms with: jingoism, racialism, fundamentalism, calls for the death penalty.

That summer our hopes for peace were laid in ruins. We had an air-raid drill at RU and I with one other refused to take part. There was a gentle, idealistic young man in, of all places, the accounts department. His name was Laurie and I had only very recently spoken to him. He and I alone sat at our desks one July mid-morning as all our workmates marched round the outside of the building, practising speedy evacuation to certain assembly points. It was eerie being the only sentinels amid a sea of once clattering desks. I had been warned the directors of RU would take our nonco-operation very ill, but I had reached the approved pacifist position that maintained any preparation for war entailed the coming of war. And I had recently taken the plunge and joined the Peace Pledge Union. I had done so uneasily, not because I had any doubts about their views but because I'd never joined anything but the Crusaders and even that I'd jettisoned. Joining anything seemed a sacrifice of one's precious individuality.

At the end of August came a memo from the directors to all the staff. It told us that in the event of war the London premises would be evacuated *in toto* to the printing house and bindery in Hertfordshire. It was regretted that only a much reduced staff could be entertained, and of those only the ones that could make suitable housing arrangements. Appended were the names of those to be considered, if they so wished. I didn't wish, but I didn't have the pleasure of declining for my name was not to be found on any list of the chosen. So the directors and I were at least agreed on that. For there in the heart of London was my ever-vulnerable family, who had no rural bolt hole, or even the wherewithal to move to one. Who except me could be trusted to catch the bombs before they fell on their feckless heads?

We knew all was up if Hitler marched into Poland. On that Friday afternoon in the office the news came through on ticker tape that he had done just that. I phoned home to tell mother the news and to say that I'd be leaving the office in a few minutes. 'Be careful,' she said, as if the enemy bombers would be over before tea.

I put my few belongings in my briefcase, covered up my typewriter, and then looked around for Jimmy Armstrong. But he was in a crowd round the ticker tape machine, so I left without a word to him. Or to JB. Or to Katie or Johnny or Tom or Clifford or any living soul.

34

I was nineteen and had no idea how long it would be before my call-up papers arrived and I was arrested for tearing them up. (I had the vaguest and luridest ideas of how it would all work out: only a very faint hope they'd let me do ambulance work or something in Streatham.)

But the war seemed more than reluctant to materialize. It had kicked off dramatically enough. On a bright Sunday morning a day and a half after the total collapse of my RU world, Chamberlain had broadcast the news that we were at war with Germany, and within ten minutes the air-raid sirens were howling all over London. We hadn't waited for the broadcast. It was a nice sunny morning and it seemed a necessary gesture for Terry and Brian and me to set out for our usual Sunday coffee in Streatham High Road. We were taken aback by the sirens and crying people running for public shelters and whistle-blowing wardens on bicycles. But led by the ever-dignified Terry we continued to march sedately along the High Road. I remember one warden swore at us and Terry rather oddly told him he was exceeding his duty as a public servant. We reached Howard's restaurant where our favourite old waitress was sitting on a chair wearing her gas mask. I think it was our entry that emboldened her to whip it off. 'Sooner be blown up than suffocated,' she sniffed. Then, after an uneventful half-hour had passed, she remarked contemptuously: 'Trying to make fools of us, they are.'

We didn't hear another siren for many months.

Terry's insurance world had evacuated itself to Norwich and he had elected not to go with them. It was, for him, an eager release from bondage. He had vague ideas of farming till he was called up. Brian also needed a stop-gap job. The bottom had all but fallen out of his encylopaedia hawking, so when a friend of the family, a clothing manufacturer who was to get rich making army uniforms, offered him a job driving one of his vans he jumped at the chance. He drove to army camps all over the southeast, including places on the coast you now needed passes to visit, and had never enjoyed himself so much. He got on well with the troops, often staying the night in camps to which he delivered late in the evening. He liked the working-class world, its beer and its skittles, and they liked him. He was practical and a good mixer.

A few weeks later some of Terry's eccentric friends offered him a job on their farm in Jersey and he took it with alacrity. The Cotswold Bruderhof hadn't drained Richard Jefferies and Thoreau and W. H. Hudson from his blood. I saw him off sadly from Waterloo, but never thinking it was to be many years before I saw him again. Mother sensed it, though. She even cried a little, which was unusual for her. She suspected break-up.

Pam's school was evacuated and she, too, flatly refused to accompany them. We were none of us aiming for 'the done thing,' the sensible and the compliant and the patriotic thing. As usual, we were being awkward, out of step, obstinately independent. Now fifteen, Pam was, as even I could see, a very attractive girl, and she knew it. In that last year of peace adolescent boys had almost swarmed to our house, and I pretended to take in them nothing but an older brother's lofty interest. But I don't think she was fooled. She not only looked older than she was, but she thought and acted older. In her intelligence and, above all, in her sense of humour, I was taking an ever growing delight. We would elaborate fantasies about friends and relatives and neighbours until we were both well-nigh helpless with laughter. She would gasp: 'Stop it, stop it or I'll wet myself.' She would run for the lavatory. I'd hear the door slam and her still shrieking behind it.

Apart from some certificates in elocution and verse-speaking she had finished her schooling with nothing to show for it. This worried me. She had not been a satisfactory pupil at any time. Quite early on she had been sent home by her rather humourless headmistress for singing in assembly: 'Jesus loves me, this I know; So does ragtime cowboy Joe.' I had to soothe the good lady's sensitive feelings with a well-larded letter from my experienced father.

Among Pam's teenage beaux were some who intrigued me, and I could never understand her indifference to them. The more handsome they were, the less she seemed to fancy them. I felt that, unable to furnish her with introductions in the manner of a normal, dutiful brother, I could not descend to preying on those boyswains who often appeared unbidden and unencouraged.

But it wasn't easy. Even the plainer ones could be amusing company. There was Angus, not really very attractive to my eyes, but a perpetual tease to me because he often wore a kilt. And Dennis, a lanky, feather-brained creature of whose existence at Montrose we had scarcely been aware. He would never go home, and was superbly uninsultable. 'For God's sake go, Dennis,' we'd say as it drew on to midnight and we had tired even of pontoon with a threepenny limit. 'You have now outstayed your welcome.' He'd beam and say: 'Oh, it's early yet.' Once, Brian and I picked him up and dumped him bodily in the garden bushes and locked the front door. We heard him calling a cheery 'See you tomorrow.'

But Donald *was* attractive. He liked poetry and was the only one I felt attuned to. Most days they would spend hours at the local tennis club. I'd sometimes go and watch, and with a kind of shy good manners Donald would drop out of a set to sit and talk to me among the thridding grasshoppers. He thought Rupert Brooke the greatest poet in the world, and I'd try hard to agree. A master at his school had given him a presentation edition of Brooke's poems, telling him he bore a resemblance to the frontispiece portrait of Brooke. Which was true, though I privately thought Donald was handsomer. He would read me, slowly and solemnly, some gem from this treasured volume, while I, under the pretence of studying the text with him, would lean close and study instead his bright eyes and sculptured cheek.

Pam, like Brian, was clever with her hands. She could ply a needle or a delicate watercolour brush and was equally skilful in wielding a hammer and chisel. If a chair needed strengthening or a book recovering she'd do it, quickly and thoroughly. I cheerfully left to her any punctures my bike suffered.

One day I was idly trying to teach a neighbour's child to read, but I found it was no good without a primer of 'The cat sat on the mat' variety, on which I had myself been weaned.

Pam was quiet and busy most of that day. In the evening, a repressed gleam in her eye, she handed me a little, home-made book. 'Here's your primer,' she said.

It was entitled 'The Strange Adventures of Mr Hogg, a Lavatory Attendant, and his Faithful Dog.' The text, which is brief, I can reproduce for posterity, for it lies before me now:

> Hogg sat outside his bog
> On a day thick with fog.
> With Hogg was Mog, his dog.
> Mog did not like Hogg,
> For Hogg, when full of grog,
> Would often flog poor Mog.
> With mouth all agog,
> Like a fish or a frog,
> Hogg sat in the fog
> Outside his old bog.

There, she admitted, her invention ran out. I can't, unfortunately, reproduce the bright and lively miniatures which depict Mr Hogg in all his ugliness and show genuine compassion in their treatment of his trembling little terrier.

But sometimes Pam's behaviour was too much even for me. Mrs Wallace was a local Conservative agent who had decided to become a regular caller, always around teatime and always with little cries of astonishment at the opportuneness of the hour. She was simple but cunning, had no shred of humour in her, and bored us all to distraction with her idle gossip. Pam disliked her. I just felt rather sorry for her.

Once she was describing to us at wearisome length some exotic meal she had taken in a Chinese restaurant: 'And then there were those delicious lobster balls.'

Pam leaned forward. 'How interesting,' she interrupted. 'I had no idea lobsters had such parts to their anatomies.'

'Oh yes, dear,' said dim Mrs Wallace. 'Little rissoles, you know, made of lobster meat. Scrumptious.'

Pam glanced at me despairingly and I had a horrible suspicion she was cooking up something else. For Mrs Wallace was now making snide comments on the so-called friends she had shared this treat with.

'Well, I say 'Mr and Mrs' but, really, my dear, I don't think - I mean, I've never seen a wedding ring on *her.*'

Pam was now sitting bolt upright in her chair, her hands clasped in her lap, her thumbs twiddling furiously, her lips pursed in Puritan disdain. I frowned at her deprecatingly but in vain.

'And, well, it's no secret: *he's* got a wife in Huddersfield. If you ask me...'

Pam rose to her feet and boomed in a voice worthy of Mrs Fraser: 'Come, brother. Let us hear no more of this *filth.*' And then, of course, dramatically swept from the room.

'Oh dear,' said poor Mrs Wallace. 'Oh, I hope I haven't shocked her. I didn't mean... I didn't realize... Of course, she's still a child.' Her weak, earnest eyes were larger than ever behind her powerful glasses. She was rising in some agitation.

I tried to soothe her. But how? No good saying it was a joke. She didn't know what a joke was. She left, full of apologies.

I told Pam it was rather a rotten thing to do, but she was quite impenitent.

'Scandalmongering old bitch,' she said. 'Well, she won't call again in a hurry.'

'Thank God for that,' mother laughed, and returned with a sigh of contentment to her newspaper.

Nor did Mrs Wallace ever call again. Even passing in the street, she was positively furtive.

And there were others who ceased to call, but for different reasons. I had, not without some relish, told Joan I intended to register as a conscientious objector. 'Well, you've always had pretty appalling views,' she sniffed. 'But I didn't think you were a coward.'

'Don't be childish, Joan,' said my mother, with the half-attention one might give to a vaguely irritating child. 'Perhaps it would be better if there were more objectors.' Mother had no knowledge of or interest in pacifism, but it was sufficient for her that I had espoused it.

A little later that week, Joan ostentatiously walked twice past our house on the arm of her uniformed father, who had been recalled from his cinema to his naval command, and also, presumably, to his rights as husband and father. Poor, nice Joan. I never saw her again, for in no time they had moved to a safe retreat in Worcestershire.

My mother philosophically lost one or two of her friends through me. 'If their minds are so small,' she concluded, 'they're not worth knowing anyway.'

One evening two burly men called at the house to see me. They said they were CID officers from Streatham police station. I wasn't really alarmed for I knew I'd done nothing wrong. Well, almost nothing. They took some time getting to the point, which was that I might be an enemy agent. I burst out laughing and one of them rebuked me pompously with talk of 'extraordinary powers' the police now possessed. It seemed that Special Branch had for the past few years kept a careful note of each packet of Nazi propaganda I'd received. They also knew the local Mosley Blackshirt agent had called on me, and that I was a member of the Peace Pledge Union. (They saw no clash between the BUF and the PPU: they were both subversive and threatening.)

At this moment mother entered, unable to restrain her curiosity. The men annoyed me by not rising. They continued with their questions and wrote everything down laboriously. I explained all the material had been unsolicited. 'How did Berlin get your name and address?' 'Oh, I wrote to Hitler when I was about sixteen.' The men exchanged triumphant glances, wrote down this damning confession and underlined it. They received with cynicism my insistence that the propaganda, like the Mosley agent, had been dismissed with contempt.

Mother entered the conversation - unhelpfully, of course. 'This is a free country,' she said witheringly, 'although some of you seem unaware of it. You can have what correspondence you choose and you can join what organizations you choose.' She looked at me with distinct satisfaction. I felt no one could more surely effect my internment. If I didn't bring the interview to a speedy close, she would reminisce about all her German friends and relatives.

After more dark hints, and some rather offensive bullying, they took themselves off. As the door closed behind them mother said: 'Now if I were you I'd phone the superintendent at Streatham police station and lodge a complaint.'

I was more than dubious.

'Well, I'll do it if you like,' she volunteered. 'We can't have policemen treating the public like that.'

'No, thank you,' I said firmly. '*I'll* do it.'

I did. I was not prepared for the superintendent's reaction. He was full of apologies, explaining that they were now, with the call-up, having to employ officers of the wrong calibre. He assured me he would 'give them a good talking to.'

I suddenly felt rather proud of my country. Full marks to them for knowing all about the beastly propaganda. And full marks for such an apology at such a time of national crisis. I glimpsed for the first time why some people might think such things had to be fought for.

But Pam had the last, chilling word. 'The apology is of course all part of the plot. To get you off your guard. They'll strike again, when you least expect it.' Then, lapsing into giggles, she added: 'Mrs Wallace is in it. Up to the neck. A copper's nark. I suspected it all along.'

35

In vain I try to recall some sense of desolation at the sudden and total collapse of my wonderful RU world. I seem simply to have accepted it and cast round for a fresh pasture. I suppose the coming of war destroyed all idea of a rational future. Even the new pasture I had to find was not likely to be an especially fair field, or even a nourishing one. I found it in the personal column of *The Times*:

> Junior master urgently required for boys' private school. Non-residential post. Subjects by arrangement. Apply: Rev Augustus Alton, Cunningham House School, Wimbledon.

So I wrote and was called to an interview. Cunningham House was another Montrose, but tattier. The Reverend Augustus was unique in my limited experience. In his seventies, lean and tall, with a hatchet face and a patrician bearing, he possessed a restless, burning energy whose source I came after only half an hour to believe was diabolic. The interview was a grilling followed by an execration. Under his inquisition I revealed far more than I had intended: not simply that I was awaiting call-up, but that I had registered as a conscientious objector. He greeted this confession in terms of disgust so immoderate that I responded with equal warmth. Having now no hope of the job, I expressed my own disgust that a minister of the Gospel could so react. He snapped: 'Christianity's got nothing to do with it. It's a question of defending one's country.'

This quite took the wind out of my sails. I had never spoken to a clergyman before. While I didn't expect them to be pacifists, I did expect a measure of mealy-mouthed sympathy for the position. Then he suddenly chuckled. His smile, as you would expect of any Mephistopheles, quite charmingly transformed his features. 'Well,' he said, 'at least you're not pernickety. You speak your mind.' He chuckled again as he added: 'Your unformed mind.' As I opened my mouth for another volley, he gabbled on: 'I can offer you thirty shillings and lunches. Can you start tomorrow?'

I gulped and said I could. He was extremely vague about what I should teach. Indeed, he didn't seem interested as to whether I could teach at all. I pressed him for more information and he said: 'Oh, teach anything and

110

everything to a class of 10-year-olds. And you can do the English with the seniors. School Certificate. I think they're doing *Macbeth*. But no divinity, of course. Or at any rate only OT.'

And so I became a schoolmaster, just as fortuitously as I'd become an editor, or a first-class commuter. My 10-year-olds loved me and I loved them. I took great pride in teaching them well. What I think I taught best, because it was my own worst subject, was maths. They got on like a house on fire, so much so that I couldn't help wishing I'd had someone like me to teach me.

But with the seniors it was quite a different story. They didn't like me, and no one could blame them. Basically unsure of myself, I made with them every mistake in the book. I was defensive and aggressive, I was sarcastic and rigid, repressive and vainglorious. But the Reverend Augustus was delighted because I kept order. They sat in sulky silence as I dictated notes. Shakespeare was affronted and they were affronted and, although I didn't know it then, I was horribly affronted myself. If one of them got out of line I heaped punishments on his head. Gus, as he was called, chuckled evilly and said: 'Not much of the pacifist about you, is there?' And to myself I had to admit uncomfortably that there wasn't.

France fell and Gus cast vituperations on it and on Plum, one of his oldest friends, who seemed to be getting on too well with Vichy. I discovered Plum was P. G. Wodehouse.

Then came day raids, with skirmishes in the lovely summer skies and spent cartridges sometimes falling round our feet. Half the school disappeared to safety in Somerset under the senior master. Gus despised the lot of them. Fanatically captained and harangued by Gus, we who remained were pledged never to desert in the face of the enemy. I think he envisaged a spectacular suicide for all of us if the Huns came. Cunningham House was to be a modern Masada.

The heavy night raids began and I'd cycle to school through rubble, and skirt huge piles of masonry which the day before had been homes. I formed the habit of saying a silent prayer that the occupants had escaped death or mutilation in the Underground, now a network of subterranean bunks. Often I'd arrive at school to find a wild-eyed Gus coming off duty as an all-night air-raid warden. Almost euphoric, he gave the impression that his whole life had been a march to this last glorious stand. I don't think he ever slept.

Terry had phoned from Jersey to say the Germans were expected there any day. We urged him to come home, but he said he wanted to see the *Wehrmacht* at close quarters. I wondered if a bit of the Gus had entered him.

Brian had been called up into tanks and was apparently enjoying his life as an instructor at Bovington. He managed to get home for frequent weekends, often without a pass and running the gauntlet of redcaps. He seemed to find the exercise stimulating.

A clever system of food rationing allowed for everybody to get something under the counter and to imagine only she was getting it. Pam, whose ability to twist any man round her little finger was becoming a challenge she relished, kept us all going whenever it was a question of another egg or two, or a bar of chocolate, or a few clothing coupons. 'Just leave him to me,' she'd say of some salesman victim.

One Saturday night when Brian was home there had been a particularly heavy raid and we felt that one stick of bombs had landed in the vicinity of the Frasers' latest home. We didn't see them now but we would have been very sorry to hear of their destruction. So, an hour before dawn when things were rather quieter, Brian and I walked towards their house, only to find it, with sickness in our stomachs, a heap of dust-capped wood and stone. I stood on the mound and brought out a cigarette. I asked Brian if he had a light, but he hadn't. Not even a fag to soothe our nerves. Then my already queasy stomach did a lurching leap as I felt someone plucking at the turn-ups of my trousers. I didn't want to reach down for those desperate, dying fingers pushing up through the rubble. But I knew I must. I groped and prodded and searched, feeling sicker and sicker. It was a full minute before I realized that I was standing on a fractured gas main, the force of which was madly fluttering my trouser end. The relief was great. Until I thought of the box of matches Brian mercifully didn't have.

As for the Frasers, we learned soon after that not one of them was harmed, for they had all gone to the public shelter before the raid started. I hope they were well compensated for the snug old Edwardian home they'd lost, and put down roots in some snug old Edwardian milieu where the shrine and its votaries were appreciated. We heard no more of them.

Brian teased me for years about the entombed hand I felt to be tugging at my trouser ends. 'Sheer panic,' he said, 'bred of air-raid neurosis.'

We still saw Pam's youthful beaux from time to time. Angus, despite his kilt, was in a parachute regiment. Dennis had blossomed astonishingly as a bomber pilot and positively collected decorations. Each leave seemed to find him with another bar to another medal. I asked him once if he ever felt pity or shame as he dropped his bombs on hapless civilians, as did his German counterparts. He didn't really know what I was talking about. Lacking all imagination, he was as incapable of compassion as he was of fear. He survived the war as one of its glamorous heroes.

Donald was now in the merchant navy and after each transatlantic voyage he would call on us, his pockets bulging with fivers, and take Pam out to some absurdly expensive cabaret dinner. And to hell with the bombs. He always stayed the night and shared my room. We didn't use the top floor of the house now. I slept on the first floor in what had once been Brian's and Terry's room. The others, during the incessant night bombardments, slept in chairs in the breakfast room, which was, in the design of the house, the least vulnerable spot.

Donald and I would lie in our beds talking for quite a while, then I'd put out the light and take down the blackout. I kept the large sash windows open, even on cold nights, for I liked to hear my bombs coming. There was an anti-aircraft gun in the fields at the back of the house, so the noise was ceaseless and deafening. We were quite cynical about this gunfire, as we were about the protective balloons. The guns never hit anything and the balloons never protected anything, but both were rather psychologically comforting.

The steady, throbbing drone of the night bombers persisted like some divine affliction, untroubled by the frantic stutter and chatter below. Then there would be the scream of a falling bomb, and one listened with all one's ears to see whether its two companions would descend hither or thither. For, like the Eumenides, they descended in triune majesty. I found it easier to lie in bed noting it all with eye and ear, as if by attending so scrupulously to it I could affect its course.

On this particular night, I removed the blackout and returned to my bed, only to find that a giggling Donald had pulled all my bedclothes on to the floor. I returned the compliment and then replaced the blackout and switched on the light so that we could see to make up our wrecked beds. Donald, dressed only in underpants, impressed me with the athletic beauty of his body, but my admiration was carefully concealed. Was not this the body of my sister's suitor?

Once more I put out the light and removed the blackout. Once more I found my bed stripped and once more I moved to my revenge. I tickled his ribs and his feet mercilessly as he squirmed and gasped beneath my hands. Then, so suddenly and so naturally that I could scarcely register it, his arms were a vice round my neck, he was covering my face with kisses and in sobs more than words telling me over and over again: 'I love you, I love you, I love you.'

Full of wonder, I released his passion and kept him in my arms. 'What about you?' he whispered. 'Not now,' I replied. 'I'd sooner talk.'

I asked him when, why, how on earth... For I had never believed that I could be an *object* of love, and I could not doubt that on his part this was love. I didn't know what to do with it. It awoke in me a great tenderness and a great sadness, and only with these did I seem to be able to respond.

Courtship and seduction were the roles nature had assigned to me and I had never experienced any others. Nor, I am afraid, desired any others. And even deeper had my maker cast the foundations of despair, and with Donald I first glimpsed them. In the ensuing years I came to recognize that I could never really desire a body that desired mine, that even a reciprocated kiss was detrimental. I was to be forever enslaved by the unattainable. For Donald I had hereafter a deep, even a more abiding, affection. But I no longer burned with desire for him.

That morning, before he left, Donald pushed his *Rupert Brooke* into my hands. 'Just to look after. I'm not giving it to you, mind, but you're the only one I can trust it with.'

Two or three times more Donald came home to us with his argosy and heaped much of it on Pam. He told me he looked on her as a sister and she on him as a brother. It was becoming clear to me that Pam, for whom each day was a source of sheer Rabelaisian fun, could be drawn only to men much older and much less attractive than herself.

Each night of each visit Donald would spend in my arms until the first wash of dawn stilled the business above and below and sent us back to our deceitful beds.

We often chuckled over life's little ironies. 'You come,' I said, 'as a prospective husband and end as an adopted brother. You come as my future brother-in-law and end as my lover.'

Then one day he came no more and his *Rupert Brooke* was cruelly and indisputably mine. Coral he has become, his eyes are pearls, and nothing of him fades.

36

About this time I appeared before my first conscientious objectors' tribunal. I wasn't at all well briefed and they disposed of me very quickly: into the army, into the noncombatant corps. Well, that was the expected conclusion to round one. Also expected was my appeal, now duly filed.

Gus was retiring ever further into a fantasy world of his own, as he strengthened his Masada against all possible comers. With estimable self-control he supervised the digging of trenches all over his sacred cricket pitches. With fiendish glee he piled sandbags higher and higher against his walls. Soon I expected him to issue us all with passes.

He left ever more of the running of the place to me. I had seldom been happier. Each day was too short for all the pleasures I wanted to share with my little charges. My feelings for them were purely paternal and paternally pure.

There were a few vague visiting staff, and a sad, short-sighted resident master who played an unceasing Tom Pinch to Gus's Pecksniff. He could keep no order and his misrule was both Gus's bane and Gus's delight, for convention required poor Tom's persecution and sadism relished it. I once saw Gus, drawn from his sandbagging by the hubbub, stick his malevolent features through the window of Tom Pinch's classroom and scream approvingly to the boys: 'Shut up or I'll flog the lot of you!' To Tom he said: 'You, you standing uselessly there. What the devil do you think you're paid for?'

Gus had favourites, and a madly unpredictable sense of humour. They were his redeeming features, if redemption be for devils. He marched about the school at odd times with a long cane with which he'd tickle the rump of any boy who crossed his path. There was one mischievous little rogue who I suspected Gus found as attractive as I did. On one occasion Gus entered the classroom to punish him for skipping detention.

'Cripes!' shrieked the boy. 'He's after me!' And he dived beneath the master's desk and wedged himself in its furthest recess.

'Come on out!' shouted Gus. 'Come out and take it like a man.'

'No,' called the boy. 'You come in and get me.'

This struck Gus as delicious. He collapsed in a chair and shrieked with laughter. When it subsided he once more felt the call of his sandbags and the boy went home triumphantly unscathed.

Even my relations with the older boys were improving. I had, thanks to their syllabus, discovered Shakespeare and I took such joy in hamming him up with them that they began to respond. I went on a Shakespeare spree as once I had gone on Haggard and Dickens sprees. I marvelled that never during my own schooling had anyone shown me what intoxicating fare his Roman plays and his great tragedies were. I learned by heart reams of them. I quoted them to Brian. I remember once spouting some of *Lear* to Brian, who as was his wont pretended to mishear certain elements. 'That's beautifully expressed,' he said. 'Which? Which bit?' I asked eagerly. He looked salacious. 'That phrase: "the flies of wanton boys".' The joke was a bit too near the knuckle for my liking. I rather quickly changed the subject.

37

One morning I arrived to such an encounter as that with Jimmy Armstrong in the far-off days of peace. In the asphalt yard a new figure had created an oasis of his own: a slender boy of about fifteen with that lank fair hair which has once been waving gold. A boy with high cheekbones and somewhat almond eyes that were dustily enrayed. A boy with full, pouting lips which seemed to tremble on the brink of a sorrow too heavy for his frame or his years. 'The faun look' Cyril Connolly has called its instant, spellbinding appeal.

Seldom had both compassion and desire been so instantly aroused in me. He stood there, forlorn and dejected, and even his clothes branded him an alien, for he wore the kind of continental plus-four suit in which young Emil Tischbein looked so appealing.

115

'Who on earth is he?' I asked Tom Pinch in tones that seemed somehow suitably hushed.

'A Belgian refugee. Poor souls, they were machine-gunned fleeing to the coast. I think his father was killed. The boy and his mother are billeted down the road and we've been ordered to give him schooling. Gus is furious because there are no fees.'

I went out to him. 'What is your name?' I asked, and then, as he looked confused and alarmed: 'Comment t'appelles-tu?'

'Je m'appelle Julien,' he replied in a low, uncertain voice and French little better than mine. 'Je suis Belge.'

I held out my hand to him but almost had to insist on his. It was cold and limp.

'Moi, je suis Monsieur Gamble. Parles-tu anglais?'

'Un peu, un petit peu,' he murmured, lowering his eyes and withdrawing his hand.

I took him in with my 10-year-olds, set them something to do and called him up to my desk.

'Est-ce que tu veux apprendre l'anglais, Julien?'

'Oui, si c'est possible.' He didn't seem at all sure.

'Mais certainement c'est possible, mon petit ami.' I decided to risk the apostrophe and looked in his eyes as I proffered it. For the first time he showed the ghost of a smile.

'Bon!' I said in as businesslike a tone as I could command. I was sitting sideways on a stool at my desk and I cast around for some seat he could take beside me. There was nothing. The place was furnished like a derelict station waiting room. I gave a comic shrug of bafflement and suddenly heard a voice murmur: 'Seulement, les genoux.' If the words were *mine* they must have been intended as a joke, for I was truly anxious to bring a smile to his sad face.

But mine or his or simply the voice of fate, the words were followed by action so apparently natural that I did not at first think to question it. With perfect composure he perched himself on my knee and said: 'Commencez, monsieur, s'il vous plaît.'

I glanced quickly, guiltily, round the room. My 10-year-olds showed no surprise. A few even smiled their approval. I looked out of the window. Gus was sandbagging furiously in the distance. No one would come in. Julien was as light as a feather on my knee. I bounced him a little, like a baby, and he smiled very slightly to himself.

Was it absolute innocence on his part, or calculated exploitation? As I gazed across some inches into his sky-blue eyes and scanned his lank, flaxen hair, I decided the question was possibly unworthy, certainly irrelevant.

I don't know what that first English lesson consisted of, but I know he definitely impressed me as intelligent. I sent him to his desk with some sentences to copy, and as I did so I formed a plan. I had already decided I must go up to Foyle's and get him a good textbook. It was a half-day, and now I made up my mind I'd risk an invitation. Unwise, perhaps, to bid so high so soon, but I felt all reality was crumbling from me. He only was real, he and my hunger for his company.

I asked him if he would like to come up to town with me to buy the book he needed. He hesitated, and I felt a first little chill. Had I blundered badly?

'Ma mère...' he began, and I interrupted him to say in desperate French that I'd explain to his mother and seek her permission. And at this he smiled, really smiled for the first time, and gave me an emphatic 'Alors, avec grand plaisir, monsieur.'

His tragic-looking mother in their lodgings up the road thanked me for my interest and said something to her son in Flemish. Julien showed me he could manage some English: 'She say, you are very good for me.'

The faulty preposition touched me and I vowed silently always to be good for him.

We had one of those days of pure joy which come once or twice in a lifetime, days which burn themselves into the mind as on to a Grecian urn: inviolate, incorruptible, never to be forgotten, never to be told. Ostensibly walking and talking and looking at shops and having coffees, but in reality quaffing that headiest of human brews, the exploration of a new and heart-catching personality. The greatest thrill for me was to see him gradually blossom into the lively, affectionate, even rather impish, boy he must have been before the hordes of Satan goose-stepped through his world.

Sitting at the back of a bus, I took his hand as if idly to emphasize some point: a cool hand, dry and fragile, a waif's hand. I raised and regarded it. 'Poor cold hand,' I said. And he produced his first English joke. 'Poor warm mister,' he murmured. And again I wondered: how knowing is he?

We wandered around London, he endlessly curious and active, I as in a dream. There was a lull in the bombing and even the birds seemed to be making the most of it with their chatter. As we walked he would unthinkingly link his arm in mine. But I, with all my accumulations of guilt, could not accept it. I told him such things could not be in England and hoped he would gather why. But he just sulked, and his sulking, too, enslaved me.

I knew I was not alone in feeling his charm. All my family fell under his spell. Brian liked him and he liked Brian. I even knew for the first time some twinges of jealousy as Brian played all manner of trumps that were never up my sleeve: teaching him old chestnut jokes, showing him card tricks, making

117

him a radio, endlessly trying to put a rusty motorbike in running order with some black-market oil and petrol.

Pam got me some clothing coupons and I bought him some trousers, for he wanted desperately to look like any English boy. He let me put them on him. I surveyed him admiringly at arm's length, then drew him to me and kissed him. The first of so many kisses, which he received without surprise or distaste, only a delightfully conspiratorial 'Look for the door' or 'Take care that window.'

And I was always feeding him, 'fattening him up for the slaughter,' as Brian put it. Even Gus would playfully tickle Julien's rump with his cane, forgetful of the unpaid fees.

He was a real boy, I saw, who liked to kick a ball about and told me Pam was a 'nice tasty dish, yes?' His English improved by leaps and bounds without ever losing its broken charm. He easily got bored. His restless 'Pete, what we go doing now?' taxed my limited resources. He seemed to have a predilection for monosyllabic names. I became Pete just as Brian was always Brine.

Sometimes he stayed the night. He needed no prompting to get into my bed, snuggle up and say 'Now you tell me good English jokes, yes?' When I kissed him he played his own little joke, which was to affect great boredom, yawning, patting his mouth, saying 'Oh, excuse you me.' Then we both dissolved in giggles. Increasingly, if we were alone in a room for a moment, I would embrace him, and he would often politely endure it, although more and more he would terminate it with a nervous: 'No more, Pete. Brine is coming.' I got a little fed up with the proximity of Brian, I must admit.

Brian was in fact taking absurd risks with unauthorized leaves and bought or borrowed passes. He seemed, too, to have lost his old fulfilment as a tank instructor. He became moody and nothing I could do would shake him out of it. After one especially miserable weekend, when it had rained incessantly and Julien had been unable to come, I accompanied Brian as far as Guildford on his return journey. We were in an unheated station buffet sipping Bovril, all they could offer. His train for Wool was late and he seemed to think exposure of his absence without leave was inevitable.

'You *are* damned miserable lately,' I said. 'It's not that bad, is it?'

'No, it's all right. The job's rather fun.'

'And there are some quite decent fellows, aren't there?'

'Yes. Some very nice ones, in fact. It's not that.'

I was silent, at a loss.

He took a sudden breath and blurted out: 'Well, you might as well know. It's Julien.'

I didn't understand. Had they had some quarrel I knew nothing about?

'You mean...?' I fumbled.

118

'I mean,' he said deliberately and looking out of the window, 'I mean I'm just hopelessly in love with him.'

I had to go on resisting. There were such walls to scale, longstanding walls of secrecy on my part and of normality on his. 'But - but you've always liked girls.'

'I suppose I like any flesh that's young enough and lovely enough,' he said hopelessly.

As it all dawned on me, I felt nothing but relief. At last. At last someone to talk to about the things which, for as long as I could remember, I had locked in my heart. And after the relief, the delight. We could share him.

'Yes, he's beautiful,' I said happily. 'The way he has of pouting when he's annoyed. And the way his voice still suddenly goes all falsetto when he's excited. And did you see him try to smoke a cigarette?'

We pooled our love. Then I risked: 'Have you... Have you ever...?'

'Oh yes, I've kissed him. Lots of times.' He suddenly laughed. 'But you, damn you, were always somewhere at hand to spoil it. Or at any rate he thought you were.'

A sudden huge suspicion struck me. 'What did he say? I mean when you were kissing him and I was coming?'

'Oh, it was always "Stop it now, Brine. Pete's coming," or "No more, Brine. I hear Pete".'

And so it all came out. We had a hilarious half-hour comparing notes, with nothing but soaring admiration for Julien and a marvellous new intimacy with each other.

Of course, I taxed Julien with it at the first opportunity. He was entirely unabashed, indeed, gloried in it. 'Was a good joke, yes?' He mimicked himself: '"Oh Pete, Brine is coming. Oh Brine, Pete is coming." I make it all up but it worked good, yes?' He had somewhere acquired the trick of polishing his nails on his lapel and examining them proudly as a gesture of triumph. He did it now, and said: 'A very clever boy.'

After a moment I said to him: 'Do you know what a tart is?'

'Of course. Something nice to eat. Apple tart.'

'It is also,' I told him severely, 'a bad woman, what we call a prostitute. A girl who gives herself to men for money.'

He feigned innocence, then shock, then great interest. 'Oh, you give me money, yes? How much you give for a kiss?'

'You really are, aren't you?' I said. 'A wicked, scheming, lovely little tart. And proud of it, too. Oh, if you were younger, I - someone, somehow - ought to give you a good smack bottom.'

'Like Gus,' he chuckled. 'He like to smack my bo'om.' (He always pronounced the word with a resounding glottal stop. It came out like stage

119

Cockney: bo'om.) 'Next time he do it I say, "Gus, you must pay to smack my bo'om. Pete say so".'

I looked at him with boundless indulgence. 'I like to see you happy,' I said. 'I like it more than anything in the world. But sometimes, you know, sometimes I wonder. Do you really like me? And Brine?'

'You and Brine,' he said, now very serious, and emphasizing each word with a gentle punch to my stomach, 'you and Brine are my best friends. For ever and ever.'

He never really learned the difference between public and private behaviour. It was this that caused the rift.

We were in a transport café. Brian had given him a taste for them. A real man's world. I never wanted to go in the places. Still less did I like squiring Julien in them, for I'd discovered (or thought I had) that these burly, basic men were by no means blind to his charms. Or, indeed, to those of any attractive youth. I'd notice how they would affectionately chaff some boy apprentice in their own gang, and more than once they had cast their nets wider to ensnare Julien.

I went to the counter and fetched him a cake. 'Oh,' he said in his curiously penetrating broken English. 'You bring a little tart for your little tart, yes?'

It seemed that a hush fell on the whole room. It seemed to me that every head was turned to examine this little catamite's master. I blushed crimson.

'Come on,' I hissed. 'We're going.'

He looked utterly at a loss and pointed dumbly to his untouched cake. I seized him by the arm and dragged him into the street. I knew I was hurting him.

Flushed, uncomprehending, almost in tears, he accused me bitterly: 'You big pig. You hurt my arm. I go home.' And he ran off.

I went through four days of hell. He had no phone, and each day I grew feebler in my resolve not to fetch him from Wimbledon.

Then he phoned me. The relief was almost unbearable. 'Pete, you come out with me?'

'Yes, yes... oh yes.' There was a world of words to tell, but the family were within earshot. I had to find prosaic words and a casual tone. I arranged to meet him at three o'clock. At our usual bus stop in Streatham High Road.

I was tortured by doubt as I hurried there. Would his mother tell him not to come? Was it just a trick of his, to punish me further? Would a car knock him down as he came to me? Would my heart give out as I went to him?

Then, from afar, from the top of the avenue that led down to the High Road, I saw him at our bus stop. Oblivious of all passers-by, he was practising overarm bowling with an imaginary ball. Very slight and alone he looked.

I felt a sudden pain within me and wondered what it could be. I was slow to recognize it. After all the false alarms, the unmet first steps, the starved feelings, it was new to me. But when I did diagnose it I was astonished by my own obtuseness.

So this, at last, was it. *This* was what it felt like to be in love.

I kept my eyes on him, a blurred figure now.

As I hastened on, I thought of all the changes and chances that had brought me to this moment, and of how essentially unchanged I was. Conditioning had no doubt reinforced my dreams of beauty and of joy, but it had not created them.

And if by any chance the words of Carter in the showers long ago had come then into my mind, I should have dismissed them. For it seemed now so unimportant that I should be 'a bloody mess' when the whole warring world was one.

PART TWO: EXPLORATIONS

1

It was a warm, sunny day in early October. We all sat round the table, breakfast done, and discussed the day ahead. Except for father, who lay on a couch with his leg in plaster. Pam, now sixteen and even comelier, sat at one end of the table with pencil and pad. Mother sat at the other end in charge of the tea and coffee pots. Julien, Pam's peer in age and beauty, sat beside me, and opposite us, tall, tragic and speechless, was Vrouw Vanderzee, Julien's mother. She always made me feel vaguely guilty. She had no English and little French, so Julien was the rather undutiful Flemish interpreter. I'd learned more about the sad family. Tom Pinch had been mistaken. They had not been machine-gunned on the road to the coast, nor had Julien's father succumbed to enemy bullets. He had died from a heart attack not long before the Nazis arrived.

I still found it hard to believe that a long-cherished dream had come true, that the kindly gods had sent me an adored younger brother. For that is how I, and even the rest of the family, had come to see Julien, especially now he and his mother were living with us.

'Hope all goes well with your court martial this afternoon, Peter,' said my father pleasantly. 'If you're not back for dinner, we'll know they've shot you. No need to send a wire.'

'Funny,' I replied.

'It's nothing to joke about,' said mother with a frown.

Father was waving his cup aloft behind mother's back.

'Captain Grimes wants a refill,' I said, by way of getting my own back, for I knew that father, like Evelyn Waugh's Captain Grimes, wanted people to think his gammy leg was due to a gallant war wound. Actually, he'd been knocked down by a van in the blackout. Strangely, it was the van driver, not father, who'd been overimbibing, so father had at least acquired some rare respectability, as well as some quite generous compensation. I scarcely remember this windfall. It must have been quickly exhausted.

'Well, what's today's programme?' asked Pam. To her, each new day was a bid for more derisory adventure. 'Apart from Peter, who's probably going to be shot, it's just another old wartime day. And still no sign of that dashing Luftwaffe pilot grounded in our garden.' That was an old fantasy of hers.

'What you go doing with him, Pam?' asked Julien mischievously.

'I'd take him up to my room and put him to bed and wait on him devotedly for the duration.'

'You know it would be his duty to escape,' I told her.

She narrowed her eyes and shook her head confidently. 'Not from my clutches, old boy.' She sighed, then declared briskly: 'Ah well, I'll just go shopping. A whole morning of shopping. I'll rejuvenate Streatham.'

'It beats me,' said my father, 'how you can go shopping for hours a day when everything's rationed. You could collect the whole week's rations in a couple of hours.'

'Oh, easily,' Pam agreed. 'And for the rest of the week they're diving under the counter for me.' Most shopkeepers pretended to fish from under the counter some scarce item for the very favoured very few.

'Or *with* me,' she added under her breath for the amusement of Julien, who was half shocked, half bewitched by her.

'All very wrong,' intoned father piously, 'very unpatriotic.'

'You eat it all,' mother rejoined, for his odd unctuous remarks irritated her.

I felt another little dig at father would not come amiss. 'Major Jupp,' I said severely, 'is wondering when you'll be fit enough to go back on the roster. He says he's badly short of men.' Major Jupp was our neighbourhood gauleiter, charged with maintaining an adequate fire-watching roster. He was always telling people that never since he assumed this grave responsibility had he taken his clothes off at night. We used to say: 'Major Jupp, Major Jupp, Goes to bed with his trousers up.'

Father groaned. He felt he ought to admire Major Jupp, but in reality he found him quite as big a bore as we did. Father's life was largely compounded of stances he felt he should adopt but couldn't.

'Fire-watching with Jupp,' he said finally, 'is a real ordeal. He holds forth at length, and usually on something he knows nothing about.' Then he brightened. 'I'll ask old Robinson to take my place on the roster. I think he enjoys such work. I think he even enjoys Jupp.'

'All very wrong,' I said. 'Very unpatriotic.'

Father chuckled, for he never really took his own role-playing seriously. For some time now he had been very well behaved. It had taken a world war to do it. Blackouts and bombs had cured him of protracted pub crawls. I almost found it hard to remember how as children we had constantly urged mother to obtain a divorce, or at least a legal separation, because of his fractious and costly drinking. She would vaguely agree but she never did anything about it. In time we came to see that she never would. But it took even longer for me to see why: because they had never actually fallen out of love with each other. Neither ever looked at anyone else, and their last twenty years together were quietly happy. And I, so proud of my acuity, didn't see it till almost the end.

'Well now,' said Pam, sitting up with a show of brisk efficiency, 'what's everyone want on the black market?'

124

'I've never really enjoyed shopping,' mother mused. 'I can't see what you find to like about it.'

I interposed: 'It's a case of "she didn't like shopping but she loved shop assistants".'

Pam laughed. 'Quite right. I've got my eye on Mr Perrett now.'

This was a private joke that got both her and me chuckling. Mr Perrett, who served behind the bacon counter, was small, balding and fastened to little, steel-rimmed spectacles. His very respectable exterior was the classic guise of the Victorian murderer. We had created his lace-curtained, antimacassared home parlour, the carving knives he lovingly sharpened, the acid stored in the garden shed. We got in well before Dylan Thomas.

'Where's Nora?' mother asked suddenly. 'She's not been seen for the past hour.'

Poor self-effacing little Aunt Nora, it was easy to overlook her, especially with two new additions to the family. Julien and his mother had been unhappy in their Wimbledon billet so I'd easily obtained my parents' consent to incorporate them in our lot. Vrouw Vanderzee had the maid's room at the top of the house. Julien shared my room.

I went to the door and called Nora. Presently she appeared, and in her usual odd working garb, which seemed to have been inspired by the Marchioness in *The Old Curiosity Shop*. But we all gasped, for this time she'd excelled herself. She resembled the golliwog on the marmalade jar.

'What on earth have you been doing?' asked mother.

'I've been in the coal cellar, of course,' she replied defensively. She was always on the defensive before mother's questions.

'In the coal cellar? What do you want coal for? On a warm day like this?' Mother pursued her doggedly.

Poor Nora had been getting distinctly odd of late. We felt we could almost date the first clear sign. It was one day when Nora had been to tea with Aunt Madge. Returning about six o'clock, she had hammered at the front door with such repeated force she had dislodged a coloured tile.

'Whatever's the matter?' asked mother, opening the door to her and already on the warpath as she did so. 'What are you hammering like that for?'

'I didn't think it would matter,' Nora replied evasively.

'Not matter? Why not matter?' Mother was prepared for an inquisition.

Nora thought for a moment, then vouchsafed: 'Because I was quite sure there was no one in, that's why.' And she had brushed past mother with some satisfaction. She had produced an answer to be pondered.

That was the first time, we decided later, that she had answered mother back. Long ago, perhaps in childhood, she had learned the futility of that exercise.

But this October day was full of surprises. She now confronted mother with a sarcasm she'd never evinced before.

'Well, if you must know,' she said witheringly, 'I've been in the coal cellar because I like playing with the coal.'

There was a moment's incredulous silence. Then we all exploded, Nora eventually joining in the cackle.

'Well, your breakfast's getting cold,' said my mother at last, wiping her eyes.

'Don't want any breakfast,' Nora replied, and left the room with hauteur intact.

To break the silence, I said: 'We must all watch out: the natives are getting restless.' And to Pam: 'See if you can wheedle some minced beef and we can make a spaghetti bolognese. We've a drum of spaghetti unopened.'

She considered. 'Yes, I can probably get that off Leonard, *if* his wife's not in the cash desk.'

'And,' added mother, by way of tying up ends, 'it'll be something to look forward to after your tribunal, Peter.'

'What a family,' murmured father. 'Traitors and tarts.' And he laughed at his little sally.

'Pete,' piped up Julien. 'Pete, what we go doing today?'

'*We* go doing nothing today,' I told him severely. 'You'll have to amuse yourself. Go shopping with Pam.'

He pouted. 'Pam don't want me. Not three under the counter. I come with you to the justice and see you damnated.' He was never at a loss for English words. If he couldn't find the accepted vocabulary he just invented it.

'No, you won't, you little sadist. Stay and look after your mother.'

But I was already weakening. I invariably did with him.

2

As we walked to the bus stop Julien said: 'Poor father. He don't like his bad family. Traitors and tarts, he say. Poor man.'

'That included you, you know.'

'Me? I'm not a traitor.' He grinned at his feigned misunderstanding. 'A very patriotic Belgian boy. That's me. Soon I go in Free Belgian Navy.'

My face clouded, but I said nothing. Several times lately he had spoken of going into his country's navy.

To change the subject I said: 'Now just you behave yourself this afternoon. No talking in court. No clutching hold of me. Or they'll damnate you, too. I should never have brought you.'

I half meant this, but said it also to make him sulk. Which he did, most prettily, until he became intrigued by two old Chelsea pensioners we passed in the King's Road. I told him things were now so desperate for Britain that we were having to call up octogenarians. He wasn't entirely sure whether to believe me.

We spent the morning wandering round junk shops in Fulham. I bought him an old bulldog lantern, a police issue of a bygone age and still wielded by cops in the cheaper comics. Then we had a snack and made our way slowly to the courthouse. My hearing was fixed for 2 pm, but I knew that meant any time between two and five. To my relief, Julien was put upstairs in the public gallery, and I took my seat downstairs with the other victims.

I was surprised to find myself so philosophic about it. If they pushed you from A to B, I felt, you just waited a while and then returned to A, and in the end they got fed up and left you alone. That was what I'd done at school and it had worked pretty well. Strange that I hadn't realized how very different the position now was.

My papers told me the composition of this appellate tribunal. A real judge presided, flanked by a trades union official and a man described simply as 'J. Ashdown, Esq.'

The first appellant was a young man so scruffily dressed and so red of eye that it seemed he had for weeks been trying unsuccessfully to sleep rough. He scornfully dismissed any suggestion of a religious affiliation. No, he was an atheist and an anarchist and he was not prepared to undertake any kind of national service.

They asked him if he knew what Hitler did to people like him and he said we were supposed to be fighting Hitler, not imitating him. I felt this was quite good, but the trades union man swelled and reddened like a turkey cock. 'Not you,' he barked. 'Everybody else is fighting Hitler, but not you. And fighting to save the likes of you, they are.'

The young man began to say something about Tolstoy, and I would have liked to hear him, but already the inquisition were whispering together, nodding together, then telling him his appeal was dismissed. The usher tapped his shoulder and he was hurried out, his mouth open in mid-sentence. I wondered if he'd go to prison or accept the army. I couldn't see him as a misfit in either.

I felt sorrier for the next appellant, a young Cockney with a scrubbed and shining face and buttoned up into an even shinier blue suit. I decided he was a Jehovah's Witness. He seemed the usual mixture of naivety, earnestness and implacable faith. He stood there, an utterly insignificant candidate for martyrdom, as the bench flicked contemptuously through his papers.

Then all three were suddenly transformed. They beamed at each other and at him. Judge P. Hoskins enlightened us. The young man had, like most of us appellants, been registered for noncombatant duties in the army. But he'd had a change of heart. He was appealing against his registration as a conscientious objector. He now wanted to go in the army, like his dad before him.

'Well done, lad,' murmured J. Ashdown, Esq.

'The appeal is allowed. And the court wishes you the best of luck,' smiled the judge, less at the youth than at his own rare descent into the vernacular.

'Now that,' bellowed the trades union man, glaring straight at me, 'that's a real conscience.'

I was rather shocked that they should not make even a pretence of impartiality. I wondered if the trades unionist had ever heard of Keir Hardie or George Lansbury. I felt sure my own appearance would inflame them, for I was tall and healthy, couldn't help carrying myself well, and even sported a somewhat raffish moustache. It was, of course, just my luck to follow this young hero.

They read through my brief statement with silent disdain. Too late, I felt it was a rotten statement. I could think of all sorts of more telling points to make.

'So you're a Quaker?' asked J. Ashdown, Esq.

'Well, I wasn't brought up one,' I began, determined to be truthful.

'Since when have you called yourself a Quaker?'

'For about two years.' (That was right, wasn't it?)

A masterly sneer from the trades unionist recalled me. 'Since 1938, eh?' he said, and gazed round to see if the damning significance of this was apparent to all. 'Since the first real threat of war, in fact?'

'Well, naturally that first made me think seriously about...'

J. Ashdown, Esq. interrupted me sibilantly. 'And what did Jesus say about peace?'

I thought wildly. I remembered one thing. 'He said "Blessed are the peacemakers".'

'Yes,' he hissed. '"Blessed are the peacemakers." Peacemakers, see, not pacifists.' He made the point triumphantly as I wondered what the point was.

'And he said, didn't he,' added the trades unionist with great satisfaction, 'he said, "I come to bring not peace but a sword".' This was so silly I wondered if it was a joke. I toyed with the idea of producing 'They that live by the sword shall perish by the sword.' But was it Jesus who'd said that? In any case, I couldn't imagine old turkey cock wielding a sword. Words he could manage. He was positively yelling some at me now: 'And he used a whip to cleanse the temple, didn't he?' What kid's stuff it was, I thought, as his bigoted, fiery face was inflated with a coughing fit.

With relief I saw the judge lean forward. He asked me politely, quietly, damningly: 'Tell us, Mr Gamble: what sacrifice have you ever made for your conscience?'

I was floored. I could think of nothing to say. What a damned unfair question. What sacrifice could I or anyone have made for his conscience before all this started?

They seemed pleased with themselves. They'd won. They were whispering together now. I felt sure they would indeed have me shot if they could. As if to compound my infamy, an air-raid siren began at that very moment to wail on the courthouse roof.

Judge P. Hoskins was speaking again, quite dispassionately: 'The appeal is allowed. For the original order are substituted the conditions: "ARP, AFS, or landwork".' I stared at him. He waved me away as if the mere continued sight of me was nauseating. But probably he just wanted his tea.

I walked away into the sunshine, trying to work it out. A sort of game. If you let them humiliate you, they'd decide in your favour. Score off them and you were lost. A game they played without pleasure, even without much interest. Just a necessary duty.

Julien capered beside me. 'Was good for you, Pete? You get what pleases you?'

'Well, yes. Yes, I suppose I have.'

'What you get?'

'I have to do ARP, that's work in air raids. And AFS is the fire service. And the other thing is farming, growing food, cows and cabbages and things.'

He opened his eyes wide. 'All that? Oh, Pete, you going to be very busy.'

'Not all of them, idiot. I just choose one.'

'Oh.' He registered disappointment. 'Not much then. Which you choose?'

'I don't know.'

I really didn't. Landwork would be healthy and leave one intact as a civilian. But it would take me away from London, and then who'd look after my awkward family? The other options might keep me in the metropolis, but they had uniforms and perhaps drilling and marching.

Julien was talking again, seriously now, cajoling. 'Pete, why you not go in the army like everybody else?'

That was harder to answer. *Was* I a pacifist, still less a Christian pacifist? Did I really believe Jesus was one? How had I ended up with this hatred of regimentation, this loathing of jingoism? Again I reviewed the shaping years in search of an answer. Two teasing older brothers had quite early on taught me that hearts should never be worn on sleeves, that to be vulnerable was to be lost. The family setting seemed to provide my armour: agnostic, cynical, instinctively committed to debunking. Ideals were suspect, the stance required for survival was that of aloof mockery. This attitude to things was one that I liked to think I shared. But I didn't really. At my heart's core was that stubborn little romantic who wanted causes and friends to die for. This had produced in me a strong adolescent ferment, which the coming of war had in a curious fashion seemed to resolve. For it seemed sense to die for peace, not war, to aim all the scepticism and contempt at the perpetrators of war, and all the tragic, romantic love at its victims.

'Pete,' Julien was repeating, tugging at my elbow to bring me back to him, 'why you not go in the army?'

'I suppose,' I said, suddenly weary of it all, 'I suppose I just don't want to get hurt.'

'Nobody like to get hurt, Pete,' he said gently. 'But if a German hurt Pam? Or your mother?'

'Yes, yes,' I replied testily, 'let's talk about something else.' Two tribunals in one afternoon were proving too much.

But he halted, facing me, and insisted. 'Pete, what if a big German try to hurt me?'

I gazed at him. He had this ability to look so utterly defenceless, so bare and alone. His question was, he knew, a real challenge. I could deflect it only with an attempt at humour.

'I'd grab the nearest knife or fork off the table and plunge it in him.'

Julien at once resumed his crisp and mocking tone. 'OK. Now we know it good. You are not a conchie. Not one bit. I go back and tell the justice: "Put him in the army".'

I kicked his behind and we went on our way, laughing merrily. The all-clear howled and Julien loudly chortled his triumph.

3

I had taught at Cunningham House School in Wimbledon for a year. It was, for me, a time of rich explorations. I was learning to be a teacher, and I was learning the meaning of love. I was also trying to cope with life, which was suddenly new and strange and demanding.

I'd done some voluntary relief work. I'd organized a weekly get-together for the refugees billeted in Streatham, a surprising number of them. I'd talked a local vicar into lending me his church hall for one afternoon a week, and not without once more being sadly disillusioned by the clergy. I had more or less accepted Gus as a sort of ogre disguised as a clergyman, and now this Streatham parson showed every reluctance to do a few modest good works. Having been brought up in total isolation from churches and clergy, I had a very good opinion of them, almost an awe, as people and places of a higher order of things, remote, holy, almost ethereal.

Shopkeepers, too, were mercenary to the core. I would call on various bakers and explain that I needed dozens of sausage rolls and bread rolls and cakes: *for charity*, for poor refugees, for a weekly lifeline of my devising. I actually thought they'd *give* them to me. But I had to buy them: yesterday's stuff, a bit stale, a bit knocked about, and with very little off. I charged each refugee threepence, and the rest of the money was my own, or cadged. What was more, the refugees themselves weren't above grumbling. I was incredibly naive. I thought people were eager to dispense charity and terribly grateful to receive it.

After the initial chaos that September, 1939, had brought to one's wage-earning abilities, things had settled down somewhat. For all of us young people, of course, the jobs had gone (my magic world of publishing), but Reader's Union struggled on, evacuated from the Strand to Hertfordshire, and I kept in touch with it and JB. Tom Glover was now doing farm work in Wiltshire, living with wife and three small children in a stone labourer's cottage. I shuddered at the very thought of it. Clifford Dyment was doing something at the new Ministry of Information. I rather envied him. Johnny Ryder, of course, was doing the unexpected. Like me, he'd registered as a CO and, like me, been given noncombatant duties in the army. But, quite *un*like me, he'd accepted the ruling and was now a medical paratrooper, well versed in first aid and hair-raising drops.

My brother Brian was getting acclimatized to the Royal Armoured Corps. He'd always been good with vehicles, and now he was reasonably contented with his lot, namely, two stripes, an armoured car, weekend passes and, above all, Julien to look forward to every time he got back to London. Just after I'd had my appellate tribunal he was given a whole two weeks' leave, I imagine as a pre-embarkation gift. He got in touch with the friend who made army uniforms and who was only too glad to have more help in delivering them. So off we set, day after day, to call at great army camps all over the southeast. I went with him and, unbelievably, so did Julien. Nearly all the south of England, within fifty miles or so of the coast, was forbidden to all but those who had permits to travel there: official permits all stamped and dated and embossed with the holder's photograph. Brian, of course, had one, but I hadn't and Julien hadn't. Moreover, Julien, as an alien, was forbidden to travel more than a few miles from his billet (previously Wimbledon, now with us in Streatham). How we got away with it I don't really know. I remember bayonet-bearing soldiers poking their heads in the car and demanding permits. Julien was hidden under piles of uniforms in the back and I was sitting bold as brass next to Brian. I sat and smiled agreeably as Brian explained I was his brother who had come just for the ride. There was never any trouble. I even felt those poor conscripts rather enjoyed bending the rules and regulations. We saw beaches festooned with barbed wire and roads blocked with pillboxes. We more than once had to drive off the road and under trees as a lone enemy bomber looked for an easy victim. And often after late deliveries in Kent and Sussex we drove back to London as waves of bombers droned overhead and anti-aircraft fire rattled every piece of glass in the car. As in my bedroom at home, I liked to have the windows down so that I could hear the closely whistling bombs. We had several near escapes, but we always pressed on, waved forward by air-raid wardens and illuminated by fires rather than our own well-shuttered headlights.

It is strange to think of it all at this far remove, not only the mad world but our mad selves as its denizens. We all three enjoyed the thrill of it and for many years reminisced about the crazy things we then took so lightly. Often Pam said to me in those explosive years: 'I bet we'll look back on these days and say "Isn't life damned dull and boring now?"'

The new term at Cunningham House had started in mid-September, and with very few pupils. Parents had at first felt their children should be removed from London. But gradually many children officially evacuated in the first panic had returned to their homes in the metropolis when enemy bombers failed to materialize. Now they were off again in greater panic. It was obvious I'd soon have to find some other school if I was to earn my living so. Yet how on earth could I when the tribunal had specified 'ARP, AFS or landwork'?

I took myself to the headquarters of the fire service in Streatham. At the back of my mind was the wild notion that I could do fire service by night and teach somewhere by day. So there I stood one bright autumn afternoon in the great training yard of the fire station while a pleasant officer enthused about the spirit of camaraderie enjoyed by the AFS. It was all wrong, I knew, that he should be trying to sell the whole thing to me. He'd taken me on a tour of the station and outlined in glowing terms the wartime training programme. He was so persuasive I felt I could swallow the uniform and become a good fireman. He was pointing to a monstrous ladder uprearing itself before an artificial tower. 'Now how would you like climbing up that, Mr Gamble?' he asked in tones which showed he had no doubt that I would love it.

And I knew that I could never do it, not without crashing to the ground once I'd risen more than man-height. I'd never had a head for heights. Even to gaze from the ground to the top of some tall building made me giddy. Sadly, I told him this, and his disappointment was greater than mine. Did all firemen, I asked fatuously, have to climb ladders? Was there not a specialist ladder corps and a specialist hosepipe corps and a specialist digging corps? I felt I could douse the flames and dig out the entombed. But ladders, no.

There seemed to be a real struggle going on within him. Had he succumbed I might have revolutionized the fire service. At last he said with a sigh: 'I'm terribly sorry, Mr Gamble. We'd love to have you, but...' He spread his hands in sad defeat.

Now the extraordinary thing was that after this I really set about finding another school job, just as though all National Service had rejected me as unfit. I couldn't really have believed anything so crass, but I wanted to believe it. Just for a bit.

Meanwhile I abandoned my refugee tea parties and became a marshal at a big rest centre in Streatham. As the night bombing grew worse, the rest centre grew more crowded. I went there on my duty nights just before blitz time and left in the morning to the sound of the all clear. Sometimes I took Julien with me, although heaven knows how I explained his presence. But he sort of helped me with my chores during those interminable, cacophonous nights. I would receive the dazed, sometimes hysterical folk who had just been blasted out of their homes. I had to get their essential particulars on to the official forms, even before dishing out tea and blankets, and they were in no mood for it. God knows I understood that. Especially the old people, who had seen the destruction in one minute of all that a lifetime had, patiently, lovingly, built and tended. I was almost glad when a stick of incendiaries fell in the spacious grounds of the centre and I had to go and help extinguish them. This one did with long-handled scoops and buckets of sand.

The centre was an old, wooden-roofed orphanage. Only its cellars were anything like a refuge for these poor people. Yet they had defiant fun, too: singsongs and 'Knees up, Mother Brown,' and the kids happily running all over the place until they sank in sheer, cherubic exhaustion.

Once something very heavy fell, shaking the ground but accompanied by no explosion. I went out with a torch to locate this unexploded bomb. The sky was bright with searchlights and the land with dancing fires. I flashed my torch beam in all directions. Suddenly a voice close at hand bellowed: 'Put that bloody light out, you effing maniac.' An air-raid warden loomed up among the trees. 'I am the deputy marshal of this centre,' I said haughtily, 'and I'm looking for an unexploded bomb.'

It was soon after this that the awful, expected blow fell. Julien told me his mother had heard that he was accepted as a cadet in the Free Belgian Navy. I had helped him with his work for the exams, or more exactly just with his English, for at the other subjects he was far more knowledgeable than I. And I'd taken him down one day to the School of Navigation at Southampton to have interviews and tests. I told myself it could never come off, he looked so young, so innocent, so ill-equipped for such a life. But now they had notified his mother of his success. In a fortnight he was to report to the cadet barracks at Swaythling, near Southampton. And at the same time his mother was leaving us to join some compatriots at a sort of commune near Watford.

I had to hide my grief, for he was so excited, so proud of himself. And his pride was justified, for there were many boy applicants and few places. Moreover, as he told me in an effort to enlist my high jinks too, his English language results had been the best of the whole entry.

I tried to make it a jolly fortnight. I took him out for trips and meals in the safer, daylight hours. And in bed at night, above the hubbub, I'd let him rattle on happily about life in the navy. Then, on one appalling occasion, to change the sea-talk I was so tired of, I said: 'What about after the war, Julien? Do you think you'll stay in the navy or will you choose some good career, say, in industry or commerce?'

And suddenly, in a voice unlike his, as though he were making a matter-of-fact forecast, he said: 'Oh, I don't think... you know, Pete... I don't think I'll be alive after the war.'

I told him very sharply, very angrily, not to say such stupid things. They were not funny, not heroic, just plain stupid. But he repeated it, very quiet, very matter-of-fact, and we never discussed the subject again.

We went up to the Belgian embassy and collected his uniform. I dressed him in it in our bedroom that evening. He looked, I need hardly say, stunning.

Brian came up for Julien's last weekend, and I let them go out and about on their own. It was almost a relief to hand him over and stop my light-hearted dissembling. Four days later, a Wednesday, was his last night. Wednesday has always been a wretched day for me, both as boy and man. We stayed in, shut in the drawing room, blackout up and gramophone on. He loved the gramophone. And certain records of ours became his special favourites: 'Begin the beguine,' 'Che gelida manina,' 'Ave Maria,' 'Painting the clouds with sunshine,' Al Bowlly, the Inkspots, Bing Crosby. And he would join in singing them in his awful cracked, oscillating treble.

This night, as he mooned around in tune with the songs, he suddenly stopped and looked at me despondent on the settee. 'Oh, Pete, you so bloody miserable,' he said, and it was the first time I had ever heard him swear. But he was a man now, a sailor. He caught my hands and pulled me to my feet. 'Now we dance together,' he said, making me shuffle round in his arms. He looked happy, mischievous. Then he stopped and very deliberately planted a kiss on my lips, the only unsolicited kiss he had ever given me. And he concluded seriously: 'Your best friend. For ever.'

4

Gabbitas-Thring, for so long the lifeline for jobhunting young schoolmasters, were sending me their rather exciting slips, all urging me to write 'promptly yet carefully' to some unknown headmaster. I sensed their prep school notices sometimes hovered on twilight worlds, especially when the headmaster had a double-barrelled name but no qualifications, and proffered as a magnet the fact that 'the headmaster's wife personally supervises all domestic arrangements.' I envisaged the penny-pinching busybody directing her unhappy minions. Brian, of course, took particular delight in his detailed embodiment of these jingoistic heads and their oligarchic wives. Some of his creations I met in later years.

But Belvedere Lodge School, Esher, and its headmaster sounded sane and sensible. The notice was unpretentious and made no mention of a ubiquitous spouse. I had just heard from Gus that he very much regretted there were almost no pupils left in his school to justify retaining me. He wished me well. Somehow I felt he meant it, despite my detestable pacifism. I never saw him again, but he and his funny old school survived the war.

So down to Mr Barnes of Esher I duly went for interview. I found he was quite young, about 35, and wasn't going to be there at all. He was an army captain, working at the War Office in Bath. Instead, there was his wife, Jill. She was someone I took to at once, friendly, humorous and kind. He would be paying visits, of course, and Jill would keep all the business side of things going. The school was entirely 'day.' There were about sixty pupils, another fifty being evacuated to Somerset with his much older partner, and all the rest of the teaching staff 'visited.' I'd live in and be virtual acting headmaster. I'd teach, as I suggested, most subjects to the juniors, and Latin and English to middle and top school. Did I want the job?

Did I! I think they'd taken to me as I had to them. I jumped at it, even though I wondered how I was going to earn a living until the new term started in January. Another surprise. 'We're pretty desperate for help. The sooner you can start, the better.' I found that by 'soon' he meant, half-jokingly, 'tomorrow!' It was a Thursday. I said I'd move in on Sunday, and start work on Monday.

They showed me my quarters (two delightful rooms with dormer windows) and took me round the school. It was, for me, love at first sight: the house and grounds, the jolly staff, and, above all, the boys. It seemed an oasis of all gracious living. The boys, in those far-off days, were radiant with prep school polish: eternally rising to greet one, ceaselessly sirring and capping, flattening themselves against walls as one approached, vying with one another to run and open doors, uncannily anticipating one's every wish. All entirely without servility, as a sort of tongue-in-cheek game, as a quadrille that never inhibited their devilry and charm.

Monday morning began with a succession of bouncy young lady teachers with scarves round their heads and rich Home County voices. Those were the days of manners and accents.

Jill Barnes had one baby and was expecting another. Her husband David gave me full instructions as to the care of her. I was to see that she 'put her feet up and rested every day after lunch,' all of which she thought silly. And I was to see she drank a pint of milk a day, which she disliked. I took my duties seriously, and claimed my share of the credit for the healthy baby that in due course arrived.

Belvedere was my first flesh-and-blood Eden. Over half a century ago, and fresh as yesterday. There are sharp pictures in my mind of days haloed in sunshine as we pretended to play cricket. Traitor as I was to the school's ethos, I reared a whole brood of boys to treat cricket as no more than a giggling, and rather boring, game. Likewise I recall days covered in crunchy snow as we played football to our own created rules, just for twenty minutes before getting down to serious snowball battles.

But no such travesties were exhibited in the classroom. I got some of the seniors sufficiently aware of Latin to become moist-eyed over Nisus and Euryalus and scornful over Dido's efforts to entrap Aeneas. I romped through Shakespeare's tragedies with them, always wresting as much from the text as I could and never forgetting he was a popular dramatist who had to grip and hold a comprehensive audience. Some of the staff thought the boys' delight in Shakespeare was rather unnatural. On wet games days they wanted nothing better than to ham him up in the gym. As rare treats I'd take them up to London matinées, hanging agog on each golden syllable Wolfit or Gielgud uttered. After seeing his *Macbeth* several times at the Piccadilly, I dared to send Gielgud my thanks and my praise, and also my own tentative views of the play. He wrote me a long letter, all in his beautiful, minuscule hand, setting out his thoughts and experiences as an actor and a producer of *Macbeth*. His letter even overflowed on to the envelope. It was typical of his courtesy and generosity to take so much trouble over a piece of ebullient fan mail.

And there were halcyon days when we would have lessons out of doors. Sprawling in the grass, the young ones would squabble like pups to nestle up against me and fall asleep, while older ones lay on their stomachs, their chins in their hands, as I read them ghost stories by de la Mare and M. R. James and Algernon Blackwood.

Perhaps I am idealizing it all. Probably not one of them remembers it in gold as I remember it.

Not only the boys but also some of the fair ladies seemed content to pivot around me, as I felt my usual guilt in dominating. Brenda was intelligent, even a little avant-garde for this junior establishment world. We became great friends. She would have me to tea in her elegant flat, where we endlessly discussed and laughed over our charges and our colleagues, as she curled up in a large, becushioned leather chair opposite and displayed her shapely legs. I thought her very like G. B. Stern, with her bobbed hair and long cigarette holder. Inspired by her, I first began to smoke cigarettes regularly: Turkish, of course, at first, then Wills' 'Passing Clouds,' then serious Player's.

One afternoon in her flat she patted her capacious armchair and said: 'Come and sit beside me. Don't be so unfriendly.'

The world dissolved, then recombined in shapes I could not deal with. I muttered something about a pile of books I had to correct. I fled.

How utterly our relationship was destroyed. I became a mere colleague, treated coldly, politely. And never again asked to tea. It all upset me, for I liked her. Now she was insulted, a woman scorned. But so, damn it, was I hurt and insulted.

I confided all this to Jill during one of our interminable after-dinner chats. It was her turn to be astonished. 'Really, Peter,' she said. 'You can't be so innocent. She was after you. Everybody knew it.'

So now I felt coarse and insensitive on top of everything else. Jill was my consolation. I had no fear of misunderstandings with her. She and David were still very much in love, and in any case Jill was a genuinely loyal, uncomplicated person. We were fond of each other and lived in complete harmony in this large house with Jenny the young maidservant and Rosemary the young nursemaid. David, too, trusted me. Perhaps he guessed my true bent. Perhaps even Jill did. Slowly it dawned on me that only with happily married women could I have a safe and successful relationship. While meantime I careered on, loving young boys and desiring older ones.

I used to go home each weekend from Belvedere. Home Friday night and back Sunday night. At such times, and in the holidays, I'd keep on with my Civil Defence activities. I can remember fire-watching on an Oxford Street roof, but just where I don't know. And for a while I belonged to something called Pacifist Service Units, with battledress and 'PSU' shoulder flashes. My job was to go down the crowded Underground stations and weave my way among the bunks and mattresses and blankets, flitting the recumbent figures with disinfectant. I soon abandoned this bit of war service as unwelcomed by the great British public, who found my Flit gun both irritating and insulting. I remember clearly, though, one rollicking old woman who called to me: 'Come and flit me boa, love,' and as I did so she asked me; 'What's PSU, ducks?' It was a question I had been rather dreading, for I didn't want to get involved in a fight with some drunken bruiser who wanted to prove patriotism and prowess in the secure setting of a subterranean bolt hole. 'Pacifist Service Units', I murmured hurriedly as I passed on. She turned to her friend and said: 'Oh, now isn't that nice? It's "Passenger Service Units".' I was very glad to let the London Passenger Transport Board have all the credit.

Then, back in Esher, I took on the administration of a large and really rather secret gas shelter. I had to maintain all equipment and emergency food supplies, and I had to make a roster for use if the shelter was ever needed. I used to cycle all over the place wheedling retired bank managers and schoolmasters and nurses and lady clerks into joining my ghostly roster. I never got anything like enough, for nearly all retired people were already involved in something or other. But I was really quieting my conscience, which periodically troubled me as a conchie who wasn't doing quite what he ought.

One holidays I remember I suddenly wrote a short story and sent it to John Lehmann, of Penguin New Writing. Of course, he sent it back, but with a kind and helpful letter which I still have and from which I now quote:

> I liked your story quite a lot, and thought it had real freshness and vigour, and a dramatic quality that makes me want to see more stuff of yours. My criticism is that you muck the whole thing by going one step too far in your self-consciousness. Chris, to my mind, is wrong, and the end rather a flop. I wouldn't say that so frankly if I didn't feel you will very soon write something much better. And when you do, will you send it to me? I very much hope so.

Now you'd think so very nice a letter, from a person as distinguished as John Lehmann, would have spurred me on to write more. Quite the reverse. My ingrained lack of all self-confidence seized on it as proof positive that I had no ability whatsoever. So I wrote very little more in the way of imaginative writing.

The senior maths at Belvedere were taught by a rather forbidding elderly man who had a crammer's in Walton-on-Thames and came over to us two afternoons a week. He also didn't teach Latin and asked me to take on two of his pupils: one 16-year-old for School Certificate set books (which were, I remember clearly, *Aeneid III* and Cicero's *In Catilinam*), and one 13-year-old for Common Entrance. The older boy came to me twice a week in the evenings. The younger one, Henry D, at first had a sort of correspondence course with me. As he couldn't come over in person he sent me work at regular intervals, which I returned liberally annotated. The older boy, Bruce, was very nice, but not attractive, or not my type. Henry was clearly both intelligent and amusing. Our written exchanges in his exercise book were quite witty, I thought. I wondered what he was like: he couldn't have looks as well as wit. Life was sparing in such things.

Henry bore a very distinguished name, almost a household name in the worldwide annals of learning. When one day our visiting maths master asked me to take Henry personally I readily agreed. The boy himself, it seemed, wanted personal lessons with me, and so did Lady D, his mother, who felt the bike ride from Walton to Esher after school wouldn't be too much for him.

Before he was due I dashed down town on my bike to beg some cakes from the pleasant lady who owned a chintzy teashop and baked little cakes whenever her rations allowed. They were like gold dust, but that day she let me have six when I explained I had a hungry schoolboy to tea. I rode back to Belvedere at speed, for I was late, telling myself what a fool I was to think that a boy with a bright mind would have a bright face.

And I almost fell off my bike as I whizzed into the drive and saw a bright vision indeed propped rather languidly against the posts. It was like my first sight of Jimmy Armstrong long before.

Henry sprang to attention, smiled, bowed, shook my hand, said: 'Hello at last, Mr Gamble.' Tall for his age, with a high forehead, slightly parted lips, and eyes that shone with intelligence and fun.

He sailed ahead with the Latin, and he scoffed almost all the cakes. And we peppered the lessons with jokes and leg-pulls. I found myself looking forward to those lessons almost with excitement. I knew my unreliable heart was melting rapidly. I hoped he liked me with just a fraction of the liking I had for him. One day Lady D phoned to ask me if I could as a great favour have Henry for lunch and the whole afternoon (it was a bank holiday). I almost laughed unbelievingly into the telephone.

We set off on our bikes for the finest hotel in the town (courtesy of Lady D, of course). As we sailed carelessly along the hot, unpeopled lanes, Henry suddenly placed one hand on my shoulder. I thrilled at this evidence of affection: but it was only to show he could cycle with one hand, even (he now proved it) with no hands at all on his handlebars.

The term ended, the lessons ended. For three more days he came to me, for I was to invigilate all his Common Entrance papers. As I packed the last lot up for posting, he yawned luxuriously and said: 'Oh, thank heavens it's all over.'

He shook hands, thanked me and mounted his bike. A careless wave as he sped down the road. I never saw him again.

Some thirty years later I had to speak to him on the phone regarding some charity I was trying to promote. He, in his turn, was inevitably distinguished. I asked: 'Do you remember, when you were about thirteen, cycling over to a prep school in Esher for Latin lessons?'

A little pause. 'Er no, no I'm afraid I don't. Was it...?'

I wanted to get it over. Quickly. 'Yes, I remember teaching you. Just before you went off to Marlborough. But of course you can't remember. It was just a few lessons. Of Latin, which you probably hated.'

I affected to laugh at the triviality of it all. But he added: 'Well, you must have taught me jolly well, because I got an exhibition in Latin at Cambridge.'

Polite, you see, to the end.

When he went from Belvedere on that last day I did something I had never done before. I wrote a poem. Or rather, it came, almost all complete, into my head. I never forgot it. I doubt if it has ever been written down. Or mentioned to a living soul. I'm going to put it down here, in memory of Henry. And, of course, to show how thankful we should be that I was scarcely ever tempted to write another.

> Pedal away and wave your hand,
> Show me you and the world are wise
> Not to suffer the parting time,
> Not to notice how cloud-drunk skies
> Oppress my heart, how stars will mock,
> O my darling, your star-got eyes.

5

My family coursed along in their rather aimless fashion. Father was on his legs again, and seldom as unsteadily as of yore. Mother held all together that was left to be held together. Terry was in German hands, transferred now to an Ilag in Bavaria. We had had one postcard from him, through the Red Cross, and by the same good offices we had sent him two parcels of clothes, food and cigarettes. We had no idea if he had received them. Brian was getting rather browned off with his army life. Now that it was no longer punctuated by weekends at home with Julien it presented a rather dreary vista. One friend he'd made at Bovington was eventually transferred and that made the daily round duller, the prospect bleaker. No talk of drafting overseas. Julien had written to me several times to say the work was very hard, the training very tough, but that he was doing well. His mother, too, was settling down happily among the Belgian refugee community in Watford. I missed Julien, achingly.

I had a sudden, chilling letter from the Ministry of Labour in Streatham. Why was I not complying with the tribunal's directives? I had not informed them of any efforts I had made in that direction. They demanded to see me at once.

When I sat before some official and explained that (a) I was doing a good deal of voluntary Civil Defence work, and (b) was teaching full-time in a school that desperately needed my services, he was rather surprisingly amenable. He said it was not, of course, up to him, but he would put my case before the tribunal and see if they would make schoolmastering a further condition of my registration. I thanked him profusely and went off feeling hopeful. Not *very* hopeful because I had never heard of any CO of my age being allowed to teach, and also because in my heart of hearts it didn't seem quite proper. This was after I had been at Belvedere for a year, and I felt I was soon to be cast out of my Eden.

Meanwhile, in the school holidays, I found my circle of Streatham acquaintances was being enlarged. My pacifism had cost us a few old friends (not really mourned), and now the night bombing brought some new ones. Two in particular were to play a part in my life.

Miss Gladys Clements lived further down our road, and we had been conscious of her proximity before the war and before we ever knew her. She lived with her parents and all three of them were, we felt sure, not our types at all: strait-laced, Tory, humourless. They were all tall and thin and severe-looking. But soon after the war started we somehow fell into the habit of greeting them politely in the street. Unconsciously, people had absorbed something of the air of impermanence, of freedom from convention, that the new hostilities had brought.

One day, somehow, Pam and I were invited into the Clements home for morning coffee. I don't remember the father, but the mother achieved some eminence in our minds by her reply to our very first 'How d'you do, Mrs Clements.' Fixing us with her rather beady eyes, she said: 'I was, of course, one of the Miss Everards of Hereford.' We especially appreciated the 'of course.'

Unhappily, the poor soul succumbed to a heart attack soon after war was declared, and her shadowy spouse followed her in a matter of months.

We invited Gladys to tea soon after her father had been interred. We felt it would be sticky but decency required it. She was a spinster of forty-odd suddenly orphaned. Enough to unsettle anyone.

But even at that first tea party we knew our estimation of Gladys needed much revision. She was more than reconciled to her loss. In fact, we felt she could hardly wait to spread her wings. She was voluble, unconventional, and even a bit freakish. She had a great laugh like a horse's whinny and she clearly liked to present herself as a bit of a Jezebel. We enjoyed her. She even gave us a description new to us. 'I'm now a VAD with all her life before her,' she said with some satisfaction. The VADs (Voluntary Aid Detachment) were nurses who did good work in the war. But I didn't know Gladys was one. I asked her about them. She gave me a searching look then emitted her horse laugh. 'You obviously don't know the other meaning of the initials.' I looked blank. 'Virgins Almost Desperate,' she cried, obviously enjoying herself. 'Thought you'd know that.'

Not long before the war, the famous Locarno dance hall had opened in Streatham. It was mainly for young people. But the place had recently launched into *thés dansants* for the older folks, at which squads of rather seedy gigolos in badly stained suede shoes offered themselves to single ladies at the rate of two shillings a dance. Like the evening sessions for the youngsters, these afternoon hops also were decried by the respectable suburbanites. So we were intrigued (though no longer surprised) to know that Gladys now became an habituée of them. She bought a fistful of dance tickets and filled each weekday afternoon with the pleasures they purchased. She loudly, brazenly, recounted her daring escapades to us of an evening. All quite harmless, and really very sad. She made out she was the belle of every ball, hated and envied by the other single ladies. 'My dears,' she whinnied to us, 'if looks could kill, I'd have been dead long ago.' She soon concentrated her attentions on a particular gigolo whom she always called 'The Major'. As Brian said: 'If ever he was a major it was only till he was drummed out of the Salvation Army.' We never saw The Major but we had a good picture of him, and of his tactics. When Gladys told us: 'I gave him the glad eye as soon as I saw him, and after that the poor old major's fate was sealed,' we gave her a new name, even to her face. Ever after she was 'Glad-eye' to us, and she goes down in these annals even so: a great romantic who was convinced The Major was infatuated with her. And I've no doubt he was, for she squandered the Everard inheritance on him.

6

The other new friend the war brought us was none other than Jonathan Gray, the son of the Plymouth Rock Peeping Tom opposite, the boy I'd eyed but written off long ago. Now the bombs blew us together. One night a few small high explosive bombs fell around us, one fracturing a water main. Most of our road came out in the small hours to watch the cascades in the gutters.

The Grays called some words across to us in an attempt to be neighbourly at last, so on a sudden whim I asked them in for coffee. It didn't seem odd to ask new acquaintances in for coffee at 3 am. Mr Gray made some excuse, but Mrs Gray and her two rather pretty children accepted with some alacrity.

Now just like Glad-eye, they proved to be positive revelations to us. Mrs Gray was both vivacious and very human. I think she was a Plymouth Rock only by assimilation, so to speak. And both Jonathan and Nancy (some two years older than her brother) turned out to be compulsive gigglers who on the slightest provocation became shriekers. They had a long-starved appetite for the outrageous. All three became regular evening visitors as long as the blitz lasted. Nancy had struck a blow for freedom by joining the Church of England and attending a noted evangelical stronghold near Oxford Street. She was quite hopelessly in love, not with the faith and not with the church, but with the curate, a young man called Adrian Cholmondeley-Puttock, a name too good to be true.

Jonathan's dégringolade was a matter of no small wonder to me, from the awesome heights of assured salvation to our depths of cynical parody. When I first knew him, he was already doing well in the (to me) mysterious world of banking. He seemed as normal as could be. He had a girlfriend, read little other than *The Daily Telegraph*, liked the dance music of the day, and was a leading light of the local cricket club. In other words, he inhabited a world light years away from mine. But, I gradually learned, he had this rarer alter ego imprisoned within him behind those solid walls of Plymouth Rock.

In fact, there were two selves screaming for release, one Dionysian, the other Apollonian. He liked doing and saying rather mad things. He had a taste for the Rabelaisian and the risqué. But also, wonder of wonders, he had a taste he never knew he had until I found it: for real music and real literature. The result was that at first he hung on every word I uttered, almost surrendered his personality to mine, even became vaguely amorous. I was glad when his confidence grew stronger, when he followed his own tastes, when he no longer felt the need merely to repudiate his father's narrow, life-denying creed.

He started by asking me to give him a reading programme, and he read and enjoyed most of it. Especially Shakespeare. Like me, he had a good memory for lines of verse and we competed in learning by heart great chunks of *Macbeth* and *Hamlet* and the *Sonnets*. Similarly with music, we indulged ourselves in my song cycles and then together branched out into chamber music. We bought gramophone records of the great quartets: Mozart and Beethoven and Schubert. Then, very daringly, and not always successfully, the more modern figures: Delius and Vaughan Williams, Debussy and Ravel and Sibelius.

He gave richly to me, too. His mind, so keen and so tidy, and his head for the smallest data, proved good counters to my less disciplined intuitions. So did his husbandry. Without ever being tightfisted (which I'd have decried at once), he enabled me to glimpse that you could do other things with money than promptly throw it away.

The night raids were taking some toll of mother's and father's nerves. We spent the night sitting in chairs around the breakfast room. Even I didn't go up to my bedroom as I had done during so much of the blitz. But we never had an air-raid shelter, either a Morrison or an Anderson. Typically, no one in the family had got round to obtaining one. In the garden of an empty house opposite was a well planted Morrison shelter. The Grays urged us to use it. We did, for just one night. After that we all agreed we'd sooner be blown up in a bit of comfort.

One night when most of London was set ablaze, when from our attic windows we could see the great glow of the burning docks, we had one top room set alight. I remember mother phoning for the fire brigade. 'Be quick,' she told them, and when they didn't arrive within a few minutes she phoned them again. 'Whatever are you doing?' she asked. They told her: 'We have a few thousand fires to see to, madam. The whole of the East End is ablaze.' I know we all, mother included, had a good laugh at the sheer unreasonableness of womankind. Our fire wasn't much of one. Brian and I (it was one of his jolly weekend leaves) had chopped down a cupboard wall and had put most of the fire out by the time the splendid firemen arrived.

Then for some months there was a lull in the bombing of London. The notorious Baedeker raids were launched: Bath and York and Coventry, and several more. Mrs Gray and Nancy didn't come in so much now, but Jonathan came every night. As soon as he arrived home from the office, he changed and had his dinner at great speed so that he could sprint across to us. Once there, he would greet warmly each member of my family and ask each one how he himself looked that evening. Similarly, he would appraise himself keenly in each mirror. At first we thought this was due to sheer vanity, and we ragged him mercilessly about his eager questions: 'Not bad, am I? Wouldn't think I've been slaving in a City bank all day, would you? Weather it pretty well, don't I?'

But we stopped pulling his leg about this when we learned from his mother that he had as a child been treated for tuberculosis. It had apparently cleared up but he secretly dreaded its return, especially when he had been rejected on medical grounds for military service. So during his initial interrogations each evening we'd leave aside our ragging for a moment to give him the assurances he craved. It was good to see his handsome, rather ravaged features light up.

His girlfriend had been unceremoniously ditched soon after he got to know us. I never saw her but I pictured her from his descriptions as a rather pretty, rather empty-headed little typist. I don't think they had any affinity. Still, I was glad to hear she soon found someone else, and probably a far more congenial swain. After that, the only piece of his life that sometimes intruded into our concert-going and play-going was his cricket, which he loved and which, he said apologetically, was so good for his health. But Plymouth Rock *père* viewed with growing disapproval his son's emancipation: all the books and gramophone records that were invading his godly dwelling. And when Jonathan began to play cricket on Sundays, he issued a stern warning that the Devil was at his son's elbow. But Jonathan, secure in his new and pagan family, laughed it all to scorn.

I was summoned once more to appear before the tribunal to explain my disregard of their rulings. They were vindictive as a slighted woman, trouncing both me and the poor Ministry of Labour official who had presented to them my ridiculous case. I was ordered to comply forthwith. But I had discovered that I had a right of appeal against this ruling, too. I did so, not with any hope of success, but as a final stalling action that would allow me to finish the summer term at Belvedere. Which was just what it did.

Shortly before I left Belvedere I had a weekend in Southampton. I had for some time been planning it. I must have got a travel permit on the grounds that I wanted to visit my young ward. Julien had grown up and filled out surprisingly in less than a year. He was no longer my fragile and lovely

144

waif, but a young serviceman in the making. He was eighteen on his next birthday. He looked very handsome in his uniform and he now knew he did, wearing his large naval cap at a rakish angle that somehow spoke the flight of boyhood. It was a dark, close, rainy day as we sat on a seat beside the deserted sea front. In days of peace it had been one of those large seaside shelters so dear to the elderly, but now it was just a decaying monument to vanished gossip and laughter, to shaky limbs and old brooding eyes. As we sat there, gazing over the great coils of barbed wire on the beach to the now unimaginable wastes of Brittany, I reached down and held his hand, not now for that instant gratification but as a salute to days now slipping away for ever. He told me of a NAAFI girl he'd got to know, told it all rather defiantly as if to underline his inevitable ripening. Yet I felt that in him, too, was an unacknowledged sadness at it all.

We had a snack in a near derelict café and then he walked to the station with me. As we waited for my train to gird up its loins and run away, he said suddenly, almost desperately: 'Oh Pete, I sorry I give to that stupid NAAFI girl what I never give to you.' It was a remark so intuitive, so gentle and kind, that I had to turn my head away from him and say the guard was preparing to blow his whistle. But I had been comforted by his words. I said: 'You are still a darling. My darling.' As I squeezed his hand he replied: 'And I tell you again: my best friend. For ever.' I deliberately fixed him with my eyes as the train steamed off: rather lanky, rather top-heavy, in his cap and long, blue naval trenchcoat. I was treating myself to a bit of self-dramatization, taken straight from a film Brian and I had seen and loved a score of times: William Wyler's *Dodsworth*, in which Walter Huston stands on the train step gazing with unforgettable desolation at the Fran he is leaving behind forever. I was at the age when emotion was no less sincere for being so vulgarly dramatized.

A few weeks later I was at it again as I walked for the last time out of Belvedere. But it didn't work nearly so well, for the happy shouts and running feet of end-of-term schoolboys had injected life and health into the whole landscape.

The appellate tribunal made short work of me, as I expected. I wasn't even asked to confirm my name and address. Just told to find 'ARP, AFS, or landwork' within a week, or prosecution would follow. I couldn't blame them, nor could I regret the urgency that left me no time to grieve over Belvedere, whose boys were already frozen into the imperishable school group with my 10-year-olds of an earlier epoch.

7

My old friend James Turner, poet and novelist, had a nursery garden in Essex, not large but successful and productive. I assumed that was 'landwork.' So did he, as he agreed that I could join him. I could live in (he and Catherine were installed in an ancient and superannuated rectory), and he could pay me a regulation wage, less bed and breakfast, as he required help at that time. But he insisted I came for a trial week. No sense in registering with the Ministry of Labour until I was sure I could stick it. Wise old James. He remembered my lifelong love affair with London.

I moved in on a Saturday and I started work on Monday morning. I remember little other than great greenhouses of tomatoes, through whose streaming panes I stared in mute horror at fields of heavy mud and skies of heavy cloud. He told me what I had to do with the tomato plants, but I scarcely listened. I knew the poor things hated me even more than I hated them. On Thursday evening I told him I'd go mad if I stayed another day. I was embarrassed and apologetic, but also adamant. Not that James made any effort to dissuade me. Indeed, I think he was as thankful as I was to be packing my things. On Friday morning he gave me a bag full of tomatoes and a letter of introduction for which I've forever blessed his name. It was to a young art student he knew who was a CO now working in Westminster Civil Defence and finding it 'tophole.'

His name was Derrick Harris and I went to see him at his Berkeley Square depot as soon as I got back to London. Over lunch in the Civil Defence canteen, Derrick told me about his duties there: twenty-four hours on and twenty-four hours off, £4 a week, a few lectures on first aid and light rescue, and that was about it. You were on duty from 9 am to 9 am, and during the quiet spells at present obtaining you could get a night's sleep and a bath in the morning before you went off to enjoy whatever you had to enjoy. He himself was studying under John Farleigh at the Central School. The canteen was good, and the chaps were a decent lot: few COs, many Irish and Cockney types, several actors. Next door there was a hostel of nurses and ambulance girls, many of them clinging precariously to a showbiz life.

Derrick and I took to each other at once. The long lunch had scarcely enough room for all we had to say to each other. It only ended when it did because Derrick insisted I go to Westminster Council's headquarters that very afternoon to convince them they needed me at the Berkeley Square depot. So along to the City powers I hurried, preparing as I went all the persuasive dialectics I could think of. Actually I needed little blarney: to my surprise they seemed to want me. I signed up there and then, scarcely believing my luck. I hurried back to the depot to tell Derrick my good news.

The depot had been a large underground garage and car park, to which it reverted soon after the war. Then it was a dark, frowsty, noisy complex almost teeming with motley life. All manner of people, from the scruffy to the starchy, seemed to use its canteen, many of them, I am sure, quite illegally.

Everything seemed free and easy. Some mornings we had lectures, on first aid or tunnelling and digging in ruins. These were rather half-hearted affairs I often found it hard to follow. Then sometimes we had special assignments in the purlieus of Westminster: salvaging the contents of a blitzed engineering works, delving in Hyde Park for an unexploded bomb we never found, a joint exercise with the London fire brigade (in whose ranks was an equally bemused Stephen Spender), and other forays whose purpose I now understand even less than I did then. Otherwise Derrick and I drifted around the depot and also, I am afraid, around most of the City of Westminster, endlessly talking, endlessly curious about neighbourhoods and buildings. We were not supposed to be anywhere but in the depot on our duty days, but only the flotsam-and-jetsam types obeyed that, and very gladly, for it was dry and warm and some of them had nothing else they could call a home.

My friendship with Derrick was to prove one of the richest I had experienced, and I cannot deny it the label 'romantic,' although the term needs careful definition. It was romantic in the sense that we shared, and added to, our respective loves: mine mainly for literature and music, his mainly for art. He was a far more rewarding recipient of what I had to offer than I was of his goods. In any case he was already an appreciative traveller in my realms, while I was mostly a babe in his. To some extent I succeeded in acquiring some knowledge and some appreciation of art, but I had finally to admit that it wasn't part of my world, chiefly because most of the great painters were so aggressively heterosexual. I did much better with etchings and engravings, which were Derrick's own fields. And illustrators of children's books, too, like Randolph Caldicott and Kate Greenaway and Arthur Rackham, although I think we met there less because of the art, more because of the nostalgia. Indeed, one great bond between us was this common love of a vanished age, in Derrick's case a relish above all for eighteenth-century England. He once said to me, much later, as I watched him at work on his splendid illustrations for the Folio Society *Tom Jones*, 'You know, there was some confusion over my birth. Two hundred years too late. I really belong lock, stock and barrel to Fielding's world.'

There was no hint, no taint, of homosexuality in our friendship, which was aesthetic and ethical. He did not attract me physically, and I was usually careful to conceal from him my romantic love of boyhood and youth. Very occasionally I had to play a part. When, for example, we passed some attractive girl in Bond Street and Derrick would say warmly: 'My God, that's a beautiful young woman.' I'd hasten to agree, though probably I hadn't even noticed her. I hoped that, if he did find something less than warm in my reaction, he'd put it down to my deplorable deficiency in visual appreciation. But at times I had to let my hair down even with Derrick. I mean in the sense that I'd say 'Ugh' over Rubens' naked, buxom females and 'Ah, yes' over Michaelangelo's marvellous young men. I often wondered why the Attic sculptors should be so much nearer to my aesthetic world than were the Gallic painters of a far closer age. As Derrick generously tutored me around the Tate and the National Gallery, I did come to like and admire many landscape painters, if only because their landscapes were often settings for my exiled Edens, landscapes of my pre-existent soul. I remember becoming obsessed by Samuel Palmer's sepia and watercolour landscapes, in which Blake's barefoot boys would have been at home.

And to Derrick I gave my love of lieder, and of English romantics like Vaughan Williams, Delius, Bridge, Ireland and Elgar. He rather teased me about them, designating their work 'woosic' (that is, woolly, oozing music).

Derrick had a beautiful speaking voice, deep and rich and resonant, and an even more beautiful laugh that was unstinted in its sheer, overflowing gusto. Anything even remotely absurd sparked off that laugh: a Lyons teashop menu that read 'Ham Roll filled 4d, unfilled 2d;' a large, clean patch on a grimy wall in the Society of Apothecaries (whatever were we doing in there?) where a painting had once been and its ornate title on a block of wood remained, declaring 'Imaginary Portrait of the Spanish Armada'; a lecture on the composition of walls, given by a Cockney builder who smote the wall and mystified us by explaining: 'You see, full of air.' (Derrick, quicker and more practical, realized that the word was an unaspirated 'hair,' which was apparently part of this wall's composition.) I remember also Derrick's sense of justice and compassion when he saw a burly police constable boxing the ears of a howling small boy. He went over and wiped the floor with the man, threatening him with all manner of reports to his superiors if he ever saw him assault a child again.

We both loved cinema and theatre and enjoyed the highlights on our evenings off. Sundays on duty were devoted to the reviews of C. A. Lejeune and Dilys Powell, of James Agate and J. C. Trewin. We took their pronouncements very seriously. Sometimes Derrick and I would disagree about something and almost a medieval disputation would ensue. On and on we'd go, each hell-bent on delivering the knockout blow. It was all done with straight faces but twinkling eyes. We were neither of us quite honest about our feelings on these occasions. We were so proud of our sophistication and detachment that any breath of ill humour in our deliberations was unthinkable. But I do know that, in my case at least, there was a buried strain of genuine rivalry when we so crossed swords, for I think Derrick was the first well-matched opponent I'd met, someone whose mind was keen as mine, or keener, and whose critical antennae were as tender, or tenderer. It did me a great deal of good. We were a couple of polished boars, always sharpening our tusks on each other's hides.

Our mates were a problem I'd anticipated from the first. I remained shy and ill at ease with all but obvious soul mates. From any whose views were orthodox, whose standards were those of the herd, I stayed awkwardly apart. And with the working classes I had no rapport at all. Indeed, I'd never met any on an equal footing. I felt quite sure my new Civil Defence buddies would give me a wide berth. I expected to be an alien, regarded with some suspicion to his face and some ridicule behind his back.

But, thrown into their midst as I was, I had to make some effort to swim with my colleagues. And, to my surprise, it was all quite easy. True, they were a bit wary at first, but soon we were ribbing each other and I even felt that they quite liked me. For some pickled old Irishmen and some London barrow boys I became a sort of amanuensis, even something approaching a legal adviser, for most of them were involved in scraps with authority of some kind and I was often called on to compose letters to these vague figures, letters which occasionally worked.

The Heavy Rescue Corps were all professional navvies. Their quarters were the other side of the Square and we only saw them at mealtimes, when they came and went in dour fashion, apparently set on having no truck with us. Ditto the girls in the Ambulance Corps, who were led by a very butch titled lady, whose inseparable companion was a lissom girl called Peter (or more probably Peta), whom even I found attractive. We had three real Cockneys from around Bow who were always rather ostentatiously cooking up something shady. I believed it was an act put on for the benefit of Derrick and me, who were regarded as a couple of innocents in some need of education. The leader of this trio was Jack Jacobs, short and fat and balding, and about fifty years of age. His particular crony was Charley, whose broken nose and cauliflower ear saved him the trouble of explaining that he was a boxer. I gathered Charley had only recently regained his freedom. Jack, who was too fly ever to brush with the law, was always telling Charley to 'go careful' and to 'watch it.'

One day Charley overheard me telling Derrick I wanted to buy a second-hand typewriter. 'I think I know where I can lay me 'ands on one, Pete,' he told me in his hoarse, conspiratorial tones. 'A real good 'un. Goin' cheap. You interested?' I said I was, and Charley reckoned he could get it for me within a week. 'Just depends on the wevver,' he said with a straight face but a wink at Jack. And a few days later Charley announced the machine was all ready for me. 'A real beauty, Pete. I could get a tenner for it any old where, but you can have it for seven quid. As a favour. To a pal.' It was one of the pickled old Irishmen who told me admiringly that Charley had on a moonless night (hence it all depending on the weather) broken into some office in Berkeley Square and nicked the machine for me. I was horrified and wouldn't, of course, have anything to do with it. But Jack and Charley told me, repeatedly, they wouldn't have thought me capable of such unbusinesslike, downright unethical behaviour. ''E got it for you,' said Jack. 'You ordered it and 'e took a big risk in gettin' it for you. Wouldn't have done it for no one else. 'E don't deal in typewriters as a rule. Now you let 'im down.' There were times when I almost doubted my sane standards, especially when Derrick pretended to side with them. I told them I felt sure Charley could find another client, probably even one who would pay a better price. 'Yerss,' said Charley reproachfully, 'but I got it for you, y'see.'

Some time later Jack sold me a wristwatch. Of course I now took great precautions to insist I wouldn't touch anything stolen, and besides, it was a very nice-looking watch. Jack swore, by 'my dear old mother, God rest her soul,' his favourite oath, that the watch was virgin clean. So I bought it, for £4, thinking perhaps in some mysterious way it would make amends for the unclean typewriter.

The watch gained one and a half hours in the first week. Jack assured me it was simply a question of my getting to know it, of regulating it properly. I regulated it, which it resented, and then it stopped, determinedly and forever. I demanded my money back, but instead Jack gave me a very serious, paternal lecture. 'Now that's to teach you a lesson, Pete. Never believe nobody. And if you do get taken in, never whine. I ain't chargin' nothink for this advice.'

'Thank you, Jack,' I said faintly. 'Very good of you.'

'That's all right,' said Jack generously. Then he added: 'Y'see, Pete, before I'm done I'm going to make a right effin' bastard of you.' He nodded a warm approval of his own bigheartedness. 'Because I like you. A right effin' bastard. You've got the makings of one, y'know.'

Derrick insisted I'd been paid a great compliment. Every time I complained about anything, in shops or restaurants, for instance, Derrick would smile his approval and murmur: 'You're comin' on, RFB.'

Jack gave me more conventional lessons, or tried to. He was my Civil Defence driving instructor. In a rather handsome squad car, a Morris Oxford, he piloted me all round St George's Circus and up and down Piccadilly. He took pride in teaching me in frequented places, but it clearly took it out of him. I'd unofficially driven my father's car as a youngster and I've no doubt that but for Jack I'd have become really proficient in no time.

As soon as I crashed in the gear and lurched forward Jack became demented, and he never ceased shrieking incomprehensible or contradictory commands until we were safely back in the depot. 'No, no, no,' he screamed, 'oh my God - left 'and down - not the left, you fool, I said right - now - 'ard, 'ard, - Keristermighty, you nearly did it then - now, now - give a signal, won't you - pull over - use yer clutch, won't you - oh, don't rev up - what yer doing?' Back at base, I crawled out of the car and into a cold shower.

Then one night, I thought it all out soberly. It was clear as daylight. Next time I was out with Jack I stopped my ears to all his cries and drove perfectly. Jack was elated. 'You're a credit to me, Pete,' he beamed. 'Best pupil I've 'ad.'

8

I eagerly acquired new London territories: Mayfair and its shops, Clubland and its restaurants, the Piccadilly hub from which one radiated in all intriguing directions. And all without sacrificing my cherished old haunts around the Strand and Fleet Street. At the top of Curzon Street was the opulent Gunter's, where even in wartime one could savour heavenly gateaux and luscious cream confections, and at the foot of Curzon Street was the civilized Trumper's, where I had my hair cut and shampooed at prices as plutocratic as those of the cakes. But for lunch we often went to my beloved Vega's, the vegetarian restaurant in Leicester Square, where we munched great Champney and Bircher-Brenner salads, or devoured their inimitable nut cutlets and spiced greens. Again, Derrick affected some disdain for what he called 'farinaceous frippery,' so far removed from the prandial gustos of Tom Jones and Squire Weston, as was the delicate pecking of Sir Stafford Cripps at his table in the corner.

Then I decided I too must have some sort of a club. Not Pall Mall or St James's, of course (not yet), but the club which was part of the Arts Theatre in Cranbourn Street. When I applied for membership they told me I must have a sponsor, and alas I had none. But standing in the foyer at that moment was the actress, Margaretta Scott, who most generously said: 'Oh, I'll sponsor you. You look OK.' So that became my first club, and a splendid one, too, with an attractive lounge and a first-class dining room. Add to all this the aesthetic fare provided by Myra Hess's lunchtime concerts at the National Gallery and you have some idea of the richness of my new life in Westminster Civil Defence. Several times a week Derrick and I slipped along to the National Gallery concerts, where turbanned and fruity-voiced ladies served marvellous sandwiches at fourpence each, and where the finest instrumentalists in Europe performed for us at a shilling a time. We queued behind Benjamin Britten for our sandwiches and sat next to C.E.M. Joad for our concerts. It was there that I became an addict of chamber music, and remained one for life.

But I must explain how I could afford all this on £4 a week from Westminster City Council. The answer is that very soon after I started at Berkeley Square I felt I must, like so many of my mates, find a job to occupy me on my alternate days off. And what more possible than my old prewar employer, the still flourishing Reader's Union? So I contacted John Baker and explained the position. To my delight he jumped at the chance. He himself was busy at the Ministry of Information, like so many of those I'd known in publishing, and had to run RU in his few spare moments. So I was taken on as head of editorial, earning another £4 a week and domiciled in a small but pleasant office RU had retained in the Strand.

I was now earning £8 a week clear, more than I had ever earned, and enabling me to give generously at home and also treat Derrick whenever I could. That was not as often as I wished because Derrick had a horror of being a scrounger. I had to argue long and fiercely to make him accept my treats. As I urged with complete sincerity, I could not enjoy the meals and the plays unless he were with me. What was the point in my earning the money if I couldn't enjoy at least some of it? Besides, he was a poor and dedicated student who would one day be a famous artist who could then treat me to his heart's content.

At RU I did all my former chores: spotting likely books to become our monthly selections, writing articles for *Reader's News*, editing the magazine each month, meeting authors, dealing with all the multifarious letters from members, and so on.

I was entirely my own boss. I seemed to be wandering about London a great deal of the time, I hope legitimately. And Derrick and I were always 'spotting' people. He was quite good at it, but I was a past master, mostly thanks to Brian. For I had been scarcely into my teens when Brian took upon himself the task of training me. This was really a question of sharpening my powers of observation. He would take me for long walks, preferably in low-life Dickensian neighbourhoods. Southwark was one of his favourites. Some purple-faced old boozer would draw unsteadily near and Brian would mutter: 'Now observe this very expensive face. Chiefly the nose. Great wealth has been lavished on that nose.' Or perhaps some poor old creature with a withered arm or leg would hobble towards us and Brian would explain: 'Now draw a moral from this. Limbs made of cheap stuff don't last. No wear in them.' A thin, working-class type could be found hurrying to his factory. 'Observe the usual cheap, cardboard attaché case in which he carries his lunch: bubble-and-squeak sandwiches. Notice also the one forefinger extended over the lid of the case. Why? Because the rotten, cheap catch broke years ago.'

Only a little later Brian took me into his favourite pubs and directed my attention to the married couples drifting off from nine o'clock onwards. 'I want you,' he murmured, 'to notice the Proprietorial Hand. It is at first on The Little Woman's arm, then as she goes in front of him through the doorway it is transferred to the small of her back. That is to stake his claim, mark his territory.'

Very often he said or did things that embarrassed me greatly. A child would accidentally tread on his foot in some crowded thoroughfare, and he would hop on the other foot, his face contorted with agony, as the child looked terrified and the parent apologized profusely. Then he would smile dazzlingly and say: 'Only a joke.' It always annoyed him if people sailed without a glance through a door he held open for them. He took to saying in a loud voice with another bright smile: 'What did you say, madam?' The woman would reply in some confusion: 'Oh, I didn't say anything.' Then he'd declaim in even louder tones with an even more seraphic smile: 'My mistake. I thought you said "Thank you".'

So with this kind of training at an early age, I recognized every eminent face (Osbert Lancaster, E. M. Forster, Michael Redgrave, Rose Macaulay, H.G. Wells, Clark Gable dressed as a GI major) we passed in the street, as well as every tiny eccentricity of the nameless ones.

It was also at this time that there reawoke in me my love of Forrest Reid's work, which I had first met at RU before the war. I set about getting any novels of his that were still in print. I remember going into Edward Arnold, the publisher, and asking if they had in stock an early novel of his, *The Spring Song*, first published in 1918 and never reprinted. An old man descended to a cellar and came up with a dusty copy. The incident was somehow in complete accord with the author's work.

But many of the older titles were long out of print. I regretted this, not only because I wanted to read them, but also because I had formed the plan to write something about him. So, on an inspiration, I wrote to Walter de la Mare to tell him what I had in mind and to ask if he could possibly lend me his copies of the early works. I stressed, of course, that I would take the greatest care of them and return them promptly. It seems to me now that I had a great presumption in writing like this. But within a few days a parcel of the books arrived, together with a charming letter from de la Mare. The correspondence was to continue for about five years and to be one of the delights of my life.

I made contact with other writers, usually through something I'd written on them somewhere. Robert Graves was as friendly as he was kind. We'd done an edition of his *The Reader Over Your Shoulder*, a compendium of rather poor contemporary writing, but in an article on it I felt compelled to cite many examples of his own infelicities. He wrote to thank me, saying 'I've always been rather a poor writer of prose.' That correspondence, too, went on for some years. F. R. Leavis took umbrage, I heard from his secretary, because I had said in a review in some literary journal that 'his many quotations from T. S. Eliot serve only to highlight his own uncouth prose.' I similarly offended V. S. Pritchett by querying his critical stance.

With Mrs Belloc Lowndes I got on much better. She was delightful. I went many times to tea or lunch at her house in Barton Street, behind Westminster Abbey. She often wrote me extravagant letters, one unforgettable one beginning: 'I long to see you. It is many weeks since we met for intercourse.' I think she romanticized, in the most charming way. Once Emily Brontë's name came up, and she said (in her fluent but unenglish tones): 'Ah, dear Emily. 'Ow well I remember 'er. She gave my mother a copy of 'er *Wuthering Heights*. I 'ave it 'ere behind me.' I waited breathless as she scanned the bookcase behind her chair. But in vain. 'It is not to 'and at the moment. The war, you know.' On another occasion I mentioned Walter de la Mare. 'Ah, Mr de la Mare.' She waxed lyrical on the slightest provocation. ''E was sitting in that very chair you're in only last week.' Several years later I mentioned this to de la Mare, who looked puzzled and said: 'I'm sure I've never met the lady.'

Rather different was my contact with a young writer whose first novel I read about in *The New Statesman* and bought immediately. That was Denton Welch, whose *Maiden Voyage* I admired immensely. I wrote to him and a sort of friendship sprang up on paper. But I wanted a meeting, and said so. He never mentioned it when he replied, so I, too, never again broached the subject. Later I was to discover the reason for his odd behaviour, I think. I had in my letters accepted the view of himself he had given the world in *Maiden Voyage*, and it was a view I fell in love with. But he was in fact badly disabled as the result of an accident on his bike when he was twenty. He continued to write, marvellously, in much pain and bitterness of spirit, and died of his injuries at age thirty-three. A great talent wrested out of great suffering.

I was much involved in those days with minority, but by no means lost, causes. Pacifism, of course. And what was not in those other fighting days known as 'women's lib,' whose patron saint was, for me at any rate, Virginia Woolf. Her suicide the year before had been a shattering death at a time when death was becoming horribly familiar. But not so familiar that I could accept capital punishment, for somehow it seemed more and not less terrible to stop a life cold-bloodedly, legally, when bullets and bombs were stopping lives haphazardly.

Another cause I espoused then was progressive education. I read all about A. S. Neill, and, of course, corresponded with him. I remember telling him I had one tiny doubt about his romantic system of schooling: had he ever turned out a boy or girl aesthetically gifted, or are only the psychological misfits so blessed? He told me to 'forget all that claptrap about unhappy, maladjusted kids making fine artists. All that matters for anyone is being able to achieve a full, complete and satisfying orgasm.' I was so innocent I had to look up 'orgasm' in the dictionary.

I got on rather better with Dora Russell, ex-wife of Bertrand Russell, who had a progressive school I rather hoped to join after the war. I took

Dora to a good blowout in Vega's, where I remember her describing how she fell in love with Bertie when she saw him in the dock.

Greedy for all the agreeable experiences I could muster, I advertised in *The New Statesman* for some tutoring in English and Latin. I ended my advertisement with the words: 'CO - but not the sort that makes kids militarists,' which was a silly phrase I'd read somewhere. One lady, a Mrs Ann Fison of Hampstead, replied to say her boy needed coaching in Latin during the coming Christmas holidays. He was fourteen and had just started at King's, Canterbury. I met both of them over tea at my club. Peter was very intelligent, had a very loud voice, and was a born exhibitionist, despite which I took to him, and he to me. I taught him Latin twice a week during those holidays, and the next Easter ones. Always over cakes in the lounge of the Arts Theatre Club. Even with his mouth full he didn't stop addressing the whole room in his extremely affected accents. I had to keep quietening him down. The only time he voluntarily lowered his voice was when he told me (truthfully or as a joke) his name was really Fleischmann and his father was an Austrian count now interned in the Isle of Man.

Mrs Fison twice insisted I have dinner with them in Hampstead. Two most enjoyable evenings followed. But over the second was a little cloud I thought I recognized, in my shy, nervous, over-active imagination. I rather avoided all further invitations. Instead, I mapped out the plot of a play I thought I'd enjoy writing: about an attractive young chap who is taken on as resident tutor to a beautiful, intelligent and misunderstood youth (shades of Henry James and Forrest Reid). The tutor falls in love with the youth and the mother with the tutor. The husband becomes madly jealous about his wife's supposed adultery with the tutor. The only way the tutor can save the woman's honour is by confessing his true nature as the unspoken lover of the boy. Result: poor young tutor is despised by all three of them. Of course, I never wrote it. A pity Terence Rattigan didn't.

On the evenings of my off-duty days, when I'd finished at RU, I sometimes met Derrick and sometimes Jonathan. Both were prized friends but they were very different, feeding diverse strands in my personality: Derrick the creative, Jonathan more the pagan and practical. I loved both.

On my off-duty Sundays I still went sometimes to the morning meeting of the Friends. I found that quiet hour refreshing, and the Quakers themselves so sane and good. Then after that meeting straight up the High Road to a more gutsy meeting with Pam and Jonathan and whatever kindred spirits were free at the time. I was doing my best to 'educate' Pam: taking her to operas and to concerts, and getting her to read Isherwood and Forster as a preliminary ducking before a hoped-for wallow with Hardy and Galsworthy and Mary Webb and Margaret Kennedy and Elizabeth Bowen. Oh, I was proud of the programme I had planned for her and I wanted to be proud of her performance with it. But there were little signs of defection in her, signs I turned a blind eye to as long as I could. She was intelligent and lively and very amusing, and I was ambitious for her. The more all of us were together, the more I could build out of this fertile family of mine. Terry was in Bavaria and Brian was in the army, but these were just two temporary dispersals.

However, I had forgotten she had been deprived of steady, secure schooling. I had forgotten she was immersed in the confused, transitory world of wartime London. Above all, I had forgotten that she was a girl of eighteen. Her boyfriends and beaux I saw only as noisy, fleeting fun. Even a new and sombre and persistent one: young Martin Gregg, who was nineteen and in the army and darkly handsome. He was the only one of all these young people who hated me for my pacifism, deeply resentful that I was not forced like him into uniforms and barracks and camps far from home.

9

It was just before I signed on with Westminster Civil Defence that my mother told me the news that at one stroke smashed my family dreams: 'Pam is pregnant.'

Disbelief, horror, disgust overwhelmed me. For days, I couldn't look at her, for weeks I didn't speak to her. I assumed Martin Gregg was the father. I was wrong: the father was a chap of twenty-six who once had worked behind the dairy counter in the grocers Pam and I had shopped and clowned and laughed in a hundred times. A working-class fellow she was determined to marry. That was the final, bitter blow: my snobbery piled on my righteousness. The fellow was now in the navy and soon to join his ship for another Atlantic crossing. Attitudes then were very different to the way they are now.

My mother said to me one day: 'You can't keep this up. Not with Pam.' And I knew I couldn't: treating her like it was breaking my heart. 'Wasn't it possible,' I asked, 'to have the baby adopted? Did she have to marry the fellow?'

Yes, I was told, Pam was utterly determined to marry him. If father wouldn't give his consent, then she'd run away with him, or do herself some harm. Her words were wild, her manner coldly fixed. As for adoption, said mother, Pam would never hear of it. I didn't know it then, but it was mother rather than Pam who'd never hear of it.

So one evening 'the fellow,' named Bob Powis, was due to come to the house to meet us all. Mother and father and Nora and Brian he met. I went out with Jonathan for the whole evening.

But I *had* to meet him. Life had to go on. It was my family and she was my sister: 'a present to me' I had been told when she was born. I sounded both father and mother about him before I met him. All father said, sadly,

156

hopelessly, was: 'Not quite our kind.' Strong words for father. Mother was more coldly obdurate: 'I shall never like him, never forgive him.' Brian, of course, pronounced him 'a thoroughly nice chap.'

When I met him, together with Pam and with Brian, who got weekend passes for these family crises, I agreed with father, tried to agree with mother, but ended up in my heart of hearts agreeing with Brian.

So Bob married her. He became perforce a member of the family. And I did my best to forget that he was not polished or good-looking, and eight years older than Pam.

Then his leave was up and he sailed in HMS *Eagle*, in which he was torpedoed. He spent eight hours in the water before he was picked up. He was invalided ashore for six months and then posted to another ship. He never spoke about his experiences. He never ceased to be as nice with me as he was with everybody. He was always roaring with laughter. Father taught him to play cribbage and thoroughly enjoyed the games he had with him of an evening. Mother said grudgingly: 'I shall never like him but I must admit he's got a wonderful disposition.' He and Brian became great friends. I came to like him, too, though we hadn't anything in common.

In the spring of 1943 the baby was born. Bob was at sea. Jonathan and I waited by the phone all day and night to hear from the nursing home that all had gone well and the baby was not a girl. We wanted the boy to be born to the gramophone strains of Mozart. We felt that would augur well.

And that was what happened. It was a boy. He and Pam flourished. Mozart's great G Minor Quintet ushered him into this vale of tears. I insisted on naming him Miles, after the lovely little hero of Henry James' *The Turn of the Screw*. Even more incredibly, he wasn't like Bob but was in fact a very pretty baby. I loved him at sight, just as eighteen years before I'd loved his newborn mother.

In no time at all, it seems, Pam was up and about, with Miles in the biggest and most opulent pram I had ever seen. So, gradually, the dark cloud over my Berkeley Square year lifted, and, if I had lost the sister I had dreamed of, I had gained a nephew to whom I could transfer those dreams.

No more boys or beaux for Pam now. They melted away, even the gloomy young Martin Gregg. We heard an injury to his foot had got him his discharge. I felt he'd deliberately dropped something on it, and I certainly didn't blame him for that.

Then, almost on the heels of this upset, came something quite as sensational. It was a letter from Brian at Bovington camp to say he was wearing his own, civvy clothes and sitting in the guardhouse. He had decided he couldn't have anything more to do with 'the filthy, cruel war game played by mindless brass hats plotting the deaths of thousands upon thousands of ignorant kids.' Only years later did I learn what had finally sparked off this defiant act of Brian's. A new intake at Bovington had included a young recruit who had established an instant rapport with Brian. He was called David Ward. David and Brian spent all their spare time together. Life became good again. Even the memory of Julien became less green. Then one terrible day David was killed. Not in battle, just in a badly mismanaged exercise.

So, in bitterness and disgust, Brian opted out. From his commanding officer down, they pleaded with him, for I think he was popular, but to no avail. I went to see the Central Board for Conscientious Objectors, to make sure they kept an eye on him. He was then taken to court, where they gave him three months' imprisonment. This he served in Dorchester prison, from which he wrote to me whenever he could. I remember one letter (in minuscule writing and very watery ink) in which he told me he had got Edward Carpenter's *The Intermediate Sex* out of the prison library and greatly enjoyed it. He ended his letter: 'I remain, dear brother, an urning, yearning and burning for a letter from you.' Beside this a puzzled warder, deputed to be censor, had placed a large, pencilled question mark, then presumably given up.

After this spell of confinement, Brian had been marched back to Bovington and ordered once more to don his uniform. He had again refused, and the next thing I heard was that he had been taken to Catterick camp in Yorkshire. I immediately informed the Central Board for Conscientious Objectors, who demanded from the War Office to know the reason for this move. I think the careful watch this voluntary body, set up by the Quakers and the PPU, kept over COs did much good. I myself remembered stories of COs in the First World War who'd been spirited away to the front.

So Brian appeared again in court, and was again given three months, this time in Armley gaol, Leeds. He was scarcely settled in there when my own thunderbolt fell.

That was my almost too well filled year in Westminster Civil Defence. Just one year. It ended as suddenly as it had started. We were served with notices from the Ministry of Labour and National Service to say that selected members of the Westminster Light Rescue Party were transferred forthwith to certain regional mobile columns. These were specially formed units based near large towns that could expect bombing too severe for their local services to cope with unaided. Mr Derrick Harris was posted to column no 1, concentrating on Basingstoke and Salisbury, and Mr Peter Gamble to column no 2, concentrating on Plymouth.

'The bastards,' Derrick and I hissed to each other. 'It's only the COs they've posted. And they've deliberately split us up.'

10

Looking back, it seems to me that my posting to Devon was quite a big shake-up in my life. But I don't recall any particular traumas as I packed up and set out for the wilds, only that of leaving the family defenceless in London. I was breaking completely with an environment, a set of personal relationships and a whole way of life, all of which were dear to me. Of course, those were years in which one looked for no permanence, no security, in which one schooled oneself to take even cataclysmic change more or less philosophically.

So off I went, from Paddington to Newton Abbot, consoling myself with determined foretastes of my usual dilettante way of operating. I intended to drift round Newton Abbot, and further afield, seeking out good hotels and restaurants. I would find fast trains to London for very frequent weekends there. One great consolation was that I was continuing with all my RU work. I had a good portable typewriter with me, and lashings of stationery, and a case full of basic books.

I was met at Newton Abbot by a sleek Civil Defence car manned by two courteous Civil Defence officers: a civilized beginning, and (I thought) quite right, too. We then drove an alarming distance from Newton Abbot (which looked rather attractive as I gazed back at it ruefully) and ended up at a large country house on a mountain top. It was once a charming house, doubtless, but was now rather knocked about and surrounded by dozens of ugly great prefab buildings. Into one corner of one of these I was shown: my upper bunk bed in a distinctly frowsty barracks. When I'd dumped my things I was shown around the house, which contained dining rooms, recreation rooms, a large saloon bar and various Civil Defence offices. I was then introduced to the commandant, a pleasant man who, I later discovered, had been a tram inspector on the southwest London routes: Victoria to Purley via Streatham and Croydon. All the 'officers' (I thought the term as mild a joke as the insignia: yellow bars on the epaulettes) were kind and courteous but also rather conscious of their 'commissions.' They also seemed proud of the set-up. Rightly so, I am sure, for the amenities were good. Not their fault that they could never for one moment be my amenities. Amongst both Devonian and Cockney ex-building workers (anything from skilled tradesmen to raw navvies) were many obvious conchies: a few, big bluff ones, obviously determined to show that a conchie could be one of the boys, a few solemn-faced Jehovah's Witness types, and no less than five young men who were heading for ordination. These last were, I thought, the most intriguing. To start with they were all quite small and dark-haired: it was almost a badge of intended office. I felt the bishops, or whoever selected them, must insist on this appearance. I always thought of them as 'the little black brigade' and

159

tried not to mix with them overmuch. But they - earnest, eager to please, at times almost servile - felt they must incorporate me, for wasn't I a conchie like them, a Christian pacifist? All rather embarrassing.

At first, life was quite bearable, for we were busy. Plymouth was getting a pasting and in long convoys we would trundle there to supplement the local Civil Defence personnel. I was fairly strong and very much concerned to show that I wasn't either a coward or a bumbling softie. So, as in Westminster Civil Defence, I came to be more or less accepted, although my mates here were warier with me, for I soon put my foot down in various ways they thought distinctly odd. I raised hell about fresh air in my barracks hut, something they didn't understand and greatly resented. But they had to put up with it for I invoked government regulations and the rather befuddled commandant. Then I flatly refused to undergo drilling and marching. The 'officers' tried to insist but when they saw I was implacable they found me something else to do when the others were jumping about and foot-slogging to numbers. We were also one evening all ordered into the dining room to hear a broadcast pep talk by Churchill. I didn't attend and, when questioned about it, told them they had no right to issue any such order, for we were not one of the armed services but a nonmilitary body incorporating many recognized conscientious objectors. This clearly alarmed the commandant and the exercise was never attempted again.

I might say that I never at any time took to Churchill. I found his broadcasts vulgar. In my teens I had bought at Twala's a book called *Falsehood in War Time*, by Arthur Ponsonby, and I was indelibly impressed by it. I thus regarded all official government statements, even all BBC news bulletins and cinema newsreels, as I did any pronouncements by Goebbels: mere lying propaganda. I saw two great nations at each other's throats and each concerned to vilify the other to the nth degree. None of us then knew anything about concentration camp atrocities, or even Japanese inhumanities. My stand regarding the Churchill broadcast was approved by most of my mates, especially the Cockneys, for their memories were long with respect to Churchill the politician. Radical views of all kinds were becoming more general as the war dragged on, especially in politics and especially among the younger age groups. The Army Bureau of Current Affairs and the *Daily Mirror* and the Left Book Club all played their parts tellingly.

Those who had to run these new regional columns, known as the Civil Defence Reserve, had to feel their way rather carefully, for there were no precedents to guide them. But they had been given good advance publicity. Even when I was at Belvedere I had read about them in the papers, who quite went to town with their descriptions of the mobile operating theatres manned by selected doctors and nurses. I never saw, or even heard tell, of any such things when I was in the CDR.

Then Goering stopped his hammering of targets like Plymouth as his Luftwaffe became badly overstretched. So we were more or less confined to barracks in our sprawling, untidy camp near Newton Abbot. We were bored, frustrated, endlessly working on silly nonjobs they were compelled to think up. One was the digging of a great pit to house a mammoth static water tank for which there was no demand at all in such a place. When we'd excavated the pit to contain the tank, we were told to fill it in again, 'owing to a change of plan at the Ministry.' Amidst our derisory laughter were some ugly mutterings, fuelled by the common knowledge that we were infinitely worse off as regards leave than were the armed forces. And out of the mutinous mutterings there emerged in time a whisper: that Britain's invasion of Europe was imminent and we were to be somehow involved in it.

There were daily convoys of troops past our gates from the interior to the coast. Many of them were clowning, fresh-faced boys, full of sexual bravado: herds of poor, dragooned humanity, unaware of the cliff sides to which they were being driven. I felt ashamed of our perpetual bellyaching as I watched them rumble inexorably by.

We had one half-day off duty per week. Fine for the Devonians, who mostly got home on their half days, but we old Londoners had to kick our heels in Newton Abbot or Torquay. Many of them just didn't bother to leave the camp, for it was better to fill the time with darts or bingo in the bar. Not so with me, I need hardly say. I went to Torquay and exploited to the full its shops, then had a long, leisurely dinner in one of its four-star hotels. It was a weekly escape that helped to keep me sane: that, and the work I received almost daily from RU. I'd set up shop in the dining room after supper. I had the large room entirely to myself, and the time passed almost pleasantly as I typed away with a schooner of sherry at my elbow, almost forgetting how lonely I was. Sometimes one or more of my little black brigade would come in for some earnest powwow. They were nice lads, really, but I couldn't make friends with them, so put off was I by their hobnobbing with the Almighty.

Then it all wonderfully changed. Because of Graham Jenks. I had noticed him quite early on. Not just because he looked younger than he was (he was my age) and was also quite handsome, but because of his attitude to the whole place. Like me, he obviously didn't fit, and made no effort to. He was bored, horribly bored, with a kind of dogged self-insulation. He was incredibly slow in all he did, seldom smiled, and spoke very little. Everybody seemed after a few attempts at mateyness to write him off. Even I, apart from a smile when we met in the course of work. I rather admired his absolute refusal to become a normal Civil Defence worker. I had plenty of opportunity to observe this, for we were in the same squad.

One afternoon we were being instructed in knots and lashings, at which all the chaps were reasonably competent except the two hopeless duffers: Graham Jenks and me. I was as utterly browned off with it all as he was. I couldn't remember the various operations you had to go through with the rope ends, nor even the names of the different knots. The demonstrator suddenly asked me if I knew how to deal with a vampire. That's certainly what it sounded like, this knot called (I think) a bantyre. So I said: 'With the usual stake and garlic, and a crucifix or two.' It wasn't very funny and it wasn't very polite to the poor demonstrator. But I felt any diversion would relieve the boredom.

It fell very flat. One or two, very puzzled, queried 'Steak and garlic?', and one of the little black brigade murmured 'crucifix' reprovingly. Otherwise, they clearly treated the words as another aberration of mine. The demonstrator made as if to discuss the subject, then gave up. He dismissed the words with deserved contempt, and there the matter would have ended if I hadn't noticed the usually impassive Graham shivering from head to foot. I thought at first he was heading for an epileptic fit. Then I saw it was mirth, shattering but completely silent mirth. Surely my offhand words couldn't have caused that? When the rope trick session was over, I asked Graham what had tickled him so.

'Bela Lugosi,' he replied shyly, 'made me a vampire addict.'

I grinned. 'Are you keen on the cinema?' I asked. He nodded. 'Let's go and have a coffee,' I said.

And in that inconsequential way it all began: at first, cinematic explorations of every kind, then wicked gossip about all our comrades in the CDR, then parodies and travesties of all and sundry, as we both silently shook and wiped the tears from our eyes. Graham had been brought up, just like Jonathan Gray, in a godly household. And, like Jonathan, he had never had anyone with whom he could express all those thoughts: cynical, anarchic, scurrilous, buried so deep within him he scarcely knew he had them. I was a sort of riotous Falstaff to his young, prim Hal, a Lord of Misrule in his very respectable life. Not that I ever was, or wanted to be, a mere corrupter of innocence, for my volleys were never vicious and his set-up was never really innocent. I just wanted, with him as with Jonathan, to pull down the fake fences they'd built round themselves and let in healthy shafts of light and gusts of laughter.

Graham was a Londoner, from a modest but thoroughly decent family. They lived in Lewisham, were Methodists, and their lives centred round their church and the large, old-fashioned draper's shop in which his father had worked for thirty years and he himself for five. He reminded me in some ways of Mr Polly: in his background, his uncles and aunts and cousins, his great respectability, and his unsuspected depths of character.

162

He was a pacifist and had been transferred from Lewisham Civil Defence. I found he was not at all sure that he could continue in the CDR. Not, like me, because he was dying for the grimy, urban airs of home, but because he wasn't going to be used as a CO, used, that is, as a part of the war machine. For he was coming to believe that the CDR had never from the first been set up as what its name implied, but as a force to keep the invasion ports accessible for the embarkation of our poor invading troops. And we saw more and more of them.

There were Dionysian depths to Graham, but not unlike Jonathan, Apollonian ones. He hadn't then read much real literature or heard much real music. But he had a mind of his own, a moral and unflinching one. He also knew even more bit-part actors in B movies than I did. I never got him to smoke a cigarette, or to take a little glass of sherry with me in the evening. With a Devon accent and a Devon leer, I'd wheeze: 'Us knows a little tipple o'nights does us good, don't us, m'dear?'

Our trips to the relief of Plymouth had often been unpleasant but they had at least left us little time for boredom. One took everything in one's stride. What else could one do? Even when we were issued with some extra kit: a Cellophane packet stamped 'Gloves for handling human remains.' We never, thank God, needed to use these, although we did once have to transport dozens of evil-smelling coffins for a mass burial. And once I even earned an admiring reprimand for lifting some masonry off a poor trapped dog: not bravery on my part but sheer ignorance, for I hadn't realized that the masonry was helping to support a whole brick wall. And another time a few of us were excavating a water-filled bomb crater in a ruined block of flats when the water began to bubble ominously. We prodded it with a stick until our alarmed squad leader ordered us out at the double and summoned the bomb disposal corps. But it was only a fractured water pipe, as the Royal Engineers captain explained rather loftily. In all my Civil Defence work I never saw a dead or injured body, I am glad to say. I don't know how I would have taken it.

But the Plymouth trips were now things of the past. Graham and I therefore lightened our days with quite different 'AWOL' trips. When our morning duties allowed us some leisure by their occasional brevity we would abscond along a secret path we'd discovered: through a coppice, over a little stream, then breaking through a hedgerow on to a road that took us right into Newton Abbot. Then what joy to take coffee and doughnuts in a pretty little tea shop called, I remember, Madge Mellor's. We even got on 'Good morning' terms with the local gentry, who gallantly maintained their morning coffee routines. There was one stout lady in WVS uniform who had a curious, barking cough and round, wide-open eyes. I referred to her as 'The dog with eyes as big as saucers,' after Hans Andersen. Once, when we had to share her table, she insisted on paying our bill, a compliment I too insisted on returning later. She described to us the prewar life of the town and how 'Q' had enjoyed his early schooling there with her own father. 'Q' was Sir Arthur Quiller-Couch, whose *Poison Island* I had read before I could really understand it, but much of which I never forgot. I read so many books before I was ready for them: books which survive piecemeal in my head as flashes and glints of them rooted in my unfledged imagination.

11

So the months dragged by, still without any leave. Then we read in *Peace News* that it was almost certain that the Civil Defence regional columns in the south of England were to keep bombarded roads open in the event of an expected emergency, which everyone understood to be a reference to D-Day, as invasion day was called. Graham and I went to see the commandant and asked him point blank if this was so. He, of course, professed complete ignorance of any such plans. It was obvious that we were to know nothing about it until it was on us. Graham and I earnestly pondered our strategy. We had no doubt we should wash our hands of the Civil Defence Reserve, now to be a frank part of the war machine.

But how? One obvious course was to take off our uniforms, don civvies, and disregard all orders. I explained to Graham that this was just what my brother had done. We discussed his case, thereby apparently reactivating it, for the very next morning brought me a letter from him to say he was to appear before a CO tribunal in York ten days hence, and he wanted me to represent him. The commandant gave me leave to travel to York, and I just had time to send Brian a letter asking for a few details I needed for my brief. His reply equipped me adequately enough, although I didn't share Brian's faith in my litigious ability.

The hearing was fixed for ten in the morning, so I decided to travel all night. It was a grim, wartime journey. The train was dimly lighted and entirely unheated. No refreshments were obtainable on the train or on any station platform. The train was maddeningly slow and all my fellow passengers seemed unduly depressed. I'd set out, I felt, days before as at last we steamed into York station at about six in the morning. I'd brought some sandwiches for the journey, but nothing to drink. It was bliss to find a workman's café open near the station. I had bacon, fried bread and coffee: a dish for the gods. Then I explored York, which I'd never visited before. It overawed me.

The courthouse was only less intimidating. I'd discovered it opened at 9.15 and began its deliberations at 9.30, so ours was not the first case, as I'd rather gladly assumed.

I took my seat at 9.15 and waited for Brian to join me. But when he arrived he was flanked by two warders and kept apart from everybody else. The real shock, however, was to see that he was handcuffed. All I could do was to give a little wave and a wan smile.

There was just one case before ours, and the good Lord must have arranged it so. For the appellant was a Joshua Huntley, leading light in some obscure religious sect. The public gallery was filled with his fellow believers, most of them, it seemed, buxom, pious women. As soon as Mr Huntley ascended the dock there was an alarming series of thuds and bangs from the gallery. I gazed at it in some alarm, thinking either some of the fat women had fainted or perhaps there was to be some staged demonstration. But it was Mr Huntley's flock, all of whom had simultaneously, as at a word of command, fallen noisily upon their knees and screwed their eyes tight shut. And thus they remained throughout the hearing.

I glanced across to Brian and found that he, like me, was having some difficulty in keeping a straight face. I scanned the tribunal, to find that one of its members, a pleasant and intelligent-looking man, was having similar difficulties.

Then an elder of Mr Huntley's church rose to give a stirring character reference. 'Our broother 'Oontley,' he said in ringing tones, 'is a man (pause) of 'oose word (pause) you can place the ootmost reliance upon.' The elder waited for this great tribute to sink in. Then he repeated it, word for word, and waited. The judge asked him, very courteously, if he could give them some example of Mr Huntley's good character. The elder appeared quite unprepared for this. For what seemed a long time he stood with his eyes shut and his lips silently moving. Then he resumed his evidence, excitedly, obviously satisfied that the Lord had touched his lips with fire. He told us how, very recently, his brother Huntley had arrived at York station off the last train from Derby, where he had been on a preaching mission. There were no buses, of course, and so he had to rely on a taxi to take him the twelve miles to his home. But for ages there was no sign of a taxi. When at last one ('The oanly oon' the elder thundered) came, a young woman dived out of the shadows and into it. The driver said she and Mr Huntley could share the cab, since she was going in the same direction. 'But our broother 'Oontley said "noa, noa".' The elder held up his hand like a policeman on traffic duty, unhurriedly, magisterially. ''E walked the doozen miles.'

I glanced again at the man on the bench. He now had his hand across his mouth, and our eyes met in conspiratorial mirth. I looked quickly away, composing my features as best I could. Partly because I felt all this was very improper in a court of law, and partly because I was rather ashamed of taking sides so blatantly: allying myself with authority against another victim. Was not my poor, manacled brother in the same boat? No, one really couldn't bracket Brian with poor Mr Huntley. The latter was now praying. The former was, just as silently, shaking.

The elder had only four words to add to his testimony, but he delivered them as impressively as all his previous ones. "Twas raining that neet.'

Mr Huntley's case was dismissed. What else could they do? The judge clearly disliked doing it, but seemed rather cheered by the attitude of Mr Huntley's flock in the gallery. They rose to their feet with looks of great satisfaction, even smiles, and trooped out noisily with their less elated brother. I think they were really looking forward to his martyrdom, had perhaps been praying for it.

When they'd gone, the pleasant-looking man on the bench gave me a quite uninhibited smile, which I felt I simply must return.

Then Brian was called. He answered a series of questions, mostly about his recent experiences, and then he asked them if they would allow his brother to speak for him. They agreed, and I began my harangue in the witness box. Before leaving my CDR camp I had pressed my uniform and adorned it with a lanyard I'd bought and a Red Cross badge one of the little black brigade had lent me. I'm not at all sure I was entitled to it after my elementary classes in first aid, but it looked very nice. So I appeared, for the first and probably the only time, as a fairly normal, conforming war worker. They must have thought so, too, for they asked me several questions about the CDR.

I told them Brian had, like me, always been a pacifist at heart, but he had tried to make a go of the army, even achieving two stripes and instructor rank. But, as he became more deeply involved in the military machine, his conscience was increasingly troubled by it, until in the end he felt he could no longer play any part in it. I ended, rather lamely, by suggesting my brother would be of more use to his country in doing some such noncombatant work as mine than in sewing mailbags in a cell.

The judge, who was chairman of the panel, nodded agreement. They then whispered together and the judge pronounced their decision, which was 'Civil Defence, hospital work or landwork.' It had been the shortest, and pleasantest, hearing I'd experienced. All due, perhaps, to our broother 'Oontley and his long, long walk in the rain.

Brian had to go back to prison for his formal discharge, but they removed his handcuffs and we all four went to the same café I'd breakfasted in for an hour's chat over coffee. Brian told me all the warders he'd encountered had been very decent. Likewise the guards in the army detention barracks. I told him facetiously it was no good being sentimental about prison: he must face his new life like a man. He said he was going home initially, then finding a job such as the tribunal had prescribed.

166

He went off with his uniformed pals in good spirits. I felt I was the one going back to prison.

A week later Brian wrote to me from Grantham to say he'd got a good job driving a lorry as part of some landwork team. It all sounded idyllic compared with our depressing CDR routine.

12

At last Graham and I decided we'd had enough. We would get up one morning and dress in our own clothes, then go in to breakfast and let the Civil Defence authorities do whatever they wished. 'But not till Friday,' I said, 'because Thursday's our half-day and we'll make the most of it in Torquay.' It was Monday as we laid our plans, and that would give me time to post all my stuff to RU and tie up as many ends there as I could.

The next evening I was typing letters in the dining room as usual, with Graham beside me licking stamps and envelopes, when an inspired change of plan almost had me whooping aloud.

'That's it,' I said, sotto voce but sizzling with excitement. 'That's the way to wash our hands of this whole rotten place. No coming in to breakfast and standing there, hands out, waiting for the handcuffs. Oh, dear no. Not on your life.'

'Oh, do tell me, for heaven's sake,' begged Graham, not knowing whether to laugh or cheer.

'We'll just walk out.'

Graham frowned at the anticlimax. 'Oh, just desert, eh? Pursued by police with Alsatians, and troops with Bren guns.'

'Yes,' I agreed. 'We'll take 'em all on. We'll make a last stand in a log cabin in those hills! Now, stop rubbishing and listen carefully. We'll go to bed as usual tomorrow night. We'll rise at 3 am, don our civvies, make up mock figures in our beds, creep out with our cases (we'll pack them tomorrow afternoon and store them in the hall cupboard), cut across the fields, get a lift to Plymouth, then London, home, freedom.'

'It'd never work,' said Graham. 'Someone'd see us. Besides, deserting's a criminal offence.'

'It'll work,' I said emphatically, 'if we plan it carefully. And I don't mean desert. Not a bit of it. Just before we slip out we'll leave letters in the hall rack for the commandant telling him exactly what we're doing and why, and exactly where we're going: our home addresses, where we'll wait to hear from him. We'll be home by the time he reads those letters. And with luck we'll have four or five days there before they collect us.'

So Graham agreed, although not as wholeheartedly as I'd have liked.

I don't think I can make a convincing narrative of this because even as I write it I am astonished that everything worked as smoothly as clockwork.

No one saw us: not in our huts, not in the ablutions, not in the corridors of the house, not in the grounds. The commandant didn't even see our letters till the afternoon, and then he didn't act on them at once. We thumbed a lift in an oil tanker to Plymouth. We got an express train to London within an hour, had a lovely, civilized breakfast on the train (as one could sometimes, even in those days), and were home for lunch. When we had parted at Waterloo it was with the promise to contact each other as soon as we heard from Nemesis.

Three days after I arrived home, the commandant phoned. I was out, but he had a long talk with my mother, who seemed to have a way with such people. He told her if we went back at once, the whole thing would be overlooked. She said she'd tell me, but she knew we'd never agree to go back. Then, he told her sadly, he'd have to inform the police and we'd eventually be summonsed.

All this cheered me considerably, for I knew it would take a week or even more to issue summonses. I went over to Lewisham to tell Graham this (he had no phone) and met his nice parents, both exactly as I'd envisaged them.

It was three weeks before the summonses arrived. They gave us two weeks' notice that our case was to be heard at Plymouth county court. I packed those five weeks with business and pleasure. I called on the Central Board for Conscientious Objectors and briefed them carefully as to our position. They in turn contacted a young solicitor in Plymouth who would represent us, and they must have paid him for we certainly didn't. Once more I had good cause to be grateful to them.

Almost daily I went into my RU office and cleared off all backlogs of work, as well as writing various bits and pieces that would help out *Reader's News* during my coming incarceration (which the Central Board thought would be for three months).

Also almost daily I went to the National Gallery concert and lunched in my prized vegetarian restaurant in Leicester Square. The rest of the time was given to greedily cherished hours with Pam and Jonathan, and to a couple of undimmed landmarks in the strange, crowded tapestries I was weaving at that time. One was a day I spent with Derrick in Salisbury, a day too short for all the gabbling, laughing, exciting news we had to share. He was half-alarmed, half-impressed by what Graham and I had done. His CDR camp sounded less deadly dull than ours, or, more likely, he was not so hopeless at adapting himself as I was.

My other landmark was a day with Julien. We met in Reading, which was about our halfway mark. It was a happier day than the last one we'd spent in Southampton, partly because it was a brighter, sunnier day, partly because amenities in Reading were so much better. Mostly, however, it was because of something I hated admitting to myself. He was older, more manly, less attractive, and although my affection for him was as great as ever, it was not the aching void of love it had been. Less tragic, less romantic, it was also less painful. We were now deeply knit friends, indissoluble brothers. He was still training, a senior cadet, but not yet seaworthy, thank God. I hoped the worst of the war would be over before he had to walk any planks.

Pam, as the mother of a baby, was now exempt from call-up. That was a relief, for she'd all along insisted she'd be an objector. When Brian went to prison she spoke almost regretfully about her inability to do the same. I think she would have enjoyed taking such a rebellious stand for a principle. She would have been in her element as a suffragette.

Much of my life in those weeks was also filled with Miles, a very pretty baby who seemed to take to me almost as much as I took to him. I was rather surprised to find how much I liked babies. I'd found that with Jill's at Belvedere. Now I as good as had one of my own. My mother, of course, adored him. She rather than Pam gave him all the loving, all the nursing and rocking, that a new life needs. Pam was entirely unexceptional as a mother, doing all the feeding and washing and dressing and nappy-changing that was required. But, I secretly observed, without delight. Nor did she really play with him. Sometimes she would fling him quite high in the air and let him land on the settee beside her. The rest of us would be terrified, but she'd only say: 'Good for 'em. They're tough as old boots. None of this cooing and slobbering nonsense.' This was really said to stir up mother, who'd say: 'Oh, you hardhearted bitch. Give him to me.' Very gladly Pam would hand him over with a laugh. I think in those weeks I nursed him more than his mother did. I used to walk him all over the house, pointing out and naming things. I had only to enter the room for him to hold up his arms to me and begin crowing in anticipation. I think I would have made a devoted father if things had been different. Perhaps too devoted to let go when the time came to fly out of the nest. Yes, perhaps it is as well that my life as a schoolmaster has been given to other people's children.

I actually had Miles in my arms when the policeman arrived with the summons. 'Mr Gamble?' he enquired. 'Mr Peter Gamble?'

'That's right,' I said pleasantly. 'That's the summons I've been expecting.' I glanced at it. 'Yes. Plymouth county court. In a fortnight. Thanks very much.' I knew he was itching to know more. He couldn't understand how this young father was taking it all so calmly, so unlike a criminal facing sentence. I thought he could go on wondering.

Graham phoned later that day. He had had his summons, too. We agreed to meet in town the next day to finalize plans. RU were proving very kind. They wanted to engage a solicitor for us, but I had to tell them the Central Board for Conscientious Objectors had already appointed one. But they did tell me later they had found us an official of the Missions to Seamen in Plymouth to act as 'prisoner's friend,' or something like that. I had to seem grateful but I really couldn't see the point. We had no intention of pleading anything but guilty, so what could anyone, friend or foe, say in mitigation?

On my last night in London I put the finishing touches to a long article on Virginia Woolf that I'd been working on for *Reader's News*. I was glad to finish it and get it off to John Baker before prison doors clanged shut on me.

13

Graham and I set off in quite good spirits. Even saying goodbye to Miles and the family wasn't as bad as I thought it would be. Perhaps I felt I was at last doing something positive and correct in the pacifist cause.

As arranged we arrived at the court in good time to meet our solicitor and have a discussion about our 'defence,' as he insisted on calling it. He was a very earnest young man with a big, black beard and very little evidence of a sense of humour. He was a Quaker and, I believe, an offshoot of the Foot family. He was clearly very anxious to put up a good defence for us, so I was keen to know what defence there could be. I never found out.

The case he presented was almost a joke: a few trite observations about 'ideals' and 'integrity' and 'example,' really rather embarrassing. The prosecuting counsel quickly dismissed him and us. The bench absolutely refused to hear our nautical friend. The chairman sentenced us to a month's imprisonment and, just to encourage our poor counsel, added he was deeply sorry the law did not allow him to impose something meatier. Then we were taken to the cells below the court, where we were to spend the night before being shipped to Exeter prison. An elderly policeman was on duty in the cells. He said to me; 'You could have knocked me down with a feather when I heard you get a month. I thought you were a young army officer up for a traffic offence.' He told us he was a Quaker, and he very decently let Graham and me chat for an hour before locking us in separate cells.

We agreed it was quite an achievement for our lawyer to get us the maximum in five minutes. And we told ourselves, repeatedly, that a month inside followed by a glorious month at home wasn't a bad solution – but a waste of the state's time and money, let alone our capacities for better things.

In the morning we were unlocked (after quite a reasonable breakfast) and told to make for the yard where the Black Maria awaited us. To our surprise, our solicitor had come to see us off. Which was decent of him. He shook hands and wished us luck, but rather spoiled things by saying in a loud and hectoring voice for all to hear: 'Now these two men are not convicted prisoners but detainees under Defence Regulation 29B, and don't you forget it.' Said the leading prison officer who'd come with the Black Maria: 'That shall be carefully noted, sir.' We were the only prisoners from these cells to enter the Black Maria, which already had half a dozen or so prisoners in it. They had craned their heads out to see and hear all that went on. They heard our solicitor add: 'That means no handcuffs or fingerprints.' So when he had gone and we were seated inside the vehicle, and the officer had handcuffed us, saying such were regulations, a great shout of laughter went up from our fellow convicts, and we couldn't help joining in. They obviously didn't see why they should be handcuffed and enemy agents like us should not be. 'Detainees under Defence Regulation 29B' was indeed the correct description of Graham and me, but to the average person it was a mere variant of 'detainee under Defence Regulation 18B,' which was the title of 'spies' like Lieutenant Baillie Stuart, imprisoned some years before in the Tower of London.

The Black Maria was rather intriguing. How often as a child they'd fascinated me. How often, but how vainly, I'd tried to see through their dark, smoky windows. How luridly I'd imagined the murderers with their chains and iron balls skulking within them. Now here I was, one of them, and glad not to be seen.

There was desultory chatter among us. I learned my first prison lesson: that it was all right to ask a chap how long he'd got, but definitely bad form to ask what for.

It was a long drive to Exeter, and rather strange to gaze *out* of those funereal windows at ordinary, law-abiding citizens going about their acceptable, even enjoyable, routines.

Then we stopped, and from the drawing of great bolts and the creaking of great hinges we knew that we'd arrived.

The reception procedure was familiar to us from many low budget thrillers we'd sat through in the cinema. When we were dished out our prison clothing by a distinguished-looking elderly prisoner, I plucked up courage to say: 'Could I have a well-worn shirt, please?' I could see that the older ones, after countless launderings, were comparatively soft in texture. With a smile he chose me one.

The suit wasn't arrowed, nor did it have bands round it, so I couldn't see myself as Gerald du Maurier in *Escape* or Paul Muni in his chain gang.

We had a shower and a perfunctory medical and were then presented to the governor. He was a small, birdlike man who clearly didn't know what to say to us. Then we were taken to our cells and given twenty-five mailbags, some bundles of thread, a lump of black tallow, and some brief instructions about what to do with them all.

Brian had advised me to describe myself as a vegetarian, and I was gratified to see both 'Veg' and 'Quaker' beneath my number on the cell door. I thought this showed some unexpected consideration.

I was then locked up for the night, since it was too late for the workshops. My cell had a camp bed (a wooden base and a biscuit mattress), a wooden table and chair, and a chamber pot. On the table was a fork and something clearly not intended to be a knife, plus a large jar of salt. There was also a pitcher of water and a hunk of carbolic floor soap beside a metal wash basin. I found all this quite satisfactory, not least the privacy of it. Solitude was the punishment for most of them, who longed for the time when they went 'on stage': that is to say, when they had the great privilege of spending two evening hours all together in a draughty hall listening to a blaring radio. I was greatly relieved to learn that as a four-week guest I was not eligible for 'stage.'

Things brightened even further when my landing officer brought me a Bible and three other books. One was *Pilgrim's Progress*, another Oman's *History of England* and the third a novel called *The Men of the Moss Hags* by S. R. Crockett. I started on the last. The Oman I read in unco-ordinated chunks during the coming week. The Bunyan I never read (nor have I, to this day). The Crockett I found rather fascinatingly strange. I knew nothing in those days of the kailyard school, not even by repute. This one example of it remains quite sharp in my memory, embedded in a penal setting remoter than any kailyard.

Then at seven or thereabouts a warder brought in my supper: a steaming mug of cocoa, a lump of cheese and pat of margarine, a baked jacket potato, and a miniature loaf called a 'cob.' I cut the large potato open and filled it with pieces of marge and cheese, sprinkled with salt. I then closed it firmly together and ate it like a sandwich, making it last as long as I could. I did this every night of my time inside and never grew tired of it. I still sometimes make myself such a dish. The cobs (we got two a day) I never ate. Whenever I'd collected half a dozen I gave them to my next-door neighbour. To the consternation of my warder, who declared it both against all regulations and also plain unnatural.

I found that by standing on my chair I could gaze out of the high, barred window and command a view of Exeter railway station, its platforms and its passengers. I found that at first rather sad, rather wistful. Then I decided it was comforting. The sane, familiar world was still there, awaiting my return.

14

I was for a while in the light workshop, sitting at a desk folding and stitching pieces of cloth. That was altogether too like my cell task of stitching handles on to mailbags. It was clear that my own particular punishment was to be hours of screaming boredom. I was glad of any break from the workshop, such as walking round and round a large circular plot of ground, hands behind one's back, talking sotto voce to Graham. (I never really discovered whether conversation during exercise was utterly forbidden, or rationed, or purely a matter of warder's whim.) At all times, in workshop, chapel, assembly, exercise yard, we as first offenders were scrupulously segregated from the old lags. All we did was occasionally to stare at them across some great divide and recognize a different species: the semidefiant slouch, the unco-operative stance, the permanently aggrieved expression.

Sometimes during exercise I spoke to a frail chap in his thirties, who was, he told me, a Scottish baronet inside for hotel bills he could not meet. His name was Noel Cameron-Dee and he was both very candid and very convincing. The more I listened to him the more ashamed I grew of my scepticism. He told me no one would listen to his explanations: of how the war had tied up the revenue from his estate so that he could get only an intermittent and insufficient income. What was more, the family seat had been requisitioned by the army, so he and his elderly mother had to exist in hotels, and hotels which were certainly not what they were.

Sir Noel's anecdotes were most entertaining. It was quite impossible to decide whether he himself saw humour in his situation. Only very occasionally did I see the ghost of a twinkle in the blue eyes above the uncompromising mouth. I learned much later, to my utter surprise, that the Cameron-Dee baronetcy was a fact, although whether he were the true baronet I cannot now know. I am inclined to think he was. Certainly it was the means by which he and his mother had diddled from Land's End to Carlisle every sort of hotel and guest house. *This* I had from one of the warders I grew friendly with. (I must stop calling them warders: nobody inside used the word. They were one and all 'screws.')

In his thin, pained tones Noel would describe to me the harshness, the sheer vulgarity, of the hostelry world. 'It was designated a four-star hotel,' he said, 'but they expected mother to run her own bath. And when we complained they ran one too cold for a penguin.'

'Disgusting,' I said. 'Of course the war is made an excuse for lowering all standards.'

'You are so right,' he sighed. 'Beds not turned down, shoes scarcely cleaned, never a finger bowl...'

'And it is idle even to enquire if your morning paper was ever ironed,' I commiserated. (One of the occasions when I *thought* I detected a dawning twinkle.)

I was released before him. I asked him if he would like me to visit his mother, currently residing in a guest house in Torquay. He seemed genuinely touched by this offer. Later, I did visit her, armed, thanks to some sweet coupons from Pam, with a box of chocolates: a precious gift which brought a little moisture to her eyes. I deliberately asked the hotel receptionist for 'Lady Cameron-Dee,' which elicited a sniff of defensive pride but not of disbelief. She was a nice old lady. I couldn't decide whether she was Sir Noel's accomplice or his dupe.

'It really is quite wicked,' she said, with sorrow but no bitterness. 'In and out of prison he goes. For me, you know. He will not allow me to "rough it," as he says. So we only stay at fairly good hotels when we are together. And so often the monthly cheque from our bailiff is late: sometimes very late, and the management hate waiting a moment.' She sighed. 'This war, you know. And I beg Noel to stay somewhere cheaper next time. I am not proud. I am adaptable. But not Noel, oh, not Noel, bless him.' She brightened. 'I am so glad he has found a friend in you, Mr Gamble. If ever a man needed a friend...' I felt the time had come for me to depart.

Noel and I corresponded for a while after we had regained our freedom. His pen was elegant, his paper crested, but headed only by some seaside hotel address. Then his letters ceased. I have an idea someone told me he had died in Canada.

No, you mustn't ask a man why he is inside, but there is always someone to tell you. Thus I discovered that a handsome and soldierly young man with whom I exchanged courtesies was serving nine months for undue familiarity with a sheep. This was so beyond my ken as to seem quaint rather than criminal. I could only visualize the kindly, knitting sheep in *Alice in Wonderland*, but she seemed too elderly for him.

There was also a very pleasant Pickwickian gentleman who whenever he caught my eye drew in his lower lip and bit it, in the manner of a slightly naughty child. I learned he was in for incest with his young daughter. I saw myself as pretty worldly, but these were new types to me.

Cuthbert (it really was his name) had a cell near mine and I gave him regular cob deliveries. He was, he told me, an ex-head waiter, and certainly his respectful manner accorded with such a job. 'Morning, sir,' he greeted me when we met on our landing. 'Did you sleep well?' Yes, his manner suited, but his appearance certainly did not. For he had only one eye and a face drawn awry by a long scar. He looked horribly villainous, a Phiz illustration to some lurid Dickens. I was thus pretty flabbergasted when he once said to me; 'Thank Christ I don't look an effing criminal. If I looked like some of these sods I'd bloody well do meself in.'

Chapel on Thursdays and Sundays was something I approached with cynicism but soon found myself anticipating with a secret joy. The words were new to me and I thrilled to their majesty and beauty. 'We have erred and strayed from thy ways like lost sheep'; 'Whereby the day-spring from on high hath visited us'; 'The mountains skipped like rams; and the little hills like young sheep'; 'When thou hadst overcome the sharpness of death.'

Tunes of canticles and psalms stirred me, too. Hymns less so because usually the words were trite and the melodies rather childish. Still, one or two, like George Herbert's, were charming, and one or two rousers gripped me in spite of myself, and in spite of the frequent ribaldry of my companions.

As officially a Quaker I had regular visits from local Friends, good people that I was glad to see. But Cranmer's liturgy so enthralled me that I asked to see the Anglican chaplain. He was a nice old Devonian, a bit disenchanted and wary. Gradually, though, we established a sort of rapport. One day he staggered me with an utterly unforeseen question: 'Ever thought of being ordained?' I laughed incredulously. 'Me? I've never even been christened. I come from a family of atheists.' He didn't mind; just told me to keep it in mind. His question caused as much mirth to the family as to me. Even to Graham.

On Wednesdays we were herded into a sort of lecture room, so that the prison governor could give us a précis of the week's news. The theory was good (keeping us in touch with the outside world to which eventually we must return). But the practice was somewhat different. Most of the news was inevitably about the progress of the war, and the governor saw his role as a propagandist, a militarist, a nationalist. I found it, of course, Churchillian in its jingoism and vulgarity. The denunciations were not simply of the Nazis but much nearer home: of those in his captive audience who preferred a prison cell to the glory of a battlefield, the few conchies, of course, and the large contingent of young naval deserters from Plymouth.

15

I had two brushes with the governor. And I won both. The first was caused by my refusal to shave. At about 7.30 in the morning a screw would open one's cell and hand one a safety razor. He waited for about two minutes, then reclaimed it and handed it to the occupant of the next cell. For several mornings I had scarcely finished examining the thing with great distaste when he wanted it back. One shared it with the whole landing (about thirty men) and wielded it in association with cold water and the carbolic soap aforesaid. Some men used their morning tea instead of cold water. Of course, nothing short of forcible shaving by a screw would get the communal razor near my face. Not least because many of my fellows had pockmarked faces and some evidence of dermatitis.

My growing facial crop was at length challenged by a screw, to whom I asserted, quite warmly, that I wasn't courting disease. I was expecting an interesting discussion, but I learned no screw ever embarked on any debate with a prisoner. His instant reaction to any sign of awkwardness was: 'Fall in to see the governor.' Which I did, and found him scarcely more amenable than any of his screws. 'Prison rules,' he told me, with the distaste he seemed to reserve for COs, 'require a man leaves here as he enters.' I told him I'd gladly shave if I could have my own things. 'Prison rules do not allow it,' he snapped. Then he sought to conclude the interview in the approved manner. 'Application for own shaving kit refused.'

But I hadn't concluded if he had. 'Are we going through this procedure every day?' I asked. 'Or are you going to shave me by force?'

The escorting screw told me in an outraged bellow: 'Prisoner not to speak unless first spoken to by the governor.' I ignored this Gilbertian remark and gazed obdurately at the governor for an answer.

In all this I knew I was being a nuisance, but I had decided that where necessary I would confront the system with its surest deterrent: sweet reasonableness. The governor bit his lip and asked me if I were seeking permission to grow a beard. He surprised me by presenting this as an entirely new development. I caught on and told the governor that was indeed my urgent request. He responded crisply: 'Prisoner's request to grow a beard granted.' As he spoke he inserted the momentous words in a great ledger open on the desk before him. I learned from this that one should never seek information or hint at a right or seek a privilege or make a complaint: just give them a way out and they were much obliged to you.

The beard, by the way, was a sad disappointment to me. I had envisaged a handsome Van Dyck affair in which I could play a modest King and Martyr. But the wretched thing grew in all the wrong places and directions. It seemed to favour especially the chops, so that I ended up resembling the elderly Ibsen. But to the young naval deserters I apparently suggested something Messianic. If I passed along their gallery as they all sat out making ships' fenders, one or two would extravagantly cross themselves.

My second brush with the governor was more serious. The weather became rather cold and so they decided that our exercise time should be devoted to drilling and marching. Their intentions were good and I really didn't like standing stock still, upsetting the whole show. But I had this genuine detestation of drill. I saw it as an attempt to make a man a machine. Even at school I'd refused to play ball.

'Do you refuse to obey orders?' barked the screw in charge, who had an unpleasant reputation for keenness. 'Yes, Mr Lander, I refuse,' I replied. (It was another ploy of mine never to 'sir' a screw but address him politely by name.) I was told to fall out and was then marched away and locked in a punishment cell. I was told that the Chief (the Chief Officer and the governor's right-hand man) had in the governor's temporary absence put me on number one punishment. This meant twenty-four hours of solitary confinement on bread and water. It all sounds far worse than it was. One day on bread and water would be positively healthy, and a spell of uninterrupted reading (I knew they couldn't refuse me a Bible) a rare privilege. I read two whole Gospels, from which I tried to remain cynically aloof but couldn't.

But my little holiday only lasted for that day. In the evening I was unlocked and marched (the escort marched, I didn't) before the governor. I formed the impression that the governor had arrived and quickly countermanded the Chief's orders: mainly because the poor chap had broken the law by condemning me without a hearing.

Said the governor after I had stated my objection to being drilled: 'I suppose you want me to make a martyr of you? Your type always does. Well, I don't intend to oblige.' I knew he was wanting to get himself off the hook, and I felt sorry for him. I also knew they were rather afraid of conscientious objectors in prison. 'So you object to a little healthy exercise?' he prevaricated, still seeking a loophole for himself. I was now able to show how much I had learned: 'Oh no, governor. I am seeking permission to take my exercise in the form of walking.' It worked. The governor pronounced: 'Prisoner given permission to take exercise in the form of walking. Case dismissed.' Then it got a little warmer and nobody was drilled any more.

After a few days I was, to my great relief, taken out of the tedious workshop and put on 'Stores.' This meant humping food from the larders to the kitchens: hard work and never a crumb by way of perks. But it did mean one moved all over the prison. Two or three times I even had to take supplies into the adjacent women's prison, which I didn't hitherto even know existed. I hated this, hated the women's ogles and muttered obscenities as they sat sewing outside their cells, scores of them. I hurried by with never a glance and told my screw I didn't want to go in there again. Nor did I.

Graham was quite content to remain in the workshop. It was warm, and not unlike his draper's emporium in Lewisham. He had dealt in his own way with the drilling and marching. He never refused, just maintained a snail's pace and a bizarre routine that was much more destructive than my nonco-operation.

I sent and received the usual ration of family letters. And I read masses of books that I would otherwise never have read. Including many dear, faded novels of bygone ages. The librarian was another elderly, gentlemanly man, like the baths attendant who always found me comfortable shirts. Both these men, I was told, were in for quite long spells through their involvement in the same case of major swindling.

16

And so the month wore by: really little worse than the CDR camp. And at last dawned the day of our release. Graham and I had a shower, got into our own clothes, collected our few belongings and said goodbye to the nicer convicts and the nicer screws. We stepped outside into the freedom of a chill near-dawn. We had planned a good breakfast in the Clarence Hotel and then an express to London.

Oh, what a pair of innocents! We walked straight into the arms of a couple of our former CDR officers, who led us straight to a Civil Defence squad car. The officers were as nice as could be: shook hands and asked us if we were OK. And in the car the dear fellows produced a positive little hamper of good food: mouth-watering things then, like cold chicken and sausages and boiled eggs, and even some warm doughnuts they had bought at a baker's opposite the prison.

Back at the camp we were handed our uniforms and requested to put them on. It was all very polite. With similar courtesy, we declined. So we were taken to see the commandant again. The kind soul begged us to toe the line, pointing out that this wretched cat-and-mouse game could continue for the duration. But we were regretfully obdurate. I don't know whether there was already a whiff in the air of the final showdown in hostilities. Hitler was faring badly in his mad Russian campaign. The Allies were successfully fighting their way up into Italy. Even in the Far East the tide was turning. Perhaps the end was in sight and we felt we should maintain our stand. D-Day must come soon, and the Nazis could not resist both British and American spearheads.

After another day of cajoling and threatening, the commandant had to call the Newton Abbot police. A squad car arrived early on a fine May morning and off we went, between quite a concourse of waving ex-comrades. Having been duly charged and arrested, we were quite ready for the local magistrates' court in Newton Abbot. It was all so efficient and expeditious that the camp and the police and the bench must have worked it all out on the phone. We were whisked from CDR camp to police station to court room in a matter of hours.

And on the bench, to our mutual embarrassment, sat none other than the lady with eyes as big as saucers with whom we'd had coffee in Madge Mellor's. We all three naturally razed such memories from our minds. I was glad that the unpleasant old man who was clerk to the justices, and who clearly ran the whole show, demonstrated his desire to remove us from his court before we contaminated all within it.

They gave us the expected month but this time added 'with hard labour.' Our Plymouth solicitor, from whom we'd decided to keep all knowledge of this second bout, had told us that hard labour was not permitted for this offence. I therefore said in ringing tones that didn't sound at all like me: 'I understand that it is not permitted to impose hard labour in this case.'

This threw the bench into what I can only describe as a near panic. Saucer-eyes put her hand to her mouth as though she had uttered an unwitting blasphemy. Her fellow beak rose and draped himself dramatically over his desk in order to confer with the clerk below him. He was distinctly agitated and tried to convey something of this to the clerk, who began to

178

flick sneeringly through the pages of, I imagine, Stone's *Justices' Manual*. His contempt for the bench seemed to be little less than his contempt for us. He looked familiar to me. But how could he be? Then I got it and whispered to Graham: 'Good God, it's Gustav von Seyffertitz': a distinguished German actor who had long descended to bit parts in low-budget American movies. Not one of my readers, I imagine, will know him. But Graham did, and a dangerous giggle escaped him. Perhaps Gustav heard this, for he repeated venomously, without further scanning of his manual: 'One month with hard labour in each case.' And he gave that disgusted, dismissive flick of the hand so dear to all such gentlemen.

So the curtain rose on our second performance. Not quite the same. For one thing, I wore my beard as of right, for I entered the prison with it. As we were led along the naval deserters' gallery there were mock cheers, further signings with the cross, even a couple of genuflections, and the cry of one young Scottish wag: 'Och, it's the Second Coming indeed.'

This infuriated the screw who was taking us to our cells, one Principal Officer Fletcher, who was known as 'the one-eyed c**t' because one of his optics was of polished glass.

The story went that his great delight was to check on the prisoners through the spy holes in their cell doors, and that he had driven one man to the extremity of removing the piece of glass from the spy hole and greeting Fletcher's next snoop with a knitting needle.

This very unpopular screw screamed first at the sailors to shut their mouths and attend to their fenders, and then to us that we should be bloody well ashamed of ourselves for returning within a week. The uncalled-for abuse of prisoners was strictly forbidden, so I said: 'We're *not* ashamed of ourselves, Mr Fletcher, and you have no right to tell us we ought to be.' This daunted him a little, as I knew it would, and he confined himself to muttering: 'Ashamed, that's what I'd be, downright ashamed.' Another screw took Graham to his cell while Fletcher ushered me into mine. He took relish in slamming and locking the door, and then instantly checked on me through the spy hole. This struck me as so funny, as if I might have further Messianic powers to demonstrate, that I sat down and silently shook with laughter. A bit hysterical, I imagine. For it was not pleasant to be back here, to be classed as a sort of social outcast. Especially when one's contemporaries were being set up, rightly in most cases, as young heroes.

As if to rub all this in I discovered with a shock that we were no longer 'stars,' or first offenders, but were flung without discrimination into the midst of hardened criminals, even a murderer. Interesting as this might prove, it seemed rather hard to be downgraded to 'old lag' after so brief an apprenticeship.

A nice, elderly screw called Mr Barnsley then arrived with my usual cell task. He threw in twenty mailbags, then, just as I was about to say an ironic 'Thank you,' another twenty, and another, and another. 'Mr Barnsley,' I protested in real enough horror, 'I can't possibly do all those. Twenty was bad enough.' 'Governor's regulations,' he replied, poker faced. I wondered if I were being framed. Said Mr Barnsley with a tremor of one eyelid so slight that it could never be mistaken for a wink: 'Sleep well, Lofty.'

Slowly it dawned on me. 'Hard labour' had by now lost almost all its meaning. All it retained of its original penal intent was the loss of one's mattress. Sure enough my cell contained the bare board and the two blankets. But no mattress. So kind Mr Barnsley had compensated with a veritable shower of mailbags.

It was surprising, I thought, that there should be such a range of types among screws. From an almost paternal Mr Barnsley to an old bastard like Mr Fletcher. (Yet even he, I suppose, prided himself on his sense of duty.) I remember Mr Barnsley had once said to me, almost with tears in his eyes: 'I've heard stories in here, Lofty' (apparently anyone taller than three feet was called 'Lofty'), 'absolutely heartbreaking stories.' He paused, then chuckled. 'And not a bloody word of truth in any of them.' I thought to myself: he must tell himself that or compassion would quite undo him.

I was back in the workshop, I discovered to my regret. Still, the old lags' workshop was at least more colourful. In front of me sat a burly man with a cropped head who told me he was in for seven years' preventive detention. He was a real kids' comic burglar. I could with ease picture him on the job: black mask, jemmy and big sack labelled 'swag.'

He spoke to me out of the corner of his mouth every time the duty screw glanced or walked elsewhere. His opening remarks were surprising:

'How old's your mother?'

I pondered for a moment. I was twenty-four, Terry was seven years older, so mother must be... 'Oh, early fifties,' I whispered.

'My age,' he sighed. Pause. Then: 'Slim? Or a big woman?'

'Oh, pretty well-built.'

A deeper sigh. 'My build,' he breathed. Another pause as a screw perambulated by. Then: 'Fair or dark?'

The questions were getting easier. 'Oh, definitely dark.'

He squirmed. 'My type,' he groaned.

I didn't know whether to laugh to myself as I thought how mother was going to enjoy my account of all this, or shudder at the thought of his long, long frustration.

In the chapel I sometimes found myself sitting near a segregated young man under sentence of death. He was an RAF officer who had survived a suicide pact with a young WAAF. One Sunday morning he caught my eye and smiled. I was shattered by the thought of him, tormented by visions of the execution obscenities. For the first time in the prison, I really prayed.

Then the governor discovered that a dreadful mistake had been made in our case: conscientious objectors, no matter how many times incarcerated, were always to be classified as first offenders. We were plucked back into a less melodramatic world, and the governor actually apologized to Graham and me for the mistake. 'He's not a bad old stick,' I said. And I was emboldened to ask him if there was hope of a reprieve for the young RAF officer. He struggled for a moment with himself, then murmured: 'He has been reprieved.' I came out of his office walking on air.

One evening I was settled down to my evening read. It was the best part of the day. I'd slowly eaten my jacket-potato-and-cheese sandwich, my book was spread out on the table before me, and I was warming my hands round the mug of (so they said) bromided cocoa. Far beyond the little window, trains belched and whistles blew, while through my cell door came the more insistent patter and guffaws of the on-stagers' radio stars: Vic Oliver or Ben Lyon and Bebe Daniels. Then it all quietened down. I heard the on-stagers shuffling off and cell doors being clanged to. The bell rang loudly to signal fifteen minutes to lights out. I regretted one could never read in bed, not even on boards and mailbags. Then, as I was washing, my door was unlocked and there stood the Chief himself.

'Come down to my office, Gamble,' he said in somewhat troubled tones. 'I have something for you.' I sat facing him across his desk as he held up, rather accusingly, a large envelope addressed to me and marked 'Proofs - Urgent.'

'Now, you see, Gamble, you've had your letter ration for this week and so I shouldn't give you this. But it's marked "Urgent" and looks official. Something about your case, I suppose.'

I laughed and told him what proofs were and said it could wait till Monday when my next letter ration was due. But his interest was aroused. He insisted on my opening the packet. I did so and handed him the galley proofs of my Virginia Woolf article. He listened with almost reverent attention as I explained how galleys became page proofs and pages were bound into sections and so forth. He said I could read and correct these and let him have them back tomorrow for posting.

The conversation then, though I don't know how, got on to the difficulties of running a prison in the face of wartime shortages. He seemed grateful to have someone to talk to, someone who would sympathize. I was well aware how bizarre it was to have a convict commiserating with a top-notch screw about the difficulties of his job. He was another pleasant soul.

17

Whether as a result of this I don't know, but within a few days I was told that Graham and I were to be put on a 'farm party' for the rest of our sentence (about seventeen days). This was looked on in the prison as a great privilege. For 'trusties' only. You went out in a convoy after breakfast, worked all day on some remote Devonshire farm, and returned exhausted about 5 pm. For this you and the screws in charge of you were given a good supply of sandwiches and ten Weights or Woodbines by the farmer whose potatoes or whatever you were getting in.

There was one other CO: a Jehovah's Witness I had little to do with. Otherwise we were composed of young naval deserters, decent enough fellows, who didn't mind killing for their country but didn't see why they should die for it.

And, of course, Cuthbert. I mustn't forget him, for we worked in pairs and he was my mate. Here, as before, he appointed himself as my protector from exploitation. Each pair had a stint in a great moorland expanse of potatoes. A tractor would drive along turning up earth and spuds. As soon as it had passed, each pair worked quite feverishly to gather in its harvest before the tractor returned. (Graham was quickly put on to holding the sack open.)

I told myself that the work would become less back-breaking as one became acclimatized to it. Yet the reverse seemed to be the case. It became more and more difficult to clear one's stint before the tractor was on one again.

Then suddenly all hell, or a goodly part of it, broke loose. I saw Cuthbert leaping about waving his arms in a parody of boxing while he shouted obscenities at our neighbours. 'Bastards,' he screamed. 'Dirty, crooked sods.' The screws had to separate him from the others and try to calm him down. Gradually we learned what had been happening. As Cuthbert and I were on all fours frantically picking, our neighbours moved the sticks separating our stint from theirs. They did this several times, so that our stint got larger and larger and theirs correspondingly shorter. The eagle eye of Cuthbert, loner as it was, had detected the fraud, and, being a man of honour, he was naturally outraged.

The screw adjusted the sticks, but Cuthbert was never mollified. His life was founded on suspicion, on the fear that every fellow creature was trying to do him down. The remainder of my potato-cropping was done to the accompaniment of Cuthbert's ceaseless warnings. 'Watch that stick, Piddur, watch that stick. Keep an eye on them bastards, Piddur.'

We had an hour for lunch. We sat on logs or bags of potatoes and ate our sandwiches and drank the tea our farming host provided. I had decided not to smoke on these farm days. Instead, I gave several of my cigarettes to

Cuthbert and pocketed the rest. It was absolutely forbidden to take any of them back into the prison: all ten had to be smoked before one returned. Graham gave me his ten.

During the lunch break my mates regaled the few farm hands who worked near us with harrowing accounts of their crimes. How much of their preposterous stories was believed, I don't know, but they were certainly entertaining.

I had planned to smuggle my dozen or so cigarettes into the prison for the benefit of my former old-lag mates. On our way back to our cells we passed a corridor in which these men were sitting picking or twining something. I had wrapped my fags in my handkerchief. We were searched when we got back but in my case at least the search was little more than perfunctory. I think they assumed I was too high-minded to indulge in anything underhand. As a screw led us along the old lags' corridor, I let fall cigarette after cigarette in their laps and round their feet. Like lightning they gathered and secreted them. I've always been glad I did this.

One day (it must have been a Saturday, for we didn't have a farm party on the road), we were all assembled in the great hall, surrounded by screws and to be addressed by the governor. I wondered uneasily if it was to be an enquiry into cigarette smuggling. It seemed rather a to-do for something so trivial, but you never knew.

Actually, it was for the governor to tell us that a few days earlier had been D-Day: 'Our glorious invasion of the continent of Europe.' He waxed quite Churchillian about it all, as I remembered all those joking fresh-faced youngsters I had seen being driven to the coast in endless convoys. I never heard that the CDR had been involved in this exercise, as we'd assumed they would be.

On the morning of our release, we passed a line of old lags. In defiance of barking screws, several broke ranks and came to wring my hand and wish me luck. I was very touched by this, by their doglike eyes and smiles on faces that had forgotten how to smile.

We were again met by a CDR squad car, again feasted, again brought back to the camp and asked to don our uniforms. We did so, to the astonishment of our more radical mates and the delight of the officers. But it was all part of our dark design, of the plot we had hatched when inside. For some time ago Graham had told me that volunteering for the coal mines took precedence over all other forms of National Service, even over the armed forces, so dire was the shortage of men in the pits. We knew that all we had to do was visit the nearest labour exchange and sign on for the mines, and no one could gainsay us. We just had to convince ourselves that coal mining was a normal peacetime activity. It wasn't our fault they chose to misuse some of the precious carbonaceous material in the war effort. No, we could dig for it with a black face and a white conscience. So on our first afternoon off ('You will come back?' asked the poor commandant anxiously, little knowing that we now had wickeder plans than absconding), we made for the Ministry of Labour in Torquay and both signed on the dotted lines. We were given official notices directing us to report to Cresswell colliery, on the Derbyshire-Nottinghamshire border, in two weeks time. We celebrated with a slap-up dinner in a four-star hotel in Torquay, then returned to the camp and went to bed, taking off our uniforms that night for ever and ever. In the morning, we dressed in our civvies and reported the whole matter to the commandant. He was furious, but he could do nothing about it. I told him in all sincerity that I was sorry we'd been such a nuisance to him. I hoped there were no ill feelings? But there were. He scarcely shook hands before we left, and he couldn't bring himself to wish us luck. I was sorry, for he'd been very decent, really. Lots of the chaps, even all the little black brigade, wished us well and waved us out of sight.

So, we had another two weeks of urban bliss. I greedily picked up all the prized old threads: the family, Jonathan Gray, RU, Vega's, the National Gallery concerts. And I called at the Civil Defence depot in Berkeley Square to see my old mates. I must say I got a very good reception, not least because my fame as a mutinous convict seemed to have forerun me. Jack Jacobs greeted me with extravagant tributes, all larded with his usual self-congratulations. 'Here he is, boys,' he called out, 'my right effin' bastard. Long time ago I told him I'd make him one, and I have. A real effin' bastard if there ever was one. And a credit to his old Uncle Jack, he is.' And my current transition from convict to collier was an added bonus.

It was all quite heartwarming. I left in almost a glow. But over tea in Gunter's, I began to feel uncomfortable about myself. London Civil Defence had been largely staffed by Cockney misfits and shady dealers, but I'd fitted in. In prison, especially as an old lag, I'd likewise fitted, been accepted, even been quite popular. I didn't really like this. Deep down I'd always prized modesty and decorum. Indeed, respectability was my keynote, real middle-class morality my modus vivendi. But no, that wasn't really true, either. Not altogether. For I was, had always been, flawed. From the first, erotically flawed. Then, later, sociologically flawed, because I couldn't live patriotically, respectably, conventionally. Once more, with a sigh, I recognized that I was, after all, just a muddle, a bloody mess.

18

Another send-off, another leave-taking of family and friends and London town. This time not west but north, not Paddington but St Pancras. Both venues were alien to me but the Midlands and north more so. Still, we set off in good spirits, for we were to remain civilians, without uniforms or barracks or insignia.

We spent two pleasant but not very productive weeks at Cresswell. We lived quite comfortably in Nissen huts and were free to eat and drink wherever we wished after about four in the afternoon. The trouble was that there was nowhere to go. Only umpteen little pubs, which never in those days served food. We ate in a quite reasonable pit canteen. But Cresswell was a small pit, not really adapted to a trainee influx. There weren't provisions for these imported 'Bevin boys,' several of whom were regular conscripts drafted by lottery into the pits. Many resented it, for there was no appeal against it, and to them it offered none of the glamour of the armed forces. I remember how odd their resentment seemed to me.

Our first day at Cresswell was so awesome that we felt the Almighty had personally stage-managed it. There had been a roof fall in which four men had been killed. The very afternoon of our arrival, suitably dark and drizzling, four flower-laden hearses and scores of black-clad mourners on foot wound slowly amid all the pithead gear: the great winding wheels, the slag heaps, the long procession of tubs. It was an introduction to our new world that left an abiding impression.

Down the pit, which seemed surprisingly shallow, we learned main-and-tail haulage, which was something we never encountered again. Above ground, we learned how to test for gas with our little incandescent lamps. I was rather proud of my certificate for this. I have it still.

We knew our stay at Cresswell was limited to two weeks. Then we were posted: Graham and I to Markham No 1 pit near Bolsover. They told us at Cresswell that this was a lucky posting, for Markham was a modern pit with splendid baths and canteens.

We were driven to Bolsover and at once taken to meet the town clerk. My impressions of a mining community (so far as I had any) were derived from D. H. Lawrence and from vivid bits of Rhondda reportage in *New Writing*. All mixed up with *Wuthering Heights* and *Cold Comfort Farm* and films like *The Citadel* and *How Green Was My Valley*: hip baths before kitchen peat fires, and beshawled, consumptive women nursing their thin and sickly bairns.

But I found myself in a clean, not unattractive suburb of respectable thirties vintage, whose houses had all mod cons. To one of these the town clerk took us and introduced us to Mrs Sadler, an expansive and pleasant housewife. She had actually agreed to take just one Bevin boy, and that merely to oblige. But she must have noticed the appeal in my eyes as the town clerk told her we were friends who very much hoped to be billeted together. So she took us. It was a three-bedroomed house. She and her husband and the baby girl had one, and her two boys, Stevie aged seventeen, and Brian aged fifteen, another. Graham and I shared the third, on canvas beds supplied by the Ministry of Fuel and Power. Our bedroom looked out on lovely rolling dales and hills not made of slag. There was one large sitting room, and Graham and I had this more or less to ourselves. The children were well behaved: Stevie at a polytechnic in Chesterfield, studying to be a draughtsman, Brian in his last term at school and not sure what to do. Father, chuckling and often a bit tipsy, was a steel erector. They were very well off: something that quite astonished me. Their National Savings had reached the maximum then permitted. After a day's work erecting steel, father would grab his dinner at home and set off with a partner to house decorating. I used to type out his bills for him. He was very proud of these official-looking documents.

But the most impressive figure was mother. She had when young been in service to a ducal family, and I think she was pleased to acquire in me a young man she could pretend was something ducal. She served our food in the sitting room, waited on us hand and foot, and never once in two years did she sit in my presence. We had endless conversations, for I was intrigued by her memories and her standards, but always she leaned against the wall by the door as I sat in an armchair. I would beg her to sit, for often these late evening reminiscences lasted two hours, but it was in vain. 'No,' she said. ''Tain't reet.' She told me once her father had worn 'one of them black dresses and funny hats you have on in a photo.' She referred to a Belvedere snapshot of me in a borrowed cap and gown. I inferred from this that her father had been the son of some grand household her mother had been in service to: a Tess Durbeyfield set-up that seemed somehow appropriate, for Mrs Sadler's education had obviously been much less than her natural intelligence deserved. Her life had fashioned her to serve: first as a domestic, then as a wife and mother. If I ventured to carry a plate into the kitchen, or even make up our grand coal fire, she was so put out that I learned to desist. But I never ceased to be shocked by the way her husband and sons never lifted a finger to help her. It was the alien ethos of a family where the males slogged outside the home and never impinged on the women who slaved within it.

Markham No 1, known as 'Black Shale,' was then one of the deepest pits in the country, and down that we at last had to dive. At the unreal hour of 5.30 am we left Bolsover in the miners' bus and were very soon disgorged into the most impressive pithead baths. I was told by the older colliers that they'd never really got used to these newfangled places: my pictures of hip baths before the kitchen range were apparently their cherished memories. But I revelled in these spacious, steaming ablutions. You had a locker on the clean side where you left your own clothes before crossing to the dirty locker where you donned your pit clothes and helmet and water bottle and snap tin.

You then called at the lamp cabin, exchanging for your lamp the numbered coin that was your identity disc. After that you were all set for caging.

These cages normally carried the coal tubs, and the only concession made when they were winding men was a pair of horribly inadequate little gates. There wasn't an inch of level floor for a foothold and nothing but your mate to cling to. 'Perk oop, lad,' said a burly shotfirer with kindly eyes. 'Tha'll find it a neece, easy ride.' And at that moment the thing simply *fell*, hurtling down in sheer, wicked abandon, as my breakfast somersaulted within me. 'This is it,' I thought bitterly. 'Terrible pit cage disaster. Bevin boys killed on first day down.' Then, suddenly, the thing began to lose speed, to shudder, to falter, and finally to land with feather-like grace at the pit bottom. The shotfirer chuckled: first leg-pull of a Bevin greenhorn.

But our first acquaintance with down under was reassuring. We found ourselves in a tunnel as lofty and well lit as any subway on the London Tube. The whole pit bottom area was similarly light and spacious. There, outside the undermanager's office, we waited to be deputed to our various jobs. Graham and I were apprenticed to the haulage gaffer, and with him we tramped a short way to our clipping-on station. Between the rails on which the tubs ran (empty ones heading for the coal face, ones crammed full with coal heading for the pit bottom cage to be wound up) was an endless, moving steel cable, on to which the leading tub in each linked set of eight had to be securely locked. It was locked by means of a cumbrous, weighty contraption possessing steel jaws below and a polelike handle above. You hooked this vicious thing to the leading tub's coupling link, set its jaws around the moving steel cable, and descended with all your weight on the handle. As soon as the jaws bit, the tubs jerked into motion, so that at one and the same time you had to bounce your behind up and down on the handle and walk backwards in front of the advancing juggernaut. You had to be something between a marionette and a crab, knowing that if you slipped and fell in front of those relentlessly advancing tubs you'd be mincemeat. Once the tubs were firmly clamped to the cable you had to fling yourself out of the road, again emulating a crab. It seems to me now a needlessly clumsy and dangerous process, but I accepted it and even became reasonably proficient at it.

Not so Graham, who was far too slow at it. Foreseeing a fatal accident in no time, the undermanager took him off it and put him on to running full tubs two at a time on to the cage. But that, although not fatal to life and limb, was certainly fatal to the smooth running of the pit. So poor Graham was moved far from the pit bottom to a coal gate nearly under our digs in Bolsover. There he was trained to work the loader end. This meant pulling a lever which raised and lowered a great chute bringing coal on a conveyor belt from the face. This even Graham managed to do with passable efficiency.

Until there came the incident that was to achieve no little fame for him and for Bevin boys. But I mustn't anticipate that.

I was consoled for the loss of Graham as a haulage mate by the arrival of Geoff. He was a youth of sixteen, well-built and good-looking, and I liked him. What was surprising, as well as very gratifying, was that he seemed almost pathetically pleased by my offer of friendship. In time I came to see that others cold-shouldered him, almost avoided him. I set out to discover why. I learned that his gaffer had been killed in some incident that threw no credit on Geoff. I never found out the details, and didn't really want to. I just felt sorry for him, as well as glad to have *his* friendship, for I knew as well as he what it was to be pretty lonely. He lockered near me and soon began to take his shower with me, to my delight. I admired his body, and I think he knew it. It was, I must add, normal to have a companion in the shower cubicle with you, to wash your back and then give you his to wash. Coal dust was pretty well engrimed by the end of a shift, and you needed much practice in getting it off. I remember how astonished I was to discover after my first shower (which I thought had been exemplary) that I was still blackened in all manner of places. In particular my eyes were haloed in black, like a Mack Sennett bathing belle of the early twenties. So Geoff and I worked vigorously on each other. And thoroughly enjoyed it.

These showers were the great consolation of my new life, just as privacy to read in had been my great consolation in prison. For in 1944 the coal mines were still largely a boy world. Yes, a century after Shaftesbury, after the act forbidding women and small children in mines, I found my pit abounded in 14-year-olds who, with stunted growth and shrill trebles, seemed younger than the top forms of Belvedere. They aped the swagger as well as the vocabulary of hardened colliers, but really they were innocent kids, and very nice ones when they'd accepted you. But it was, of course, their somewhat older brothers who most intrigued me.

Graham had no such consolations. I wondered, unhappily, how much longer he would last. Evenings and weekends gave good scope for enjoyment, which really meant a film and a dinner somewhere pleasant. But since we had to get up in the middle of the night for our day's work we didn't feel much like an evening out. Except on Saturday, when we went to Chesterfield and made the most of it.

Mr Twining, the undermanager, was a source of great amusement to Graham and me. He is the only man I have ever seen (outside a two-reeler) throw his hat on the ground and jump on it in a fit of screaming fury. It was all simulated, I am sure. *Pour encourager les autres.* Graham and I once met him in Bolsover on a Sunday morning. He was dressed in the most respectable of clothes (including a black bowler) and was clearly on his way to chapel with his hymn book. He raised his hat to us and said, almost demurely: 'Good morning, Graham. Good morning, Peter.' We could only contrast it with the foul-mouthed whirling dervish we knew in the pit.

19

Mr Twining had a sense of humour, and he gave full rein to it. He thought Bevin boys (especially the London ones) wanted taking down a peg or two, or even three. One Saturday there was more absenteeism than usual, so jobs had to be reshuffled. He didn't quite know what to do with me, as I stood waiting and feeling as usual an ungainly misfit in my great, steel-toed pit boots, and my far too big helmet, which the weight of my cap lamp was always pulling over my eyes. He looked at me. 'What's tha' do in civvy street, Peter?' he asked me pleasantly.

'Oh, I was a schoolmaster,' I answered, rather diffidently.

'Was tha' now?' he said reflectively. Then he brightened as an idea struck him. 'Tommy Jackson's doing his rounds this morning. He's safety inspector. Tha' can go wi' him. See the whole bloody works. Something to teach tha' lads about coal mining, that'll be.' I jumped at the idea. A welcome change from haulage, which was getting a bit tedious.

So off I set with Tommy, a nice, portly old man with a great fund of innocent, Chaucerian dirty stories, most of which I remember when so much of wisdom I have forgotten.

We left the chilly, breezy main road we were in, along whose rails lines of full and empty tubs endlessly rattled, and passed through several doors on a crossways road until we emerged on to another and parallel main road that was very hot and rather foul. We had passed from the intake road to the return road. Along the former rushed in cold, fresh air, out to the furthest workings, whence it returned sultrily to a great shaft for expelling used air. If, Tommy told me, one propped open those many doors on the crossways road one would be cutting off all fresh air from the coal faces. With fatal consequences.

In this return road were also rails, but on these no tubs ran. Instead, they carried a nice little passenger train that would have been quite at home on Brighton front. This took colliers to their various working stations and to the gates, as the now mostly disused roads to exhausted coal faces were called. Tommy and I travelled to the terminus, where we recrossed to the intake road. I well understood how those fitters whose work took them to and fro between the two roads, intake and return, needed constantly to don and doff clothing, or else risk pneumonia.

Here was real pit. Here were real miners. These were the coalfaces. Here laboured the coal getters and the shotfirers, the roof shorers and the safety men. The actual coal pickers were mostly bent, curiously dehydrated men whose skin and bones seemed harder than the elements they wrestled with.

We trudged on. The roof was getting lower, the air warmer. Occasionally, Tommy would stop to test for gas. Once he indicated a bricked-up entrance, telling me it was a gate in which some twenty years before seven or eight men had perished. Because they couldn't be recovered, they were sealed in: entombed forever in the vault they'd daily sweated in. I wanted to believe this was another Bevin boy spoof.

Tommy gave me a large brown bag of fine, snow-white powder for me to chuck all around me. 'That's stone dust, sirrah. Tha' puts it on top of coal dust to stop it igniting when they're shot-firing.' Then, as a grim afterthought: 'That's what kills, tha' know. Not coal dust.'

He was interrupted by a hoarse cry ahead, which made him drag us both into a refuge bay. A muffled explosion. I thought: 'Roof fall. Entombed. Buried alive.' Tommy said, as he calmly took snuff: 'Shotfirer, tha' knows.'

We were now bent double. A few feet further and we were crawling on hands and knees. I wondered how much longer this could go on before I turned round, then crawled, scurried and bolted. But even worse was to come. We now began to drag ourselves on our bellies between the men and the face they were hacking at. My pit boots seemed like fetters, my water bottle strap was choking me, my helmet and cap lamp had to be kept in place with a hand I couldn't spare. I knew I was very close to panicking. I wanted to. I wanted to scream and lunge out with my fists. Or just die. But I didn't, I wouldn't, I couldn't. And with an astonishingly clear head I knew just why I couldn't. Because of a greater fear than that bred of claustrophobia. The fear of looking a booby, a coward, a risk: a real, southern, urban milksop. The end of the face was in sight. I would make it. I *would*.

And I did. Of Tommy I had for so long seen nothing but feet and rump. Now he was no longer widdershins. Now he faced me on his knees. Now he extended a hand to haul me, but I proudly refused it. He said simply: 'Well done, lad.'

Nothing else we did that day is even worth mentioning. Routine stuff in gates that were old and disused but still had wonderful roofs designed for *homo erectus*. Our last port of call was at the pit bottom cages. Tommy (how was he so agile at his age and size?) asked me if I wanted to accompany him on his last job, which was squeezing yourself under the cages' landing places to inspect the machinery. I told him I was going with him. It was nasty, but not as nasty as the coalface had been.

As we trudged back to the undermanager's office, Tommy told me: 'Tha's seen things, been in places, those who've worked down here all their lives haven't seen.' And so ended the worst day I spent below in all my mining life. But it was only much later that I think I discovered why Mr Twining had done it. It was those pegs he wanted to take me down. It was a lesson the snooty little Londoner had coming to him. And all because of my innocent misuse of vocabulary there. I'd told him I was a schoolmaster. I should have said 'a schoolteacher.' To them, a schoolmaster was the master of a school, a headmaster, and that I could not at my age be.

20

My twin enemies at this time were catarrh (or sinusitis) and insomnia. I was once sent by my doctor to Chesterfield hospital outpatients to have my sinuses pierced. As I waited my turn, a sister came up and whispered: 'Take my tip: don't have it done. You'll regret it.' So I left, very gladly. I've blessed that kindly sister many times. A much bigger problem was getting some sleep. I was, still am, a light sleeper who can never manage a daytime doze. I could never get used to rising in the middle of the night and going to bed in summer months when the sun was shining and kids were playing happily in the street. I staggered on for a long time, hollow-eyed and yawning, with frequent visits to the doctor for days off. I was reported once or twice for absenteeism.

Graham went on working half-heartedly at his loader end. Until the memorable day when he had a nasty cold in the head. Solemnly, determinedly, he stopped the loader end, which caused the conveyor belt from the face to stop, followed by the coalface conveyor belt, then by all the tubs throughout the pit. Very soon the entire Markham No 1 pit was at a standstill. Thousands of tons of coal stood idle. Deputies and undermanagers and safety officials were scurrying everywhere like ants.

When they reached Graham to learn what terrible disaster had caused their world to stop turning round, he obliged them with a quiet and factual explanation: 'I stopped the machine to blow my nose. I can't work this loader end *and* blow my nose, can I? I have a bad cold in the head.' And he went on wiping and mopping the guilty organ as deputies frothed and even Mr Twining could get no words out.

I think this conduct of Graham's was perfectly natural. He was without guile. He was reported to some government board, but I couldn't see what they could advise other than a firing squad. But alas! there was something they could do and they did it. To my great sorrow, they chucked him out of the pit, out of anything remotely connected with coal mining. He was told to wait at home for another tribunal.

I couldn't for his sake lament his release. But it was with a heavy heart that I saw him off. We'd been through a good deal together. I liked him. I was now to face real loneliness.

He soon had his extra tribunal. They added hospital work to his conditions. He took up some pen-pushing job in one of the great London hospitals. There in due course he met a pleasant, practical nurse who became his wife and the mother of his four sons.

191

By another of the coincidences we were taking as normal in those days, Brian wrote a little later to say that his lorry-driving in Lincolnshire had finished and he, too, had found hospital work in London. But not, of course, pen-pushing. As a stoker. He described his stokehole to me in glowing terms. Typically, he had furnished it and was living in it. Such pictures of life in London for both Graham and Brian filled me with an envy that made my solitude even harder to bear.

My doctor recommended I be taken off the day shift on health grounds. I was put on 'afters,' the afternoon shift from about 2 pm to 10 pm, and things were much easier. I now had a real night's sleep, and I had mornings free to go to Chesterfield for shopping and libraries and morning coffees.

I also made a request to move to another locker in the showers. I had seen an empty one in a bay near the doors, which was far breezier and cooler than my present one. This was a genuine request, for after my shower I found I couldn't stop sweating as I dried and dressed, so warm were the ablutions buildings. But with dastardly cunning I had an additional aim. I wanted to get to know Colin. With my posting to 'afters' I had lost old comrades like Geoff and gained new possibilities. Moreover, I found there were more boys and youths on 'afters,' and fewer grizzled miners.

Colin lockered facing me. He had an upper locker, so he stood on the steel balustrade in front of his locker to dry himself. He was fifteen and looked like one of the striking cherubs on a medieval print. He was friendly and he seemed to know, without in any way resenting, my attraction to him. He would stand aloft, towelling himself, his anatomy aswing, as I asked him about his life and his home and his job in the pit. He had a fine head of chestnut hair, so thick that it took much drying. I often helped him to scrub it with a dry towel. Then comb it, which sometimes made him yell. Then one Friday I gave him half a crown. He was delighted. And astonished.

'What's it for?' he asked.

'For being a cherub,' I replied.

'What's a cherub?'

I smiled and said: 'A sort of angel.'

He laughed. 'My mam don't think I'm an angel.'

I gazed and gazed. 'It takes a special sort of person to recognize one.'

So for all the rest of my time in the pit I gave him a Friday half-crown. He accepted it, politely, naturally, never greedily. Just as he'd accepted that he was a cherub.

He had a week's summer holiday with his family in Llandudno. So I gave him five bob that week, and I said: 'Wouldn't it be nice if you sent me a postcard? But you won't.'

He was almost indignant. "Course I will. Write down your address for me.' And he did: one of those super big seaside views that open out like a toilet roll. I still have it.

That was all.

My jobs on 'afters' were more varied than before. I was taken off haulage. I suspect this was because I grew rather slapdash about it, rather overconfident. A long way beyond my clipping-on station was a section of line known as 'the roller turn,' where many of my tubs became derailed as they rounded the bend.

So I was mated with Jack in the task of 'bringing down tackle.' Jack was wild and tough and despised his new mate even more than he despised his poor pit pony. (This wasn't what I imagined a pony to be at all, but a large horse with a mind of its own.) I had to woo both Jack and the horse: the former with bright ideas, the latter with most of the lunch in my snap tin. We would make for an old, long-abandoned gate, or road, down which we had to bring rails and roof girders which wartime shortages had made precious. At the bottom of the long gate we'd harness the horse to a waggonette on rails and set off up the pitch dark, utterly silent, increasingly steep incline. At the terminus we had to turn the horse round and fasten the waggonette to a chain across its chest. We then loaded the chariot with great girders and props, carefully retreating as we hammered down the roof girders and ripped up the rails. Often the roof would crumble and rumble ominously as it lost its supports.

Jack, I could see, was revising his first opinion of me, initially because I worked with a will at loading the heavy steel tackle. This was because I had discovered how quickly time passed if one kept at it. Jack and I proved a good team, an appreciable amount of tackle was brought down, and, in such hot, stale conditions, I was losing flesh and gaining muscle.

I hated seeing the distress of the horse during the descents, trying to restrain the chariot chained to his chest as his feet slithered, his nostrils flared, his bloodshot eyes rolled wildly. As we inserted wooden lockers between the spokes of the chariot wheels and saw how little effect they had, I wondered how long before the poor beast's legs buckled and he was dragged ever faster to a mangled death.

So I made a suggestion to Jack which appealed to his daredevilry. 'Let's put the wagon, fully loaded, on course, and just let it go on its own!' Faster and faster, until finally we saw it and heard it, far ahead and far below, fly off the rails and, with a noise like a bomb, scatter its load in all directions. We and the horse, who like us watched it all appreciatively, walked at a leisurely pace to the 'accident' and calmly reloaded.

We betted on the distance the thing could travel before derailment. All quite exciting. But we gave it up when we discovered the showers of sparks we were causing: an insane thing to do in a pit. Also how nearly we killed Steve, our deputy, who often laboured up the gate to see how we were getting on.

Yes, Jack was a wild one. When we knocked off, Jack wasn't having the long, hot trudge to the pit bottom. He did what was utterly forbidden: he rode the horse back at a fine gallop the length of the return road. I can see him now, crouched like a jockey, smacking the horse's rump, his water bottle and neckerchief flying in the wind, as he disappeared to the sound of thudding hoofs and amid dense clouds of dust.

I wished when I came to the end of my coal mining days that I could buy that horse and take him with me. Just to pension him off in some green meadow.

Less humane, but infinitely more exciting, were my dreams of similarly rescuing Colin: of taking him with me to London and setting him up in some grand apprenticeship.

Mrs Sadler sent the canvas beds supplied for Graham and me back to the depot and got me an excellent divan. She also got a few more bits for the sitting room, now recognized as almost exclusively my parlour. In that I sat and read and did my RU work, and my long critical essay on Forrest Reid. This was engaging me more and more. I had read and returned the novels Walter de la Mare had lent me, and had borrowed some more. Graham's departure made me work rather harder at these tasks, out of sheer boredom and loneliness.

The latter condition prompted a venture that brought a fine return. I had, in a vague, half-hearted way, been observing Mrs Sadler's boy, Brian. He was quite a handsome lad, and one of his chief hobbies was muscular development. He took postal courses in such things. He was smouldering of eye and, so far as I was concerned, utterly mute of tongue.

One Friday evening, he and I were, as usual, alone in the house. Mam had gone to the pictures with a neighbour, Stevie was at night classes, Dad was decorating or 'supping ale.' I went into the kitchen where Brian studied one of his manuals in front of the fire. I asked him about it. He made no attempt to reply. I decided it wasn't unfriendliness but chronic shyness. 'How are your muscles coming on?' I asked. I squeezed his arms, then his legs. 'Not bad,' I commented. Then, because I couldn't think of anything else to say, I asked: 'Like to feel mine?' To my surprise he nodded vigorously.

He made much of his testing of my person. I asked: 'Like a friendly wrestling match?'

More vigorous nodding. I cleared a space in front of the fire and we began to circle round each other with arms extended. I hadn't the faintest idea how to wrestle, nor had he, but soon we were both on the floor and at close grips. I knew he was after exactly the same thrills that I was after.

We must have played for a couple of hours. Throughout which he never uttered a word, as usual. But that didn't matter. We were communicating otherwise. I spoke, teasingly, laughingly: 'Come on, Heathcliff,' I said. The game became ever less of a wrestling match. Hugging and tickling and squeezing and clasping. We were both sorry to end it, but we knew it was time for the others to return.

A week later: same day, same time, same place. He was waiting for me. I said: 'Look, let's go up and wrestle on my bed. It'll be more comfortable.'

Silently, he assented. A more frank and serious set of bouts now.

I discovered that he took a very real pleasure in my body, as I did in his. We were perfectly attuned, and also I had complete confidence in him. Our Friday night sessions (which lasted a full year) were our affair, entirely. He was a very nice lad and our intimacy did us both a power of good, weaning me from my rather gloomy solitude, him from his morbid shyness.

My RU work often took me to London for the weekend. Not really necessary from the commercial point of view, but certainly necessary for my sanity. I would go up Saturday morning and come back Sunday night, unless 'business' detained me until Monday night. Whether Sunday or Monday, I arrived back at Chesterfield on the last train, long after all buses had packed up for the night. So I had to walk back, all the way from Chesterfield to Hillstown, which was a southern outcrop of Bolsover. About nine miles. At night, alone, sometimes in foggy or freezing weather. But I didn't mind at all, it was so wonderful to see the family again, and to savour my London.

21

However, as 1944 wore on London was being ever more battered by Hitler's V1s, the awful flying bombs. One of my weekends in London had been particularly bad. The hellish things were coming over ever more frequently. The family spent a large part of each day and each night under the stairs: Miles in his cot, Nora in plaster of Paris after one of her falls, mother and Pam, and father at night. I used to be mostly up in my bedroom leaning out of the window, waiting for each droning machine's engine to cut out. Then I'd shout down to make sure they were all under the stairs, while I crouched under my bed and listened. Some fell very near and shook the house and cracked the glass of the windows. Mother couldn't take much more, I could see. We had to get out of London. We had nowhere to go, no money to go with. But desperation bred quick decisions. I presented my bombshell almost matter-of-factly. And not one objection was raised. Our lives depended on instant action and the one I proposed was the only possible one. 'We must sell the entire home, then you must all come up to Chesterfield with me. I'll insist they house or billet you: that is, if they still want me as a miner.' Father said he must stop behind because of his work, but he could easily stay as a paying guest with a colleague who lived in Chesham (which was a trifle less vulnerable than Streatham).

The next day, Monday, was one of almost frantic activity. While they worked like Trojans to pack up belongings in suitcases, I went to a large local firm that moved whole homes and also bought them. Their valuer came up that afternoon with a great pantechnicon and bought the lot. People were well used in those blitz days to sudden requests and instant action. I got the money from them (a pitiful, a disgraceful sum for a whole home) and watched everything going: all my childhood and youth, a thousand memories, mostly happy, for that is the way of man at such times. It is now more than half a century since that cataclysmic day, but regularly in those years I have dreamed of that home, of that family, of a million buried incidents, of a lifetime's early mosaic.

Glad-eye, good trouper as ever, took in a few coveted sticks for us: a little sewing table which had belonged to mother's mother, a small rocking chair in which most of us had been nursed as babies. I have them still. She also took all my books which I hadn't already humped to Bolsover. I then found a taxi that would (for a good fee) take us to St Pancras to catch the slow evening train to Chesterfield. It was due there at 9.30.

Brian had come over as soon as his stoking shift had finished to help with final arrangements and to liaise with Glad-eye in any contingencies. I also saw Jonathan and bade farewell to his family.

Miles' de luxe pram was fastened to the taxi roof, half a dozen large cases stowed next to the driver. Then in climbed mother, Nora in plaster, Pam nursing our swearing cat in a basket, and last of all, with a long, hard look at the house, I myself with Miles. Droning V1s and distant explosions accompanied our whole journey to St Pancras. It would be an irony dear to the gods that we should all be killed after selling the home: even the modest wad of notes blown to kingdom come.

But no, we escaped. Father and Brian weren't with us, but were safe for the time being, while the family nucleus was in my hands and I was going to fight for it. Fight savagely, if need be. My blood was up.

A long, cold, foodless journey to Chesterfield. I got in at the Station Hotel without any trouble, but they were adamant against babies and pets. So I tried a large commercial hotel nearby. Same story there. But the young undermanageress took pity on us. 'Mrs Simpson isn't here at the moment. She's the manageress. Can you be out by 9.30 in the morning? If so, she need know nothing about it. Don't you tell a soul.'

I thanked her humbly, profusely, and swore no one would ever hear a word of it pass our lips.

As soon as she was out of earshot, Pam did her Jane Murdstone act, drawing herself up, pursing her lips, folding her hands on her stomach. 'I trust, brother,' she hissed to me, 'that come the dawn and our effects removed, you will report this *traitress* to her employer.'

'Can you doubt it, sister?' I replied. 'Loyalty must be honoured as a cardinal Christian virtue.'

I settled them in their rooms: Pam and Miles in one, mother and Nora in another. I was talking to mother about the next day's programme, when Pam appeared, hanging on the door. From the door she sank to the floor, holding her stomach and silently shaking. 'Now what is it, you couple of fools?' asked mother, beginning to laugh before she'd even heard the joke. I begged Pam to keep quiet, for experience told me shrieks were only too likely to follow the mute contortions. She did her best and finally managed to tell us what had happened. Sam, our cat, had escaped and she'd pursued him all over the establishment: past dressing-gowned commercial travellers who gazed in wonder at this fleeting, bent figure, past an elderly man who staggered on the polished corridor floor and nearly went flying, into a room where a man was just getting into bed, and finally into a gents, where she'd shut the cat and locked him in. 'Here's the key,' she gasped, 'go and rescue him.'

I unlocked him, and found him crouching beside a little puddle he'd made. I picked him up, gave him a tiny shake by way of rebuke, followed by a tiny squeeze by way of reconciliation. He responded by swearing a little, then purring. He was the dearest, cleverest cat we ever had. A gentleman, too. For as Pam was frantically seeking him, he himself was urgently seeking a gents.

Next morning, early, I collected them and all their gear, and rewarded the kindly undermanageress. I took them to the café in the Odeon cinema, where the manageress was a friendly soul I knew quite well after regular morning coffees ever since I was put on 'afters.' I left the family with her while I went to the town hall. I had decided to find the Lord Mayor and bully and threaten him into housing my family.

I discovered Alderman Moffatt was indeed in his parlour and it was unheard of for him to see anybody without an appointment. 'Then I'll make one, right now,' I said, brusquely. An altercation ensued, from which they deduced that I was a determined, sharpshooting, trouble-making immigrant who claimed to be a collier. Well, I was finally ushered into Alderman Moffatt's presence. There I explained the position: I was a Bevin boy. From London. To which I'd been on Saturday. There I found my family at the end of their tether with the flying bombs. I'd sold up everything and brought them here. The council must house them all. Two middle-aged ladies, namely my mother and aunt, and my young sister with her 10-month-old baby. (I didn't mention Sam.)

Alderman Moffatt said he could do nothing because we weren't official evacuees. I brushed this objection aside. Contemptuously. No time for such red tape. I said I had to extricate them from blitzed London before my mother cracked up with trying to care in such conditions for an invalid and a baby. I repeated: they had to house them, at once. Damn the pettifogging rules and regulations.

I must have convinced him we'd all camp out in the mayor's parlour if he didn't do something. He summoned the chief billeting officer for a confab in another room. When he returned he told me they had a few condemned cottages behind the Odeon cinema. These were for one-night stays only, usually for evacuees who arrived in Chesterfield on late night trains. The billeting officer would put us there for one night, while he sought billets for us.

All this was done. The condemned cottages behind the Odeon were quite respectable, and decently furnished with all necessities. I left Pam discussing things with the billeting officer (a very correct official of about forty-five), as I got the others somewhat settled in the very temporary haven. Then I went out for some things for tea. We all felt how wonderful it was to be relaxing, making tea, cutting bread and butter, talking, with never one moment's thought of a roaring machine overhead that would suddenly cut out, then blast to eternity hapless strangers or near neighbours or even *oneself*.

I left about eight, promising to return next morning, early. There were the billets to move into, ration books to reregister, cases to unpack. 'If only we could stay here,' sighed mother. I thought the same. 'The billeting officer would never allow it,' I said sadly. 'Rules and regulations.' Pam looked mysterious. 'Just leave him to me,' she remarked darkly, and refused to elucidate. But I had such confidence in her as an organizer that I went off feeling more hopeful.

My optimism was justified. Somehow she got a stay of execution from the billeting officer. Grumbling, and telling us he was taking a considerable risk, he just let things slide. He was during the ensuing weeks always referring to billets he had found for them, billets that somehow never materialized.

Meanwhile we got ration books and local shops organized. I shall never forget our first Sunday roast in the condemned cottage: delectable, both in itself and in its ambience. Pam then set about a greater triumph with her complaisant billeting officer. He had to sign a form to say that we were official evacuees, so that we (that is, the family) could get the official allowance: not much, but a necessary help. It was really just a formality, and Pam carried that off, too. Of course, the BO (as we soon came to call him) made out he was taking even greater risks, but as I pointed out we were true evacuees, who merely lacked a chit from Wandsworth Borough Council to say so. The BO took Pam out to lunch once or twice. I felt she was making noble sacrifices for us all, for I found the BO a somewhat dreary and unprepossessing man. But she maintained: 'Oh, he's rather a honeybun, really.' She often referred to such types as 'honeybuns.' Perhaps she meant it. Her tastes were, I thought, distinctly odd.

They were happy days. I once more had the family to shepherd. The condemned cottage was ever more appreciated: the scene of endless chatter and laughter, of wild experiments with wartime rations, of highly critical comments on all sorts of radio programmes. For I'd bought a secondhand set that worked when it felt like it and elicited reams of curses when it didn't. Often we wandered over the town, mother and Pam arm in arm, Miles in his pram, with me pushing it and Nora clinging to it. And when I had to dive down of an afternoon, well, that, too, was not without its compensations.

Some time in December 1944 brother Brian wrote to say he wanted me to go up to London on a certain day: he had something urgent in hand, something which needed my presence.

'I know,' said Pam eagerly. 'He's found us a house.' To tell the truth, there were little hints, the merest clues and insinuations, nothing at all explicit, that we were all pining for London.

So up to town I went, fighting down as usual my guilty qualms about absenteeism. Brian had not found us a roof but something even more astonishing for himself: nothing less than a wife. The marriage was taking place at Chelsea registry office that very afternoon of my arrival.

And the wife, the last kind of wife anyone could imagine for Brian, was the assistant matron of the hospital in which Brian was the stoker. I liked her, but I don't think Brian did. She was everything Brian could never be, in fact despised to be. She was a little older than Brian and had long worshipped at every shrine of bourgeois respectability. She had her standards and I didn't in the least blame her for defending them against Brian's mounting onsets. She had a nice little flat in one of those ugly old Edwardian houses in Oakley Street, Chelsea. Into that Brian moved, as I secretly wondered if one reason for this marriage was disenchantment with his hospital stokehole home.

What a bombshell I had for the family next day. For a moment they gazed at me open mouthed. Then they all roared with laughter. After they'd got over it, they felt a bit ashamed and decided they must write their congratulations. Pam, of course, went a step further: in a junk shop she found and spent two whole shillings on a large Victorian card of an old Darby-and-Joan couple in a riotously luxuriant cottage garden. It was entitled: 'Down All The Changing Years Together.' Brian, of course, appreciated this, but I don't think his wife did.

This family convulsion, plus growing evidence that the V1s were fizzling out, plus hints of poor father's increasing dereliction, brought their urban nostalgia to a head.

We were all sitting in the Odeon café one morning, chatting to the manageress, now a good friend and known to us as 'Sparrow' because of her birdlike legs and feet, and her rapid, bouncing movements. She often had Miles crawling all over the café while we went shopping. I said, not really seriously: 'Do you want to go back?' Pam pounced on it. 'Yes,' she said. 'When? Now?'

I sighed. 'You can't go back until you've got somewhere to live.'

Mother, too, seemed resolute. 'Well,' she said, 'we must just go back as we came up. You managed all right then.' I was flattered by her faith in me.

'All very well,' I replied. 'But I can hardly pull that one on the Lord Mayor of London. And I suppose the Mansion House has better defences.' I was at a loss, rather despondent. 'If only there was someone we knew who could put you all up while you looked around for something.'

Silence. Then Pam and I sat up and yelled out in almost the same breath: 'Glad-eye!'

Another moment's silence. 'Unless The Major's moved in on her,' Pam added.

The only thing was to find out. I phoned Glad-eye that afternoon. I said I was coming to London for the day and would like her to meet me at the Army and Navy for lunch. She was, of course, delighted.

She was even more delighted to think we would all be going to stay with her. I arranged suitable terms, having by devious means established there was no major. (I learned much later that he'd made off with quite an amount of loot, and cured poor Glad-eye of the Locarno forever.)

So within a matter of days I had them all packed and entrained. There were quite emotional farewells taken of Sparrow and the BO and a few friendly shopkeepers. Not mother or Nora or Pam or Miles has ever seen Chesterfield again, but it has shone handsomely in our memories ever after.

I went with them to London, of course, and saw them all comfortably established in Glad-eye's sensible, old-fashioned house. I found it very sad to see again our house, our garden, our road. Now an alien land. Strange people trampling my boyhood dreams.

Seeing Jonathan and his family again was an added delight. To Pam I confidently left the task of finding us a house. And when Glad-eye suggested father join them all under her roof, it seemed our cup was brimming over. I went back to Chesterfield that night, very aware of my new loneliness there, but also grateful to the powers above that all had worked out so well for the family.

22

Whether as a result of the recent upsurge of solitude and discontent I don't know, but my health began to show signs of disrepair. Mild spells of dizziness accompanied my pit work, especially when I stooped. I confess that I hoped this would lead to my release from the mines, to the substitution of a different condition in my CO registration. After all, Graham had got hospital work simply because he couldn't work the loader end: why not me for delicate health? I knew my local doctor, though nice enough, was not equal to this challenge. I needed an eminent Harley Street man. As I pondered, other possibilities declared themselves. I had heard of a young man released from the army by a CO tribunal on the grounds of homosexuality. Surely it was bad for a person like me to be segregated in this largely nude world of men and boys?

Now where was the Harley Street man, and how could I get to him? Well, I was equal to that, too. At RU we had selected for one of our monthly choices a book for which I had much respect as also for its author. It was called *Diagnosis of Man*, half philosophy (western and eastern) and half medical science, and its author was Kenneth Walker, by profession a genito-urinary surgeon, by nature a sage, a guru. I had corresponded with him at RU, but he wouldn't, of course, remember my name. I just wrote to him asking for a consultation, which I was duly given.

He was extraordinarily kind, but puzzled. Had a GP sent me? Why had I chosen him? So I told him all about RU and *Diagnosis of Man* and dizzy spells and homosexuality. He gave me a medical exam and told me I really needed an endocrinologist. Did I know Dr Raymond Greene? No, I didn't. So Mr Walker phoned him there and then and asked him if he could see a young man who needed his help, a coal miner, a Bevin boy, with various problems which were more up Dr Greene's street than Mr Walker's. Astonishingly Dr Greene said he would see me in an hour. 'He's only over the road,' said Mr Walker, brushing aside any question of payment, and still looking rather mystified.

Dr Greene (a brother of Graham Greene, the novelist) was charming. I told him all. I asked him if there was any kind of medicine one could take to reduce sexual energy. I remember he threw back his head and laughed long and loud. 'You're the first man ever to sit in that chair and ask that,' he said. 'They all ask the exact opposite.'

He felt the homosexuality was a less likely course to pursue with regard to the mines than the giddiness. He was going to arrange for me to have a series of tests at the Courtauld Institute of Biochemistry. He phoned them, and asked me if 2.30 pm in a week's time would be possible. It certainly would: another trip to London, and medical necessity overriding all objections from the labour enforcement officer of the Ministry of Fuel and Power, with whom I'd had another brush recently.

As a result of the medical tests, Dr Greene diagnosed me as suffering from 'hypothyroidism associated with spontaneous hypoglycaemia.' He prescribed medication and he put me on a diet, which meant a rather sharp correspondence with the Ministry of Food regarding alterations to my ration book. I was a little taken aback to find I really had something wrong with me. Dr Greene didn't at that stage feel he could take on the Ministry of Fuel and Power and the CO tribunal, but he'd keep me under strict surveillance and see how we got on. And again all fees refused. I was well satisfied, and very grateful.

The family had returned to London just in time for the V2s, the rockets. The damage caused by these was greater than that wrought by the V1s, but their terror was far less. This was mostly because you had no warning of them, no siren, no engine and its terrible cutout. All you heard was a large explosion, which mercifully seemed to be some way off. There weren't so many of the things and they didn't seem to have a penchant for southwest London, as their predecessors had. So we all coped with them, more or less.

Besides, the new year, 1945, was thick with rumours of victory in Europe, rumours we dared scarcely believe, rumours that seemed too wonderfully good to be true. We had almost forgotten what a world at peace was like: the sheer magic of pavements over which streamed the bright lights of well stocked grocers' shops. So we didn't allow ourselves to hope too much. And there was never a word about derationing or demobbing. Those dreams didn't even enter our minds.

But, quickly, almost diffidently, it came. The impossible overtook us. The black, evil shadow that was Hitler began to shrink, shrink to a bunker in a mass of rubble that was Berlin. May 8th was VE Day. So unbelievable we couldn't rejoice as we felt we should. Besides, the attempts at rejoicing were sternly seasoned with talk of the great conflict raging in the east, of the Japanese beast still to corner.

So on I went as an attempt at a coal miner. To lighten my days I wrote reams of letters: not just RU ones, but countless letters to friends and acquaintances, especially friends from those far-off thirties: Robbie and Tom Glover and Johnny Ryder and Clifford Dyment and James Turner. Somehow, keeping in touch with them was keeping my finger on my teenage pulse, my capricious Streatham roots.

And many later contacts. Not least the intriguing principals of Hadley Manor School in Scotland. I had been in touch with them, or mainly the distaff side, for quite a while. I'd written an article about progressive schools in a journal called *The New Era*. I was under the impression that I had great faith in such schools, chiefly because I worshipped at the shrine of the Romantic Child: all Vaughan and Traherne and Rousseau and Wordsworth and de la Mare. And, of course, Forrest Reid. And one Mrs Cassandra Pike had liked my article, or said she did, and wrote to me to suggest a meeting and, perhaps, eventually a position on their staff. So I had recently said I would go to spend seven days with them in summer, in 'Stand Week,' when the pit was more or less shut down and most men took their annual holiday. This suited me well for I needed to get away, but I could hardly add another Gamble to the horde that had invaded Glad-eye.

23

In mid-June I arrived with my bags at Peebles station: my very first visit to Scotland. Cass met me there, very tall and thin, wearing a large black cloak, extending to me both beringed claw-like hands. As I heard her slow, rather husky American drawl (another first in my personal experiences), I made jumbled comments in my head about these rapid first impressions: 'A real Yankee Edith Sitwell, Tallulah Bankhead dropped amid Scottish heather, and an ugly, overexpansive American jalopy to match.' She stowed me and my bags in the car.

We drove miles. Peebles was soon quite out of sight. Beautiful scenery, nothing but rolling hills and blue-clad mountains and in the distance a silent, shimmering loch. I had forgotten Edith and Tallulah now and could only compare all this with Dracula's coachman meeting Jonathan Harker and whisking him off to the distant, shrouded family castle. I stole a glance at Cass. Yes, she could very well be a vampire: gaunt, patrician, and lips red with (I hoped) lipstick.

She was telling me how eagerly John Roland Dove had been awaiting my arrival. Counting the days, in fact. She had mentioned him in her letters: a young man of twenty-three, a Londoner, a CO, a student of religions, now invalided out of his wartime service into schoolmastering. She smiled darkly and said: 'You'll find out all about him. Intelligent. Courteous. But something of a defector. Like all of them.' She laughed outright. 'You've come to a colourful community, Peter.'

The school was a rather lovely small manor house right below that hilly loch I'd been watching for miles. It had a paucity of furniture. My bedroom consisted of a camp bed, a rickety chair and an upturned packing case as a table. No floor covering other than dust and fluff.

Cass showed me into this with the words: 'I'll leave you here to unpack. The bathroom is just down the passage. Then you may find Roland. He'll be pacing the ground floor. Euan and I will see you and Roland for drinks in the salon at eight. You are very welcome, Peter. Perhaps this is the beginning of a saga. Who knows?' With another Mona Lisa look she swished off.

I couldn't unpack because there was nowhere to put anything except back in my case. Not even a cupboard. I wandered down to the bathroom for a wash and brush up. It was an untidy muddle of pupils' things. I presumably used the same ablutions. I thought of Belvedere and became forever disabused of progressive schools.

I went downstairs and wandered about looking for Roland Dove. I went into a large kitchen filled with hissing, steaming pots tended by a bearded young man who was clearly having nasty words with a young woman who equally clearly was a vegetarian, a pacifist, a fresh air fiend and a martyr. They quite ignored me, so I backed out and continued my Dove hunt.

Then I met him. I knew him at once. A handsome, well-built young man, a trifle clumsy in his movements. But quite at variance with this was the manner of his greeting. After a lightning, almost imperceptible shadow of disappointment, he smiled, he bowed, he held out his hand, he exuded welcome and delight. 'My *dear* fellow, how *wonderful* to meet you at last. Cass has told me almost *daily* all about you, and needless to say I've been absolutely *dying* to meet you. How *are* you? Did you have a good journey? Shall we go for a little stroll before supper? This is *such* a pleasure.'

This effusiveness more than made up for that fleeting cloud on his face when I first appeared. I felt the effusiveness, though unknown to my circle, though even a touch unenglish, was genuine. And as for the cloud, well, I had my own ideas about that, which time might or might not corroborate.

We wandered about in the grounds and ended up on higher ground by the loch, on the banks of which were one or two benches. There we sat and began the stimulating thrust and parry of mutual examination. Yes, he was intelligent. But it wasn't my intelligence. He was well read. But it wasn't my reading. He was interested in philosophy, or rather, theosophy. And in the great Hindu and Buddhist scriptures. And, at that stage in his development, his literary gods were two: Proust and Henry James. I'd never read Proust, and not much James. These differences were an advantage rather than an obstacle. But the ligaments that even on this first meeting began to make themselves felt were supplied by a shared London background (his home was in Wandsworth Common, quite near Streatham), by a bourgeois rebelliousness, by a common, wickedly satirical sense of humour. By the time a great gong boomed incessantly for supper we had sufficiently resolved our relationship to explain its blossoming as the chief friendship of my life.

There weren't many children: about twenty of them, of all sexes (including, it seemed, hermaphroditism) and ages and sizes. Mainly maladjusted, unpredictable, 'difficult,' as were most of the adult community, I felt.

Quite a reasonable supper. And some pleasant enough chats with the kids. One boy of about twelve was very attractive to look at and, with his broad Scots, to listen to. He was known to all as Mitchie. In one week I grew very fond of him, have never forgotten him. He took to me, too. I don't think he knew much affection in his life at that time. I hoped with all my heart he later found it.

After supper, the bearded young man said to us: 'You two off to the witch's cave, I suppose? Don't get burned by the cauldron. Bed at dawn I expect.' And laughing rather scornfully, he went off to the kitchen while we mounted aloft to the salon.

'Mounting aloft' was quite right, for we were entering a more rarefied atmosphere, a more celestial domain. The room was huge and, as if to make up for the bareness of all the other rooms, was positively crammed with every sort of exotic furnishing, but mostly of the Near East: chairs and tables and couches and rugs from Arabia, Persia, Turkey. And almost every inch of wall space lined with books, with large and beautiful books. On a brass table before the great chair in which Cass lounged was an intricate, appetizing coffee machine, surrounded by long-handled brass dispensers. There in a less impressive chair sat, uncomfortably, fretfully, Professor Euan. He was a rather insignificant-looking man, but perhaps only by comparison with his wife, who seemed even more expansive, in a voluminous kaftan with colourful, trailing appendages. Euan, too, was American, but of Scottish extraction. He had been a professor of humanities in America and in Persia. Now he was retired, but how and why they had ended up here I never did discover.

The coffee was delicious, and real Turkish, but the glory of the occasion, of all these late sessions in the salon, was the conversation: the conversation of Euan and Cass. They both knew they were great performers and they both loved a worthwhile audience. Roland and I felt flattered that they presumably felt we were worthwhile.

Discovering I smoked cigarettes, Cass made me some. Not only Turkish, like the coffee, and entirely hand made, but also bearing my name: 'Peter' beautifully inscribed where one's lips would press.

Alas, I don't recall the conversation in any detail: just rich recollections and pronouncements and explorations. And they encouraged us to talk, too, though what of interest I could have said I cannot imagine. We stumbled off to bed at 3 am.

And that happened every night of my week's holiday. Sometimes outside my bedroom door in the morning I would find elegantly tied bundles of my inscribed cigarettes, and sometimes attractively wrapped pieces of Turkish delight and montelimar.

On the top of the beshawled grand piano in the salon were two large framed photos: of two handsome, clean-cut American boys in military uniform. Roland told me these were the Pike boys, but no reference was ever made to them. I wondered if they were war casualties, and their parents had emigrated to Scotland to ease their grief.

Roland and I seemed to spend more and more time on the bench by the loch. One day Cass met us returning from one of our long, deep dialogues there. 'Been up on the conspiratorial bench?' she asked with a little laugh that had no mirth in it. We both felt very guilty, for we had long reached the stage of evaluating Euan and Cass and their really rather questionable school. And we knew they knew it.

Cass got odder, rather silent and depressed. One day she disappeared, hadn't been seen since we all parted at 3 am. Euan spent the day wandering round the grounds with an old shepherd's crook, poking bushes and plumbing pools. He was still doing this some time after we'd seen Cass gliding back into the house. We told him we'd seen her: she was all right. 'She never told me she was back,' he said in his usual querulous tones. 'After all,' he added, 'I am the principal, aren't I?'

All classes at the school were voluntary, so I did no real teaching there. No one did. Cass told me of the apparently marvellous young man into whose shoes she hoped I would one day step. He was called Hugo, and he was a transvestite. 'Sometimes he would come to teach them dressed as a young man, sometimes as a girl, and I must say he looked very nice as either. There was nothing slovenly about Hugo. Always clean and neat. So good for the children. The element of surprise, you know.'

That conversation put the lid on Cass's school so far as I was concerned, although I had already decided it was not for me. Perhaps I was not worthy of it.

On my last night, they had a grand ceilidh. I remember Mitchie doing a Scottish sword dance, which I thought was absolutely enchanting. And Cass and Roland gave a performance of the *Ballad of Lord Randal*, Cass as the mother and Roland as the son. I thought it was pretty good. I remember being privately astonished that Roland could act upon a stage: something I could never in a thousand years encompass.

When I left on the Sunday, it was with vows of reunion between Roland and me. At the same time it was clear between Cass and me, though unavowed, that I would not be joining her staff. Indeed, I never saw her or any of them again. I have always regretted losing touch with them.

24

That was Stand Week, 1945. I went back to the pit with more reluctance than ever. Not only because of the work but also because of the loneliness. Brian Sadler still enlivened Friday evenings, thank goodness. And I had a new job in the pit and a new mate. The job was running in empty tubs under the chute from the coalface, and running out full ones. Not a bad job, but very boring. Mick was my mate: aged sixteen, with high cheek bones and rather almond eyes that reminded me of Julien. I taught Mick Roman numerals. He had to chalk up the number of tubs we filled and he became adept at doing it classical fashion. The deputy was very angry when he saw it, but when we explained the system he too studied it till he could do it well. Like so many miners, he had a real hunger for education.

Mick had all the swagger of a hardened miner, with vocal tones and vocabulary to match. He always referred to his girlfriend as 'our woman,' and had a sort of caveman attitude towards her. He told me his girlfriend had said his Roman numerals were 'just daft.' 'What did you say to that?' I asked. 'Nothing,' he replied with grim satisfaction. 'I belted her one.'

But even Mick couldn't reconcile me to the pit. Then one day I received a blow that made it all ten times worse. For half my income disappeared. All my RU work ceased. I had had to read and report on a certain novel RU was considering as one of its monthly choices. I was late in reporting, and when I did send in my report it was definitely thumbs down. I remember the novel well, for I disliked it so much. And it cost me so much! It was *The Power House*, by Alex Comfort. Part of my irritation with it was due to my genuine desire to like it. I certainly liked, and approved of, Alex Comfort. But worst of all, my nasty report arrived at RU after the book had been bought and paid for. JB, tired of waiting, had assumed my recommendation. In a fury, he wrote sacking me.

I poured out my bitterness to Roland Dove in Scotland. We were now prolific correspondents. Where and how he unearthed the bizarre people he wrote such rich letters to and about, I don't know. Some were distinguished academicians, some were fringe philosophers, some unorthodox clergy. His comments on them and their views were hilarious. In one letter I asked him if I had been right in my interpretation of his first fleeting glance of disappointment when we met. It took much soliciting on my part to get the truth from him, for above all else he hated passing an uncivil remark. His reaction had been purely aesthetic. 'You are, my dear fellow, a very handsome man. But, well, to be honest, I think it was that moustache of yours.'

He also told me he was leaving Hadley Manor for good. In a fortnight. He was going home, to London, and was looking for another, but saner, school job there. He'd had schoolmastering added as a CO condition after he'd been invalided out of some guinea-pig medical work he'd been embroiled in. I was envious of his teaching condition, something I longed for. He suspected this and filled his letters with extravagant predictions of my imminent release. Then London, and a school job, and endless meetings and conversations and adventures.

About this time we had the great postwar general election. I found I was quite passionately left-wing. Everything liberal and humane I saw in the Labour Party. Only they could direct this brave new world that beckoned us. I remember the feverish excitement down the pit as the results began to flood in. On the sides of the tubs at the pit top the men would chalk each set of results, and as soon as the tubs arrived at the pit bottom a great cheer would go up from the men working there. And these cheers would be raggedly echoed all through the pit as the tubs rattled on. I identified myself completely with my mates in not wanting a postwar Britain run by Churchill.

The loss of my RU income, plus the worldwide stirrings of armistice, goaded me on to seek other part-time employment. And on only one kind was my heart set. Surely, I said to myself, surely there is not far from Chesterfield a nice prep school that will jump at my offer: morning, nine to twelve, every day. I could get back to the pit in time for 'afters.' So in Chesterfield public library I pored over *The Public & Preparatory Schools Year Book*, and all sorts of maps and all sorts of timetables. I found a school I liked the look of and which seemed reasonably accessible: bus to Chesterfield, train north from there, then another bus. So I wrote to the headmaster (noting approvingly that he was not only an MA Cantab but a Hon: what glory!), and he replied by return, calling me to an interview.

Of course, any prep school would have been nectar to my long-deprived, coal-encrusted lips, but Kingsholme was a truly nice school, and the Hon Head was also most agreeable. I told him I was a miner and a CO: two pills he never thought he would have to swallow. He took it well, making it clear he could never share my views, but he had a hundred boys desperately in need of good tuition in Latin and English, and their Common Entrance due next summer. Could I do it?

Oh, magnificently! So it was clinched (subject to his contacting Belvedere). Could I start next month (it was August, 1945)? Of course I could.

So he took me round the place. There was one classroom with about a dozen boys in it, for holiday coaching. I remember that classroom for something almost uncanny happened there. The Hon Head knocked on the door and briskly flung it open. And I found myself gazing, instantly, unerringly, deeply into a pair of blue eyes. Neither of us had to find the other's eyes. It was as though we had found them, fixed them, before ever the door was opened. We had made contact through several inches of oak. No other person or thing did I see in that first instant, nor did he. I had the strangest sensation that all had been fixed for us in advance. So beautiful was the owner of these eyes that I felt only he could break the spell. He did so by colouring perceptibly and lowering his gaze to the ink-stained floorboards.

Very soon the Hon Head wrote to say that he had received a most satisfactory letter from Belvedere, and that he herewith formally appointed me to his staff. He only hoped I could manage both jobs without cracking up.

How long the new term took in coming. And how terribly that August was stained by the unleashing of humanity's first atom bombs. I could not

208

for one minute accept the argument that such hideous destruction and maiming were justified in terms of all the Allied lives saved. But who was I to say so? Or to express my outrage that the new Labour Government, that Clem Attlee and his men, could be the purveyors of near genocide.

Civil Defence, prison, mines. It seemed the long pilgrimage was drawing to its end. V-J Day had followed V-E. Now reconstruction must succeed devastation. It had never comforted anyone I knew to be shown the terrible destruction of Hamburg, Dresden, Berlin.

25

Mid-September came at last and I began my mad journeys, rising now almost as early as I had when on the day shift. But now not only up with the lark but as blithe as he. Even scooting back down at 2.30 pm was light-hearted enough, for in about sixteen hours I would be once more winging my way back to the light. Like Uriel. To be teaching again was the remedy for all ills. It was simply, but marvellously, a matter of sharing one's joys.

They were delightful boys, mostly the sons of doctors and solicitors and clergy. Full of impish fun, but also working with a will. I got my seniors enthused, like me, on Vergil and Shakespeare. To the others I introduced Rider Haggard and Sherlock Holmes and every good ghost story I could lay my hands on. All between dashes for buses and trains. I liked to get to school in time for assembly, for at that the Hon Head, who was also an accomplished musician, taught the boys hymns I often liked. One such I have never ceased to love, especially if sung, as then, by a group of good trebles. That was the setting of Masefield's 'The Everlasting Mercy' to the tune Gonfalon Royal.

About halfway through the term I heard from the family that father and Pam between them had secured a little furnished house near the Crystal Palace, at a rent that needed us all to pull together. I was able to send them some money, Brian a little, and Pam got a part-time job in a riding school. It was all going to wait for me when the term ended: I couldn't get away before.

I became obsessed by the thought of a real holiday at the end of term, in fact, of getting out of mining altogether and re-entering full-time schoolmastering, as, indeed, the Hon Head greatly desired. So, assisted by him and Dr Raymond Greene, I applied for a new tribunal to add teaching to my list of conditions.

My tribunal was fixed for November, in Derby, another town I had never before visited. I wasn't too hopeful. It seemed too *sane* a thing to come about, for the world had been mad and cruel and dark for so long. Still, the doctor had written the tribunal a letter to say I was medically not much use to the pit, and the Hon Head had written one to say I was a very successful teacher and my charges desperately needed me. To my surprise it all worked, quickly and easily. Not only that, but to my astonishment the chairman added these words before I stepped down: 'We should like to say, Mr Gamble, that you did your best for as long as you could.'

I really wondered if I had heard aright. I was so used to disapproval and contempt from CO tribunals that these words of theirs seemed wholly out of character. My surprise was followed by guilt, as if I had in some way cheated them.

I came out of the courtroom into the unfamiliar streets of Derby as into an auroral landscape, a new and hope-filled world. I was free. Peace had come.

The Hon Head was delighted. He arranged for me to move in next term. And I had to break the news to my wonderful landlady that I should soon be leaving.

I remember my last day down under. At the end of the shift I pulled Mick on to my knees in a dark corner and said: 'Take your helmet off.'

'What for?' he asked, in his gruff but expectant tones. He was used to crazy assaults from me.

'Because,' I said, taking off my own helmet, 'I'm going to kiss you goodbye, and you can't kiss properly with helmets on.'

He guffawed. 'Tha' mad booger, Pete. What tha' want to kiss me for?'

'Because you're nice. Now come on, I haven't got all night.'

Laughing but fully compliant, he removed his helmet, embraced me and began a series of quite rewarding kisses. In one of the intervals I said: 'You're a dear Mick and I shall miss you very much.' And he said: 'I'll miss thee, too, Pete.'

I mention this not only because it is a sharp, vivid memory, but also because it exhibits how ready, how gentle, how natural, such an encounter can be with the unlikeliest person.

I never saw Mick again, nor was I able to say goodbye to Colin or Geoff. I did take my farewells, surprisingly kind ones, of many old mates, even of Mr Twining the undermanager. Neither of us even hinted at our last brush, some six months earlier, when I'd led a little strike, refusing to work in water, and leading a posse of men and lads to tell Mr Twining so. It was, I knew, artificially created work to keep busy those men who had *not* absented themselves to attend a big football match. I didn't see why we should be penalized just for reporting for work. But Mr Twining was, of course, equal to the occasion. 'That's all reet, Peter,' he said kindly. 'I'll find thee something else.' Which he did. Eurystheus didn't do better by Hercules.

It meant lying on one's side before a deafening machine at the end of the coalface: a machine which worked the conveyor belt and ground to a halt whenever (roughly every ten minutes) it became clogged with coal dust.

Freeing it again made the Augean stables kid's stuff to my mind. I was released from it after three weeks, wondering who normally did the job. Was it reserved for criminals?

But my fame spread after that little strike. I think it marked my acceptance in the pit. I became 'the booger with the 'tache.' So my farewells when they came were more than perfunctory. Alf, one of the deputies (the one who had learned to use Roman numerals) said: 'I suppose at home you've got a study? With a beroo?' I had no idea what a beroo was, until further questions elucidated it: 'With lots of drawers? And a flap you can pull out?' I didn't want to laugh. It was somehow both touching and gallant.

I wrote a long letter to *The Derbyshire Times*, paying my grateful respects to all the miners I'd worked with, all the folk I'd lived with. They printed it on the front page headed: 'Schoolmaster's Tribute to Miners.' Several years later I met one of my old mates having a day in London, and he told me that letter was pasted up in the pit bottom. Perhaps it's still there!

As soon as the term ended, the Hon Head drove over to my digs in Bolsover and collected all my things for storage at the school, ready for the new term in January. That left me a few days with the Sadlers. Not a final Friday night with Brian. But perhaps that was as well, for a change had been coming over Brian of late. He had started work, and he had actually managed to exchange two or three words with me. All along his communion with me had been made up of half-nelsons, slaps and tickles, not words: eager and demonstrative and full of giggles, but too shy for any verbal intercourse. But on my last night with him, as we sat on downstairs after all the others had gone to bed, he became almost eloquent, telling me all about his job and his girlfriend and his hopes and plans. It was astonishing. And I felt very happy for I was sure I had helped to bring it about. All those silent communings on Friday nights had loosened the terribly shy boy's tongue. I genuinely felt I had done him good. I hope he can look back and feel the same.

Mrs Sadler's last words included a sudden challenge that alarmed me: 'Eh, tha' wicked booger, what tha' mean by telling everybody I was fat?'

'Whatever do you mean?' I asked.

'Tha' knows. In t'paper. I'll show thee.' She produced *The Derbyshire Times* with my 'tribute' in it. And among the tributes I paid was one to 'my indefatigable landlady.' I explained and we had a long laugh over it. They were a fine family.

As I packed on my last morning in Bolsover, I told myself that this was another watershed in my life and I ought to be experiencing it more acutely. There should be at least a few twinges of regret, of sadness, of gratitude, for this had been my home for two years, the setting for some pretty indelible incidents. But the plain, and not very pleasant, truth was that I could only rejoice to be leaving forever a place where I had known more essential loneliness than ever before. Now I was a schoolmaster again, now I was starting my Christmas holidays, now I was off to a new home, the family's home, in London. No, silly to pretend I was anything but excited and very happy.

I liked the new home the instant I first saw it: fairly small, rural-looking, with quite a sizeable garden and a crop of rather attractive outbuildings. But I liked it even more when I lived in it, for it had a happy atmosphere. I was told that it had been the home of a Miss Lodge, a relative of Sir Oliver Lodge, who had himself often stayed there. If this was correct, they must have been very agreeable people, as also must have been any spooks Sir Oliver invoked, for he was the noted spiritualist. The house was called Harmenleen (I don't know why), was pleasantly furnished, and was, I think, the happiest place we ever lived in. It was in a quiet cul-de-sac but a stone's throw from the shops, and only a few minutes away was the great Crystal Palace Parade. I remembered the exciting days Billy and I had spent there long ago, and how in my teens, from the top of our road, I had seen the poor old Palace savagely ablaze.

We soon exhausted what the district had to offer in the way of shops and restaurants and cafés, which was not much. Usually, Pam and I would catch the bus to our old stamping-grounds in Streatham, there to meet up with Jonathan, or sometimes Robbie, who was now in some military establishment's drawing office and got most weekends at home. Once Roland Dove had joined us all for our long-established Sunday morning coffee session. He had clearly not enjoyed himself, but his farewells were congenial and effusive as ever. Indeed, only I could tell from the narrowed eyes and the toothpaste smile that he was seething, though what about I could not imagine. When I met him that evening he told me he thought my friends were uncouth: they had not given him the attention, the consideration, the courtesy, he had tried to give them. Moreover, the whole occasion was clearly an opportunity for them all to pay court to me. Well, he would never attend such a function again. It took me years to realize that he could never share me with anyone, never even fit occasionally into any ambience that was mine. I found it very strange, but I had to accept it.

I saw much of Derrick, too. He was now, just like Graham, just like Brian, doing hospital work. I wondered if I could have changed to such work long ago, instead of knuckling down to the mines. Oh well, too late now. What's more, *now* I didn't regret a moment of it: Colin and Geoff and Mick and the showers. Already the nostalgia was beginning to work.

My life was once more shaping as a repository of friendships. And the bleak background of war-scarred London just made those friendships the warmer and more precious. London's dirty, ravaged face was in itself lovable. There it stood yet, my dear metropolis, with every fourth or fifth house a gaping wound, a rotten tooth among serviceable ones, with static water tanks on bomb sites, and with already a prefab home or two springing up. My city, fairer to me in all its afflictions than the loveliest, heather-clad hills of Yorkshire or Derbyshire.

26

In mid-January, straight from the feast of London to the feast of Kingsholme. Now resident and full-time. I positively threw myself into that teaching. My timetable was expanded, of course: a little more time with my seniors, and nets cast wider in the lower school. But I had no friendships among my colleagues at the school. Prep-school masters were a definite type, and it wasn't my type at all. They clung to Toryism, to every kind of conventionality, because it was all they had. And even if their lessons rubbed shoulders with culture, they were essentially Philistines. Church, women, beer, organized games. Well, so they seemed to me. If they were middle-aged or more I could accept, even mildly enjoy, their moulds. But not if they were young men in their twenties or thirties. Like Price, who was about twenty-eight and insufferably, stupidly, of the Establishment. An admirer of militarism, capital punishment and the Boy Scout movement, he was destined to clash with me. I saw in him every unhealthy threat to boyhood. He saw in me not only a despised radical but a challenge to his whole standing in the school. I can feel sorry for him now, and dislike my own exploitation of the new young master's popularity. But I couldn't then.

For my fifth and sixth form boys this was their decisive year, its climax being Common Entrance or scholarships. Their Latin was pretty ropy, even that of the bright boys, for they'd had years of poor and broken teaching. In those days Latin was still one of the star subjects for public school aspirants, and really wise parents chose prep schools whose headmasters were classicists, for headmasters rarely change. Otherwise, Latin is taught by a succession of young chaps who don't know how to teach and are often just filling in time before going to university. That's how it must have been at Kingsholme, for the Hon Head was an historian. So I had a great deal of undoing as well as a great deal of doing in my Latin classes. The bright ones responded easily and well, while the less able found it hard going. But they nearly all worked with a will, and I think I got more joy out of the lame ducks' first flights than out of the clever ones' little triumphs. The less able often had evening tuition with me: good for them and extra money for me.

And the boy with the blue eyes who had first seen me right through the heavy classroom door? He was one of my fifth-formers: not very bright where Latin was concerned, but, like nearly all of them, a worker, a trier, a boy with a goal. And *very* beautiful.

His name was Janssen, Carl Janssen. His father was Dutch, his mother English. He was a tall boy who remained in shorts rather beyond his years. He would sit in my class, his shorts hitched up, his legs wide apart, and glower at me behind lashes that with maddening skill offset those blue eyes. But he kept his distance. He never seemed to enter the classroom without half a dozen fellows, and he was the first to leave it at the end of a period. I felt sure I knew why: adults had wooed him from early years, schoolmasters had petted him, unwelcome attentions had often come his way. So he was very cagey. I should never get to know him.

But the Eumenides, carefully concealing their other identities, were positively eating from my hands. For Carl's parents felt he badly needed extra tuition from me in the evenings. Rather to my surprise, Carl himself seemed quite agreeable. But I was intrigued by his arrival for the very first lesson, at 5.30 pm on a balmy day in early spring. He was for the first time in long trousers, and he carefully decided where he would sit: not on a chair beside me at my master's desk, but in a pupil's desk facing and abutting mine, so that I had to gaze for an hour into those eyes.

We worked hard, but our labours were, as was my custom, interlarded with little jokes and pleasantries. Surely he had from the first known I was attracted to him, and now knew that I was wanting to flirt with him verbally? More surprisingly, I felt he wanted to flirt with me, was in fact capable of positively coquettish behaviour. As the weeks went by I became intrigued, then bewitched, then enslaved. I knew I had fallen, fallen badly. I didn't know the danger I was in.

Still, I got through that Easter term without mishap and went home for another happy month with family and friends in cherished old haunts. Yet even there I often mused on, and pined for, that little jewel I'd left behind. I could talk to Jonathan about him, and, of course, to Brian, who was now driving some heavy goods vehicle and fretting in his wildly unsuitable role as a husband.

I didn't like leaving London, but I loved the school and I loved my work. And, in a variety of ways, I loved my pupils. I vividly remember having elevenses in the staff room on that first day of term, and gazing out of the window at hosts of boys kicking about a tennis ball in the playgound. I had an eye only for Carl's rather elegant eurhythmics. So it seemed had the plump young matron who suddenly said: 'That Janssen's far too pretty for a boy. Such looks are wasted on a boy.' Apart from my involuntary blush of guilt, which I hoped no one noticed, I felt extremely irritated by the woman's conventional judgment. As if the gods had slipped up in giving beauty to a boy, when in fact they had distilled something rarer and finer.

Not, I must here be at pains to explain, that Carl's looks were at all insipid, doll-like, over-smooth. He had just enough disorder of feature to

214

create a wantonness that was an essential part of his allure. His mouth was slightly crooked when he smiled, there was a small, age-old scar on one cheek, and he commonly focused one with lowered head and eyes uptilted in their sockets. He had that curious sultry, cadlike charm that had distinguished Carter many years before.

The school was really too 'pi' for me. The Hon Head said prayers at assembly with rather more fervour, and at rather greater length, than I could stomach. I used on such occasions to feed my irritation by watching awful Price with his tightly screwed eyes and blubbery, moving lips. They all trooped off to church on a Sunday. The Hon Head had asked me if I'd care to join them, and been rather taken aback by the readiness of my refusal. He had an elderly, faded sister-in-law who taught French and who died daily, and extravagantly, to sin. And, of course, Price had regular earnest sessions with his Scouts. He would spread a large Union Jack over his master's desk and on it place one lighted candle. Over this they would pray, meditate and then confess their sins to one another. I had this from one of my seniors who had attended once but was too intelligent to continue.

I was initially rather a puzzle to the boys (and even to myself): an undoubted disciplinarian, but one with an unquenchable hankering after subversive fun. I loved a joke and even 'cheek' from them, provided it was affectionate and never ill mannered.

All my after-tea coaching sessions seem, as I look back on them, to have some romantic aura to them. It was a lovely summer, the classroom was cool and intimate, and in through the window drifted a summer music: the sounds of the remote cricket nets mingled with those of birds and bees and far-off dogs. But the most romantic sessions, of course, were those with Carl. And one day, one fatal day, I said to him: 'If you get the next sentence wrong, you'll have to pay a forfeit.'

He looked at me with a smile. 'What sort of forfeit?' he asked.

'Oh, I don't know,' I replied rather shakily. 'I suppose something awful like a kiss. That's the usual forfeit in party games.'

He worked carefully at that sentence. The faulty subjunctive in it was certainly not deliberate. Neither of us mentioned the forfeit, not until the lesson was done and he had picked up his books and was heading for the door. Then, closing my ears to the warning bells that clanged within them, I said: 'Oh, but don't you owe me something?' He stopped, leaned smiling against the wall, and very deliberately pursed his lips to receive mine. I leaned forward. Our lips had almost met when with great deftness he inserted his exercise book between our mouths. So deftly that it was too late to prevent my lips from brushing Messrs Philip and Tacey's limp green cover. I had to laugh at the skill with which he did it. 'That's cheating,' I said. But already he was through the doorway, and his merry 'Night, sir' was ringing up the stairs.

Next morning I was taking the fifth, Carl's form, first period. He sat next to his friend Hawkins, a pleasant enough boy of a rather unprepossessing appearance (do beauties deliberately choose plain friends?). I became aware that Hawkins was trying to say something and Carl was trying to stop him. Both were suppressing giggles. Never guessing, I paused and said to Hawkins: 'Well, come on, share it with the rest of us.' And Hawkins blurted out: 'Please, sir, did you enjoy Janssen's kiss?'

The blood at once suffused my cheeks, so I turned quickly and began to cover the board with a lot of unnecessary Latin. As I did so, I said in tones as offhand and unconcerned as I could command: 'Oh, don't be silly. Now, come on, get this down.' Only when my face was nearer its usual colour could I turn back to the class, and then with a sickening conviction I'd behold a set of knowing glances and nasty smirks. But there was no hint of any such thing. Their smiles and giggles had died away: they were seriously intent on copying from the blackboard.

Was it because they all genuinely thought the episode so trivial as not to be worth another laugh? Or was it a gentlemanly concern for my embarrassment, a loyal awareness that the matter should never have been broached? Were they utterly innocent of the implications? Or only too aware of them? I could not then and cannot now decide the answers to those questions. All I knew for sure was that I had had a lucky escape. Or so I thought.

The next day after lunch the Hon Head asked me to call at his study in a few minutes. He often did this. He liked to discuss with me the boys and their problems.

So it was that I entered his room with my usual ease and self-confidence, and settled myself in the brown leather chair. He came instantly to the point.

'Now, Gamble, what's this I hear about you kissing Janssen?'

For a moment that seemed suspended in eternity my mind raced up and down corridors of thought. But my voice, almost disembodied, was obeying the call to utter *something*. 'Oh that,' I heard myself saying, even with a little easy laugh, 'I didn't think anything of that.'

'Well, I'm afraid I do. Good God, Gamble, you must know what people will say? Price heard some boys talking about it.'

'But I didn't kiss him,' I replied. I told him of the forfeit game, of the interposed exercise book. I knew it was no excuse, no exoneration.

'To Janssen perhaps just a silly joke,' he replied with more astuteness than I'd given him credit for. 'But to you? What was it to you?' Before I could think of a reply, he hurried on: 'Any parent hearing of this will assume

Three Brothers: Peter aged three with Terry and Brian, *c.*1923

The same three brothers at Peter's farewell party at Harrow School, 1982

Peter and Pam at Ripon Hall,
Oxford, 1950 or 1951

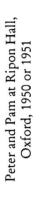

Mother with Peter,
aged four, c.1924

Father and Pam, 1950

Peter Gamble, *c.*1948

Harvey Guthrie and Peter, at Harvey's wedding, 1951

John Roland Dove, 1944

David Lockwood, Jersey, in 1983

Bishop E. W. Barnes, Bishop of Birmingham,
in conversation with Professor Ryle in 1952.
Photograph courtesy of the Hulton Deutsch Collection Ltd.

Milton Abbey and School, *c.*1960

Milton Abbey School: headmaster and housemasters, 1957

Milton Abbey School: athletics team, 1958

Walter de la Mare (1873-1956), photograph by Howard Coster
reproduced courtesy of the National Portrait Gallery, London

Forrest Reid (1876-1947), photograph reproduced
courtesy of Hulton Deutsch Collection Ltd.

Harry Guest at a Poetry Reading, Durham, 1975

Derrick Harris, c.1957

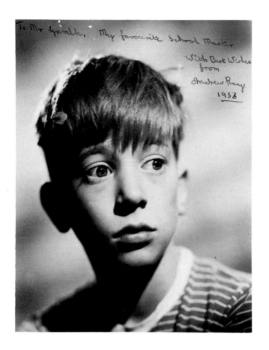

To Mr Gamble, My favourite school Master
With Best Wishes
from
Andrew Ray
1953

Pupils and Friends, 1940-1980

Pupils and Friends, 1940-1980

Harrow School: a small new boy encounters the Head of School (the small new boy is Randolph Churchill, great-grandson of Sir Winston Churchill), in 1981

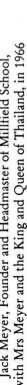

Jack Meyer, Founder and Headmaster of Millfield School, with Mrs Meyer and the King and Queen of Thailand, in 1966

Opening Ceremony of the Anglo-American College, 1968, by the Hon. Cornelius Van H. Engert, CBE. From the left: John Roland Dove, David Carver and Peter Gamble. Extreme right: John Paxton. Photograph courtesy of the *Oxford Mail and Times*

Anglo-American College: the Quadrangle

Adrian Room and Brian Gamble
at Anglo-American College in 1970

Nikolas Jon Powis
during the Anglo-American period

Christopher Headington, c.1970

Terry Gamble with Robin
Miles Powis, in 1970

Roger Mills, on location in the desert, during the Moroccan-Algerian War
in the late 1960s

Harrow School: Farewell party to Peter Gamble in 1982

John Ryder and Peter, *c.*1985

I have on my staff one of those, those...' He stumbled over the terrible word and could produce it only sotto voce: 'Those homosexuals.'

Now I reached a decision. A new pride sustained me. I had been beginning to despise myself. Not for what I essentially was but for the crafty dissembler events were conspiring to make me. Almost with self-detachment, I decided he should never pin on me the label of liar beside that other label he'd just decorated me with. Coolly, I made a mental comparison of myself with Wilde, refusing the royal yacht in which to make his escape.

I said quietly: 'Well, that's just what I am.' Now my whole world must collapse: school and home and all I held dear.

But with a sudden impulsive gesture, that good and circumscribed man leaned forward and touched my arm. 'Oh, my dear Gamble,' he blurted out, 'I am so sorry... so sorry.' It was as though I had confessed to having terminal cancer.

'What a waste,' he was saying. 'What can we do?'

'Well,' I said with complete truth, 'I just want to go. At once. Tomorrow morning.'

Perhaps they were Eumenides after all? For I couldn't, without ever meaning to, have more surely saved myself.

'Oh no,' he was saying. 'Not that. You mustn't go. These boys need you. Their exams... You must finish the term.'

He became more practical. 'It would be absurd to make a song and dance about this. That would do more harm than good. I'll see Janssen and tell him it was all a silly joke. Best forgotten. He's a sensible boy. Er... do you really... I mean, are you really fond of him?'

'Yes. I'm afraid I am.'

'A pity. In many ways it would be better if the attraction were purely... I mean, were not in any way emotional.'

So many of his words were sensible, so many were straight out of the *Boy's Own Paper* of an earlier age.

'The parents. Now, should I tell the parents?' I knew I really would leave in the morning if he did any such thing. 'How culpable would I be if I failed to tell them?' he mused. 'If I don't tell them and the boy himself does?' Then he abruptly demanded: 'You will, of course, give me your word that nothing like this will ever happen again here? With Janssen or any other boy? And these private lessons. I think if you have the window and door wide open: a cool draught right through the room, you know. And if you are, should ever be... ah, um, tempted as it were, a brisk walk round the garden, perhaps.'

All this while I was staring at the carpet in acute discomfort. I just longed to escape. I assented to all he said, confirmed my desire to leave at the end of the term, and extricated myself at last more intact than I would have thought possible.

217

The Hon Head never told anybody about it. No boy ever mentioned it again, so far as I knew. And Carl certainly never told his parents. With me, he continued much as before: industrious, teasing, seemingly unaware of all that had passed.

As for Price, he confined communion with me to the merest salutations, and carefully avoided my eye. I was glad that at least he couldn't write me off as a gay deceiver.

27

The term, for the first time in any school, dragged for me. I wanted to be away. Well, my pupils all passed their Common Entrance, and there were two scholarships. The term ended with sports day. After the athletic chores were done, I rested on a great roller in a corner of the sunlit field. It was hot and everyone was agreeably fatigued.

The scene was colourful and the atmosphere one of indulgence. The mothers had enjoyed their dressing-up, their surprisingly successful defiance of the clothing coupon. The fathers had enjoyed their displays of jolly good sportsmanship in the fathers' race. And even the plainest boys were charming studies, with their tanned and rounded limbs draped in virginal white.

It all took on the kind of beauty I loved best. It was suffused with valediction. The happy day was now declining. The sun's rays, still powerful, were oblique through the great elms and oaks that skirted the field. For me, it was farewell not only to the school but also to a region fair and hospitable. And for all my seniors, bound for their public schools, it was goodbye to untrammelled boyhood.

Suddenly, Carl came and perched beside me on the roller. With an instinctive and guilty reaction that irritated me, I looked around for the Hon Head. He was the other side of the field, busy with the presentations table.

Carl looked at me. The sun had tanned his skin and bleached his hair. And in scanty shorts and with bare feet he seemed as leggy as a newborn colt.

'Well, goodbye,' he said cheerfully. 'Thanks for all the help.'

'We're both leaving all this,' I said. 'You for Uppingham and me for London. Are you sorry?' I was fishing, I knew, for just a hint of regret in his goodbye. And I knew it was dangerous.

'No fear. I'm glad to get away. Had enough of it. Uppingham's pretty good at rugger, you know.'

'I shall miss you,' I murmured. (Would I never learn?)

'Will you?' He was surprised, but clearly pleased.

'Look,' I said desperately. 'I'm here for a few days yet. Will you come out with me one day? We could have lunch somewhere nice, then see a film.' It was the same old game: the striving to sound casual, offhand, when every nerve of heart and head hung on the response.

'That'll be super. Thanks very much.' He seemed genuinely enthusiastic.

'But your parents must give their consent, you know.'

'Oh.' He jumped up. 'That's what I came over for. They want to meet you.'

The parents were... just parents. Mother was very pretty, father quite plain. They laboured their gratitude: I had been a great help to Carl; Carl thought very highly of me; how extraordinarily kind of me to take him out on Tuesday; would I come to dinner that evening, or any evening that suited me? I arranged to dine with them on the day after our outing, which I didn't want to spoil with other duties.

Now we were to gather round the pavilion for speeches and prizegivings. After reviewing the school's year, and saying they had never had a more successful record academically, the Hon Head went on: 'I want, of course, to thank *all* my staff for their hard work, but I know they and you will want me to single out for special mention Mr Gamble, whose work in Latin and English has played a leading part in this year's successes. The boys have greatly enjoyed his teaching. They will miss him. He leaves us to return to London where his home is, his family are.'

Quite a volley of applause followed this. In all my embarrassment, and my sense of the Hon Head's great kindness and generosity, I was secretly rehearsing a sardonic response: 'Grateful as I am to the headmaster, I must set the record straight in one particular. I am not leaving here because I wish to live in London but because I love your sons too well. Indeed, I arranged to kiss one of them earlier in the term.'

But no. Just endless handshakes, and many presents. And one little boy, now a leading GP in that town, came up to say goodbye and burst into tears.

For our day out, Carl and I went to Leeds, partly because I didn't know the town, and partly because it had more than one five-star hotel for lunch. I also thought a real change of scene would help us lose our master-pupil relationship. But there was no sign of it. We were just friends. Carl was completely uninhibited and thoroughly enjoyed himself. He stuffed himself in the Grand Hotel and laughed his head off in the cinema.

In the train coming home he was rather sleepy and at one point laid his head on my shoulder as the preliminary to a snooze. It thrilled me. It appealed to the fraternal and even the paternal, which was always an element in these friendships. But before we arrived he suddenly sat up and did something even more unforgettable. He kissed me firmly on the lips and said: 'Thanks for a super day.' I instinctively, gently, recoiled. I was so unprepared for it. And so nervous, too, for though we had the compartment to ourselves it was a corridor train.

He seemed a little surprised, even a little hurt. 'Didn't you like it?' he asked anxiously. 'Didn't I do it properly?'

219

'You were splendid,' I rejoined. 'Ten out of ten. I just thought my moustache might tickle you.'

He laughed. 'You know what they say: a kiss without a moustache is like beef without mustard.'

It was my turn to be surprised. 'Where on earth did you hear that?' I asked.

'Oh, it's one of mother's sayings.'

I glimpsed a new picture of that pretty mother. And of her surprising son. I'd always had this idea of him as basically aloof, guarded, unapproachable. Now he seemed suddenly to have accepted me, lowered all defences, gladly paid the forfeit. Or was I exaggerating everything?

The next day I had dinner with Carl and his pleasant parents. In the hall I said goodbye to them all.

'Good luck at Uppingham,' I said to Carl as I formally shook his hand. But even there I couldn't resist one tiny appeal, dressing it in tones as indifferent as a comment on the weather. 'Drop me a line some time and let me know how you're getting on. If you feel like it.' And he said: 'Sure.'

And that, I said to myself, rubbing salt into my wounds, was that. The end of the Janssen saga. He would not write. How could you expect any boy, amid the thrills and fears and wonders of his new public school world, to remember a fleeting figure from his childhood? In spite of the kiss. In spite of my London address I'd given him on the train.

But I was quite wrong.

28

Back to Miss Lodge's Harmenleen for the remainder of a fine summer. Indeed, in my memory it is always summer there, and doors are always open on to the garden, and Miles runs in and out, and cats have litters in the outhouses.

I had no difficulty in getting another prep school job, using as testimonial the letter the Hon Head had written to my last tribunal. I selected carefully from the *Public & Preparatory Schools Year Book*. An IAPS school of course, with an Oxbridge head, and no suggestions of a bossy wife or imperialist staff or unnatural kids.

This new school, Walton's, was near Banstead. I took a trolleybus from the Crystal Palace to Sutton, and another bus from there to Walton-on-the-Hill. Quite a journey, but I didn't mind that. Especially after I'd met Jimmy, as I later came to call the headmaster. That was Mr Jamieson, who was ancient and huge and very much 'one of the old school.' I took to him, and I felt he took to me.

He is the most memorable in my gallery of headmasters. A bachelor, he lived in Edwardian splendour and guarded seclusion. The school was mostly a day school, and his house adjoined the sprawling buildings which taught and fed the hundred and fifty boys in his care. The manservant, Salts, tended his master's well-dressed but frugally tasted board, for Jimmy never ate with school or staff. When I knew him he did no teaching, either. He was eternally emerging from, and disappearing into, his dark, lace-curtained house. He was about seven foot tall and very heavily built. He wore at all times a trilby hat. When he went into his house, his hat brim was correctly lowered and his face mild and sallow. When he emerged, his hat brim was absurdly turned up, like a Yankee comedian's, and his face was puce. We all knew, staff and boys, that he entered the house to quaff whisky, and we also knew that when he came out he was dangerous, on the warpath, roaring, and cuffing heads. Staff disappeared into their common room and boys scattered to playground recesses. We knew that if we had anything at all to say to him, it must be done on one of his homeward journeys. Woe betide any master or boy who accosted him when the drawbridge was lowered and the dragon came forth. The master was bellowed at and the boy had his ears boxed, that is, if Jimmy could aim straight, which was mercifully not often on such occasions.

He despised most of his staff and nearly all his parents. He told me once: 'That boy's mother said to me: "I want my boy to go to Heton", and I said: "What's the matter with 'Arrer?"' He assumed that all the world lived, like him, for cricket. He physically assaulted members of his first eleven who lost a match, and once, before my eyes, he impulsively raised his hand to a shrinking young master who had coached his losing team.

Once, long, long ago, rifle practice had figured in the curriculum, and in Jimmy's befumed, emergent head it still did. In one corner of the playground still stood the old, decaying, rifle butts, and to get between the phantom marksmen and those butts was the most heinous of crimes. Not, I imagine, because of danger to the victim, but because of obstruction to the marksmen, all in training for the Indian frontier. Jimmy would shake his poor culprit like a rat as he bellowed: 'Keep away from those butts!' I don't think any boy questioned the sacrosanct nature of those butts. It was just one of Jimmy's laws, as unquestionable as the Almighty's.

In cold weather Jimmy wore a long, tubular overcoat, so long and so unvented that he could take only the shortest of steps in it. Once he told me the story of this overcoat, of the difficulty he'd experienced in getting his tailor to make it just as he wanted. 'Fellah said I'd never be able to walk in it without a proper vent at the back. Said I didn't want to walk in it, just sit in it.' Apparently it was intended for chilly days at Lord's, whither, so the legend ran, Salts chauffeured him in his prewar Daimler, and then carried him in his arms to his seat. A story hard to swallow.

There were two older masters who were institutions of the place. Both had come, or fallen, from good families; both were near alcoholics and cadgers; both had a social charm I found it hard to resist. Cornwallis had been an actor. He had a long nose, lips that seldom met, and a 'silly ass' drawl. He also wore a monocle on a silk ribbon round his neck. I never saw it in his eye, but he was always playing with it, in imitation, I always thought, of Leslie Howard's Scarlet Pimpernel. Before he had been an actor, he had been a barrister. From both professions he had, I imagine, been jettisoned as a confirmed boozer. Like many a player manqué he found a classroom some compensation for the loss of the boards. He hammed it up in all his lessons, and the boys loved it. He was invariably entertaining, and they never questioned his vainglorious yarns, peppered with careless references to Old Vic and Stratford and Larry and Peggy. Sometimes he would vary the recital with dramatic anecdotes about the Old Bailey and 'my old friend, the LCJ.'

Once I was waiting for a train with him on Banstead station when he suddenly asked: 'See that fellow over there raise his hat to me?'

No, I hadn't. 'Is he a friend of yours?' I asked. He shook his head, his face deadpan. 'Never set eyes on him before.' I waited. 'He was saluting the silk,' he explained.

Clovis Dace was a different proposition. No exhibitionist like Corny: wryly amusing, utterly unashamed in his confessions. On my very first day at Walton's he asked me if I could take his class, as he had a date with Mary. I agreed, and as he left the room, patting me appreciatively on the shoulder, Corny looked up from his paper and told me: 'Fucks like a stoat, y'know.' From this I gathered that Mary was some sort of mistress. Both Dace and Cornwallis were in their sixties. All such a change from the Hon Head's set-up. I wondered if Jimmy collected eccentrics, or even down-and-outs.

Clovis (I had always assumed the name was Saki's invention) was seedy to look at and at home in any company, unlike Corny, who knew what he owed his public and invariably retained his dignity, if not his balance. Corny was always cued for an entrance, his eyes always seeking audience reaction. Clovis was altogether blander: a round, rather fleshy face, and the assured expression of a gentleman who never doubts it. He was always cadging cigarettes. I bought ten Player's a day in paper packets, and impossible to get except from your one regular supplier. So each one given away was one smoke less that day.

Clovis lived in Clapham with his good-hearted, fast-fading shop assistant (I met her several times with him). Mary mothered, wived and whored him, all with a kind of twinkle-eyed resignation. Even so, Clovis occasionally had trouble with his shirt. He seemed to have only one, and when it grew too grubby even for him he would remove it during some free period he had and carefully wash just collar and cuffs in the washroom hand basin. Often I'd enter the staff room to find him sitting stripped to the waist over the gasfire, drying a cuff. Quite unabashed. Usually saying: 'Can you spare me a cigarette, my dear fellow?'

Yes, I enjoyed Walton's. The boys were a treat (but then they always were), and my work grew on me. At first I felt deprived of top English and Latin, which had long ago been bagged by Corny and Clovis, and not adequately compensated by all the divinity. But I had to work at it, for the sixth were particularly bright and raised many questions. I began to find this amateur theology rather fascinating. And the Old Testament narratives I found superb as literary studies. Soon I started to know my way about the Bible and to appreciate its treasures. The OT passages were often deeply moving, sometimes riotously funny. And with the Gospels I set out to show the splendour of Jesus without sacrificing my rationalist convictions.

At the end of my first term one young master left and Jimmy had to find a replacement. I suddenly had the idea of suggesting Brian for the job. I knew he got on well with young people. I had a strong hunch that he could teach, and I could see him shaping into a successful prep-school master. The vacancy was for French and maths. Brian had always had a flair for languages, and he was by nature a practical person. Jimmy interviewed him and he got the job. There were little hiccoughs at first, but I gave him all the support I could, which wasn't much where the maths was concerned.

But he swotted, he prepared every lesson carefully, he worked out all his maths problems in advance. In short, he made a distinct success of it all. The kids greatly appreciated him. He had always had a fund of tricks to delight youngsters with. Now he collected a whole box full of conjuring tricks and semi-scientific apparatus. He always had a crowd of fascinated boys round him out of school hours. He loved the work: it was as if all his odd and often rather crazy jobs had been leading up to this fulfilment. We were both very popular and very happy. When our respective half-days came round, we moped, and indeed often agreed to do another master's duty afternoon. The chap would scoot off with a chorus of grateful thanks, while no doubt thinking we were a bit touched. Said Brian to me once: 'To think Jimmy actually pays *us* to come here. We should be paying *him* for the privilege.'

Jimmy was quite bowled over by Brian's practical skills. He repaired the antediluvian lawn mower and serviced the school bus. He talked Jimmy into buying a film projector. Jimmy told the mystified boys: 'Mr Brian has not only got you moving pictures but talking ones as well.' I don't think Jimmy had ever seen a talkie. Indeed, I think he'd stopped short at the bioscope.

29

So the terms rolled pleasantly on. I had, apparently, no real ambitions as a schoolmaster. I supposed I was ineligible for any, having no degree. I may have had a few secret ambitions as a writer, but I couldn't take them seriously. It seems so odd to me, looking back, that I could have accepted so grey, so commonplace, a lot.

Most of my spare time was spent with Roland Dove. Our Saturday evenings were especially formal in their composition. Almost ritualistic. His parents then were out at bridge sessions, so we could talk freely. Roland had prepared a modest vegetarian supper, for which I had brought a little contribution (eats, not drinks, in those strange days), and then we cleared away and settled down to our eagerly awaited, richly indulged discussions. The absorbing, recurrent theme, of course, was our own composition: our tastes in literature and life. This entailed many elucidating anecdotes about our families. Roland's family seemed a richer mine, or at any rate he a more imaginative prospector. He was an only child, but he had many half-brothers and half-sisters. After his first wife's death, Mr Dove had at quite an advanced age married Roland's mother, and thus created a family circle of breadth, uberty and dissidence. From this foison Roland had drawn all the material a precocious child's developing imagination could wish for. Not only anecdotes but also old family albums illustrated his narratives.

There were sufficient disparities in our situations to give our conversation an edge. Roland didn't much care for his large brood of demi-siblings, while for me my restless family was everything. This was a difference of sentiment to which Roland has never quite reconciled himself. Again, my taste for youths was something Roland just couldn't understand. Many a time he deplored the fact that I couldn't change my tastes. I would say 'as vain as asking you to covet goats and monkeys.' Still, I accepted that my own amorous tastes could not be shared with him.

Roland was a great one for creating 'jolly afternoons' and 'nice evenings,' in a kind of mischievous send-up of bourgeois respectability. We would go to Kew Gardens and end with a set tea at the Maids of Honour, or solemnly tour Harrods and then take tea in Derry and Toms' rooftop garden, or take a trip up to Oxford in a Thames pleasure boat. Or more homely forays to Putney or Wimbledon or Richmond, with always a 'nice tea' (with pastry forks and tea strainers and paper doilies) in some Zeeta or Cadena or Fullers. All tinged with mockery and valediction.

For even in those immediate postwar years there were already hints of the coming social revolution, of the new world that was on its way, a world where all shrimps became prawns and all prawns became scampi, where workers dined out somewhere once a week, and even took a glass of wine with their basketed chicken and chips, where second-hand cars began to multiply (as yet untrailered by boats), where state schools faltered in their discipline, and children called Kevin and Tracy started to grow unhealthily fat. All mostly embryonic as yet, and none of it impairing my fervent loyalty to the secure Attlee government.

My two years at Jimmy's school are strewn with milestones, some marking sad stages on my journey, some bright ones. Poor Aunt Nora, bowed by Parkinson's disease, died at last: in a cot in an almost Dickensian infirmary in Croydon. I went to see her there just before she died. She couldn't form words but she tried. Urgently, almost frantically. I thought it best to supply them for her, for I knew what they were. 'You're trying to tell me that you want to come home.' She nodded vigorously. I said: 'We'll soon arrange that.' She began to rub one hand along her arm, now little more than skin and bone. 'You want to show me how thin you're getting.' Again she nodded with urgent appeal. 'We'll soon fatten you up when you get home,' I said, loathing myself for the deceit and lies of my tongue. But I didn't know what else to do. She died that night. For a year afterwards I would sometimes awake suddenly to find myself sitting up in bed, rubbing one arm with my hand. It was my first encounter with death, and it upset me. Especially its grim, solitary, alien setting.

One day I answered the phone to a voice I scarcely dared to say I knew, a voice from long ago, from my boyhood, from a world no bomb had blasted. 'Who is that?' snapped the voice impatiently. 'Who am I speaking to? Oh, Peter. Well, this is Terry.'

I could scarcely believe it. 'Oh, how marvellous,' I gasped. 'Where are you? How are you?'

'Quite all right,' he answered, sounding testier than ever. I knew he hated any show of emotion. So did I, really. So did we all. But I felt this really was something rather exceptional. After six or so years. He went on: 'I'm at Dover. I shall be in London in about three hours. Just tell me how to get to the house. I've no idea where it is. I got the phone number from the operator.'

'Well, I'll meet you at Victoria. Tell me when your train is due there.'

'No, no. I don't want to be met. Just tell me where you are.'

I gave him the address. 'You get a number two bus outside Victoria station to the Crystal Palace. That's the terminus. And we're just a step from there.'

I waited, we all waited, in a fever of expectation. What would he look like? Act like? Even speak like? After so many years in the hands of Hitler, he must surely be emaciated, bitter, perhaps even a left-wing activist?

225

Well, he *was* thinner, but in almost every other way he belied our expectations. He was waspish as ever, and to our eager questions returned not one anticipated answer.

'Were you treated badly?'

'Treated badly? Who by?'

'By the Germans, of course.'

'Got on splendidly with them. In Jersey and in Bavaria.'

'But... but the Nazis. The camp guards. The... the Gestapo.'

'Oh, mostly meaningless labels where I was. They had to belong to the Party, of course, but it meant very little. They all behaved very well. The commandant was an Old Carthusian.'

'But the lack of food, the loss of liberty?'

'Well, there wasn't much to eat. We were often pretty hungry. But the local people came up trumps.'

'You mean they brought you food?'

'They didn't bring it. We had an arrangement with the guards. On a sort of rota basis we went out to dinner once a week with families in the village. A delightful family sort of adopted me. I must send them a food parcel.'

We were nonplussed. Then Pam said: 'To think of all the pity we've been wasting on you these last few years. While we were starving. And being bombed day and night.' She threw up her hands with a mock-pious ejaculation. 'God in Heaven, how we suffered.'

'I can imagine,' said Terry, laughing for once. 'You all look as if you did.'

So Terry came to live with us, and, very soon after, Brian came, too, having finally decided that he could take no more married bliss. I felt rather sorry for his wife, but I think she was glad, and we all remained on good terms.

As for me, I felt that the good God had at last given me what I had long dreamed about: a united family. True, poor Aunt Nora was gone. And true, boisterous Bob Powis had now joined us. But essentially the family unit was intact. And the more we were together, the merrier it would be. Mrs Mackenzie's painting was coming true for me at last.

Family, friends. Then, as if that were not more than I deserved, a little throb for the heart: a letter from ·Carl at Uppingham. Not much of it, obviously at rather a loss to find news for me, but proudly ending with a phrase he'd no doubt just learned and was anxious to use. He signed off with a flourish: 'Yours till Hell freezes, Carl.'

I replied at once, telling him I had to be in his area next holidays. How about another day out together? Not without a twinge did I write 'had to be,' but then all was fair in love, and as for war in that context, I never envisaged it. He wrote back with the usual tag of 'super' and the usual invitation to dinner from his parents. I took him out to lunch and to a film as before, but we had to dine with his parents the same day, for I couldn't afford two days at the best hotel in town. Over dinner, his mother said to me: 'Now next time you must stay with us. No more hotels, please.' And when they were both out of the room, getting the next course, Carl said (as he did his usual unnerving tricks under the table): 'Do stay here next time. Then when they're asleep I can come into your room.' For an instant the lovely picture flashed across my mind, but I told him I'd do no such thing. The temptation would be too great, succumbing to it really rather low, as a guest, in his parents' house. He didn't understand this at all. He was growing up all too fast.

30

That summer (of 1947) Roland and I went to Switzerland for a fortnight. It was, of course, done on a shoestring, and we so fell in love with Basle that after two days in Zürich we returned to it. It was the first time either of us had been abroad. We revelled in the brightness and cleanliness of everything Swiss, especially in one much-loved vegetarian restaurant. We now decided to become lifelong vegetarians, on humanitarian and aesthetic grounds. On our way home we stopped off in Paris for a few hours. The train taking us there was crowded, but (not without artifice) I wedged us in a corridor next to a party of French Boy Scouts in the care of a young, soutaned priest. I sat on the corridor floor next to a particularly attractive boy and struck up a conversation in my awkward French. His name was Ramon and he was fifteen and he'd just love to have an English pen friend. We carefully wrote out and exchanged our names and addresses. All this while the young priest was eyeing me rather suspiciously, so I stood and spent the rest of the time chatting to him. All went well until my final remark, which was intended to show concern, compassion. I told him I thought there must be much hunger in Paris. He looked at me sharply, said 'Yes' and turned his back to me. Not till much later did I decide he had mistaken my '*faim*' for '*femmes.*' And no doubt written me off as a villainous, Anglo-Saxon bisexual.

I sent Ramon a rather fine penknife with umpteen blades and other gadgets to it. He was delighted with it. I never saw him again, but we corresponded for some years. He would be around sixty now.

Erosion began, gently, to eat at my dreams of family togetherness. Terry had re-entered the insurance world and then told us, with great satisfaction, if not triumph, that he was about to get married. He had met in London, at the Quaker Relief Service headquarters, an attractive French girl, and they were going to live in a basement flat in Chelsea, in the very house where Brian's marriage had been domiciled. Janik was indeed an attractive girl, and they soon had two daughters. After which they departed for Paris, where they have lived almost ever since, following successful careers (British insurance is well regarded in France), bringing up the two girls, and finally retiring to a lovely house in the Dordogne. Terry and I stay with each other every year. As the years pass we seem to become more, not less, close.

Then the owner of Harmenleen wanted it back for his son, who was also about to get married. This was a blow, but we had no time to feel sorry for ourselves. Brian and I found a large luxury flat in Banstead, one of four into which a fine Edwardian house had been converted. It took much persuasion to get the lease, in the names of father and Brian and myself. We succeeded mainly, I think, because Jimmy allowed me to use him as a referee (he owned a large slice of Banstead).

But, of course, we had no furniture. I left that to Brian. He was an authority on junk shops and rather seedy antique dealers. We got a bedroom suite on the never-never for mother and father, and Bob got one on the same terms for himself and Pam. We collected chairs and tables and cupboards, and for ourselves two really basic camp beds. Pam got curtains somewhere and hung them, and we covered the floors with roofing felt father produced. Then on the appointed day for the move, Brian and I got some old vases and filled them with flowers, which mother loved. I know she cried with sheer pleasure when she arrived (in a taxi laden with suitcases) and saw how utterly, unexpectedly, nice it was. The suitcases were crammed with bed linen and blankets and towels and tablecloths, which good old Glad-eye had guarded for us ever since our flight from the doodlebugs.

I began to realize that we were survivors. Not gypsies, not really Bohemians, for everything had to be done properly, regardless of the cost. Somehow we always got through, though there were some more rough passages ahead.

As soon as we were settled, I decided to write to Julien. I hadn't heard from him for some time. Even his little parcels of food and chocolate, which he used to despatch from any prosperous country his ship visited, seemed to have dried up. So I wrote to his mother's home in Ostend, telling him it was time he visited us again. We now had a new home in a new town, where he could share my room (though not now my bed as he was too large for it).

It was some two months before a reply reached me, and then in a hand I did not know. The letter was from a woman friend of his mother, whose French was better than Vrouw Vanderzee's. It told me that Julien had died earlier that year of some tropical disease, and that to the very last he spoke of me and of the happy times he had spent with us all in London. Enclosed was a photo of a large, monumental grave. According to continental custom, the headstone had a photograph of Julien glazed in it. It was as I had last seen him: tall and lanky, in naval uniform with his cap at a rakish angle. In my bedroom, half choking and with eyes awash, I burned that photo in the grate.

228

I did not want it. That was not my Julien. My Julien was that lovely, faun-like boy my eyes had first fallen on in a sandbagged playground long, long ago. That was my Julien, 'My best friend. For ever.'

31

It was about this time of my life that my horror and disgust with capital punishment began to assume something like crusading proportions. I was endlessly involved in arguments about the necessity for a death penalty. I came to assess people, instantly and implacably, in terms of their views on capital punishment. I joined the Howard League for Penal Reform. I recognized that the only hope for abolition lay, politically, with the Labour Party, and that cemented even more firmly my support for the Labour government, my contempt for the hanging and flogging Tories. The Nuremberg executions strengthened rather than diminished my beliefs. I got all my family and all my friends to aid and abet me in my propaganda for abolition. Some of them, like Derrick, needed no persuasion; others, like Jonathan and Robbie and Roland, agreed politely rather than passionately.

I spent much of my spare time during that term at Jimmy's finishing my longish critical essay on Forrest Reid. De la Mare had more than once urged me to finish it quickly and get it off to Forrest, for he was in poor health and time was running out. But I didn't. He died in January 1947, and it was late summer before I had completed it, typed it out and sent it to de la Mare. To tell the truth, I was not sorry that I could not show it to Forrest, for I did not think it was worthy of him. I thought nothing I wrote was any good. So my astonishment, even my incomprehension, was great when I had this letter from de la Mare:

> I believe nothing could have given him greater delight of the rarest kind than the paper you have sent me. It is, I think, a most admirable and a beautiful thing in its imaginative insight, and he would have valued it for its own sake, as well as for his. You won't think it is intended as a mere compliment when I say that anything so delicate and intuitive in judgment and appreciation is quite beyond me, even though mine is the advantage of having known him so well.

Later he wrote:

> Stephen Gilbert tells me 'he seems to have found out and understood the side of Forrest which Forrest himself considered most important. I don't think I ever before read anything about him which brought out, or rather penetrated to, that side of his character... It was almost as if he were talking to me, walking through a particular field, which for a long time was part of his regular route on Sunday afternoons'... I agree with everything he says about the paper as a whole. I think it is a wonderful piece of work and wish indeed that FR could have shared it.

In another letter some months later, de la Mare wrote: 'The revisions and additions to your appreciation of FR have been, I think, all to the good. It has been a real delight to read it again.' This letter shows me that I did improve the thing, though now all I have is a tattered first draft. De la Mare induced (if that is the word) Denys Kilham Roberts to accept it for his miscellany, *Orion*: 'Kilham Roberts was delighted with the essay: "It is a penetrating and sensitive study and beautifully written." A few words, but every one "of the gold".'

I could never, at any time, then or now, believe it deserved such high praise as de la Mare gave it. I believed his words sprang from his wonderful kindness of heart, his desire to encourage a little scribbler, and also, perhaps, from the rather precious prose in which I wrote it, from the arch and whimsical allusions in which (I now think) it too freely abounds. Perhaps my revision of it was better. I hope so. Anyway, Kilham Roberts' *Orion* collapsed before he could publish my effusion, and nothing ever came of the project de la Mare told me about: of 'a collection of papers on Forrest Reid to submit to Geoffrey Faber... I hope very much that you'll let this be *your* contribution to the collection if publication is secured.'

But perhaps the greatest thrill in all this came when de la Mare asked me to dinner with him at his flat in Montpelier Row, Twickenham. I accepted, of course, and with gratitude and pride. Yet also with some misgivings, for he was to me one of the greatest English lyric poets, and I felt that I was a mere bundle of ignorance and gaucherie.

I was due to arrive at 7 pm, and I was pacing to and fro along the main road some thirty minutes before then. At a minute or two past the hour, with a thumping heart I ascended what is in my memory a great winding staircase and rang the bell. I had fixed my gaze at eye level and prepared my little opening speech: 'Mr de la Mare, it is so kind of you to invite me, and I am honoured to meet you at last.' Not, one may be sure, what Rimbaud said when he knocked on Verlaine's door.

The door opened, and instantly I had to lower my gaze. For he was shorter in stature than I had, from head-and-shoulder portraits, ever imagined. That disconcerted me, and so did the next shock I had, for he spoke in a huntin', shootin' and fishin' voice that I was quite unprepared for.

The opening words were his, not mine.

'Gamble,' he boomed, 'thy name is punctuality.'

Now I loathed being called by my surname. Courteous, even flattering, as it was, it called up visions of school, and of all that was hearty, extrovert and uncaring. I pulled myself together and realized I must say something.

'Actually, Mr de la Mare, I have been pacing the main road for half an hour so as to be punctual.'

He smiled. 'Come in, come in. Let me take your coat. And... and scarf.' (Was it wrong to go out to dinner in a scarf? But it was the start of that bitter winter of 1947.) He continued: 'Come by the fire. Or as much of a fire as I can manage. Not at all adequate for such a night.'

I felt indignant that such a person as Walter de la Mare should have to endure fuel rationing. Still, feelings of inferiority and embarrassment kept me, at least, warm, as we chatted about Forrest Reid. I asked many questions about this doyen of paedophilic novelists (though never the ones I wanted to ask so much). But I was coming to see that de la Mare and Forster appealed to different sides of Forrest, and that I could understand well enough. I am sorry I never met Forster to talk about Forrest (though we did correspond interestingly). I am sure I could have asked *him* what I wanted to know. Forrest's involvement in *Maurice* has now made that clear enough.

I was not doing well. I thought I must say a little about de la Mare's own poetry. But I felt very inadequate for that. Instead, I found myself telling him I was a vegetarian, only to realize too late that he had probably got a chop under the grill. On the other hand there was no suggestion of a meal. There was a dining recess but nothing but books on the table, and no aroma of cooking in the flat. Perhaps he hadn't asked me to dinner. Perhaps I was asked for sherry, and had already stayed too long?

Now he was booming (the word is absurdly wrong, but so it seemed to me then): 'The London Vegetarian Society once wrote to ask me if they could use in their literature that poem of mine about a butcher's shop. You know, the one beginning...?'

It was a trap. The horror of it was that I *did* know the poem, had even quoted it to Roland. But not one word of it could I call to mind. Suddenly he moved his large head a little nearer and said: 'Gamble, I don't think you've ever read a poem of mine.' It was said with a pleasant laugh, but I was hurt to the quick.

Before I could find words for a reply, he had fallen on his knees and begun prodding the fire with a poker as he muttered: 'Bloody Shinwell. Bloody Labour government.'

I was shocked. All such light years away from Tartary and Cathay and Lyonesse and Thule. But he was on his feet again, kind and courteous as ever, and now (glory be!) telling me: 'We are going in to Richmond for dinner. A nice, old-fashioned restaurant I sometimes go to. Not vegetarian, but they do excellent omelettes.'

On the way down the stairs outside his flat he paused to draw my attention to a giant and impressive tree which filled the view from the great staircase window. It was white with hoarfrost and possessed a quite unearthly beauty in the cold moonlight. 'I call that my haunted tree,' he said, 'and this is my haunted staircase.' Then he added with a chuckle: 'Two special de la

Mare props.' And I laughed, too, quite loudly, uninhibitedly. 'He is a dear,' I thought. 'He can laugh at himself.'

We had to wait quite a while in the now perishing cold for a bus. I hoped he could stand it. Guilt was now added to my sense of inadequacy. We were the only passengers. We sat on the long seat by the entrance. Opposite sat the poor conductress, raw and dew-dropped, counting her tickets. My companion said: 'My dear, you look very tired. And cold. Is this your last run today? I do hope so.'

This sympathy won her quite, and soon she was telling us some of her life story. If only she had known who her audience was!

I don't remember the dinner, or the conversation. We went back to the flat for a welcome brandy, and I left very soon after and, as usual, with great relief. I remember so vividly the kindness of de la Mare. Even more keenly, though, do I recall the shallowness of his guest.

32

I would in the normal course of events have recounted the whole de la Mare story to Roland the next Saturday evening. He was dying to hear it all, as I was to relate it. But alas, he had gone. Not very far and not for too long, but it was a break we ill endured. For Roland had gone to Oxford. For three years. To read English.

He had often discussed with me this dream of his, for a dream it initially seemed. But he had determination, and he knew how to play his cards when his mind was made up. In the end he was accepted by the Unitarian Church (which he favoured) to receive a scholarship from them for Oxford graduation, followed by Unitarian training and ordination. They offered this to commence in Michaelmas 1948, but at the last moment they found him a place for Michaelmas 1947, and he jumped at it, for he was already twenty-three.

I was delighted for his sake, and not envious of it for it never entered my head for a moment that any such future was possible for me. Soon after I had met de la Mare I visited Oxford at Roland's insistence to see his new ambience. He was living at Manchester College and reading English at an unglamorous college. I was enormously impressed by all I saw. It was a world entirely new to me. I didn't know the difference between the colleges of the university and all these theological colleges, or between the Roman, the Anglican and the Nonconformist seminaries. Manchester College, like so many, was huge and grand and staffed with highly qualified dons. It was also half empty. Despite this, the splendours of dining in hall were gallantly maintained.

Roland found me digs for the night in an ancient and glacial house nestling beneath New College. He listened avidly to my account of the de la Mare evening, of course, but I felt he had something up his sleeve.

He had. It was nothing less than a proposal that I should do just as he'd done: somehow get to Oxford to read English. He was deaf to my hoots of laughter, my incredulous dismissal of his idea. 'If I can do it, you can,' he kept insisting. In vain I pointed out how different our situations were: I was three or four years older, and I had no hope of any theological college to back me.

'No, of course not,' he countered. 'Not a theological college. Something quite different: an ex-serviceman's grant.'

I really thought he was becoming a little unhinged. Perhaps it was all the studying. But he was adamant. 'I know a CO who has got such a grant. And he'd not done anything as impressive as coal mining. Now what you've got to do as soon as you're back in London is to go to the Ministry of Education, get the necessary forms, and put them in at once. Meanwhile, I'll get working on my tutor, and you get working on de la Mare.'

I agreed, just to please him. I got the forms, and also a shower of cold water from some disdainful official at the Ministry. He told me that as a former conscientious objector I was not exactly in a strong position, and that in any case the deadline for all such applications was quite a year ago. Something in his manner roused my spirit, and I said: 'Does that mean that you will refuse to accept the form when I have completed it?'

'No, I cannot do that. Complete it if you like. I am merely trying to save you unnecessary disappointment.'

I typed out a rather telling brief: how war came when I was still in my teens, how I wished to make schoolmastering my life's work, how I served in Civil Defence and coal mining for the duration. Then I got de la Mare's permission to use him as a referee, and finally Roland arranged for his English tutor at St Catherine's (Chesney Horwood) to read my Forrest Reid essay and interview me. He then obligingly wrote to the Ministry to say he could find me a place if they awarded a Further Education and Training grant.

It had all happened so quickly I was almost dazed by it. I still could not believe it would ever materialize.

33

Meanwhile, in the Easter holidays, I again had important business in Carl's part of the world! I arranged to dine with his parents on the evening of my arrival, leaving the whole of the next day free for our outing. This time I recklessly gave myself two expensive nights at the best hotel in the town. Dinner with the parents was pleasant as ever, and Carl himself, in blazer and

233

flannels, was even more eye-catching. He was doing *Jane Eyre* at school for his coming School Certificate, so I said we'd go on the train to Penistone and see something of the Brontë country.

It was a fine spring day and the moors were, I felt, scarcely less Elysian to me in my present mood than they habitually were to Emily. After an impressive hostelry lunch, I told Carl something of *Wuthering Heights* as we tramped happily on. He liked walking as much as I did, and he still seemed, to my surprise and pleasure, absolutely at ease in my company. So relaxed, so carefree, were we that we forgot to observe the clock. We knew the train we must take back from Penistone, and we knew we couldn't make it. Not that we were unduly concerned. There must be another soon. We rested for a while, for it was warm and we were rather weary. We romped in the heather, 'in memory of Cathy and Heathcliff,' though I doubt if either would have approved our frolics.

We had strayed much further from Penistone than we had realized. It was dusk as we still tramped. We tried to thumb a lift from the very few cars that we saw. Not one seemed inclined to stop. I remember we were resting for a moment by the wayside when we heard an engine in the distance. Carl jumped up. 'Leave it to me this time,' he exclaimed devilishly. As the vehicle approached, he stood half in the road, pulled down his sock and hitched up his trouser leg as far as he could, then thumbed with a face full of coy invitation. The car swerved and sped on. Carl collapsed beside me, laughing his head off. 'He actually revved up when he saw me,' he cried. 'You are a devil,' I replied. 'You'll be arrested for soliciting.' And I pictured my reaction if I'd been that motorist.

It was quite dark when we reached Penistone station and learned the next (and last) train was an hour and a half later. The wait was chilly and interminable. The train when it came was a maddening tortoise. We arrived around 11 pm. 'The old man will be furious,' said Carl. 'He said nine o'clock at the latest.'

It was a bus ride from the station to Carl's house. 'You needn't come with me,' he urged. 'I'll be OK. I can handle him.'

But I wouldn't hear of it. I insisted on delivering him to the door. Mr Janssen was actually pacing the road outside his house. He cut short my apologies, my explanations, with a brusque 'Good night.' He almost pushed his son into the house. Carl managed to give me a last, deprecating glance over his shoulder. I felt very guilty. I wondered if I would ever see him again.

Soon, all too soon, after I was back at Jimmy's I had a letter. I knew from postmark and handwriting that it was from the Hon Head. He wrote: 'I am horrified to learn of your continued association with Carl Janssen. I must insist that you tell your present headmaster the whole Janssen story, and ask him to write to me to confirm that you have done so.'

234

It was a blow that could, I knew, finish me quite. I showed the letter to Roland, who hadn't yet returned for his Trinity term. He was shaken by it, but full of sympathy and sound advice. 'You must write to this head asking him what has caused his action.' I had already decided on that.

I also showed the letter to Brian, who was quite deflated by it. 'It's the end,' he declared in a voice of uncharacteristic doom. 'It's the end for both of us.'

The Hon Head replied, more moderately, to say that Mr Janssen had contacted him that night, heard the Tale of the Undelivered Kiss, censured the poor Head, and insisted they both go at once to the hotel, fearing, I suppose, that Carl and I would be caught in flagrante delicto in my room. The receptionist told them no Mr Gamble was staying there. They described me, and she said: 'Oh, you mean Mr Granville. Yes, he arrived yesterday. He has been out all day today. His key has been on its peg since ten this morning.'

True, the hotel had misread my squiggly signature as 'Granville.' This I discovered from the bill they gave me, but I hadn't bothered to correct it because the room number was mine and the amount correct.

All this I explained in a further letter, even trying to introduce a lighter note with this presumed picture of me as 'the villain of a Gothic novel, touring incognito the hotels of Britain for his own nefarious ends.' I told him of the trouble we'd had with trains and how I'd insisted on taking Carl home to explain to his father. I suggested the whole thing was too trivial to deserve such dire action as he proposed.

Roland thought it a good letter. I could see he knew how much was at stake. He was at our house when the reply appeared. I had to tear it open and read it in front of him and the family.

My appeal was not allowed. The Hon Head apologized for his misunderstanding. He said he wanted me to know that he still had a high opinion of me and deeply regretted that he must insist on his request. If he did not hear from my present headmaster within a week that I had told him the whole story, he would have to write to him himself. Then he added a phrase which, even in the circumstances, caused me to smile by its very crudity: 'I am sorry thus to throw sand in your gearbox.'

With a chuckle I did not feel, I put the letter in my pocket and said to Roland: 'Well, let's get going if we're to be up in town for lunch.'

Roland has always said that my reaction to that letter was superb in its sheer self-control, its perfect camouflage. Indeed, it had convinced him all was well. His face fell when on the train I produced the fatal letter for him to read.

So, with sinking heart, I asked Jimmy for a private interview. It was fixed for lunchtime the next day. Behind those dreadful, heavy lace curtains.

In that grim, intractable setting of Edwardian propriety. As I walked across to his forbidding house, all I could think of was George V's remark: 'Good God, I thought such fellows shot themselves.' Beside this, Roland's incurably optimistic attitude was merely irritating. He was, though, nature's answer to every Cassandra, every Job's comforter.

Since it was before lunch and Jimmy himself had only just come in, he was expansively kind. 'Now, Mr Peter, what can we do for you?' He no doubt thought I wanted a loan.

I blurted it all out quickly: the private lessons, the teasing about the kiss, the walk on the moors, the misunderstanding about the hotel. Then I handed him the Hon Head's two letters. I never glanced at him during all this. I couldn't. Only too well I could picture the mounting puce of that patrician face: a puce now rightly engendered. At last he exploded. 'Poppycock. Never heard so much poppycock in my life.'

It seemed he was rejecting my account out of hand, and even in my misery I felt some resentment.

He rasped on: 'Boy upset. What more natural than to comfort him with a kiss? Nothing in it.'

Were these words really coming out of Jimmy's mouth? Or was it some cruel trick played by the gods? He went on: 'What a fuss this fellah is making over nothing. Are you fond of Carl?'

'Yes,' I murmured, still in a daze.

'Quite right. Sounds a nice boy. I'll write and tell this headmaster I am dismissing the whole thing.'

Suddenly he put his arm round my shoulders and gave me a hug worthy of any grizzly bear. 'Seems to me, Mr Peter,' he said in tones of finality, 'that you've had a very worrying time. All over nothing. Now you just go and forget all about it.'

I left him in a dream, sought Brian in a dream, and, in a dream, recounted the wonders that had passed.

'Does Jimmy really kiss boys that are upset?' I asked Brian.

'No doubt about it,' he replied happily. 'Just thank your lucky stars we urnings hang together.'

As I told Brian, I had never for a moment suggested Carl was upset or that the kiss was meant to comfort him. These were Jimmy's inventions, presumably deliberate ones designed to let me off the hook. So Brian interpreted it all, and Roland concurred.

Some years later, after Jimmy's death, Clovis told us of a scandal Jimmy had been involved in at the school in the early thirties. Said Clovis: 'Corny and I stood by him, and of course he remembered that.' Said Brian to me: 'Now we know why those two old rogues never got the push. Well, good for Jimmy.'

236

And that, any rational person would assume, was the tightly secured end of the whole Janssen story. But no, there was to be a sequel, after more than twenty years. I think I'll recount that in its place.

34

About this time I saw a stage play which, in its theme and by its opportuneness, had a strong effect on me. It was called *The Hidden Years* and it told the familiar but viable enough story of a deep affection between an older and a younger boy immured in a public school. The younger boy was superbly played by a very handsome 15-year-old called Ray Jackson. I fell for him and was moved by the well constructed play.

I call this play opportune because I saw it when I was in the midst of my negotiations with the Ministry of Education. As I have said, I was not building even the ghost of a hope on their outcome. But, such is the vulnerability of even the most cynical, I had my occasional secret dreams. Dreams of teaching in a public school: the marvellous prize to be won by a miraculous Oxford degree. Only a small, modest public school (I was not greedy), but a boarding one exclusively, and set somewhere remote and rural: a male preserve, a monastery suffused by male ideals, a place where innocence was always nobly guarded by the enlightened few. Now I was not such a fool as to take this farrago quite seriously. I was a schizoid dreamer, half ridiculing my fantasies, half lost in love with them.

I was not alone in making of such schools my little Utopias, while being entirely devoid of any personal experience of them. It was so with the Greyfriars of Frank Richards. It was so with R. C. Sherriff, who casts the glow of such a school, its boys and its masters, over his *Journey's End*, because he himself never went to one. Even Ernest Raymond was a dayboy at St Paul's, but for his *Tell England* has dreamed up an ancient boarding school of rustic beauty, filled by boys of aristocratic pretensions and personal grace.

Thus I dreamed, and thus I laughed at myself for dreaming such dreams, as I walked to the Ministry of Education in Belgrave Square for their final decision.

I saw the same rather disdainful man I had seen throughout. He seemed to enjoy keeping me on tenterhooks as he shuffled and sorted the papers on his desk. He almost stressed the effrontery of my application. I wondered if he'd once longed to go to Oxford himself and ended up redbrick.

'Your application was made eighteen months after the FET lists had closed,' he said severely.

'I am sorry,' I replied frigidly.

'And it went to the highest level for a decision. In fact,' he lowered his voice as if betraying a state secret, 'to the Minister herself.'

'I am grateful for the trouble you have all taken,' I said, hoping he could detect the irony in the remark. I took the sheaf of papers he now handed me and began to stuff them into my briefcase.

For the first time he looked rather puzzled. 'The Minister has treated your application as exceptional,' he added, then said loudly as if to someone mentally retarded: 'Your application has been allowed. *You have your grant.*' Then, as if rather ashamed of himself, he said: 'Congratulations.'

I don't know what I then said to him. I don't remember leaving the building. The next thing I clearly recall is standing in Belgrave Square holding the roadside railings. Like Wordsworth trying to recapture reality.

No young person today can understand my feelings then. Today, grants fall like autumn leaves and university places are grasped as a right. But I, as a child of the thirties and the Great Depression, as a youth to whom a degree was little more attainable than a knighthood, I was as incredulous, as transported, as poor Jude would have been by such news.

As I walked slowly on in the bright sun of early summer, other thoughts crowded, jostled, in my head. I was twenty-eight, ten years older than an undergraduate should be. I had been earning my own living since I was seventeen. In between I'd been a conchie, a jailbird, a miner. How was I going to adapt myself to Oxford? I went into Lyons for a coffee and to scan my papers. I hadn't even discovered how much grant they'd give me. Or what I was supposed to do with it.

It was £210 per annum. £70 per term. For board and lodging. The state was to pay all tuition fees. I thought how incredibly generous this was. I couldn't see why they should pay anything. No state handouts of any kind had figured in my life.

Then I realized that the Minister herself, to whom I owed this grant, was Ellen Wilkinson, 'Red Ellen,' leader of the Jarrow march to London, of the marchers who had so affected me when, a greedy little boy, I was told they were hungry. I was glad to know Ellen had helped me, my brave Labour government had sent me packing to all those dreaming spires.

Roland was elated. I owed a great deal of it to him. Jimmy was full of congratulations, though sorry to lose me. He wrote me a charming letter, telling me the lives of the boarders especially were to be much poorer. This was because whenever I was on duty in the week Pam made me a great, workaday fruit cake for their tea. Jimmy, not out of meanness but from a belief in old Spartan values, more or less starved the poor little devils. And when I was on Sunday duty I took them all to Chessington Zoo or the South Kensington museums or Hampton Court, instead of letting them endlessly kick a tennis ball in the cold, damp yard. Yes, I'd miss them, as I had missed so many others over the years.

238

The family were pleased because I was pleased. Mother said: 'But you should never have left Reader's Union.' Always, to her, publishing was much preferable to schoolmastering or Oxford. Pam said: 'Well, now we must all pull our belts in so as to support you.' She didn't mean it, but there was truth in the remark. She herself, with my help, got a job in a local prep school teaching eight-year-olds. She stayed there some years and made a success of it. That summer I tried to study English literature, all of it. Impossible, of course, but a foretaste of my chaotic life as a student.

I had to go to Oxford to find some digs, preferably vegetarian. I didn't like any of those I saw. So I went to a theological college which was, to my surprise, on the list of approved lodgings I was given. Such venerable institutions were short of students and short of money. The one I visited, Ripon Hall, on Boar's Hill, was very beautiful, and the aged principal (the great Dr Henry Major) was a delight, with his ear trumpet, his wicked sense of humour, and his elaborate Trollopian manners. I liked his description of lodgers as his 'dear lay brothers.' I felt I must become one of them, even though it meant surrendering my vegetarianism.

And so at last Roland and I set off for the immortal city. In it we took a taxi each to our seminaries. As I sat in the very large, very old automobile, so utterly unlike a London cab, and so redolent of generations of undergraduates, I felt I really had arrived at the Mecca Jude had only glimpsed.

PART THREE: WANDERINGS

1

I entered two new worlds at once: that of the university and that of an Anglican theological college. Coping with both was not easy, for in both I was a stranger. And both intrigued me, although in the latter I was supposed to be no more than a guest in a pension.

So far as my three years reading for a degree in English was concerned, I was from first to last a hopelessly disorganized student. My tutor was too kind, and I had no idea what was expected of me. Twenty years of undirected reading was now followed by a weekly attempt to read everything written by and about the particular literary giant we were devoting that week's essay to. My tutorial was on a Friday morning and every Thursday evening late I finally despaired of conquering that week's giant. At about midnight, sick at heart, I would start to scribble an essay for which I felt largely unprepared. At about 3 am I could no longer keep my eyes open. I fell on my bed, alarm set for 6 am, when I had a shower and shaved. I continued scribbling before and over breakfast, on the bus, even up the stairs to my tutor's room. There, at 11 am, despising myself, I began to read my effort. Oh, usually true enough, and *literate*, which most of the students, I gathered, were not, and which during all my time at Oxford led my mentors to assume I was short of time rather than material. Week after week, I would break off after about a quarter of an hour with a sick, shamefaced mumble: 'I'm afraid that's as far as I got.' And my all-too-courteous tutor would say: 'A pity, Mr Gamble, a pity.' He should have reprimanded me. But then I was nearly thirty and, I dare repeat, *literate*! Only twice can I recall finishing an essay. Once on Shakespeare's history plays, when my tutor said: 'An excellent, indeed an illuminating, survey.' And once on Milton's Satan, when he said: 'That really is worthy of publication, Mr Gamble, and I hope you'll see to it.' Of course, I didn't.

On Tuesdays I had my language tutorial, which had no such despondencies. I enjoyed working at the Anglo-Saxon and Middle English texts, although there was a horror of a paper called the A4 which I never made head or tail of. I apparently lacked ear. My tutor would say to me in vain: 'Surely, Mr Gamble, you can hear the difference between (blank) and (blank)?' pronouncing two vowels that sounded to me utterly, exquisitely identical. There were one or two others like me. We knew all tutorials on the A4 as 'the great bowel shift.'

I was a rotten student. My tutor never ceased to hope for better things. He entered me for the Charles Oldham Shakespeare scholarship. I withdrew myself ignominiously. Passing me on the stairs just before Schools (that is, finals), he whispered: 'We're expecting great things. A first, you know.' Poor man.

I had the chance to transfer to a grander college, namely Balliol, where the English tutor was John Bryson, whom I had met through my interest in Forrest Reid, a close friend of his. But I didn't, for it would have been a slight to the excellent and indulgent tutor I was already disconcerting. Another Reid connection I availed myself of was Lord David Cecil, who was Goldsmiths' Professor of English Literature, a fine biographer, a delightful man, and not a very good lecturer. I remember one of the clerks at the Examination Schools (where most of the lectures took place) telling me at the beginning of one term: 'We always put Lord David in the very big lecture room, and Mr Dyson in a small one. Then after a week or so we swop them over.' Hugo Dyson was indeed the finest English literature lecturer during my time: on Shakespeare he thrilled us all. He was the only lecturer I can recall being long and loudly applauded. My tutor sent me to a weekly seminar he and C. S. Lewis took jointly, and to which each college was allowed to send a favoured student.

I had a most enjoyable session with Lord David in his rooms over tea and (no doubt) muffins. We talked about all Forrest Reid's books. Lord David's favourite was *Pirates of the Spring*, which is all about schoolboy loves and loyalties but is not a school novel, for they are all dayboys and scarcely anything happens within school walls. Reid didn't like schools.

Lord David agreed to take me for a B Litt on Reid and his ilk. 'Come and see me as soon as you have your results.'

It was a stifling hot summer when I sat my nine papers. I knew I was performing terribly: on few papers did I do more than one and a half essays. I quite expected to be failed. Roland had sat the summer before and made a similar hash of it all. He was suicidal. 'If they fail me I'll never go back, never resit. Oh, for God's sake go to Horwood and tell him so. He'll listen to you. Tell him he's got to tell the board I must be given some sort of a degree, it doesn't matter what.' So with enormous misgivings I did tell my tutor all this, without, of course, ever suggesting he try to influence the board of examiners. And Roland got his degree. He sent me a telegram to say: 'A Glorious Fourth,' and he meant it. Degree classes so often were no true evaluation of a student. Roland went off to America, got a Ph D and finally a professorship, and has taught and written nobly in America and Scandinavia.

To my surprise, I was called before the board for a viva, that is, a gruelling oral quiz. When I told my tutor, he was delighted, saying: 'That means a first, Mr Gamble. Most of those they call to vivas are possible firsts or possible fails.' That still he didn't know which *I* was astonished me.

The Inquisition were extremely kind. I translated some *Beowulf* not too badly and one of them said 'Well, why didn't you do that in the exam?' The literature questions I somehow blundered through, not very respectably. I remember the last question was something on Dr Johnson's *Dictionary*, which entirely flummoxed me. So one of them said: 'Can you give us just one fact about the *Dictionary*?' I was hot, fed up, and past caring. I said: 'Other than that it is, presumably, in alphabetical order, no, I can't.' At this they all laughed, and one said: 'I don't think you have seen a copy of Dr Johnson's *Dictionary*, Mr Gamble.' I said with a wan smile: 'I'm afraid not,' and left. They gave me a third.

I humbly apologized to Chesney Horwood and took him out to dinner. I tried to explain my deficiencies as a student, partly so that he'd never feel it was his fault, but also in an effort to unravel myself. It was not only the silly notion I had that I must know all that had ever been written about my subject, otherwise I might perpetrate some naive blunders. It was also a niggling belief that it was a waste of everybody's time for me to write an essay unless I had at least a few original ideas to propound, some fresh lines of approach to plot. I was almost ashamed to mention this, it seemed so presumptuous. But it was so, an ingrained relic, I suppose, of Mr Bullock's advice to me as a little boy: 'Get out of the rut. Be original. No good just repeating other people.'

I don't think my kindly tutor understood what I was trying to elucidate. And, of course, I didn't have the face to go near Lord David again.

2

So much for my English studies. This is all I shall say at the moment about them. On the other hand, very different, and almost imperceptibly growing in influence, was my simultaneous life as resident in the really rather extraordinary theological college.

I was among the last trickle of wartime veterans to come up. Boys and girls straight from school were beginning to reassert their sway. Quite right, for it was essentially their world. I didn't find either intake very endearing. A noisy exhibitionism seemed to characterize most of the young ones. Where were the old, touching charms of adolescence: the shy and the gauche, the coltish limbs and quickly colouring cheeks? They seemed to have died when Europe died in 1939. Or perhaps they had never existed outside my sentimental dreams.

Andrew was an 18-year-old straight from public school with an Exhibition in maths and, like me, a rather befogged lay brother. He was a nice boy with a fine socialist idealism the University Labour Club was to erode. In my room about half a dozen undergraduates (ordinands and lay) would often congregate of an evening for coffee, and we'd chatter till the small hours. One such causerie hovered around homosexuality. I was, of course, careful to remain quite noncommittal, for I felt I was a loner there.

Suddenly Andrew burst out: 'If any man tried anything like that with me, I'd smash my fist into his face.' I felt Andrew could be dangerous.

The only chap who had a sane and liberal approach to the subject (apart, of course, from me!) was a handsome young American called Harvey Guthrie. I took to Harvey at once. He had appeared in Oxford, unheralded, unintroduced, in late summer of that very year, and then gone round banging on college doors until one took him in to read theology. His looks and his charm ensured a fairly brief search. He had a degree in history in the States, and he was further equipped by some respectable national service as a naval lieutenant.

Very early in our friendship I learned just what Harvey was and was not. He was not homosexual, and he was not at all narrow or prejudiced. We were strolling through Magdalen Deer Park when we met an elderly theology don Harvey knew slightly. This person did not shake hands with Harvey or take any notice of me. He responded to Harvey's 'Hi, sur' by running his hand heavily down Harvey's back and on to his buttocks, at the same time murmuring: 'And how is my Adonis today?' Harvey jumped back as if he had been shot. The don walked on with an enigmatic smile and Harvey hissed to me: 'That old bastard.' I thought I'd add my own bit of teasing. 'Now you must remember, my dear Harvey, that you have entered a land steeped in chivalry and tradition. No gum-chewing, fornicating GIs here. No campuses littered with copulating bobbysoxers. Just the gallantry of man to man. Here, on the very turf where Oscar sauntered with Bosie, honour that tradition.' Harvey said, grinning from ear to ear: 'You're just as decadent as the rest of them, you old son of a gun.'

So it was easy to let my hair down with Harvey. I told him the kind of physical beauty I admired, and I could do so because I wasn't in any way attracted to Harvey myself. Sexually attracted, I mean. In terms of character, disposition, temperament, I was enormously attracted. I was aware of his good looks, but he was too old for me. I soon found myself expounding this to him, telling him that as far as I was concerned he was almost senile. No one had ever spoken to him like this in that brave, macho New World that had bred him. Or at least its highways were aggressively 'normal.' Of its byways he seemed to know nothing. He was an innocent, uncomplicated he-man. That was what I loved about him. That, and his good, generous mind, his warmth and spontaneity, his essential liberalism. In politics and religion we were twins.

I was learning my way around in theological discussions. For a while I just listened. Then, as I got to know the terms, the positions people took up regarding articles of belief, I tentatively waded in. Actually, I knew my Bible better than most of the ordinands did, since I hadn't taught divinity in prep schools for nothing. But my biggest surprise, and pleasure, was to discover what theological modernism was. I found that this college not only held views like mine, but also propagated them. I couldn't help getting immersed in the controversies engendered by staff and students, by lectures and sermons and books and protests and gossip. The views I thought were daring, heretical or just *démodé* were being tossed all around me. I no longer hesitated to declare my doubts regarding Virgin Births and Resurrections, my disrelish for the barbaric elements in the Eucharist. I was more shy about advertising my great love and admiration for Jesus of Nazareth, for all he did and all he taught. Or almost all, for there were darker references in the Gospels, references I came to dismiss as passages far smaller minds had foisted on him.

Yes, artful old Oxford played its age-old tricks even with such poor intellectual material as I was. Gently, insidiously, it got me to unfold a bit, grow a bit, expand a bit. I now had an utterly 'straight' friend with whom I never need be devious, and I dwelt in an ecclesiastical environment where I could be quietly, modestly assertive. My Oxford blossoming was less in English literature than in this new discipline where I was a babe, but an eager one.

Harvey's great hero was Albert Schweitzer. I hadn't been able to take over Roland's heroes very easily (Proust, Yeats, Krishnamurti, von Hügel), but I could take over Schweitzer all right, especially as Harvey enthused over him. 'Reverence for life' became a sort of watchword of ours, and we vowed one day to make a pilgrimage to him at Lambaréné.

I couldn't be shocked by textbook heresies, but I certainly could by some of the young ordinands. Not by their habits of worship, which struck me as often silly or amusing. We had some High Church brethren (I never really discovered what they were doing there, unless it was a desire to carry their war into the enemy's camp). They burned incense and lit candles and adored garish Virgins in their study bedrooms. When the bishop of Oxford visited us they would not shake hands with a respectful declension of the head, as most of us did. They would fall upon their knees and kiss his episcopal ring. All this was done to upset the now principal, Canon Richardson, who merely viewed it with a pitying smile. He had this disconcerting habit of gazing with pity, even clemency, at anyone whose views he regarded as juvenile. I remember once we had a dignitary to inspect us, an ex-colonial bishop who had become a power on church selection boards. I was sitting next to him at the high table. He said, between rather noisy mouthfuls of soup (which caused the principal to look martyred), 'I wish, principal, you had a Sanctus bell at the Eucharist. To mark the stages of our blessed Lord's approach.' The principal gazed at him with infinite pity, infinite mercy, and said: 'I have never thought of him as approaching on a bicycle.' Some of the High Church brethren within earshot all but choked.

I was sorely disillusioned with most of these ordinands. If they really were devout, they tended to be fundamentalists. If they were not, they tended to be quite shockingly worldly. They were, these embryo apostles, extremely ambitious. They endlessly discussed the likeliest places and persons to offer them preferment. Who was a rising star among vicars to whom you could attach yourself? Which parish was closely watched by its progressive bishop? Did the mission field offer the surest path to a mitre? They were bitchy, and they were true academic snobs, who ransacked *Crockford's Clerical Directory* in search of honour classes more frequently than they scanned their Bibles.

Perhaps I am exaggerating it all. Perhaps, now I come to think of it, they weren't so very different from those original apostles. And of course there were some good people among them. It's just that I expected so much: both I and Harvey certainly did.

Towards the end of my first term, after much agonizing about it, I decided I must move into the centre of Oxford, perhaps to some hard-up theological college there, or to an institution with a few rooms to spare. I didn't really want digs again, such as I'd had in the mines; I needed some sort of collegiate life to stop me getting lonely. If only my present abode wasn't so off-centre, its bus services so skimpy. So I told the principal I had with great regret to be moving on. He, too, was sorry. Harvey was quite woebegone. So, really, was I, but I tried to cover the regrets with talk of putative gains.

At the end of term we students had a little party. We lit a great log fire in the junior common room and had lots of sherry and snacks. After a few sherries, Harvey came up to me and said: 'Aw shucks, Peter, you can't do it, you old bastard. Scrub out the whole idea. Go and tell the principal you want to stay. He'll kiss his prodigal son. So will I, if you insist.' I looked at him. We were both a bit squiffy. Harvey chuckled out our usual parody of ourselves: as sentimental old Teutons (like me, Harvey had a bit of German as well as Scottish blood in his make-up), as extravagant old pals locked in camaraderie and schmaltz.

'We'll sit in the chimney corner and reminisce,' he giggled.

'We'll wipe our eyes, and light our meerschaums, and philosophize,' I added.

'Go and tell the principal before it's too late, buddy,' he repeated, shoving me in the back towards him.

The principal was delighted. I was enormously relieved. Harvey was incoherently happy. We really did sit in the chimney corner by the log fire and ridicule the deep affection we had for each other. It was, on my part, a sudden snap decision, a wild about-turn, I'd been longing to make. A decision that changed all the rest of my life. A decision I've never regretted.

3

I had, of course, taken Harvey along one morning to Roland's rooms in Manchester College. Roland had gone into his kitchen to brew some coffee, and I'd followed him with some buns I'd bought en route. Hissed Roland to me: 'Who *is* he?' I said: 'He's one of the theologs at my place and he's a dear.' If any newcomer had a good and attuned mind to offer, which Harvey had, then Roland threw himself into the conversation, as eager to receive as to give. The two of them very soon became immersed in fringe theological pursuits. I sat and listened, glad I'd brought together two people so excitedly.

So in that first vac (Christmas 1948) Harvey came and stayed for a week with me and then for a week with Roland. He fitted in with my lot quite easily. They fell for his loud, artless, affectionate ways; he liked their easy, rather unconventional kind of behaviour, their tolerance, their ready acceptance. I think he assumed they were a typical English family, which they certainly weren't. It was a less successful week he spent with Roland's family. Mrs Dove especially, whose sense of humour, and later friendship with my mother, helped both to come to terms with life, found Harvey's brash backwoodsman manner needed some getting used to. Night after night these two young men, almost exactly of an age, sat up till the small hours, washing down endless discussion with endless lagers until their speech became too muddied for service. And in the daytime we went about *à trois*, introducing Harvey to our London kaleidoscope, or to as much of it as we could afford.

When Harvey had gone off, bumming around England (with which he fell in love for life), I found I must earn some money in a hurry. So I went to see our local town clerk, who took me on in the legal department of the town hall at the splendid salary of £8 a week. As a shorthand typist. I thoroughly enjoyed it. My boss was a rather dry, worried man with a stammer. But I soon found he stammered only if you looked at him. I took his dictation down in my own invented 'shorthand,' which was mostly initialled longhand, such as I'd used with JB long before. And if my boss ever went too fast for me, I gazed searchingly into his eyes as he coloured and stammered and sometimes dried up completely. Rather cruel, but it was a question of the fitter surviving. I did this town hall work during many a vacation from Oxford. And when I did my last stint there, some four years later, the town clerk called in a time-and-motion team to check on all my former colleagues. I've always felt rather a worm about this. But the large office in which I worked spent endless hours chatting and sending out for doughnuts and making tea and coffee and swopping letters and snapshots. I just got on with my work because I hadn't much to contribute to the gossip, and time went faster if you had some work to do. I also had a bit of a conscience about my £8 a week.

I kept all my friendships in good, running repair. I always have, being a confirmed romantic. I introduced Roland to Derrick, who was now married, but that meeting wasn't a success. Derrick had married a nurse at the hospital where he was portering. She had been an art student and she made him a good wife. Derrick's work was prospering, aesthetically rather than financially as yet. They lived in a large studio room in Hampstead, and Mavis helped out with frequent bouts of private nursing. Life wasn't easy for them, but I had many good times with them: at concerts and at the opera, and even at one or two art galleries.

I didn't let new friends take me away from Robbie or Jonathan. Both were doing quite well: Robbie at a well-known architect's and Jonathan at his bank. Roland quite liked Jonathan, but it was not a relationship that developed.

I had some amorous encounters. On a tube train one day I found myself sitting opposite a most striking young man. Not a youth, but in his very early twenties, and bronzed and athletic and extremely good-looking. I just assumed such a person was far too desirable, too swish, for me to know. But I couldn't help gazing. And then, to my astonishment, the eyes and corners of the mouth signalled that this lovely creature was actually interested in *me*.

At Oxford Circus he got off, giving me a look of concentrated invitation as he did so. I followed him. At the end of the platform he stopped to examine a poster. I joined him and said: 'You're not in the least interested in that poster. Come and have some tea with me.' He was very willing to do so, but first he had to go to the BBC to collect some fees: he was an actor.

We went somewhere opulent in Mayfair for tea. He chose a table well sheltered by palms. If he hadn't, I would have done.

We chattered away. He was very bitter about a well-known actor with whom he'd had an affair but who now had turned against him and was preventing his attempts to get work. I commiserated. I then told him I was a student. I saw it was a shock to him, for a student is far removed from a sugar daddy. A little later he gave *me* quite a shock. I said: 'You really are rather beautiful.' He replied: 'I think you're nice, too.' Emboldened by this, and by the secluded corner in which we sat (side by side on a sofa), I kissed him, quickly but firmly, on the cheek. He recoiled and cried irritably: 'Oh, do mind my make-up.'

It was my first contact with male make-up, and it rather unsettled me (that lovely Riviera sun tan!).

Still, we arranged to meet again soon. It was one evening for supper. We went somewhere fairly costly in Soho. He quite assumed I'd pay for everything, always; I might be a student but I could obviously afford to pay or I wouldn't do it.

His name also was Peter, and I grew quite fond of him. We never had any physical relationship. All he ever did, sitting on a bus or in a restaurant, was to take my hand and push up my cuff, murmuring: 'Lovely wrist, lovely, lovely wrist.' I mention this as an example of the sexual fetishes one may meet.

What he needed was a friend. Someone to grieve to. He endlessly, compulsively, vindictively, condemned the actor he felt was ruining his career, his life. I began to suspect it was a neurotic delusion. After a whole year of painful listening and even more painful financing, I began no longer to look forward to our meetings. He seemed to become remoter, too, ever more immersed in his thespian vendetta. I never repudiated him, but somehow it all ended. I have never forgotten him, never ceased to lament that so lovely a vessel should be so flawed.

During that first Christmas vacation from Oxford someone else turned up unexpectedly. That was Nigel Day. He had been at Jimmy's when I taught there, but I had scarcely noticed him. He had left at the end of my first year at the school and become a dayboy at St Paul's. One day in the next Easter holidays he had called to see Brian, with whom he'd kept up a relationship based on a mutual affection for vintage motorbikes. I noticed what a handsome boy he had grown into. But his friend was Brian, to whom he was not attractive. They went camping together in Spain that summer, and Brian said he was a very nice kid and very good company. 'Did you...?' I asked Brian, well aware that there was no need to finish such a question asked in such a context. He laughed. 'Good Lord, no. He's a galumpher.' That was our descriptive name for awkward adolescents who had temporarily lost control of growing feet and hands and lurched forward with the aid of flippers.

Nigel was indeed one such, and he possessed other pleasant attributes commonly associated with galumphing: a frank, sunny nature and laughter ever on tap. I think his burgeoning mind attracted me quite as much as his burgeoning body. I sort of wooed him. He didn't talk about the things a boy of that age and type might have been expected to drool about: sport and girls. He didn't even discuss motorbikes with me. He seemed to want from me opinions he didn't get from Brian, or indeed anyone else. He endlessly argued about politics and even morality. He resisted at first my admiration for the Labour Party and scorn for the Tories, my passionate condemnation of capital punishment and repression of any kind. But it was merely a token resistance: soon he was as unsympathetic as I was to any thoughtless conformity, in religion no less than in politics.

We went for long walks and talks, in the nooks and crannies of the metropolis and in the Surrey hills. We were utterly frank with each other. We discussed homosexuality. He said he wasn't, and that was true. But when I told him he attracted me, he said: 'Ditto.' So amorous play became as normal, and habitual, as eating. He never evinced the slightest guilt about it or reluctance for it. His healthy, cheery attitude to all such things was a breath of fresh air. Like me, he could mock and parody what he enjoyed so readily. But he also smiled with pleasure when I serenaded him in my version of Cole Porter:

> Nigel Day, you are the one;
> Only you beneath the moon and under the sun.
> In the roaring traffic's boom,
> In the silence of my lonely room,
> I think of you,
> Nigel Day, Nigel *Day*...

Which soon came to be quite true. He brightened all those Oxford vacs, and many, many years to come.

4

The Oxford terms flitted by. Eight weeks at a time was a small span in which to hang so great, so rich, so miscellaneous a tapestry. There was the official degree course, where I made few new loves but added depth to the old ones: to Chaucer and Shakespeare and Milton and Wordsworth. I was breaking little new ground, and few students shared my enthusiasm for the Lady of Christ's or the Seer of the Fells. Spenser and Donne and Pope I acquired. The course stopped with Keats and Shelley and Byron, none of whom I cared for.

Then there was all the unofficial exploration of theology, via gossip and hearsay and argument and report, and Harvey's excited rehashing of his tutor's learning. Harvey had enormous respect and affection for his tutor. With Roland I remember sharing only snide and often hilarious comments on the university and its dons, not any literary loves. In fact I don't think Roland had any real loves in our curriculum. Perhaps the ceaseless grind of study killed any he once had. Roland liked all the byways and alleys and hidden courtyards of literature (preferably not English), but really he should never have read English at all; his heart was in philosophy and theology. Just as I have always regretted not reading Greats.

I had another friend who was reading English and could never think why. That was Bruce, an ex-service student of about my age, and like me a lay brother at Ripon Hall. I remember he had made a rather final contribution to our discussion of homosexuality. He'd drawled: 'Can't see the need for it, ol' man, so long as there's enough floosies about.' He was not merely at sea in English studies: he actively and unashamedly disliked literature. He was a seven-foot, utterly cynical, utterly Tory, utterly decent old Philistine. Getting through the requisite texts was an agony to him. I can see him gangling moodily before my bookcase and saying: 'Got anything here on Dickie Three-stroke, ol' man? I've an essay coming on Shakespeare's bumped-off king with the looking glass.'

'Richard the Second,' I said.

'Oh, was it? Sure it wasn't Edward the Second? Didn't he make up in a mirror?'

'Marlowe,' I answered rather shortly. Since it was early in the week I was writing letters.

There was a rather long silence. I looked at him. A certain rheumy nostalgia had entered his eyes. 'Never forget a weekend I had there once with a floosie I'd met at a rugger match. A real sport.'

'Who?' I asked, mystified. 'Where?'

'Marlow. Regatta. God, you're ignorant, ol' man.'

After Oxford, Bruce wandered half-heartedly into schoolmastering and implanted in a few desperate kids his own hatred for poetry. Then he chucked it, or was chucked, and became a travel agent. At the same time he took a general science degree by correspondence and went back into schoolmastering in an entirely different, and infinitely more rewarding, capacity. I must say I greatly admired this.

Roger was another part of my theological college world. He was a genuine ordinand, of working-class extraction, who by his own unaided efforts had got to Oxford to read theology. He'd been brought up in an Anglo-Catholic family, had been a rather pretty altar boy and choirboy, then a server, then a scoutmaster, before doing his National Service as a naval rating. It was an evolution as different from mine as can be imagined. It rather intrigued me. I often questioned him about his family (his younger brother, whom I never saw, alas, was a telegraph boy) and about his progressive churchgoing, and life in the navy, and how he taught himself to play the organ (quite well), and finally how he got to Oxford. It was quite a romantic story, but rather spoiled by the fact that he was utterly unaware of its romance. Religious faith was nothing you had discovered or wished to discuss. It was a *donné*. So was almost everything that had befallen him. The only spark of interest I found in him so far as his vocation was concerned was a sartorial one: how many buttons to have on a cassock and how many frills on a surplice. It was all a mystery to me. As were all the crossings and genuflections that were second nature to him, and his total unawareness of mental ferment as an ingredient in faith.

Andrew spent more and more of his time with drinking pals and less and less with his mathematical studies. This worried me and I spoke to him about it seriously. But I was in no position to do so. I too was endlessly seeking

THE MORE WE ARE TOGETHER

reasons and persons and places to escape my studies. Many evenings, when even Roland and Harvey had to refuse my luring invitations, I sat alone in the lounge of the Randolph Hotel with a book and a pot of coffee and a votary's anguished eye for a certain lovely pageboy. The books I had with me were all germane to the coming Friday's essay. All allayers of guilt, purveyors of self-deception, stalking-horses behind which the sorry eyes forever darted. I can't remember the books. The boy I vividly do, although I never said so much as 'Good evening' to him.

One morning Andrew and I were having a bit of breakfast in the Town and Gown. The place was noisy. The Cypriot owners were forever yelling out orders ('One eggy, spammy, chippy tomato'), and at a nearby table half a dozen young men were talking loudly and affectedly for all to admire. Said Andrew to me as one of them went up to the counter for a refill: 'He's one of the brilliant set. You know, Ken Tynan and Tony Richardson and the C.S. Lewis crowd.'

'I know,' I said, viewing the back of the young man at the counter. 'Would you like to meet him?' I asked, knowing from his hushed and awed tones that he would like nothing better.

'How?' he asked breathlessly. 'You don't...?'

For answer I went up to the counter and said to the young man: 'Remember me, Peter?' He wheeled round, stared at me for a second in wild astonishment, then shouted out as he threw his arms round my neck: 'Peter, *darling!*'

Yes, it was Peter Fison, the bright and amusing 14-year-old I had tutored in Latin at the Arts Theatre Club some six or seven years before. I must say his greeting, though it touched and pleased me, was also rather embarrassing for such a reticent creature as I. But Andrew was enormously impressed, especially when Peter insisted on taking us back to Magdalen for some mead.

For many years Peter intrigued and amused me. He seemed to have distilled for himself all that was most captivatingly extravagant in Firbank and Fitzgerald and Waugh and anybody else who could be grist to his wildly whirring mill. He was very gifted, becoming a bright young don who founded his own small extramural university. His early death was a great shock.

By sheer accident, I was able to impress Andrew on another occasion. We were passing the Playhouse when Andrew said he'd like to see Shaw's *Pygmalion*, which was billed as the current attraction. I saw that the lead, Eliza Doolittle, was played by my old boyhood friend, Hy Hazell. So I said casually to Andrew, as we gazed at the stills outside the theatre: 'She's an attractive girl, isn't she? I think you ought to meet her before we go to a performance.' I guessed Hyacinth would be there, resting before the evening house. So, followed by a goggle-eyed Andrew, I walked in and asked the stage

252

doorkeeper for Miss Hazell, giving my name. Sure enough, we were asked into her dressing room. She was charm itself. After this Andrew almost revered me for my connections.

One day we had a lecture at the college by Dean Inge, and the dining hall was cleared of tables and filled with chairs for the many guests. We frequently had prestigious visits, often from distinguished Boar's Hill neighbours like Gilbert Murray and John Masefield. On this occasion, we students were packed into a little gallery. Several had to stand, including both Andrew and Roger. I said to Roger, who was right beside me, 'You can sit on my knee if you like.' With a grin, he did so. I thought nothing of it, and completely forgot the incident.

Andrew used to arrive back at the college well after lock-up, having walked up from the city, often rather the worse for wear. I told him there'd be trouble if he were caught: not just trouble for himself, but also trouble for the college, which could lose its licence as a hall of residence. So he promised to be earlier, or at least very careful. He formed the habit of getting into pyjamas and dressing gown and coming to my room (I had a grand room at the top of the tower) to report in to me as I read in bed.

Doing this one night, he was, I sensed, unusually uncommunicative, almost sulky. 'What's up with you?' I asked.

'Nothing.'

'Oh yes there is. Come on, out with it. I may be able to help.'

He was sitting on my bed. Suddenly he flung himself on me, his head smothered in my chest and pyjamas and bedclothes, and blurted out: 'You asked Roger to sit on your knee in the gallery, not me.'

It was so bizarre I couldn't believe my ears. I wanted to burst out laughing but realized in time that such a reaction would be cruel. So I soothed him by protesting my innocence of any slight. 'I never dreamt you would take such a thing to heart,' I murmured. He didn't reply, didn't raise his buried head. Then he said, in an odd faraway voice: 'I want to get into bed with you. Can I?'

To be honest, I didn't really want him to. Partly because I wasn't attracted to him in that way. Partly because we could be caught by some late caller. But I had to say: 'Of course, if you want to.'

So in he got, and in he stayed for about an hour. Nothing happened. I don't think he wanted it to, any more than I did. He wanted to snuggle and talk and feel wanted.

That happened on many nights, and always I remembered one of his first remarks: 'If any man tried that with me, I'd smash my fist into his face.' I was learning how full of surprises people were, life was.

Two other incidents I associate with Andrew.

One concerned a girl he had got to know at the university Labour Club, where she was, apparently, a star, destined for great things. Andrew proudly said he was going to bring her to tea with me. It was his chance to impress me, and I welcomed it. I gave them tea in my room, having bought some rather special things to eat. After tea I gave them a little recital on my gramophone, of which I was rather proud. I had only recently acquired it: a fine EMG with a great horn and fibre needles you had to cut with special scissors. I also had some new records I was growing very fond of: songs by Richard Strauss and Villa Lobos, and Wagner's Mathilde Wesendonck songs, beautifully sung by Kirsten Flagstad. I can't think the visit was very successful. No doubt it was a mistake to inflict my songs on a stranger, but perhaps I did so because the conversation was a little sticky. I vaguely felt the girl had not taken to me, and that, of course, was the surest way to see to it that I didn't really take to her. I think I was a trifle surprised that we had so little in common: her attitude to Labour governments and Labour politicians didn't seem as idealistic as mine.

A day or two later, Andrew and I were talking over the occasion and he said casually: 'Oh, I'd already told her you were queer. Didn't I tell you that beforehand? Thought I had.' The girl was Shirley Catlin, today better known as the Labour politician and cofounder of the SDP, Baroness Shirley Williams, and to me even more intriguing as the daughter of Vera Brittain (an old star of mine).

The other little vignette enclosing Andrew was a summer's foursome on the river as the day was dying. Bruce, Harvey, Andrew and I. In a punt. On the Isis near Magdalen. And Bruce was punting, because he was as long as the punt pole. Harvey and I lay soporifically, trailing our warm hands in the sticky water. And all the while Andrew played his recorder beautifully. When he'd finished, the occupants of other boats applauded.

It was the only typical, traditional Oxford cameo I gained in my four years at the university.

5

Neither Roland nor I entered into the normal swing of university life. We neither of us joined any society, although I did put my foot into the spokes of one. It was called the Heretics Club, and it specialized in lectures on fringe, off-beat, unconventional subjects. I wrote to the secretary and issued a challenge. I said: 'You won't really earn the title of Heretics until you get someone to speak on homosexuality.' He rose to the challenge, and was positively enthusiastic about it. But, could I suggest a speaker who was eminent enough and respectable enough to placate the proctors? I suggested Kenneth Walker, a very distinguished surgeon *and* philosopher. Walker agreed to come. But the proctors were as obstructive as they could be.

Finally, and grudgingly, they agreed only on condition the lecture was entitled 'Maladjustment.' Of course, it spread around like wildfire what the real topic was, and it was the most crowded meeting the club ever had.

Walker gave a fine talk, and I, yes I, was one of the undergrads who asked a question from the floor. It was the first time I had spoken in public, and so shy was I that my knees knocked, my tongue clave and my heart well-nigh burst in my chest. But I did it, determined to eclipse Hazlitt (I think it was) who forewent a pension he desperately needed because he was too shy to tell a large and eminent concourse how deserving he was. I don't remember what my question was, or Walker's reply, but I asked it. It was a triumph, a landmark in my life. Walker didn't, of course, remember me.

The Heretics Club asked me to write the whole proceedings up for *Isis*, which I duly did. I was secretly rather proud of the achievement. Eight years before the Wolfenden Report was published. Seventeen years before the Labour government brought in the act permitting homosexual relations between consenting male adults in private. Few now can realize how savage was the law in 1949, how intense the suffering, how high the suicide rate. Before we went to Oxford, a friend of mine, a noted BBC producer, had taken his life, as had a bright young solicitor's clerk I had helped to gain his matric and win a place at Cambridge. No subsequent swings of the pendulum too far the other way can ever make one wish those cruel days back again.

Sometimes Harvey and I would go for great bike rides. I had brought up my old bike from London: large and gentlemanly and painfully heavy and slow. The principal had lent Harvey a bike, and the two of us went exploring very old, very remote churches.

In the college grounds was a large, artificial lake on which were moored two old rowing boats. Both lake and boats had seen better days, gracious and festive days. They must have grieved at the use to which Harvey and I now put them, although it was probably better than being ignored. We soon tired of rowing demurely, each in his own ungainly craft. Instead, each tried to ram, rock, flood and finally sink the other. Always in the shallows near the bank (I was no swimmer), and always to the raucous accompaniment of oaths and yells. I am astonished, looking back, at our juvenile behaviour. But we loved it, often getting into old clothes and sprinting down to the lake before we had digested our lunch. I expect it did us a world of good.

I remember once we were floundering in the weeds, Harvey stripped to his underpants, and the air blue with our oaths, when the principal and his wife appeared on a gentle afternoon promenade. He looked very pained and adroitly steered his lady off course. I told Harvey he looked upset because he couldn't join us, or at any rate become a spectator of Harvey's near-nude antics. The scene reminded me of a similar aghast encounter in Forster's *A*

Room With a View. But it all seemed just the setting for Harvey: Huck and the Mississippi *à l'anglais.*

Our other great recreation was table tennis in the cellar. Usually foursomes. For the first and last time in my life I became really quite a champion at a sport. I even wondered if I had been silly to decline so promptly an invitation from my Oxford college to report to a greater waterway for a greater sport: someone felt I had the makings of an oarsman in the college eight.

With Roland were sedater pleasures: trips to Woodstock for 'nice' teas with boiled, new-laid eggs. We were still four years from the end of food rationing. There were even large, and basic, 'British restaurants' to tempt one in High Streets. I don't think I ever went in one: Fuller's and the Cadena would have missed me so much. But a really new-laid egg was then a treat. They were all free-range too, I think.

At some college 'do' I met an impressive old lady from a nearby village. Lady Toogood was the self-appointed Lady of the Manor: unconventional, amusing and almost too true to her name. Among other things she ran the village boys' club and, I discovered too late, was forever scouting for undergraduates to help her run it. I found myself volunteering, and in due course I was tramping across fields and over stiles and among cowpats to the village hall where the kids met once a week. There were some nice enough boys among them, but also some horrors who knew quite cynically that they were on to a good thing with Lady Bountiful and her long-suffering aides.

Sometimes we all went to a fixture with a more professionally run boys' club in north Oxford: the boys in a bus and Lady Toogood and I in her chauffeured car. This Oxford club was run by a girl who had recently graduated in English at Somerville and was training in social work. I discovered Helen's father, Canon Power, was a very successful parish priest in Birmingham, and a well-known modernist to boot.

I tried to involve Harvey in the village youth club with me, but his two visits there had scarcely enamoured him of the work. Very often on a Sunday afternoon I would have the boys up to the theological college. We played ping-pong in the basement and barged about on the lake. And I'd give them a bumper tea in my room, with lashings of stuff I'd bought the day before. I don't remember many of these boys: only Ben do I recall clearly. Because, of course, he was very attractive, and also nicer than most. I remember an occasion when both Ben and I were being driven back from somewhere by Lady Toogood. I stole a glance or two at Ben, thinking what a lovely boy he was: dark-haired and tanned and lithe. Suddenly Lady Toogood put her arm round his neck, hugged him hard, and said to me: 'Oh, isn't he lovely? Don't you love his bright eyes and his wonderful little face?' I don't know who blushed deeper, Ben or I. And I wondered again if my inmost thoughts could advertise themselves aloud.

I eased myself out of the village club. I talked Harvey into coming to the north Oxford club with me. I thought it might make a better impression on him. Which it certainly seemed to do. He even asked when was my next visit. Some time later, when I had all but severed my connections with the village club (and not without a sense of guilt), one evening I saw the desirable Ben, all poshed up in his best suit, hanging around the bus station at Gloucester Green. He didn't see me, and I didn't speak to him. He looked as if he were waiting for someone. I thought nothing of it, but when the same thing happened again in more or less the same spot, and I saw an undergraduate I knew by sight stop, speak to Ben, and then walk off with him, well, then I did wonder. Probably not what I thought, but it was titillating to think so. I once wrote a long series of rhymes about Ben's putative profession. The rhymes are now lost, but I remember the refrain:

> So higgledy-piggledy, my dear Ben,
> Once such a joy to gentlemen.

There was also a long lament, penned some years later, when, on a return visit to Oxford, I saw Ben serving behind the dairy counter in a large grocer's. All the glamour had gone from him. I imagined a nagging wife and whining children with none of the beauty that had once been his. One section of the lament ran:

> Gay little huntsman, lithe and lean,
> All decked up in Gloster Green,
> You would raise your horn
> To salute the morn,
> In that mullioned window
> Just off the Corn.

I should have read such things to my tutor as occasional respites from mangled essays. I wonder what his reaction would have been.

There was another, infinitely more conventional, meeting in Oxford. Around lunchtime, in the High, as I decamped from a lecture. It was a young man, walking along hand in hand with Helen, the girl who ran the north Oxford boys' club. The young man was Harvey. I took care they didn't see me.

Back at the college later that day, I drifted into Harvey's room for a chat.

'We must go to that north Oxford boys' club again soon,' I said casually.

'Oh, yes, I suppose we must.' He was even more casual.

'Remember that rather nice girl who ran the show? What was her name...?'

'Don't remember,' he said. 'Got a cigarette?'

I leaned forward, fighting to keep a straight face. 'No, I haven't got a cigarette. Not for such a rotten, lying, hypocritical old roué. Oh, you slippery, underhand, two-timing, double-dealing...' I was running out of epithets, as well as of an appropriate cast of countenance. Harvey was lying on his bed with a book. 'What the hell...?' he began.

'You don't remember the name of the girl at the north Oxford boys' club. *You*, that I saw walking along the High hand in hand with her. You toad, you rat!'

Harvey buried his face in his hands and went into shrieks of laughter, followed by me. When we'd subsided a bit, I said: 'And you wanted me to believe it was the boys' club that mildly interested you. What a snake.'

So that was how Harvey began his courtship, spied upon by the very Pandar who had brought them together. I was glad to have done so, for two nicer people you could not wish for. But the ping-pongs and the Mississippi games and all the long bike rides and the even longer talks became fewer and briefer.

Harvey was doing a wartime shortened degree, and Roland had come up a year before me, so both were taking their finals at the end of my second year, that is, in summer 1950. This was a sad deprivation for me. Nevertheless two happy events illumined that time. One was Harvey's securing for Roland a place as Instructor in his old university, in Ohio. This elated Roland, who wanted to work anywhere but in England, and accounted for his desperate desire to get 'any sort of a degree.' I was glad that Harvey had done this for him, and that I had introduced him to Harvey, thus in some measure repaying Roland for getting me to Oxford.

Harvey got his degree and said that his marriage to Helen was to take place that July, at her father's vicarage in Birmingham. I was to be best man. It was all done in style, with Moss Bros finery and marquee meals. Canon Power married his daughter, and her brother gave his sister away. It was a joyous occasion with lumps in many throats, including mine, for Harvey and Helen were to fly off very soon after the wedding to their new home in the States, where Harvey was to be ordained. And Roland was to fly off to Ohio very soon after. That was a summer of valedictions for me.

6

It was as well that in my friends' final term something had happened to make me concentrate more seriously on my own future. The principal had said to me one evening in his study after dinner: 'Peter, dear boy, have you considered being ordained? I should rejoice indeed if that were to happen.' I smiled and shook my head. 'You know, principal, that suggestion has been made to me before.' He nodded appreciatively, as if I were agreeing to his suggestion, and as if that were the only necessary preliminary to my ordination.

I told him I was from a family of sturdy disbelievers. 'We are not ordaining them, brother,' he replied urbanely. I told him I was myself no orthodox believer. 'Nor I, dear boy,' he rejoined. I told him I had not even been baptized. 'No trouble at all,' he smiled. 'I can do that any time in the chapel. And we can get the bishop to come in one evening and confirm you.' It was all beginning to seem so easy. Could it really be so? 'But I have never been a churchgoer. I am not familiar with church life in any way.' He chuckled and said in conclusion: 'Think how wonderfully fresh will be your approach to it all.' I tried one last, desperate shot as he rose to his feet: 'But I've no call to parish work. I think I'd be awful at it. In fact, I'd hate it. All I'd really like to be,' I said it wonderingly, as for the first time the idea really gripped me, 'is a school chaplain.' He opened his study door for me, saying: 'And that you could certainly be, dear brother, after two years' work as a parish curate.' And he didn't actually say as I left, but certainly conveyed: 'So that's all settled.'

That long vacation at home was rather different in tone and texture. After the crowded days of Harvey's wedding and the God-speeding of Roland, I sat down to recover my breath and comfort myself with the family and friends remaining. From the family nest both Terry and Brian had flown, but, I stubbornly told myself, enough were left for me to cherish and preserve my vision of a happy, united household. Yet the dust of the years was beginning to settle even there. Mother could not battle on as gamely as she had. Legs could not walk as far, hands fashion as much pastry, eyes thread so many needles. Father, too, was ageing perceptibly: travelling to and from the office was an effort. There were pains in the chest we all hoped would respond to milk of magnesia. Miles was now seven: a difficult child who did badly at school and was unbiddable at home. He adored his grandmother and resented his father. And Pam? She had beaux again, and less legitimately. Bob, her husband, was a fly trapped in a web. He seldom asserted himself: partly because he was intimidated by the force of her personality, but mostly because he had never ceased to love her. Nor, time was to show, had she him. It was a strange, chequered relationship which perhaps only they understood. Often Pam would go out on an evening date. If ever I asked her where she was going, she would look secretive, mischievous, provocative. Tapping her nose with her finger, Dickens fashion, she would say: 'I have an appointment with *Friend*.' And burst out laughing. This was an affectionate echo of Glad-eye, who always referred to her liaisons as '*Friend*' (with a whinny and always without an article, definite or indefinite). Pam never came out with me as she once had. Very sadly I remembered our hilarious walks and talks, our interminable evening coffees in far-flung cafés.

Then one evening, as we returned from the theatre, Jonathan blurted out to me something he had great difficulty in formulating, something that, I now saw, had been clouding the whole day. 'Peter, I've something to tell you. I... I don't want to. I've been putting it off and putting it off. Peter, I'm terribly sorry. I'm going to get married.' I said nothing for I was stunned by the news. He gabbled on: 'Miranda's an awfully nice girl. You'll like her. She's so sensible. And... and a good cook. She can do vegetarian food, too. You can come to dinner whenever you like. She'd enjoy that.' There was a silence. Then I said: 'Of course, I'm very glad for your sake. I hope you're both very happy. That's the proper thing to say, isn't it?' Jonathan was nearly in tears: 'I must get away from my father, you see. He's getting worse: condemning everything I do. Oh, Peter, it won't make any difference to our friendship. We've got a nice flat in Highgate, and you're welcome there always, *always*.'

For Jonathan's sake I acted delight in his good fortune, said I looked forward to many a happy evening in Highgate with them, told him not to be so absurd as to present such splendid news lugubriously, apologetically.

Miranda *was* a pleasant girl, intelligent, with nothing flighty or shallow about her. She was also a good cook, and I did indeed have several well-fed evenings with them in Highgate.

But... well, *but*. Friends can't talk in front of wives as they once did. Wives hate friends who talk about matey days they've known before ever the spouse came on the scene. Yes, they had all disappeared into marriage, or were about to: Derrick and Graham and Harvey. And now Jonathan. This, I saw, was to be the pattern of my life, and I must come to terms with it. Only homosexual friends might remain, and I had very few of them.

And then a piece more of the past broke, dissolved, reformed. Good old Jimmy died one day: quickly, quietly, seated in his chair with a whisky behind those heavy lace curtains. The school was inherited by some distant married nephew. Brian didn't want to stay. He fixed himself up in a beautiful, very superior boarding prep school in Sussex. In the holidays he lived on and off with a nurse who'd been at his stokehole hospital, younger than his wife, under whom she had served, and much more Brian's cup of tea: a bit of a beatnik, like him. One day Brian told me, quite casually, that they had a son, whom he named Julien. This girl changed her name by deed poll to Gamble. And Julien Gamble has turned out a very pleasant and successful young man.

What a tangled web we have all woven.

7

As soon as the Michaelmas term of 1950 opened, the principal hastened to get me baptized and confirmed. All very quiet and private, according to my wishes. He baptized me in the college chapel one evening. I don't recall any godparents: perhaps he and his wife filled these roles. I do remember his asking me before the ceremony: 'Now, brother, do you wish to be baptized with the trinitarian formula?' This was said with an almost imperceptible wrinkling of his nose, a fleeting hint of distaste. 'Or...?' His face cleared and a little seraphic smile played round his mouth. 'Or "In the name of Jesus Christ," just like the first gallant Christians?' I was so ignorant of all such usages that I thought these were legitimate alternatives. Well, to be quite honest, his manner of presenting them was so weighted one way that I had a tiny suspicion he was following some cherished aberration of his own. Even so, I shared his liking for the simpler and more ancient words. So those I chose and in those I was baptized. A week later the suffragan bishop very kindly came up to the college and confirmed me, very soon after which I was told to apply for all the necessary forms from CACTM. This was the Central Advisory Council of Training for the Ministry, the awesome body who vetted would-be ordinands and gave the thumbs up or down.

In all this I was prompted and guided by the principal, who had clearly set his heart on getting me dog-collared. I mustn't suggest any lack of spiritual sincerity on his part in all this. Or, indeed, on mine, even though I knew myself far, far better than he knew me. There now very quickly developed in me a sense of vocation: a genuine, earnest desire to minister to boys both aesthetically, teaching literature, and spiritually, as a school chaplain. I felt that I could be absolutely sincere as a priest because of my love for the person and teaching of Jesus. All else was second to that.

The principal now gave me occasional (very occasional) tutorials on doctrine. I enjoyed these, for they reinforced my growing belief that most heresies had a long and attractive history and the dear, sane, liberal Church of England could accommodate them. I knew that after I had done my degree I could be given a grant for a one-year postgraduate Diploma in Education. This was all in order, but not at all in order was my decision to combine it with my rather haphazard studies towards (as I hoped) ordination. But what else could I do? I couldn't find the money or, frankly, the energy to tack on a fifth year of study.

There were other obstacles to surmount, but I had another backer in addition to the principal. This was the Ripon Hall tutor. He was a devout, but liberal, High Churchman (or 'spike', as I was learning to call them). As may be imagined, he was not quite on the same wavelength as the principal. Nevertheless he was impeccably correct: respectful, loyal, supportive. He also had a distinctly off-beat, sequestered sense of humour. Things tickled him, I noticed, but he did not try to share them, as though he had long ago discovered the futility of attempting it. He endeavoured to be invariably straight-faced, but his eyes and even sometimes the corners of his mouth betrayed him.

On one occasion we were both reading some things on the notice board when a rather stuffy, complacent ordinand passed us: a middle-aged man of oppressive respectability who did not doubt that he possessed a rich sense of humour. His routine was clockwork. A quarter of an hour after each meal he would solemnly traverse the grounds. His route was invariable, as were his sartorial quirks. He always carried in one hand a pair of brown leather gloves, as indissolubly compressed as a pair of kippers. When he had passed us, our tutor murmured to himself: 'There goes master for his constitutional.' And I murmured: 'In his elastic-sided boots.' The tutor's face creased and he said hurriedly: 'Do please come into my study for a liqueur, Mr Gamble.'

In that rather grotesque fashion we inaugurated one of the odder friendships of my life. He, like the principal, but for soberer reasons, I feel, was also convinced that I was worthy of ordination, and his assistance was likewise invaluable. For on my CACTM forms it was necessary to give my 'home parish priest,' conjuring up pictures unknown to me of a little boy brought up in some domineering, all-fulfilling local church. What was I to put down: 'Never gone to church until I arrived at my theological college, except for a few weeks in prison'? The tutor came to the rescue. Near me in Surrey (he told me) he had an elderly friend, a man of intellect and sanctity. In the holidays I must attend his church and get to know him. I liked Father Lubbock: a celibate, highly disciplined parish priest. I couldn't share the views of such men but I respected them, not least their austere programmes of a mass each day around dawn.

So the principal and the tutor and Father Lubbock were all going to sponsor me. I was beginning to look almost orthodox, when one day the rather agitated tutor asked me: 'Mr Gamble, may I ask you a personal question? You need not answer, of course, but I hope you will.'

'Of course,' I said, wondering what was coming.

'Can you tell me what words the principal used when he baptized you?' (Was that all? Phew!) I replied brightly: 'Oh yes: he baptized me "In the Name of Jesus Christ".' And I added loyally: 'He asked me if I would like those words or the usual ones.'

The tutor said gravely: 'Your baptism is quite invalid. Therefore your confirmation is also. So also will be your ordination.'

'Oh dear,' I said, trying to sound as appalled as the tutor, but in reality wondering what all the fuss was about. 'What can we do?'

He pondered solemnly for a while. Then he proceeded more brightly, as though suddenly enlightened. 'I shall ask Father Lubbock to baptize you in his church next holidays and then put you forward as one of his candidates at his next confirmation. That would be best.'

'Thank you,' I said with appropriate fervour. 'Thank you very much.'

And so that holy hurdle was overcome and I tried to address myself keenly to my Dip Ed work. Rousing any enthusiasm for it was difficult. Teaching is a gift, one of the very few I felt I possessed. I found the attempt to impart it to these young people who had never done any quite unconvincing - in my case, decidedly irritating. As for things like 'Psychology' and 'The History of Education,' I found them dry bones, lifeless, unreal. My specialist subjects ('Teaching of English' and 'Teaching of Divinity') were more rewarding, for I had an excellent tutor in each. Miss Wilkinson took me in the divinity and Harold Loukes, the University Reader in Education, for the English. Loukes was a delightful person and a fine, stimulating lecturer; a Quaker and a Liberal and everything that appealed to me. Sadly, both Loukes and Miss Wilkinson died a few years after my time at the Department.

8

The whole of the second term of my Dip Ed year had to be spent teaching somewhere away from Oxford, at a school chosen by me and approved by the Department. I chose a famous public school in the far north of England because its headmaster was a noted modernist cleric I thought I'd take to. That was Canon Luce, headmaster of Durham School.

I travelled up to Durham by coach, money being so short, and Brian came with me for company. This was crazy, because he was poorer than I was, but I was very grateful to have the backing. We arrived in the ancient northern town at 9 pm, with the prospect of finding digs. We knew that was impossible at such an hour, and we must check in at some modest, probably commercial, hotel. We crawled creakingly out of the coach and collected my huge and heavy suitcase. From a notice in the bus station we took the name and address of a suitably seedy hotel and looked around for a taxi. But a small, fair-haired and attractive youth seized my case, hoisted it on his back, and said: 'Where's tha want, sirrah?' Brian murmured: 'Everything laid on. Most agreeable.' I told the youth the hotel we wanted, but said we were going there in a taxi. The youth took not the slightest notice of this, but set off at a spanking pace, calling over his shoulder: 'I'll get tha theer.' Brian and I were obliged to sprint behind him, for fear both he and the case might be eaten up by the murky night.

But at last we saw the name and lights of the hotel. 'Before we go in, let's call in there for a pint,' said Brian, indicating an unprepossessing pub across the street. Over our drinks, we asked the youth his name and how old he was and what he did for a living. He was Jackie, aged eighteen and awaiting his call-up. He did any old jobs he could find and he was going to mutilate himself just before his medical was due. He concluded by pointing out of the window and saying: 'We live down along theer.'

I nodded, anxious to convey interest and no shocked surprise. 'You live at home with your mam and dad?' I was slowly drifting back into the language of my coal mining days, though this was considerably farther north.

He said rather contemptuously: 'Na-a-a. Live with me woman and our bairn.'

I felt this was quite enough eye-popping revelation for one night. I said we must be going, and thanked him for his help. I gave him five shillings.

'What's tha doon a-morrer?' he asked. Reluctantly, I told him I had to find digs and then inspect the school I was joining. I didn't want to tell him much, or, in fact, to see him again, attractive though he was. 'What time's tha start?'

I told him, 'About ten.' He nodded. 'I'll be theer,' he said. 'No, no,' I countered. 'We've a lot to do. And' (lamely) 'we mustn't take up your time.' He grinned, rather savagely, and repeated: 'I'll be theer.'

When we were ensconced in the drab, cabbagy hotel, Brian said with a smile: 'Well, you've made a friend already.'

'One I could do without. He won't be exactly a recommendation at the school.'

'Oh, I don't know,' went on Brian. 'He's really rather nice.' Then he added wistfully: 'More than a hint of Julien about him.' I'd noticed the same.

The next morning we emerged into snow and Jackie. He was leaning against a wall whittling a piece of wood with a vicious-looking knife. He took command at once, leading us to a council office where I could get a list of lodgings. Then to inspect the school: a small part of which was quite old, the rest rather depressingly Victorian. All the streets were pretty alpine and the school itself was set on a high hill. Term had started and boys were milling around behind rather penal-looking walls and iron gates. It was my first sight of the type of milieu in which I was, perhaps, to spend the rest of my working life.

Then we descended and found a café where we all had coffee and buns. The lower you descended, the seedier it became. Around the school, however, there were broad roads filled with large houses that betokened Edwardian industrial prosperity, while around the university and the magnificent cathedral all was impressively grand.

I had been told when to present myself: at 11 am in the headmaster's study three days after the official opening of term. That was tomorrow. Brian had to leave early the same morning. We got rid of Jackie with difficulty, and an assurance (or threat?) that he'd be whittling outside the hotel at the same time in the morning.

I saw Brian off on his coach early the next morning gloomily, for I didn't much care for my new location. Perhaps, too, I had forebodings. Still, Brian had to go, for his term started the next day, and he was in any case flat broke (as usual). I didn't go back near the hotel for fear of meeting Jackie. I kicked my heels all around the school locality until it was time for me to call on Canon Luce.

There are some people you take to at first sight. And some you don't. That's how it was with Canon Luce: tall, spare, and with a permanently clouded expression. That, at least, is how I remember him. However, I showed none of this but was (I thought) suitably respectful. But I don't think Canon Luce considered me so. It also became clear very early on that the canon's impression of me was as unfortunate as mine of him.

Now I wish to be just about this. I think I behaved naively. I was so delighted to be teaching again, and in a noted public school, that I made every effort to be efficient, reliable, successful. This offended the headmaster and other leading masters. They expected someone innocent, inexperienced, touchingly grateful for all their patronizing expertise, their lofty instruction.

I was expected to sit in on certain lessons and be overwhelmingly impressed by their skill when in fact I thought most rather poor. With a clear sense of the enormous privilege he was conferring, the headmaster let me attend one of his divinity periods with the sixth. It was one of a series of lessons on comparative religion. He was speaking on (I think) Islam. He outlined a popular picture of an eastern paradise: a place where luscious maidens with bowls of sherbet indulged every whim of the (apparently all male) elect. As he etched the picture I stole a glance round the room: those boys who were struggling to conceal their grins vied with others who were obviously entranced by such a vision of paradise. Canon Luce may have made converts, but I suspect they were to religions other than Christianity.

9

I made a disturbing discovery. All the lodgings I called on were already bespoke, for the town possessed a great number of undergraduates. I couldn't afford to stay on at the hotel, so I went to see the headmaster in an appeal for help. He told me: 'This is the first time you have approached me civilly.' (I think he meant 'servilely.') Then he astounded me by adding: 'The other day in the town you cut my secretary. A despicable thing·to do.' I told him, rather warmly, that I had not seen the lady, and was not sure that I would have recognized her if I had. He simply remained silent.

However, he passed me on to a quite affable young master who found me an elderly couple who could let me their spare bedroom and even give me a continental breakfast, but I would have to be out all day. I took it gratefully.

I then fell rather foul of the head of English because I dared to suggest some texts I'd like to take them in. Nothing doing. 'You will use the literature texts I have chosen for them.' I took some lessons in Latin for the head of classics, who was quite different. He told me they were the best Latin lessons he had ever heard. They were Caesar's *Gallic War*, and I worked hard preparing them. One of my delights always had been to show en passant the derivations of English words and the structure of the related Latin ones.

Then the quite affable young man was laid low for weeks with flu and I took over his entire timetable. I thoroughly enjoyed that, and so, I think, did the pupils. I could not but be aware that the school was getting an experienced teacher and unobtrusive disciplinarian full-time for absolutely nothing. That was quite acceptable to me, for I was enjoying the work, but I did feel the school could manage rather more friendliness, not to say a meed of hospitality. But there was none. Two rather kinder housemasters asked me in to lunch with their boys on one day a week each. Otherwise I had a sausage roll in a café.

There was a common room which, I was told, no one ever entered. It was dark, bitterly cold, and its stone walls ran with damp. It had one small, old-fashioned gas fire. In there I crouched perforce if I had a free period between lessons. The evenings were the most deadly times: I couldn't go in before nine, and then it was straight to bed. Once a week (more only if they sent me a pound from home) I had dinner in a delightful hotel that had a good dining room and a lounge with a great log fire. I made my dinner last as long as I could, then sat by the fire with a pot of coffee until I crawled 'home' to my bed, which I had to load with my jacket and overcoat, so bitterly cold were almost all the days of that term. My hotel dinners were paradise, exceeding all the curvaceous maidens and all the bowls of sherbet. Not once during that term was I offered hospitality by anyone. Not once did I see inside any home of any master.

Jackie continued to dog me. Most days I treated him to coffee and buns. Again and again I gave him shillings that he said cold and hunger and unemployment craved. He was about the only person other than the boys I taught that I had conversation with. I remember once telling him the headmaster was not very nice. He said: 'Shall I stroke him for tha?'

'Stroke him?' I asked, puzzled.

'Across the face, with me nails, or me knife.' I had often remarked his very long and pointed finger nails.

I never knew if he really did like me a little, or if he had no feelings but mercenary ones. Once he said to me: 'You can have me if you like, OK?' I looked and sounded utterly mystified. 'Whatever do you mean?' He said no more in that strain, either then or ever. Of course, I knew well enough what he meant, and knew also how utterly dangerous it would be to touch him even if I wanted to, and I certainly did not.

One day I found him outside the school gates at lunch time, accompanied by his 'woman' with their child in her arms. They all three looked drawn, peaked, bloodless, like a vampire's victims. He told me they were going off to Newcastle in search of work and must have some money. I gave him thirty shillings, almost all I had, and silently vowed that if he met me again I'd threaten him with the police. I'm very glad I never had to, for I never saw him again.

Towards the end of the term Harold Loukes arrived to see and hear how I was doing. He told me Canon Luce had given me a bad report. I told him what I thought of the canon. He said: 'Don't worry about it. These headmasters very often have god complexes. And if they're clergy to boot, there's often no holding them.'

At the end of term I bade fond farewells to some of the boys, and escaped at the earliest instant. Leaving prison was not more ecstatic. I have never seen Durham since, and I find it easier to recall my loneliness and cold and hunger there than the rather barbaric splendour of it all.

10

Easter was early that year, and still very cold. But I was back in the arms of family and Surrey, and warmed also by the thought that this was my last vacation as a student. I had never believed in that role for myself, or enjoyed very much of it. Still less could I see myself yoked to the Church, so that it was with something of a shock that I received a letter from CACTM calling me to a selection board very soon after the next term opened. This entailed spending four days at a clergy retreat house in Lichfield. With my heart in my mouth I scanned the Department of Education's timetable for the coming term to see if a clash between my two lives would result in sudden and shameful exposure, for it will be remembered that neither the Church nor the university knew of the other's hold on me. Happily, the four days with the selection board were spread over a weekend. I had no tutorials on the Friday or the Monday, and a bad cold could explain any lectures I might have to miss. It did not, in the circumstances, seem at all appropriate to say to myself 'The Devil looks after his own,' but I did say it, and thankfully, too.

Behind me in the Education Department's lecture theatre sat a young man who irritated me with a recurrent single barking cough. He seemed almost by design to choose a place from which he could bark right in my ear. Several times I turned round and glared at him. Finally I said: 'Could you control that cough, so that I can hear what the lecturer is saying?' After the lecture he said: 'I'll have a laryngotomy if you like.'

'An excellent idea,' I answered. 'Would you like me to do it for you? I have a pretty sharp penknife. You know that is not a necessary cough. Just sheer thoughtless habit.'

'Yes, teacher,' he said, then astonished me by saying: 'My name is Clough, Basil Clough.' As he spoke he held out his hand to me. Wonderingly I took it: it was limp, elegant and inverted, almost as if he expected me to take it and raise it to my lips. Then, as though it was the most natural thing to do, he added: 'Will you come to tea with me? My digs are in Longwall Street.'

Not knowing why, I said: 'Thank you. I'd like to.'

When I got there three days later, I noted with approval that the table was decently laid with what I assumed was his landlady's second-best stuff and that he'd bought a batch of Kunzle cakes from Grimbly Hughes, Oxford's famous high-class grocers.

Over tea he asked me, as if by way of polite conversation: 'Are you a member of the Glorious Brotherhood?'

I responded with a little smile that matched his. 'I take it you're not referring to a religious order?'

'Indeed not.'

And that was how it began. In a surprisingly short time we were exchanging confidences like long-standing friends. And not once did he cough.

The confidences were at first about our literary tastes. He too had read English. He told me, almost apologetically, that he'd got a first. I was greatly impressed, not only by his academic distinction but also by his indifference to my own lack of it. (He treated degree classes as no indication of merit.)

He had similar maverick ideas about Shakespeare. He maintained Shakespeare himself was in love with Romeo, not Juliet. 'All the men in the play are in love with Romeo,' he explained, 'from Mercutio and Benvolio to Friar Lawrence, and nobody except Romeo loves Juliet.' I countered by denigrating Hamlet: 'Only the sentimental Horatio falls for Hamlet's adolescent posturings: his self-pity and his self-righteous murder of the innocent. Shakespeare no more falls for Hamlet than he does for Brutus. The real hero of *Julius Caesar* is Cassius. Brutus kills the man he loves; Cassius sacrifices his life for the man he loves.'

I remember the excitement and the pleasure of such propagated ideas. No less stimulating were our first steps towards solving the great mystery of our beings: why we were what we were. Here our tastes were less congruent than in our Shakespearean adventures. I liked youths; he was sexually indifferent to them, his own attractions being toward men of his own age or older.

I asked him why he'd made a point of sitting immediately behind me in the lecture theatre.

'Can't you guess?' he asked.

We said no more about it. He has always from that moment behaved like a perfect gentleman. In forty years of friendship there has been no physical contact between us. Only to the very knowledgeable does he betray any hint of homosexuality, mainly in the way he uses his hands.

He lived with his widowed mother in Roehampton. His father had died when Basil was about ten, leaving them moderately comfortable. He had an older brother and an older sister, both now married. I think my encounter with Basil was especially apt, filling as it did painful gaps left by Harvey and Roland.

I had been advised by everybody not to mention to the church selection board, nor, indeed, to any important churchman, that I had set my heart (and head) on a very special sphere of ordained work, namely that of a school chaplain. You were, I was told, a candidate for ordination. Full stop. If you were accepted, the Church in its wisdom would direct you to the work it felt suitable. But I didn't like this at all. I had no call to parish work, and I wasn't going to pretend I had. I was quite happy to face an initial two years of it, and to do my best there. I made up my mind to say this frankly. If they didn't like it, they could reject me. Far better for all concerned to reject me than to trap me.

There were about twenty-five of us aspirants, most of them rather younger than I was. The whole set-up was modelled on the army's officer selection boards. The panel of assessors consisted of an archdeacon as chairman and three other men: two clergy and one lay. One parson was an experienced parish priest, the other a university don, and the layman a retired lieutenant-general. All were very pleasant, the archdeacon and the general particularly so.

The evening we arrived, after supper, we gathered in a large assembly room at one end of which the panel sat in some state with us ranged on chairs before them. The archdeacon told us that 'to break the ice and make us all friends' we candidates were to take it in turns to rise and in not more than seven minutes to say something about ourselves: a little of our recent past and in conclusion why we were there. Fortunately, I was about tenth, so I discovered the way nearly all of them tackled it, which was very earnestly, very piously, and, I am sure, very truthfully. All of them, in some manner or another, asserted that the Lord Jesus had sought them out and called them hither. I knew I could do no such thing. I'd be as honest as they were but that was about all. There seemed to be a preponderance of very pleasant, very 'Protty,' very churchy believers. I didn't fit in with them one little bit. If they were the desired material, I had no chance of making the grade, or even of wanting to. So when my turn came I gave a brief review of my rather unappetizing past (I think the panel already knew about my 'war service'),

269

then spoke of my more or less lifelong admiration for Jesus and ignorance of churchgoing. I felt this was not winning friends, but I thought I would top it all with what I had been advised to keep quiet about. I said I had no real desire for an orthodox parish ministry, for which I honestly didn't feel suitable, but I felt I could do good work as a schoolmaster-priest. I sat down as dispiritedly as I'd so often sat down after CO tribunals. But was it my fancy or did no member of the panel look disapproving, and one or two even a little relieved, as if they'd had rather a basinful of piety?

The next days were quite busy. There were five services per day in the chapel: Mattins, Holy Communion, Litany and Intercessions, Evensong, and Compline. I decided two per day would be enough for me, three if I felt like it. Most of the candidates attended all five, and at the conclusion of each most remained on their knees in silent prayer for a further ten minutes or so. I, however, departed more briskly, being more economical with my prayers. By this time I had come to a few conclusions of my own, not without twinges of conscience. I had decided the panel were too intelligent, perhaps even too worldly, to be overimpressed by impeccable behaviour. They must, I thought, know that a somewhat more peccable parson would be closer to his flock, especially a schoolboy one.

To my surprise, and without putting on any act, I got on quite well with my fellow aspirants. The only recreational diversion was ping-pong, at which I wasn't bad, and which I played with a young chap I took rather a liking to.

On the second day we were all gathered in the large assembly room for some special briefing. I regarded this with some trepidation. I was always afraid something was going to happen that would reveal my ignorance of church matters. We were told that we would be split into five parties of five each, and that each party was to go off into a small room on its own and choose one of its members as its chairman. Each chairman must then return to the panel to be told the subject for discussion by his group. My group chose me as its chairman (I could only think on account of my seniority in years) and I returned to learn the topic we were to discuss and I was finally to report back on. Our topic was: 'The present divisions in the Church are simple.' It seemed to puzzle one or two of my group, but I maintained quite warmly my own agreement with it, for all these divisions created by purblind and bigoted men were chaff compared with the real, the challenging, the difficult teaching of Christ. I seemed to carry them with me and by the end of an hour I had quite a nice little report jotted down.

Back in the assembly room I placed myself so as to be called upon third or fourth (I was getting craftier), and was feeling almost assured. Some of the reports were good, and this despite being, to my mind, on deeper topics than ours. Still, no cause to be ashamed of ours.

My turn came. 'We will now ask Mr Gamble to report on his group's topic: "The present divisions in the Church are sinful".' The bottom seemed to fall out of me. I saw my group gazing at me with panic in their eyes. Well, I was the captain. I could not abandon my crew. Mine was the ghastly error. None other should shoulder blame. I gazed bravely at the archdeacon and said almost airily: 'I'm afraid there has been a rather ridiculous misunderstanding. Entirely my fault. The topic we have been discussing was: "The present divisions in the church are *simple.*" I... I'm sorry.'

A deathly hush as the crass, the sacrilegious error flaunted itself. Then it came: a positive roar of laughter from the whole panel. When he'd recovered, the archdeacon said: 'Now, Mr Gamble, do read your intriguing report.'

And the report, too, went down well, almost as well as its misconceived subject. Truly, an angel of some sorts was watching over me.

Each of us had a searching private interview with each of the panel. They asked me if I felt I had to preach pacifism or modernism. I quite truthfully said I had no call to convert anyone to either creed. Nevertheless, I wouldn't conceal my views if they were sought or if I felt it necessary to make them known. They asked me if I understood that I must at least begin my ministry in parish work. I said I was perfectly happy to do that.

11

It was almost with regret that I said goodbye to them all. It had been an impressive and rewarding experience. Diving back into the sluggish waters of the Dip Ed was almost an anticlimax. After two or three weeks the CACTM report to the principal arrived. Beaming, he told me: 'A triumph, dear boy, a triumph, as I knew it would be.' He gave me the report to keep (which I don't think he should have done). It is before me now.

'We believe,' they wrote, 'that his spiritual concern for the schoolboy is a sincere one, and that a full and rewarding ministry awaits him in such work.' I read that almost with awe. It has sustained me through many trials and tribulations.

Yes, they passed me. First go, too. I gathered that well-nigh half my batch of aspirants was turned down. It was with great relief that I learned all were entitled to three attempts, three selection boards. How many of my fellow candidates were even then on second or third essays I did not, of course, know. I had the rather novel experience of feeling humble as (at last) a genuine ordinand. But not for long. Other and stranger adventures awaited me.

I somehow scraped through the Dip Ed and then discussed the next steps with the principal. I had for the past year considered Canon Power, Harvey's father-in-law, as a possible vicar to join if ever I became ordained. I liked him and felt I could work for him. He was a good modernist and a very successful parish priest. I had never told him of this, for I had no real faith I would achieve a dog collar. But the crafty old principal had discussed it all with Canon Power and found him more than willing to have me. 'So you see, dear boy,' said the principal, 'you must get yourself done quickly.'

I looked dubious, even rather alarmed. 'But I'm supposed to have two years training in a theological college, and then take all that GOE.' That was the General Ordination Examination of the Church of England. Quite a formidable hurdle to jump.

The principal smiled in his inimitable manner: half inspired and half indomitable, half prophetic and half exasperating. 'You have already, brother, had four years in a theological college.' That was both quite true and also definitely hyberbolic. 'As for GOE, you know that as an over-thirty candidate you can take a shortened GOE that won't require much more than a little intense mugging-up. Now we have no long vac term here this year but I have found a college, Queen's College, Birmingham, that has one and is willing to take you. I have also spoken to the bishop of Birmingham about you, and he is quite happy to take my recommendation.'

My head was almost reeling. 'You mean take GOE at the end of this coming long vac term, in about three months' time, if that?'

'Quite so, brother,' he beamed. 'Then the bishop will make you deacon in September.' He obviously thought I was academically bright. Also perhaps something of a magician. Like many modernists he had a mystical streak that nothing could daunt.

So that was what I found myself up to the neck in: the principal's great net, woven of faith and sheer impudence, of sublime assurance and downright legerdemain. In due course I arrived at the new theological college, found everybody much saner, much more orthodox, much more disciplined, and settled down with a pile of books and a programme so wild I never for a moment believed in it. As usual I found two or three young men I liked, and who liked me. And in Birmingham I found a city with much to admire and enjoy. I also found my principal had told this principal I was not requiring any tuition: only a study in which to swot and a library in which to consult.

The eight-week term went by with horrid ease. In no time I found myself on the brink of GOE. I knew it was hopeless. I was nothing like ready. And I was worn out. So on an afternoon some three days before the first GOE paper (ethics, I think), I sat down and wrote a mind-made-up letter to the bishop of Birmingham. This was the great Dr Barnes, whom I admired enormously as pacifist and modernist, and of whom I went in some awe. He had no small talk, suffered fools not at all, least of all gladly, and was by then both wounded and fatigued. I told him how grateful I was for his patronage, how ashamed to have wasted his time. But I was not anything near ready for GOE and must probably give up all hope of ordination.

I delivered that letter by hand at his house and then went off to a solo dinner in the Grand Hotel. I felt immensely relieved, free as the air. I'd go home tomorrow. I'd try to get a schoolmastering job for September. I'd banish from my head all thought, all memories, of my crazy, my impudent, brushes with the Church.

When I got back to the college late that night, more euphoric, more liberated, than ever, it was to find a note from the college bursar to say that Canon Power had been trying all evening to contact me. He would be phoning me again early in the morning. I was to make sure I was there. I spent most of the night wondering what it could all mean. Before nine in the morning I found out. Canon Power told me that as soon as the bishop read my letter he phoned both my English tutor at Oxford, and the Reader in Education who had supervised me. As a result he had told Canon Power to ensure that I was in attendance at the episcopal residence at 11 am. Wonderingly I went, wonderingly I sat before Bishop Barnes and wonderingly I tried to drink in what he said.

He told me he had spoken to both Oxford dons about me, frankly and at some length. As a result, he had decided to make me deacon in September even though I had not taken GOE. Canon Power was willing to have me on those conditions, well aware that there was no question of my ever being priested until GOE had been passed. 'And as you know,' he said sternly, 'it is the priest's ordination that is the real ordination.' I thanked him humbly, half-believing. As I left, he said, more to himself than to me: 'As long as I have breath, I'll ordain liberal men, for God knows who'll do it when I'm gone.' Words I have never forgotten.

12

To cut a long story short, I was indeed ordained (that is, the 'first ordination', properly called 'the being made deacon') by Bishop Barnes in his cathedral in Birmingham. I swotted up both GOE and the diocesan priests' exams during the ensuing fifteen months and somehow got through them. I remember the bishop's examining chaplain, marking my priest's papers, said acutely: 'His answers on Bishop Gore's book would have been outstanding if he had ever read it.' To my great sorrow, Bishop Barnes died and I was priested by his successor. I was made deacon in September 1952 and priested in December 1953, so even my entry in *Crockford's Clerical Directory* maintains the facade of respectability, saying simply 'd 52˙p 53,' and letting on to no one that more than the normal one year separated the two landmarks.

Canon Power told me I had a dual job: as assistant to him at the great parish church, and as chaplain-in-charge of a daughter church, a real old tin and wood tabernacle I came to love as my own baby. He also found me digs with a fine family near the daughter church. I was the only young man of the dozen or so Bishop Barnes ordained that day who had not a soul present in the way of family or friends. I told myself I didn't mind. If any member of my family had been there, he or she would have had no idea what was going on, would not have known what to do except dissolve in mirth.

After the service, we were all invited to lunch with the bishop. I sat next to him at the table. He said almost nothing, but I didn't notice the fact, being too immersed in my own tortured thoughts. For Canon Power had told me: 'You'll be back from the bishop's by about three. Be up at the parish church by six for Evensong. You'll have to take the service as well as preach, for I'll have to take Evensong at your daughter church of St Chad. I expect the lay reader will be at the parish church to give you any help you need.' Long afterwards I was told that Canon Power said to a colleague who remonstrated: 'I believe in throwing them in at the deep end. If they can't keep afloat, they're no good to me.'

It wasn't the sermon so much that was petrifying me. I had quite long ago found a text that appealed to me and that I wanted to develop when my first dose of pulpitry arrived. (It was Paul to his trying little band in Corinth: 'Ye are not your own.') No, it was taking the actual Evensong, with all its expansions and interpolations and, above all, the versicles I had to intone. Almost from birth, Brian and Terry had heaped derision on my attempts to sing. I felt I had no pitch, no tone, no volume, nothing. Fortunately, a friendly chaplain at my long vac college took me in hand, dismissed my doubts and fears, and simply made me intone all the usual versicles. I found I was quite passable and in time almost jaunty. But I couldn't read music properly and so I have never dared sing a mass in my life. I have always recalled, wistfully, Lady Catherine de Bourgh's appraisal of her daughter: 'Lady Anne would have been an excellent pianist - if she had ever learned to play.'

Somehow or other I got through it all, and the vicar told me a few days later that he had received 'excellent reports from many people, including the churchwardens.' He added: 'If you can get churchwardens even to listen to a sermon you've done pretty well.'

I got £350 a year, out of which I had to pay everything. A friend who considered it sheer exploitation told me to insist to the point of violence on parish expenses, that is, anything I spent on fares and telephones and postage as part of my work. I kept a scrupulous account, which came to about twenty-five shillings every five weeks or so. Whenever I presented it to the vicar I was treated to a lecture which as good as asked me if I wasn't ashamed to expect such an emolument. 'We had no such thing when I was ordained. We didn't expect it. We were paid less than you and we gladly provided our own expenses. If we hadn't money for fares, we walked.' I got used to this harangue. In time I sat, silent and impassive, almost drumming the table with my fingers as he unlocked a box in which he kept the money some trust gave him for clergy relief. And every Sunday morning, when I assisted him at Holy Communion, I had an inward chuckle as he faced the congregation before the collection and declared in ringing tones: 'The Lord loveth a cheerful giver.' Well, he belonged to an earlier generation which no doubt starved with equanimity. He was a good chancellor of both his own and the Church's exchequer. He had a wife and a maid and three children, all of whom he sent to Oxford. And he was known as something of a wizard in raising money for his church. All qualities I sadly lacked. All my ordained life I have been embarrassed and ineffective in money appeals.

I have endured pain in another respect all my ordained life. That is, in preparing sermons. I was intellectually incapable of preaching doctrinally, of holding forth about the orthodox faith. My preaching (which, I must add, could be challenging, even rousing) was by temperament moral, psychological, political, but never credal. I was as crucified by sermon preparation as I had been by my weekly essays at Oxford. And for a similar reason: I just felt I *must* try to find something fresh to say, some new slant, some unexpected ray of light. And, as with the essays, I worried at the thing most of the week but hardly ever got anything jotted down until I was frantic on Saturday night. Often I would give up and fling myself on my sleepless couch at midnight, knowing I must rise before dawn to renew my batterings at inspiration's door. Thousands and thousands of wretched Saturday nights I have somehow weathered. If I felt I had something reasonably worth hearing, I could deliver it with some aplomb. If not, I hurried through it, scarcely concealing my own distaste for it. But never, whether it was good, bad or indifferent, could I ever gaze at any member of my audience while delivering it. I also disliked going to the church door after the service to bid goodbye to the people. I felt it must seem I was waiting for congratulations. I was also embarrassed by processing, at which I kept my head down and my eyes averted. I concluded that I felt quite sure I was a bogus priest, a charlatan performer. I have never lost that sensation.

I found that by sheer instinct I was aware of the necessary histrionics: when to pause, when to change pitch and volume, when to have the right facial expression. The same with reading the lessons. I had quite a good reading voice and I was almost as accomplished as Dickens at making each lesson a little dramatic performance, without ever overdoing it. I seldom kept to the Lectionary, for I refused to read subchristian passages, which so many of them were. I chose readings for their religious truth, their dramatic power, their verbal beauty. Quite often I was so moved by the passage that I had great difficulty in delivering it because of the lump in my throat, the catch in my breath, the moisture in my eyes. All these things I found out for myself. Untrained and unstudied, I learnt in the best possible way, by actually *doing*. It has been the same with my teaching. I master my texts by preparing them assiduously day by day. That, I feel, is the best way. It is also an intensely enjoyable way.

13

When I arrived I found my little daughter church could boast a small and elderly congregation and two small choirboys in cassocks which were once black, now greening with age, and long enough to trip them up on each entry and exit. I was determined to transform this situation. First I got the parochial church council to raise the choirboy pay from sixpence a month to half a crown. I then gained entrance to the local secondary modern school by going to talk to their assembly once a week. There I got the headmistress's permission to appeal for choirboys. The response was a little overwhelming: thirty of them came to the first audition in the church. I somehow got that down to twenty by deferring (not, I explained, rejecting) those who were not very keen or whose voices were practically nonexistent. I admit I let in one or two whose faces compensated for their vocal cords, or who were almost pathetically eager. It was a largely working-class parish and some of the kids rather desperately needed someone or something to belong to.

The next job was to get them robed. A gallant band of ladies rose from the pews and seated themselves in the vestry at long trestle tables burdened with their scissors and patterns and sewing machines. They all said they'd never seen a pattern for a cassock and didn't know where to find one. But, not at all daunted, they got a pattern for a very similar girl's frock and adapted it. They chose a suitable material and I chose the colour. I had set my heart on red, because it looked cheerful and I thought the boys would look rather sweet in it. For a week or two the church became a sort of sweatshop, but much happier than any that Thomas Hood portrayed.

In a surprisingly short time these holy garments were ready. We had to buy the surplices and ruffs. I took every choir practice; not as a musician, of course, but as a disciplinarian and cheerleader. We had an old harmonium and a splendid old rough diamond as organist-cum-choirmaster. We trained them long and hard. There were several with quite good voices and we set them standards and gave them challenges. There were the Sunday psalms to learn and always quite an ambitious anthem. Half a dozen ladies and gentlemen with powerful voices were also garbed and enrolled. The result was a choir that made up in gusto for any aesthetic deficiencies and was largely responsible for a greatly expanded congregation.

These choirboys of mine were models of good behaviour. I had several elderly, long-standing members of my congregation who did not really welcome this influx of the young, nor of all the newcomers who usurped traditional pew places. But not even they could find fault with my choirboys. When the ecclesiastical gear arrived from Wippells, I heard one or two of the old stagers murmur sardonically: 'Ruffs for the roughs.' But so well did I train the little roughs that they acted almost demure, without ever losing their native gaminerie that was (to me, at least) their charm. They arrived at church with scrubbed hands and faces whose tidemarks were well hidden by their garments. Their hair was flattened with water and their shoes polished with spit. And when they were all robed, they sat quietly on benches in the vestry until I gave the word for them to rise, form up and bow their heads devoutly for the bidding prayer. All this was possible because they enjoyed and coveted their role, as also their salaries and other perks. After Evensong the whole congregation repaired to the church hall for refreshments and gossip, and occasionally little talks or gramophone recitals.

Very often on a Saturday morning I took the boys to games of football against other church choirs. I could never referee these games, but I loyally attended and cheered and commiserated. And once a year, out of the choir and the youth club and the Sunday school and the four winds I got together a goodly group of candidates for confirmation. After instruction that was as full of Christian guidance (and fun) as I could make it, they were confirmed in the parish church. The next Sunday at 8 am in my tabernacle they made their first communion (taken in my first, unpriested year by an old, retired parson who arrived with some trepidation and left charmed). After communion, at which after several rehearsals they could behave naturally and reverently, we all adjourned to the hall for my greatest triumph: a Grand Parish Breakfast. We had eggs and bacon and toast and marmalade, and baked beans and cornflakes and tea and coffee. All provided and prepared by the good ladies of my church. I wanted the kids to have a confirmation they'd not forget. Perhaps for some it was indeed that.

The youth club was for local over-fourteens of both sexes. I got much extra equipment and some good leaders out of my congregation (which was becoming almost imperceptibly a little younger), but I felt it never really took off. I think this was because of a rift in the PCC between those who felt every member of the youth club should attend one service on a Sunday, and those who felt no such commitment should be required. The second group was smaller, and worse. I could never make up my mind which side I was on.

I realized I must divide my time with some show of impartiality between the various organizations. There was a Mothers' Union and a very evangelical gospel meeting and a Guild of Healing as well as a Boys' Brigade and Girls' Friendly Society. I more or less got by. I remember speaking to the

Mothers' Union on cookery, to the gospel meeting on Mary Magdalene, and to other bodies on more or less appropriate subjects. Most of my flock were kind and tolerant with their ignorant curate, and not until my second year did I have some stormy meetings of the PCC. One was when I proposed disbanding the Boys' Brigade and forming a Scout troop (mostly because the latter weren't so 'pi' and would not be expecting me to take regular Bible studies with the boys). And on another occasion we almost degenerated into a PCC slanging match when I quite passionately demanded the closing down of a time-honoured weekly session that was one of the church's biggest money-spinners. That was the whist drive, which I assumed was a pleasant little social for our more senior congregation. But I heard fairly persistent rumours that not all the money that should have come to the church was getting there.

So one Saturday evening I went in to look at the whist drive. I was distinctly offended. The hall was jammed with card tables and gamblers, the atmosphere was thick with tobacco smoke. And, worst, there was scarcely anyone from our church present.

But the loss of money entailed in calling a halt to all such drives would be considerable. I said it was a sad thing if we relied on money from such a source. Better to give more, economize more. I won the day, and I think there was general agreement that our church and our hall were healthier, happier places from then on.

I got some good extra helpers for the Sunday school, and an excellent scoutmaster and cubmistress. I also realized my now bulging tin tabernacle could do with rather more publicity. I had the services of a good poster artist locally and I saw that times and purposes of Sunday services were well displayed. The local press was also used to good effect. But more of them later.

I am not claiming credit for all this: I could not have done any of it without a marvellously loyal and responsive congregation. I was astonished to discover that all that was needed to galvanize such people was a leader, someone to please and be thanked by.

14

Of course, there were all the usual clergy duties to perform: visiting (which I didn't enjoy, being convinced I was an awkward mixer), funerals (which I dreaded, for human grief ravaged me) and weddings (which I loved because they were so joyously touching). From the word go, I took funerals and weddings galore, to the surprise of friends in more orthodox parishes who didn't get either until they were priested. I must admit I sometimes secretly wished I earned a penny or two from these chores when I saw how much others were making from them: choirs and organists, sidesmen and bellringers, vergers and parish clerks. I knew one poor old parson in a downtown parish who positively rubbed his hands when he had a funeral and its fees. 'What I always say, brother,' he told me gleefully, 'is "Where there's death there's hope".'

But my real agony came on a Wednesday, old dark and gloomy Wednesday. It was my day's duty at a very busy crematorium in the Black Country. I had services usually at twenty-minute intervals, with hearses often queuing round the back of the large, chimneyed building. I had been told: 'Don't take these occasions personally, or you'll not get through them.' I never learned to heed that advice. Each funeral was some family's, some individual's, great loss, great grief. I would scan the undertaker's certificate in the vestry before the service to discover the age of the deceased, always fearing dreadfully that it might be someone young.

Many of the crematorium clergy went straight from their sanctuary places back into the vestry when each service was done, pleading that the cortèges came so hot on one another's heels. But I just couldn't do that. I went to the chapel door and waited to squeeze a hand and murmur a few loving words. It was all quite sincere: I couldn't but share their sorrow. And, I discovered later, it was more appreciated than I had ever guessed. Even the crematorium directors wrote to tell me so. I know at the end of each Wednesday duty I felt positively drained: physically bathed in sweat, emotionally racked with grief. And, of course, not one penny of crematorium fees came to me.

At harrowing moments, I found only the age-old words of Christian hope would come, however my rationalism normally bypassed them. Nor were they perfunctory. Deep within me, resistant to all the enlightenment, the modernism, the free thought, were bottomless wells of feeling: feelings that man was not made to die, that beyond death was reunion with loved ones, that intense human affection was imperishable. Sometimes such intellectual and emotional muddles left me stranded, speechless. I remember visiting one old lady in hospital who was in tears because her sister had just died. 'Don't take it so much to heart,' I said, with too ready comfort. 'She was a good person. She'll be having her reward.' The old lady looked at me with astonishment. 'Oh no, she weren't,' she replied. 'She were an old bugger. That's what I'm crying about.'

I felt I had to say something pretty arresting when I preached to six hundred people at the parish church Evensong. In that diocese, in that parish, they were not shocked by pacifism or modernism. I was lucky: I could more or less speak my mind. Quite soon, there came the opportunity to speak on a cause even dearer to my heart: the abolition of the death penalty.

Christopher Craig, aged sixteen, and Derek Bentley, aged nineteen, broke into a Croydon warehouse one night in November, 1952. The police were called and on the roof of the warehouse Craig shot one constable dead. (Bentley was actually under arrest at the time, being held by another constable at the other end of the roof.) The police had repeatedly asked Craig to throw down his revolver. Bentley (it was claimed, but has frequently been denied) had called out: 'Let him have it, Chris,' which some said meant 'Fire at the constable' and others claimed meant 'Let the constable have your gun.' At the Old Bailey in December, the Lord Chief Justice, Lord Goddard, sentenced Bentley to death, passing on the jury's recommendation to mercy, and Craig to be detained during Her Majesty's pleasure. The LCJ had no alternative to sentencing Bentley to death as accessory to murder, and equally he could not so sentence Craig (who had actually committed the murder) on account of his age.

As the time for Bentley's execution drew near and (to the astonishment of nearly all, including Goddard) it became clear the Home Secretary was not recommending a reprieve, extraordinary and unprecedented scenes took place in the House of Commons and throughout the country. I myself sent telegrams to the Queen and to the Home Secretary, Maxwell Fyfe, urging mercy. In spite of this, Bentley was executed.

I was sickened, outraged. I felt I must do my best to register my disgust. I went to see the Bentleys. How indelibly impressed on me is my interview with Mr and Mrs Bentley and their daughter in their little home in Thornton Heath. They told me all about Derek (who was mentally retarded and had been injured in a wartime bombing) and Craig and other friends. They produced a box filled with letters of sympathy (hundreds of them) from home and abroad, and also a telegram they had received from the Croydon police after the execution. It said simply 'Justice has been done.'

I preached a blistering sermon at the parish church the next Sunday morning. I outlined the case, I paid tribute to the courage and self-sacrifice of the police, I spoke with contempt of the prosecution and (above all) of Maxwell Fyfe, and I utterly condemned the system they administered as barbaric, obscene and an insult to Jesus Christ, who had once interfered to prevent the fulfilment of a death sentence, and was himself the victim of legal execution. I knew from the dead silence in which I was heard that my words had struck deep. The next day the local and even the national press gave me not over-sensationalized publicity.

On Tuesday the vicar told me the bishop had been on the phone to him. He had received complaints about my sermon and desired my vicar to speak to me about it. A day later the vicar told me he had reported back to the bishop. This, said Canon Power, was the actual conversation: 'Bishop: Well, Power, have you seen Gamble about his sermon? Power: I have, my Lord. Bishop: And what did you say to him? Power: I said "Well done," my Lord. Bishop: Quite so, Power, quite so.'

After this, the press did not leave me alone. More importantly, I had many requests to speak on capital punishment: at churches, at schools and at public meetings. I accepted them all, and I also made it my business to learn as much as I could about the whole sickening business. I lunched in the Commons with a former Home Secretary (Chuter-Ede) and I talked to barristers, MPs and a retired prison governor. I learned that Maxwell Fyfe was told the loyalty of the police could no longer be guaranteed if Bentley were reprieved. (It was disgraceful that the same government minister should be responsible for the police forces and for recommending reprieves.) Scored deep in my brain is what I heard about the execution of the 18-year-old youth Forsyth, in what was known as the Towpath murder case. He was dragged to the scaffold screaming: 'I'm too young to die! I'm too young to die!'

Yes, I am glad to have made my small contribution to the eventual abolition of the death penalty in 1965.

15

To turn from legalized murder to life preservation, I must tell of an experience that greatly impressed me in the first month of my curacy, and that has never left some musing corner of my mind. My vicar said to me: 'I want you to visit old Mrs Jones. Her husband is dying. Just say some comforting words and prayers and that you'll take the funeral if she wishes.'

I had had no instruction on the correct clerical procedure for visiting the sick, the dying, the bereaved. At the little council house, the door was opened by frail, red-eyed old Mrs Jones. She led me straight into the parlour, which was almost filled by a double bed in which lay a heavily built man fighting for breath.

Mrs Jones had no hesitation in talking about her husband in front of him. He seemed too distressed to pay any attention to our words. She told me he hadn't much longer. He had been a foundry worker and a lifetime's labour there had rotted his lungs. He had been such a good man. In the old days, exhausted at the end of a shift, he and his mate would travel homeward on the tram and he would carry his mate from the tram stop to his front door on his own broad back. That was a vivid picture I have not forgotten.

I badly wanted to say and do something that would bring comfort to them. Suddenly, I heard myself saying: 'Now, Mrs Jones, I want you to kneel on the far side of the bed and take your husband's hand in one of yours. I'll kneel this side and do the same. Then you and I will reach across the bed and hold our free hands. So we will make a chain of prayer.' I heard myself saying all this, but in a detached manner, as if I were listening to someone else. The whole situation seemed unreal. All that was real was the compassion I felt.

I said some prayers (and even those I had to invent), and knelt in silence for a few moments, grasping those hands that had weathered half a century's hardships together and were now to be parted forever. I left, saying I would call again in a few days. I caught the bus straight to the city centre so that I could have coffee somewhere cheerful and bustling: my regular anodyne in moments of depression.

I visited again two or three days later. I did not expect to see the dying man again. Sure enough, the bed (which I could see from the front door) was empty and covered over. Before I could voice my sympathy, Mrs Jones burst out excitedly: 'A miracle, that's what it is, a miracle. The doctor said the same. He began to pick up soon after your visit. Next morning he wanted some breakfast, the first meal he'd had for days.' She paused, looking at me brightly, even a touch reverently.

'How wonderful,' I said. I was quite as excited by it as she was. 'But... but where is he?'

'In hospital. And he says he's going to come home soon, *better*.'

I was rather shattered by it all. That I'd been in some way involved in 'the miracle' was clear. Equally clear (to me) was that, sceptical, doubting, even resentful about the injustice of it all, I was utterly ruled out as a channel of divine mercy. Unless... unless the good Lord could use a true compassion and ask no further questions.

I visited Mr Jones in hospital. He was sitting up in bed, bright-eyed and breathing normally. Even more excited than his wife, he told me in a torrent of words and laughter: 'I'm not staying here, y'know. Not on your life. Why, some of these chaps are just here waiting to die. Not me. I'm going home. Soon. I'm cured, y'know.' And go home he did and had another lease of life.

I kept this experience to myself. I never said to anyone what I scarcely liked saying to myself: 'Had I a gift of healing?' I deliberately avoided the question, fearful that the answer was 'Yes' and my duty was to stay in a poor parish laying on hands, with never again any thought of a school chaplaincy, of teaching, of a boy world. I will add only that I have had three such experiences of healing by the imposition of my hands, my compassion, my hope. Three in my whole life. But I avoided always any call to a healing ministry.

The second Christmas in my parish was drawing near. I was now priested, and the choir was getting quite good. I had got them enrolled in the Royal School of Church Music and they now proudly wore ribbons and medals to tell the world so. I conceived the idea of going round the big local factories so that my lusty and colourful choir could give a concert of Christmas carols. Several factories gave us permission to call during the workers' lunch breaks. I was in a cassock and played the part of compère. I had a few jokes that went down quite well, and the kids looked and sounded quite angelic. I explained there would be a collection: half for specified charities and half for our own church. There were many communists among our audiences, as their contemptuous indifference showed. Several continued to play snooker rather noisily during our carols until their mates told them to shut up. At the end of one concert, the factory workers' spokesman made a little speech. He thanked and praised the choir, then added: 'But I mustn't finish without congratulating them on the resident comedian they have brought with them. I mean the vicar. Give him a hand, boys.' All quite a success. And another wildly unforeseen role for me. (One never repeated, I may say.)

Not long after this, I decided I must begin to plan my future. I had never envisaged staying more than the minimum two years in a parochial appointment. No, it was to be a school chaplaincy for September, 1954. I told very few about my projected departure. I knew a great many people would be sorry, not least myself, for I had forged many friendships, many affections. Above all, I grieved to think I would be leaving my choirboys. I wondered sadly how many would remain loyal.

However, life must go on, *my* life. I decided to have a big service of thanksgiving and renewal. Several people had suggested this, for there really was much to thank God for in the growth of our little mission church, the bigger part it was now playing in the local community. So the archdeacon of Aston was invited to preach. He accepted and we all worked hard preparing a grand Evensong. I had told the choir they were to be seated on their vestry benches as usual, and as soon as I brought the archdeacon in they were to jump up and stand respectfully at attention. The Hitler Jugend were not better trained. But as soon as the distinguished visitor entered and they all jumped to their feet, I saw his face register surprise, even shock. He turned to me and said ironically: 'I had no idea, Gamble, you were a royal foundation.' I was so ignorant I had no idea what he meant. He saw this and elucidated: 'I mean your red cassocks.'

However, he swallowed his sense of offended etiquette and we had a most inspiriting Evensong. And afterwards in the hall he conveyed the impression that he was enjoying himself. He was Clement George St Michael Parker, afterwards bishop of Bradford. An Anglo-Catholic and a pacifist, he did fine work as Bishop Barnes' archdeacon and then suffragan.

I was glad his visit had been so rewarding, both for him and for us, because I must admit I wanted a good recommendation when I moved. It was therefore rather to my dismay that I heard from my vicar that the archdeacon had sung my praises to him in the words: 'Whatever we do, Power, we mustn't lose that man Gamble from the diocese.' I had to laugh to myself about this quite unexpected outcome, even as I set about looking for a school chaplaincy.

I was well aware how uncomfortably I might fit into the typical public school world, and to such a niche in it. Nevertheless, I was determined to try. I had two sources from which to draw applications. One was the Oxford University Appointments Committee and the other the clerical vacancy columns of the *Church Times*. My two educational referees were my two Oxford tutors. With my application I gave a brief sketch of my parish experience and my prep school teaching before ordination. My vicar and the Ripon Hall principal were my clerical sponsors.

I was very heartened to discover that I was invariably shortlisted and called for interview. But the optimism was short-lived, for always the result was rejection. Was I a bad interviewee? I didn't think so; nothing in my past encounters suggested so. Was it the degree, the lack of sporting prowess, the wartime record? No, for these things had either been stated in my original application or were not discussed. Could it be that the Birmingham diocese was queering my pitch because it wanted to keep me? I couldn't believe anyone in the diocese would be so dastardly.

After many interviews followed by rejections I suddenly thought: Can it really be old Canon Luce up north following me like a Fury to damn me as a school chaplain? I became more and more convinced my guess was accurate. I asked one or two of those headmasters who had rejected me if they felt they could possibly say whether Canon Luce had blacklisted me. None did, until at last one honest headmaster wrote: 'All I can say is that you have been most unfortunate to offend Canon Luce, for he is a very senior member of the Headmasters' Conference.'

So that was it. Well, I'd fight him to the end. But meanwhile I'd have to find some more congenial church post from which to combat his efforts. But what? I really must leave Birmingham, fond as I was of many there. The thought of another year of crematoria and sermons and near poverty was more than I could countenance. Hospital chaplain? No. Prison chaplain? No, no. Army or navy chaplain? Ah, that indeed had its attractions but was quite impossible.

Then one miserable Friday I saw a notice in the *Church Times* to say that a young priest was sought for work in northern Europe, ministering to our embassies and English communities. I applied. I was interviewed by a bishop and by some civil servants. It was clearly rather an important appointment. I awaited the usual rejection, since no sane man would post a wartime conscientious objector to European embassies! But I learned that they were pleased to appoint me.

Well, it wasn't what I wanted, but it was infinitely better than another curacy. I was sad to be leaving so many kind people, so many nice kids. I even wondered if I ought to have made less of a splash, knowing I had determined on a mere two-year stint. But I couldn't honestly weep to be leaving Birmingham: a nice enough city, but not London. And there was another reason to escape as soon as possible: one or two young females felt I was a desirable catch. One was even phoning me anonymously, presumably for the pleasure of hearing my increasingly irate voice. In the end I contacted the police, and told the houri next time she mutely dialled me that the calls were being monitored. I knew quite well who she was. It astounded me that anybody should think I had remained a bachelor to age thirty-three only to come to a wooden tabernacle in Birmingham to find a wife. I was pretty exasperated by it all.

There was a heartwarming and touching send-off after my last Evensong. Even the poorest little choirboy brought me some sweets. I wanted to kiss them all goodbye. I had never felt anything but paternal towards them. And I have not been able to forget Canon Power's last words to me: 'Well, Peter, if ever a man entered the church by the back door and left it by the front, it's you.'

16

I arranged things so that I had about a couple of weeks at home before I set out to minister to the British diaspora. I found some changes on the home front. Father, having reached his sixty-fifth, was now retired. We wished he could enjoy it more after waiting so long for it. But, after a lifetime's dedication to the bottle, he had neither the money nor the health to do so. On the other hand, he now evinced not the slightest desire for liquor. It made me wonder if he had ever really liked the stuff for itself. Brian, who sometimes went off for a drink with him, told me his modus operandi throughout those lonely, cheerless, expensive years. He would enter some saloon bar, stand at the least frequented part of the counter, and down his whiskies as quickly as he decently could. He made no attempt to talk to anyone. If someone spoke to him, he would answer politely but not encouragingly. Then he would leave to repeat the operation elsewhere. His inebriated homecomings had always been met with a wall of disgust. Just once, in our later years, Brian told me he put much of the blame for father's alcoholism on mother's intransigence, her utter lack of understanding, her implacable contempt. But I rather cut him short, as I'd done once before, when he'd said he thought mother liked him least of her children. They clashed because he had much of her independence, her self-assurance. Anyway, I just couldn't take any criticism of mother. I had grown up seeing her as always beyond reproach, and I wanted to keep it that way, even when she castigated Miles too seldom and his poor father too often.

Another change was brought about by Pam's new, and almost revolutionary, possession, her companion, soul mate and comforter: an Alsatian puppy with an enormous pedigree, a creature as costly as aristocratic. I think it was a gift from some well-heeled admirer, and it was typical of Pam to choose a canine rather than a sparkler offering.

Emil was a lady, but she came to us craven, snarling, neurotic. We never thought of her as female, and certainly not as a bitch. To us she was above such vulgar classifications, and in any case she had a masculine name, that of a pleasant German prisoner of war that Brian and Pam had known.

I remember clearly my first meeting with Emil. I had arrived home rather late, and they had all retired for the night. Emil was on a cushion on a chair in the doorway of Pam's bedroom. There she lay, one eye open, a growl in the throat and lips already baring her large teeth. I knelt beside her and spoke very quietly, very chattily, very patiently. After about half an hour, she stopped nibbling my fingers and rather wonderingly suffered them to stroke her head.

Next morning, suspicious, aggressive and skulking, she yet remembered Pam was her saviour and I her friend. Before the day was out, her tail gave the first hint of a wag. At the end of a week she had given to the whole family a lifelong devotion, with an overplus for Pam and a special remembrance that I was *primus inter pares*, all because of our midnight chat on her day of arrival. All her life she was highly strung (thunder reduced her to a quivering jelly), but she took very seriously her duty to guard us all. She was the most beautiful, the most loving, the most intelligent dog I have ever known. We could, as a family, do what we liked with her. The household largely revolved around her, which, without any trace of arrogance, she took as her due. Only Sam, our much travelled cat, was indifferent to her. As distinctly senior to Emil in years and wisdom, Sam kept her in her place, only very occasionally cuffing her when she became too boisterous. Even when she was fully grown Emil never took a liberty with Sam. Wary respect was the rule.

She had a great sense of humour, even of dramatics. If we murmured to her: 'What is the correct way to treat the working classes?', she would draw herself up, gaze haughtily at the ceiling, and even contrive to look supercilious. If we bid her be a 'savage, snarling wolf,' she would crouch and bare her fangs in a manner that could terrify a timid visitor. When Pam and I played ball with her on the lawn, I would sometimes run on all fours, seize the ball in my mouth and take it back to Pam, who would pat my head and say: 'Oh, you clever, clever dog.' Emil would set up a howl of protest and then take the ball from my mouth, always as gently as a lamb. We did sometimes wonder if she was doing all this to amuse us.

I hope the good Lord will take note that, in the heaven earmarked for all my family, places are to be provided for Sam and Emil.

As usual, I spent much of my fortnight's freedom seeing old friends. That is, such old friends as remained. There were fewer of them, for I was robbed, by distance and death and marriage. Jonathan had visited me several times during my curacy in Birmingham. At first the visits had been sheer delight, even though they were crowded one-day affairs. But I had felt something alien intruding on the last two visits. He had seemed remote from me in a way our friendship had never known before. One curious incident stayed in my mind. I wanted him to come into my little tabernacle to see some improvements I had made and of which I was, to tell the truth, rather proud. He made some excuse, and when I tried to brush it aside he became rather agitated.

And now, when I phoned to suggest a meeting in London, he put all manner of obstacles in the way. So many, in fact, that I gave up rather brusquely. Ah well, I thought, marriage has removed him, too. He and his wife were the last friends I expected to lose like that. It hurt me. I was now becoming more of a cynic, less of a romantic, even in the matter of friendships.

Except for one. One friendship which might turn out to be tough and shockproof: the friendship with Nigel Day. In its durability it was already unlike any other friendship I had had with a young person. Nigel was now past twenty-one and as affectionate as ever. Also unique was my feeling for him, which remained as intense now he was in his twenties as it had been when he was sixteen. So when he told me he was madly in love with a girl called Heather, and determined to marry her, neither he nor I saw it as any impediment to our friendship. She was a pleasant, rather proper girl; a South African, and some two years older than Nigel. She took a lot of wooing. I think she felt it wrong for a woman to marry a man younger than herself. And I think it was her reluctance that kindled Nigel's ardour. Well, I married them in a fashionable Kensington church just before I left Birmingham.

At the wedding, I met for the first (and only) time Nigel's father. He and his wife had separated when Nigel was about ten, and quite early in our friendship I wondered if I were, fractionally, a father substitute. Nigel had grown up in an entirely female environment, for he had two older sisters. Yet I never discovered any trace of the homosexuality you might expect, unless it were the relationship with me. No other male figure played a part in Nigel's life. He told me, and I certainly believed it, that he had never even had a passing liaison with another boy at school. While still in his teens he was girl orientated, and quite successfully so.

Nigel's father had been a handsome man, but his looks were now fading. I learned he had been a successful businessman (in estate management, I think). Even now he had an entrepreneur's charm, and that he had passed on to his son. Nigel went straight from school into oil, where he was already doing well. He was something of a go-getter, in his amours no less than in business. Why, I wondered (and went on wondering through all the years), did I endure as his only male entanglement?

17

I flew off to my new sphere of work with no very clear idea of what to expect. It seemed my activities were to be centred on northern Europe, effectually on France, Belgium and the Netherlands, so I could get by on French, which was in any case the only modern foreign language I had, and that but ill. I found I was to minister not only to the expatriate communities of Britons, but also on occasions to various NATO and Common Market gatherings. Everything about the set-up was amorphous. I had no official standing of any kind, yet was frequently welcomed on the periphery of official bodies. So far as the Church of England was concerned, I was functioning in the jurisdiction of North and Central Europe, and I was under the bishop of Fulham. I was paid neither by HM Government nor by the Anglican Church. I was paid by a noble and long-established missionary society, who were kind and supportive but could give me only the equivalent of an English curate's stipend. My expenses I had to pick up where and as I could. Of course, the English communities and official bodies I ministered to were wonderfully hospitable, but that wasn't quite the same as having some money in my pocket. Only after weddings and funerals did I have a fee which enabled me to relish some indigenous gastronomic treat. I existed in embassies and expatriates' homes and seedy hotels, often running a whole social gamut in a very brief space of time. I was frying sausages over a spirit stove in a run-down *pension* (and running the taps in my washbasin to drown the hissing, for it was forbidden to cook in one's room), when a flunkey from our nearby embassy arrived with an impressive invitation. I was summoned in a few days to attend a reception in honour of Her Britannic Majesty's birthday. There I duly went, and unobtrusively, even elegantly, made a meal off the very attractive cocktail snacks.

I went to many such formal gatherings. There was something a trifle Ruritanian about them, with their decaying European royalty, and their statesmen and diplomats and generals and cardinals. At one, I remember, a famous politician's lady (who was perhaps a trifle tipsy) decided I was a certain Canon Gamble who had prepared her for confirmation as a young girl. As such she introduced me to several people, who (if themselves soberer) gazed at me in surprise, for my good lady was quite twenty years older than I. I gave up trying to set matters right, and settled down to enjoy the mild wonder I was causing. At another, very crowded, reception I was irritated by a man behind me who was talking so loudly in a transatlantic accent that I could scarcely hear my own interlocutor. I therefore turned round with an expression of strong disapproval to fasten on the offender, only to discover it was the Duke of Windsor. I gazed at him for a moment, trying to see in the rather small, rather wizened creature that young and handsome Prince of Wales of my boyhood. It was all rather sad. The Duchess was at the other end of the great room, surrounded by clearly charismatized men.

But I mustn't give the impression that my activities were confined to such circles. There were many poor expatriates I visited, often with very welcome gifts of tea or preserves or whisky, or, once, a fine canned hock of gammon. How could I afford such things, you may well ask? Well, quite early on, I discovered that each diplomat in one fair city had access to a wonderful Aladdin's cave known as the commissariat, where one could buy a whole Harrods Food Hall tax-free. I asked why I had no such privilege and was told that I was not a member of the diplomatic corps. This raised my hackles and I went to see our ambassador, who was well disposed to me because he enjoyed my sermons. I told him how enormously helpful it would be to have access to the commissariat. The upshot was that I was granted the privilege, but was told not to advertise the fact. I wonder if my successors have enjoyed such amenities? It would be nice to think I established such a rich concession.

I also saved two marriages, as I had saved one in Birmingham, and was to save one later on. A strange ministry for a person like me. I always found something genuinely sad about the break-up of a family.

And I also had someone released from life imprisonment. I was introduced to the convicted murderer by Princess Maria.

Those are two arresting sentences which must now be elucidated. I met the Princess as a parishioner of one of my little, historic English churches. She attended only Mattins there (she was a Roman Catholic), and she did not seem on particularly friendly terms with the rest of the congregation. She was in her fifties, always 'sensibly' dressed (tweeds and brogues), and she rode an equally sensible bike with everything except a crossbar. She was the daughter of one of those petty Teutonic kings. Both king and kingdom had now disappeared, and she had been interned by her countrymen during the war because of her family's long opposition to Hitler. Now she was a displaced person in France, refused citizenship by the Germans (East and West) and barely tolerated by the French. Without a passport and with very little money, she was aggressively pro-British. She said her mother had been Scottish and her own heart had in earliest childhood been implanted in the Highlands. Her little flat (where I often had tea with her) presented visitors with a tattered Union Jack pinned one side of the hall and a large portrait of Churchill pinned the other. She tried to conceal any gutturalism in her rather gruff accent and to exhibit a familiarity with English idioms, neither aim altogether successful. I remember I was once due to take a friend to tea with her, but he had to cry off because of a bad cold. When I told her this, she commented: 'Poor devil. God help him.' Still wilder was her judgment on the French gendarmes, whom she was comparing unfavourably with the well-groomed English bobbies. She spoke slightingly of the gendarmes' lack of smart uniforms, with their 'frayed handcuffs.'

I liked Princess Maria, or Mary, as she preferred me to call her. She loved any English contacts she could make, especially English girls at finishing schools or studying at the university. The consul general once asked me to call on him 'for a little chat,' which turned out to be a stern word of advice. He told me to have as little to do with Princess Maria as possible. When I asked him why, he said he was not permitted to say. I told him she was a parishioner of mine and I should not dream of repudiating her without a reason (or even with one, I added to myself). I met the same mysterious antagonism to the Princess in one or two of the English community, and I never discovered why. Which is not to say that I had no ideas of my own. I suspected that she was a lesbian, and perhaps once had been indiscreet. As may be imagined, such bigotry cut no ice with me.

The Princess did much good work among the English poor, and especially among English ex-servicemen who were for one reason or another washed up like jettison in France. Among her flock was one Sidney Curle, who as a British Tommy had in 1918 been convicted of the murder of a French girl. He had been more or less rotting in a French prison ever since. The French wanted to repatriate him, but the English didn't want the worry and responsibility of him. I visited him two or three times with the Princess. He wrote poetry and did drawings and now as ever protested his innocence. The Princess knew *she* could do nothing with the English authorities, but she begged me to. I tried with the consul general, but he would have nothing to do with the case when he heard of the Princess's connection with it. However, I knew a young man who was the French correspondent of a great English newspaper. I interested him in poor Sidney, and took him to see the conditions he was living in. The upshot was a long and hard-hitting report in the English press. This, as hoped, spurred the English authorities into action, for they were being charged with a shameful negligence. Sidney was quickly repatriated and spent less than a year in a provincial English jail before his release. I corresponded with him for two or three years. I heard he ended his days as a model old age pensioner. I was glad about that. Full marks to the Princess.

18

I was asked to call on an elderly English lady in Brussels. She was a Miss Inez Halliday. She lived in a large garret room in a millionaire's mansion, her sight was failing rapidly, and she was reputed to be a spitfire, who even caused a breakdown in the commandant of the Nazi camp in which she had been interned for the last two years of the war. I was also told that she had been a missionary who from age eighteen or so had worked among lepers in the Belgian Congo. Thus briefed, and with some trepidation, I climbed to the top of the millionaire's house and knocked timidly on a door labelled 'Mlle Halliday SEULEMENT.' An impatient, irritable voice that seemed just right called: 'Qui est là? Que voulez-vous?' I replied in English: 'I'm a clergyman. I've called to see how you are.' A pause, then a torrent of words: 'You cannot call on me without giving me notice of your visit. You must write making an appointment. I am not in a state to receive you.' For some reason this did not put me off at all. If anything, it rather endeared me to the owner of the voice. It seemed somehow gallant to maintain one's standards in a garret in a foreign city when one was ageing, solitary and going blind. So I called back: 'Oh, please don't send me away. I've been looking forward to meeting you. I'll wait as long as you like.' Distinctly mollified, she said: 'Oh, very well. Enter when I tell you to.' I waited, not too long, as furniture creaked and footsteps pottered behind the door. Then it was opened, and I had my first sight of Miss Halliday: frail but indomitable-looking, lean and wiry, tall and upright. (She wore a steel corset to offset calcium deficiency.) Her grey hair was neatly pinned in a bun, her grey flannel costume (long skirt and military jacket) was brightened round the shoulders by a silk shawl. The pupils of her eyes were colourless and questing.

I said: 'Oh, Miss Halliday, it is good to see you. I've heard so much about you.' And she replied: 'You know how to conquer the old dragon, don't you?' And at this we both burst out laughing.

I called the next day and took her out to tea. We became great friends. Whenever I was to visit Brussels I wrote to her well in advance to arrange our tête-à-tête tea party. I admired intensely the skill and courage with which she faced her awful handicap. Soon after I returned to England her sight failed completely. I got her into a pleasant old people's home in Eastbourne, and I obtained for her a grant from the Distressed Gentlefolks Association. Several times a year I visited her in Eastbourne and took her out to tea. Once I had to visit Eastbourne on business and didn't tell her about it. But a nurse from the home saw me in the town and told her. I received a long and censorious letter, and a sharp dressing-down when next I saw her. (She wrote with a frame, defeated only when her pen ran out of ink.)

Not long before she died she walked me round a large cemetery to choose a burial plot for her. I must say it seemed to me a task involving neither good cheer nor diligence, but she found it a most enjoyable outing. When I suggested a nice shady spot near the wall, she said: 'No, it'll be near the road. Too noisy.' Then, as the absurdity of it struck her, she went into peals of laughter.

291

THE MORE WE ARE TOGETHER

We were friends for twenty-five years, and I remember her funeral as the only cheerful one I have ever attended.

When I walked round Brussels I thought of Charlotte and Emily and M. Heger's academy. But more poignantly I thought of my Julien and how he would have loved to show me proudly round his metropolis as once long ago I had shown him round mine.

In The Hague I made contact with a family called Simpson, of jealously English extraction but speaking their native tongue with a marked foreign accent. They were Anglicans and they wished their 15-year-old son Robert to be prepared for confirmation in the Church of England. He was a nice boy and we became good friends as I gave him two-hour lessons once a month for three months. He attended a Roman Catholic lycée and spoke both French and Flemish far better than English. My lessons had to prepare him for baptism as well as confirmation. I arranged to baptize him in the local Anglican church on my third visit. But on the second visit, he told me I needn't bother about the baptism because it had already been done. I was rather disconcerted by this. I asked him where it had been done. 'In the Roman Catholic church near my home,' he told me. I asked him if he had told the priest he was to be confirmed in the Church of England. 'No,' he said, looking embarrassed. I told him it was rather deceitful, and I had better, as a matter of courtesy, call on the priest to explain. Then, blushing, he told me the facts. He had been baptized by a friend on their way home from school.

'But why,' I asked, 'when you knew I was intending to baptize you in the Anglican church?' Stammering, he told me his friend didn't think the Anglican baptism would be the real thing.

I asked him where exactly his friend had baptized him and what words he had used. 'In the stoup of holy water by the entrance to the church. And... and he used the proper words: "In nomine patris et filii et spiritus sancti".'

'Was it a joke?' I asked severely.

He was quite shocked. 'Oh no,' he told me. 'My friend was worried about me.'

Well, I consulted a wise colleague, who told me if the intent was serious and the trinitarian formula was used, then the baptism was valid. So I duly entered it in the baptismal register and signed the entry as the officiating minister. Just by my name I put a well-disguised 'p.p.'. So there it stands for posterity. And Robert was so pleased that at his confirmation he added a name: mine. So the record stood: 'Robert Louis Simpson: Baptized p.p. Peter Gamble.' And in the confirmation register: 'Robert Louis Peter Simpson: Confirmed George Fulham.' I thought the whole thing was really rather beautiful.

In Paris, on the first Sunday in the month, some cultural offshoot of the British embassy or the British Council held a cocktail party for resident British students, the venue being either at the Sorbonne or the Alliance Française or else at some finishing school. They roped me in as a host. I felt at first that I'd be more likely to put young people off than enfold them in affectionate, expatriate arms. But I suppose I did little worse than most people would have done in such circumstances.

I used a kind of patter designed to thaw as I approached each group of happily chattering students, who fell self-consciously silent as I bore down on them. One student told me afterwards: 'Oh, you were smooth. And intimidating. Up you came, smiling blandly and toying with your sherry glass, and said with awful self-confidence: "Now, come, come. I'm supposed to promote conversation, not kill it".' How different the impressions we create from those we think we're creating!

I'd ask each one where in England he or she came from, then go on to inquire about studies and job plans and grander ambitions. Chatting thus to one young man I learned that his home in England was in Belmont, which was close to my place in Banstead, although I didn't at first let on about this.

'Where were you at school?' I asked him.

'At Malvern.'

'No, I mean prep school.'

'Oh, you wouldn't know it. It was in Banstead. Called Walton's.'

With insouciant expression, I remarked: 'And no doubt Jimmy taught you maths, and Corny English.'

His mouth fell a little open. He looked at me as if I were a seer. I felt I must explain. 'I taught there for a while. Oh, years and years ago. I must have missed you.'

The young man, Henry (or Harry) Guest, was enchanted by the coincidence. So was I. Especially when I added: 'I hope you kept away from those butts.'

Well, that was the start of another great friendship. As rich and warm as so many that I've been blessed with. And as mortal. Perhaps because we were at the time both somewhat uprooted, cut adrift, relocated, we found in each other and in the accident of our shared memories something comfortable, even luxurious. Then the final cementing was a common sense of humour, a parity in our literary and dramatic loves, an affinity in political and religious matters.

Harry had read modern languages at Cambridge and was now doing a higher degree at the Sorbonne. So I tried to be in Paris as often as I could. We had marvellous evenings together, combing *Une Semaine de Paris* for cultic films and avant-garde plays, seeking out delicious, recherché restaurants and bohemian bistros, exploring all the famous corners of the Latin Quarter,

293

sipping exotic nightcaps in every other café we met, and talking as fast as the words would come, laughing hysterically until the breath choked, and drifting homeward only when Paris, even Paris, had no more ports of call to accommodate us.

We even exploded into guffaws at the unquestioned rituals of our patient, tolerant Church of England. That is how I instinctively remember Harry: spangled through my tears and the rays of streetlamps, doubled up with mirth, clutching a *pissoir* stand, as he slowly sank groundward. He had been nicely brought up and conventionally educated, so there was just a modicum of starch to be washed from his system.

Before we returned to England, his parents moved to Thanet, to gorse and cliffs and sea, and there I often stayed with them. I grew almost as fond of his family as of my own. Harry and I went for protracted country walks, even for one or two week-long pilgrimages. He taught at Lancing, where I often stayed with him and met his bright pupils: Tim Rice and Peter Jay and Ian Huish and Christopher Hampton.

Then one day (of course) Harry told me that he was going to get married. They lived for a while in the orient, then returned to England to settle in Devon. Both Harry and his wife have written work that is commended and admired. They have three children, now busily carving their own careers. I have never seen them.

Our embassy restaurants were a godsend whichever European country I happened to be in, and the American ones were even better. I was delighted to discover that my UK embassy pass was good also for the US embassies. The latter were also safer, for the young women there seemed rather less VAD (to use Glad-eye's description) than our own heftier misses. As I sat alone in one UK embassy, eating my lunch and reading my paper, I was chatted up twice in one week. The trouble was that I liked both the young women and was often so lost and lonely that the friendship of a congenial compatriot was welcome.

Both were educated, intelligent girls, but otherwise very different. Wendy was neat and prissy and habitually played the competent but defenceless little woman. She often accompanied me on a Sunday excursion when I had to administer to some rather remote English community. I was glad of her company, and not least because several years' residence made her much better than I at dealing with buses and trains and restaurants. But several things began to make me less grateful and more irritable. If when crossing a busy road we had to pause halfway to let the traffic swirl round us, she would seize my arm and tremble and cry and stamp her feet dementedly. I thought, rightly or wrongly, it was an act.

One evening, returning from a Sunday engagement, we came to a bifurcation we hadn't met before. Said Wendy: 'Shall we go that way or this way?' I replied, abstractedly, unthinkingly: 'You sound like the old dance song:

> Let's walk a-that-away,
> Not a-this-away,
> This-away only leads to home.
> Don't throw our chance away
> To hug and kiss away:
> This-away only leads to home.'

No reply. I continued in complete innocence to consider our itinerary. Then from close beside me I heard a little twee, coquettish voice: 'Then why do we?' I didn't immediately know what she was talking about. So determined was she to leave me in no doubt that she added, in a coy little whisper: 'Why throw our chance away?'

When the penny dropped I was quite horrified. I said sharply: 'Don't be ridiculous.' And I strode ahead (along the more populous road), leaving her to catch me up. After that I cruelly starved the relationship of all sustenance. In a very short time thereafter poor Wendy was passing me in the street with never a glance. The Brenda travesty all over again. How could I be so stupid as to involve myself in such a painful misunderstanding? And now I was almost fifteen years older!

With Dora things were, I comforted myself, very different. She was more intelligent, more sophisticated, more worldly. She also had a rather raffish sense of humour I liked. I introduced her to my favourite restaurants, and often she cooked me excellent meals in her little Latin Quarter flat. She was half French and a Roman Catholic. She also suffered privately from a cruel sense of exile. Not from England, but from her church: because of a male lover she had (whom I never met), she dutifully, but agonizingly, cut herself off from mass.

Yes, I liked Dora, and I felt safe with her. Especially when one night, sipping coffee and Ricard in a noisy pavement café, she said to me: 'I want you to know, Peter, that I quite understand, and accept, why you have no emotional affairs with women.' I musingly smiled on this. I thought it was both sensitive and humane of her to speak so. I wondered: should I tell her something of my tastes, my experiences, my bright and darker memories? It would be good to unburden myself of many things to a sympathetic if not identical ear.

She was speaking again: 'Yes, do believe that I respect greatly your duty as a priest to renounce such things.'

I re-entered my reverie, but in an entirely different mood. Supposing I had opened my heart! I didn't know how to react: in gratitude for a lucky escape from exposure, or with shame for accepting a virtue I didn't possess.

Well, either way I could continue to feel secure with Dora. What a hypocrite I was compelled to be.

The life of one's imagination can itself act as a lifeline when the daily round is not too congenial. Especially when a book activates the imagination. This was vividly the case when I was browsing idly in a British Council library in Paris or Brussels. Searching for something by Henry Green, whom I was impressed by at that time, my eye suddenly lit on a novel entitled *An Air That Kills*. Calling your book by a line in Housman was, to me, in itself a recommendation, so I took it up and glanced at its opening words: quite enough to tell me it was my cup of tea. I knew nothing of its author, Francis King. I read it all that evening and finished it in bed about 2 am. Not merely because it was in its writing full of life, gripping, humorous and moving, but also because I discovered its plot (and more than its plot) was lifted from a very fine novel by Forrest Reid called *Brian Westby*. I was sure this was so. I felt I must ask this Francis King to confirm my hunch, and must also tell him how impressed I was by his book. I felt it was a young man's book, and a young man would not take anything I said amiss. So I wrote to him, care of his publisher.

I very soon had a most rewarding letter. 'Your remarks about *An Air That Kills* were far more perceptive than any reviewer's and you were the only person, apart from Robert Liddell, to note the parallels with *Brian Westby*... Do you merely write brilliant letters? I know nothing about you. What do you *do*?... I hope we shall meet soon.' Yes, we met and corresponded for several years. But then our paths diverged and our jobs were at variance. But I remember him with pleasure and have followed his career with admiration.

19

I was granted occasional weeks' furlough, when I hared off home as quickly as I could: first of all by air, because it was quick, but later by train and ship because it was far cheaper. In such spells of freedom I would, of course, bask in the company of family and friends, and also try to fit in any calls to interview from schools. For I never gave up seeking a school chaplaincy, although actual interviews were now both rare and fruitless.

On one leave I had a sudden phone call from Jonathan. I had, with real sorrow, more or less given him up. Nor did this phone call hearten me, for his tone was even more nervous, more constrained. He said he wished to see me, for he had some things to give me. I sensed they were books and records I had lent him. Just like an engagement ring returned, I reflected bitterly.

We met in a café in Mayfair we had once been fond of. (He didn't want to journey all the way to Streatham.) He was already seated there when I arrived. He was pale and drawn, and there on the chair beside him was, sure enough, the carrier bag of pleasures we had once quaffed together. A barren cornucopia.

He made no effort to begin with a few friendly, or even sociable, remarks. Picking at a paper serviette, and not looking at me, he said: 'Peter, I'm letting Miranda divorce me. She's found somebody else. She's been unfaithful. But I don't mind playing the guilty party. It doesn't matter. Anyway, I *am* the guilty party.'

I murmured perfunctory protests, but with an impatient wave of his hand he cut me short. 'Yes, I really am. I should never have married her. I just used her. Now I'm being punished for it.'

I felt lost, groping. Perhaps somewhere in the recesses of my mind was a hope that now we might return to the happy days of our friendship. But his manner suggested that nothing was further from his own thoughts. He went on, speaking quickly, as if he wanted to get an unpleasant task over and escape.

'My father was right all the time. He has shown me the way. God has given me a fine father who has shown me my sins. Sins like playing cricket on the Lord's Day, and... and chasing worldly pleasures at the Lord's expense. This divorce is my shame and my penance. But God will put away my sin. I am the lost sheep he has found.'

I could think of nothing to say. I just stared at him as at a stranger. He went on: 'I've given away all my books, all my records. These here are yours that you lent me. All baubles, the Devil's baubles.' If his face had not been so adamant against it, I would have thought it was all a parody, like our old, mocking, laughing parodies.

He added: 'I am going to join the Exclusive Brethren, and there, if the Lord will, I'll find a true wife and become a true husband.'

He waited for me to say something, but I was still fighting to take it all in, to receive it as a sober fact. So he said in conclusive tones as he pushed back his chair and prepared to rise: 'I felt I ought to tell you this in person.' This prompted me to blurt out the question I must ask before he went. 'And I suppose I have played a prime part in your corruption?'

He said, in hushed tones that sounded as appalled as appalling: 'I... I think you are Antichrist.'

I deliberately finished my coffee, put the money for both on the table, picked up the carrier bag and left. I was shattered. Oh, not by the name he'd given me. It meant nothing to me. Only that he was sick.

But I grieved, grieved with every step I took. Not simply that he was lost to me, but that he was lost to humanity. I went back to my ecclesiastical duties more aware than ever before of the evils that can be perpetrated in the name of religion.

Then the unbelievable happened. I applied, almost mechanically, for a school chaplaincy advertised in the *Church Times*. I was called to an interview, and with no little cynicism I went. I met the headmaster and his wife at the Hyde Park Hotel for lunch. I liked them. Even more I liked what he told me about the school, the job, the boys. But most of all I liked, no, I fell in love with, the picture postcards of the school that he showed me. Of cricket matches and sports fixtures and rollcalls, all set in glorious West Country landscapes of high summer. There and then he offered me the job. A week after I was back on the Continent his letter arrived confirming my appointment and setting out all the needless details.

It was early in 1955. I wrote at once to give my Society six months' notice, and for most of those months I lived in a dream, ever and again pulling from my wallet the postcards he had given me, and gazing long at them with expectant, shining eyes. More often than ever before I would say a silent prayer of thanks to the good God who had listened at last.

As in Birmingham, my love for my job was never so great as when I prepared to surrender it. So many kind people, so many pangs at parting, so many little, meaningful gifts.

I left the Continent with regrets smothered in glorious expectations. I arrived back in England in early August. As the train bringing me home sped through the Home Counties, I gazed out of the window at vale and down and stream and said over and over again to myself: 'I love you, I love you, I love you.' I was astonished to find in myself this great love for my native land. It suggested a patriotism I never knew I had.

Soon after I reached home, I went on a visit to the school at the headmaster's request. Its ageing stones and rolling fields made me feel as I had never felt before (not in London, not at Oxford): that I was to be incorporated in a great maturity, and in that I was to be blessed.

But the headmaster greeted me with a coolness that flawed my very heart. 'I am afraid, Gamble,' he said, 'that I have not had a good reference from one senior cleric. All your other references were very good, but his wasn't, and I am bound to take notice of it.'

His words told me who the villain of the piece was. But I was not going to give up now. I said, scarcely hiding my bitterness: 'It is Canon Luce, who has been pursuing me to damn me ever since I embarked on a Dip Ed. Are you so unsure about me, and about your own instincts, and about all my other referees, that you are going to reject me on this one man's prejudiced word?' He looked uncomfortable, torn, irresolute. I said emphatically (for my blood was up): 'Will you come with me right now to the bishop? To lay the whole thing before him? To see if I must throw back to the bishop his licence which he has already sent me?'

He couldn't refuse. To the bishop of Salisbury we went, after phoning to request a vital audience. And there, in the Bishop's Palace and before the bishop's face, I finally laid to rest the ghost that had been haunting me so namelessly, so cruelly, so long.

At the end of my passionate defence, the bishop thought for a moment (only a moment), then turned to the headmaster and said: 'I advise you to ignore Canon Luce's stricture and go ahead with your appointment. I myself am quite satisfied.'

I am glad to recount this, for the often anonymous machinations of a headmaster on the Headmasters' Conference is a cross beneath which many a young schoolmaster has sunk without trace. And so for the rest of August in that fine summer of 1955 I prepared myself for the school chaplaincy which had for so long been the Grail I was pledged to grasp.

21

Milton Abbey School was for me a jewel set in a golden scene. It had been founded only a year before and its founder, the Rev Dr C. K. Francis Brown, had lavished much of his private fortune on it and equipped it extravagantly and conventionally, with all the boys garbed just as in Frank Richards' Greyfriars. Such was their appearance in the postcards the headmaster-elect had given to me. Dr Brown had left after it was revealed that he had vastly overspent his resources. I don't know the story but it was clearly a tragedy for him and many others associated with the project. A consortium of new governors, led by the Hambros (of Hambro's Bank), had taken over and appointed a Hambro nephew, one Lt Cdr Hugh Hodgkinson, DSC, as headmaster. He had spent a year teaching at Gordonstoun under Kurt Hahn and brought with him such Hahnian ideas as clothing all the boys in shorts and blousons and beginning every day with a morning run and cold shower. Moreover, the ethos of the school was now largely technical and industrial, in place of the traditional military and imperialist slants.

So the set-up was 'the new public school for the new age,' but housed in the loveliest medieval and Georgian buildings erected on the site of a Benedictine monastery whose abbey was the school chapel.

There was beauty abounding: the beauty of the setting, the beauty of the job I was given, and the beauty of the boys. The setting was Wessex, but with none of those clouds of fatalistic gloom that Hardy had cast over it, rather, a sort of Camelot of my own. The job was magic: the magic of my prewar Reader's Union combined with the magic of wartime Belvedere.

As at RU, I zoomed upward and onward too fast for my own good. As at Belvedere, I made a little kingdom in which I was inevitably to topple. I was at once made a housemaster, and I set out to make my house the best, not only in work but also (surprisingly) in games. I had, as usual, to learn as I went along. My congenial colleagues, most of them friends to this day, were themselves the products of public boarding schools and so knew all the ropes I had, by the judicious use of eyes and ears, to acquire. I was very anxious to guard against any hint of conceit, which is why I rather emphasized my ignorance in certain fields. But my colleagues had no resentment, and my growth was due in part to the headmaster's connivance, in part to my ready acceptance by the boys.

Hodgkinson was not academic. He was never so happy as when taking a group of boys beagling, or to point-to-points, or spotting roedeer droppings in the surrounding woods. I think social milieu, plus a gallant war record, had got him the headmastership, and he rather gladly left the academic side of things to me and the other housemasters.

Milton Abbey was rich not only in boy beauty but in innocence. But perhaps 1955 was a more innocent age, before the kicking over of teenage traces, before the example of pop idols, before the cult of drink and drugs, before the enthronement of the all-knowing, streetwise, sophisticated adolescent.

The school had one large complex of communal showers, and we housemasters took it in turns to supervise them. The boys showered and towelled and chatted to us with a complete absence of self-consciousness. I was aware of their beauty, but I was free of temptation. Since I had been ordained I had yielded to no amorous intrigues with youths. Not because I felt homosexual love was wrong, was forbidden to a Christian. Long after I was ordained I continued to love Nigel Day. But a dog collar helped me to see that any of those boy-centred lubricities I'd known in my twenties were now literally unthinkable. A real affection, a true pastoral care, had now supplanted all such thoughtless self-indulgence.

I threw myself into the chaplain's work. As in my Birmingham parish, I persuaded them all to change to a better hymnbook, to the unexceptionable *Songs of Praise*, which avoided all excesses of either High Church or Low, and which sought the aesthetic in words and in music. At Milton Abbey, it had offended me to find a chapelful of healthy boys singing 'Who is this with garments gory, Triumphing from Bozrah's way?', and the fact that they neither knew nor cared what it meant made it more, not less, offensive.

Our annual confirmation was the outstanding event it should be. I put the religious life of the school on the map. I had a chapel fixture card printed each term to rival the games fixture cards. I took the boys on a three-day retreat before their confirmation. They were so good that I myself was as spiritually uplifted by it as I think they were. Even the little hitches caused what one old school chaplain I know called 'holy laughter.' This happened in

300

one retreat house we stayed in where the rooms of the nuns were named after St Paul's 'fruits of the Spirit': Love, Mercy, Peace, Hope, Charity, Longsuffering, and so on. I was thus horrified to find one not terribly bright boy about to barge into a room labelled 'Gentleness.' Just in time I seized him by the seat of his pants and dragged him back. His surprised explanation (quite sincere) was: 'Oh, I thought it said "Gentlemen".'

The bishop confirmed them on a Saturday afternoon, and I had already told all parents that they were expected to stay in local hotels that night and be promptly present for the boys' first communion at eight o'clock the next morning, followed by breakfast in our great hall. This was, of course, based on my Birmingham confirmations and it was just as joyous an occasion.

For the end of the Hilary term I arranged other memorable events. First there was the carol service, which displayed the voices and the faces of my large and handsome choir. Each person at that service had a candle in a gold-painted block of wood and a box of matches. As soon as the 'Once in royal' solo began each person lit his candle and the service proceeded by candlelight, in which ancient walls and pillars swayed and stained glass stared eerily on. Beautiful, but too dangerous to repeat. Then came a fine Christmas dinner in which senior boys wore dinner jackets and made witty after-dinner speeches. Some of the speeches I wrote myself and many of the deliveries I coached them in, not because I wanted to but because a producer was needed and no one else would do it.

Soon after I arrived at the school I was called on by a charming man who had once been bursar and was now the self-appointed custodian of the abbey. An ex-army officer, he was a devout High Churchman and a friend to each boy and master in the school. He was also deaf, with an inadequate hearing aid. I don't think he heard a word of any sermon, but this did not prevent his calling on me each Monday morning and saying with the sweetest of smiles: 'Too long, padre, too long.' He also made good, if not legitimate, uses of his hearing aid in chapel by causing it to whistle quite loudly after ten minutes of preaching. I often had tea with him in his honeysuckled cottage in the adjacent village.

About halfway through my first term, he told me something of his life: 'When I left the army I became a prison governor for some years. Couldn't stand the thought of doing nothing useful.'

There stirred within me tiny echoes, rustling whispers, long-buried tones from days long past. Scarcely wanting to, I asked casually: 'Which prison were you at?' Carelessly he gave me what I had somewhere, somehow, known to be the answer: 'Exeter prison.'

I communed with myself. Should I tell him? Wasn't it sheer common sense to let such old, sleeping dogs lie? But the dogs were now yapping to be heard. I wanted to talk about it all.

THE MORE WE ARE TOGETHER

So I told him, trying in vain to see in this kindly old man that governor I'd been hauled before as a rebellious old lag, as a troublesome conchie who wouldn't shave and wouldn't march.

He wasn't surprised, wasn't shocked. But he was anxious: 'My dear padre, tell me truthfully, was I well disposed? Tolerant? Sympathetic? Oh, I do hope I was at least just?' He seemed very concerned. And when I reassured him, his relief was almost absurdly apparent. He never told a soul, although I wouldn't have minded if he had. Guy and his wife Molly were dear friends of mine for the rest of their lives. One of those odd little tergiversations fate sometimes enjoys.

I ran the school tuckshop, as a consequence of which a few boys tried to popularize the obvious soubriquet of Friar Tuck for me (although it never caught on). Every month I had to drive to my wholesaler in the school bus to replenish supplies, and I always took a few boys with me. On spring days we would en route visit a lonely and beautiful piece of coast, where the boys changed in a cave for a swim, or once when they had no costumes swam in the nude. I usually contrived to have Jeremy with me, and that set the seal on such halcyon days.

Jeremy was in my house, and I think he was probably the most beautiful boy in the school, which was praise indeed. He was often in trouble: kleptomaniac trouble, not just normal schoolboy high spirits. He wasn't naughty, he hadn't a great sense of humour, and he wasn't particularly popular. But two little incidents deepened my love for him. He was one of my servers at Holy Communion, and like all the band he took his job seriously. One Sunday I arrived as usual very early for the 8 am service (I always had a fear of being late), and didn't expect anybody, server or communicant, to be there before me. But going into the Lady Chapel for a book, I found him there, kneeling in prayer at the altar rail, a shaft of sunlight gilding his fair hair. I had never suggested he should pray in the Lady Chapel before our service. No other boy did. It was entirely his own idea. It touched me, deeply. I have never forgotten it, but I expect he has no memory of it at all.

On another occasion, I was awakened by a knock on my bedroom door at about three in the morning. I quickly donned slippers and dressing gown (always to hand, for one was always on call) and opened the door. Outside was Jeremy in tears. He came in and told me all about it. Before lights out he had had a fight with another boy in his dormitory, and had sworn at him. Then he couldn't sleep for thinking of it. After several restless hours (I use his own words): 'God told me: Go and tell the chaplain all about it. Do it now, don't wait for the morning.' So we sat on my bed and talked about it, and then said some prayers together, simple, straightforward, commonsensical prayers. Then he went to bed, quite happily, leaving me even happier, even daring to feel 'wonderful, counsellor, a prince of peace'!

I was earning a little more now. Not so very much more, for public school salaries, like clerical ones, were in those days supposed to be above vulgar commercial considerations. But enough to take on both the rent and the rates of the family flat in Banstead. Now father was retired, money at home was very tight. I was glad I could help, for they had seen me through Oxford, and even Birmingham, with money they could ill afford.

And I bought my first car. It was a sort of van which had been fitted with extra seats. I bought it off the school at £20 a month, and I loved it. I think I cherished it as I have never cherished a car since. It was a Jowett and it was marvellously reliable. I wish I'd never risen above it.

22

Halfway through my time at Milton Abbey, the family reached an absurd decision to move. For some years they'd been taking a modest holiday at Selsey in Sussex, and they'd rather fallen in love with it. So when one summer they found a very nice house to let there at a reasonable rent (less than the Banstead flat), they told me it was only sense to move. The flat rent was due for another increase, and the house was large and handsome and almost on the edge of the sea. I was as captivated by it as they were. I was almost as naive as they were, too.

So one summer holiday we upped and moved to Selsey. At first all went well. They loved the sea, and the proximity to Chichester. Only gradually did it dawn on us that the rent was low because the situation was an impossible one for a family without a good private income. Bob could find no work down there, so had to go and live with his mother in London. Pam could get nothing either in a riding stable or a prep school, so was forced to become a part-time hostess in a club. And in the school holidays I lived there with increasing dissatisfaction, because it was lonely and boring.

I was glad when the holidays ended and I could once more immerse myself in my Eden. Yet there, too, the skies began to lour, and the heavens began to reverberate with the spiteful chuckles of those Eumenides.

Hodgkinson, the headmaster, was a pleasant man. Initially, and instinctively, I liked him and his wife. But I liked the school, and my house, and my colleagues, and the boys, even more, and I just couldn't approve of his way of governing them, or, more accurately, of not governing them. It seemed to me that he was not very interested in the most important elements, such as the education of the boys, and too consumingly intent on things like architecture and landscaping and all manner of country pursuits. Most of the blame for what happened was mine. I must confess I came to resent his position as headmaster. I think it was a Gamble family trait, or at any rate a fault of Brian and Pam and me. We none of us could gratefully accept working superiors unless they were grand old men like Jimmy, and these were rare. Both Brian and Pam had brushes with headmasters and headmistresses, but none as dire as mine.

Yes, most of the blame for the bad blood between Hodgkinson and me was mine. But not all of it. If I resented Hodgkinson, he no less certainly came to resent me. I was aware of this. From the first I looked in vain for a word of appreciation from him. He was incapable of giving it, probably because he felt no man was less in need of approbation. But I longed for a hint of praise.

He soon came to see that my wings urgently needed clipping. I don't think there was much doubt that in the eyes of the boys Hodgkinson was the titular headmaster, while I was the actual one. It was an impossible situation, and Hodgkinson was justified in tackling it head on. First he engaged a new man in a new position, as second master, which had not hitherto been a part of the school's structure. This new man was a courteous and reasonable person, but we housemasters made his life miserable. I saw to that. After this, Hodgkinson created a new house and housemaster. The latter was a former wartime comrade, another lieutenant commander (we now had five on the staff), who was not a success as a housemaster but who was for long championed by Hodgkinson against me. Then Hodgkinson said he thought it was time I resigned as a housemaster because no man could be expected to go on wearing that hat as well as a chaplain's. I had been thinking this myself, although I must say the boys had never found any difficulty in the situation. But I was getting tired of doing all the work and taking all the blame, for that was how it seemed to me. So after three years as a housemaster, I settled down to teaching and to running all things ecclesiastical. I felt I'd lost a limb. If I hadn't had my little war with Hodgkinson and the second master to wage I think I should have found myself rather at a loss. Unfortunately, I hadn't then read *The Lanchester Tradition* (most splendid of school stories, although there isn't a boy in it), for I'd have dissolved in laughter as I inevitably identified with the unspeakable Mr Chowdler. I might even have come to see that in this paradise I was not only a keeper of the Tree of Knowledge but was also the serpent coiled round it.

The new housemaster was both very devout and a confirmed flogger. (I never had corporal punishment in my house.) He also had a bee in his bonnet about homosexuality. He rather obsessively looked for it in his house, and if he thought he'd found any he would seek to exorcize it with his cane. Once he was overheard to ask, in a manner reminiscent of Henry II, 'Where's that bloody priest?' The crunch came when he cornered a boy in his house who had consulted me as chaplain and demanded to know what the boy had said to me. The boy refused to say, and I told the housemaster he had transgressed every religious rule. He bellowed and blustered, so I invoked Hodgkinson, who could think of nothing better to say than: 'I'm not coming between you. You two are always at loggerheads.' I reported it all to the bishop, who did nothing, perhaps because he knew oil slicks on troubled waters were ecologically dangerous, or perhaps because he felt the serpent was the last citizen of Eden that he was in a position to champion. Or perhaps even because he was a former Royal Navy chaplain!

One boy I had in my House still visits. Even at school he was a very useful (if over-sensitive) organist. Now he is the talented musician and composer Francis Shaw.

At the end of that summer term, when all the boys and most of the masters had left, Hodgkinson sent me a brief note to say it would perhaps be better if our ways parted at once. All that term I had felt that such must be the end, but to make the break was something I could not initiate. Hodgkinson could, however, and gladly.

For me the blow of losing Eden seemed mortal. I was heartbroken, but no one knew. For me, grief has always been an intensely private emotion. I merely set about the making of my future, such as it was to be. It was too late to find something suitable for September. A stopgap was essential, and that meant something less than fulfilling. I told Hodgkinson I expected every backing from him in my search for a worthy new berth. I knew he was willing to do almost anything to see the back of me. Besides, I felt that for all my cussedness I had given the school a great deal, in fact all the good that was in me. I told Hodgkinson I wanted from him an open testimonial he could not gainsay. Twice I returned what he wrote. Twice, with pretty clenched teeth, he recomposed it. The bursar, who had every confidence in me and less in Hodgkinson, later told me that at least two of the school governors were on my side, and that if I'd stayed and made a fight for it things might have been very different. But I'm glad I didn't, for I quite liked Hodgkinson, and I couldn't admire what my pride and possessiveness had made of me. In the event, Hodgkinson went on to make Milton Abbey the fine school it is today.

I left a goodbye letter to the boys, which Hodgkinson said he would post up when the new term opened. I heard the boys were very shaken by it. Several wrote to tell me so. One boy said: 'The school will go downhill quickly now.' But, of course, it didn't. Soon I expect my name was seldom mentioned, seldom remembered.

For some years I met former Milton Abbey pupils in the school holidays and took them out to theatres and dinners. Jeremy I saw several times a year even when he had left school and was dallying with a profession. I remember well our last evening out together. I had taken him to *A Village Romeo and Juliet* at Sadler's Wells, for in him and several boys at Milton Abbey I had implanted an abiding love of opera. As we then drove to Kettner's in Soho for a late dinner, he said suddenly: 'Did you put me in charge of all the tuck shop takings and... and make me chapel treasurer because you knew I'd, well, had troubles that way?'

I smiled. 'Of course I did. And it worked. I knew such troubles weren't a real part of your character.'

He seemed very surprised. 'I never guessed,' he said.

Thinking back how fond I was of him when he was such a lost young boy, I glanced at him beside me in the car and said (thoughtlessly): 'You know, you're still very beautiful.'

To my surprise he was most offended. He said, angrily: 'That's not what you say to a man. "Handsome," if you like. But not "beautiful".'

I, too, was annoyed. It seemed such a ridiculous reaction to my little compliment. I didn't stop to think he saw it as an affront to his dawning manhood. I said, coldly: 'I choose my words with care. "Beautiful" I said and "beautiful" I mean.'

He sulked all the way through dinner. I drove him home to his parents' flat in Chelsea. He said: 'Will you come in and see mother and father?'

I answered: 'I think not, thank you. It's rather late.'

And I have never seen or heard of him since.

23

I found a temporary job at a boys' private boarding school in the Midlands. It was a depressing experience. I felt sorry for the headmaster, an ex-army man who wanted to make something worthwhile but hadn't the income or the intake to do so. I remember three incidents. One boring Sunday evening I agreed to have a friendly game of rummy with two or three colleagues. We were playing for matchsticks, each representing a halfpenny, so that one or two sixpences and shillings were lying on the table. I had, to be honest, forgotten it was still Sunday, and even that I was a parson, since I was never asked to take a service or even say a grace. (These were little duties the secular headmaster coveted.) The school boasted a very devout matron, very starchily uniformed and, like Malcolm's mother in *Macbeth*, more often upon her knees than on her feet. She entered the room, saw me, cried in horror and ran. Ever after she avoided me as though I had the evil eye.

There was little discipline in the place. On one's duty day one had to rise in time to get everybody else out of bed. The duty prefect had to call the duty master and together the two toured the whole establishment, the boy ringing his handbell and the master checking all was in order. On my first duty day the prefect, as I expected, was himself still snoring. So I put him in detention. This incensed a rather neurotic master who had taken a dislike to me. He told me to remove the boy's name from the detention book. I refused. From the other side of the staff breakfast room, the enraged master screamed: 'All right for you. You're going on somewhere else. We're left to run the place.' I ignored him. He shrieked: 'Do you hear me?', and he seized a sharp knife from the table and hurled it at me. Colleagues grabbed him as I picked up the knife, which had quite narrowly missed me. All worthy of *Mr Perrin and Mr Traill*.

My third sharp recollection of that school is of something I did not witness but which the headmaster described to me with much self-satisfaction. He found a boy carving his name on one of the desks: a time-honoured occupation. The boy's great hobby was making model aircraft, at which he was quite gifted. Sometimes he brought a particularly successful model to the headmaster, at his request, for he prided himself on being able to share his boys' own enthusiasms. On this occasion he admired one such model quite extravagantly, even asking the boy to set it on the floor so that he might walk all round it. The boy looked very proud. Then the headmaster suddenly jumped on it, saying, as he stamped it to smithereens: 'Now you know how I feel when you destroy my furniture.' (Who knows what psychological trauma that boy may have suffered as a result?)

I applied for two school chaplaincies that term. For both I was called to an interview. For both I was turned down. It was the same old story. I wrote to Hodgkinson to ask if he had been approached by these headmasters. He said he had, and that he had recommended me. I didn't doubt him. Was Canon Luce active again? Or even perhaps the bishop of Salisbury? As I was applying for a chaplaincy, it was only natural that my last bishop should be consulted.

I was extremely downcast. I wasn't accepting the school I was at present in as my fate. If I had to be a vicar, it would be in a City of London church. Not quite Dean of St Paul's, but one of those historic old churches of my beloved city. So I wrote to the bishop of London to ask if I could call and see him. He graciously granted me an interview. He lived in Fulham Palace, which I had much difficulty in locating, for taxi drivers thought it was a music hall.

The bishop of London was then Montgomery Campbell, whom I had never seen but had heard much about. And all I heard intrigued me. He was said to have a tart tongue and a ready, acidulous wit. When he'd been made bishop of Guildford and all the aged canons and clergy came processing to greet him, he'd murmured to his chaplain: 'The see gives up its dead.'

So I thought I'd like the bishop. I did. He said that he'd see what he could do, and I left considerably cheered.

Then, in the *Times Educational Supplement*, I saw that the famous Millfield School wanted someone to teach senior English. No mention of any chaplaincy, but that might be to my advantage, as a sort of overplus. So I wrote, and was called to an interview. I wondered if the spell cast by Canon Luce might be broken here, for I knew that Millfield had a somewhat eccentric, highly individualistic headmaster, R. J. O. Meyer, who rather prided himself on his ability to read men shrewdly and rapidly, and to make snap judgments and stick to them.

I found Meyer (as he intended) not only an eccentric but also something of a showman. I didn't gather that he had contacted Hodgkinson. He seemed satisfied both that I could teach and that I wasn't likely to create a gulf between young people and their Maker. He seemed able to offer me whatever I wanted in teaching terms, and although he had a chaplain (in fact, three) the man was soon to retire and the job would be available.

Then he astonished me by saying suddenly: 'You've got a brother Brian?' Giving me no time to reply, he added: 'He was here a couple of days ago. Can he teach?'

'Yes,' I replied. 'I think I can say he's a good teacher.'

'You two get on together?'

'Yes. We always have.'

'Good. That's fixed then.'

'You mean...?'

'You both start here next term.'

I was delighted. The campus and its hundreds of students looked attractive, exciting. As soon as I got home I phoned Brian and learned his story. A fairly elderly classics master at his prep school had applied for a job at Millfield and had been called to an interview. Since he hadn't a car, Brian drove him there and sat outside in his Morris 1000 while the interview took place. Soon Meyer came out with the nice, bumbling chap I had met once, and insisted on being introduced to a very perplexed Brian. He took him in and cross-questioned him. Brian said: 'But I haven't a degree.' Meyer ignored the remark. A week later two letters arrived: one for the bumbler, regretting, and one for Brian, offering a job teaching maths and French. Brian had at once written to tell me the fantastic news, and I received his letter after I had myself been appointed.

So we were back as at Jimmy's, teaching together and sharing the hundred and one impressions, jokes and discoveries the situation begat.

The image of Millfield, as compared with Milton Abbey, was rather more on the side of the parvenu than of the gentleman, of money rather than breeding. Even so, it was studded with Anglo-Irish peerages and European ex-royalty, as well as most of the famous showbiz names. Its students ranged from the pleasantly dim to the outstandingly bright, for the headmaster operated a Robin Hood system of entry and a steep sliding scale of fees. Classes were small, discipline excellent, manners impressive. Brian began in some terror, for his classes consisted of some gentle giants of boys, and he feared they might be heavy with brain as well as with brawn. He soon discovered his mistake and settled down to teaching that was predominantly happy and rewarding.

Millfield's buildings, unlike Milton Abbey's, were undistinguished. My classroom, a sort of small chalet in the grounds, was the best I have ever had, for no one was overhead or on either side. I have always been ultrasensitive to nearby noise in my teaching rooms, I think mainly because in a subject like literature it is essential to have an uninterrupted milieu in which one can create atmosphere, build up tension.

Typically, where on parents' day Milton Abbey had to provide a spacious carpark, Millfield had to lay on a heliport.

On the whole I liked Millfield. My teaching there was perhaps the most enjoyable and rewarding I have had.

I had many pleasant and interesting pupils. Two amusing boys I once took out to dinner were Crown Prince Alexander of Yugoslavia and Robert Arias. I remember Alexander had a crazy plan of visiting Yugoslavia under an assumed name. I talked him out of it as highly dangerous.

But the reader will perceive that my praises are qualified, and rightly so. First, no accommodation at the school was provided. We were compelled to find digs. Brian soon found something more his line: a caravan parked on the forecourt of a small country pub whose ambience he liked and whose old regulars soon became prized friends. There every night he had his sandwich and beers, did his *Telegraph* crossword, and played shove-halfpenny (at which he soon became quite a champion).

As often as I could afford it, I drove to Bristol or Bath for good food in a good setting. But I had to limit myself in such matters for, although I earned a little more now, I still had to pay rent and rates for the family, and these increased more penally than ever my salary did.

There was virtually no masters' common room at Millfield, certainly no common room life. Nor could I imagine or desire any, for the large staff was not very friendly. I think I must hold the headmaster responsible for this. He seemed to have more respect for his prefects than for most of his staff. Soon the main chaplain, whose motto was assuredly 'anything for a quiet life,' retired, and Meyer made me senior chaplain, with several misgivings that were clearly apparent.

For I had not been getting on very well with him. He and his secretary thought (or hoped) that I would be as compliant as my predecessor, in short, nothing but a doormat. He seemed to assume that his prefects would run the chapel with the senior chaplain as a sort of messenger boy. As can be imagined, I did not accept this for one moment. His prefects were always complaining to him about this chaplain who seemed to think he was, well, the chaplain.

THE MORE WE ARE TOGETHER

Things reached a head when my first confirmation service had to be planned. I was told airily by Meyer's secretary: 'Oh, the prefects and I stage-manage all that.' Acidly I replied: 'Not as long as I am chaplain.'

It was a mammoth service. There were almost a hundred candidates, with about four or five guests for each. I had thought the one previous confirmation service I had seen there was pretty chaotic. This was going to be different, even if it was to be my only one. I dismissed prefect after prefect who would not do as I told him, and in his place I either appointed a willing boy I taught or did his job myself.

Meyer was fuming about all this, but he was astute enough to know that it was too late to undo me and all my arrangements. The showdown came in the hallway of his house, when he shouted at me (in front of a terrified small boy): 'My prefects hate the sight of you!'

Now, I'd had enough. As always in such circumstances I seem to get quite outside myself and to view the scene and all its actors with an entirely detached, dispassionate and realistic eye. I knew exactly what I was going to do and what it would cost me. I walked right up to him and held my hand in front of his face. And I said in quiet and deadly tones: 'Don't you dare talk to me like that.' Then I waited for Jove Meyer to hurl his whole thunderbolt arsenal at me.

I seemed to wait ages. As I watched, his face changed from rage to wonder to compliance. 'All right,' he said in mild and even respectful tones. 'All right.' That was all.

The scene was never referred to. His attitude to me changed completely. We never again had an unpleasant word, although I was there for another four or five years. What is more, my attitude to him changed. I had always known that he was, as a pioneer and an organizer and a headmaster, nothing less than a genius, even if a genius rather corrupted by too much undisputed power. I had always known, too, that he was far too intelligent for the roles he assumed: the eccentric, the showman, the oligarch. No one, I think, had ever stood up to him before, and he appreciated it. Also, he was a son of the manse who had a little, buried respect for a parson. Of course, all was not entirely plain sailing from now on, but there was mutual respect. He offered me a housemastership, which I would have liked, but I was obliged to stipulate that there would be no corporal punishment in my house, for the school was free with the birch. It was the only school I've taught in where boys still flogged boys. He could not accept my proviso. Then he asked me to take lunch each day in his house. I did so for a while, but finally asked to be excused when I found I acutely missed the freedom a lunch break from schoolmasterly supervision provided.

24

In my first year at Millfield two sad and heavy blows hit me. One morning at Selsey, when I had already set out for Chichester and some shopping, father died in Brian's arms. As he fell back on his bed, he looked at Brian and said with a smile: 'I'm going now. Goodbye, lad.' That scene never left Brian's mind, nor did his description of it fade from mine.

We were all filled with silent, unshown grief. Much more so than I would have thought possible. I'd no idea I was so fond of him. He had been agreeable for so long that I think we had all but forgotten his Jekyll and Hyde days of our youth. And he had so enjoyed Selsey. He and mother actually wandered to shops and cafés arm in arm, like a normal husband and wife. Indeed, mother never really recovered from the shock of his death, which induced in her a tendency to diabetes.

We knew we must leave Selsey and return to London where we could all find employment. Also, we didn't want to stay there now. So Pam and Bob were detailed to look around for something in London. For sentimental reasons we decided to look first in Streatham, and in a very short time Pam came up with a large mansion flat in the High Street. How she managed it, I didn't ask. Anything to let was like gold dust, but Pam was equal to any Yukon prospector in such matters.

I wondered if there was enough money in hand to meet all the expenses. The wretched Selsey estate agent insisted on charging us more to get out of the house than he had charged us to get into it. Then came the cost of the removal and the advance rent on the Streatham flat. But more immediate than all this was the cost of poor father's funeral. Brian said: 'Pay nothing to damned undertakers. Insist on a parish burial.' This seemed eminently sensible in the circumstances, for we none of us, including me, believed it was moral to spend money urgently needed by the living on the disposal of mortal remains. Although I had officiated at hundreds of funeral services, I knew nothing at all about the business side of such things. Brian led me to believe that a 'parish burial' was a permitted alternative, and I therefore went to the council offices in Chichester to arrange it all. To my astonishment, there was no such provision, and officials could only gaze at me in stupefaction when I said 'Of course you must have conditions for burying a body from municipal funds when there is simply no money otherwise available.' Each person I saw made an excuse to fetch a more senior colleague. Moreover staff kept coming into the office to look up things in filing cabinets. I knew quite well that these were mere excuses to catch a glimpse of this monster, this Parson Who Won't Bury His Own Father. In the wonder, the awe, I was causing, I felt like Christy Mahon in *The Playboy of the Western World*.

At last a broken, almost a tearful clerk said to me: 'But Mr Gamble, *Reverend* Gamble, what you ask is done only in the case of an unknown body washed up on the seashore.'

Well, they finally agreed to ask the cheapest undertaker they knew to do a cut-price burial with no trimmings at all, and with this I was compelled to make do.

The funeral was quietly and reverently done for £40. Terry came over from France for it. Miles and I were the only other mourners. Mother and Brian and Pam would not on principle attend. I remember we three mourners, in my old Jowett van, passed them shopping in the High Street, as we drove to the cemetery. And there, in an unmarked grave no one has ever visited, father lies quietly waiting for us all to join him in the Great Beyond.

25

In the Christmas holidays, just after all was fixed for Brian and me to join Millfield, and I was in a happier frame of mind than I had known for many a day, I had my delightful, time-honoured, Yuletide dinner with Derrick and Mavis. Derrick relished all the preparations for a Dickensian (or even Fieldingesque) Christmas, with holly wreaths on the front door and tasteful decorations within, and hot punch and roast goose and mince pies and chestnuts. For some years they had enjoyed the ideal setting for all this: lovely old Hunt Cottage, reputedly the home of Leigh Hunt in the Vale of Health, and a frequent port of call for Keats. But they had recently, with heavy hearts, to leave this Shangri-La when its owner wished to sell it. They were now in a pleasant, but unatmospheric, flat near the BBC. Their seasonal plans were heart-warming as ever, despite their more mundane setting, and despite a tinge of melancholy I ascribed to the loss of Hunt Cottage.

I myself had recently acquired a new milieu: the Junior Carlton club in Pall Mall. Inside those august Tory portals I wined and dined myself with a secret smile for my alien location. Actually, I was not a member of the Junior Carlton but of an ecclesiastical club which had lost its premises in the war and was now kindly housed by the Junior Carlton. And here, in January 1960, on the day before I had to drive down to my new job at Millfield, I gave Derrick a good, festive lunch. It was a happy occasion. He was in high spirits, and so was I. I remember that we finally sat by the great log fire in the vestibule for a few words before he left. He told me he had other friends he wanted to call on that afternoon, so he couldn't stay any longer, much as he'd like to. I remember he slapped my knee as we sat there side by side and said: 'Fine lunch, old boy.' I walked to the door with him and then waved him out of sight up Pall Mall from the club steps. The next morning I set out for Millfield.

I had been there only a few days, staying initially with Brian in a snooty guest house while we sought digs, when at seven in the evening, just as we were going in for dinner, I had a phone call. It was Mavis, Derrick's wife, and she was scarcely coherent. She told me that Derrick had committed suicide: in some seedy hotel on the very day he had lunched with me.

This news was as shattering as it was unbelievable. I helped Mavis get through the crematorium service, and then back at her flat we searched our hearts and Derrick's and then all the universe to account for the tragedy. Not one shred of explanation could we find. Mavis told me that Derrick had tried to commit suicide in their new flat not long before my Christmas visit there, and she had longed to tell me about it. But Derrick was adamant that she was not to breathe a word about it, made her swear solemnly that she would not. He saw a psychiatrist to please her, but in the light of what later happened she knew that his mind was made up and because it was made up it was content. On the day he set out to have lunch with me in my club he was especially happy, she said. He was looking forward to seeing me and, afterwards, some artist friends he was fond of. Then he went straight to the hotel and gassed himself.

Was he worried about his work, I asked. On the contrary: he had recently had an exhibition in America which had been a great success. They had both enormously enjoyed America and the many delightful friends they'd made there. Well, was it, I wondered, his eyesight, for he had short sight and wore very strong glasses. I had seen how in his work he had to cut with his nose almost touching the block. No, he had never once complained about his eyes. Was it depression at leaving Hunt Cottage? That had, admittedly, been a shock to both of them, but they had got over it, and with all the new commissions coming in they were too busy to mope.

So we could only grieve in pain and wonder, and comfort ourselves with the many tributes paid to Derrick and his work. It was several years later that Mavis said to me: 'May I ask you a personal question?' 'Of course,' I replied, for we had remained good friends and there was nothing we could not talk about. 'I've been wondering,' she mused. 'Was Derrick homosexual?' I had no hesitation in telling her that he was not. In all our close and intimate friendship there had never been any suggestion that he was, nor any clue given by me that I was. So that explanation, too, had to be rejected.

A year or so later, after another visit to America (where, as in England, she devotedly kept Derrick's memory green with little exhibitions and references in art journals), Mavis returned to the subject of homosexuality. She told me she had asked an American friend of Derrick's (a professional artist) the same question she had asked me. He looked at her, wide-eyed with astonishment, and said: 'Didn't you *know*? Yes, oh yes, he certainly was.'

313

It was my turn to be astonished. And I have remained so to this day. How was it that we never confided in each other? How was it that neither ever guessed? As I have said, I made no definite attempt to conceal my tastes. Nor to exhibit them. It all seemed less important than the exciting views and experiences we did share in those days. But if Mavis had told me of his suicide bid, and if we had spoken freely to each other at last, would that have saved him? I doubt it. The real pain for him would have remained: that of telling Mavis and hurting her beyond all balm.

Mavis remarried and had a charming daughter, who is my goddaughter and a talented actress. So out of the strong (we three were all in our separate ways strong: we had to be) has come forth sweetness.

Then, as I weathered on, agreeably, on the whole, at Millfield, there came new life to offset the grievous deaths. And it, too, was hard to believe. For Pam, now aged thirty-six, was again pregnant.

It was just like Miles's birth eighteen years before. It was by strange coincidence also in Streatham. And Pam took it all as coolly, as matter-of-factly, as before. Very soon she was up and about and coping with her maternal duties as efficiently, and as coolheartedly, as she had done amid the wartime bombs.

It was another boy, and this time very like Bob, while being at the same time quite attractive. In character, too, he was like Bob: good-natured, laughing, friendly. Quite unlike the disconsolate, moody Miles. I, of course, became an attentive, affectionate uncle all over again. Even more captivated than I was Brian. And I think the little boy liked him more than me, for he was far more easy-going, less concerned to train him for the future than I was. He was also forever tinkering with cars and motorbikes, at which the new boy soon became surprisingly adept. He was christened (I use the word figuratively) Nikolas Jon, and even the spelling achieved a little unfamiliarity.

Very soon, with this unlooked-for increase in the family, we had to think of roomier premises. By chance I saw in the *Evening Standard* an advertisement for a fair-sized unfurnished house to let in Stanmore, Middlesex. I drove over there the next morning. I think my dog collar and chequebook did the trick. It was a nice house, with garage and large garden and such essential amenities as a hall cloakroom, in a very attractive road lined with cherry trees. I snapped it up and we moved there in the lovely, sprouting springtime of that year. It was well north of the Thames, and we had always lived south of it before, but it was so pleasant that the new locality merely added to the excitement. I know I felt that at last we were all together in an ideal setting and the future was to be sheer happiness.

26

In these years Roland spent each of his long summer vacations here in England. It was always a joyous reunion. He arrived in the midst of Millfield's summer term, with all the O level and A level hassles. I had O level groups in English language and English literature and Latin and divinity, with two A level groups in English literature. I enjoyed the need for sheer professionalism in such a heavy teaching timetable. I was now marking O levels for the Oxford Examining Board, as well as taking services somewhere or other on Sundays. As I had so many assistant chaplains I was not needed at Millfield every Sunday. Indeed, I contrived to escape often, for I didn't enjoy weekends there. And when I escaped and went home to Stanmore, I always ministered somewhere in the London diocese. I was on the London list of relief clergy and in great demand. I took services anywhere in the diocese and in every kind of church, from Highest to Lowest. The Low ones caused no problems, for their ritual was at a minimum and all the emphasis was on the ministry of the word. But I had to work hard at the High ones, and I invariably confessed my ignorance directly I arrived at the church. There was always a master of ceremonies who enjoyed instructing the pathetic visiting priest. As I was paid by the diocese for these services, my expenses in connection with them were reimbursed, and I greatly valued the extra income. The new rent and rates in Stanmore were even more burdensome, so I had to earn every penny I could. I found on these clerical visitations not only how I invariably enjoyed preaching to new and appreciative congregations of adults, but also how they enjoyed someone who didn't quite fit. The Low churches were rather tickled by a moderate parson who nevertheless crossed himself once or twice, and the High ones enjoyed a priest who could give them a good sermon even though his incense-swingings and biretta-doffings were distinctly erratic.

In the spring and Christmas breaks from school Basil Clough was often my companion. I found him not only refreshing after twelve weeks of teaching, but also something of an eye-opener. I knew, of course, that there was an active homosexual demi-monde in central London, but I had never entered even its fringes, nor really known anyone who had. Not until Basil set out quite deliberately to educate me therein. At first his revelations were purely verbal. He told me of his Friday and Saturday evening encounters in Chelsea and Fitzrovia. What a gallery they were: wild-eyed poets and soaring philosophers and earnest, impious clergy, and what he called 'charming young flits up from the provinces.' I must say I found his descriptions very amusing yet frighteningly dangerous. Their locations I could scarcely imagine: gay bars and seedy bedsits and cramped automobiles and inadequate park bushes. But I could not help admiring the skill with which he manipulated such props and his determination to lead the life his instincts demanded.

Then he insisted on my accompanying him to some of his haunts, claiming I was absurdly bourgeois for an intelligent young man. I didn't, of course, fall for such nonsense, but I was curious to see this world he'd painted so graphically.

He took me to his favourite gay bars and gay pubs. I disliked them, especially the rather vicious aura of the pubs. It was soon a question of my sitting in *my* club while Basil paid flying visits to his haunts in search of any 'nice' contacts he could make. 'Nice' meant well-spoken and well-mannered and reasonably intelligent. If he met any such he would later in the evening introduce me to them. One such was Michael K, who was twenty-five and very personable: dark and handsome and well groomed. I wondered that he should find us interesting, and soon discovered that he was after good minds and conversations. He himself was quite bright and distinctly artistic. We soon became a high-spirited social trio.

Eventually, urged by Basil, I joined a gay club that was well known in its day. It was in Soho and extremely piss-elegant, to use a vulgar epithet then popular: that is, elegant in a somewhat self-conscious, unconvincing, even tatty fashion. All behaviour there was extremely correct: one made the discriminating social contacts between those veloured, print-hung walls, but went elsewhere for any closer contacts one desired.

Michael told us about himself. He had read philosophy at Cambridge, worked now in an estate agents, and had a sugar daddy who was a fabulously wealthy American film producer. Michael had a nice little flat in Bentinck Street, Mayfair, or 'Beatnik Street' as we called it.

From the first, Basil and I had our doubts about Michael, but since I was very fond of him and Basil was very much in love with him, we allowed all such doubts to lie dormant. Even when one evening we were walking to a favourite restaurant in Kensington and passed a charming house with a plaque on the wall. Basil and I were fascinated by all streets and all houses, and we stopped to read the plaque. 'Oh,' I said, 'It was John Stuart Mill's house.' Michael, who wasn't particularly interested in houses, and was wanting his dinner, said frivolously: 'Who on earth was he when he was at home?' Basil and I exchanged glances and Basil covered up quickly by saying: 'Oh, just a very minor poet of Victorian times.'

When Michael had money he was generous with it, but when he hadn't (which was usually) he expected us to finance him. As his tastes were expensive we had to train him rather carefully not to expect too much from us. I remember once he phoned to ask us to take tea with him at the Westbury, 'where,' he added airily, 'I'm staying at the moment.' We did so, more out of curiosity than anything. We had a delightful tea in his room. He phoned down for some smoked salmon sandwiches, and after tea he phoned down even more impressively: 'Room 108 here. Bring my car round to the front in fifteen minutes, will you?' Bring it round they did (the latest Ford tourer: impressive without being at all vulgar) and Michael drove us all off to the piss-elegant club. The following week there was no mention of hotel or car and we had to pay for his dinner.

Michael intrigued and delighted us. But I grew tired of the flash-in-the-pan stories and exploits. 'We must have a showdown,' I said to Basil. 'There can't be a real relationship without some honesty.' Basil begged me not to. 'What does it matter?' he asked. 'Why hurt him?'

But I felt it must be so, especially after his latest story: of his widowed mother's engagement to an Italian nobleman, whose tedious heterosexuality bored and offended Michael's own tastes.

So one day, when I was having tea with Michael in his latest rooms in Hampstead, I broached the subject. 'Michael, dear,' I said gently, 'there's no need to spin yarns to Basil and me. We don't believe them, haven't done so for a long time. But that doesn't matter at all, because we're both very fond of you and there's not the slightest need to try to impress us.'

He went very red and turned his head away. He said nothing. I saw that he was crying. I felt a brute, Ibsen's Gregers Werle. I pulled him on to my knee and put my arms round him. 'I'm sorry,' I said. 'Forgive me if I've hurt you. It's only that we both care so much for you and for our friendship, that we want to get rid of all pretences, all acts, and just be utterly frank, as true friends are.'

I laboured to redeem the situation, but nothing was ever quite the same again. Not so very long afterwards, Michael disappeared and all our efforts failed to find a trace. Perhaps he went to America. Perhaps he went to prison. That was all many years ago. Michael was from a humble background and he had never been near a university. Those who have cannot envisage the sense of inferiority that once crushed those who hadn't, or the Herculean attempts which in this snob-ridden society the lowly-born took to paper over the cracks. Things are rather better now, but perhaps too late to comfort Michael.

27

Not long after this, Basil became enamoured of Amsterdam, and sold it to me.

Our first summer break in Holland, in their 'Venice of the North,' was a great success. We stayed in a very pleasant gay hotel, and Basil took me to the famous homosexual clubs of which he had heard so much: the COC and the DOK. I was surprised to find how eminently respectable they were. Gays and lesbians socially enjoyed themselves, sipping lagers and chatting, and dancing together without embarrassment, with complete naturalness. The clubs were state run by committees of psychiatrists and clergy and social workers.

The hotel was managed by two friends. With some perplexity they prepared for me a single room, the only one they had, and that was not really part of the hotel. 'Why do you come to Amsterdam if you always want to sleep alone?' they asked me. I told them I'd never liked sharing a bed, and in any case my wild youth was past.

At one of the clubs, Basil and I were as usual sitting at a table by the dance floor watching the fascinating assortment of couples. One pair rather intrigued me, especially the younger partner who danced with a vigorous, springing motion I'd never seen before. On concluding one dance, the handsome young springbok came up and asked me if I had a light. I knew this was the recognized way of striking up an acquaintanceship, so Basil and I asked them both to join us. The older of the two was a barrister, and the younger was still at university. We had a very interesting chat (almost everybody in Holland speaks English), and arranged to meet for dinner the next day. The younger, who was nineteen, said he'd like to go to bed with me. I said I was too old for him, and possibly he was a little bit too old for me. He thought all this quite hilariously English and odd. Basil liked the mind of the older one, Raymond, and I liked the attractive, youthful personality of the younger, Tony.

This encounter soon led to a firm friendship, with Tony coming to stay with me in England, where we shared all things except (I still laughingly insisted) a bed. Tony now has his Ph D and is a noted journalist. Raymond is on the way to becoming a judge.

On another visit I asked Tony to take me to a gay club which specialized in men who liked teenagers. (Sixteen was then the age of consent in Holland.) I had no intention of forming any liaison, but I wanted to chat to some of the boys. The club he selected was clean and orderly, and there were some very attractive 16-year-olds there. Before long the two most winsome ones responded to my smiles by coming and joining us at our table. We bought them drinks and I got them talking. I was fascinated by their origins and lifestyles. One rather beautiful German boy called Erich told me he had left home in Germany to seek his fortune in Amsterdam. His parents believed he was learning to be a waiter. He sent them money each week. He was not himself gay (he had a girlfriend), and he and his boss were extremely careful in the choice of customers, all of whom had to be contacted on these premises and passed by the boss. ('That's him, standing over there. He's already nodded to say it's all right with you.') I asked him if he wasn't afraid of contracting some disease. He said he took great care with condoms and washing with germicides. I asked him where he went with his customers. He told me there was a nearby hotel with which they had an arrangement.

I thought I could become very fond of Erich, without ever becoming a customer. I asked him if he could meet me for lunch one day: I'd love to treat him to a first-class meal. He told me, rather sadly, I thought, but perhaps I imagined it, that he wasn't allowed to. In any case, after working all night he had to sleep by day, otherwise he wouldn't be fresh for the next night's patrons.

He begged me to go to the hotel with him, but I insisted I couldn't and wouldn't. He said he would be 'good to me' (they all, apparently, say that) and he wouldn't charge his usual price, which was then about the equivalent of £20.

Before we went, I asked him what his future was to be. 'Oh,' he said with rather brutal realism, 'boys don't last long at this game. I'll get a steady job. Then I'll marry and have kids.'

I tipped him handsomely, on the basis that one should give a boy at least the equivalent of the money he could have earned while he was talking. When we left he said: 'Come and talk again.' I suppose to him it was all a novel and enjoyable experience. It was good of Basil to accompany me there, for it wasn't really his scene. I wouldn't have dared go on my own. I never went there again.

28

Things in Stanmore went well enough for a while. But Miles was a worry. He had had no schooling to speak of and had never passed any exam. But he always found himself a job, because he had great charm when he chose. At present he was working in a West End record store, a rather superior one where he specialized in classical recordings. He surprised me not only by his love of music, especially sacred and choral, but also by his knowledge of classical works of a wide variety. All self-taught.

Mother idolized Miles, as he did her, but she was becoming ever more antipathetic to Pam's husband, Bob. Now it is true that money was tight at home, and that Miles was a spendthrift. It is also true that Bob was by nature and upbringing rather stingy. He always paid his way, but he gave Pam very little for herself. I suppose he felt she could with a teaching job be self-supporting. He never took her out, never bought her clothes, seemed entirely unaware of the common practice of husbands in making little surprise presents. *I* bought Pam presents and took her and mother out to lavish dinners whenever I could. All this disgusted mother. She was convinced that Bob was hoarding quite liberally, subsidized by all the rest of us. Her denunciations of him grew more frequent and more vitriolic. The nice house in its pleasant setting grew ever less like the dream house I had so long envisaged for us.

Added to all of this was the suspicion I tried to stifle, but couldn't, that Pam was growing fonder of alcohol. At first it seemed innocuous enough: her obvious enjoyment of a glass or two whenever I brought in a bottle of sherry. Then, once Nik was bedded down, she liked to go out with Bob to some drinking club she had induced him to join. He didn't like spending his money there, but I think he liked to escape from a home that was less and less welcoming.

Naturally, I introduced Basil and Roland to each other. They got on well as long as we were all discussing literature or theology or related topics, but Basil was essentially a self-contained person, detached and quite happy with his own company, whereas for both Roland and me personal relationships were the great joy of life. Basil was also frank and at times even explicit about his sexual tastes. That was fine when he and I were on our own or in declared homosexual company. But I was as embarrassed as Roland when the company was less select.

Basil and I enjoyed discussing whether our parents had any inkling about our lives. I told him I felt my father was too innocent to guess, but we both felt less certain about our mothers. At any rate, if they half-divined it they were sensible enough to put it away from them, perhaps in some little corner of their minds, perhaps grateful that they had sons they were not going to lose to younger women.

Before Roland had left for America he had given me his revered twelve-volume Proust, the Chatto edition, mostly translated by Scott Moncrieff. On the flyleaf of volume one he had written: 'For Peter Gamble, the only man I know who could have spoken to Proust as an equal.' Although disregarding the extremely inflated compliment, I was very touched by it, for I knew the high opinion in which he held Proust. I treasure the volumes still, but am ashamed to confess that I have never read them, although I have dipped and browsed frequently.

Basil was doing a Ph D at London University. We had discussed a subject for his thesis. He rather wanted to do 'The Greek Tragedians and Shakespeare Compared,' but I talked him out of this, saying he'd have to add 'to the distinct detriment of the latter,' which might prove unacceptable. I sympathized with his views, but couldn't echo them. So Basil wrote on 'The influence of Schopenhauer on Ibsen.' I had grown to know and admire Ibsen almost unreservedly, but I must say I couldn't really understand Basil's thesis. However, he got his Ph D, and it would be absurd for me to wonder if he got it because his examiners couldn't understand it either but felt they must give him the benefit of the doubt.

Basil became very keen on Algeria. I went with him one Easter holidays and thoroughly enjoyed it, especially his conducted tours of places Wilde and Bosie and Gide had lived and loved in. I'm not sure that all Basil's literary landmarks were reliable, but it was nice to think so. I liked the Arabs, too, and admired one very handsome youth Basil had made his own.

One summer holidays I spent two weeks in Amsterdam, not with Basil but with Roland. It was a very different Amsterdam from the one to which Basil had introduced me, with no gay or 'red light' quarters, but a city of historical and architectural allure and great natural beauty. Roland and I stayed at the Hilton and 'did' the art galleries and museums.

It was in the café of the Rijksmuseum, a favourite haunt for our endless coffees and talks, that we decided to write a play together. It was to be about someone who had for some time been fascinating us: the philosopher and psychologist Edmund Gurney, reputedly one of the most gifted, handsome and charming men of his day. He was a friend of George Eliot, who confessed that his good looks haunted her and that 'his mind was as beautiful as his face.' She made him the model for her *Daniel Deronda.*

Gurney was a founder and first secretary of the Society for Psychical Research, as well as a friend of William James, the father of Henry James. He became involved with George Smith, an 18-year-old Brighton stage hypnotist and mind-reader, and brought him to London, where Smith worked for both the SPR and Gurney himself. A few years later, keeping some assignation in Brighton, Gurney was found dead in a hotel bedroom.

Smith went on to become a pioneer of the motion picture industry. In 1955 he was made a fellow of the British Film Academy, and two years later, at the age of ninety-three, was honoured at the opening of the National Film Theatre and presented to Princess Margaret. He died in 1959.

Gurney's friend Frank Podmore was one of the chief luminaries of the SPR, as well as an important official of the Post Office in London and founder (and namer) of the Fabian Society. Staying at a guesthouse in Malvern in the summer of 1910, Podmore met a young man whom he invited back for dinner. After dinner, both Podmore and the young man went for a walk, but separately. Podmore never returned, and five days later his body was found in a lonely pool. The deaths of both Gurney and Podmore could not satisfactorily be ascribed to accident or suicide. Inquest verdicts were challenged, and have continued to be challenged. Smith seems in later life not to have spoken of those days when at eighteen he had greatly impressed Gurney and many of Gurney's friends with his good looks and intelligence.

Roland and I were intrigued, for a time almost obsessed, by this saga. We did a lot of research and made some interesting discoveries, and endlessly planned our play over Rijksmuseum coffees. I eventually wrote a projected first act. From then on, to my puzzled regret, Roland seemed to lose interest

321

in the whole idea of the play. I can only think he didn't like my Act One but equally didn't like to say so.

Meanwhile my life was branching out in various little ways. I was ministering during interregnums at two or three well-known London churches, and my spells there led to several interesting connections, not only with private individuals but also with institutions that an ambitious man would have exploited. For example, Toc H asked me to an enjoyable dinner at their headquarters with the famous Tubby Clayton, the object being to see if I'd accept some appointment with them. But, pleasant as they all were, I felt it was not my scene and I gratefully declined. Then some rather distinguished college of preachers asked me to join them: not a job, of course, just a sort of honour. For some reason or other I turned this down, too. Perhaps there were some strings attached I didn't really like.

Some time later, someone at the BBC urged me to apply for a post up for possession in the Religious Affairs department. I applied and was asked to construct half a dozen radio programmes for teenagers. This I did, and enjoyed doing it. I was short-listed and then called for an interview. A panel of not exactly engaging men asked me a number of questions I was unprepared and unfitted for. The last, I remember, was: 'Tell us, Mr Gamble, which books of a religious, a devotional, nature have you read recently?' I stared at them, hummed and hawed, and muttered something about C. S. Lewis' *Screwtape* and Joad and Blamires. Then I dried up. I was rather witheringly dismissed. They even made bones about paying my expenses.

The plain truth was that I had no ecclesiastical ambitions. And I have never been a reader of devotional books. What ambitions I had were in the educational field. And the books I read were literary.

Perhaps it was the void left by the Gurney play project that led Roland and me, at first casually, then with increasing earnestness, to explore the possibility of founding a school of our own, a British-cum-American school. We were serious about the need, the demand, for such a school, which we saw as located in England and as combining the best in British and American education. Roland felt he was in a position to contact and explore the world of American secondary-level independent schools, and I was fairly well informed as regards the British equivalent. I am sure I was inspired by all I knew of the way in which Meyer had started Millfield. Roland wondered if he should not teach in such a school, but might rather be an American-based governor of it. At first all our plans for it were lodged in the craziest castles in the air, but the more we talked about it, the more firmly it gripped us as a plausible, even desirable, undertaking.

Aunt Madge's husband John died after a brief illness, in which he was as quiet and resigned as he had been in his uncomplaining life. He had an appropriate Roman Catholic burial, at which I shepherded Aunt Madge, in whom it awoke memories of her youthful flirtations with religion. Said mother to me once: 'Oh, she was always rather weird. As a girl she seldom joined the rest of the family in fun and laughter. She sometimes stayed shut in her room reading the Bible.' After Uncle John's demise I did notice an old family Bible was for a short while in evidence. But her reading soon reverted to the novels of Hall Caine and Mrs Henry Wood. She was particularly attached to a novel called *The Channings*, which she reread every two or three years. Otherwise, she scanned every inch of *The Daily Telegraph* with a reading glass. She was a splendid press cuttings agency for all of us. Anything even remotely connected with my life was meticulously scissored and stored for me.

Also after her husband's departure she hung on the wall a large crucifix with a transfixed Christ figure. The first time I noticed this I was astonished to see that from the Christ's back rose two silver branches I assumed were wings.

'What an extraordinary crucifix,' I said, going over to examine it. 'I've never seen a winged Christ before.' Then I found what it actually was: behind the figure's back Aunt Madge had wedged a sturdy silver horseshoe. 'Why on earth have you put this here?' I asked her. 'Oh,' she replied, rather indifferently, 'just for luck.'

I never forgot this testimony to the pragmatism that underlay her shafts of piety, this very practical desire to blend the divine and the pagan.

Her determination was never to enter a hospital or home. 'I'm not having these chits of girls, these nurses, ferreting out all my private affairs.' Whatever her private affairs were, Lord knows, but she successfully safeguarded them to the end. She passed away triumphantly seated in her own armchair in her own little flat. At her feet, just where they'd fallen, were the reading glass and the *Telegraph*. And I thought: 'Well done, Aunt Madge.'

I should mention another family death that occurred soon after that of Aunt Madge. It was that of our cat, Sam, partaker of so many of our adventures over the years. He died of old age and he died singing. We all felt the loss, and Brian, to our surprise, was particularly affected. He had a rather special relationship with Sam.

29

It was at about this time that I wrote a few literary articles which appeared in academic journals. When I had typed out an essay on *King Lear* (for so long my King Charles's head), I sent it to Dame Helen Gardner to see if it was any good. She had been Merton Professor of English Literature at Oxford, and I had long admired her and her work. I remember I posted her my essay on a Monday afternoon, and at about noon the next day she phoned me. I was quite bowled over, not merely by the speed of her response, but that she should phone me at all. She asked if I could visit her to discuss the essay.

'Y-yes, of course,' I gulped. 'When?'

'This evening?'

I pulled myself sufficiently together to say: 'Oh yes. Thank you. I'd... I'd be honoured.'

She lived not far away. As soon as I arrived, she plunged, curled up in a big armchair, into a viva on the typescript she brandished.

'Now,' she said, 'I'm going to see if I can shoot you down.' She smiled. 'We'll soon see if you've done your homework.'

Well, I knew I *had* done my homework. I would never have sent the essay to her if I had not felt assured of that. At the end of about an hour (and even at the time I felt: this is how my tutorials at Oxford should have gone), she leaned back and said with obvious satisfaction: 'Yes, you've proved your points. Get it published.'

At home, in the school holidays, things came to a painful, a once unthinkable, head. So rancorous and so repetitive had become mother's denunciations of poor Bob Powis, that Pam said it would be best for them to leave, to find some home of their own. After more than twenty years of married life!

I remember that my private thoughts hovered on the edge of admitting: 'Now at last you must bid farewell to your lifetime's dream, for now the first real family cracks have appeared: the cracks that will become crevasses that will shatter into dissolution.' But I pushed the thought away, hoping desperately on.

For ever since Aunt Nora's death, mother and Pam had been well-nigh inseparable. Each day, in Banstead and in Streatham and in Stanmore, began with protracted morning coffees in some favourite restaurant, coffees that, as friends and neighbours dropped in and out, often merged into lunches at the same table.

When Pam acquired her MG, she often drove further afield, mother beside her in front, and Emil rather uncomfortably jammed in the back. She was uncomfortable for two reasons. One was that she much preferred the front, next to Pam, which she had only when mother was not with them. She resented being demoted. But her main discomfort was due to the wind in her eyes, for mostly Pam preferred the hood down, and even when it was up there were more or less no side panels. Then Pam solved Emil's troubles with a nice pair of goggles. These Emil quickly accepted as a natural part of motoring. When the hood was down, she would sit imperiously upright, goggled and disdaining every other creature abroad. She was greatly admired by all who saw her, and Pam of course loved the exhibition. She said to me:

'I think after the goggles I really must get Emil a toque. She sits there for all the world like Queen Mary in her Daimler.'

On other days, Pam and mother used to set out arm in arm along the High Street to do a little shopping before the coffee rituals began. Like all the rest of us, they (and Emil) could never envisage a day that kept one immured. Life was on pavements and in cafés. Sunrise beckoned one streetwards and not to heed the call was not to heed life.

So now Pam and Bob were going. And Nik and Emil were going with them. The last two were losses mother felt more keenly. Miles, of course, was staying, for he disliked his father and was not attached to his mother as he was to his grandmother. In any case, they were moving only to a furnished house they had found in Edgware, ten minutes away by car.

So that was the new set-up, and I liked to believe it was an improvement on the old. Pam brought Nik over each morning and did the shopping, often taking mother out in the car, for she was now too infirm for walks. Miles loved having his grandmother to himself and being virtually the head of the household, for my visits were less frequent in termtime. Bob was now seldom seen or mentioned at Stanmore.

It was also at about this time that I revived a practice of my past: I wrote letters ('fan' letters I suppose one would call them) to eminent people I admired. Not now to literary giants. So many of those letters of my teens, and their exciting replies, have passed into oblivion (long replies from Isherwood and Richard Aldington and Compton Mackenzie and Warwick Deeping). I now wrote only two grateful letters, and with deprecatory smiles for my ageing precocity.

One was to the actor Fredric March. I had for so long admired his full-blooded performances, starting from my childhood relish for his Jekyll and Hyde, and now I had just been greatly impressed by his characterization of William Jennings Bryan in Kramer's excellent film of the notorious 'monkey trial,' *Inherit the Wind*. I thought I must express my thanks for the thrills and pleasures he had given me over so many years. His reply was delightfully appreciative: amusing, reminiscent, informative. He told me his forebears were English, and of good Bedfordshire stock.

The other letter I wrote was to Benjamin Britten. I first became impressed by his musical genius before the war. Later, during the actual war years, he and Peter Pears became my heroes, not only for their artistry but also for their courageous stands as conscientious objectors. Unlike Auden and Isherwood, they returned from the States to spend the cataclysmic years in their native clime. I bought their recordings and went to their concerts. As we emerged into peacetime austerity, I went to first nights of Ben's great operas: *Peter Grimes*, *The Turn of the Screw* and *Albert Herring*. I also knew that Ben had for many years been a devotee of Forrest Reid's work.

So I wrote to Benjamin Britten, expressing my love for so much that he had composed, sharing our mutual pleasure in Forrest's work, and even telling something (tactful and tasteful) of lives like ours dedicated to the shrine of boyhood. But I would not have written to say just this, much as this was. I had a serious aim. I wrote: 'I am a man of modest means but I will donate a token one hundred pounds to any cause you choose if you will compose a tone poem - say, in the manner of your wonderful seascapes in *Peter Grimes* - entitled something like *The World of Tom Barber.*'

Tom Barber is Forrest Reid's finest creation. He wrote three books about him: *Uncle Stephen* in 1931 (where Tom is fifteen), *The Retreat* in 1936 (where Tom is eleven), and *Young Tom* in 1944 (where Tom is eight). *Young Tom* was (belatedly) awarded the James Tait Black memorial prize. *The Retreat* is an exquisite book, its symbolism absolutely right (the grandfather clock that ticks away Tom's innocence; Henry the mysterious cat whose claws represent the dawning of Tom's sexuality).

Equally exquisite is *Uncle Stephen*, which E. M. Forster in his *Abinger Harvest* calls Forrest's masterpiece, an opinion with which I entirely agree. Like Alain-Fournier's *Le Grand Meaulnes*, it is a superb blend of fantasy and realism. But behind it all is an attempt to answer the painful question that haunts lives like Forrest's: Is true friendship possible between a boy and a much older man? Caught in a time warp, Tom unknowingly falls in love with his elderly and affectionate Uncle Stephen as a boy of his own age, but of so different a character: the handsome and very pragmatic Philip. Tom's devotion slowly tenderizes Philip, who finally agrees to vanish in order that Uncle Stephen may rematerialize. Tom learns that his relationship with Uncle Stephen is more pure, more abiding, more spiritual than the largely physical relationship with Philip. There is a great deal more to the book than this inadequate description suggests. It was also extraordinarily outspoken for its time. If there is a flaw it is an unavoidable one: simply that Philip is so engaging that the reader cannot surrender him as readily as orphan Tom can.[1]

Britten replied charmingly and frankly, but saying that he had so much work in hand that he couldn't envisage tackling my proposal in any foreseeable future. He did not say, but I later understood, that he knew his time was short. Some time after his death I heard that among his papers were some sketches for a setting of Tom Barber's world, but I do not know if it was so.

A long-standing friend of mine, the distinguished musician and musical biographer Christopher Headington, took me to a first performance of Britten's splendid *Death in Venice* at Covent Garden. Ben was himself present

[1] See Brian Taylor's excellent *The Green Avenue. The Life and Writings of Forrest Reid, 1875-1947* (Cambridge University Press, 1980).

with Frau Mann. After the opera was over, Christopher took me backstage to meet Peter Pears, who was, as ever, courteous and charming, despite his exhaustion. The lifelong affection that Ben and Peter had for each other was very touching, and is movingly described in Christopher's respective biographies: that of Ben appearing in 1981, and that of Peter Pears in 1992.

People like Forrest Reid and Benjamin Britten are but more recent stars in a whole galaxy of creative men who have sat at the feet of boyhood and youth: Plato and his Aster, Edward II and his Piers, James I and his Steenie, Verlaine and his Arthur, Wilde and his Bosie, Housman and his gondolier, Forster and his policeman... not to mention Milton and Edward King, Matthew Arnold and Arthur Hugh Clough, Tennyson and Arthur Hallam, and all the 'Uranian' poets of 1889-1930 whom my friend Timothy d'Arch Smith has chronicled so excellently in his *Love in Earnest* (1970). When I sometimes feel more 'special' than I wish to be, I comfort myself by thinking how sturdy is my lineage!

PART FOUR: BUFFETINGS

1

All this time Roland and I were actively pursuing our great goal: the founding of an Anglo-American school. We had decided on a programme which contained six key targets, as follows: (1) To set up a small committee of friends and ourselves to further the project; (2) To prepare an appeals letter to be sent initially to selected Anglo-American firms in Britain; (3) To print a handsome prospectus; (4) To register 'The Anglo-American School' as a limited company; (5) To seek suitable persons of distinction as patrons; (6) To seek wealthy backers.

Roland's half-brother was David Carver, the secretary-general of PEN, the international association of Poets, Playwrights, Essayists and Novelists. After a distinguished career in music he had devoted himself to PEN's objectives in promoting international literary co-operation and championing the writer's freedom of expression wherever it was threatened. After much enquiry and debate, both David and his wife joined us.

Then we were joined by Colonel Forrest Agee, an American who had followed up a notable military career by taking his doctorate at Yale and specializing in academic administration. He was a friend and colleague of Roland and a man whose charm was not merely native American but native Texan too.

Our sixth member was Paul Christophersen, a distinguished scholar who at that time occupied the chair of English at the University of Oslo. Paul was a dedicated Anglophile and a person of shrewd and judicious temperament. He and his family spent part of each year in England, and he also knew the American academic scene as a visiting professor in the States.

Each of us put £50 into the kitty. I opened an account for 'The Anglo-American School' with Coutts Bank in Old Park Lane, where the almost avuncular kindness of the tail-coated personnel boosted my morale as surely as I hoped it would inspire confidence in prospective donors.

I visited the leading educational agencies who assured me that the best market was for a school of secondary age range: the recent selective employment tax was hitting many prep schools very hard, and one heard of the tragic demise of many old and honourable schools.

It was clear that we should have to charge high fees and thus cater only for the rich. Neither Roland nor I felt happy about this, but we resolved to institute bursaries and scholarships progressively, as and when we could afford them or donors be found to establish them.

I toured the headquarters of all the political parties and obtained their educational programmes. Harold Wilson's Labour government was in office at the time and seemed set for a long innings. I admired a great deal of its legislation but obviously hoped it would not legislate independent schools out of existence.

At the time no one knew whether the more radical elements in the Labour Party, and particularly the trade unions, could compel legislation against fee-paying schools. I had once dined à trois with Antony Crosland and a mutual friend and remembered an evening of especially good conversation. Crosland was now Minister of Education. I rather diffidently wrote to him, recalling the occasion and asking if I might put to him a few questions concerning our proposed Anglo-American school.

Crosland courteously (and correctly) referred me to one of his chief assistants at the Ministry. I remember entering a quite palatial room at the far end of which, at adjoining and identical desks, sat two strikingly similar gentlemen, as polished as their heavy furniture, as deep as the pile carpet I waded over to solicit their unattainable confidence. I expounded our project in the most general terms, while they listened with a kind of benevolent irony. My every instinct was to thank them warmly and escape. But I knew how I should regret leaving as empty-handed as they no doubt wished. I forced myself to say: 'It would, perhaps, be immoral, or at least improper, for me to ask here if Her Majesty's Government intended to legislate against independent education?' (I tried to catch their own tone of lofty amusement.) Tweedledum glanced at Tweedledee, hesitated, smiled a little. Said Dee (or Dum): 'It would perhaps, Mr Gamble, be even more immoral for us to let you leave here to open an independent school if we knew Her Majesty's Government intended forthwith to close them all.' Said Dum (or Dee): 'I think you need not fear, Mr Gamble.' Both beamed and at once resumed their inscrutable masks. We shook hands, and I left, thanking them warmly for their kindness and encouragement.

It therefore seemed safe to go ahead. I had already typed and duplicated some dozen foolscap sheets, setting out our aims and ideals and a detailed three-year costs analysis, based on realistic mortgages, a student intake of somewhere between 50 and 100, and a reliable breakdown of all overheads and running costs. This in itself had proved quite a formidable task for one's scant leisure: it had meant picking the brains of school bursars and housemasters I knew, as well as interminable night hours devoted to the typing and running off of stencils. Of course, I had no help in all this spade work, and didn't want any. It was an exhausting but exciting private life, shared in the main with only one other person, and then usually across the Atlantic in air letters that tended to cross ever thicker and faster as we kept each other informed of each little forward step, each disheartening reversal.

The time had now come to expend our modest capital on a quality prospectus and on the registration of a company. But what sort of company?

One with a share capital, or a non-profit-making corporation registered as a charity? I think some of us were human enough, and needy enough, to wish to derive some kind of return from our labours. Already Roland and I were spending more and more of our own limited savings on promotion, and both of us, perhaps, might be faced with the hazard of giving up our present jobs to become joint headmasters of the proposed school. We also knew that there was the kind of entrepreneur who would invest in a sound scheme but not donate to it, and such a person would have no interest at all in a charitable trust. On the other hand, we all felt that we could not promote our project with any real enthusiasm if personal profit were the smallest part of it; nor would we be so likely to interest men and women of disinterested goodwill.

In the end we decided to set up a charitable trust. I never regretted this, but harder-headed friends have told me it was the initial blunder which sealed our doom.

Through personal introduction we had obtained some excellent solicitors in Bond Street, who saw to all the initial formalities of company registration and dealt with the Charity Commissioners and the Department of Education and Science. These solicitors, let me say here, neither then nor later charged as much as they might for their well-tried services.

John Ryder, my old friend from Reader's Union days, agreed to design and print our prospectus. I was delighted by this for he had now become a leading authority on print and a distinguished typographer. He generously donated his services as a designer and charged only modestly for the whole production job.

I then settled down to the challenge of composing this all-important prospectus which was to be at once our manifesto and our grand appeal.

This prospectus had to sell an idea: sell it compellingly, but with some dignity. It would be a harder sell to Britons than to Americans, I felt. Any idea that we were proposing one step nearer the incorporation of Britain as the 52nd State of the Union had to be avoided tactfully and totally. And indeed no such thought was in our heads.

We envisaged a school where there should be no self-conscious élite of any description. I had seen many pleasant boys become less pleasant once given the status and the powers of school prefects. If intellectually bright, they sometimes added a further dimension of arrogance to their characters. If the 'training for leadership' were too intense, humourless, shallow, in its insistence on the sins of the flesh and its pursuit of virtues more stoic than Christian, then an unlovely and unlovable creature could result. Add consciousness of class and rank, and the conception of privilege as a right rather than a responsibility, and the ruin could be complete. Of course, I doubt if any public school this century has *wished* to fashion such a young man, or has rejoiced when it has done so.

331

Roland and I had felt it was unrealistic to expect American citizens, even avowed Anglophiles, to help set up an institution which, for all its Anglo-American aims, would be planted firmly on British soil in a British culture. We thought it both necessary and right to aim eventually at *two* linked schools, one in each country. It seemed best, however, to establish the British school first and try to forge a link with a good independent school in the States.

Our somewhat Platonic concept of the two schools ('one soul in two bodies') was, I think, a good one, and really essential to the whole project if the label 'Anglo-American' were to mean anything educationally.

Another concept, that of the boarding school, was scarcely a matter of debate. With a great part of our intake coming from overseas, we would *have* to be a boarding school. But we were well aware that the concept was distinctly more unfamiliar to American than to British minds. The British middle and upper classes have long accepted that it is good for them and their children to part company for some twelve weeks after each Christmas, Easter and interminable summer. Their American counterparts do not generally accept such periodic migrations of the fledglings as a manifestation of natural law. A nation of settlers is deeply concerned to take root, become assimilated, achieve good neighbour relations in the immediate habitat. Even so, we felt that as a boarding school we could aim for a worthwhile balance between the British and American emphases: a boarding school well integrated with the surrounding community and organized in houses that would rather resemble a group of individual families enjoying neighbourly relations on an open campus.

And not monastic. Which raised the question of co-education. We discussed this at length. After eight years at Millfield I was well used to a co-ed community. There it had worked well, confirming my theoretical approval of it as a sane, healthy and valuable type of schooling. But I knew it worked because the control was tight and the discipline tough: tighter and tougher than I wanted for our school. Moreover, several Americans told me, with apparent authority, that they felt the type of American parent who would consider a boarding school in England was likely to be the one turning his back on co-ed schooling as he knew it in his own country. And so we decided that, at any rate in our early years, we should be a boys' school.

Discipline was the next subject to discuss and Roland and I reverted to it on many occasions. On one thing we were agreed: there was no question of corporal punishment. We both abhorred it. At Milton Abbey, as already mentioned, I had been the only housemaster with a declared policy of no corporal punishment. For the rest, there was little agreement. Roland was really averse to any kind of punishment, any repression, any intimidation of the young by the old. This, I felt, was largely sentimental, a product of his

332

humane and idealizing instincts, which had never been empirically tested, for he had spent almost all his professional life teaching undergraduates, not schoolboys. After further discussion, Roland finally contented himself by saying: 'Well, that is your area. You have had the experience. Do what you feel best.'

I decided to keep a diluted form of the 'prefect' system of discipline. At Milton Abbey I had tried the experiment of allowing my house to vote for their own house prefects. After I had explained to them what responsible voting was, and how they themselves would be the ultimate sufferers if they voted for the merely popular senior who might be expected to turn an habitual blind eye, they always chose their prefects intelligently: not always the ones *I* would have chosen, but I don't think I ever refused an electee of theirs, or ever really regretted one. I accordingly wrote in our present prospectus: 'The English prefectorial system of discipline and character training will be employed, but in a form manifestly reconcilable with democratic procedure. Prefects will be neither policemen nor informers: they will be encouraged to see the responsibility rather than the privilege of office, and to hold themselves answerable to those below as well as to those above them. The School does not envisage the use of corporal punishment in any circumstances.'

Curriculum and examinations posed less of a problem. British education then encouraged early specialization and the study of a few subjects in depth; American education tended rather to stress the study of a wide range of subjects in less detail. We felt there was a great opportunity for the Anglo-American school to strike a valuable compromise here, surrounding our major subjects with a generous battery of minority ones, nonexam electives of wide general appeal. We decided to prepare for the British GCE exams at O level and A level, since these were obligatory for entry to British universities and warmly welcomed by American ones.

As for games, we said the chief national games of both countries would be played, and fixtures would be sought with US diplomatic staffs and the personnel of US defence bases. But, perhaps with visions of the British at baseball and the Americans at cricket, I cagily added in the prospectus: 'Games will be played for their own sakes, for personal fulfilment, for the promotion of healthy loyalties and rivalries, and as a release from tension. It is not intended that they should become fetishes.'

The section in the prospectus headed 'Religion' stated that worship in the school chapel would centre on both English and American prayer books, and that freedom of worship would, of course, be extended to other denominations and faiths on a basis of mutual respect. I wrote: 'The thoughtful agnostic will be able to state his case. The School will consider itself to have failed if it does not present Christianity as a faith satisfying no less intellectually than spiritually, and interpreted afresh in the symbols of our time.'

Such was our blueprint. However, that was not quite all. Our prospectus needed to conclude with some convincing arguments that such a school was both needed and viable. After a great deal of homework, I wound up with three sections that represented the best I could do by way of selling an as yet nonexistent commodity to a largely unknown market.

In the first, 'The Demand,' I pointed to the general demand for the provision of independent schooling, quoting appropriate statistics with regard to the upward curve on the graph for the numbers of senior pupils in schools in both England and Wales and the United States. In the second, 'The Supply,' I indicated that the school should appeal to parents with diplomatic, cultural or commercial associations with both countries, emphasizing that company executives in Britain and the United States should welcome for their sons such an education as the proposed Anglo-American school would provide. Finally, in the third section, headed 'Unique,' I triumphantly declared that no comparable educational establishment then existed on either side of the Atlantic, adding that the school, by virtue of its contacts in both countries, would be able to offer its leavers unique opportunities for further education.

A bold claim indeed! Little could I then foresee how our aims and ambitions would be grievously shattered by the events that ensued.

2

We existed, then, as a legal entity, our handsome prospectus enshrined our ideals and the practical means for their attainment, and we had already attracted the patronage of some eminent people, assuring them that we sought only the presence of their names on paper if they honestly felt they could support our project: we were not after their time or their money. So far, so good. But, having sailed that distance, we became horribly becalmed: 'painted ships on a painted ocean.' Gradually we realized that we were not going to be considered seriously for donations until we had some pragmatic existence, some bricks and mortar, some staff and students.

A good friend, Robin Crockett, had become our company secretary. A barrister and a lecturer in law, he attended to all the important, time-consuming legal niceties, kept the minutes of all board meetings, and met the requirements of the Charity Commissioners and of the Department of Education and Science, all without a penny in payment. He had sent out an appeals letter, with our prospectus, to most of the large Anglo-American business houses in Britain. This had brought in about £300: a help, but scarcely the response we needed or had hoped for. And one tycoon had told us frankly that we would not be taken seriously until we had some measure of corporeal existence.

But how to do that? How to break that Catch-22 situation: no money without premises, no premises without money? Was there an established private school enduring some lean years which would welcome incorporation in the Anglo-American school idea? We inserted advertisements in *The Times* personal columns, and we consulted one or two school transfer agencies. As a result I travelled over half England, trying to sell the idea to various independent school headmasters who had handsome premises and dwindling numbers. I met some interesting people and heard some sad stories. Once or twice (incredibly, it now seems to me) we came within an ace of success. 'Incredibly' because we had nothing to offer but an idea: no capital, no pupils, no goodwill. One headmaster with a beautiful building and lovely grounds was so keen that he committed himself verbally, and we thought we had achieved our longed-for breakthrough. But at the last moment his solicitor advised against it, feeling the risk was too great. In fact, there was little or no risk, and I believe we would have proved the ailing school's salvation. In the event, it collapsed altogether within two years.

Another scheme would be to rent suitable premises. I called on a leading West End estate agent, who produced two or three likely properties. At one stage the manager called to his assistant: 'Now what was that great mansion that poor old Major Yardley wanted so badly?' With some foreboding, I asked: 'May I enquire what the poor old major's tragedy was?' The reply was breezy and chilling: 'Oh, same as yourself. He wanted it for a school. He's dead now.' I resolutely rejected my vision of this bowed, military figure, pockets stuffed with unpayable bills, placing the gun barrel to his head in dripping woods at dawn.

I visited all these sad houses. Several were badly decayed, going at peppercorn rents to anyone who would spend a fortune on making them habitable. One was magnificent, in perfect condition, ideal for our purposes, but they wanted a year's rent of £3,000 in advance, and we simply could not lay our hands on so much.

Roland had for some time been advocating a castle by the sea: this, he was convinced, would hold an immense appeal for an American Anglophile millionaire. I therefore had further recourse to the columns of *The Times*: 'Anglo-American educational project (charitable trust) seeks lease on castle or similar stately home. Write Box —.' This produced a small crop of anticipated weeds: decayed country gentry existing in one corner of some ancestral home that was falling about their ears, crushed by death duties and impossible running costs. But amid the weeds was a possible healthy bloom: a letter from the Countess of Sutherland described briefly her own Dunrobin Castle on the east coast of Scotland. I knew how dangerous for a school sheer geographical remoteness could be, but advantages in this case might be sufficient to outweigh that consideration. I went to see Lady Sutherland in London and liked what I heard of the castle. I arranged to visit it in the summer when Roland would be in England.

Two of my fellow housemasters at Milton Abbey were more than a little interested in our project. One was Michael Fletcher, of whose abilities I had a high opinion. A man of unusual integrity, he was moreover a biologist, a first-class housemaster, and had had a distinguished athletics career at Oxford. For these reasons, and because we had worked together and liked each other, I very much wanted him to come in with us on the Anglo-American project.

Thus it was that, in July 1963, the three of us set out for Scotland in Mike Fletcher's car, my own being now too aged for such a journey. In Edinburgh we called on a Scottish lawyer to be briefed on the main differences between English and Scottish law, especially in the matters of property and finance. We arrived at Dunrobin Castle in the late evening, and we had to echo Roland's first raptures: it certainly was eye-catching and atmospheric, and its coastal setting gave it a wild splendour that would have gladdened the heart of any precursor of the Romantic Revival in his search for the 'sublime.' Two elderly retainers were in residence and they welcomed us with all Scottish hospitality. Man and wife, brought up in service to the Duke of Sutherland, they eventually overcame their reserve to the extent of regaling us with some reminiscences. It seemed that one of the husband's duties had been to play the pipes on formal occasions around the Duke's dining table: a privilege not, alas, extended to us. Now his main task appeared to be walking the castle ramparts at regular intervals throughout the night, setting burglar alarms. He presumably slept by day.

We had several sessions with the Sutherland agent, asking all the basic, unromantic questions about soil, sewerage, services, damp rot and dry rot and so on. We also visited the area officer of the Scottish Development Board, who welcomed us with open arms and made our mouths water with his descriptions of grants and subsidies likely to be available to us. We made sketches of the Castle's interior and grounds, calculating the numbers we could accommodate, the uses to which rooms could be put, the fields suited for cricket and baseball pitches. At dawn on our last day, we walked down through shrieking peacocks and a shrubbery maze for a dip in the sea. Then, well primed, we departed, both retainers bobbing on the steps in traditional fashion, pocketing their tips and doubtless epitomizing us in the dourest Gaelic.

The trip had been leisurely, with a halfway overnight stay in Yorkshire, so that we had plenty of time for discussion in depth of our proposed school's ethos, and of our respective roles in it. Mike Fletcher held that corporal punishment should not be rejected in a merely doctrinaire fashion as one possible element in overall discipline. Roland and I would have none of it. On the other hand, I felt constrained to present to Roland a clutch of concrete examples of breaches of discipline about which something must be done, the more so since we were agreed that rules and regulations would be kept to that sane minimum without which no community could survive, no boys be happy, no parents retain confidence in the school. His answers were, it seemed to me, vague to the point of wilful blindness. Nor, I added with some heat, was I prepared to be Wackford Squeers while he drifted around all honey and light. And that spelt early disaster. Roland countered this by claiming sadly that he had always known that we two could never pull together in joint harness and hinting that I had never really wanted this, anyway.

Now it was untrue that I had not wanted us to be joint headmasters. Nor, to be fair to myself, did I ever cease to offer this. But in my heart I knew that he was right in foreseeing the impossibility of such a working relationship. Each was in his own way a strong character. Each had his peculiar integrity which was different from the other's. In this matter of young people and discipline, he saw me as too unyielding, too egotistical. I saw him as too ostrich-headed, far too afraid of unpopularity. And I think we were both right.

'I'll be a governor of the school,' he concluded. 'I'll be of more practical value staying in America, promoting it, recruiting for it. All I ask is a few rooms in one of those turrets which I can furnish to my taste and occupy during my vacations in this country. That is, if you'll deign to lower the drawbridge for such an old and sacrificial friend.'

This martyred tone was designed to provoke me, and did. 'I've never really believed, when it came to the crunch, you *would* give up your lucrative American career for this. So don't pose as a martyr to the *real* martyr-elect, who must give up *his* career on this hazard. Nor, I may say, do I much relish the role of indigent Ludwig playing host in his own castle to a rollicking Wagner whose every visit shakes its foundations.'

'As I've so often told you,', he countered, 'you're the one who exhibits all the less admirable Teutonic traits, as well as all Wagner's ruthless egotism with none of his creative industry.' (This was two unkind cuts: my maternal grandmother was a Wagner, and I was a devotee of his music; and Roland was forever chiding me with an accidie that stifled my vague literary aspirations.) 'And what's more,' he finished as he reopened his book, 'if we do get Dunrobin, and if there is a Götterdämmerung there, you as usual will prove the Phoenix and I'll be the poor, wronged Ludwig at the bottom of the loch.'

Well, it ended, as our frequent clashes invariably did, with ineluctable laughter. In due course he moved from America to lectureships at Marburg and Trondheim and finally a Professorship in Finland. He never did join me as fellow principal.

On our return to London we told Lady Sutherland we were certainly interested in the possibilities of Dunrobin Castle for our project and she invited us to a family discussion on the matter. We went fairly exhaustively into ways and means: everything, I remember, from mortgages to manure, from the pros and cons of kilts to the wisdom of a school helicopter. It all went swimmingly, so far as we could tell. Then Patrick Maitland arrived, as, we gathered, a friend of Lady Sutherland's whose judgement was greatly valued. He seemed to like us very little and our project even less. Over the politest of cucumber sandwiches, the atmosphere became progressively glacial. I got the distinct impression, which I am sure he did not mean to give, that he saw himself as a dedicated lifeguard battling to save the incautious bathers from a trio of sharks. I showed my cold resentment and the meeting ended with an air of polite and unmistakable finality all round.

So there we were once more, three little Aladdins whose genie had decamped together with the castle he had so briefly conjured up.

Sometimes we asked ourselves if we should abandon the whole idea. But we couldn't. It was becoming compulsive. We were addicted. One never knew what the post might bring, what might come of some introduction. Looking back in old diaries of those years, I am astonished to see how many people we corresponded with or met, how many avenues we explored. And the most trivial gain was enough to convince us that the project was moving slowly ahead, some puff of wind trembling those becalmed sails.

All the time we were adding judiciously to our list of patrons and our advisory council, both of which were becoming quite impressive: resounding names that could lie fallow on our letterheads, never to be disturbed by cries for cash or credit, kindly names to whom I solemnly reported at regular intervals in progress bulletins of optimistic enthusiasm I was hard put to feel. Oh, the millions of words I wrote: and the thousands of eyes too busy or bored to read them.

I was becoming increasingly troubled by a serious desideratum: I had never been to America. This must, I felt, be put right. So, exhorted by Roland and financed by Lombank, I flew off to New York in April, 1965.

3

I stayed for a while with Harvey in New York State, not far from the Canadian border. It was good to see him and Helen again, and to meet his children for the first time. He had two girls and a boy. They had a charming house and a lovely church all in white slatted wood. It was clear that Harvey was greatly appreciated there.

I preached for Harvey and met most of his congregation, as well as entering into his various church groups. I couldn't help noticing, with a private smile and no comments, how much plusher was Harvey's way of life than mine had been with his father-in-law. The parish provided all manner of perks, including a monster car. The church vestry was quite luxurious in its furnishings, with a large coffee pot always on the hob.

I had an impression that Harvey and Helen were less in tune, less close, than at first, but I told myself this could only be expected after a dozen or so years of married life. But before I left I received a great, well-nigh unbelievable shock. Harvey told me he and Helen were to separate: he was finding his life suffocating and he must escape and have time to breathe, to think. I did my utmost to resist such a state of mind, but to no avail. In my heart of hearts I thought I could glimpse what he meant (but I never expressed my thought). He was still alive with ideas and enthusiasms, but wifehood and motherhood had inevitably given her more maturity. Moreover, Harvey had met a young woman (a musician) with whom he had a deep and rewarding rapport.

Well, Helen divorced him. Harvey suffered sheer agony over it all. They remained good friends to the last and Harvey never lost his respect, almost his reverence, for Helen's character. She never remarried but devoted the rest of her life to her children and to a career as a college lecturer. Harvey married his lady musician: a very nice person who has made the marriage an undoubted success. Harvey has never ceased being a devoted father to his children.

Despite his Bishop's assurance that a move to some distant parish would ease all these painful events, Harvey insisted on placing his religious Orders into some personal interregnum and becoming a college instructor. When Helen died in 1989, deeply mourned by countless people, I told Harvey he should reactivate his Orders. I am glad to say he did so, becoming like me a College Chaplain as well as a lecturer.

Such was the shock and sadness into which I walked on my first visit to America. I left Harvey's parish with a heavy heart.

I flew down to Texas, where Roland was teaching. He and his colleagues fêted me as generously as had Harvey's friends. I did some preaching and some teaching, met many academics, and returned to England with affection for Americans. A reticent Englishman myself, I cherished their warm, outgoing friendliness. Yet Roland had surprised me. He was rather cooler in his feelings for America than he had been. I hadn't expected his first euphoric reactions to persist, but I wasn't prepared for the hunger for Europe that I found in this expatriate.

A friend in America had suggested I contact Lord Bossom of Maidstone in London. He had behind him a lifetime's labours in Britain and America and elsewhere as an architect. He told me I could use his name as an introduction and on our letterheads. His kindly, practical encouragement, gave me new heart at a time when I badly needed it. Sadly, he died not long afterwards. His son, Sir Clive Bossom, later wrote me: 'I'm so glad you have those nice memories of my dear old dad. It is astonishing how many people seem to feel like you about him.'

Roland, who was infinitely better at promotion than I, did succeed in catching the interest and patronage of Douglas Fairbanks, who wrote a charming letter of acceptance and was duly inscribed on our letterheads.

It was through Millfield that we obtained the playwright Robert Bolt (who had been a predecessor of mine there) as a patron, and, more importantly, another ex-member of the Millfield teaching force became one of our governors. Dr John Paxton had been head of the economics department, and had recently left to become a consultant in his own right. In addition to all his professional commitments, he had the formidable task of editing *The Statesman's Year Book*. He made it clear that he took on this extra chore with the Anglo-American school only out of personal friendship to me, and that, having taken it on, he would not be a mere rubber-stamp governor, a sleeping partner. For several years, despite his ever-growing practice, he honoured those declarations.

Then Paul Christophersen, another of our governors, introduced me to Peter Utley: i.e., T. E. Utley, the distinguished leader writer and political commentator of *The Daily Telegraph*. I agreed with very few of Peter's political views, but I have always relished his company. Erudite, witty, unfailingly courteous and helpful, he always seemed to me so much better than many of his opinions. I spent many a delightful evening with him in my club or in his favourite Fleet Street tavern, and I invariably begrudged time devoted to discussing our project when there was so much else to explore in the company of his fine mind. He was totally blind, yet at that time was commuting daily between Fleet Street and his home near Newbury. With such a handicap, achievement in any profession is remarkable; in the tough world of daily journalism it was little short of miraculous.

Peter Utley duly joined our board of patrons and was most helpful in the way of introductions and, of course, publicity. Then at David Carver's house we met Stephen Spender, at that time working in the US as Director of the Library of Congress. He, too, agreed to give us his backing.

I asked Lord Gladwyn (whom I had known and liked when, as Sir Gladwyn Jebb, he had been our ambassador in Paris) if he would become a patron of our Anglo-American school. He felt he could not: he wouldn't take on anything he had no time to do properly. I had much the same response from other retired British ambassadors to Washington, most of whom were now working even harder in the worlds of high finance or academic government. One of them, Lord Harlech, sent his son, Francis Ormsby-Gore, to Anglo-American College. Francis was an attractive personality, and Harlech himself proved a true friend in need.

4

Roland had been very busy in Texas. He wrote to me that he could get the national American press to say a few words about us and the Texas press to say quite a lot about us, *but* that it required some actual event as the peg on which this publicity could be hung. So, after a great deal of discussion and planning, we gave at David Carver's London house a cocktail party 'to mark the inauguration of the Anglo-American School.' Handsome invitations were sent out to anybody and everybody who might be interested, and, of course, to our patrons and colleagues likely to be in England at that time. We had a fairly good response, and Peter Utley brought with him some important journalist colleagues. A press hand-out had been prepared and distributed in Britain, and Roland had seen to it that the American press received this in good time.

I was not much in evidence at the party for the telephone rang interminably. The British press. The American press through their London representative, Reuter's. Then long distance from Texas: an editor wanting from me the low-down on the whole project. In a couple of minutes. In a couple of sentences. But hadn't he received the press hand-out? Yes, but he wanted something extra special from the horse's mouth. Anything a bit sensational. Anything funny. Well, I did my best, but he wasn't satisfied. 'Say,' he shouted suddenly, 'put me on to Doug Fairbanks, willya, Reverend?' I explained Mr Fairbanks had been unable to attend. That, I thought, was that. But Mr Editor astonishingly replied: 'Aw now, Reverend, don't give me that stuff. Just put him on for a couple o'minutes, willya? Willya do that little thing for me, Reverend? Willya go get him for me?'

I finally hung up on him, hoping he'd believe we had been cut off. He had his revenge. Some weeks later Roland sent me a half-page article from this man's paper: the tone was faintly but perceptibly derisive, and the banner headline curiously facetious, screaming 'GET YOUR WICKET, JUNIOR!'

However, it was all publicity. We had more staid, more telling reports in the British press. I had driven back to Millfield after the cocktail party, apprehensive about my reception now that the cat was out of the bag. But everybody was very pleasant about it, seemed curiously impressed by it even. The always hard-pressed administrative offices at Millfield patiently took call after call on my behalf, arranging for people to phone back if I was in class. I

341

had wanted to avoid all this, but had had to say where I was currently teaching and everybody knew Millfield. Most of the leading national dailies telephoned me and printed something about the project. The BBC sent down their educational correspondent who recorded a brief interview with me. This was broadcast several times in one day.

The whole thing had made a rather louder bang than I had anticipated, or even desired. Patrons were being harassed somewhat by news-hungry journalists, and I was afraid we might lose some of our bright names. Again, I had little time or opportunity to deal with the enquiries since we were well into the spring term at Millfield. Correspondence stepped up: many parents expressing great interest, several people wanting to join the staff. I answered all these, sending out prospectuses. Several parents asked me to put down the names of their children. Some wanted to *send* me their sons almost at once. In addition to all this, there were countless letters touting for business, and two strange, abusive letters: one clearly cracked, the other (which I answered) roundly condemning us for one more step towards an American take-over of Britain.

All this: and we still had no money, no premises, no existence. It took all my diplomacy as well as half my sleeping hours to cope, quite single-handed and on an old portable typewriter.

But we had the press cuttings mounted and photocopied, using them to reinforce our prospectus when we wrote for patronage or for possible donations. And we found that we were indeed taken more seriously, such is the hallowing power of press publicity. Our board of patrons was greatly strengthened about this time by such eminent men and women as Sir George Thomson, the Nobel scientist (through Paul Christophersen), Sir Robert Mayer and Dame Rebecca West (through David Carver), and Sir John Gielgud, with whom, it may be recalled, I had corresponded some years before. Douglas Dodds-Parker joined us. As MP for Cheltenham and a leading member of the British-American Parliamentary Group, he often called on us with his American wife when we finally opened.

Roland had succeeded in interesting Lewis Douglas, perhaps the most popular ambassador America had ever sent to Britain. It had taken all Roland's considerable epistolary skill to obtain his eventual agreement, which he gave in a pleasant and amusing letter that testified to Roland's powers of persuasion.

Lord Cowdray became a patron, and sent us small, unsolicited cheques from time to time. Lord Arran came... and went.

But I was most delighted by a letter of enquiry from Dr John Phillips, bishop of Portsmouth, who had read of us in the press, liked the sound of us and wished to know more. We exchanged many letters, asked and answered many questions. Roland went first to see him, I later. We then plucked up courage to ask him to become a governor, that is, a fellow director of Anglo-American School Ltd. We felt our directorial board now needed strengthening, but we knew that this was a very much bigger thing to ask of a busy public figure than to stand on a letterhead as a patron. For this meant giving much time, taking much trouble, and, of course, it meant a definite legal involvement. His acceptance was enormously encouraging. No governor gave us more practical help.

Just about this time Roland left Texas to take up an appointment in Pennsylvania.

That summer of 1966 was to prove our busiest yet. It was five years since we'd first seriously discussed the project. We felt we had achieved all too little in that time, but also that we had achieved far too much to kill it all now. We had to go on.

5

I forget how I first heard the name of The Hon Cornelius Van H. Engert, CBE, M Litt, but it was certainly as an outstanding American Anglophile and one of the earliest promoters of the English Speaking Union. A former ambassador in South America and in the Middle East, he was elderly now but (I gathered) busier than ever, lecturing in many continents, intensely interested in world economic co-operation, still tirelessly promoting Anglo-American friendship. I wrote to him in Washington, asked him to read our literature and to consider if he could become one of our governors. He replied at length, courteously, shrewdly, helpfully, and he accepted the invitation. This was indeed encouraging, for we badly needed to strengthen our board of directors with some weighty American names, and I felt we could not have done better than this. Mr Engert (or 'Van', as he preferred one to call him) spent a great part of each year in travel (as an unofficial ambassador, he said) and always a summer month in England. Short, lean, tough, purposeful, Van seemed invulnerable to heat or exhaustion. He never let slip any opportunity to promote the school, or college, as it later became. To be honest, I was sometimes embarrassed by his determined production of photos, press cuttings and prospectuses, and I suspect he felt I never really exploited the introductions he gave me, never really invaded the territories his initial forays so conscientiously softened up for me. True enough, I suppose. At first, I felt we were too small and trivial. Later, when we *could* claim serious attention in terms of students and faculty and property and results, I felt unable to embark on any ardent eulogies, any idealistic propaganda. Van must, at one time or another, have introduced me to most of the surviving ex-ambassadors from St James to Washington and vice versa.

Another interesting contact that summer was Lord Kings Norton, who combined academic and industrial eminence to a rare degree. He had been

343

sent one of our prospectuses and an appeals letter in his capacity as chairman of the Metal Box Company. He took the trouble to read our literature and to write me a carefully reasoned comment on it. Chiefly he took exception to such apparently patronizing remarks of mine as 'humanizing the scientist' and 'if to produce too few scientists and technologists is to court economic bankruptcy, to produce uncivilized ones is to court that dire bankruptcy of the spirit.'

A bit pompous, I suppose, but I felt I could and should defend the statements, especially since I had tried to hold the balance with my equal strictures on woolly-minded arts candidates who couldn't think straight or write straight. I wrote back. He asked me to visit him at his office in Baker Street. Actually, I paid him two or three visits in his plush rooftop suite.

Lord Kings Norton underlined what I knew was our great desideratum: our list of patrons was overloaded with 'culture' at the expense of those leaders of science and industry we must somehow involve in our project. There was no balance, and my prospectus positively harped on the need for balance.

I asked him if he could suggest some likely names to approach. He gave me nine or ten, but warned me that the bigger the fish the more improbable would be any catch, for these men were already fully stretched. I asked him if I could mention his name in writing to them. He demurred a little, then generously indicated where I might and where I positively might not use him as an introduction.

Roland had been active. In his new academic environment he had heard much talk of the ambitious plans of the bishop for a great new Episcopalian high school in his diocese: a purpose-built, independent school of quality, for which the land had already been purchased and upon which the local millionaires were already smiling favourably. The bishop of Erie was known as a fighter for what he believed in, and he believed in his project. Roland convinced him how similar were our plans to his, how like in ethos the schools of which respectively we dreamed, how mutually enriching might be a liaison. I, too, began a correspondence with the bishop. Then Roland felt the moment had come to invite him to join us. He accepted, became a director (or governor), forming with Mr Engert a most valuable American element in our composition. He was too over-committed to be a good correspondent, but he did find time to visit us when in England for the 1968 Lambeth Conference.

1966 closed with an embarrassing encounter and an intriguing letter. The former was with our patron, Douglas Fairbanks. A somewhat brash entrepreneur we knew had insisted that I take him along to see Mr Fairbanks. I had rather reluctantly agreed because I did not see how to refuse. I don't have to say Mr Fairbanks is a charmer, for all the world knows it.

And the nicer he was, the worse I felt. Our entrepreneur (I'll call him Mr Wise) had told me that I could leave all 'business' talk to him, since this was clearly not my province. (I met so many people in those years who told me that: and subsequently proved more unbusinesslike than I could have been if I'd really tried.)

'You describe yourself here as a "director of companies," Mr Wise. May I ask the names of some of them?'

'Er, well, you know, that was in the past. Retired now. And too many companies to remember, really. Now I was about to tell you something of the British interest that has been aroused.'

Mr Fairbanks was as gentlemanly as cynical. He listened. Then he told us that his father, whom the world at large remembers as a swashbuckling, romantic film star, had been a most astute and intelligent businessman. 'And I expect' (here Mr Fairbanks' charm reached its peak), 'I expect in my own more modest way I have inherited some of that.'

As we walked up St James', I muttered to Mr Wise:

'Well, that was pretty disastrous.'

'Oh, you mustn't be so impatient,' he replied cheerfully. I don't know which astonished me more: his optimism or his condescension. 'You mustn't expect these people to pull out a cheque book after five minutes chat. Businessmen don't behave like that, you know. I expect we'll hear from Mr Fairbanks pretty soon.'

We did. He wrote to say that pressure of business compelled him, regretfully, to resign forthwith as a patron of the Anglo-American School.

The letter I mentioned came from Van Engert in Washington. He told me of some good friends of his who lived near Oxford: John and Virginia Tilley. They were great Anglophiles and might well be interested in helping to promote our project. He felt sure I'd like them. They lived in Alvescot, near Oxford.

So I wrote to them. I had a very agreeable reply. Van had told them something about me and they were most keen to meet. Could I come to lunch one day soon?

6

I had found a shorthand typist in Glastonbury, a married woman with a young child. She took dictation at her home, typed the letters and had them ready for collection the next day. Sometimes she could get to the library and find necessary addresses in *Who's Who*. I used her services whenever I had a pile-up of correspondence and could afford to employ her. She, I remember, wrote to the scientists and businessmen Lord Kings Norton had proposed.

Almost all declined gracefully. But Dr J. V. Dunworth, director of the National Physical Laboratory, and a member of the International Atomic

Energy Commission, agreed to become a patron. I spent two most interesting evenings with him. And so, to my surprise and delight, did Sir Charles Wheeler, who had been described to me as a talented and high-powered man of business.

I liked the Tilleys and their house. They eventually suggested it should be the nucleus of our school, far more modest than Roland and I had planned, but not more unassuming than Meyer's first steps towards Millfield.

I was now involving, as potential key personnel, Michael Fletcher and his wife, and Michael Charles and his wife.

Michael Charles had been, like Fletcher, a fellow housemaster of mine at Milton Abbey. Like Fletcher, he was keenly interested in joining our Anglo-American school, and he, too, was someone I wanted very much as a colleague. Not only for his personal qualities, but because I knew him to be a good teacher and a successful director of studies, well versed in the intricacies of timetabling, academic counselling, university applications and so forth. Moreover, he had at Oxford specialized in American history and government, which he was keen to teach more widely.

With many generous gifts and two delightful farewell dinners, I left Millfield that July and in due course I moved in with the Tilleys. We were launching our project not with the anticipated bang, nor yet with a whimper; rather with a whisper, an amused, exploratory whisper. We had just £26 in our Anglo-American School account with Coutts Bank. It was a venture of faith for the Tilleys and for me. Our governors' meeting that summer had decided that there was nothing for it but for me to seize this opportunity and work like a slave to exploit it. We felt the whole situation must be left fluid and informal for the moment. If, later, we looked viable, then we could conclude such formalities as a lease of the Alvescot premises, contracts of service, definitions of responsibility and remuneration, plans for physical adaptation and expansion. All we could do just now was, in Tilley's favourite phrase, 'play it as it comes.'

I felt we should not, at this stage, announce ourselves as the long-projected 'Anglo-American School.' For several reasons: the premises were too small; we had no money to advertise ourselves or to make any kind of splash with an official opening ceremony; if we were to fail, it was clearly better to fail as something modest and anonymous, leaving the Anglo-American scheme intact and capable of implementation in some hopefully rosier future. Roland opposed this, overtly because he was still working furiously to induce the bishop of Erie to identify his own project with ours, and also because he was planning a summer school of his own Pennsylvania students at our premises the following year. I think he feared I might become sidetracked into running with Tilley a possibly lucrative tutorial establishment and eventually lose interest in the scheme on which we'd lavished six years of sweat and toil and almost every spare penny we possessed. But I was adamant, and I think I was right. We reached something like a compromise in so far as Roland could feel free to tell anyone unofficially that a year hence the governors of Anglo-American School would adopt this present infant if it had been successfully weaned and promised healthy growth.

So, once more, I set out to write a new prospectus. I made it straightforward and businesslike, tasteful but inexpensive. I wrote simply, pragmatically, with a modest self-assurance. And, perhaps not surprisingly, this was, for what it was, the most successful prospectus I ever produced. It was devoted to selling, not an idea, not a property, not any kind of an educational novelty, but simply the theory and practice of successful teaching as I had learned them over the years.

I had obtained the prospectuses of pretty well all the British tutorial establishments which were residential and preparing for O and A levels. From these I gained an idea of the fees we could charge without, on the one hand, having to jeopardize essential standards, or, on the other, pricing ourselves out of the market. 'Good teaching and good living' might fairly summarize our basic aims.

We knew we stood to lose everything if no students materialized. I knew that I'd be jobless and broke.

We sat and waited. It was all very exciting. I felt *some* fish must bite. But I also knew that it was now well into autumn and few parents would at this stage be looking for schools.

As we grew bigger and busier, I found I had no time for that which many parents expected in a first uncommitted interview. I learned that there are more people than one would care to imagine who quite happily accept one's hospitality, take up inordinate amounts of one's time, exploit to the hilt one's professional know-how, and then disappear without even a letter of thanks. I realized that we were in danger of running a busy educational consultancy without fee or subsidy from any source. I wondered if such people would dream of consulting a lawyer on such terms. I soon saw a preliminary questionnaire was the solution, and I made it my practice to interview no one until I knew from the completed questionnaire that we could at least provide the educational programme that was needed.

As our daily post grew in volume and complexity, I learned to detect the African or Middle East student who would engage in verbose, unctuous and wildly unrealistic correspondence for a particular purpose of his own, namely to obtain a formal letter stating Mr So-and-so was registered as a bona fide student of Anglo-American College to pursue a full-time course extending over at least two years. After which the would-be student vanished from our ken. I learned, after one or two such experiences, to request a term's fees before issuing the desired credentials.

It soon became apparent that we must, all else being equal, give priority consideration to a potential student who came by personal recommendation, since on all those who came from agencies we had to pay ten per cent of the first year's fees. In vain did I point out to the agents that this was fair enough when they were sending 13-year-olds to a school for a five-year programme. But since most of ours were coming for a one-year concentrated course, it seemed more reasonable to charge their commission on only the first term's fees. I could never budge them on this issue, and I can see their difficulties, but we could ill afford the thousands of pounds we had to pay to the agents on whom we initially depended so heavily.

I had aimed the prospectus at GCE candidates, feeling that we could not, at first, expect to cope with younger children: sixteen plus or minus seemed sensible for a first intake. But I had been careful not to address myself exclusively to one sex: the more or less self-contained flats into which the house was divided made it easy enough for us to accept girls, and thus the co-ed principle was established. How could we afford to ignore a principle that doubled one's potential intake?

Tilley had introduced me to a neighbour, a Colonel Arthur Brooke, recently retired from the army and becoming ever more bored with the leisure which had come too soon. Arthur was prepared to act as honorary bursar for a term or so and cope with such important mysteries as income tax, superannuation and national insurance, as well as the usual bursarial chores. I took a very modest salary because I had to, and the Tilleys were paid a reasonable provisional rent of £2,000 p.a.

We were committed to teaching nine subjects for O level. I found locally a visiting art mistress and a visiting master for history and geography. I did the English language, English literature and divinity.

And two or three times a week my brother Brian would drive all the way from Somerset to take the maths and French. I had refused to let him leave Millfield until I could feel we were reasonably secure. Looking back now, I find it quite astonishing that, after a full day's hard teaching at Millfield, he could drive seventy miles to us, give two hours of concentrated tuition from 5.30 to 7.30, and then drive back to Glastonbury the same night. But he did it, in all weathers, and for no other payment than the cost of the petrol he had used.

7

At this time the luxuriance of boys' hair and the brevity of girls' skirts were still shocking many older people, as they were intended to do. I wanted the students, as their numbers increased, to express their individual personalities by means of their hair styles and their clothes. But I was soon to be disenchanted by the drab and scruffy uniformity of their sweaters and jeans: the badge of their teenage solidarity in despising the 'hypocrisy' of sartorialism, the 'insincerity' of subscribing to any sense of occasion. There were still quite a few boys left over from the 'peacock' era of Carnaby Street and the early sixties, and quite a few girls who'd dress to kill when we had a buffet dance or a pop barbecue. But they gradually became rarities until in the end most had achieved a uniform as durable and functional as any Poor Law institution could have devised. This, of course, came to Britain generally from the affluent, middle-class kids of America who were rejecting the 'smart boy' and 'cute cookie' image worshipped by their ignorant begetters. I once encountered one of our girls, pretty, petite and intelligent, having a furious battle in a flower bed with a pair of jeans, pounding and treading them as conscientiously as any eastern housewife on the banks of the Ganges. 'They're new: I've just bought them,' she considered a total explanation. But even our most dedicated slummers usually made some voluntary, shamefaced concessions if they were going off for a job interview or university selection or even, one or two of them, when going home at the end of term. Some of them were just getting it out of their systems. Others were playing that age-old game of adolescents: 'Let's see how far we can push him.' Others again, whose fanatical pursuit of the real freak image was more disturbing, were in effect screaming to all the world: 'Look at me. I'm different.'

Sometimes, in the midst of such a disciplinary harangue, I'd stop and gaze at them in a kind of flippant exasperation. 'Am I convincing you?' I'd ask.

'No,' they'd cry.

'Nor myself, really,' I'd admit. 'To be quite honest with you, I suppose the main reason I clamp down on your wilder excesses is public opinion. You know the label we're getting locally: "that hippie college." I don't mind that in itself, but we *are* in business and we've got to survive. We've no income but student income and I've a vast number of bills and salaries to pay. I *have* to consider the sordid cash side of it all, something you lot have never in your lucky lives had to think about. If prospective parents driving in here are met by a fancy-dress ball of freaks and drop-outs and junkies and head-hunters, they'll very likely drive right out again.'

'That's being hypocritical,' they'd counter gleefully.

'No, *you* lot are the hypocrites,' I'd taunt them. 'You and your posters of Che Guevara and your "Thoughts of Chairman Mao" when you're all as Tory as they come. You with the swagger of Bonnie and Clyde when you're really as gentle as Buddha. You dressing up as nomads and drop-outs when you've come here of your own free will to get A levels and university entrance.'

349

This was *my* little game of teasing and pushing: purposeful enough beneath all the banter. I felt they were too old for these fantasies and at seventeen-plus should be capable of some honest self-examination. But I suppose I tended to expect both too much and too little of them, overestimating their intelligence and maturity, underestimating their basic goodwill and hunger for approval. And a fanatical handful really did want to drop out and were later to show how far they'd go in order to be dropped. Not many could bring themselves to admit this, though. And one cannot blame them, the pressures to conform being so great.

And I must now relate how coming events did cast one shadow over even this first genial year. Drugs: not mentioned so far in this account of our first three terms, not even as a problem I was prepared for. For the simple reason that I wasn't. Even in 1967, I think few teachers in this country had any first-hand experience of illicit drug-taking by the young. Oh, we knew about the problem, had read about it, but I believe most of us then still thought of it as a scourge of other lands, other cultures, other social groups. We didn't see flashing danger signals in the independent schools, I am sure. Like most housemasters, I had over the years had to deal with the occasional thief, the compulsive liar, the cheat, the bedwetter, the deviate. One always did one's best to keep them in the nest if that was right for them and for the community as a whole. Most of those who more or less successfully stayed the course benefited from doing so. So very often they were saved from total shipwreck by the mere process of time, by hanging on to the community that was hanging on to them until they had spewed up most of their bile and could face the world with a rather more settled stomach. I always felt this was one of the jobs of a school, especially a boarding school, which must expect to get a higher quota of 'difficult' kids. But when I started at Anglo-American I had not, to my knowledge, encountered drug-taking pupils. I hadn't even heard of it anywhere near home. Perhaps, even then, the school that had a case swept it frantically under the carpet. For a prestigious school it was worse than an outbreak of ringworm.

There had been disquieting reports from schools during the past twelve months, but lack of evidence and publicity encouraged one to ascribe more to rumour and exaggeration than to fact. I'd detected in students of ours no such tell-tale signs as 'alternative moods of depression and elation' or 'sudden and inexplicable changes in behaviour patterns' or 'sudden decrease in academic ability' or 'general lack of concern for standards hitherto valued,' as the textbooks had it. 'The unmistakable odour of cannabis?' I've as good a nose as the next man, I believe, but I've never found the smell of pot 'unmistakable.' There were other 'signs' I'm glad I didn't know then and am sorry I know now: students who much preferred candlelight or painted electric bulbs, who burned joss sticks and incense in their rooms, who never rolled up their shirtsleeves and were always very careful to destroy their fag ends. We discouraged, but permitted, over-16s to smoke in the common-rooms.

Still, I spent some part of the summer of 1968 questioning schoolmasters, psychiatrists, social workers. And reading all I could find on drug abuse.

8

Then I found our pearl of great price. I liked the sound of Tim Clark on the phone and I liked him even more in the flesh. Until very recently he had been headmaster of his own small, boarding school in the Lake District, and I have no doubt at all that it folded up because he gave too much for too little, and thus had no reserves to tide him over the lean years. To the handicap of geographical remoteness was added the final straw of selective employment tax. His school, like so many other good schools run by dedicated men and women, fell a victim to economic squeeze and its own distaste for tough commercialism. His wife was now working as school secretary in a large northern girls' college. He was struggling manfully to honour his debts, clear up his affairs, and find a job. He joined us: as director of art, as teacher of a range of O level subjects, and as what (trying to avoid traditional titles) I called 'community director.' In all these spheres he was excellent, and not least in the last, where he was 'in the forefront of the hottest part of the battle,' often worn out, disappointed and distressed, but at all times a hundred-per-cent loyal and reliable. He knew the meaning of professional integrity.

Thus there were five of us in residence and a goodly band of visiting tutors, full- and part-time. Arthur Brooke was by now doing almost a full-time job as bursar, and taking a small salary. Our local doctor held a surgery at the college each Wednesday, and a capable nursing sister visited twice a week.

All was rolling merrily on towards our grand official opening as 'Anglo-American College', our July D-Day, when we hoped to invade the bastions of power and wealth with all the intimidating weapons of a lavish hospitality. To our delight, Lewis Douglas had agreed to perform the opening ceremony. We sent out some five hundred invitations announcing the fact.

We kept our fingers crossed for weeks before the event. New buildings that we'd ordered were a major headache: it seemed impossible to believe that they would be ready in time, prefabricated though they were.

The workmen laboured throughout the Friday night to complete the buildings. On Saturday morning I found several of them snoring on hard boards, so exhausted they were, oblivious of the final hammerings and cursings of their mates. They were magnificent. Before they left, only a

351

couple of hours before our guests were due at noon, we opened a dozen bottles of champagne and toasted their success.

Two enormous marquees had been erected the day before. Now they were red-carpeted, furnished and a dozen chefs were setting out the Arabian Nights feast. The catering firm we had engaged were on their mettle: they had been feeding the college none too happily for the past three months. Now they were out to prove that they certainly knew how to serve a royal banquet when money was no object. They clearly enjoyed themselves, running the entire conceivable gamut of a cold buffet from smoked salmon to wild strawberries and clotted cream.

The weather was more than merciful. We could deliver our speeches on the open-air platform. Mine was to begin with a sad note: a week before I had heard from Lew Douglas that he had suffered a minor heart attack and though he was progressing well his doctors forbade all engagements, all travel. This was a blow. He was profuse in his apologies and felt sure that his old friend, our governor Van Engert, would deputize for him. Which he gracefully did.

My speech, which I kept short and light, seemed to go down quite well. David Carver, our chairman, spoke with his usual elegance, and Van introduced the necessary note of serious purpose in outlining the need for British-American friendship, the strength of the old 'Unwritten Alliance,' the humble but not unworthy part 'this little new college of ours' hoped to play in furthering mutual trust and affection. Then he unveiled the rather imposing brass plaque we had had made. After the polite applause I invited all to the marquee for refreshment. Many of them were not slow off the mark.

Socially, it was all the most tremendous success. Guest after guest told me they hadn't enjoyed such an occasion so much in years, and it was obviously true. Almost the common theme of the older ones was: 'It's quite prewar. Takes me back to the thirties.'

At last it was all over and the very distinguished gathering scattered slowly, even reluctantly.

It was a day from whose success I think we never really recovered. The whole point of the operation had been to solicit donations and gain publicity. Not one penny piece did it ever bring in. The press coverage was virtually nonexistent. Incredibly, no one had thought to ensure a press photographer or any other kind of photographer recorded the gay and glittering scenes in and around the marquees. When I asked our PR men for some explanation, they promised to make hushed and tactful soundings in the darker byways of Fleet Street. They reported back: 'Well, it seems the press was a bit blasé about Anglo-American College. Said they'd heard it all before.'

We reckoned our big day cost us about £1,500.

9

The bishop of Erie (Dr Crittenden) generously found time to call on us, with his wife, in the course of a tightly-packed schedule. As I have said, he was in England to attend the Lambeth Conference, and the few extra days he had after that were understandably crowded with personal and professional engagements. I knew something of him as a courageous and impressive dignitary of the Episcopal Church. I was prepared to like him and it was certainly not difficult to warm to his attractive personality. We got on well. It was a flying visit, but we found time to discuss his project and ours, and to sound out possible areas of co-operation. He, of course, favoured our original scheme: for an Anglo-American school for boys of thirteen to eighteen years. Since his project envisaged a boys' school of the same age range he was naturally disappointed that we were now a co-ed college for over-sixteens. However, we felt we could still have a mutually profitable interchange of older pupils and, perhaps, staff. I gathered his school was approaching an actual, physical existence: the site had been acquired, some buildings erected, and donations received sufficient to complete the initial building programme. He concluded our interview with an invitation that I took as a great compliment: 'Mr Gamble, I want you to be one of the governors of our school. Will you?' I accepted with ready and real pleasure.

Alas, nothing ever came of any of it. Our own closure overtook us before the bishop's school opened. I kept in touch, and of course the bishop, as one of *our* governors, received regular reports and all official documents. I must say he was a rather poor correspondent!

So that long, busy summer wore away until the challenging new term was upon us.

We opened in September 1968 with forty-two students, about one third of them girls. From four to twenty-five to forty-two in one year: not bad going, we felt, and no indication that our growth rate would for many years to come be limited by anything but our capacity. In due course we were elected to the Association of Tutors and to the Independent Schools' Association. I was even more gratified when we were (after much corresponding and visiting) finally 'adopted' by the British Schools and Universities Foundation. To this body, established in New York, an American could donate with important tax concessions. The Foundation could then in its turn donate to a British school or university registered with it and established in this country as a charitable trust.

The first half of the term passed gently, peacefully, autumnally. No real troubles. My A level English group was (I hated admitting it even to myself) rather a disappointment: the essays were thin, and the classroom joys were not shared. Their giggles seemed private, my aesthetic dreams positively esoteric.

A parent phoned to tell me his daughter Samantha[1] had carelessly left behind a letter when she was home last weekend. It was from a former student of ours. The parent decided not to send me the letter, but he read it to me over the phone. Silly sick stuff most of it: bits of obscenity, lots of pot-and-pop-scene slang. Some sad things too. ('God, Sam, how I miss dear old Anglo. Think of the place all the time. Dream of you all sometime. Remember our great little parties - in that barn - you and me and...') And at least one sentence plain frightening: 'Get some more groceries from Eddie next time you're in Oxford. Saloon bar. I want some tea and some sugar. Lots of tea if you can. Bit of sugar if you've got the bread for it. Some dexies if you can't get anything else. Anything, Sam - you know I'm pretty desperate. Send them quick. Before I jump in the river or something. I can only send a pound now but I'm expecting a lot of cash this week and I'll send it all off to you. Honest.'

That was the gist of it. I write it now from memory, but I can vouch for the key words and the general tone. My summer reading had introduced me to the euphemistic nicknames for drugs and I refreshed my memory from some pamphlets I had. 'Tea' was cannabis and 'sugar' was LSD. 'Dexies' were, quite uncryptically, the amphetamine Dexedrine. Sam and the boy sounded like old hands at the game, complete with 'pusher' Eddie in Oxford.

Six of our students were implicated: four boys and two girls. Three of them newcomers this term, and all three in my A level English group.

10

At first I was just depressed by it all: I felt suddenly weary and rather sickened. I expect I was feeling sorry for myself.

I remembered the drugs warning I had given to all of them on the first day of the term. I thought of the trust they'd enjoyed and betrayed, the apparent callousness and cynicism with which they had so soon set about corrupting one another and the college itself. I recalled the excellent performances my three English students had given at their interviews: their excited commitment to the college (it was everything they'd been looking for!), their enthusiasm for the literature course I'd outlined to them; their own literary ambitions and university aspirations. I thought of their very disappointing performances in class and in their thin essays; the curious hint of a suppressed euphoria beneath their surface dullness. What a naive fool I had been, excusing the dullness as an initial shyness, amused and even touched by their own esoteric jokes, their own high-spirited fun world whose privacy I respected.

[1] The names of all students have been changed.

By now I wasn't so much feeling sorry for myself as plain bloody angry. Not negative or passive in my reaction but filled with all the righteous indignation of hurt pride, with a determination to strike at the enemy quick and hard. There was going to be a confrontation and I was going to win. I thought of all the work that had gone into starting this venture, all the lives that were involved in it and dependent upon it, all the honest efforts we all made all the time to be not only just but also generous and liberal with our young people. Now a bunch of spoilt, indulged, wilful kids, hellbent on 'doing their own thing,' thought they could bring us all crashing in ruins, to the music of their own vapid giggles. Over my dead body!

It is fair to say that very few indeed of our drug takers were sick in the sense of being so addicted that they could no longer be held responsible for their behaviour. Those few who were 'hooked' were, I hope and believe, treated humanely and, with the co-operation of their parents, passed on to those qualified to help them.

Most were sick by no responsible definition. Are you sick (in the sense of not being responsible for what you are and what you do) if, despite all the warnings, you choose to take drugs because you haven't the guts to refuse them when your 'friends' offer them? Is to be weak in character and yield to temptation to be 'sick'? Are you 'sick' if you take drugs just for the hell of it, because you get a kick out of defying authority, plucking forbidden fruit, identifying with an underground peer group?

I wanted, of course, to be just. I honestly believe I wanted to be merciful wherever it was possible. But I had no doubt in my mind that those certainly guilty of taking and distributing drugs on our premises would have to go. No matter who they were or how many there were.

I decided to start my investigations at once. It was almost eleven o'clock now, and that was an advantage. They'd be in their rooms, but almost certainly not yet in bed, and that reduced the chances of any collusion between the suspects. I asked Tim to be present, knowing how important it was to have a witness, and then as always I wrote down the gist of everything said in the course of the interviews.

I fetched Freddie first. He was an American boy of about fifteen. He and his older sister had joined us that term. I had interviewed the father and daughter and had liked them both: Angela was intelligent, mature and in every way an attractive personality. Freddie had not by then arrived in Britain and for some reason I now forget could not arrive until a day or two after term began. But his educational references were respectable and Angela surely an impressive guarantor. When Freddie arrived, however, he was rather a shock: thick and slurred in speech, dull and phlegmatic in manner. I suspected drugs and once actually revealed my suspicions to him, but he was so emphatic, even offended, in his denials, and I so eager to believe him, that

I gladly changed the subject. Similarly, I had, casually, almost flippantly, touched on the matter to giggling Samantha, who had laughed so guiltlessly at the very idea that I had felt almost ashamed of mentioning it.

Freddie at eleven p.m. was even less attractive in appearance and manner than usual, and his eyes were strange: red-rimmed and with dilated pupils. Just looking at him and listening to him convinced me he had taken *something* very recently, no doubt confident that he would not encounter me or any other adult until the more obvious effects had worn off. But what I found most incriminating was the practised hardness of his response to questioning: cunning, evasive, dogged and with every sign of well-rehearsed boredom. He denied everything, without surprise, indignation or any vestige of passion. I finally asked him: 'Then I take it you will have no objection to our doctor examining you? He will be able to give an expert opinion quite readily.'

For the first time he faltered. And he was intelligent enough still to realize at once that his reply was a mistake. 'When? Tomorrow?'

'Oh, certainly not tomorrow,' I assured him. 'Tonight. Within half an hour or so. You have no objection?'

He showed his first trace of desperation. 'What sort of tests?'

I was now bluffing unrestrainedly. I had no idea if our doctor would consent to examining him, or even if he were available then, or what tests if any he could carry out. 'Oh, we now have reliable means of testing for drug consumption. Urine tests. Blood tests. Something like a breathalyzer, no doubt. The doctor, of course, will explain it all to you first.'

He blinked. 'Why should I?' he muttered. And a tear ran down his cheek.

I had to swallow an enormous temptation. I suddenly saw all the pathos of this wrecked, 15-year-old bundle of misery. I wanted, quite desperately, to put my hand on his shoulder and say: 'Look, Freddie, you're basically a decent boy, an intelligent one. Just get it all off your chest and I'll help you all I can.' But he'd probably see that as the well-known police technique of the sudden switch from intensive grilling to warm human sympathy. I felt so miserable myself that I really didn't know if that was indeed my motive.

I stared at him, my thoughts racing crazily down new avenues. They were thoughts that became familiar enough later. I was, in a few seconds, exploring huge alternatives. Supposing I kept him, tried to help him? He had no mother, and his father saw little of him. But I had no idea how to treat his sickness, no training or experience or skill. I could well do more harm than good. However, couldn't I co-operate with the experts, keep him here and liaise with the clinic in Oxford in trying to effect a cure? On the other hand that would surely be quite irresponsible towards the other students. Yet I could put it to them all, invite their consent and assistance: I knew they'd give it. Of course, their parents would have to consent. And why not? I could write to them all, enlisting their sympathy and support. But, again, how could I run a drugs rehabilitation centre and a serious academic college under the same roof? Well (and this was the ultimate crazy question), why not switch from the A level rat race to the real Christian ministry? Why *not* become a centre for all the tattered and torn army of puberal slaves, calling them into a new little kingdom? Ah, too enormous an undertaking, and too risky! So back to square one.

I blinked back at Freddie. I heard my voice, horribly cold and practical, telling him: 'Why should you? For your own sake, of course. If you are innocent, then this can prove it. And no one will be more delighted than I, or quicker to apologize. So...' I was giving him no further opportunity to demur. 'So, we'll phone the doctor now.'

'Can I go back to my room?'

'No, you just wait in the drawing room until the doctor arrives.'

'Why can't I go back to my room? I want to wash.'

'Because, my dear Freddie, I can't take the risk of your contacting the other people I must now interview. And it's getting late. Off with you: into the drawing room, and stay put there until we fetch you.'

So off the poor kid went, while someone sat with him and I telephoned the doctor. I explained the situation briefly and he was with us a quarter of an hour later. He told me there were no sure tests he could make, but he'd look at the boy and take a urine sample. He, too, was met by a brick wall of denial, distrust, defensiveness. (What, really, could one expect? All the students knew I'd expel those I found guilty of drug abuse.) He took the urine sample and said he would send it to the Home Office forensic laboratories, explaining the reasons but frankly expecting little in the way of positive identification (as was subsequently revealed by the Home Office's courteous but noncommital report).

While the doctor was attending to Freddie in the sick bay, I sent for the boy known as Bugs Bunny and put him in the drawing room. I then fetched Gail to my study and asked a tutor to see Freddie back to his room the instant the doctor had finished with him. It was reminiscent of the old problem of the farmer who had to cross a river by a two-seat ferry with a fox, a hen and a sack of corn.

Gail was a nice girl: bright, warm-hearted, impulsive and easily led. I had little doubt that, if she were involved in this business, it would be at the urging of her friend Samantha, who was a more determined character of a more committed 'protest' type. Gail was soon in floods of tears and wringing her hands. She strove to be loyal to Sam, but was confused, self-contradictory and, finally, gave what I could only take as 'consent by silence.' I was tough with her because I felt in my bones she wasn't a hardened liar, was only marginally involved in a bit of pot-smoking, and I wouldn't be expelling her. I remembered a powerful essay she had written me last term about a visit she and Sam had paid to a young man who was in a psychiatric hospital after a total breakdown. She had vividly conveyed both her horror and her compassion. Discussing it with her later, I had learned this young man was a friend of Sam, who had urged Gail to accompany her one visiting day. It was an Oxford hospital, and I had learned from Gail that part of the shock it all gave her sprang from Sam's apparent inability to be shocked. I suddenly saw a gleam of light. How blind of me not to have seen it before. I leaned across my desk and barked at Gail: 'And Sam has friends who are hooked, hasn't she? Friends she'd made before she ever came here. That's true isn't it? Answer me: isn't it?'

Gail stared at me wildly, even her sobs suspended. I couldn't afford to lose this advantage.

'And some of these fine friends are so ruined by drugs that they're in psychiatric hospitals. That's right, isn't it? Like that poor young devil you and Sam went to see some months ago. The one whose condition so shattered you, but not Sam. The sort of condition you could get in, my girl. I'm right, aren't I? Aren't I? No good sobbing. I want an answer and I'm determined to get it. I'm right, you know I'm right.'

Her face in her hands, Gail nodded emphatically, repeatedly. I felt a great wave of relief but always at the back of my mind was the fear that one of these silly, desperate kids might do something dreadful, irrevocable. So I applied what comfort I could to Gail's wounds. I told her she had behaved responsibly, hadn't really incriminated Sam, since I as good as knew already what she had told me, and that I believed she herself was so little involved that I didn't see her having to leave us.

Then, while the still wailing and shivering Gail was taken back to her room, I called in Bugs Bunny. He was an American boy, loud, brash and 'difficult,' with a violent temper which earlier that term had impelled him to thrust his bare fist through a glass partition. On the other hand, I had never found him to be a liar. Indeed, half his troubles seemed to spring from his uncompromising honesty, with himself and everybody else. He seemed not to know the meaning of tact, gentleness, forethought, silence. He wasn't very popular with students or tutors, but I rather liked him: he got so mad with himself after each misdemeanour, admitted his faults so savagely, responded to forgiveness and trust so totally.

When I asked him about drugs, he reacted first with stupefaction, then with indignation, finally with a kind of exasperated amusement.

'Look, reverend,' he confided in ultimate candour. 'I've got a kid brother. He thinks I'm one helluva guy. Sort of hero, I s'pose. D'ya think I'd let him have a... a junkie for a big brother? Tellya something else. I've got an uncle. Quite young. He's been put away. Not drugs, an alcoholic. I liked him, he was a kind of hero to me, I guess. And I saw him go to pieces. Like I said, put away, locked up. So what sort of a moron would it make me to go the same way?'

I felt relieved. 'All right, Bugs,' I said, 'go straight back to bed. And don't wake the others up with those big feet or that ear-splitting voice.'

He paused at the door. 'They're all up, reverend. All downstairs in the common room, waiting for me to get back.' He grinned. 'We gotta good grapevine, reverend.'

I found myself grinning. 'Oh, go to bed, you horror. You and your beastly grapevine.'

It was nearly 3 am. We decided to call it a day, or rather, night. If they had such an efficient grapevine there was no point in continuing now. Besides, it would be fairer to all concerned to tackle the others in the morning.

Before turning in, I tiptoed across the lawns and into the girls' cottage. I shone my shaded torch into the room Gail shared with Sam. Both seemed to be sound asleep, breathing heavily. I then crept into the new block where Freddie lived. His roommate was snoring, but my torch revealed a Freddie squatting on his bed, his arms cuddling himself against the cold, his eyes fixed on the faint glow through the Venetian blinds. I searched quite desperately for the right words but could find none. 'Come on, Freddie,' I said lamely. 'Get into bed. Get some sleep.' He lay down. I pulled the chaotic bedclothes over him. 'Good night, Freddie,' I said. 'Night, suh,' he answered. It was the first, and the last, time I ever heard the casual 'sir' pass his lips.

11

I cancelled my class and at ten o'clock the next morning was back at my inquisitorial bench.

I saw Hugh first: a quiet English boy, rather plump, bespectacled, harmless. Anxious to please and to be accepted, I felt that he, like Gail, would be only peripherally involved. And that, like Gail, he would be a poor liar. In fact, he folded up like an old deck chair the moment I sat heavily on him. I told him I had an incriminating document in which his name appeared. It was sufficient grounds not only for expulsion but for police intervention. This was perhaps stretching it, but I felt justified in view of the need for a variety of evidence. Evaluating that evidence would be difficult but by no means impossible.

Hugh's concession to schoolboy codes of honour was minimal, his resistance a mere token. Yes, Sam had said he could join one of their sessions: in the long grass in the churchyard, after supper. Only twice, just smoking cigarettes, 'drugged ones.' Nigel hadn't wanted him, said he was too young, too chicken.

'I expect he meant "too dangerous",' I volunteered, but the irony was lost on Hugh, whose cue now appeared to be 'the bigger the stool pigeon, the bigger the pardon.' He rattled on in an orgy of confession, revelation, recrimination. I took it down more or less verbatim, stopping him only when he was in the third repetitive cycle. How much of it I ought to believe should become apparent later. His exit was almost too good to be true: he paused at the door, all but squinting with ingratiation, to say: 'You won't tell the others I told you anything, will you?'

His 'evidence' had suggested that Sam and Nigel were the leading lights: sponsors of regular pot sessions and members of occasional acid parties. Hugh had said: 'Freddie's the guy who's always got acid. Everyone goes to him for it. Well, I don't think Sam does, but Bugs always gets his from Freddie. Nigel did once, I think.' His own first reefer hadn't done anything for him, the second had made him feel sick, and he'd already pulled out of the clique altogether. No, he'd never taken any acid. Because I'd warned them of the dangers and the consequences. He thought they were stupid to take it. Well, they were stupid anyway: bigheads, show-offs. He'd finished with them.

Hugh, again like Gail, was from a home background unlikely to produce really mixed-up kids. Gail's parents were relaxed, easy-going people, emotional but not repressed. The parent-child relationship struck me as healthily affectionate. Hugh's parents were like Hugh: dull, unimaginative, rather selfish people, with four other children making up a family group probably too loose and too placid to create tensions.

I didn't know much about Bugs' home environment. His father had impressed me as a strong character: possibly too strong, too ambitious, for his little Bunny. Mother I hadn't met, but I had gathered the family unit was still intact, legally, at all events. But Bugs Bunny Senior was a successful diplomat (one clearly in line for an important posting), and the children of diplomats and soldiers tend either to lack roots or to put them down firmly in a terrain distant from their parents. I was disturbed by all Hugh had said about Bugs. Was I so gullible, or Bugs so accomplished a liar?

Sam was actually the daughter of a distinguished psychiatrist of an academic rather than clinical bent. He was of the conventional mid-European background, racily fluent in English, but unmistakeably alien in accent and gesture. His wife was English (I had met her only once, by chance) and she struck me as an unhappy person, lost, unable to cope: with her husband or his work, with her home or her two girls. Not surprisingly, perhaps, the psychiatrist himself seemed remote from his family, overcompensating by means of his multifarious professional activities. He told me his wife had almost from the first showed herself incapable of establishing any rapport with Sam. He smiled wryly as he recounted his family problems, as if belying his professional dogma that diagnosis is nine parts of the cure.

So Sam had become a loner, seeking other loners far from the family hearth. Cannabis was more or less inevitable in her case, I suppose: if a dozen or so encapsulated kids get into a huddle they can achieve the delusion of social communication. (To be fair, the same might be said of most cocktail parties.)

Nigel was the only son of a wealthy businessman of some culture, a patron of the arts and an impressive amateur painter. Nigel had come with an acknowledged background of 'difficulties.' He was very intelligent, well-read, sensitive, sophisticated. He seemed to be the student with the mostest, for he also possessed considerable charm and was, quite literally, 'tall, dark and handsome.' Even his surname of Carruthers was rather ridiculously true to a romantic novel. He had been to several schools. I had seen his reports from all the recent ones and had corresponded with their headmasters. I had also had two long sessions with his psychotherapist, who was almost as anxious that we should take him as Nigel himself was to come to us. I had hesitated long before accepting him: bed-wetting, persistent underachievement, theft, refusal to co-operate, lies upon lies, more theft, truancy... But, significantly, never any insolence, violence, aggressive opting-out, just a quiet, sad withdrawal into himself. All his previous mentors spoke of their affection for him, their regret at losing him.

Why did I take him? Because, of course, I wanted to help him and thought I could. I had questioned Nigel closely about drugs, and he told me he never took anything his therapist hadn't prescribed. The therapist herself felt convinced this was so, that she would be the first to know if it were not.

Nigel had contacted me himself. I had sent him a prospectus, and answered his queries, under the impression that this was a preliminary postal enquiry from a parent. And only after several sessions with Nigel and his therapist had I finally met father, who had deliberately kept out of the picture because he wanted Nigel to feel that *this* school was his very own choice. I liked the father. He was frankly worried about the boy and frankly in need of help. And as soon as I saw him getting out of his car in our drive, I felt I understood a little more of Nigel's problems. For, as I have said, Nigel was not only intelligent, sophisticated, charming, tall and handsome: he was also dark-skinned, and his eyes had the faintest hint of remoter origins. It was obvious that Mr Carruthers was Anglo-Indian and old enough to know something of the tensions inherent in that status. Had Nigel somewhere, somehow, in his first years, unconsciously absorbed some of those tensions? Were all his subsequent misdemeanours trials of the love of those who, he felt, could never totally accept him for himself? I had to recognize that this diagnosis was rather crudely obvious. I never discovered if it was trite because true.

So I now had to confront both Nigel and Samantha, well aware that they knew the screws were on and had had ample opportunity for collusion. I saw Sam first, and with her I tried a different, if less respectable, line.

'Sit down, Sam,' I began affably. 'I know you're intelligent enough to realize full well why I want to see you, and to have your story all prepared. So I'll come to the point at once. I have good reason to think you are taking drugs here, on our premises, in termtime.'

She smiled. 'I know you think that. I don't know why, though. It's quite untrue.'

'Well, it all began with a phone call. From Eddie.' I scanned her face. A trace of concern, guilt? I couldn't be sure.

'He didn't, of course, want to speak to me, but to you or Nigel. Unfortunately, he got me. And announced himself and spoke about "groceries" before he knew who he was speaking to. I didn't at all like the sound of Eddie, Sam.' (Yes, perhaps there were some flickers of alarm.)

'Well, Sam, *do* you know anyone called Eddie? In Oxford? Do you have an account with him? For... groceries?'

She hesitated momentarily. Perhaps she was debating with herself which was wiser: to acknowledge Eddie and legitimize the groceries, or to plead mystification? Wisely, she chose the latter.

'I've never heard of any Eddie. And why should I have a grocery account? I can get all the groceries I want in the village shop.' Then she giggled. I knew that giggle. I had come to hate it. I decided to leave her in midair for a while.

'Well, that's fine then. No Eddie and no groceries. No tea, grass, sugar, nothing. Good.' I smiled at her.

'Is that all?' she asked, seeming for the first time disconcerted.

'For the moment, Sam, yes. Thank you. Of course, I'll be wanting to see you again when I have all my evidence in. There's not much more to come.' And I patted the little wad of notes before me.

She shrugged and went. Tim and I discussed it. We felt she was unlikely to admit anything but also seemed indifferent to our suspicions and her own possible fate. Such indifference was itself symptomatic.

I next saw Nigel, and with him I tried yet another line. Not really as tactics, more because I wanted to be direct with him.

'Nigel,' I said, 'you and I have had many frank talks, even about drugs. I think we respect each other. I hope we like each other. I don't think we've lied to each other. I wonder if you'll lie to me now.'

He looked at me steadily, but he was darkly pale now. 'No,' he said at length, with a considerable effort. 'No, I won't.'

'Thank you,' I replied, though I thought: 'How I wish you would.' For I didn't want to have to expel Nigel, or anyone, for that matter. He needed us, and it's good to be needed. In an odd way, I needed him, needed all these little lost sheep, so that I could feel myself a real, saving shepherd.

'Have you taken drugs here? I mean, illegal drugs, cannabis, LSD?'

'Well...' He faltered. 'Not *here*.'

'No, not in this room. Don't be silly. Perhaps not technically on our premises at all. Let's say: in the long grass, in the churchyard, after supper?'

'You seem to know all about it,' he murmured unhappily.

'That's not the straight answer I want - and you promised.'

He sighed. He looked strangely old for his years now. Only sixteen. 'Yes, I have. Perhaps half a dozen times. In the churchyard, as you say. Now I suppose you're going to expel me?'

It was an appeal, of course. I pretended I hadn't heard it. I kept my eyes fixed on my notes. 'What drugs, Nigel?'

'Pot, cannabis. You know, reefers.'

'And?'

The pause was so long that I repeated my question, looking him in the eyes as I did so. He looked away, shook his head, opened his mouth. I said quickly: 'Don't spoil it, Nigel.'

In place of his denial came, almost inaudibly: 'You know. You know.'

I stood up, said quickly: 'That's all now. Thanks. You can go.' I really couldn't take any more.

We adjourned for lunch, over which we discussed the suspects and their respective performances, and collated all the evidence now to hand. I felt Sam and Freddie and Nigel must go. Gail and Hugh I was inclined to blister with my tongue and suspend for a week. I felt both were rather more sinned against than sinning, and that I myself had sinned against them by putting them into a drugs scene they couldn't cope with. Bugs remained an enigma. I needed to know more. I had also decided to make a point-blank appeal for help to about five senior boys and girls of whose integrity I felt as sure as one can feel of anything or anybody in this world. Promising them, of course, unbroken confidence. Since, however, anybody could find out, merely by traversing the path outside my large study windows, or the hall outside my study door, just which students I had interviewed in the course of my investigations, I knew it was necessary for me to see every boy and girl individually and before the day was out. I asked each one: 'Have you yourself taken drugs here?' and 'Have you anything further you wish to tell me in confidence?' I drew the expected blank from everybody.

Just before supper I had another, and far tougher, session with Bugs. He was, if anything, more convincing than before, finally begging me, as a great favour, to get his father on the phone. 'Ask him if what I said about my kid brother's true. About that uncle of mine, too. Ask him if anybody's ever found me having anything to do with drugs. Get him over here. I'll tell him the same as I've told you. And he'll want to know what bastard here's been telling lies about me. Gee, I'd like to get my hands on the bastard.'

I had so arranged the interviews that my five seniors would be seeing me after supper, interspersed with a few neutral students as a blind. One of the five adamantly refused to say anything, and I couldn't help admiring his stand. The others, to each of whom I recounted in confidence all the evidence I had collected, but not mentioning the sources, proved, after much soul-searching, more helpful. From one I learned that Freddie had arrived at the college with £150-worth of LSD, successfully brought by him from America and through our customs. With this supply he had apparently been quite generous. But the spectacular revelation concerned Bugs. Said one senior boy who lived in the same outlying unit as Bugs: 'Of course he's hooked. I'm surprised you even ask. He gets violent when he's had some. That's how he put his fist through the partition. Once, his friends had to sit on him for a couple of hours, literally.'

'Well,' I sighed, 'I suppose I really am a naive old fool. But if you'd heard him, in this room, yesterday, and again today, not a couple of hours ago, sitting in that chair you're in...'

The student leaned forward and said to me with a kind of exasperated intensity: 'I was in our unit common room, with the others, when he came back this evening. Straight back from that very interview. He told us everything you'd said and he'd said. And then, you know what? He laughed and said: "I was high all the time he was talking to me. But he never guessed."'

Again I went to bed in the small hours, but this time with all my decisions taken. Bugs would join the three expellees. Four cast out and two suspended. Only six weeks after the new school year had started.

At ten the next morning I told the four (individually) that I was expelling them and they were to go and pack while I phoned their parents. I won't recapitulate the pain and distress of those final interviews, those telephone conversations. Bugs and Nigel went off in a taxi to catch a specified train to London, where their parents would meet them. Sam's broken mother collected her after much ado. With Freddie I had greater problems: his father was in Africa, and the London doctor who was named on our registration form as his bona fide guardian in this country flatly refused to take him until I was compelled to deliver an ultimatum: 'As I have said, doctor, I am putting him on the 1.30 from Oxford, which arrives at Paddington at 2.50. I am sending his sister with him. I regard it as your moral and legal duty to meet him and provide for him until his father can be contacted.'

I phoned later in the day to satisfy myself that all had arrived home safely. Hugh and Gail were similarly despatched upon their week's suspension.

Then I addressed all the students, giving them all the facts, warning them once more about drugs abuse. They were silent, stunned, resentful. The general gloom didn't lift for weeks. The old cheerful camaraderie was gone forever.

Bugs Senior flew over from his continental embassy to see me. He said he would sooner believe his son than me and demanded to know the names of his accusers. I said I had every sympathy with his feelings but had no intention of revealing any names. I admitted that I had been so convinced by Bugs myself that I still thought he was two people, probably sincere in his protestations of innocence when he was actually making them. In other words, that he was schizoid. My words didn't help: I was a fool to think they would. A week later I was told that Bugs was haunting the village, and that in the pub he had shown a knife which he declared was for sticking the pig who'd shopped him. I drove out in the dark, found him, told him I'd call the police and have him charged if he didn't get back to London within an hour, then wrote to his father to the same effect. I never heard any more.

I don't know what happened to Freddie, except that he returned to the States. His sister, who was torn apart by it all, stayed with us and fulfilled her promise as a student and as a person.

Nigel and I corresponded for a while. He seemed to have had the right kind of shock at the right moment in his development. I hope things have gone well for him.

Some six months later an officer of the Thames Valley drug squad was talking to me in my study. Suddenly he asked if he could have a closer look at a group photo of the college. He pointed to Sam. 'She's not still with you? I thought not. We know her and her friends only too well.' Poor Sam. I like to think she learned something useful with us.

I never, then or later, heard anything to suggest that I had acted unjustly. I don't think any one of the four could have been helped by remaining within our fold, and I am quite certain they would have corrupted others.

Tilley seemed, as my investigations were drawing to a close, to fear I might bale out so many kids that the financial boat would be rocked to the point of capsize. Even of the four I expelled he remarked uneasily: 'Now be careful, Peter. These are important parents.'

Within two days of the expulsions I sent out an explanatory letter to all parents, to the governors, and to everybody involved in the college. I wrote as follows:

THE MORE WE ARE TOGETHER

From: The Principal, Anglo-American College

November 12th, 1968

Dear Parent,

I feel it is my duty to report to all parents that we have in the past week uncovered cases of drug-taking among the students here, and to tell them of the action I have taken. As you will know, this is a new hazard in education and some of our most respected schools are already suffering badly from it. One small consolation in the whole sorry business here is that we have been small enough to detect it and cut it ruthlessly out of our community. These are the facts:

I warned all students at the beginning of term of the dangers of drug-taking. I told them that I did not countenance any distinction between so-called 'soft' and 'hard' drugs, nor subscribe to any woolly-minded claims that 'soft' drugs are no worse than cigarettes or beer, because (a) the cigarette smoker or the beer drinker is not surrounded by utterly unscrupulous 'pushers' whose sole aim is to get the stupid experimenter off the 'soft' and on to the 'hard'; (b) all drugs interfere with one's ability to study, with their alternating moods of euphoria and depression; (c) they are destructive of moral fibre in that they present the quick and cheap path to pleasure and are a flight from reality; (d) as the law stands at present, *all* such drugs are illegal. I warned them of the dangers not only to themselves but also to the future of this college, and I said that any student detected in drug taking need expect no mercy from us.

You will appreciate that detection is enormously difficult, not only because the symptoms could equally well be due to other causes, but also because the character-rot drugs produce is such that the nicest boys and girls become liars so accomplished and plausible that one is left doubting one's own sanity. Several times this term I have questioned one or two students about whom I was having suspicions but their performances were so consummately convincing that, for lack of anything approaching even circumstantial evidence, I could take no action.

Last week, however, some students not involved volunteered vital information. I then set about interviewing many of the students, and, for the first time in my professional life, I asked boys and girls to 'split' on their fellows. I hated doing it and they hated responding, but after I had explained the gravity of the situation, and had told them that this action was necessary to save the unfortunate individuals from worse addiction, and to save the college, very many of them furnished me with names, times and places. We all owe these students a debt; I know what it cost them to speak up, and I am of course keeping their identities secret. I may add that the names supplied were the same in every case: four students definitely participating and two others probably tolerant onlookers.

As soon as these enquiries were complete (after ten hours of questioning), within twenty-four hours of the first definite information laid, I had expelled the four students: their parents were informed by telephone and they left in taxis the same day. Most lied to the last, but one or two have subsequently admitted much. The other two I have placed on the strictest probation. I think they may well redeem themselves, their chief crime being spinelessness and irresponsibility.

I am now as certain as one can hope to be that we have removed this poison from our midst. I can also say that all four students had formed introductions to drug-taking before coming here. I wish I could say that none had indulged on these premises, but latterly they had extended their activities from a weekend at home to at least one session here. There is also some evidence that one or two of them had already begun to experiment with LSD. I do not need to say how much I sympathize with their parents, and with the pathetic youngsters themselves. I have for some time now made it my practice to ask all prospective parents point-blank if there is any interest in drugs on the part of their offspring, and I also of course check with previous schools. I am prepared to believe that parents and headmasters are as unaware as anybody of these activities, so cunning are these teenagers in concealing their wretched habits.

I will close with the expressed determination that such habits are not being tolerated here in any shape or form. If we had not been able to crack this group on our own I should have had no hesitation in calling in the police, since I would sooner have no college than such a one. I have tightened up on all exeats and informed all students of the situation.

Yours sincerely,

Peter Gamble, Principal

No one quarrelled with the line I had taken. No parent withdrew a child. Many parents, and others, wrote to commend my action. Only Roland, in a mood of somewhat bitter recrimination a year later, referred suddenly to 'That dreadful letter you sent out after you'd expelled the boys and girls: the smug Pharisaism of it, the crocodile tears, the hardness... Oh, you're changing, and not for the better.'

12

In one respect at least I was no Pharisee: I was not displaying my righteousness in public. Quite the reverse. I withdrew more and more into my study shell. I more or less gave up eating in the college dining room and appeared less often in the bar. My late evening visits to students in their units became less and less frequent. I had enjoyed those informal common room chats when the kids brewed coffee and talked freely. I missed them badly, but I felt I was now *persona non grata* to them. The innate horror of inflicting myself where I was not welcome was given free play. I am now quite sure that I got it all out of perspective. Perhaps somewhere in me were unacknowledged depths of guilt and shame. No good telling myself the four expellees had asked for all they got, and it would have been positive misprision on my part to keep them. I couldn't forget that I'd liked them and had cast them out instead of ministering to them. I thought I saw all this confirmed in the vigilant eyes of the remaining students, some resentful, some reproachful.

I ought to have known enough about young people to recognize how mercifully brief is their resentment, how minimal their capacity for imagining adults, too, can feel hurt. I discovered later that very few indeed reacted to me as I believed they did, that several made themselves rather unpopular by too vigorously defending me, that most put the whole scandal behind them with a shrug, and that *all* of them thought I was avoiding them because I disliked them so much.

I had in Oxford bumped into a young man I had taught when he was a very bright and very likeable schoolboy. This Michael (or Mick as he now preferred to be called) had recently graduated at Oxford with a good first in mathematics, and was staying on, he told me, in the hope of admission to a junior fellowship. The great thing, he assured me, was to be seen on the doorstep when these things came up. But he was by now almost completely broke: his grant had dried up and his father (a schoolmaster) couldn't afford to keep him. Could I give him *something*: just full board and pocket money would do? I didn't really want anybody for maths, although most of our A level students in this subject could do with extra help. But I remembered him as a nice person, industrious and responsible. And I also felt we needed more young blood in our faculty: some tutors nearer in age to our students, who could speak to them freely, release through them the moans and groans of which they seemed to have an inordinate supply. So I made a job for him, with the full consent of our resident tutor in maths and physics, and I gave him a good preliminary talk about the possible dangers of his youth in such a place as ours: the obvious danger of getting emotionally entangled with the girls, and the less obvious danger of being pushed into the unhappy position of playing a double game. I gave him a résumé of our basic rules, which I believed to be minimal, necessary and rational, and I assured him the kids would rail against the rules and against me as the source of the rules. His most valuable function, I said, was to act as a pressure reliever, to give a sympathetic ear, but also to justify the rules wherever he could. Where he couldn't himself believe in them, he was free to argue them with me privately, with the staff collectively, and at the weekly meetings of our student council.

My excuse now is that he seemed intelligent, rational and well-disposed. It didn't take long to discover that he was horribly conceited, emotionally immature, had no respect for reason and no inkling that even elementary loyalty was due to the place supplying him with excellent living conditions and very much more than pocket money. He spent all his spare time in the girls' private common room, to such an extent that they told me it was embarrassing. They couldn't move from bedroom to bathroom without meeting him. I told him of this as nicely as I could. Very nicely he assured me he quite understood, and did nothing at all to rectify matters. He then asked me if he could take a couple of our girls to a Saturday evening party in Oxford. After much enquiry into the circumstances of this party I refused. The girls, of course, sulked and he himself took the decision with little better grace. I was careful to see that the girls did *not* go, for I felt they and he would have no compunction about disobeying if they felt they could get away with it. But one Sunday, two or three weeks later, I noticed that both girls had been given weekend exeats, stating on their forms that they were staying overnight at the home of one of them. Nothing unusual in that, and it could be mere coincidence that young Mick had also had a rare weekend away. A phone call revealed that one of the girls had indeed gone home as stated. I spoke to her mother, who told me Daphne had arrived home at the usual time on Saturday and was in fact still in bed then (it was about noon on Sunday). However, she had brought no friend with her, nor had ever suggested she would. The two girls returned to the college together at the proper time that evening, and clearly worried about my phone call.

I eventually got the truth out of them. Daphne had been used as a cover by her friend Judy, who had in fact gone to an all-night Oxford party with the ineffable Mick. I sent them to bed, promising them they'd hear more the next day, and sat up to intercept Mick as soon as he crossed the threshold. That was at 2 am, and he clearly didn't want a chat at that hour. But I insisted. He gave me all the expected lies until he found I knew the truth, and then he changed to a rather juvenile pretence at defiance. Finally he said: 'I don't see why Judy and I shouldn't please ourselves. She's sixteen.' I realized that in his conceit he really couldn't see himself as dispensable. Or he banked heavily on my (real enough) distaste for all the troubles and chores involved in sacking a tutor in mid-term. Rather to my own surprise, and to his stupefaction, I found myself saying: 'So you don't see why? Probably, you will never see why. And I can't any longer risk this place while I probe you for signs of better nature. So you'll kindly pack and be out of here by nine o'clock tomorrow morning. I'll order you a taxi for that time. Perhaps the best thing would be for you to go home and start looking for a job. But I expect you'll prefer to rejoin your lively friends in Oxford. That's up to you. You have three weeks' salary due to you. The bursar will give you this before you leave in the morning'.

'You - you can't do that,' he blurted out.

'Why not? It's as easy as what you did. And one other thing: don't you make any effort to contact any students before you leave. You've done enough damage. No doubt Judy's parents will take effective measures to prevent you seeing her again'.

'I - I can't pack and leave by nine. I - I *won't*.'

I felt I must bring this interview to a speedy end, for he was getting quite human and likeable again. 'If you aren't out by nine,' I said, in tones meant to be ominously dulcet, 'I'll call the police and have you put out for trespassing.' He looked at me wildly and for a moment I thought he was going to call my bluff. But all he said was: 'You old bastard!'

It was such a comical remark, and it was so refreshing to see him reacting naturally after the five weeks of pretentious posturing to which he'd treated us, that I found my perverse inner voice (or goblin or angel?) whispering its usual enormities: '*Couldn't* you keep him somehow? Won't he be OK now?'

Fortunately he lurched out after firing his naughty shot. And he left at nine in the taxi I ordered. About six months later I saw his name in the local press as one of a dozen or so young people charged with drugs offences after a police raid on a house in Oxford. Probably the same house and the same friends he'd introduced Judy to.

I seriously considered sacking Judy, too, but felt she was more sinned against than sinning. I suspended her for two weeks, gated Daphne for a month, and tried to get both of them to see how nasty the outcome might have been perhaps: even a corpse by a river bank. Judy assured me she'd slept in a big bed with two other girls and 'nothing ever happened.' I'm sure this was true. I could believe it even if she'd slept in the big bed with two boys. I think it's very often the grosser adult mind which assumes a wild sexual promiscuity in the student population because it is baffled by the earnestness with which such young people cultivate physical proximity, tactile 'language' and overt displays of casual affection.

And, as usual, I made painstaking efforts to explain the whole matter to the college at large and to invite their views. As usual, too, those who in whole or in part agreed with me said nothing at all, and those who didn't could express nothing but a frankly irritated attitude on the lines of 'nasty-boss-man-spoils-our-fun-and-denies-our-rights-again.'

I wanted as much democracy as the situation permitted. I enjoyed and valued discussion with faculty and students. It was obvious that any decision reached by common consent stood a far better chance of being implemented. Indeed, my prolonged quest for student participation began to irritate some of the staff and, eventually, many of the students. The student council met weekly with me, John Tilley, Tim Clark, Arthur Brooke and any other staff who cared to attend. Tim's minutes of these meetings make rather depressing reading. Many of the kids' ideas I knew could never work in our set-up. Some of them we had tried and found impractical. A few I had offered to try if the student council would take responsibility for their smooth working (and usually they had refused the offer). The basic trouble was simply that they felt I was playing at democracy and, when it came to the crunch, never allowed it. I then once more embarked on my tedious spiel: I had never at any time offered them full democracy and had no intention of doing so in a situation where one and only one person was finally answerable for everything to everybody. But I did want the greatest measure of democracy I could get within that set-up, the measure being closely related to the measure of their own sense of responsibility.

Their idea of a student council's function was to demand more and more self-determination while leaving the total weight of responsibility squarely on my shoulders. Their idea of democracy was capitulation to a militant minority who themselves revealed their innate contempt for democracy by declaring all discussion useless, all confrontation a waste of time. Rereading the minutes I am surprised to see how rare and timid and tentative were the contributions of the reasonable majority of the council, how obsessed the few militants are with grabbing-without-giving, how many of their proposals were in fact adopted, and (to tell the truth) how astonishingly patient I was in setting out the reasons for any refusal!

13

Spring that year seemed to be uncommonly imbued with nostalgia, lyricism, romanticism. Or perhaps I was in my new status abnormally deprived of affection and idealism. At any rate my thoughts seemed to play repeatedly around Carl Janssen and the deeply-scored events of twenty years before. He would be entering his upper thirties now. What was he like, in appearance and in character? Did he remember our relationship with pleasure or with disapproval, or, more likely, now scarcely remember any of it? Was he married? Had he children? I felt I must ask, even if the response was cold silence, or a brusque rebuttal. I found from his telephone directory that he lived in the same house, his parents' house where they had entertained me, although now he was presumably the householder.

So I wrote, factually, apologetically. I said: 'If this letter is unwelcome, and you ignore it, I shall quite understand.' A very few days brought a reply. (Oh, how well I knew that handwriting; how my heart once leapt to behold it; how it leaped now!) He wrote warmly, even excitedly. When could we meet?

My reply was as prompt and as glowing. I proposed we have dinner ten days hence in the town's newest and grandest hotel, in which I should be staying for the night. I warned him that the years had marked me down, so that he might not know me. I should be seated in the cocktail lounge at 6 pm clutching a *New Statesman*.

Promptly he came in and my first incredulous impression was how little he had changed. He was slim and he was very handsome, and his opening comment to me as he advanced with hand outstretched took the very words out of my mouth: 'You haven't changed at all. I'd have known you anywhere.'

In no time at all we had erased the intervening years and were chatting as freely as ever. And after a while I felt able to ask what I eagerly wanted to know: 'Do you bear me any ill will? I mean, did I harm you in any way?'

He opened his eyes then knit his brow. 'Harm me? What do you mean? What harm?'

'Well,' I said, finding it for once difficult to phrase my thoughts. 'Well, the world would think I was a bad influence on you, surely.'

His face and his voice changed. There was a surprising bitterness, almost scorn, in them as he mouthed: '*The world*... The world's just a lousy hypocrite.' I wondered how the world had hurt him to cause such a judgment.

We took three hours over our dinner, reliving, reassessing, amplifying all that had been. He learned for the first time the Hon Head and Jimmy saga.

'Gee, I'm sorry,' he said.

'Good Lord,' I replied. 'It was all my fault. I was lucky to emerge so unscathed.' And what a burden of sorts had now been lifted to know that not then, or ever since, had he felt guilt or regret regarding our relationship.

He was now quite a tough businessman. I gathered it from his conversation before he described himself as such. He was also a connoisseur of wine. He brought me a rare vintage claret.

His childless marriage had ended in divorce some three years before. He hoped to remarry very soon. I walked from the hotel to his house with him. Outside that well-remembered portal through which a scandalized parent had thrust him long ago, he said: 'Do come in. I live alone.' But I said: 'No. Forgive me. It's late and we both have busy days tomorrow.' I paused and looked at him as I held his hand. 'I'll just add this, if I may. You're remarkably well preserved. And... you're still a dear fellow.'

He laughed and said: 'Nice to hear one's well preserved. But I'm certainly not a dear fellow.'

About two years after that reunion, Carl phoned me to ask how I was and, he explained, to ask a favour. 'Peter, you remember I married again about two years ago? Well, I've just had a son.' I told him I was delighted to hear it. He went on: 'Is it OK if we christen him Peter, after you?' I told him it was probably the nicest thing that had happened to me. I still think so.

That happened over twenty years ago. We have met only twice since: both very happy occasions, of reminiscing and chaffing and political arguments. (I was pleased to find he still on occasions growled.) Otherwise it's just Christmas cards, but prompt, and affectionately inscribed. I have never seen Carl's wife or children. When young Peter was the age Carl was when we walked the moors together, I did wonder. But no: unlike Gide's Edouard, I was not '*curieux de voir le petit Caloub.*'

Things at home were gloomier. Pam, we all knew but didn't acknowledge, was an alcoholic. Her descent was at first gradual enough, but one event in particular accelerated it. That was the death of Emil. We had to have her put down when age and infirmity no longer made life the joyous gift it had been. Bob had the rotten job of supervising the vet's visit. Just before he came, I murmured a few words in Emil's ear. I told her there was a new life to come in which we'd all be happily reunited. Her ghost of a tail-wag may have signified her assent.

Pam went out on the day Emil was put down. She couldn't be there when the vet arrived with his lethal equipment. I knew where Pam had gone: to the local pub. I had just once seen her there, and it was an unforgettably painful picture. She sat on a high stool at the bar and people avoided her. She whom men had courted for so many years was now shunned as an embarrassment. I bottled up the tears I could have shed for her.

One Saturday, she called at Stanmore with Nik, and they went off in the car to do some shopping mother wanted. (All this I heard later, for I was at school.) She brought back the shopping and settled Nik down with a painting book and a large box of paints she had bought him. She then said she'd forgotten something: she wouldn't be a moment, and there was no need to take Nik. But it was more than a moment, and mother's suspicions grew. At first she thought she had gone to the pub. But something (mostly, perhaps, the unusual gift of paints) made her fear otherwise. With great presence of mind she phoned Pam's next door neighbours in Edgware and asked them if Pam's car was in the drive. It was. Mother then at once phoned the police and asked them to call at the house, where she suspected a suicide attempt.

The police broke in. She was lying in front of the drawing room gas fire. They only just saved her. Beside her was a note for Bob. It said: 'I have no wish to live on and be a burden to you all. I'm not in the least afraid of dying. (But I don't like to think of anyone else having you!) Brian and Peter will have Nik. Love, Pam.'

I went to see her in hospital. She looked awful. I told her she could have treatment for the drink problem: I had heard wonderful stories of complete cures. She smiled disbelievingly. Then, with something of her old sense of ridicule, she whispered: 'Look at the person in the next bed. Surely it's a man. But in a women's ward?' I looked at the poor, senile creature. Pam added: 'No, it must be an aged, balding lesbian. I wish we could hear her speak.'

The doctor at the hospital told me he would try to conceal that it was a suicide bid (in those days, a criminal offence). I took Nik back to my school with me, for Bob's work took him away for much of the time, and even when Pam was home again we felt she was no longer capable. She was glad to hand him over, for she knew she could not look after him. He lived with me in my school house, and I fixed him up as a day boy in a pre-prep school in Burford. I had all the domestic care of him, and Brian all the other care. I washed him and bathed him and dressed him and fed him. I heard all his news and I read to him at bedtime. Last thing at night I cut his sandwiches for school next day. Brian took him to school and fetched him home again. He took him out on his half-days, and I took him home to Bob and Pam and mother at weekends. And Brian took him on wild camping holidays all over Europe in the long summer vacations. I remember his form mistress saying to me: 'Oh, he is such an entertaining little fibber. He described to me his summer holidays. All about camping with his uncle in Italy, living in a tent in all sorts of places, and drinking in bistros till ten at night. Oh, such stories.' I of course concealed from her that the stories were undoubtedly true.

One weekend I took him as usual to Stanmore. Bob was home that Saturday, and until Sunday lunchtime, so Nik slept there, and Pam was to bring him over to me at teatime on Sunday, when we had to set out on our return journey to Oxford. But at four o'clock Pam phoned me in tears to say she had set out to bring Nik to me, but she felt unwell and couldn't continue. Could I come and fetch Nik? They were parked by the roadside some way off.

I went and found them. I stopped behind them and sat in her car with them. I begged her to come back with Nik and me. A change of scene, some company, my work: all this would do her good. She looked at me incredulously. She even laughed at the very idea. I was seated beside her, my hand resting on the gear lever of her car. Suddenly, she put her hand on top of mine and squeezed it. 'Thanks,' she said. 'But I'll be all right.' I mention this, a stark, clear memory, because as an undemonstrative family we had never touched one another. That affectionate hand pressure in that car on that afternoon was a unique and unforgettable experience.

I followed her as she drove slowly and shakily home. She parked the car in her drive. She kissed Nik, which was certainly not her custom. I made her promise that she 'wouldn't do anything stupid.' We both knew what I meant.

She stood at the door of her house waving us out of sight. Three days later, on a Wednesday in November, Bob phoned me at ten in the evening. It was some time before he could speak, but before ever he did I knew exactly what he had to tell me. He had just arrived home to find Pam dead in her bed. There was no note this time. Just a two-thirds emptied bottle of gin on the floor beside her.

I went for a long walk that night, along desolate moonlit lanes over which snowflakes blew. I didn't want anyone to see the state I was in.

Life to Pam had always been laughter, and when the laughter had to stop, she stopped the life. By so doing she extinguished in me a light that has never rekindled.

I think Pam kept her promise. Her end was not suicide. She choked to death, and her doctor (who liked her) put down cancer of the throat as the cause of death.

I had the dread task of breaking the news to Nik. I had to do it before the next weekend when he was expecting to see her. He was only eight.

One grey afternoon we were seated in front of a log fire in my study. He had just come in from school and we were having tea together. He liked making toast with a long fork he held to the fire. I said to him: 'What became of Emil?' A sudden impulse gave me that opening, but I had no idea how he would reply. He said: 'She went to Heaven.' I wondered who had dressed Emil's passing in such terms. Probably Bob. I was grateful for the phrase. I said: 'Well, the same thing has happened to Pam. She had been ill, you know.'

He didn't cry, or even register disbelief. He paused thoughtfully for a few moments, then said: 'That's very sad.'

We talked about it just as much as he wanted to. Then I took him to Brian's garage, where he was as usual tinkering with one of his old bangers. With our eyes he asked if I had told him, and I said I had. I left him with Brian for a few hours, feeling that to be busy and not companioned by the fatal messenger would be the best treatment for him.

After I had put him to bed, I returned quietly several times to listen outside his door. I wanted to know if there was any delayed shock. I heard what it crucifies me afresh to record. He was talking aloud. 'It wasn't my fault, was it, Pam? I wasn't a bad boy, was I?'

Next day I took him to a bicycle shop and let him choose a junior bike he could ride all over the school grounds. It was a splendid medicine. And some time later Brian bought him his first long-trousered suit. It was dark blue corduroy, and, like Julien in his uniform long ago, he looked very good in it. At any rate Brian and I thought so. He himself was not so sure.

Then I had to find him another school, for the happy little pre-prep didn't keep boys older than nine. I managed to get him into Christ Church Cathedral School, Oxford, a school I had long earmarked for him. But that meant he had to board, for it was too far for Brian to fetch and carry him each day. This was my next agony. He cried when I left him on his first day and I could scarcely speak for the lump in my own throat. I told him I'd fetch him on Saturday for his weekend at home, for he was a weekly boarder. 'It's already Tuesday. Saturday will be here in no time. And you've lots of other boys to play with. You'll soon make friends.' I kept up the empty patter that so many broken mothers have mouthed. But I wasn't a mother. Not even a father. And he said nothing, just gazed at me with eyes large and wet with reproach. Once again I had to walk, walk for ages along the narrow back streets of Oxford until I'd recovered some composure. I was grieving not only for him, but (I knew well) also for myself: I was going to miss him more than he would miss me.

Of course, he did more or less settle down, and with merciful speed. He wasn't a good pupil. So many times I had to visit the school to reason with form masters and placate the headmaster. I was terrified they would ask me to take him away. He wasn't badly behaved, just always in little scrapes that disappointed him and his teachers. Nor was he any good at his lessons. Like Miles, he was not at all academic, nor (to my sorrow) at all literary. I never knew either of them to curl up with a book. The ups and downs of their childhoods, plus the floodgates of television that soon engulfed Nik, saw to that. Yet the same causes have given both of them a resilience, even a certain toughness, that has ensured survival.

After two years at Christ Church, I got him into the junior house of a minor public school in Gloucestershire. I did this because I knew that such an arrangement would provide him with an education for as long as was necessary.

At his public school Nik at last showed some signs of self-confidence and stability. He seldom if ever mentioned Pam, to me at any rate. I felt he bottled her up within him. Perhaps he spoke of her to his father, for he and Bob were extremely fond of each other. I can say with my hand on my heart that I was very glad about this and did all I could to encourage it. The same was true of Brian. But it was also true, and I was aware of it and pushed it to the back of my mind, that Nik was being brought up in a world and in a fashion Bob had never known. He never visited Nik at any of his rather posh schools, and all he could do was laugh rather sadly when Nik told him that a little girl at his pre-prep who was his special friend had a daddy who was a lord. (This was not one of Nik's romances: I had to take Nik to their place when he was invited to the little girl's birthday party.) Perhaps, I mused, the day would come when Nik saw and suffered from the difference between his school and his life with father.

On mother's lips, too, the name of Pam was seldom if ever heard. Yet she must after a lifetime of companionship have grieved silently, even if her temperament bade her see alcoholism as sheer weakness and suicide as sheer selfishness.

14

In recounting anecdotes about errant tutors and feckless students one risks giving a distorted picture. Each little drama rocked our small community at the time, and even in retrospect each tends to stick out like a sore thumb, but communities have a tough survival instinct and even a sore thumb leaves one with nine efficient digits. That proportion is about right, too: only one tutor or student in ten proved calamitous. The rest of the tutors (including several young ones) ranged from good to outstanding; the rest of the kids ran the gamut from half-broken colt to Derby winner. And most of the time we lived together in a state more positive than uneasy truce, less dynamic than common resolve. More happy and busy than not.

It was about this time that an old friend and one-time pupil gave us the benefit of his professional advice.

Peter Lander, founder and managing director of ManPlan, the marketing consultants, conducted an exhaustive enquiry into our assets, liabilities, commitments and prospects, finally producing a most impressive set of tables that would enable us, at any stage of our growth, to ascertain our viability, maintain a realistic contingency fund, and become aware at an early stage of any danger signals. He charged us nothing for this generous help, with which Tilley in particular seemed delighted. Arthur, the bursar, and I gazed at it askance, I'm afraid. We used it for a while but it proved fearsome in its accuracy and honesty. It's no good seeing danger signals if you lack the courage or means to deal with them. So I rather did a Moses with Peter's inexorable tablets of the law. 'If you'd really applied them,' he said to me on several occasions afterwards, 'you'd probably be still in business.' Perhaps. My own feeling is still mild astonishment that, starting with no capital and expanding as lavishly as we did, we should have endured so long.

It was now early June and only three weeks to the end of term. Under the pressure of public exams and their own imminent release from *in statu pupillari* bonds, some of the older students were kicking over too many traces. Knowing how they needed nursing through this period, I appealed to them to be sensible, not blot the last page of their copybooks, not drive me into some action which would upset all of us. I turned a blind eye to much that was of a less serious nature. Some things (a couple of boys rolling drunk one night, a boy and a girl roaring round the countryside on a motorbike in the small hours of the morning) I penalized more gently than I might otherwise have done. I dared to hope we could come through the last week or so without disaster.

Then Perdy did it. Perdy was a friendly, scatty, almost amoral American girl whom you couldn't help liking. The boys liked her, especially. But she was proving more and more of a headache. A responsibility, too, with a father no longer living and a mother resident in America. One weekend she'd fail to go where her exeat form claimed she was going, one night she'd be missing from her room from 11 till 3 am. But she was either brilliant at covering her tracks or had the devil's own luck.

One evening I spent two hours talking to her like a Dutch uncle, and the apparent cause of all her ills emerged. She had adored her father and was his own special favourite. She had suffered acutely when, as quite a small child, she had overheard her parents' frequent quarrels. She blamed her mother for these and tried by every means to make up to her father for the affection his wife denied him. The situation was aggravated by her father's serious and prolonged illness. Perdy saw herself as official nurse and resented the laudable efforts of her mother and the resident nursing sister to make her lead a normal life, attend to her studies, go out with her friends. Her schoolwork began to suffer, her teachers to complain. Mother decided she must go to boarding school and her father, too, tried to get her to see this was best for her.

'But I knew,' she sobbed, 'I knew he didn't really want me to go. And I felt so sure he'd never get better without me there to look after him. But they *made* me. It was horrible. Just like taking someone off by force, to prison or something.'

She wrote letters daily to her father, most of which her mother never showed him. 'She opened them and read them herself and burned them. She said they were selfish, all about *me* and how unhappy *I* was, and she said they'd just have made Daddy worse. And I suppose they might have done, though I never meant that, I was only unhappy because I knew he was unhappy and wanting me to talk to him and read to him.'

At last she ran away from the school and went home. Before her mother could stop her she had rushed into her father's room and into his arms, and only when her first passion had subsided did she realize how appallingly changed he was, how weak and emaciated. She stayed at home that night, and that night her father died.

I remember vividly that harrowing two hours in my study: harrowing but stimulating, too, for I knew, I could see, that the very process of getting all this out of her system was a healing agony. At certain points of her narrative the child was so upset that I feared the vomiting might be physical as well as psychological. She more or less picked the braiding from the arm of the antique chair, and I hadn't the heart to tell her so.

She said she had flatly refused to return to her boarding school: if they sent her back a hundred times she'd only run away again. So they decided on a total change of environment as the best means of rehabilitation. She'd once been to England, had happy memories of that holiday, had an aunt and cousins here, and wanted to get away from home and all its associations.

That was how she'd come to us. But, it seemed, neither space nor time had healed as they should, partly because the memories she carried were too bitter, but mostly owing to the incredible, crass stupidity of her mother and elder brother.

'You see, Mom's always said Daddy wouldn't have died that night if I hadn't run in to him and upset him. But... oh, I didn't upset him, I really, really didn't upset him. I'm sure I made him happy. He was so glad to see me. And if his heart was so bad he couldn't have lived, could he? But Mom still says things like it when she writes to me. If I've not had good reports, or you've written to them about me, and I know, I know, I'm stupid and do silly things, then they say things like "Remember what you did to Daddy and try to behave yourself." And last week, Barry, my brother - he's very clever and a college professor - he sent me a horrible, horrible letter.' Then she unfolded and read from a damp wad of paper from her pocket: 'I hope heart disease isn't hereditary, otherwise the shock of your school reports Mom's just sent me will add another victim.'

She ripped the sheets of the letter apart and stuffed them back in her pocket. 'I didn't kill my Daddy, did I? Oh, did I?' All her fingers crammed into her distorted mouth, her red eyes horribly protuberant, she seemed to be tearing my reassurance from my heart.

I talked long, gently, deeply. About her dead father. About death. About love. About life. In the end she was calm, strong, smiling. I told her she'd had a raw deal but it was now in the past. She mustn't ever again use it as an excuse for silly, selfish behaviour which could only hurt her far worse than it could hurt mother or brother. I told her she had already half won the battle by getting all this out of her system and she must win the other half by talking just as frankly in any future moments of stress, to me, or to any of us. She promised she would. She said she'd say her prayers as soon as she got into bed and she knew, she just knew, she was going to have nice dreams that night. I think all my paternal feelings were stirred. I remember that, in saying goodnight, I kissed her forehead and added: 'God bless you.'

The next morning I wrote at length to both Mom and big brother. I was gentle but firm. It surprised me that they had not told me all this background history when they brought Perdy for interview, and it more than surprised me that they could ever be so cruel or so stupid as to suggest she was in any way responsible for her father's death. However, I concluded: 'All's well that ends well, for we have managed to objectify all her self-lacerating guilts and fears, and I now look for every co-operation in developing her many good qualities.'

About ten days later I had a reply from Perdy's brother, thanking me for all we were doing for her and saying that he and his mother would be coming to England soon and hoped for a long talk with me.

THE MORE WE ARE TOGETHER

Perdy kept to the straight and narrow for a while. Then several sums of money were missed and all the evidence pointed to her as the culprit. After another long, upsetting interview she finally confessed, though insisting it was all a joke, a diversionary drama: she was going to give it all back, because she hadn't needed any of it. This worried me a great deal. It was true that she had a very generous allowance, and such merely 'sick' stealing is indicative of personality problems that require the analyst's expertise and patience. So, very reluctantly, in view of all that had gone before, I told Perdy she must go, but that she could leave quietly towards the end of term, providing she gave no further trouble.

The following day, two of the most responsible students brought me a petition, signed by every student (for Perdy was almost as popular with the girls as with the boys), begging me to reconsider, to give her another chance. I met all the students (only Perdy being absent) and discussed the affair with them at some length. One and all were convinced that it *had* been a joke on her part. They spoke of her value as a popular community member, of her real efforts to do well, of her love for the college, of her various family disasters. I replied with similar frankness, freely acknowledging the credit items they had enumerated and trying to show them something of the debit column. I said nothing about the 'family disasters' they'd referred to, feeling this was too confidential, but I asked them to try to understand the responsibility they were asking me to shoulder in retaining her. I had already decided what I would then say and I said it:

'I don't think there's any virtue in sticking stubbornly to a decision after any shadow of doubt has arisen in your mind. There's no question of anyone losing face, no idea in my head that it's bad for me to do an about-turn on such an important matter as this. You *have* raised a doubt in my mind. I do respect you for bringing me this petition. And I like Perdy as much as you do, and want to help her as much as you do. It's simply this: will you share with me the responsibility of keeping her? I mean, really, seriously share it by giving her your creative friendship, your constructive help and advice all the time, encouraging her to discipline herself and raise her standards? None of which you can do without disciplining yourselves and raising your own standards. Can you? Will you?'

The response was immediate, universal and wholly sincere. 'Then I rescind my decision. She stays: on probation to all of us.'

I felt much happier, not only about Perdy, but about all of them. Alas for the gulf between spirit and flesh. Only a week later I caught two boys red-handed in Perdy's bedroom at 3 am. Perhaps they *were* 'only drinking coffee and larking about': that, now, was not even the main point. I expelled both boys, which really meant very little since only two weeks remained of their final term and I was allowing them to come back to sit a remaining A

380

level each. Perdy's mother and brother had arrived in England and were due to visit me in two days. I had the unpleasant task of phoning their hotel in London to say that they must take Perdy away with them, for good.

The students were especially sulky and resentful. It was easy, but unhelpful, to say that they felt guilty, too.

But it was left to Mom and Barry to add those finishing touches that converted the little drama from pathos by way of farce to something like tragedy. For Perdy had dreamed up all the tale with which she had harrowed my soul during those two late night hours. Her father had been killed in an automobile accident when she was two. She could scarcely remember him at all, though Mom and Barry still keenly lamented a good husband and father. For a wild moment I wondered if I could accept *their* story. But it was impossible to doubt these two sane and sorrowing people in front of me: especially Barry, who impressed by his intelligence and integrity. (Afterwards, too, the relatives in England confirmed it all to me.)

This made Perdy at once more intriguing, formidable, frightening. I was glad to see the forlorn trio drive away. I felt Perdy had a great future as an actress or a romantic novelist.

The students were due to have an end-of-year barbecue dance the following Saturday. We had all been working busily and happily on this for several weeks. Now one of the most senior boys came to me to say that in view of all the expulsions they wanted to cancel the whole thing. 'Certainly,' I said, 'it was for your pleasure. If you don't want it we're saved a lot of time, trouble and expense.' It was a cheap enough attempt at insouciance. But how else could I react?

At last came what I had for some time been thinking was likely: the sad rift between me and the Tilleys. Roland and Van Engert laboured long and hard to heal it but to no avail. The Tilleys saw me as far too rigid a disciplinarian whose growing number of expulsions was a sure recipe for total economic collapse. So we decided to part. The Tilleys told us we had to leave Alvescot at the end of the present academic year.

I was then introduced by a wellwisher to the Revd John Underwood. I liked him, as I think he liked me. He was a gentle but ambiguous soul: often frank, but sometimes oddly reticent, often very vague, but sometimes disconcertingly practical. Several meetings followed. I found him less of a mystery, more of a puzzle. He seemed to want me to solve him, and to enjoy my difficulty in doing so. His passion was music, to which he wanted to devote himself (he was no mean pianist), and our tastes here coincided most agreeably. I lent him records, he played me Schubert on his concert grand, we went to *Götterdämmerung* together.

I told him the story of the college from its arrival at the Tilleys to their rejection of it only yesterday. He proved almost as good an audience as

Desdemona, seeming to like me for the dangers I had seen, as I liked him that he did pity them. And if I wasn't quite such an opportunist as Othello, I was now less sensitive than I had been when it came to talking money. I had decided that perhaps there *was* something worth salvaging.

And we had a property in view. This was the impressive Barcote Manor. Its position amid 83 acres and on the Great Golden Ridge that runs from Swindon to Oxford, was one of unquestionable splendour.

Barcote had been, for us, a name to conjure with long before it became a living presence. There had been an independent boarding school for boys there until two years previously. I've no reason to think it wasn't a good one, its ideals real enough, if conventional. It had collapsed suddenly, leaving debts and ill will in the locality. Two of the boys from there had come on to us, and people had often sung to me the praises of Barcote.

Tim Clark had seen it and pronounced it ideal for our purposes. Arthur was equally enthusiastic. I went over one fine, hazy June afternoon: hot, but with a threat of thunder and cooler, darker days to come. I drove in, with Roland (then over for his Summer vacation), between the great stone pillars supporting massive wrought-iron gates. A long, winding driveway led us first between sheep-decked fields, then amid giant trees of all varieties, homely and exotic, a positive arboreal feast. A last, sharp twist between high banks and there, rather dramatically, was Victorian lead, iron and timber, laid out expansively in a great L. Behind the base of the L was a sober ornamental garden. Adjoining the longer arm were two handsome courtyards enclosed by stables, storelofts and a three-storied residential wing. Any suggestion of merely vulgar size or ostentatious display was entirely absent. It had clearly been built for the comfort and perpetuation of a large family and its army of servants. There was no sound but a medley of birdsongs. Nothing moved but these singers and a resentfully lolloping convention of rabbits on the lawn. We entered the house: straight into the great vestibule with its splendidly carved chimneypiece and unforgettable hand-tooled wall coverings.

Roland took to it all instantly. I was rather less enthusiastic, I remember. Houses speak to those who can hear. The older the house and the more dramatic its story, the more it has to say, though sometimes its vocabulary must be slowly learned. There was nothing hostile about this house, nothing remotely evil. But it was, to me, unmistakably a sad house. It suggested a melancholia bred of too many comings and goings, ends and beginnings, of too much hope lost in resignation, dream dying into unfriendly day. Perhaps I'm falsifying my first impressions, colouring them too strongly with what I subsequently learned of its history. However that may be, it was certainly not love at first sight between Barcote and me. But it grew on me: grew with each visit I paid it while still an alien with no real hope of possession.

BUFFETINGS, CHAPTER FOURTEEN

But what a Marie Celeste we seemed to have boarded on that first visit! The place was fully furnished: all the staterooms with the original period furniture, all the others with desks, chairs and blackboards or those auctioned lots that fill the common rooms of schools. On one desk was an exercise book, open at a boy's unfinished composition; on a blackboard some idle graffiti; on a wall, in red chalk, a brutal 'Goodbye and good riddance'; and, somehow saddest of all, on a bedside locker a mug half-filled with green-mantled cocoa.

In what had been the headmaster's study were other relics: stacks of his prospectuses, school rules, clothing lists, fixture cards. All the paraphernalia of school administration, all compiled (how well I could imagine it) with such high hopes, awaited from the printers with such excitement, distributed with such quiet satisfaction. So much that was of purely personal relevance or sentimental value had been left behind that the order to abandon ship must have come as a bolt from the blue. Or perhaps there had been no warning at all and disaster had rained on them like pumice on Pompeii. Only a gallant and prescient Major Hutchings appeared to have made a last-ditch bid to defend his property, sticking upon a pompier watercolour and to the back of an attractive prie-dieu labels so smudged and thumb-marked and slap-dashed they spoke horrible volumes: 'THIS ARTICLE IS THE PERSONAL FAMILY PROPERTY OF MAJOR ED. WM. HUTCHINGS. HE WILL COLLECT IT. DO NOT REMOVE. *PLEASE.*'

Yet it wasn't this scholastic graveyard that I found dispiriting. It was rather the house itself, so fuscous in appearance, so elegiac in mood. In a drawer I found a short history of the mansion, nicely printed at the instigation of the vanished headmasters. I scanned the first few pages.

In 1870, a young man who had arranged to get married began building his dream house. Nothing is known of him except that his name was Raleigh, and that his plans were never brought to fruition because his fiancée jilted him and he left the district in despair.

On his abandoned foundations, I learned as I read on, a Lady Theodora Guest (daughter of the Duke of Westminster) had erected the house we now stood in. She had spent eight years and ten thousand on it, lived in it for a few months, decided she didn't like it and never darkened its doors again. Then a wealthy man called West (head of the Great Western Railway) moved there from London and he and his family stayed there for many years.

'Do you know,' I mused to Roland, unaware he had wandered off and I was addressing the empty air, 'do you know that if, by some miracle, we do get this place, we shall be moving in exactly a hundred years after this young Raleigh laid the stones all this stands on?' My too ready imagination saw Raleigh bubbling with enthusiasm, directing with his ivory-topped cane the dour labourers who secretly despised him.

383

I was quite glad to get out into the sunshine again. We surveyed the whole place from a nearby knoll. It seemed to be in excellent condition within and without, though empty for two years or more. A mercantile bank had acquired it in 1951 as a possible retreat in the event of war, had stored many of their records there, but had moved out in 1964 when they leased the house and its grounds to the school that died so soon.

I made a conscious effort *not* to become involved with the house, for I was convinced we hadn't a hope of ever acquiring it, and I was sick to death of carting my pipe dreams round splendid mansions in rolling acres. We had paid a silly, token £25 to the local agents to secure first option to purchase. But the agents had insisted that the bank who owned it would not again consider leasing it, nor were they interested in leaving any of the purchase price on mortgage. Was there, I had asked, any point in my seeing them to discuss the matter? 'None whatsoever,' the agents had assured me. 'They are adamant in seeking an outright sale. Never another lease. Once bitten, you know.' The asking price was £30,000, and a mere £500 for the entire contents. This was certainly a bargain, but £30,000 on the nail was as far beyond our hopes as three million would have been.

15

We settled down to what was obviously going to be, for all concerned, a very difficult exercise in temporary coexistence of Anglo-American College with the Tilleys.

The American summer school went well. Its members clearly enjoyed both their work and their planned and unplanned leisure. Before their departure they treated us to a very talented and amusing revue.

This summer school occupied Roland's day, and mine was filled with all the usual chores: interviewing new students, planning new courses, restructuring the faculty, and so forth. But all this must now be done against a most unusual (and unpleasant) background: my firm belief that we had a life expectancy of one year. This meant that I could not possibly lead any new student or tutor to envisage a goal, academic or financial, further off than twelve months. I took only those students who required a one-year course, or who aimed at next summer's exams and left entirely open the possibility of a further year with us. Visiting tutors came on one-year agreements anyway, and even full-time tutors were on the usual 'one term's notice either way' basis. Moreover, all these safeguards had to be taken without ever betraying by word or gesture, nod or nuance, that we were under a sentence of death due to be carried out within nine or ten months. Of course, our 'inner circle' knew all about it, but were pledged to secrecy. My aim was to earn as much and spend as little as possible in this final year, in the hope that, with the sale of our assets, we could close free of debt. I was even aiming for a packed one-month school of English for Foreigners between the end of our own academic year on June 24th and our ejection on July 31st. But this meant the continuation of running credit with our suppliers, who would almost certainly insist on payment on the nail if they caught so much as a whiff of an impending closure.

Michael Charles, my old friend from Milton Abbey, had felt our position strong enough to justify the risk and start with us in September of 1969. He had bought a house which, as luck would have it, was quite near Barcote, and moved in that summer: Michael, his wife and three children.

By another stroke of good fortune I had dinner about this time with Adrian Room, another Milton Abbey colleague with whom I had kept in touch since I had left there ten years previously. He had been teaching in Cambridge for the past eight years or so. I knew him to be not only a very good teacher but also a first-class schoolmaster in the same sense that Tim Clark was one: someone who, in a residential community of young people, would be as totally reliable and responsible out of the classroom as in it, ready to give his time unstintingly to extracurricular work, able to cope with emergencies and deal sensibly with adolescent upheavals. A gifted linguist (Russian his chief foreign language), he was at this time contemplating a gradual move from teaching to lexicography. He was then working on a new Russian dictionary of the British way of life, and he had decided to give himself a year or two away from teaching (full-time teaching, at any rate) in order to complete his formidable task. After explaining our present shaky position to him, I induced him to join us as senior tutor in modern languages and as a counsellor in residence. I told him his timetable and his salary would be light, which, in the first year, was certainly true of the latter. He taught French, German, Russian and English with equal success and proved of invaluable help to Tim and me in running our always explosive little community.

With Adrian thus ensconced and Michael a new pillar of strength as director of studies, with all the talent we already had in our faculty, and one or two lucky finds in the way of visiting tutors, I felt we had as good a teaching force for our needs as could be found anywhere. All of which merely underlined the irony of it all: fortifying a position that was so soon to be abandoned, buttressing an edifice scheduled for demolition. There was no acceptable alternative, however, and it is astonishingly true that man habitually lives from day to day like the immortal he is not.

And so our new academic year got under way. We were full, with a large number of new faces, and we still found it impossible to begin a new session with anything less than optimism, that ingrained dominie's hope that springs eternal as he regards all the new faces and nurses his ineluctable belief, despite all cynicism, that this lot really will be rather better, just a little more eager to learn, just a little more responsible, trustworthy, *friendly*. Just as (of course) they all look at us with the optimism of their youth, eager to find this new set of stuffy beaks a little less bored and boring, rather more willing and able to bridge the great divide.

Whatever my inner sense of fatalism I had not been idle in the matter of survival efforts. We had our accountants prepare a detailed statement of our current position and a forecast budget for one year, based on our present income and expenditure, in some hypothetical new premises. Both statements showed a paper profit, and the document went on to underline our rapid and continued growth rate, and to point out that in new premises we could expect to accommodate almost fifty per cent more students at about thirty per cent less cost.

I sent copies of these statements to the mercantile bank that owned Barcote, with a covering letter that asked (or rather, begged) them to study them carefully and to consider either leasing Barcote to us or allowing a very substantial mortgage. In due course, I received their courteous and regretful refusal. All very dispiriting.

But Mr Underwood remained on the touchline, an enthusiastic and involved spectator. I sent him, too, these statements our accountants had prepared. He told me how impressed he was by them, how he never doubted our viability once we were free of the uneconomic situation at present enmeshing us. But, he felt, he could not be the *only* one to advance a loan: surely with that brave array of wealthy names in our list of patrons I could induce some others to put up money? This was an entirely reasonable question, to which I could only make the same sad response: when inviting these people to become patrons I had assured them we were not, and never would be, after their cash, and I simply could not renege on that. So, another depressing stalemate.

Then the bishop of Portsmouth told us that a charity of which he was a trustee had agreed, after lengthy consideration of all the facts and figures, to make us a donation of £5,000. This was the first ray of sun to pierce our clouds: a modest enough beam, but sufficient to bedazzle our sight, and (hooray!) that of Mr Underwood also, who agreed to advance £10,000. We now had half the purchase price of Barcote. I wrote again to the mercantile bank, asking them to consider leaving half the price on mortgage over three to five years. I implored them not to reject this idea out of hand: would they at least agree to see me at their offices in London to discuss the matter?

It was now March of 1970, almost at the end of the second term of our last academic year *chez* the Tilleys, four months before we were due to be evicted. Worse than that, the whole staff now knew the position. It had become clear that no such secret could be kept and I had found it more dignified to make a frank statement to them of all the facts. I had promised them that I would do my utmost to achieve our salvation by the end of this present term. If I could not, they were free to consider themselves in receipt of the statutory one term's notice and to seek other jobs for next September. Gloom settled on all of them and, as the weeks dragged by, was succeeded by all the marks of strain and stress. Tim would come to see me at regular intervals to ask if I had any news, any grain of comfort, any ray of hope for a staff which, he assured me, was rumbling with ominous rumours and showing signs of disintegration. I had to swallow my exasperation and explain once more that the instant I had an optimistic word to relay I'd shout it to them from the housetop. But until then I could not and would not say anything. Did he expect me to *invent* signs of hope, feed them with quite deceitful crumbs of comfort?

Then the student council asked me outright if it was true the college had to leave these premises at the end of the term and had nowhere to go, would in fact be winding up. I gave them, too, all the facts. Although they were not personally at risk, since they'd all be taking their exams next term and most would be leaving anyway, they were rather surprisingly sad and sympathetic. I discovered then that in their own funny way they were rather fond of the college, even rather proud of it. 'There's nowhere like it,' they said. 'It'll be rotten if it closes.'

Then the tutors asked me if I could guarantee their salaries to the end of the academic year. All very well, they said, to regard themselves as under one term's notice, but could I assure them they'd be paid all next term? This was the final nightmare. If any of them left at the end of this term it would be next to impossible to continue the students' education next term, in those vital two months before they sat their A levels and O levels. 'I think it will be all right,' I answered wearily. 'There's all next term's fees, and the summer school should bring in a fair amount. But I can't *guarantee* your salaries in the sense that I give you my solemn word they're safe. All I can say is: do what seems to you best. It will be horrific if any of you don't return next term. But I won't blame you.'

For they didn't know what I knew: that twice recently the end of the month had come and found us with insufficient funds for their monthly salary cheques. This was simply because so many parents were dilatory in paying the fees (overseas cheques often took weeks to clear), but I felt that even this quite reasonable explanation would sadly undermine staff confidence. And so on each occasion I turned to good Mr Underwood, who, without a murmur of reproach, handed us a cheque for £1,000 in return for a similar postdated one from us. The staff had unbounceable cheques on the due date and Mr Underwood was repaid within a fortnight.

Then a letter from the mercantile bank: yes, they'd see me. I think I did then let out a whoop sufficient to bring Arthur in from his adjacent office.

However, they'd fixed an appointment two weeks' hence, the day after our term ended. I phoned them and begged for an earlier date. Nicely, they consented to see me the following week. I wanted to say: 'And is it hopeful? Are you likely to agree to a lease or a mortgage? Oh, say something to put us out of our misery.' But the tone had to be insouciant as I thanked them for this minor readjustment of schedule.

Early on the bright, crisp morning of March 18th 1970, I set out for London, all the last minute words of advice, warning, pleading and good wishes buzzing in both ears. For this was surely it. If I failed to win over the mercantile bank directors to agree a lease or a fifty per cent mortgage on Barcote, then we must bow to the inevitable. The chances of finding another property so suitable in every respect, and so moderately priced, were almost nil. Barcote was a chance that doesn't come twice. Property prices were rocketing up, and time was dead-set against us.

I met three directors and two chief executives of the bank. We all went into a huddle over sherry in a rich, dark-panelled room overhanging those streets paved with ancient gold. They questioned me closely about our facts and figures, the philosophy of the college, the reasons for so early a move, just what we proposed to do with Barcote and its 84 acres. I tried to combine complete frankness with unbounded optimism, and must somehow or other have succeeded. For the atmosphere quite suddenly became more relaxed, friendlier, kinder. Said one director: 'I know all about the pains and joys of running a school: my father was headmaster of an independent school.' Whereupon another director capped this with: 'My father was a schoolmaster *and* a clergyman.'

'So...?' I breathed, hopefully.

'Yes', said the chief spokesman, 'we will agree to fifty per cent remaining on mortgage over, say, five years.' Involuntarily I closed my eyes for a moment as I said a simple 'Thank you.' To think I could return to them all with cries of victory to dispel all those months of keening gloom. No, I'd phone Arthur the good news the instant I left the bank. But what was the director saying now? What *was* he saying?

He was saying: 'But of course we must get the agreement of our head office, you understand.'

'But... but...' (my dismay must have been comical), 'I thought you *were* the head office.'

'Oh no. The head office so far as Europe is concerned, but our actual head office is in Hong Kong.'

'Oh Lord,' I said, all my little act in ruins, 'and how long will *that* take?' Before me floated childhood visions of oriental inscrutability and timelessness, of communication by rickshaw and junk.

'Oh, not long. A few weeks. Not more than a month, I'm sure.'

388

I took a deep breath. 'Look,' I hissed, 'can't you phone them, cable them, get an instant decision?'

'Of course not. We have our report and recommendation to prepare, then we have to send this together with your accountant's facts and figures, to Hong Kong. By post. They must consider it all, put their decision in writing, then post it to us.'

I groaned, then flung all my cards on the table, told them the strain we'd been living under, told them the term ended in eight days' time, told them there was a risk of losing some of the tutors and jeopardizing the students' exam prospects if I couldn't give a definite yea or nay by the last day of term. I thought this might erode whatever confidence I had inspired in their commercial breasts, but I really didn't care now. Strangely, my words evoked sympathy, understanding, even a suggestion of admiration. Emboldened, I hurtled on:

'Today's Wednesday. You could do your report tomorrow and post it by the evening mail, and before you close phone through the salient points and stress the urgency for a decision.'

The chief spokesman looked at me in some astonishment, then threw back his head for the indulgence of a rare guffaw. 'You're a hard man, Mr Gamble,' he laughed, 'a hard man. Well, we'll do our very best to get the decision to you by your end of term. I suppose we can use telex.' He mused a moment then, rising, said: 'Hong Kong isn't likely to turn down our recommendation. I think you'll be all right.'

They were absolutely charming. I solemnly shook hands with them all as they insisted it had been a pleasure to meet me.

And they kept their word. They phoned me on our penultimate day with the news of Hong Kong's ratification. It was quite an emotional occasion announcing to the staff their reprieve, and to the students our grand new address. But any undue elation on my part was limited by the knowledge that we had less than six months (and very little cash in hand) for the enormous task of adapting Barcote.

16

As soon as the term ended, almost before the dust raised by the last coach had settled, our little convoy set out for the first blitz on Barcote: Arthur and Tim and Michael and Adrian and Brian and I. The first thing was to plan in detail the minimum structural and decorative work needed for a September opening with seventy students and about eight staff in residence. My vision and inventiveness surprised me and the others. I realized what a lot I'd learned about the art of adapting and converting bricks and mortar.

We had decided that Tim's wife, Betty, should join the college as my personal secretary and as registrar: posts in which she had already demonstrated her prowess, as her testimonials and my own intuition told me. In any case, Tim had been a grass widower quite long enough and I accepted it as my duty to provide accommodation for them both. They, naturally, with two student sons as fairly frequent visitors, stipulated three bedrooms and two living rooms as a minimum. As we roamed Barcote trying to plan this it became horribly clear that their accommodation alone would cost us about fifteen residential students, fifteen deducted from our necessary target of seventy, since Barcote couldn't as it stood take more than that. Not if we were to preserve intact our policy of small living units with no overcrowding, each with its own kitchen common room where students could prepare their own breakfasts. So Tim told me sadly that he and Betty felt they couldn't ask the college to provide so much accommodation for just two staff members and must therefore seek other jobs.

This was a blow I felt the college (and I personally) couldn't take lying down, for Tim was invaluable on so many fronts that I couldn't imagine the place without him. So, somehow or other, the college managed to find the deposit for Tim to put down on a charming little house in a nearby village. It still left him with considerable mortgage repayments to make, but he felt that he could manage this on their joint salaries, especially if they took two of our students in with them as a fairly painless means of reducing the college loan. Of course, I was sorry to lose him as a resident, which his vital post of community director really required, but Adrian agreed to become resident deputy community director, and Tim readily undertook to be on call by phone all round the clock. In fact, he was so fond of the place, and so wholly committed to his job, that he usually stayed till close-down at 10.30 and always arrived within ten minutes if a crisis arose during my Saturday or Sunday overnight absence.

This matter of the loan was the only decision I took which (as I well knew) was not really mine to take. It was a decision for the governors, but I confess they heard of it as a *fait accompli*, and then only some time afterwards. I just felt at the time that they would not understand the vital necessity for Tim in his role as community director, much as they liked and respected him. Or, more precisely, they would not have considered it responsible of them to sanction so appreciable a loan in our present circumstances. Nor, perhaps, have understood how incredibly difficult it would have been for me to find a second Tim, and to train him in an entirely new and enlarged set-up with five other new tutors-in-residence. And it was certainly not a post I myself could fill: I hadn't the time, for one thing, and in any case the essence of the job was to walk this unenviable tightrope between principal and students, retaining the confidence of both sides.

I don't regret that decision. It was certainly worth the financial cost, but I suspect it played a part in a cost I was subsequently to feel more keenly: the resignation of two valued governors who publicly made the excuse of other heavy commitments, but more privately complained of being regarded as 'rubber stamp' governors.

I had only two regrets in leaving our present abode: the loss of our good doctor, and the loss of 'Oxford' from our address, which would in future be 'Faringdon, Berkshire.' For there was no doubt that the name possessed a certain magic attraction, both for overseas students with academic ambitions and for certain English students who had heard of it as a centre of swinging youth. So when Mr Underwood, who seemed full of surprises, sprang his next one on me I was more than interested. He told me, almost casually, that he had the lease of a suite of offices in the centre of Oxford, near Carfax, where he had once run a secretarial college. One evening he took me to see it. Because of his somewhat diffident references to it I was prepared for something small, dark, poky. Not a bit of it. Occupying the entire first floor above reputable shops, it had great windows commanding lively views of Carfax, five lofty rooms of various sizes, lavatories for both sexes, and nightstore heaters and strip lighting he had himself installed quite recently. I thought the rent and rates must be considerable, but they were surprisingly low. Did the college want to take over the lease as from September?

I had no doubt we should acquire it if we could. I discussed it with the governors and with our senior staff, and they agreed with me. We had discovered that there was a ready market for serious instruction in English for Foreigners, not only to vacation students, but to our own ambitious students from the Middle East, who (we felt) would react enthusiastically to a package deal of one year in digs in Oxford, perfecting their English and taking minority background courses in such subjects as economics and mathematics, followed by a guaranteed year in residence at Barcote in full one-year A level courses. The idea was exciting and viable. I told Jack Underwood it was a deal. And I further rejoiced that we would retain the magnetism of the name 'Oxford,' with one foot planted firmly amidst those psychedelic spires. A few years later, ironically, the reorganized county of Oxfordshire took Faringdon from Berkshire, so that we would have had the prestigious name in our address after all.

Another use to which I felt the Carfax premises might be put was the housing of our long-projected courses in art identification and art restoration. This was something Tim and I had long discussed with my old friend, John FitzMaurice Mills, writer and lecturer on art. His frequent visits to us were always something of a tonic for me: most irrepressible and infectious of funsters, he wore lightly his learning, expertise and very shrewd entrepreneurship. Again, the courses we planned together were without doubt the surest of winners, since there was a growing demand for them. But the equipment was costly, our vicissitudes abundant, and, alas, we never got off the ground with these grand schemes.

I had hoped that our last term *chez* the Tilleys would not be marred by student upsets.

But the students were worrying me more and more in this last term at Alvescot, not least because I felt in some measure responsible for their ills. About a half-dozen of the worst seemed to be afflicted by 'accidie,' that state of mind which the medieval theologians so wisely categorized as one of the seven deadly sins. A state of listlessness, torpor, ennui, it affronts the gift of life and can make a man finally something less organic than a cabbage. This handful of kids worked only when driven, had little or no interest in their impending exams, took almost no exercise and, all through the long summer evenings, advertised their lethargy by sprawling in armchairs, in and outside the common room, slowly puffing at cigarettes and very occasionally conversing in scarcely articulate mumbles. As I say, only about half a dozen were as bad as this, but they were horribly prominent, and, I felt, infectious, too. I felt guilty about them because of a niggling sense that I had failed them by not keeping them busy, active, occupied. And I had a horrible fear that the group was slowly, almost imperceptibly, enlarging itself as certain students who worked well enough in the day drifted in the evening hours around its outskirts. Oh, they were no trouble: often I wished they *would* show some positive awkwardness.

All those months, both in my own mind and in long discussions with colleagues, I was planning the remedies we could apply in our renaissant life at Barcote. Most of these remedies were the concessions I knew I must make to the hedonism of youth and the wisdom of traditional school policies. They were concessions that seemed uncomfortably like defeats, but I wasn't so purblind as not to recognize the crux of the whole situation; namely that so-called 'progressive' means were not enabling all the kids to achieve our entirely conservative ends of healthy community living and ultimate exam success. For my unfortunate and overweening perfectionism didn't like any failures: it worried and irked me to see the fallers by our wayside. I think I've now learned a gentler wisdom. But gazing on these half-dozen torpids I found myself, rather to my annoyance, thinking in such clichés as 'one rotten apple in the barrel' and 'the devil finds work for idle hands.' For these kids, I felt, were just plain bored, had too much time which *they* were required to fill profitably but couldn't. Organizing their out-of-class periods and their official leisure hours was something I had not wanted to do. During the former they were supposed to work in their own rooms, and *not* to the accompaniment of radios or record players. I believed they were old enough to learn to organize sensibly at least parts of their day. And to work in their own rooms, unsupervised, during the one-and-a-half-hour prep period in the evening.

As for the official recreation times in the afternoon and later evening, I disliked the idea of compulsory activities organized by us. We had facilities for basketball, football, croquet and swimming on the premises, and we made provision locally for horseriding, driving instruction, tennis and the like, for those who wanted them. Tilley, in earlier days, had been good in supervising more recondite pursuits like weightlifting and fencing, while a judo instructor came twice a week to the village hall to instruct a group of our students in the mysteries of his craft. In addition to all this, Tim was excellent in offering the facilities of his art shops at all hours. Once, exasperated by the tendency of several kids to waste the evening hours on TV programmes, we had organized several weekly courses to fill profitably and interestingly those leaden-footed hours before bed: photography, chess, bridge, first aid, car maintenance, and so forth. But these were soon starved out of existence by their backsliding and my refusal to *order* anyone to attend. In this final year at the Tilleys we were missing badly our excellent young director of activities and entertainments, who had left the previous summer to get married. A young lady of great character and charm, highly qualified in physical education, she had succeeded in making everybody enjoy some kind of exercise and had organized 'cultural excursions,' such as theatre trips to Oxford.

So I had decided that at Barcote we must have another full-time, resident tutor with special responsibility for activities and entertainments. I was resolved also to have a full-time chaplain if I could find the right sort of man: someone who could feed the spiritual hunger they all had, however vehemently they might have resisted the thought, and who could supply their acknowledged demand for instruction in comparative religion. And I decided each student must have a counsellor, someone who took a personal interest and held a kindly and unobtrusive watching brief on each individual. I wanted to increase the number of 'electives': nonexam subjects for minority time. With a fairly wide range of these from which the student could select, there would be fewer out-of-class periods for those who abused them. A boy who had used his work and leisure time to good effect said to me at this time: 'You know, when you get to Barcote you really ought to have a general, supervised prep period in the evenings. This studying in your own room just doesn't work. People do have radios and record players on at low volume, they're in and out of one another's rooms all the time, tea and coffee are being brewed every five minutes. Frankly, I found it very difficult to get any work done in the prep period.' I felt he was right. We had a large assembly hall at Barcote and somehow we'd get seventy extra desks and chairs to fill it. We'd need them anyway for invigilated public exams.

These were some of our New Year resolutions for Barcote. Pondering them was some comfort as I contemplated the torpids and blamed myself for them. *Some* comfort, but not much. And not for long.

17

A visitor I took into the common room and bar one evening quite threw me by remarking casually: 'It just stinks of cannabis in there. You didn't know? Oh, I quite thought you were turning a blind eye. You must have a blind nose then.'

Poor innocent, I certainly had not identified the general fustiness of that common room with pot smoking. If I remarked it at all it was to associate it with the obvious aversion of a few scruffier boys to soap and water. Now it clicked. Now I thought I understood the torpids' rather odd preference for sitting and smoking *outside* the common room even on quite fresh evenings. Now and only now I felt I could diagnose correctly their habitual air of gentle, vesper lassitude. Not any natural accidie but the unnatural inhalation of cannabis resin.

Perhaps I can be forgiven for my blindness. I felt they really had learned something from those traumatic expulsions the previous year, the memory of which had certainly not died. Students still with us from that time described it graphically enough to the new intake. I myself had referred to it in the brief warning about drugs abuse which I incorporated in each opening-of-term talk to the students. I had placed in their common room (without comment) the excellent pamphlets on drug abuse which had been prepared by the British Medical Association and by the Advisory Centre for Education, and had silently replaced missing copies. I had invited a lecturer from the Oxford health department to give a talk on the subject, illustrated by a video. And I had been very conscious of the need to eschew both pitfalls: both the conspiracy of silence and the obsessional emphasis.

Then it seemed a local resident with a keen and tutored nose said something to somebody in Oxford about the smell of cannabis on the last bus back from Oxford to our village, implying or stating that it emanated from the students of 'that hippy college.' The Thames Valley drug squad came to see me again. They asked if they could return with a couple of trained officers (one male and one female) to search a few likely rooms. I agreed.

I lay awake later than usual that night, thinking of the kids who were likely to be incriminated: not just the handful of torpids but one or two others who were clever enough to cover their tracks and clever enough to be on the brink of two or three A levels. I thought of what it would mean to them if I had to throw them out now, a few weeks before they sat their exams, what it would do to their careers, their parents. And I reached a decision.

Now I had always co-operated with the drug squad, who had always been very fair with me, agreeing readily to my insistence on being present whenever they searched a student or a room, and keeping out of the press any reports they felt would damage us. I hated breaking the mutual trust, but I decided to leak the news of their impending visit. It was deceitful, but I couldn't feel anything but happy about the decision I'd reached.

Next morning I spoke privately to the likeliest student. 'Tomorrow,' I told him darkly, 'we are having visitors: visitors who could cause much trouble to some of our students. They will be looking hard at certain rooms, and maybe certain people. What I'm telling you is *not* confidential.' He grinned, thanked me and left. The searches were duly made and everything and everybody pronounced 'clean.' When the detectives had departed I assembled all the students and tried to show them what a tragedy it would have been to the individual and his family if anybody had been charged with possessing cannabis. I begged them not to spoil their records and chances at this eleventh hour, but to get down to the final revisions for their exams. 'Which,' I concluded with solemn emphasis, 'you know as well as I you can never do if your heads are fuddled with pot fumes.'

Perhaps it did some good. I know how strangely pleasant it was for me to think that they felt I was on their side for once. Not only that but, as the mother of one boy reported his words to me: 'At least Rev Gamble cares about you, cares what becomes of you.' Writing this now makes me very sad, as from this perspective I see all those kids as hungry for my approval and affection as I was for theirs, and all of us so full of resentment whenever I was forced into some punitive action.

And how nice if I could say the remainder of that term was plain and happy sailing, at any rate so far as student troubles were concerned. But the Fates and the Furies had apparently decided long ago that Anglo-American College's voyage should be as tempest-tossed as it was brief.

One Wednesday (their half-day) a party of students returned from Oxford on the last bus, checked in, said their goodnights and went to their rooms. Half an hour later a white-faced girl from the cottage unit fetched Tim and me to her roommate, Alison. 'She's very ill. I don't know what it is. She looked dreadful when she came in off the bus, but she's getting worse. Screaming and hysterical.' She panted this out as we hurried across the moonlit lawns.

We found Alison standing on her bed, clawing at the window, sweating and shouting. We forcibly laid her down. She was largely incoherent but clearly terrified. Her quite ferocious aim was to get out of the window, away from something that was threatening her very existence. Tim held her down, speaking soothing words all the while, and I went to summon the doctor. Our own doctor was not available but his stand-in (whom I didn't know) arrived within twenty minutes. We left him with Alison. Tim and I walked the lawns, talking in low tones. We both felt this was a case of LSD ingestion. Half an hour later the doctor emerged. 'I think she'll be all right now. She's calm. I've given her a sedative. She'll probably go to sleep very soon. Keep her in bed tomorrow. I'll get Dr Hill to call.'

'We feel pretty sure, doctor,' I replied, 'that she's taken LSD. These seem typical symptoms.'

He waved a deprecating hand. 'Oh, I don't think so. Just stress - she's got her exams soon, hasn't she? - leading to mild hysteria.' He sounded most unconvincing, and seemed in a hurry to be off.

When Alison was her usual pleasant self, two or three days later, Tim and I questioned her about her visit to Oxford that evening, about the onset and nature of her attack. We drew a blank, as also from her companions. They'd seen a film, had a snack, then sat in a pub for an hour or so, where she'd had nothing but cider. She begged me to say nothing to her parents, who were such awful worriers. She was all right now, she said, and she'd certainly not drink cider again.

I didn't tell her parents. There was nothing really to tell. Nor could I blame the doctor for being such a clam. After all, it's no part of a medical man's job to involve his patient needlessly in trouble with the authorities.

The final nasty memory I have of that term is the strange affair of Karen's ankle. I arrived back late from London one Sunday night. Tim was sitting up to give me the facts.

Karen had been sitting quietly in the common room, looking at some magazines and drinking a cup of coffee. Just before dispersal time she had suddenly leapt up with a horrible cry and dashed out into the night, right down the drive and into the unlighted road. There she had fallen heavily on the grass bank and into the gutter, breaking her ankle. It was a mercy that she did, for the village had no speed limit, the drive gave on to a sharp bend, and cars were fast and frequent.

Like Alison, she could throw no light on her behaviour, which was, in her case, wildly out of character. For Karen was a reserved, dignified person, rather too mature and 'ladylike' to mix in well with our generally boisterous gang. Many months later, long after Karen had left us, I said to Tim: 'You know, looking back, I feel pretty sure it was LSD that sent Karen crashing out into the ditch. Although she's the last person on earth to take it, I would have thought.'

Tim frowned, took a deep breath, and said, 'Yes, it was. I heard the story much later. In a roundabout sort of way, and unintentionally, too, I think. It *was* LSD. But Karen didn't take it knowingly. I don't suppose she knows to this day she'd had it. One of the kids somehow got her to take it without knowing. I don't know who.'

I thought I had a pretty good idea. I suspected Henry and Trevor, two English boys, roommates and close friends, both from well-known public schools which had had little or nothing to say for or against them, both very bright, both invariably polite and co-operative. The key word in that sentence is 'close': both pretty uncommunicative, very softly spoken and remarkably unobtrusive. And both, it must be admitted, most agreeable if one did encounter them. I liked rather than disliked them, but always with reservations.

I felt quite sure they would have been found in possession of pot but for my timely leakage of information. And my thoughts homed straight to them in Karen's case. It would, I mused, be their kind of sick joke to watch someone like Karen react unawares to something like LSD. Perhaps I do them an injustice. I'd certainly like to think so.

They were moderately friendly with a pretty 16-year-old called Rosemary, who had come to us not too enthusiastically in January of that year. She could be marvellously sweet and winsome, and all those who taught her spoke well of her. Her heart was set on going to a stage school in London, but her parents felt she was too young for London and probably too ungifted for a notoriously overloaded profession. I agreed with them, but changed my tune when the child revealed her obsessional urge and quite frightening wilfulness in this matter of 'doing her own thing.' I eventually advised her parents to let her have her way and find out for herself. I tried to help them locate a respectable London hostel for her to live in and a reasonable stage school she could attend. I remember, vividly and reluctantly, how she conducted herself once in my study as with her parents we discussed her future. To the mildest, most tentative suggestions of father and mother she responded with a passion and contempt so withering that they seemed to crumple before it. They were clearly afraid of her tongue, her temper, her iron self-will. It was so distressing to watch that I sent her out of the room quickly. Yet the parents loved her, and she herself cried out to be loved.

I met Henry quite recently. As we chatted, he said almost casually: 'By the way, did you hear about Rosemary Lawrence? No? Oh, she committed suicide. She and Trevor set up house together, you know. Old Trevor tried to commit suicide too. Twice, in fact.' Poor, stage-struck Rosemary. Poor, broken parents. Poor old Trevor and the Cambridge Exhibition he'd won and spurned. I rather envied the nonchalance with which Henry seemed to take it all.

And so, with bangs and whimpers, ended our last term in our natal home. We had just over a month to our D-Day, and it was devoted not only to a more determined attack on Barcote but also to a last-gasp winning of our bread-and-butter *in situ*, the summer school. I had written to selected boys among our past and future students, inviting them to join us for some part of the summer vacation, either here or at Barcote, or both, for 'full board (alfresco), limited pocket money, limitless hard labour.' There was a sufficient response, and invaluable they proved as tough, cheery packhorses.

With our own cars, the school vans and a mammoth hired lorry, we moved everything across in good time. I left till last the books and papers in my study, piling them into my car as the final act of the last, lone person from the old régime.

As I drove out, there was little room in my head or heart for relief at what I left behind. I was far too preoccupied with the exciting challenges that lay ahead. But now, reliving it, all I can think is: I wonder if the Tilleys will ever know, ever believe, how much I liked them both, how void of all bitterness my memories are now?

We had an enormous task before us at Barcote and well we knew it. We had to believe it was possible, for it was largely our faith that had literally to move mountains of stone, wood and iron, as we stripped room after room in readiness for its new role. Little local labour was available, at least, not on our terms. For we had now scarcely any cash in hand, so it was a case of 'wait until the fees come in,' or even of three termly payments spread over the coming academic year.

We had bedrooms, common rooms, showers, offices, reception rooms, kitchens, dining rooms, laboratories, classrooms to adapt, repair, decorate, furnish. And most of it we did ourselves: Tim, Arthur, Brian, Adrian, four boys and I. In fact, I did least, for all day and every day I was interviewing parents and new staff or racking my brains with Michael Charles before the hundreds of multicoloured pegs stuck in the huge, impressive and efficient programming board which Brian had made: a computer-type instrument that was in effect a fluid master timetable for everything we did. As parents and prospective students positively queued up in drawing room and hall, Michael would phone my study in agonized tones: 'Don't take one more for sociology. Remember it is now impossible to offer Russian with French, economics with German, any A level science *except* biology and zoology with any A level subjects. And try to get more for phys-chem: these groups are well understocked. And it looks as if botany and statistics may have to go altogether, so don't take anyone for *them*.'

It was enormously exhausting and exhilarating. It would have been totally happy but for the speed with which our deadline approached and the daily frustrations as suppliers failed to honour their commitments and various technicians fell sick or went on holiday or just disappeared mysteriously for days on end. But somehow we did it. Somehow everybody seemed to come up trumps in the end. Of course, on opening day we could have wished a hundred things looked better, worked better. But it was passable, and the countless finishing touches could be applied at a less white heat. Brian (to whom carpentry was, I think therapy) also made a fine language laboratory, a delightful bar (lager and wine and soft drinks) and a long serving counter outside the kitchens.

In many ways I was sad when the first day of term finally overtook us, for it marked the end of a happy if feverish camaraderie. We had all come and gone as we pleased: drifted into the kitchen at any hour of the day or night to fry our eggs and brew coffee. The two past students proved far nicer companions than they ever had been when *in statu pupillari*. Equally, the two new students would never be as nice again. I remember saying to Brian: 'What a delightful couple of boys Paul and John have been. Isn't it rotten to think they'll soon be the usual sulky, bolshy students and we'll be our usual nagging, niggling selves?'

'*Must* it be so?' Brian asked. 'Why need it be so?'

I shrugged. 'You know as well as I do they're going to turn sour under the heat of work and routine and regular hours.'

'If only,' Brian murmured, almost to himself, 'if only we could all be here, just *be* here, without any of those things.'

18

I was well satisfied with the new staff I had engaged. Three were fresh from university: two young ladies, teaching between them history, government, sociology and geography, and a young man who had graduated in both English and physical education. These three, together with a young chaplain, who taught divinity, history and music, were all resident, and all counsellors. I had had very few suitable applications for the chaplain's post. It was more than easy to short-list two.

I also engaged daily visiting tutors in chemistry and linguistics, and biweekly ones in philosophy, psychology, ethics, logic, world affairs and Spanish. These, with a nursing sister who attended daily, and a resident housekeeper, made up a task force of twenty-three people all directly concerned with the welfare of the seventy students. They also made up a formidable salary bill, to which, of course, were added the wages of clerical, domestic and outdoor staff. But all had been nicely calculated in relation to the seventy students we aimed to enrol, and we actually achieved seventy-five if we include a handful who lived out.

I duly organized the evening prep periods in the hall. All students were required to attend and the whole session was supervised by the duty tutor. Of course, students were allowed to work in the library or the labs, and I extended the carrot of allowing students of proven ability to work in their own rooms, during the evening prep sessions, and during out-of-class periods in the morning, when again the general rule was for such periods to be taken in the hall.

THE MORE WE ARE TOGETHER

Each student met his counsellor formally each week, with a sacrosanct period built into the timetable for this. Every other week in this period he discussed with his counsellor his fortnightly grade sheet. This was a foolscap form on which tutors recorded the fortnightly grades for effort and achievement in each subject taken by each student, adding any comment they chose. After going through this sheet with the student, the counsellor would add his comments concerning the student's reaction to his grades, and to his college life in general, then pass them to the director of studies, who passed them to me, so that one or other of us could interview any student especially deserving a brickbat or backslap. The grades for achievement were very carefully geared to public exam grades, so that each student could see his progress as the grade sheets multiplied. It was gratifying to see how seriously almost all of them took these grade sheets, often challenging a fall in grade with the tutor concerned. This grading had also to be related to each student's psychology, requiring in some cases a concession to morale-boosting, in others a concession to hubris-puncturing.

Full-scale, formal mock exams were set early enough in the academic year for us to diagnose and treat such imponderables as 'exam nerves,' demoralization by the clock or the silence of the invigilators, lack of the stamina required for a diverse, three-hour paper, and so on. These 'mocks' were also graded on the public exam scale.

I redesigned the termly report forms so that parents could supplement with such statistics the verbal reports made by the tutors. And I added now what I had come to see as a vital statistic: the number of teaching periods the student had missed or curtailed, usually through late risings after late nights, or sheer medical malingering. Of course, we cracked down on those who missed first (even second and third) periods because they couldn't get out of their beds. On the other hand, we weren't going to drag them out, wash and dress them, and pitch them into the classroom. Again, it is simply not worth the risk involved (as some of them well knew) in brusquely dismissing the alleged ills of the regulars on the morning sick parade outside the surgery. Better safe than sorry, whatever one's private exasperation or even contempt. However, I was determined that the parent should know the position, so that the right party could be blamed for the eventual exam failures.

Although I had now initiated Saturday morning classes, the students still had ample and well-spaced leisure. They were free from teaching each evening from 8 till 11, and free to visit local towns on Wednesday and Saturday half-days and any time on Sunday. Those over eighteen weren't required to ask any permission or give any information regarding such visits or regarding visits to local pubs. Moreover, they had a large and pleasant mixed common room (complete with jukebox), a television room, a table tennis room, a congenial bar, and 83 acres of captivating gardens, woods and

400

fields. I had interesting friends come to speak about their careers: Andrew Ray, the actor, who had been a good friend ever since I had taught him at about age twelve and he was the star of that charming film *The Mudlark*; and Christopher Hampton, the dramatist, whose *Total Eclipse* was especially a play I cherished.

No, I felt we had at last found the happy medium in the work/play ratios, and we had good games fields and a young sports tutor bubbling over with enthusiasm. Frankly, I couldn't help being proud of our set-up so far. Not complacent: just pleased to feel that now at last we were giving excellent value for money and each kid was getting a very fair deal.

We had a first-rate staff and a very responsible academic structure; housing was comfortable, food good, leisure well catered for. But what about the students for whom it all existed?

I had, as ever, been careful in my choice, checking with past schools, refusing those whose records in any way suggested the bad apple. I had redesigned my registration form, now requiring a parent to sign below this additional assurance: 'to the best of my knowledge and belief the student has no character defect that would render him/her unfit for college life (including, and especially, drug dependence or addiction).'

Early in the term one boy came to me in some distress to tell me he had not been honest at his interview: he had in the past smoked cannabis, but had broken with the stupid habit some time ago. He'd been ashamed of his lie, and more and more ashamed as time passed and he found all of us so nice and himself so happy with us. He just had to get it off his chest and beg me to believe him and forgive him. He promised me he'd do his utmost never to bring any pot on our premises, or accept any if offered, or smoke any at weekends, or tell any other student of his past indulgence in it.

So what, at that stage, could I do about it, but accept his assurances? He was a nice lad, and (yes, I admit it) I was touched by his urge to make a clean breast of it all. But all in vain, for this boy, Kevin, quite early showed such emotional instability that I felt sure he was either still on drugs or showing acute withdrawal symptoms. In later talks with me he admitted that he had in the past habitually used not only cannabis but LSD, and had actually been placed on probation by a juvenile court for such offences. And so he had to go: quietly, undramatically, and with sorrow all round, disappearing at the end of the first term. I remember too well the near despair of his parents in my study when I asked them to 'withdraw' him in December. I liked his parents as much as I liked Kevin himself. And I remember that I just hadn't the heart to ask them the obvious: 'How on earth could you so dishonestly have signed that registration form?' Anyway, I knew well enough why: they were desperate, and this was their last hope, a hope they prayed would be fulfilled. But keeping him would not only have put the rest of the community at risk: it was also doing harm to Kevin himself, as he grew ever more bitter and frustrated through his own inability to make any progress, even when we retailored his timetable to give him the minimum academic and maximum creative subjects.

A shrewd and telling critic of my policy of expelling the drug abusers was later to challenge me in these words: 'You say you took very seriously your *in loco parentis* role. But what mother would ever expel a sick and needy child from her family?' Well, Kevin's mother did just that. In my last talk with her, on the phone, she said: 'It breaks my heart but I'm sending Kevin away: to a small, residential clinic where they seem to cope with young people like him. You see, I just can't any longer face this terrible fear that he'll corrupt his younger brothers and sisters.'

Of course, I hoped that Kevin's troubles would be kept so confidential and unpublicized that he could weather the rest of the term and fade gently from our ken. And I think that in fact happened, the more easily since the rest of the students seemed to have written him off as too bizarre for any real friendships.

Then, late one night, I had a phone call. 'This is Detective Sergeant Cooper here, sir. Thames Valley drug squad. May we come along and see you sometime tomorrow?' I fixed a time, feeling sick in my stomach. Was it all going to be re-enacted here, in our bright new home? Was it going to happen every year, every term, of our lives?

The next afternoon they explained. One of their men had happened to be in our local pub a couple of evenings ago (in plain clothes, and actually off duty) and he overheard a group of young people quite openly discussing the drugs they used. It wasn't difficult to find out where they were from. So could they see if they could recognize some of them and search both them and their rooms? I agreed, and we set off across the quads (filled with knots of students) for the mixed common rooms. We had twenty or so students who had been with us in our old quarters, and as we strolled along (the officers glancing keenly at faces as we went), I noticed several of these students nudging one another, whispering, moving off with an alacrity they tried to conceal. Three boys were selected, questioned, admitted they were in the pub at the relevant time, and one even blurted out the name of another boy who'd been with them, but who was this afternoon quite legitimately absent in Oxford. In my presence, these three boys were searched and found 'clean,' and all three accompanied us as their respective rooms were searched. Again, nothing. I breathed again.

Then, almost as an afterthought, the officers asked to see the room of the absent student. And there, up the chimney, they found a pipe, a smoker's pipe of rather exotic workmanship. One of them sniffed it and nodded grimly.

'When will this young man be back, sir?'

Since he was due back within the hour, I agreed they should wait for him. Thus it was that Dave walked, on time, into the midst of these four intruders in the privacy of his room. I don't know if he had been tipped off by another student. He was in any case a cool, self-possessed young man. He was cool now. Yes, it was his pipe. Yes, cannabis had been smoked in it. Yes, he had himself smoked in it the cannabis he had bought. But, and here he was not only a little defiant, but a little triumphant, too:

'Not in England.' He'd bought the pipe in Mexico, and the cannabis, too. And he'd smoked it there. Never in England.

'You didn't intend to smoke it in England, David?' asked Cooper so nicely that someone less cocksure than our 19-year-old American Dave might have been on his guard.

'No, of course not.'

'Why "of course not"?'

'Because I know it's against the law here.'

'So why bring the pipe with you?'

A tiny hesitation, then: 'Well, it's a rather unusual pipe, rather attractive.' I was watching him closely. I saw him almost bite his lip as he saw the mistake he'd made.

'I see. You brought it back as a decorative ornament for your room? And keep it up the chimney?'

I felt sorry for him. He was so obviously unaccustomed to any need for bluster, equivocation, embarrassment. But he did quite well.

'I... I did keep it on the mantelshelf at first. And one of the other guys borrowed it. I mean, without me knowing. So I decided it was best to hide it. I didn't want some English guy to get himself in trouble with it.'

But it was no good. Dave had admitted it was his pipe and the dried remains in the bowl were cannabis dregs. And he didn't know that, as the law of this land stood, mere possession was an indictable offence.

So they asked Dave to accompany them to the station. I privately asked Cooper if they were intending to do anything more than ask for a signed statement, because if so I'd come with him, awkward as it would be with a group of parents coming to see me and probably already here.

Cooper assured me they didn't intend to do anything more than take a statement on the lines of the conversation they'd just had. He wouldn't be required to state anything more than he had already stated in the presence of the detectives and myself. So, telling Dave (in front of them) to be sure to say no more than he'd said already, and to think very carefully about his statement, and to sign nothing that he *hadn't* said, I rather wistfully let them take him off in their official car.

Knowing his parents were still in London, I spent a couple of hours locating them, and asked them to visit me as soon as possible. I didn't alarm them with the facts or with any hints of disaster.

Dave was duly brought back (suitably impressed by the courtesy and fairness of the British police, but adding wryly: 'I guess there's no call to grill a crazy guy who accuses himself'), the pipe was duly pronounced by the forensic laboratories to contain cannabis, and Dave was duly summoned to appear before the local bench. Knowing him for a seasoned international commuter, and understanding how strong might be the temptation simply to abscond from this mess, I asked him to give me his passport until his court case had been heard. He handed it over with a shrug and leaned back in the chair, an ungainly, scruffy, gangling youth, all arms and legs and glum defeat, encased in dirty jeans and sweater, blinkered with riotous sideburns and crowned with shocks of auburn hair.

As we chatted rather aimlessly on (it was late and he seemed to want to talk), I idly flicked through the pages of his passport, and experienced a jolt so sudden and so astonishing that he noticed the start I gave. For I was gazing at a remarkably vivid passport photo of a boy I seemed to know: a boy whose fresh face beneath modest, groomed hair, gazed back at me with uncompromising, honest eyes. A face whose every feature conveyed alert intelligence. Yes, it was the Dave of three years ago. Nothing has so poignantly crystallized for me the lostness of so much modern youth as merely to gaze across three years from what my hands held to what my chair held. Perhaps the shock betrayed me into mere sentimentality. We all have somehow to carry our fragile innocence through muddy seas of experience to some projected maturity. Perhaps the Dave I knew was a deeper, richer person than the ghost caught immutably by the camera. But it was hard to think so. The boy in the photo didn't look green, nor the boy in the chair look ripe.

Dave was fined and returned to the States with his parents. And I sighed with relief. Dave as a student wasn't a great loss, and the dramatic nature of his exit, via a police court, might be the one salutary shock that would do them all good. As usual, I spoke to the students all about the case: told them what fools they were to talk so recklessly and publicly about what were actual criminal offences. 'But,' I concluded, 'I'll assume that most of it was simply talking big, keeping your end up in front of your pals, boasting about things you haven't really done but which you think they'll admire you for having done.'

I would have liked to believe that, but lacked the necessary powers of self-deception. And, as the weeks of that first term slithered by, one could no longer ignore the old tell-tale signs as several students deteriorated (gradually or fitfully) in their work, their appearance, their personal hygiene, their essential vitality.

19

Then the inevitable explosion came. Margaret, one of our new young tutors came to see me in a state of some agitation. I was aware that for some weeks now these young tutors who had joined us at the beginning of term were going through the sort of hell they just had to go through. Dedicated and conscientious teachers, they sweated away half the night preparing their stuff and grading their students' work. They also gave themselves unsparingly as counsellors. I had warned them at the outset of the two great dangers: (a) identifying so closely with their charges' real or imaginary woes that they would become emotionally exhausted, and (b) they would, with the entirely laudable aim of vindicating their own youthful idealism, lend too ready an ear to the perfunctory subversive talk of the kids, taking far more seriously than its perpetrators that constant, querulous murmur that goes up from all members of all institutions.

But these warnings, of course, meant little or nothing: they had to find out for themselves, the very hard way. Often I would sit and chat at length with Margaret and Jean and Bud about our college rules, defending them as a necessary, basic minimum which were nevertheless always open to discussion by staff or students. At first they were shy about speaking. Said Jean: 'Well, it doesn't seem right somehow for us to criticize your rules: I mean, you being the principal.' I couldn't resist the mischievous reply: 'Not right, you mean, to criticize them to my face.' She grew somewhat pink and I had to hasten to explain: 'Perfectly natural. I *know* they bitch and moan and groan about me and my rules, because all students do. And I *know* you can't help listening sympathetically, because I did when I started in teaching.'

Thus encouraged, they *would* query, challenge, speculate, put forward alternatives. And I would try to explain how, after much trial and error, much experiment and failure, we had arrived at our present code. Invariably, they would nod their agreement, but rather unhappily. Their heads were with me, their hearts with the kids. Naturally so, for they were intelligent, responsible and warm-hearted. In addition, they had all been at university in those peculiarly turbulent sixties, when student protest was so often more instinctive than rational.

So they served harrowing apprenticeships with us. Adolescent self-pity drenched their compliant shoulders to a most unhealthy degree. Familiarity, licensed then regretted, began to offend their self-respect. They saw their credulity manipulated, their generosity exploited.

Poor Bud, in charge of PE, activities and entertainments, began with an enthusiasm so explosive that it simply had to abate. He came to me after a few months, his eyes brimming with tears of rage, mortification, frustration. It was the final straw. With great difficulty he'd trained something like a soccer team. With equal difficulty he'd got them a fixture with a local village team. And half our louts hadn't turned up or let him know. He had suffered the humiliation of cancelling the match on the pitch.

I shared his indignation and comforted him as best I could. I told him he was in no way to blame. I knew he had laboured to make something of them, infect them with some part of his own enthusiasm. But no, I was *not* going to apply any compulsion. If they didn't want a team, that was it.

The odds against him were unfairly loaded, he felt. I suggested gently that perhaps it was a mistake in our set-up to attempt anything so formal, and so hazardous as a fixture. 'But they'd *asked* for one.' He almost squeaked in protest against the injustice of it all. 'Well, perhaps their spirit was willing,' I murmured, 'but you know what their flabby flesh is like. I'd confine myself in future to spontaneous knockabouts here.'

On another occasion Jean came to me, very upset, to complain about three boys in her A level sociology class. They'd asked for an extra class so that they could go more deeply into a part of the syllabus that especially interested and taxed them. She'd agreed to take them in a free period she had the next morning, and she'd sat up till three o'clock preparing three sets of exhaustive notes for them. And not one of them had turned up. Tim told her later that they were still in bed.

I gave the three boys hell and told them they would work in the library, under my eye, the whole of that evening. This was a penalty that hurt, for they were going into Oxford that evening with a group of friends.

That afternoon, rounding a corner into one of the quads, I saw Jean in the midst of these three. Eyes and ears told me that they were not blaming her. Oh, not at all. On the contrary, she was commiserating with them against the tyranny which had spoiled their evening's fun!

It is perhaps best, in defiance of chronology, to conclude my tale of these three novice tutors by recounting how they took their final farewells of me. All three, quite individually, and with varying emphases of disillusion and embarrassment, said something like: 'Sorry I took so long to see your point of view about the students. Sorry I was so gullible with them.' And I record this in order to pat, not my back, but theirs. I hope their disenchantment was only temporary. I hope they stayed in the profession, for it badly needs such good material.

To return to Margaret, who, tense and nervous, asked for a private word with me. We strolled in the gardens, I remember, as with much difficulty she unburdened herself.

'I've been awake most of the night worrying about this. I mean, worrying whether I ought to tell you what I heard yesterday. Two of the boys told me in the bar last night. I don't think they meant to: it just sort of slipped out. Then they tried to get me to promise I wouldn't tell anyone else. I hate splitting on them. I don't suppose they'll ever trust me again. I did mention this to Brian, and he said I certainly ought to tell you. In fact, he said if I didn't he would. Which made it sort of easier.'

She paused. I prompted her: 'Drugs, I suppose?'

She nodded. 'Yes. It's young Chris Maclean.'

I was shocked. Chris was our youngest student, and pretty innocent even for a bare sixteen. I was in for a worse shock. 'Smoking pot with some other fools in the woods?'

She shook her head. 'No, not pot, LSD.' I halted in our perambulations of the lawn. She spoke quickly now. 'Oh, he didn't take it. I mean, he did, but he didn't know what it was. Another student gave it to him, dared him to take it, said it was just a little pep pill or something. And he got the horrors. Rushed out into the woods that evening and began fighting and screaming.'

I interrupted her. 'Fighting? Fighting whom?'

She gave a mirthless laugh. 'The trees. He said the trees were trying to kill him. Then some students went out and tried to calm him. He fought them, too. But somehow they dragged him up to the house and got him to bed.'

'Do you know who gave him the acid?'

'No. No, not really. I heard a name mentioned but it was only a guess on their part, they said, they didn't really know. And I don't want to say that name because it could be terribly wrong, and then I'd never forgive myself.'

'Will you tell me who told you this?'

'No. Please. I'd rather not. I'm only telling you any of this because I get so mad every time I think of what they did. Chris Maclean is such a nice kid. It was a filthy thing to do. I remember what you told them all about the effects of LSD.'

'All right, I accept your reservations. Thanks, Margaret. And... don't worry,' I added grimly, 'I'll find out. if it's the last thing I do.'

I talked about it to Brian, my brother, that night.

I said: 'This is the third case we know of where acid's been given to one of the kids unawares. Anyone so vile, so amoral, so...' (I was fighting for epithets) 'so pathological as to do this is obviously getting a real kick out of watching his victims scream. A sense of power, you know, the real sick criminal streak. And it could snowball.' A new, nasty thought struck me. 'I could be the next. An obvious target. And I often have coffee with them in their rooms.' I stared at the bar of the electric fire, the only light in the room. And a far more horrific thought struck me. 'My God, they could slip one to Nik.' (Nik, it will be recalled, was our little nephew, now slowly progressing at boarding school in Oxford, but still pathetically vulnerable. He often came to stay at Barcote over the weekend and mingled freely with the students.)

'If one of them did,' said Brian slowly, and in a tone I hadn't heard before, 'I think I'd strangle him with my own hands.'

I had no doubt that I must and would root this poison out of our midst. I set to work early the next morning, after preliminary discussions with Tim and Adrian and one or two other counsellors.

And I worked more or less alone. I've been asked since why I didn't call back the drug squad. Quite simply because I knew they couldn't get anywhere. They needed tangible evidence, and I felt quite sure our criminal or criminals were too shrewd to supply that. Also, they couldn't 'put the screws on,' as, quite frankly, I was prepared to do if necessary. Again, they were the law, who, rightly, had to convince a bench of magistrates in open court. I wasn't so inhibited. I was within my rights to expel on the basis of merely circumstantial evidence. Indeed, on the basis of strong suspicion alone. If I called in the drug squad to deal with this, and they drew a blank, then they effectively prevented me from further action. No, I was determined to go it alone.

In the ten beastly days that followed I interviewed almost every student in the college and, as before, always with Tim present as a witness, and always taking careful, dated notes of what they said. Almost fifty pages of them. Many of the kids I interviewed again and again, as my dossier grew and new facts had to be thrust in old faces.

And at the back of my mind lurked, once more, that sickening question: 'Were we to be faced with this sort of thing every year, with each fresh intake?' Still further back in my mind, at that stage, was the further thought: 'If so, this is not how I intend to spend the rest of my days.'

In the middle of it all I went up to London to dine with an old friend. I welcomed the opportunity to escape for a few hours from the progressively putrid atmosphere, to discuss it all with someone quite detached from it, to gain a different perspective. I sat in the club room of the Television Centre, well aware that I was not the liveliest of guests, as my host soon detected. In response to his query, I told him the cause of the despondency I was so ill concealing.

I had known Roger Mills and his family for about ten years. He was a talented producer in the documentaries division of the BBC, already with much good work to his credit, and clearly even better things to come.

He was silent and thoughtful for a while as my wretched spiel trailed off, then he said: 'Peter, what would be your reaction to the idea of a documentary on drugs in schools? It's something I've long wanted to do, but, as you can imagine, no school that's had this trouble will let me in to film it.

It seems to be swept under the carpet, and any publicity is shunned. Would that be your own reaction?'

I didn't have to ponder that one. 'Far from it,' I rejoined, quite warmly. I'm *proud* that we fight it, not ashamed that we have it. All schools have it, and they're liars if they say otherwise.'

And so the seeds were sown. We entered on a long, hard-headed discussion. I pointed out that I'd have to obtain the governors' consent on so important a matter of policy, and that I should sound the staff, since they might be involved in certain filmed scenes. I wondered if I ought also to test parent reaction. Clearly there would be much preliminary work before any go-ahead.

The next time Roger and I met, I had closed my dossier. Five students had been expelled on the spot and four more put on the strictest probation. In less than two months after our almost miraculous opening at Barcote, with seventy students in high spirits and promising high endeavour, with a third of the resident faculty embarking excitedly on their teaching careers, and the remaining two thirds enthusiastic enough to forget the exhaustion of their summer-long labours; yes, within mere weeks of that happy, purposeful inauguration, the whole atmosphere had been soured for ever. Was it because a handful of spoilt, wilful, mindless brats had insisted, almost as soon as they had unpacked their cases, and in defiance of all their assurances and my warnings, on taking and distributing pot and acid? Or was it because I had made the initial, catastrophic error of declaring publicly that drug abusers would be expelled, and had in the event done exactly what I had threatened? Over all those dark days loomed that ugly, insistent question mark.

Over the Christmas holidays Roger and I met frequently to thrash out the shape of the proposed documentary. He had to submit a substantial outline to the head of his department. My half-a-hundred sheets of evidence taken from the kids, and the careful logbook I had kept of the whole operation, provided the nucleus of the script. I knew Roger to be a person of integrity and idealism. I knew also of the fine reputation enjoyed by his chief, Charles Cawston, who had recently earned general acclaim for his pioneering film of the Royal Family. I knew both of them realized how delicate my position was and would be fully co-operative. I believe I was only the second person to be granted the right which had been granted to the Queen: of vetting the completed film before it was televised. I had stipulated that nobody (student, parent, tutor, governor) must suffer hurt from the film in any identifiable way. Obviously, professional juveniles must play the parts of any students found implicated in drug abuse. For the rest, the film was to be shot entirely at the college. All others appearing in it, with the exception of the drug squad officers who also had to be professional actors, would be the actual individuals involved, and the reconstruction was to be as meticulously accurate as we could make it. I insisted that not only names and nationalities of the culprits should be changed, but also personalities interchanged and genders reversed. Roger felt that this was, perhaps, somewhat overcautious of me. But in the last few days before the programme was screened, when several people made great efforts to have it banned, and there was even talk of applying to a judge in chambers for a restraining action, he told me he blessed my name for that decision, which enabled him, with a clear conscience, to tell any parent: 'Your son/daughter will be totally unidentifiable, I give you my word.'

Despite this scrambling of all the material, the film scrupulously portrayed the types involved and followed the hourly course of the actual drama. When I saw a preview of the finished film, I asked for only one change to be made: one student made a remark to the effect that the college was so isolated that they seldom saw people outside their own student and faculty bodies. This was such arrant nonsense that I could not have our image so unjustly damaged. I asked for those words to be deleted, and they were.

I believe the film created another precedent. The professionals were acting parts as they would in any filmed play or novel. The rest of us were re-enacting our own professional roles in what must surely be a documentary. The professionals were paid professionals' fees. We others were given token payments (determined by the BBC) for our time and trouble. This alarmed Equity, the actors' union, who at first insisted on a clear-cut and familiar definition. Was this a television drama, a work of the imagination? If so, all appearing in it must hold Equity cards and be paid the full professional rates. Or was this a documentary? If so, no professionals must appear in it. A compromise was reached after much anxious negotiation and this new 'docudrama' form duly recognized.

Early in the New Year it was fairly certain that the BBC wanted to go ahead. I therefore wrote a brief account of the proposition to each governor and invited his reaction. Then we were hit by a national postal strike, so that none of the letters could be delivered by the Post Office. Several of the governors lived abroad, and those who did not lived out of London. The BBC stepped in and had the overseas letters taken to Calais for posting, and all the others delivered by hand.

There was no dissent. And the senior staff, too, felt that the programme could do us no harm and could very well do us much good. It was filmed over five weeks of the summer term, 1971, cost £30,000 to make, and attracted a record viewing public for the Tuesday documentary series. A record response, too, in letters and phone calls to the BBC. I myself received almost 200 letters from total strangers.

It was shown at peak viewing time on BBC 1 and its running time was extended from the standard 50 minutes of the series to an unprecedented 100 minutes, and this at the express command of the Great White Chief himself.

As most of the professional critics recognized, it was a first-class piece of film-making in an original and intriguing genre. All this I can say because the credit for all of it belongs to Roger Mills. I played the lead and I supplied the script, but neither of those contributions accounted for the film's remarkable style and impact. I hated myself in it, and I had assumed from the outset that this mangy old dog-collared wolf sticking his fangs in his own poor cubs would be torn apart without mercy by the sharper fangs of the younger wolves of Fleet Street. And so it was indeed! But, and this astonished me, the voice of Fleet Street was no vox populi, at least not to judge by the postbag response through the BBC's letterbox and mine.

20

The BBC film team arrived on June 2nd and departed on June 25th, and were thus filming throughout the GCE period. I had had to face squarely the possibility that the re-enacting of what was still, after seven months, a bitter memory might adversely affect the students' exam performances. I decided no harm would be done, provided I explained in advance just what the BBC were doing in our midst. So I told them the kind of film that was to be made, and also told them that only the over-eighteens might appear in it as voluntary extras. In fact, I think the whole filming operation proved of positive help to them. It gave them the opportunity to refresh their memories of those traumatic days, to gain some perspective on them, and to reconsider rather more objectively the issues involved. Yes, I think it had a generally cathartic, salutary effect on all of us.

I had never at any time of my life done any acting, not even at school or university. But any preacher who aims higher than the crooning of pulpit lullabies must have in him (or acquire) some basic histrionic ability, must be sensitive to audience reaction and possess some audience control. I knew I had a little capital of this kind, and that I must exploit it, for it was the only capital I possessed. In some ways it was easy to play oneself, in some ways very difficult. Especially since it was oneself of seven months earlier, and already I wasn't sure that I was now quite the same person. There was a temptation, too, to project a rather more favourable image of oneself. I was so determined to resist that one, that I think I actually overdid it. Moreover, two 'softer' sequences, in which, after grilling a student pretty fiercely, I said I was sorry I'd had to do it and applied what generous balm I could, were both cut from the film. Both sequences were almost literal reconstructions of what I'd done and said, but Roger told me there was just something a little bit unconvincing about them.

411

I'd always rather prided myself on being able to see myself as others saw me, but this experience of repeatedly watching myself on film playing myself was quite an eye-opener. I saw how easily impartiality could be taken for coldness, detachment for aloofness, advice for pontification, remonstrance for condemnation, inquiry for inquisition. And, though I speak quickly enough in the excitement of dialectic, I found I was dreadfully, irritatingly, slow when formal circumstances demanded every word be chosen with care. The penalty, I suppose, of being *too* word-conscious.

The film was shot out of sequence, and this required scrupulous attention to setting, wardrobe, mood, tone. Moreover, there was no real script, just my basic, specimen dialogue, and this proved quite a challenge, especially to the young professionals, who had not my advantage of being able to recall the living situation. I could see that this was policy on Roger's part. He was more likely to get verisimilitude if our words broke spontaneously forth from a felt situation. Usually, I'd go into a preliminary huddle with the boy or girl professionals, seeking to kindle them into a mutual combustion. This was almost second nature to me after a lifetime of English literature in the classroom. Though I've never trodden the boards, I've hammed half the characters in Shakespeare, striving by means of dramatic readings with my pupils to impart and elicit that incandescence of the psyche which Keats called 'burning through *King Lear.*'

I was lost in admiration for most of these youthful professional actors. It wasn't just a joy to work with them, but was a genuine privilege, too. And at least once the combustion was real. I had to play a scene in which a student (Jeremy Cook) attacks my attitude to drug-taking by the young as prejudiced, ignorant, obscurantist. There was no prepared script whatsoever. The young man playing the part said he didn't want one. Nor did we have any rehearsal. I sat behind my desk. Opposite me sat Jeremy, and behind him were the cameras, trained as usual full on me. Came the clapperboard and I began this reconstruction of my first conversation with Jeremy by asking if he had ever taken drugs. No, he never had, and he wouldn't do so at the college, *but* he felt this was a matter young people should be left to decide for themselves. It was absurd for adults to feel they could apply some total embargo. I asked him why he felt that way about it. And the boy launched into a heated barrage of defiant questions. His flushed face, angry eyes and explosive utterance were just too good to be untrue. I suddenly realized that this was from the heart of the young actor: a very bitter and personal attack. I guessed that he had talked freely with our more radical students and had identified himself completely with what he saw as their gallant resistance to persecution and tyranny. I knew this was 'for real, man,' and I warmed to the combat, conscious that I was sitting forward aggressively, even flushing with the heat of battle. He argued well, while I parried rather than

412

counterattacked. We left that bit of real-life drama intact in the film. When we'd finished shooting I tried to continue the discussion, for he was obviously a sincere and intelligent young man, and I admired his spirit. But he didn't want to talk to me at all.

There were two scenes requiring the student body more or less en masse. One was a rebashing of the occasion when I entered the dining room as they ate their lunch and told them of the visit of the drug squad. The other corporate scene took place in the assembly hall, a re-enactment of the later occasion on which I told them that more than cannabis was involved, that I now knew some students were taking and passing LSD and I was determined to find out who they were. In the first scene, I had asked any who had taken cannabis to come and tell me about it. I said I couldn't make any promises, in view of the police involvement, but I'd do my best to help anyone who owned up to pot-smoking and was not implicated in anything worse than puffing at the occasional reefer.

In the second scene, having gained greater and uglier information, I had told them once more of the dangers of LSD and asked anyone who could give me any information about it to see me at once. 'Yes,' I said, 'I'm doing what I loathe doing and have never done in any other context: I'm asking you to become informers. Informers, moreover, who know I'll expel any boy or girl against whom the evidence, or even the suspicion, is very strong. But knowing, too, that in so doing you may well be saving the victims and potential victims from acute physical and psychological damage.'

Now I felt these two scenes would prove the most difficult to shoot, simply because our students knew this was play-acting and someone was bound to grin or giggle or otherwise impair the realism. But quite the reverse. As I stood on the dais, willing myself back into the mood and manner and delivery of that distant autumn day of our infancy, as I launched into my grim and distressing ultimatum, I gazed around at all those tousled heads and realized with quite a shock that every one of them had, naturally and unconsciously, slipped back into his original role. Oh, I remembered well enough their individual reactions at the time, and I was convinced that this was no skilled play-acting on their part now. The clock had just whizzed back eight thousand hours, and there they were again, the sullen ones, and the cynical ones. It was a rather disquieting experience. I made a point of thanking them briskly and cheerfully, of congratulating them on their skill as players, as soon as Roger pronounced the take satisfactory.

I shall now be describing the events as chronicled in the film, but they are a true record of all that had actually happened.

After my first appeal to the cannabis users, a few students did come to confess privately to having smoked the odd reefer. One of the first to come was Troy Lefebre, an intelligent, hard-working young man who was in his second year with us and was universally popular. He had too much money, I had often thought, but was too much of a gentleman to flaunt it. He was sophisticated, but never unpleasantly so. His natural courtesy, friendliness and charm were most ingratiating, and his academic ambitions made him one of our more worthwhile students. And although I had no delusions about the essential playboy life he led when beyond our ken, I had generally assumed he had too much sense to jeopardize his future when under our very noses. Unfortunately for him, his performance on this occasion just failed to convince. He overplayed his hand. As he sat there, exerting all his charm, striving for an image of frankness and contrition, holding up a conscience sorely troubled by what I knew he must consider a very trivial offence, I felt and Tim Clark felt that the lady was indeed protesting too much. Yes, he admitted with hung head, he had once smoked a reefer in the grounds. Very stupid of him, he knew. He'd never do it again.

I thanked him for coming, but let him detect something equivocal in my manner, a little mockery in my eyes to disquiet him. When he'd gone, Tim and I agreed his was the obvious 'clever' move for anyone deeply implicated to make. But, of course, we did no more than place a small question mark beside him in our minds' eye. I didn't, at that time, envisage any severer action against him and similar miscreants than a dire warning and probationary status for the remainder of their time with us. I felt this would suffice to keep them clean till the academic year was over.

There was a girl who came with a similar confession that was even less convincing. She, too, had a winning manner, and was no less attractive in appearance than in manner. But I had never felt I could trust her. Under Troy's charm was, I had never doubted (and do not doubt today), a fundamentally very nice person, spoilt by too much material indulgence and too little spiritual guidance. But Angela (what a misnomer!) was accurately summed up by one of our American tutors as 'the toughest little cookie I've seen yet.' Her particular charm became positively sinister as soon as one sensed the hard shell encasing her and the moral vacuum within her. I never had any doubt that she was taking drugs. Nor, later, did any of us doubt that she was sleeping around pretty freely. Nor, at the last, did we doubt that she was behind the frequent thefts of sizeable sums of money from the girls' rooms.

Angela's thefts weren't compulsively sick ones. I am sure they were very pragmatic indeed, for the most generous student allowance can't meet the high cost of illicit drugs. But I don't think she sold or passed any of her stuff. She was too secretive, too solitary, too much in need herself of whatever she could get. Too clever, too, to get any of it internally. I reckon she had contacts outside and used them regularly. But it was all suspicion: no proof, not even the evidence of other kids' suspicions to add to my own. Nor could appeal or threat ever move her. She was stone. But in the end I did build up a body of circumstantial evidence against her in relation to missing money, and she knew it. Even here, though, she achieved a rather sickening triumph. For, just as I was about to ask her parents to remove her 'for generally unsatisfactory conduct,' she jumped the gun, asked her mother to take her away as she was sick of being suspected of everything under the sun. Almost every girl in the college told me, privately and individually, that she suspected Angela of stealing £20 from her roommate's bag.

21

After I had discovered that LSD was being passed around, and even given to unsuspecting victims as something fairly innocuous, I set about collecting every shred of evidence I could. On a college list I noted those students with known 'problems': broken homes, quarrels with parents, sibling jealousies, and so forth. I then marked on the same list those who had been noticeably 'awkward' while with us. Next, I turned a searchlight on Thursdays and Mondays (Wednesday was a half-day, and weekends were, of course, free). I also incorporated two important information sheets which arrived on my desk daily. One, from Tim Clark, the community director, listed those who had missed teaching periods and gave the offenders' 'reasons.' The other, from the medical sister, gave the names and ailments of those attending the day's surgery. Certain names appeared with increasing frequency on Thursdays and Mondays. So did such ailments as severe headache, vomiting, diarrhoea, and such comments as 'still in bed and asleep when I visited his room at 11 am.' Cross-checking in dead exeat forms one found most of these students had on Wednesday afternoons been to Oxford, and at the weekends to either their own homes, or to the houses of approved family friends. Or so they had stated on the forms.

In our early days I had issued fewer such forms and had destroyed such as we did have almost as soon as they became dead. But since our second year I had insisted on careful records and had filed them punctiliously. Yet never with any idea that they might one day serve my present purpose. My sole aim had been to protect our good name from parents of malingering or hypochondriac children who had failed their exams because they had missed their classes.

Finally, my clue-hunting activities took me round the students' rooms on the lookout for such seeming trivia as 'underground' magazines, joss sticks, psychedelic decorations, or posters of Jimi Hendrix, a pop singer who had recently killed himself with drugs and was now fast becoming a cult hero. Trivia, of course, but a tiny piece of a particular jigsaw puzzle might be thrown up.

We had, of course, been aware before of all these facts about the students' lives, but this was the first time they had been co-ordinated, collated on one student list. At least, all the facts except those relating to their rooms: hitherto all we'd looked for in those was a reasonable cleanliness.

The film reconstructed my tour of the rooms and, although the voice-over to this sequence insisted 'Such facts might mean anything - or nothing,' it was an obvious target for ridicule by newspaper reviewers. And fair enough: it *did* look rather absurd on film. I subsequently found I couldn't repress a grin when viewing that scene.

I'd like to mention three young actors who, I thought, did particularly well. Nigel Havers brought Troy Lefebre to life in both his earlier charm and his later panic. Olivia Whitemore finally made an excellent showing as Barbara Vane, the student who had become positively fey on cannabis. I say 'finally' because she clearly found it a difficult assignment. In the film I have a long scene with her in which I coax and flatter information from her in a cosy, chatty manner, as she burbles on with a rather mad, inconsequential gaiety. We played this several times before Roger was satisfied, but in the end she achieved a miniature portrait of a mind expanded to fatuity.

I think the hardest task fell to a young actor called Ricky Reeves, who played Chris Maclean with a conviction that was most affecting. He had to portray Chris' 'bad trip' in the woods at night when he imagines the trees are people closing in to kill him. He is at length overpowered by other students who, to a chorus of desperately well-meaning reassurances, drag him, still screaming and struggling, back to the house. Of course, I hadn't seen the original of this, but Roger had carefully gathered his evidence for it from surviving eye witnesses. Nor did I see the filmed reconstruction of this, or of any scene in which I was not actually engaged, until some three months later after all the artistry of cutting and editing had been lavished on it.

This young actor playing Chris Maclean had another lengthy and difficult scene: the one in which I force him to give me the names of those who induced him to take the LSD tablet. In the real-life drama I had waited in vain for any student to volunteer information about LSD in the college. I hoped some might but was not surprised that none did in the circumstances. It meant that I had to threaten and bully the information out of young Chris. I can only ask to be believed when I say that this was a last resort which I disliked employing. It was upsetting at the time, and strangely upsetting in the re-enactment. It seemed certain to me that, in the film, this scene above all others would rob me of any shred of audience sympathy I had elicited and transfer the entire weight of sympathy to the wretched little victim. I know that if I had been one of that audience I would have felt waves of protest rising within me against this grand inquisitor. This didn't appear to be at all the popular reaction, however, so I must assume that the film conveyed better than I knew the basic harsh facts: that I *had* to find out, and that this was now the only way I could hope to do so.

Before summoning Chris I had satisfied myself that he was in a fit state to be questioned about the incident. I had no doubt then, and I have none now, that he was fully recovered from his bad trip. It remained, of course, a nasty memory, but he was in no way still in the grip of the experience. Indeed, he was surprisingly 'normal,' relaxed, confident at first. And, upset as he became when I insisted on his giving me names, it was the natural upsetness of any boy who is told his parents will be summoned to remove him forthwith. If his reactions had been other than they were, I would have desisted immediately. I was, after all, aiming to protect young lives, not damage them.

So I was very tough with young Chris, refusing all excuses, nailing all lies, brushing aside angrily every prevarication. At one moment I banged on the desk with the flat of my palm and barked at him: '*Don't* lie to me, boy.' The poor kid almost jumped out of his chair and began to cry. I had steeled myself for this, and had predetermined all my words and actions. I told him tears would do him no good, that I hadn't the time or the inclination to play games with him. Either he told me now who gave him the tablet or I phoned his mother to ask her to come for him in the morning. He'd be expelled, and I would have to tell his parents why: for taking LSD and for shielding the supplier. He started to say something but it was lost in sobs and snivels. 'Oh, very well,' I snapped, as though my patience were at an end. I picked up the phone, said to my secretary. 'Oh, Mrs Clark, will you get me Mrs Maclean on the phone, please. Yes, right away.'

The boy took his hands from his face and stretched them wildly towards me. 'Oh no, please, please. Don't tell mummy. I'll tell you. I'll tell you.' I took up my pen. 'Well', I said coldly, 'I'm waiting.'

He fought for his words. 'I - I... it was... oh, I can't, I can't.'

'Right. Your mother must take you away.' I didn't quite know what to do if the phone didn't then ring, as arranged with Mrs Clark. But it did. I said grimly into it: 'Oh, good afternoon, Mrs Maclean.'

'*No,*' he yelled, as I quickly clamped my hand over the mouthpiece and waited, 'No, no, no, no. It was Jeremy Cook.'

As he sat moaning, I said sweetly to the phone: 'I just called to say that Chris has been rather unwell lately, but he's fine now.' I was, of course, speaking to no one but Mrs Clark with whom the whole shabby subterfuge had been arranged.

Then, with great difficulty, I tried to apply the balm. 'I'm sorry, Chris, really sorry, that I had to be so beastly. If it's any comfort, you really haven't told me anything I didn't know already. Perhaps... perhaps one day you'll see why I had to know. For your sake, and for the sake of other students. Now, don't go in to prep. Go to your room and lie down for a bit. You'll soon feel OK.' (That was the balm Roger found so unconvincing and cut out of the film.)

He stumbled out. I was annoyed to find that I didn't quite like to meet Tim Clark's eye. 'Yes, *beastly*,' I muttered, 'but absolutely necessary.' Tim said nothing. I gazed out of the window. I thought of all the school stories I'd read as a boy. Each, it seemed, had contained just such an episode: the little hero out-bullied by the odious housemaster, for whom nemesis couldn't come quickly enough.

Still, it had worked. I'd got what I wanted. Rather an easy victory, to be sure. And rather dirty play to achieve it. My collated information had pointed to Cook as the guilty party. Maclean merely tied up the case for the prosecution.

Now this scene was not only harrowing to play: it was also technically difficult. For one thing the microphones taped to my desk had to be so doctored that they would reproduce convincingly my slam on the desk. Again, Betty Clark at the switchboard in her office way across the hall had to know the exact moment to ring my phone and announce 'Mrs Maclean on the line, principal.' This meant a complicated trio of lookouts all cued to signal at the same instant.

We made many abortive attempts at this wretched scene. Sometimes the technical business went awry; sometimes Ricky Reeves or I would dry up or omit some part of the scene or just fail to get back into the mood and rhythm of it and, knowing this, have to throw up our hands and say 'Sorry, scrub it.' But at last we ran through without a hitch. Roger was more than pleased with the result. He murmured to me: 'That really had me gripping my seat.' And then the cameraman, deep in the desperate mysteries of his instruments, would cry in despair: 'Sorry, sorry. Hair on the gate.' This always produced a universal groan. I never discovered what it meant, except that the take was ruined and we'd have to start all over again.

Roger was clearly disappointed. This scene was the unluckiest in the film. For, after we'd at last got it safely and satisfactorily on film, after Ricky Reeves had returned to London, after we had waited several impatient days for the rushes to be delivered to Barcote, we received a laboratory report that the film had been ruined in the developing process. So the poor lad had to come back as soon as he could, and we all had to begin again, and twice Ricky and I ruined the take by dissolving into giggles.

I found as my enquiries proceeded that though Jeremy Cook and one of the girls (Toni Vathou) had got Chris Maclean to take the tablet (and both, to their credit, finally admitted this), there was a source within the college which those wanting LSD knew they could tap. I felt Cook and the girl were truthful in denying any such role as theirs. Much circumstantial evidence pointed to Troy Lefebre, but I knew I must have more than circumstantial evidence.

I had a hunch that some wanted to talk, if they could. I dared to believe that some, just a handful, no doubt, would give me names if they felt it would never be known. Their reluctance to come forward wasn't due, I sensed, to any doubt that confidence would be betrayed. Then, suddenly, the solution seemed so obvious that it was incredible I hadn't thought of it before. The trouble was that my summoning of any student to my study was common knowledge. He was either called over the Tannoy or fetched by somebody. In either case it was impossible to conceal his visit. In such circumstances no student could feel he spoke incognito. The next morning I therefore posted up a notice: 'I have set aside today for the individual interviewing of every student in the college. Please attend promptly at the time recorded beside your name.'

And with each and every student, even those who had admitted guilt, even those under heavy suspicion, even Chris Maclean, even Troy Lefebre, I went through the same formula: 'For the sake of everybody here, I am asking you, in the strictest confidence, to give me the name of any student you believe to be bringing LSD into the college.' With conviction, if sometimes with great reluctance, eight students gave me the name of Troy Lefebre. All the rest were virtual 'don't knows.' When the eight were asked how they knew it was Troy, they produced convincing, and often tallying, accounts of seeing him display the LSD tablets, or of catching him unawares counting them in his room, or of overhearing him talking about the LSD tablets he'd got. Several of the eight said simply: 'Well, everybody knows it's Troy.' Not one of the eight was known to have any grudge against Troy. Indeed, he was very popular and I doubt if he had an enemy in the community.

Little now remained to do, but that little was the vilest task of all: telling Troy and Jeremy and Toni that they were expelled. Ordering them to pack and be ready to leave within two hours. Then telling it all over again on the phone to their gasping, protesting parents or guardians.

It was a black, raining, windswept Saturday afternoon when they threw their ill-stuffed suitcases into the taxis I'd summoned.

22

Four had been expelled for drug abuse, two had run away, a further six 'unsatisfactory' students I eased out at the end of that first Barcote term, and two boys from overseas just failed to return in January. This meant that we had lost two terms' anticipated fees from each of fourteen students: a total lost income of over £8,000. This in our first term at Barcote, which had cost us, of course, much more to adapt to our use than we had budgeted for, even on the most generous basis, and adhering to a strict order of priorities. We had no reserve and contingency fund, I need hardly say, and it would be now almost impossible to fill these vacant places with one-year A level students. We did pick up about five students, for O level or English for Foreigners or general courses, or combinations of these. But the blow, as the bursar had warned me at the time, was so crippling that when other blows landed home later we were pretty well knocked out. (Of these later blows, by far the deadliest was dry rot.)

We had sold for £2,500 a rare and magnificent mechanical organ which had been built and installed for Squire West at the turn of the century. We obtained permission to sell many of the estate's towering trees, and the woods were in fact improved by this thinning out. We sold off a plot of land to a local farmer. We received further help from the educational charity of which the bishop of Portsmouth (now chairman of our governors) was a trustee: they offered us either a loan of £5,000 or a gift of £2,000, and we took the latter. Best of all, through the good offices of our friend Mr Underwood we had been adopted by two very reputable agencies on the Continent, who after several visits, inspections and discussions had contracted to furnish us with two summer schools of English for Foreigners, each consisting of some fifty boys and girls from Germany and Italy. Thanks to all this, and not least the two successful summer schools in July and August, we were still economically viable.

During those two months I had been interviewing parents and prospective students. True there were not as many of these as I would have liked, but we told ourselves that the rush would come, as in all previous years, after the publication of A level results in August. I had determined, after a year of drugs and vandalism, to be even more selective in my enrolments. In June and July and early August I turned away many would-be students I might in previous years have accepted: not simply those with known drug abuse records (who had always been 'out' so far as we were concerned) but also those whose behaviour at their previous schools suggested they could be part of a drug-taking 'protest' scene.

Despite the increasing precariousness of our situation, we somehow endured to the end of that academic year. Somehow we coddled and bullied the students through the ordeal of public exams. I made myself ever more unpopular in the process. Several weeks before the exams started I imposed a 'lights out' deadline at midnight. This brought a fury of protest and resentment from a section of the students who had been in the habit of doing most of their work in the small hours and lying abed half the morning. Abetted by a conscientious but misguided young tutor, they wailed that they worked better at night, they really couldn't get through all their work without this very post-midnight oil, and so forth. It was all nonsense.

Painstakingly I went through each protestor's timetable with him, pointing out the hours and hours of daylight in which he was free to study. I wouldn't budge on this issue for all their sulks. I toured the grounds regularly in the small hours, pitching in to any boy or girl I found infringing the rule. But finally I realized that I must tackle the problem from the other end: insist they arrive for a communal breakfast and proceed from that to their classes.

Even at this stage I was reluctant to abandon wholesale the self-determination I'd always taken pride in allowing them: not least that of preparing their own breakfasts in their own units, of being held personally responsible for getting enough sleep and attending their classes. But I could not ignore the fact that the reckless and antisocial minority were sitting up half the night, keeping awake those in their units who wanted to sleep, gobbling up the entire unit's breakfast supplies as they did so, and driving their tutors to distraction by missing vital morning classes. More and more of the reasonable students came to complain that they couldn't get any sleep and they couldn't get any breakfast.

In the end, I felt compelled to disband the student council when it degenerated into mere demands for privileges and a virtual refusal of responsibilities. I created special units for which any student who wanted to get his A levels could volunteer. The privileges of such units were complete self-determination as to out-of-class time; the responsibilities were attendance at breakfast in the dining hall, all classes and work assignments honoured, and lights out at midnight.

The 90 per cent all volunteered: the 10 per cent who did not were segregated in a unit of their own. It was obvious that this 10 per cent, now seeing themselves as official drop-outs, might well deteriorate further, despite my insistence that we certainly had not written them off. 'If you fall below minimum standards then you'll just have to go,' I told them. 'But we have reached the stage now where I can no longer ask tutors already stretched to breaking point to fight to save you from yourselves. You now have the liberty you want, including freedom to hurt yourselves. We naturally hope you will not. We naturally want you to pass your exams. If I am to some extent letting you opt out it is because I can no longer allow you to hurt others.'

I knew I was taking a big risk in this, but it worked better than I had dared to hope. Of course, it was Machiavellian: only the silliest were willing to declare thus publicly that they were *not* interested in passing their exams, especially since I solemnly produced printed forms that set out all the conditions and required them to sign them in front of me. And even the silly 10 per cent actually improved slightly, thanks, I suppose, to their ingrained desire never to respond as the establishment expected them to respond. A further benefit was the sweeter condition of their living units, the filth of which when they were cooking in them was fast becoming a health hazard.

It was obvious too, that the 90 per cent were much happier. Someone had ordered them to do what they knew they ought to do, and they clearly welcomed release from the burdens of free choice, self-discipline and guilty conscience.

We had no resident domestics, so the considerable added chores of serving them breakfast fell upon two already loaded backs: nearly always on that of a gallant relative of mine who (in response to a desperate telegram I sent her when our resident housekeeper decided after the briefest of trials that she couldn't stand it a moment longer) gave up her post as a hospital sister to supervise all our catering and medical care. But sometimes I would take over this serving of breakfast, and, to be honest, rather enjoyed it. It was a pleasant change from desk-work and an extra encounter with the students on a novel basis. The unlikeliest boys and girls, beholding my forays on eggs and cornflakes and toast and tea, offered to help or were profuse in their thanks or just treated me to rare, embarrassed smiles. 'Now at last,' they seemed to be saying, 'we see you doing something for us.'

There were three or four boys who had never ceased to hate me for the drugs expulsions. Most of them had also fallen foul of me for such offences as filthy rooms or persons, rudeness to domestics, public petting, acts of vandalism. All the students were free to leave for home as soon as they had finished their public exams, and I encouraged them to do so. Most of them preferred to stay on a day or two for the novelty of watching others still in the throes of those pains from which they themselves had just escaped. A young tutor said he had heard a rumour that these four planned to remain just one extra night after their last exam: during the night hours they would totally wreck their living units and escape forever soon after dawn. Perhaps it was mere bravado, but I wasn't taking any chances. While they were still in the examination hall I phoned their parents to say that they must return home that day: by train if not collected. Thus it was that, sauntering out of the examination hall they were met by their counsellors and either their parents or a taxi driver. Muttering imprecations, they packed and left almost before the ink was dry on their scripts.

The rest departed more or less pleasantly, and we at once began to prepare for the considerable influx of summer school students. By the end of August these, too, had gone, and we were beginning to face the hideous and inconceivable possibility that we could not get anything like our full complement of students for the new academic year. By mid-September 1971 this possibility was a certainty. I had an appointment at the BBC to record the voice-overs for the film (now scheduled for a mid-October showing). I remember the setting vividly: as Roger and I waited for the lift at Bush

House I told him we might well have to go into voluntary liquidation. He was incredulous, thought it was a rather sick joke on my part. I convinced him otherwise, and when the inevitable actually happened, he added to the film a voice-over of his own: 'Since this film was made, Anglo-American College has been forced to close, largely through the income lost by the drugs expulsions.'

23

We had been greatly heartened by that summer's GCE results. They were the best we had yet achieved: our 46 candidates had between them gained 47 A levels and 55 O levels, and this after only eight months' tuition (*what* an eight months!). Several of the A levels were top-grade, too. Almost every student seeking a university place obtained one. Of the ten with whom I had so enthusiastically embarked on the English literature course the previous year only one had survived to sit the A level, and she was a girl. Drugs expulsions and 'easings out' had, as usual, hit my class hardest: the rebels and the tearaways had all opted for Eng Lit. So only June was left to sit the actual exam. She had come to us from a well-known school with a battery of O levels and three failures at A level. Despite my warm praise for her industry, intelligence and sensitivity, she had received not one offer of a university place and was understandably despondent. With us she achieved 'A' grades in her English and in her history A levels. She came to see me in the final ruins of Barcote, and I told her to go out and hammer indignantly on some of the university doors and ask them if they still dared to slam them in the face of her results. I wrote her an open letter to brandish with her certificates. She got into Oxford.

Yes, those results cheered us. A much-needed boost. It was good, too, to add up our total score over the four years: 117 A levels and 198 O levels. Often with most unpromising human material. Usually against other and undeserved odds. And in the sober knowledge that most of the students wouldn't have succeeded anywhere else. Yes, I remain proud of that record and of all those who made it possible.

I had worked out those figures, and many similar statistics, in August for incorporation in our new prospectus. For six weeks and more I had been laboriously reviewing, with the senior tutors, every facet of our life at the college. We scrapped, overhauled, innovated in all areas: academic, social, constitutional, penal. I felt none of us could or should be asked to face another year like the one just ended. And out of it all emerged yet another prospectus (my seventh, I think), the distilled wisdom of four purgatorial years. In this prospectus I increased the fees to £338 per term, for it was clear that we had for the past year been giving value greater than our fees. (I remembered a county education officer who had called with a view to placing with us a boy whose fees the authority would be paying. I spent much time describing our ethos, and then Tim took him on a tour of inspection. Finally, he asked me what were our termly fees. '£298 per term,' I replied. He whistled. 'Well,' I replied with some asperity, 'you've seen all they're given, and you must know the costs.' He interrupted me quickly. 'My dear sir,' he demurred, 'I whistled because I don't know how you can provide so much for so little.' The local authority sent the boy to us, and he proved one of our major successes.)

Our two large summer schools of continental boys and girls were the subject of a little experiment on my part. I had been wondering rather more frequently than usual if I really were too rigid, intransigent, demanding, in my attitude to young people. I suspected Tim sometimes thought so, and I knew one or two other tutors did. I was not relishing the prospect of taking on half a hundred foreign kids (all in holiday mood) so soon after our awful term had closed. 'Don't worry,' said Brian, who has always been happier on the Continent than in this island, and was actually looking forward to the invasion. 'They'll not be like our own little horrors. They're more mature, more civilized, more responsive.'

I put Tim in complete charge of these summer schools. I had nothing to do with them, promised not to interfere (not unless the roof fell). The kids themselves scarcely ever saw me and had no idea who I was if they did bump into me entering or exiting. Once two young Italian girls found me scratching in some bushes. I was looking for my pen, which I'd dropped from my first-floor study window. 'You are the garden man?' they asked. I told them I was, and didn't they think I made the flowers grow beautifully?

Tim was, I knew, gifted with really beautiful funds of patience, kindliness and helpfulness in dealing with young people. Nothing was too much trouble for him. He and Adrian, who had similar enviable qualities, didn't spare themselves in keeping those boys and girls happy sixteen hours a day: in their work, their food, their sightseeing, their countless little alien problems. And certainly some were grateful, while very many of them were bitterly disappointed subsequently to find they could not return to us. At the end of their month's course they were all entered for the Pitman College exams, either intermediate or advanced, and very few indeed failed to gain their certificates. But after a depressingly brief time some familiar signs appeared: graffiti, vandalism, dirt, theft. The boys were much worse than the girls, the Italians much worse than the Germans. And as for sex and drugs: I hugged my ostrich role. I didn't ask Tim and Tim didn't tell me. Brian was entirely disillusioned. Adrian was very fed up. One tutor whose beloved vintage car had been damaged and pillaged summoned the police and preferred charges against the youth he'd caught with the spare part. I know some tutors felt Tim was far too gentle with them all. He himself seemed pretty annoyed and exhausted after a few weeks of it, and even perhaps secretly agreed with the crusty tutor who said: 'They're all the same, these kids, British, American, German, Italian or Eskimo. Spoilt brats. Too big for their boots. No manners. No decency. No guts. Whole world's going mad. No discipline anywhere.'

When in early September we began to be seriously alarmed about the fall in enrolments, I rewrote two pages of the new prospectus. On the first of these I reinstated chemistry and physics, which I had silently dropped as a tentative economy measure, for the numbers in these classes had never justified the high tutorial and laboratory costs involved. But now it was vital to preserve the wide range of subjects we offered, for even profitless places were to be preferred to empty places. The second sheet I rewrote in order to restore the termly fee to £298. At the time we could explain the sudden dropping-off only in terms of these two major alterations in our prospectus. But it seemed to make little difference.

I had to warn the senior staff that the situation would be desperate if within the next week enquiries and applications did not revert to their former healthy trends. Tim, Michael and I also spent the week tapping every likely and unlikely source of assistance. In vain. I stepped up advertising. Likewise to no avail. Then reports drifted in of a drastic recession in the number of British and American students desiring to enter universities.

On September 21st I told the staff that we were going into voluntary liquidation. That morning's post brought about £1,000 in advance fees. I returned all these, with a memorandum I wrote and duplicated in one black hour, as the dazed staff wandered about, torn between desultory talk and desultory packing. Verbally to them, and in my memorandum, I had expressed my deep sorrow and regret, and my determination to do all I personally could to help those hit by this disaster, although all financial matters were now in the hands of the liquidator-elect. I advised the staff to remove their personal belongings from the premises as soon as possible.

The previous night I had advised the governors by phone and cable of this unavoidable decision. I had, of course, warned them some two weeks earlier of our dire straits, just as I had reviewed the position with our accountant, who had said that, if the worst happened, he was willing to stand for election as our liquidator.

In her office I found my excellent secretary, Tim's wife, Betty, clearing her desk for action. I had a hundred people to whom I must post my memorandum, and the parents of those due to arrive in a few days must be told by telephone or cable that we no longer existed. In addition, I had to get all our business files ready for the liquidator and for the meeting of creditors. Not to mention the horrific task of moving myself, all my belongings and all the academic files to my home in London. I had also promised to write open testimonials for all the staff before they left. It was a Tuesday, and I thought that with Betty's help I could get through the worst of these chores by the end of the week. I couldn't decently ask her, or anyone, to stay later than that, nor would our modest petty-cash box be able to pay them. So I said: 'I quite understand, Betty, that it is now every man for himself, and I know you have to look for another job. If...' She interrupted me: 'I'm just going, principal.' With that, she put the cover on her typewriter, snapped to her handbag, and left.

This was the first intimation I received that upon my head alone was to fall all the opprobrium. Looking back, I find it odd that I was unprepared for this. I don't think I felt any self-pity: I was far too busy for such luxuries. What I hadn't realized was that another element was involved in defeat: the trial to determine war guilt. Such, in effect, was the meeting of creditors; and in countless individual minds that war crimes commission arraigned me and found me guilty. I now understand all this well enough. At the time, though, I was rather surprised and (frankly) rather hurt that almost no one thought to throw me personally a word of commiseration. I found it especially hard to understand how some people we had helped far beyond the call of duty could register nothing but a total bitterness even though they knew I was myself hit at least as hard as they were.

On September 22nd the bishop of Portsmouth called to sign, with me, the necessary instruments of voluntary liquidation. On the 26th I went to the Television Centre in London to see a run-through of the film *Expulsion*, now due for transmission on October 19th, five days after the date fixed for the meeting of creditors. All this time I was living on alone at Barcote. I kept the front of the house shuttered, my bedroom and study both being at the back. The electricity supply was now disconnected and the phone mercifully dead. Somehow I waded through the morass of work I had to do. I seldom saw anybody. At first I was cheered by the distant sounds of the timber-fellers, who were furiously removing the trees for which their boss had already paid. But the liquidator-elect soon froze their labour in full spate, according to the law in such matters. I missed their occasional shouts and the insistent whine of their saw. Now there were only the birds to be heard, raucous and triumphant all round the house. The rabbits had repossessed the lawn as a playground, lolloping off with insolent tardiness when I showed myself. The wheel had certainly come full circle.

A freelance journalist from the *Radio Times* came to see me: a pleasant soul whose sympathy was novel and welcome, though it led him to write an article that was embarrassingly near to sob-stuff. Later, two photographers called, also commissioned by the *Radio Times*. In hair and clothes and manner they were clearly part of a younger generation than mine, so that I was surprised to meet in them, too, dole for the college and contempt for those students whose excesses had helped to kill it in its prime. (I met a similar response, with similar surprise, in some young technicians at the BBC, and in opinions expressed by several younger viewers.)

The meeting of creditors was quite as unpleasant as I had been told it might be: sneers and abuse from strangers, cold animosity from professional acquaintances, a discomfited and downcast silence from friends. In all this I was greatly helped by the presence of the bishop of Portsmouth who had with courage and kindness insisted on facing the creditors with me. He was the only governor or patron so to do. Here and later he showed himself the same faithful friend.

The wealthiest creditors were generally the worst, since money to them was nothing to be taken lightly. A few days before I had learned that, in returning the £1,000 pounds sent as advance fees, I had in fact 'acted criminally,' as on another occasion when I allowed a vendor to take back some costly equipment which was unpaid for and still unwrapped. It had seemed to me that to accept those fees once I knew we were liquidating *would* have been a criminal act. Nor did I see any harm in allowing the firm to remove the equipment: was I not thereby reducing the list of creditors? I had not at that time appreciated what was meant by 'freezing all assets,' and I could indeed have been ordered by a court to pay the liquidator, out of my own pocket, the £1,000 plus the face value of the equipment.

One florid gentleman rose, with all the assurance of a prosecuting counsel in a TV melodrama, to ask me: 'You say your term ended on June 30th?' I assented. He repeated: 'June 30th,' and, gazing round portentously, paused for effect. 'So how do you explain the fact that we delivered several kegs of ale and lager to you on July 2nd, and there's not a drop of it left now?' He closed his mouth with a sudden snap and surveyed the jury to whom he had so triumphantly unmasked these tippling tutors, this reverend, roistering rogue. I explained quietly that we had held two summer schools, for whose refreshment those kegs had in fact been ordered and had in fact been consumed.

A lawyer engaged by a local tradesman suggested that it was 'downright dishonest' to use fees paid in advance. 'Are not your clients' shops filled with goods obtained on credit?' I countered acidly, 'goods they aim to sell before they have paid for them, sell on the entirely reasonable assumption that customers will continue to walk through their door as they always have done in the past? And isn't that just what we did?'

But, of course, the less I cringed, the angrier they became. I had expressed my deep and sincere regret, as well as my hope that our assets might meet their debts, but cringe I wouldn't. When I proposed, and Michael Charles seconded, that our accountant (who had already done all the initial chores, and had required the bishop and me to guarantee his fees for that in the event of his not being elected) should be appointed liquidator by this meeting, the local tradesmen at once proposed and seconded their lawyer. Two votes were then taken, and our accountant was elected by a fairly easy majority.

A small committee of inspection was then elected. This represented the various types of creditors and 'advised' the liquidator. Michael Charles was chosen to represent the staff (all due for 'salary in lieu of notice'). And so the meeting dragged on to its wretched end.

Two days later, on October 16th, I packed all my stuff into a van and two cars, and drove out of Barcote for the last time. I have never seen it since. The attack mounted against me at the meeting of creditors continued for about eighteen months. My own claim for 'salary in lieu of notice' was disputed all along the line. Then it was found that the governors' decision regarding my 'principal's car' had not been recorded in the minutes of their meeting. The committee of inspection would not therefore accept that it was mine and demanded that its value be deducted from the salary due to me (which would have left almost nothing). I said that the bishop of Portsmouth, the company secretary, the bursar and I myself were all prepared to swear statements that this well-remembered decision had in fact been taken by the governors, and that in accordance with their wishes the car had reverted to me some twelve months ago. No, they wouldn't accept any sworn statements, even from bishops and barristers and colonels and clergy, and insisted on what they believed to be their pound of flesh. There was still some stubbornness left in me. I consulted an expert in company law and, in the light of his advice, I told the liquidator and his committee that they would be behaving most improperly in setting off the value of the car against the salary due to me: that their only correct course was to sue me for the return of the vehicle, when I should be most happy to defend myself and call my witnesses to give their sworn statements in person. Since, as I guessed, they knew they could win no such case but would almost certainly be landed with heavy costs, they yielded (with how ill a grace I could well imagine) and consoled themselves by deducting from my due the road tax the college had paid on the vehicle while I was using it as principal. Such unpleasantness continued even after it must have been clear that debts would be paid in full. And so they were, thanks to the excellent price the liquidator obtained for Barcote Manor, its contents and its arboreal acres.

Some months later I learned that all creditors had been paid their full claims, and that the liquidation fund showed an appreciable surplus. This, like most things connected with Anglo-American College, is highly unusual.

24

Once *Expulsion* had been more or less completed, it had to be submitted to the BBC Supremo for a yea-or-nay decision. I had gathered from Roger's reactions that he was in no way certain the film would emerge victorious from this dread ordeal. In theory, it could be totally rejected and consigned to limbo. In fact, the boss was so enthusiastic that he not only extended the running time of the film itself but further decreed: 'Run a bulldozer through whatever's been planned to follow it, and get this man Gamble and a panel to hold a post mortem on it.' Roger phoned to ask if I'd join such a panel. Now, if I'd had one criticism of the film it was that it concentrated so exclusively on the views of the 'establishment' (in effect, of *me*) and gave little or no opportunity for the students (let alone the expelled 'victims') to state their case. I had from the outset urged Roger to incorporate in the film some spontaneous student discussion on the merits or otherwise of my handling of the case: a discussion with me, or with him, or just among themselves. I do see that, artistically, this might have impaired the film, one of whose chief merits was its clean, economical story line, its sense of inevitable momentum. Three boys *did* give their views at the end of the film: something of which I was totally unaware until I saw a preview of the finished product. I remember sitting forward at that point, thinking to myself: 'Now for it. Now I'll hear a few home truths.' I was actually rather disappointed that all three seemed more pro than anti; disappointed not only because I felt the film needed the stringency of attack, but also because I knew this little sequence could to some eyes appear suspect. One of these three students said: 'Considering the time he had, which was very short, he handled it as well as he could have done in the circumstances.' Another said: 'He was a bit unfair on some people and a bit lenient on others, but then that's just a matter of opinion, of liking. I think, on the whole - yeah, he did it pretty well.'

A third boy was a particularly honest, outspoken young man. (A few days after Troy Lefebre's expulsion, he had organized a petition throughout the college asking for Troy's expulsion to be commuted to suspension. He had presented this to me himself and pleaded his case tenaciously. I'd told him I had nothing but admiration for his motives and no doubt at all that I was justified in rejecting his petition.) Here is what I remember this boy saying in the film:

'Well, at the time I hated him - very, very much - because I thought he was... well, sort of like a father figure - isn't it? You get a whipping so you hate your father for a while after the whipping because it still hurts, and we thought a lot of what was going on was just dishonest and very, very low. This was the general atmosphere after the whole incident took place, but after a while, in the second term, I got to thinking - I think a lot of people got

429

to thinking - that he handled it very, very well under the circumstances, and I think he saved a lot of people, in fact I know he saved a lot of people from the police, and it's done some of them a lot of good.'

So I jumped at the idea of a panel to discuss the film. I suggested some people for such a panel, but my ideas were not taken up. I felt the panel finally assembled was not good. It was decided it would be more constructive to have two medical men specializing in the treatment of drug offenders, a headmistress whose declared policy was never to expel a pupil for drug abuse, and a headmaster who was known to expel in such circumstances, just as I had done. The chairman of the discussion was Ludovic Kennedy, a mass-media luminary I had long admired, especially as a longstanding opponent of capital punishment. The discussion was to be prerecorded.

We all met in the Lime Grove studios on Sunday afternoon, October 17th, two days before the programme was to be shown. I had never before met any of the other panel members. I at once took to the headmistress, who was just the kind of warm, caring, broadminded person I have always relished. Just as instinctively, I knew that the headmaster represented everything that was alien, if not actually antipathetic, to me. And it was obviously a mutual disrelish.

We entered a viewing room and settled down to watch *Expulsion*, now in its final form as it was to be transmitted on the Tuesday. It was the first time I had seen it in colour and the first time I had watched it as part of an audience. And one thing was indisputable: as a drama it gripped them all from first to last. At the tenser moments they leaned forward, otherwise there was scarcely a movement throughout, not even from so old a hand as Ludovic Kennedy. When it was over, there were one or two sudden releases of breath, otherwise no word or movement for several moments: always the highest tribute an audience can pay. I was delighted by this, for Roger's sake. It confirmed my own conviction that, whatever the reaction to me and my doings, the film itself was a modest triumph for its director. When we did rise, Mr Kennedy patted my shoulder and murmured: 'Never mind, Mr Gamble, the Old Vic will be after you in no time.'

I have no script of this discussion and must rely on a somewhat overscored memory, but I do recall twice joining the fray. Once when the medicos were enumerating all the possible private griefs motivating our adolescent drug offenders, I felt constrained to suggest one or two others: 'Or the mere self-indulgence of a spoilt child? Or the calculated defiance of those who hated all authority? Or sheer spinelessness? Or a reckless disregard of others' health and safety? Or perhaps you regard all these as sicknesses for which they can't be held responsible?' And when someone trotted out the platitudes about all of us being hooked on drugs, and how could our perhaps *more* harmful smoking and drinking be condoned, I interposed my habitual rejoinder: 'We *don't* know that cannabis is less harmful. Even if it were, it scarcely justifies it as an alternative. What's more, cannabis is smoked in tobacco, while those on LSD seek greater kicks by following it with chasers of alcohol. And finally, since there's no breathalyzer for pot or acid, we just don't know how many road deaths can be laid at their doors.'

What with my image in the film, and the ineptitude of this ensuing post mortem, I felt that evening I'd pretty well had it so far as audience reaction was concerned.

I stayed behind to have a drink with Roger and several others who had helped to make *Expulsion*. A passing Cliff Michelmore, hearing festive sounds, put his head round the door and asked if he could join us. He stayed two hours, in the course of which he and I had a long and stimulating interchange: about drugs, education, young people. He said he'd ask his son, Guy, who was at boarding school, what he and his friends thought of the film. And he thought I might make a useful recruit to a radio programme called *If You Think You've Got Problems*, in which listeners phone in their problems for discussion by a panel of advisers chaired by Jean Metcalfe, Michelmore's wife. But nothing came of that - fortunately, I'm sure, as I'm not by nature the gentle, forgiving type the programme seemed to favour.

The first review of *Expulsion* that I read was that in *The Guardian*. 'The programme I thought I might just look at,' the critic wrote, 'and looked and was hooked and irrevocably addicted was BBC-1's *Expulsion*.' The reviewer said I reminded her of a bird pulling a worm out of the ground: 'I would like to have had the worms' eye view, too.' Apart from thus thinking 'it was rather lopsided,' she had nothing but praise for the film as 'shocking, painful, and compulsive viewing. And when I came to write about it my fingers slipped off the typewriter keys, being sticky with sweat.'

The *Daily Telegraph* reviewer had similar praise for the production, similar reservations about the wisdom of my action. Again, however, the review was much milder in its strictures than I had anticipated. However, I was not to be cheated of the anathema I'd always expected from the younger and/or trendier reviewers. Said that Sunday's *Observer*: 'When the kids transgressed his fairly permissive ideas of what was acceptable, that is, when they moved from drinking at the local to smoking pot, he became ruthlessly authoritarian, rooting out the offenders and expelling them without any consideration of their circumstances.'

As a result of the publicity the *Oz* trial had brought him, Richard Neville had been given a weekly column in the *London Evening Standard* and had clearly been told his success would be measured by his ability to *épater la bourgeoisie*. He understandably pounced on *Expulsion*, saying (among other things): 'The attitudes of those in authority at the school were portrayed as so obnoxious, infantile and ill-informed that sensitive young people are bound to identify with the expelled pupils. The programme was an hour-long advertisement for soft drugs.'

It is rather interesting to find both these reviewers (and certainly not these two alone) giving the impression that the principal went berserk and hurled into perdition a few kids he found smoking pot. Since the film made it painfully clear that I was pursuing those who supplied LSD and who had given it to the youngest kid without his knowing what it was, I can only conclude that the reaction of these reviewers was so emotional that they registered or recalled not what the film said but what they (in their denigrating zeal) wished it had said.

Alan Brien in *The Sunday Times* was refreshingly forthright: 'Personally, I thought this headmaster ... vain, short-sighted, pompous and silly.' Honest, if rather negative: he didn't anywhere in his review suggest how he felt I should have dealt with what he curiously named 'the drugtakers and anarchists who were "corrupting" their fellows.'

Ned Thomas, in *The Times Educational Supplement*, wrote quite the most responsible (though not uncritical) review, such as one would expect to find in a professional journal. In the same issue, Leonard Buckley wrote at some length about the programme in his media column. Both writers found the panel discussion unsatisfactory: 'generalized clichés,' 'smooth talk,' 'a lack of frankness,' 'a complete failure to suggest how else the situation might have been handled.' (Leonard Buckley returned to the subject in later issues of the *Supplement*, in terms so cryptic I don't know what he was getting at.)

The *Radio Times* published a selection of letters under the heading, '*Expulsion*: Did Mr Gamble do the right thing?', and kindly invited me to write a brief reply to points raised. After making various points already made in this book, I concluded:

> So many simple-minded young rebels think they are gods. Suddenly affluent after the war, they were conned by Tin Pan Alley and Carnaby Street, etc, into the worship of the Teenage Idol. (How many remember the avalanche that nearly engulfed poor Gilbert Harding when he spoke of the 'spineless and spoonfed generation'?) Poor things, they've never had it so bad. I feel very sorry for them and I now just hope and pray I can live with them according to the motto they so glibly chant: 'Make love, not war'.

Most of the letters contrasted the panel discussion unfavourably with the documentary, so that the editor felt he should also invite a comment from Roger Mills, who wrote this generous and entirely unsolicited testimonial:

> Sorry. It was my responsibility to cast the panel. I thought I had chosen a fair cross-section of opinion - from a headmistress who was against expulsion under any circumstances, to a headmaster with a known record of expulsion. But every discussion programme is a leap in the dark. You can't make people say what you expect them to say. If the headmaster who had expelled for drug abuse in his own school chose not to support Mr Gamble's decision to

take similar measures in his school, it was that headmaster's right - even if
Mr Gamble appeared thereby not only jobless, but friendless, too.

The real trouble was that the headmistress (whom I liked) had had no experience of a boarding school, and the public school headmaster (whom I did not like) was far too much of 'the establishment' to second any of my views. So neither supported me. But the reviewer who got really worked up about *Expulsion* was Clive James in *The Listener*. No media man trendier than he, none more anxious to promote himself by means of broad humour and verbal pyrotechnics. He held much the same sort of brief as his fellow Aussie, Richard Neville: '*Shout* (you want to be heard as far as possible, don't you?) and *goad* (the maximum come-back is good for all of us, you see).' James spent two thirds of his long review retelling the *Expulsion* narrative in the form of a Sherlock Holmes story, with me as Holmes and Tim as Watson. Then, after giving us such dazzlers as 'the Rev had done nothing more useful than try to kill a weed by chucking it over the fence,' he produced his own little homily to lighten our darkness: 'Moral integrity ... can't be imposed by diktat on those whose morality is still forming: it has to be transmitted by persuasion.'

As a review by a professional television critic of a serious documentary on a serious subject, his article was, of course, a nonstarter. As a laugh from a journalist-entertainer, it was, I thought, *quite* funny. I suddenly felt I'd like to write a reply: partly because I thought irresponsible distortions needed correcting, partly because I wanted to cheer myself up, and partly because I needed at that time the mental exercise afforded by a reasonably intelligent sparring partner.

So I wrote a long letter in which I sarcastically congratulated the *Listener* reviewer on his 'insight, compassion and wit,' and on being the only critic to realize that *Expulsion* was indeed 'a try-out for a new comedy series' commissioned by the BBC in 'their desperate search for a rival to the brilliant *Rivals of Sherlock Holmes* on another channel.' I then proceeded to outline future episodes. My purpose was to parody the 'permissive society; the cult of youth; the irresponsible trendiness of some reviewers; the febrile quest of all the media for the Even Bigger Shock; the commercial exploitation of minority and protest voices.'

Well, it was fun to write. I was surprised that *The Listener* published it; surprised too, by its length. The editor headed it 'The Rev Peter Gamble's New Comedy Series,' under which title the correspondence ran through four successive issues of the magazine.

Clive James' reply was frankly disappointing. Where I'd hoped for some wit or some serious dialectic, there wasn't much more than *rudeness* of defiant-little-boy variety.

I have quoted from these reviews and letters because they show the reaction to the programme of people whose voices command some audience. They were, as I have indicated, almost wholly at variance with the many people who wrote me personal letters. The warmth and kindness of these were a real help during my wretched doldrum days, except that I couldn't feel I had earned the laurels they decked me with. It was even more embarrassing when they sent me money! About six good souls sent me small cheques. In my letters of thanks I said I felt unable to accept these gifts, though immensely heartened by the spirit that prompted them. I asked if I could send them on to the liquidator, to help meet our debts. They all agreed, except for an elderly lady doctor who insisted her £10 was for me and no one else. One generous young man gave his permission for me to send his £5 to the liquidator and with his letter enclosed a Book Token for the same amount, daring me to liquidize that. Otherwise, I passed all the money to the clamorous hands of our creditors.

25

Early in the New Year I was invited by the Independent Schools Association to be one of the three speakers at their annual conference, for which they were arranging a symposium on 'Drugs in Schools.' I accepted, and prepared the kind of talk they expected: an account of how I had dealt with the problem at Anglo-American College. I duly arrived in Scarborough for the reception on the Tuesday evening. We ourselves had been elected to membership of this association and I was looking forward to meeting its staff and my fellow members, all of whom were heads of independent schools other than the 'official' public schools. These were generally dedicated and conscientious people who were often very worried about the new look their pupils had acquired. None of those to whom I spoke betrayed liberal views in any direction. There seemed to be total approval for the strong line I had taken with our drug abusers (which was why I had been invited to speak, of course).

I decided, rather recklessly, to scrap my prepared talk. Of what value was it to anybody present to repeat the story told in *Expulsion*, or to sound again the truisms of that panel discussion? And to be hailed as their little hero or saint or martyr was, I knew, more than I could stomach. My fellow speakers were a detective inspector in charge of the regional drugs branch and a psychiatrist who headed the drug addiction unit at a northern hospital. I knew they would supply all the expert knowledge and advice. I wanted to do something that I, at any rate, considered both different and constructive, though I doubted whether that would be the verdict of the audience.

In my speech, I suggested the young themselves didn't want a great deal of their posturing to be taken seriously. Much of it was provocative mischief, much of it exhibitionist fun, and most of them knew they were destined soon to grow out of it. But about some things they demanded with great earnestness both a voice and an ear, for they believed they were right and time was not on their side.

'Only if we are proud of the world we've made for them,' I concluded, 'can we decently be deaf to their cries. Don't stop your ears when they tell you you're sick, just because so many of them are sick, too. Don't reject their strictures because they haven't the remedies. Don't patronize them or flatter them. Above all, don't fear them. Be honest and open with them. Share with them: share your own sicknesses and uncertainties and they'll be readier to share your wisdom. For they *do* need us, as we go in terrible need of them. Build bridges, hold out hands. I believe there are hopeful signs now. I believe we have passed the peak of their loonier antics, their more dangerous excesses. I think they see how fatuous it is to seek more abundant life by means of the lethal harder drugs. I think most of them use cannabis less irresponsibly than we use alcohol. I think they're ready for a *rapprochement* with us, their unhappy elders, but I don't want that *rapprochement* to be their capitulation. I don't want it to be at the expense of all the good and positive things they've stood for. I don't want to lose those tongues that cry Hosannas, for if we do, it's our tragedy no less than theirs.'

I sat down to muted applause and mystified faces. I was followed at once by the detective inspector, whose hardheaded, pragmatic approach and considerable skill as a lecturer was an obvious relief from my windy rhetoric. He distributed bottled specimens of drugs and a batch of 'horror' photos, shrewdly hinting at worse ones that he would prefer not to circulate.

And I was admiring the inspector's expert and informative delivery when suddenly he said: 'I want to see the death penalty brought back for pushers. And I tell you: I'd gladly give up my half day to help the hangman by grasping the pusher's ankles and hanging from him with all my weight, which isn't little.' To his credit, the psychiatrist here interposed to say that he couldn't agree with this: apart from anything else, it was impossible to define a 'pusher.'

As can be imagined, I was revolted and angered. I began to feel more and more isolated in this gathering, for the chorus of 'hear! hear!' was almost aggressive.

After a short tea break we reassembled for question time. Somebody wanted to know just where I stood about cannabis: did I or did I not think it ought to be legalized? It was an entirely just question, and I *should* be required to take some public stand here. I said: 'I can give you, with a passionate conviction, the arguments against legalizing cannabis. I can quote to you the final words I spoke in that film *Expulsion*. I said then:

I'd stick my neck out and say that drugs, soft or hard, are potential dynamite in the hands of teenagers. At best, they arrest personality development, since every human being develops naturally by facing challenges, overcoming obstacles, and not by running away from them into a fantasy world where adversity doesn't exist. And at worst they can lead to such horrors as the Manson murders and My Lai. I can't get beyond that and I think that is what is facing us today.

But in the ten months that have elapsed since I said that I have made it my business to know and speak with many young people who take drugs. I have been struck by the sane attitude of most of them to cannabis use, by their compassion for those hooked on the harder stuff, and by their antagonism to the police forces. And since you rightly press me for an answer, I say that I think perhaps the laws against the use of cannabis should be removed, though obviously its use must be controlled. The alternative is to produce a whole alienated generation whom we quite monstrously dub as criminals.'

In his summing-up, the chairman thanked the other speakers most warmly for their valuable contributions and me for an 'interesting' talk with which he felt no one present could be in agreement.

In the *Times Educational Supplement* I wrote a long article which I titled 'Between a Butlins and a Borstal.' That, so far as I was concerned, shut the door on the whole unhappy saga. Professionally, I intended now to look forward, not back.

PART FIVE: WAITING

1

After the demise of Barcote I was well and truly out of work, of course, and returned to live in my family home in London. The best chance I had of new employment was in further teaching of some kind, whether or not combined with a chaplaincy. And the school that was obviously the one to sound out, if only because it was so near, was Harrow. Fortune smiled. The headmaster had not only seen *Expulsion* but actually needed someone urgently to teach A level English, and another (assistant) chaplain would be useful. So in April 1972 I began yet another phase in my pedagogic career. And the almost indescribable joy of being able, at last, to return to *teaching*, and to leave to others all the inquisitorial and penal headaches.

Beneath its polish, Harrow was tough and sophisticated. I was quite prepared for this. The school had a reputation for giving new masters the sort of gruelling at which boys can prove so accomplished. I knew more than one young master crack under the strain and leave. If this could befall a young man at the beginning of his career, how much easier (thought the boys) to undermine a master arriving in his early fifties, and an old parson to boot. But I was ready for them, and not one little bit of defiance did they get away with. What is more, I found the skirmishes quite exhilarating, and I had a good hand of cards they didn't know I prized. For much of what I taught I enjoyed (most of all, English literature), and what you enjoy teaching you make enjoyable. Also, I liked most of the boys as well as most of the books. My brushes with them became fewer. Once I found the encounters were fun and no longer sulks or cheek or mindless rebellion I could take any amount of them. The boys had a grapevine, like all boys in boarding schools, and on this I was eventually semaphored OK. I even became almost a Mr Chips.

No Mrs Chips, of course, which rather intrigued them. I often had a boy ask, 'Sir, why have you never married?' I developed a most arresting answer. Another characteristic of boys in a boarding school is gossip: sheer scandalmongering chatter, especially about masters, and about the bachelors pre-eminently. I'd assume a serious, almost tragic cast of countenance in response to their probings, and say: 'Well, to tell the truth..., perhaps I shouldn't tell you this..., I am one of those unfortunate people...'. There was a deathly hush in the form room. They leaned forward, their breath was bated, their eyes were wide, they were rehearsing the tales they could tell their friends of Mr Gamble as gay, or at least as a eunuch: 'I must confess that I have never found a woman worthy of me.'

They were quite aware of the joke. Laughter mingled with disappointment in their chorus of 'Oh, sir!'

437

I remember especially, soon after my arrival, standing outside the chapel one Sunday morning and surveying the lines of tailed and toppered boys moving slowly in. This is, I thought, a pageant, a show put on for all the masters and all the old boys, and all the votaries of youth everywhere. These boys are before the footlights and therefore in their stage costumes. It is a re-enactment of all those old *Boy's Own Papers* and *Magnets* of my boyhood, a festival of *Tom Brown* and *The Hill* and *The Oppidan* and *Tell England* and *Journey's End*. And as the boys moved along it seemed to me they dimly glimpsed that they were characters in a very old, very English drama played amid graffitied wooden desks and newly-tenanted bedsteads and flying cricket stumps and sweating khaki battledress. And leagues away from the outside world of 1970s Britain.

There were, of course, many good-looking boys amid my pupils, but it was for Alec Scovell that I fell. As had happened with Carl, he seemed wary because he was so attractive. I had long ago learned to keep my feelings under control, to show to my Ganymedes neither more nor less attention than I afforded others. Also never to seek out or to avoid the topic of homosexuality, for this was a school aware of its incipient presence, aware of past excesses and present triflings, of a reputation that had never died, even of fathers who never spoke of their own bitter-sweet memories of escapades within those same, venerable walls.

So I should not have been surprised when one Saturday Alec waited until the rest of the form had decamped and approached me with an unbelievable question: 'Oh, I'm sick of being shut up here. Can't you take me out somewhere? Anywhere?'

My incredulity showed in my face. He went on: 'Oh, go on. Be a devil.' He put on an expression of coquettish temptation that was half a joke, half serious. I said: 'I'm certainly not going to elope with you secretly. But,' I paused and deliberately looked conspiratorial, 'if we make up a little party with two of your friends and we go to see some educational play and I get housemaster's permission in each case, well, then it might be possible.'

'Marvellous,' he said with unfeigned exhilaration. 'Who shall we take? How about Humphreys in our O level English lot? I know he'd jump at it.' He thought for a moment, quite assuming all the choices were his. Then he registered sudden excited inspiration. 'Do you know Parrish? No? Oh, you'll like him. He's one of our chief pin-ups.'

It was all so breathtakingly sudden. 'Well,' I said faintly, 'I'll leave it to you to see Humphreys and Parrish at break and then report to me so that I can approach their housemasters. I know you and Humphreys are both in Puttenham's, and Mr Swayle is a good friend of mine.'

'And Parrish is in Fortescue,' he called over his shoulder as he sped off. Fortescue was Mr Damian who was very gamesy and no special friend of mine. And I didn't know he and Mr Swayle were old enemies, so his permission was given with very bad grace.

I had already decided I would take them to *An Enemy of the People* which was being put on at RADA, of which I was a member.

So we met immediately after lunch, where I inspected them to see that they were decently suited. I also with some interest inspected Parrish, who had certainly a most deserved reputation. Most would have considered him the handsomest of the trio, but I was not deflected in my admiration for Alec. Humphreys, too, was very personable (Alec had decided that I deserved only the best), so all in all we were a rather splendid advertisement.

I told them the story of the Ibsen as we drove there, and they thoroughly enjoyed it. One at least I know has never forgotten it. What I didn't tell them was that I had booked dinner for us all at a rather atmospheric place I knew in Marylebone with excellent food. They were enchanted by and grateful for the whole day, and so was I. They were delightful companions, and perhaps because of that the play and the dinner were first-rate, too.

From then on, these three made of themselves a regular dining club, whose membership was jealously safeguarded and programme strictly confidential. I gave them dinner in my house about twice a term, and once a term we ate out somewhere rather special. The dinners I gave were generally quite lavish. I can cook, and I rather enjoy doing so if the company is agreeable. And once or twice the boys insisted on taking me out. I was a little unsure about the first assignation. Alec chose it, telling me it was very pleasant and near his home in Eaton Square. He added, because he thought he ought to: 'Actually, it's a gay restaurant. Do you mind? I've been there once or twice with my parents. Of course, mother didn't know it was gay, but father did, and told me.' He then told me its name, which was what I expected, for I had often dined there with friends. I knew it was quite respectable, but even so I was glad that the boys had their strict code of privacy. As we left the restaurant, Alec said to me with great glee: 'Hear what that man at the next table said about me as we went out? He said, "And he's got a nice figure, too".'

All these dinners of ours were entirely respectable and enjoyable occasions. I wanted to instil in them a love of good conversation over good food and a modest amount of good wine. Housemasters' blessings on them were always obtained in advance.

In addition to the forms I taught, most of whom I had to tea in twos and threes, never singly, I knew, or at least was known by, hundreds of other boys. That is one of the advantages of being a school chaplain who is always ministering to the whole assembled school. Confirmation classes were especially rewarding. I found that after instructing a group over two terms I had become extraordinarily fond of them.

I did not conceal that I was hopeless at and mostly bored by games. Boys accepted this without surprise or disapproval, but some of my colleagues found it puzzling and rather off-putting, especially those in whose studies were displayed caps awarded at school or university for prowess at games. (All I could hang up in my study was my old miner's helmet, which I duly did.)

My teaching at Harrow was not uniformly rewarding. As always, the supreme enjoyment was for me, and for my pupils, English literature, at both O and A level. The set books changed each year, as did the boys to whom I had to introduce them, and just as excitingly. At O level we offered an internal English literature exam, which was only partly from prescribed texts. Most of the course was devoted to a long thesis on a subject and texts the master himself selected. At first I had my reservations about this kind of syllabus but very soon I was wholly converted. It enabled me to choose topics that required the expansion of a boy's horizons, and texts that got his mind working over a wide range of times and genres, from Chaucer and Milton to Hardy and Beckett. The A level course demanded some Chaucer and two Shakespeare plays to be studied in depth, plus poetry and novels, and plays chosen from the Metaphysicals to the Theatre of the Absurd. Novels I rather played down, because I hadn't time to read them with the boys, which I enjoyed doing, and which most of them frankly needed. We had only a year (in reality two and a half terms) for both O and A courses. We all had to work hard, but the pace, though hot, was stimulating. I record this here because O level has already disappeared, A level may follow, and in their place will come shallower and flimsier exams.

The rest of my teaching was more of a chore. There was no English language at A level (a strange desideratum), but a semi-A level called 'Use of English' which I detested. This exam, as also, but to a lesser extent, O level English language, was designed to assess a boy's literacy, and standards of literacy had lowered since I was a boy. So also had a boy's awareness of his own poor performance. I had from the moment I learned to read had no trouble with literacy, and thus teaching it was for me a bore, but a bore to which I grimly, with a horrible masochism, submitted. Younger boys thought my corrections mostly personal fads and fancies. Older boys bitterly resented them as insults to their maturity. All of them (and nearly all the younger masters) were quite ignorant of parsing and analysis, and they were unaware in almost every sentence they composed of the necessary agreements in number and case. I expect many people reading this will think of me as a dry pedant. But I wasn't. I was just someone who insisted on intellectual clarity and precision in the shaping of sentences.

Of course, much of the trouble sprang from the decline of Latin. I started off at Harrow by teaching Latin texts as I had always taught them, by requiring verbal construes (from scrupulously unmarked textbooks!) that showed an accurate knowledge of accidence and syntax. My O level candidates were astounded by this. They pleaded for me to dictate to them the translations I laboured to construct with them. I discovered that they learned these translations by heart for their O levels. This was a commendable feat, but it wasn't learning Latin. The penultimate shock, and for the pupils their triumphant justification, was that most of them gained their Latin O levels. I aired my dissatisfaction at departmental meetings with my colleagues, amongst whom were some considerable classical scholars. But none supported me. I thought, but was, of course, too much a gentleman to say, that amid dwindling numbers of Latin candidates in all schools an old-fashioned defence of standards might rock already insecure boats.

I also taught Latin to would-be Oxbridge history scholars. These were emergency classes for intelligent boys in their final years. Together we construed aloud from countless classical and medieval Latin texts, using all the construe tips I had gathered in my teaching years. These classes were fun. Divinity I had no time left to teach at Harrow. I regretted that, for I had enjoyed much rewarding divinity teaching at Millfield.

So my schoolmastering life ended as countless similar lives have ended for countless generations, that is, shaking my hoary head and bleating: 'Things aren't what they were. Standards are tottering on all sides.'

2

The chaplain, Brian Boucher, shared most of my tastes, and we very soon became good friends. He was by training and conviction a High Churchman, but knew that any excesses in that sphere were not appropriate to a school chaplaincy. He also accepted good-humouredly my own more radical views and practices. I, like him, never said or did anything during our concelebrated Sunday masses that would stand out as too individual or quirkish. My signings and genuflections were rather less than his, but there were some devout High Church and some devout Low Church boys as well as hordes of no-church ones in our congregation. Of course, my colleague took all sung masses, and I also gladly left to him such little extravaganzas as processions and gifts of candles and signings with ashes. We made a good team, for neither was a Holy Joe. Once, in the course of a form room discussion, a boy presented some reactionary view he claimed a master had expressed to him. I said: 'I'm sure you've never heard any such thing from me, or from Mr Boucher.' The boy looked almost shocked that I could think such a thing. 'Oh, not you or Mr Boucher, of course. It was one of the religious masters.' Both Brian and I were highly flattered.

THE MORE WE ARE TOGETHER

Harrow was the most civilized, the most congenial, teaching community that I have lived in. The masters and their wives, not to mention all the clerical and domestic staff, were always friendly and courteous.

I had little time, or desire, to undertake 'extra' activities, for I taught a maximum timetable and took a daily service before school, as well as one or two on Sunday. A seven-day working week. Moreover, a coterie of masters ran the literary societies and organized the debates and producd the plays. They did not seem to require any assistance, and I was happy enough to leave it to them. I did, at the headmaster's request, resurrect a once leading society devoted to theological studies. I obtained some very distinguished speakers, but the number of boys present was embarrassingly small. I was glad to hand over to a thicker-skinned and (I am sure) more successful secretary.

Boys often asked me, even begged me, to set up debates or produce plays for them. I always gracefully declined. But one day the head boy of one house implored me to produce a play: 'Anything you like. And we'll work hard and do you credit. We haven't had a play in our house in all the time I've been here. Oh, go on. You must, you absolutely must.' Now I had never produced a play and I assumed the technique was complicated and arduous, requiring a long apprenticeship, and I had had none. This has been my lifelong reaction to any specialized challenge. What is more, I had little interest in the average house play that was put on, which inevitably involved heterosexual activity which even boys in the female parts could not in my eyes wholly redeem. Then I suddenly thought of the play which had so moved me as a boy: *Journey's End*. Not a female in it, and for all its unobtrusive humour essentially a tragedy. So I said: 'Well, I'll come along and audition a few of you for a play called *Journey's End*. That's the only play I'm prepared to do. If I do one at all.'

I had some good preliminary tips from Brian Boucher, who was a most successful producer, and so I dived in. There is not much talent available for a house play, unlike a school play which often scintillates with talent. But I was mildly astonished to find how good were the boys I assembled, how hard they worked, how resourceful and intelligent they could be in their contributions. And they learned their parts, something I am sure stage fright would never have enabled me to do. One or two of the boys gave compelling performances. I also had an unbelievably gifted team of boy carpenters and electricians and wardrobe masters. Under an experienced master they managed sound effects and lights and curtains with professional ease.

The boy playing Stanhope, the shell-shocked officer, was in love with a slightly younger boy who was in my A level English class. I had once encountered both of them mooning around a small back street that was out of bounds. They both looked very guilty. All I said was: 'Get back to school quick before you're caught.' And I added, because they looked so apprehensive: 'My lips are sealed.'

A few days later the older boy asked if he could come and see me. He came to tea, and after a while he gulped and said: 'I think perhaps you can guess what I want to tell you.' I replied: 'That you're fond of Webb? I teach him, you know. He's a nice boy.'

That was how Peter Reynolds came to tell me all. He thought the world of Webb, but although Webb seemed to like him he certainly didn't feel the way Reynolds felt. What is more, Webb's housemaster had perhaps guessed. He had at any rate forbidden either boy ever to call at the other's house.

It was a difficult situation. I saw each boy privately. Probably nothing physical had taken place, so my main aim was to remove any sense of guilt from their minds. I told them that such a friendship was quite natural, but some people felt it more deeply than others. I told Webb privately that if Reynolds valued the friendship more highly, and felt it more intensely, then he (Webb) must be kind and understanding, without ever surrendering his own personality. And I told Reynolds privately that, as the older and more mature of the two, he must be very careful never to frighten Webb by asking too much of him. That would be the surest way to kill the friendship. I knew that to Reynolds it was a Great Romantic Passion and he was suffering for it, while to Webb it was just a rather puzzling friendship.

The term was ending and Reynolds was desperately anxious to tell Webb how much he meant to him and ask him if he could write to him in the holidays (they lived at opposite ends of England). So on the last day of term I had them to tea. Webb had to leave first. I said to Reynolds upstairs in the drawing room where we had taken tea: 'Will you see Ian off for me? I must stay here by the phone. I'm expecting a call from America.' I heard their murmurs in the hall and out of the window saw Ian Webb scoot off quite happily. I hoped that in the holidays Reynolds' ardour would cool somewhat. At any rate both got through their final term without mishap.

I've told Reynolds' story because he played Stanhope, who probably felt for Raleigh, the young subaltern who had been his fag at school and was to join his company in the front line, much as Reynolds felt for Webb. I know the play greatly affected Reynolds, who played the part with deep conviction. I lent him, at his request, my copy of the novel *Journey's End* on which R. C. Sherriff and Vernon Bartlett had collaborated. I think it moved Peter Reynolds as much as it had moved me at his age.

I found producing was just common sense. I imported a touch from my boyhood film of *All Quiet on the Western Front*, where Paul's hand reaches out for some fleeting beauty in no-man's-land in the shape of a dazzling butterfly. We hear a rifle shot and see the hand jump, recoil and turn over before becoming still forever. In the last scene of *Journey's End*, Raleigh is laid out badly wounded on a bunk in the dugout. I had to let the audience know that he has died before Stanhope re-enters. So I made his darkening eyes search for the candle alight in a bottle beside his bunk, and his hand reach out for the light, then fall forever. Stanhope enters and, unaware Raleigh is dead, talks cheeringly to him and tucks the blanket around him. Slowly he realizes Raleigh is no more. Then, and this was entirely Reynolds' idea, which he had never used in rehearsals, Stanhope takes Raleigh's limp, dead hand and presses it for a moment to his own forehead. I asked Reynolds after the first performance why he had done this. All he ever said about it was: 'I felt it was right.'

The play is well constructed and avoids sentimentality. I hope my production more or less avoided it, too. Not altogether, for boys are sentimental creatures and I wanted to give them their fair share of it. All the time I was producing the play I was conscious of the keen irony of it all, for these boys were the very Raleighs and Stanhopes of Sherriff's imagination. They were the fags and heroes who were training in khaki for the next patriotic slaughter, and the play itself was a broadside aimed at the sickening idealization of war.

The play was a success. I knew from the dead silence and the ensuing applause that it had affected that mostly hearty, extrovert audience. It was, unusually, put on for a third night. Some boys told me they had gone to see it two or even three times. One elderly master told me he had never been so convinced and so shaken by a house play. That last scene, thanks to the expertise of the schoolboy lighting crew and recording engineers who so tellingly blended the whistling of bombs and stutter of machine guns with the ghostly strains of 'Goodbye Piccadilly, farewell Leicester Square,' was so powerful that (I was told) many ladies in the audience were in tears.

I want the last of all too many words about this production to be some that were addressed to me after the first night by the boy playing Raleigh. He said: 'Sir, could you see me moving in that bed when I was supposed to be dead?' I replied: 'No, I didn't. I should have been pretty mad if I had. Why do you ask?' He answered rather shyly: 'Well, you see, I was crying.'

3

On the Saturday before an exeat Sunday (of which there were three a term) I would drive up to Nik's school and take him to Stanmore for the weekend. I was thankful that his housemaster now seldom reported instances of his nonco-operation. In the school holidays he would divide his time between Edgware and Stanmore. In the holidays, too, I would take mother out to lunch or dinner somewhere. Frequently I would drive her and Roland and his mother down to Brighton: lunch at the Old Ship was always a pleasure. Once or twice we stayed at the hotel with them for a few days. I hired a wheelchair, which the ladies alternately pushed and rode in, along the front. Both Roland and I were glad to brighten up their latter days with such little treats.

It was about this time that Basil Clough quite took my breath away by telling me he was going to broach to his mother the subject of his own homosexuality. I thought at first he was joking, and when I found he was not I begged him to do no such thing. To a lady in her eighties who has never had personal contact with the condition, and who knew of it only as an unmentionable affliction, it could be a terrible shock. But he was insistent.

'Why?' I asked. 'Whatever's the point? What good can it do?'

'Just honesty,' he replied. 'You know, every evening when I'm there mother and I sit up late, chatting over a nightcap. She tells me her life story, especially memories of her childhood and of her days working for a famous charity. I find it fascinating. But more and more I resent having to edit my own life story for her. I don't want such a barrier between us. Don't you ever feel anything of that with your mother?'

'Never, never, never,' I responded. 'I have never wanted to share my private life with anybody who hasn't a similar life. I've never wanted to be relegated to a pigeonhole. Anyway, one's sexual nature is vastly overrated in importance. I find there's ample role-playing and conversation to share without introducing that.'

He looked at me with some amusement. 'Are you afraid my mother will tell yours?' (They had met once or twice.)

'Yes,' I said. 'I'm very much afraid of that. They may well have discussed their unusual sons. Speculation is far more entertaining, and often less wounding, than certainty.'

'I'll make sure she does not raise the subject with your mother. Or imagine for one moment there's any such relationship between us.'

So tell her he did. He informed me she took it very well, and that they felt closer and happier now there were no such hidden compartments in his life. I wondered.

My own mother was no innocent. In fact I think she was less innocent than Basil's mother. Perhaps she guessed what my sexual tastes were. If so, she had no more desire than I had to discuss the matter. I was comfortable in my little closet.

Basil and I were different in another way: he wished for a permanent relationship. His great desire was to live with someone he was fond of and who was fond of him. A perfectly understandable and laudable aim. But I had no such longing. This was basically because I could not have a boy to live with me, but also because I really did not enjoy sharing my living quarters with anyone. Whenever Nigel Day's wife and children (he had had another daughter now) went to stay with her parents, either I went to his house or he came to mine for the duration of their absence. This was all quite above board. His wife told me she was glad he had the company. And both Nigel and I enjoyed the break and the lavish meals out and the other pleasures, but it was always nice to be back in my house alone. I have lived alone for many years now. But Basil sought seriously for someone to share his life with, and no one was happier than I when his quest was finally rewarded.

Then another unforeseen event encompassed me: my brother-in-law, Bob Powis said he was going to marry again. This did not enhance mother's opinion of him. But I was glad, especially when he told me it was not simply, or mainly, for his own sake but so that Nik might know a mother's care. I also knew that it was because Bob did not wish to lose Nik to us as he had lost Miles, and I could certainly understand that in a father.

They settled in Essex, far from his grandmother and his uncles. And soon I had a letter from Bob to say that he had given Nik complete freedom of choice about his own future: either to stay at his boarding school or live at home with his parents and attend the local comprehensive.

I was, of course, furious. But I had no rights and my letter begging Bob to reconsider was ignored. I wrote to say what rubbish to let a child decide between home and boarding school: it was quite obvious which Nik would choose. I said that Nik wouldn't understand now, but one day he might justly blame him for spoiling his life.

So Nik went to his comprehensive. But the best-laid plans... For the new wife disliked Nik and he disliked her. I was glad he was loyal to Pam. The marriage soon ended in divorce, and all because of Nik, who (now about sixteen) triumphantly bore his father off to a new abode, where the two of them may still be living happily together.

Nik had often come over to stay with Brian in Esher, where he was now lodging with a nice young woman he had met at one of his prep schools. I also went over to see Nik on such occasions. He now spoke Cockney, but I couldn't deplore his new life because of that. Who knows? He may at a boarding school have become hooked on drink or drugs, while he was now a well-behaved working-class young man, soon to find some appropriate job and marry some appropriate girl. I cannot regret any of it. And I know it is sheer selfishness for me to lament that I, who came so near to loving a child of my own in Nik, so near to being a father, am back on a shelf alone.

4

One day about this time I answered my phone to a voice which said: 'Peter, my boy, can you guess who this is?'

If deep within me a hint of a memory stirred, it perished in the air. 'I'm afraid I can't,' I replied, even a trifle irritated by the apparent trick being played on me.

'Remember *Hedda Gabler* at the Westminster when the pistol went off too soon? And... and Robert Atkins at the Open Air when he dried and had to invent speeches for Bottom?'

I floundered still. 'Remember when we read all *Lear* together one evening on the settee at number 53?'

'It can't be,' I breathed.

'Oh yes, it can,' he went on excitedly. 'And it is. It's me, Jonathan. And why have I phoned after all these years, after twenty-three of them, to be precise? I've phoned first to apologize. Oh Peter, I'm so terribly sorry for the wicked thing I said to you when we last met. Can you forgive me?'

The cogs of my brain were whirring. Jonathan, the once dear friend. All the shared jokes and the literary gems and the musical adventures. And I was no longer Antichrist. Did this mean that he was cured, that he had spewed all the ugly nonsense out of his system? Could the magic past be re-created? Could we take up our golden days as though nothing had tarnished them?

His next words dashed my hopes. 'I've prayed to the good Lord so often to forgive me. And good he has been.'

I surrendered myself to the tale pouring through the earpiece. After twenty or so years as one of the Exclusive Brethren, he had renounced them when some scandal broke over the head of one of their elders. I dimly remembered the case, but I was no longer eating his words so greedily. All he was saying was as sordid as it was predictable, and nothing was put right by his telling me that he had reverted to the Open Brethren.

It was a little more interesting to hear his more secular news. He had remarried, of course: a wonderful girl whom he had met at a Brethren meeting. They had two boys and a girl, all very near university age and all, 'thank the Lord,' zealous Christians. He himself had retired early, on a very good pension, because of his heart condition. Still, he was fit enough to take Bible classes and contribute to wonderful gospel missions. Of course, we must meet soon, very soon. He had so much to discuss with me.

So, one Saturday a few weeks later I had him and his boys to lunch. They had come to drive the car and help him up the steps. Apparently his heart was very dicky indeed. After lunch the two boys went off to explore the neighbourhood, leaving Jonathan and me to discuss salvation. I wanted him to state plainly from what I was to be saved, and eventually he did so. Although he tried to find gentler words, he had in the end to admit that it was from eternal damnation, from everlasting hellfire. By some perverted logic, some diseased jugglings with scripture, he held that such a punishment was quite within the province of a God of love. God sent his Son to tell man the terms on which salvation was offered, namely, via Him alone and during each man's lifetime, and anyone who did not fulfil the conditions was lost forever. No salvation was possible by any other route or within any other timespan.

He knew his scriptures (but then, so did I), and could even interpret them consistently from his own premises, which were in fact the most primitive ideas of the Old Testament and the most literally interpreted passages of the New. Haste, he kept insisting, was of vital importance, in order to avoid the fire and brimstone. Paradoxically, his loving concern to save me was quite commensurate with his picture of a merciless Jehovah. I saw that there was no point in further discussion. Trembling before his concept of divine retribution, he was incapable of comprehending divine love: the infinite and eternal compassion of which Jesus was the exemplar.

Unabashed and loving, Jonathan simply looked forward to many more wrestlings with my hard heart, which he firmly believed would result in my eventual salvation. But we never had them. We never even saw each other again. He died of a heart attack less than a year later. I prayed that *my* Jesus was sufficiently valid to forgive him *his*.

It was as my fifties mounted slowly to sixty that I began to see my life as taking a gentle, downward slope. This was due in part to mother's decline. Miles could no longer look after her with his job in antiques taking more and more of his time, and, although I visited Stanmore whenever my heavy timetable allowed, it grew ever more harrowing to leave her alone in the house all day. Neighbours were kind and helpful but there were still ample opportunities for her to fall or to set the place alight: the sad, familiar story of ageing loved ones. We sent her in to the local hospital's geriatric ward, refusing steadfastly to admit to her or to ourselves that such it was. We said it was only for a spell until her walking improved, but I hated myself for lying to her. I hopefully inspected several private nursing homes, but they were far beyond my means and were in any case not interested in anyone who was becoming incontinent. Their refusal was a blessing in disguise, for the hospital and its staff were magnificent. I had no doubt that she was happier there than she could ever have been in a private nursing home. She ruled the roost there, so much so that I was afraid they would grow tired of her demands on them, such as her daily bath. But, surprisingly, they seemed to like it. She was known to them all as 'Duchess,' and they enjoyed her jokes as she enjoyed their care. Miles visited her every single day of her year there. I visited her at least twice a week. Every Saturday I took her in my car to some beauty spot where we picnicked on the goodies I had brought.

She remained *compos mentis* to the end. Her life had from the day of her marriage been geared to fighting, and as a fighter against the now unserviceable body she died. At almost ninety. And when it happened two nurses and one hard-boiled sister were in tears. Of my own feelings it is needless to write.

5

Not long after mother's death I moved out of the Stanmore house. I sold most of its contents and let Miles keep the proceeds. He found digs in town, and I with a wry smile realized that for the first time in my life I had a salary that was all mine: no rent or rates to pay for the family home. Solvent at last, just two years before I had to retire. On next to nothing.

I was, as I had always been, a babe when it came to money. All I had ever understood was that I had to pay my debts and keep my head above water. I had no idea what the old age pension was, nor if I was as a schoolmaster entitled to any pension from the church. I knew that my education pension would be modest, for I had contributed only in my last few years. I knew I must find out about these things, which I did after a fashion. It was all rather a muddle. All that was clear was the modesty of the pensions I was likely to get from so many years of preaching and teaching. Even the state pension, I discovered, was reduced because of four years at Oxford and two ministering on the Continent.

All this was bad enough, but even worse was the prospect of ostracism from teaching, which I loved, and civilized youth, whom I loved even more. All I could think to do was to find one of those *Church Times* jobs that frankly made me shudder: 'Retired priest offered free accommodation in return for assistance in parish.' In other words, back to a curacy, although this time without pay. But I had to find such a berth, and quickly. I inspected one or two, but with some shamefaced impudence turned them down. Either the accommodation or the vicar was not up to scratch. My scratch, at any rate. But at the last moment I found one which I liked as much as I could like any curacy. It was in an attractive town and offered an attractive flat, with a vicar who was pleasant and a congregation that was intelligent. I felt I could not do better.

I was to retire in July 1982. But as the Christmas term of 1981 drew to its close I began to be aware that my breathlessness and slight chest pains were increasing as I climbed the hill from my house to the school. I was not for one moment tempted to ascribe this to indigestion as poor father had done. I determined to finish the term and then at once have a thorough medical check-up. I thought tablets to counteract angina would quickly put me right, but the doctor was horrified when he checked my blood pressure. He sent me at once to a heart specialist. Who immediately ordered me to hospital.

Now most people go into hospital when they have just had a heart attack, but I, with my usual meticulous planning, went into hospital in order to have one. The specialist and the hospital and Miles' daily visits all did a wonderful job so that, after I had spent the Easter term recuperating, I was able to resume my full timetable for my final term, and to see my last pupils through all their exams.

This was the term of the annual Founder's Day sermons at Harrow, when some distinguished churchman was invited to preach on four successive days to the school. The first of the four sermons was on a Sunday and was compulsory. The other three were on weekday evenings and voluntary, a sure way of discovering if the preacher had made his mark with the schoolboy congregation. To my surprise, I was honoured by being invited to give the sermons that year. I was surprised not only because it was not usual to ask a member of staff to assume this office, but also because I had recently, in a hard-hitting sermon, attacked the government for waging the Falklands war and slaughtering countless young men in a venture that was as crudely chauvinist as it was unnecessary. As I had often found in true-blue public schools, there were always some boys who were more enlightened than most masters. It was a group of such boys who asked me if I would devote one of my four sermons to the subject of pacifism. Which I did, with great sweat and toil, and some reward.

In a little speech of thanks after a very kind presentation, I remember I said: 'I shall never return, unless wanted for some help in an emergency. Even that rather cruel Old Testament God did not inflict further pain on Adam and Eve by allowing them return trips to Eden.' Silly, really, but I wanted to make it known that retirement is not always an occasion for rejoicing.

With a heavy heart I moved out of my school house and into my parochial one. In the popular concept of British pluck I set my jaw and faced adversity, which in the event wasn't as adverse as I'd feared. Not because the parochial tasks were any less uncongenial than I had expected, but because the congregation were so delightfully welcoming and so profitable to speak to and preach to. I was asked to take on the fortnightly Bible class, and I inwardly groaned at the prospect. But the class of fifteen was composed almost wholly of graduates, and, after I had gently eased out two rather fundamentalist members, they and I settled down to stern intellectual study of notoriously difficult texts. I worked very hard at this, but enjoyed every minute of it. Not one member of that Bible class was as radical, as rationalistic, as I was, but I was very careful not to offend a firm faith, or to be as hidebound in my liberal interpretations as the literalists were in theirs. I found I was teaching again, now diving as deep into biblical texts as I had for years been diving into literary ones.

Preaching here unmistakably echoed my preaching in Birmingham when first ordained. Sometimes I wondered whether I should rejoice in the consistency of my views or deplore the constriction of them. Into my Good Friday 'Three Hours' preaching I introduced, as I always had, a denunciation of the death penalty in all ages and all climes. And in a memorable Remembrance Sunday sermon I bitterly attacked the western powers' reliance upon the atom bomb. There was a quite vociferous demonstration against this sermon outside the church after the service, with red-faced colonels shouting and waving their arms about. It got into the provincial press and caused quite a commotion. I wrote what I considered a long and benign reply in the local paper, which enjoyed making the most of it all, printing many other people who were eager to join in the fray, chiefly Tory blimps and local CND supporters.

More frank, but still kindly, was the opposition to my views on the ordination of women. I found myself in something of a quandary in this matter. All my life I had inclined to defend women's rights, to condemn emphatically any assumption of male superiority. Yet now I felt I couldn't put them on a par with men in the Church, not for the usual reason, not because I felt they were not in every way as fitted as men for the ministry. I found the two 'weighty' reasons for not ordaining women (that Jesus never had and that tradition never had) just plain silly. No, my reasons were not theological but aesthetic.

I have always thought that the ideal activity for friendship is discussion and its ideal setting is the dinner table. So it has always seemed to me inevitably right that the one uniquely Christian service should be the re-enactment of a meal shared by loving friends. On any commonsensical view, the altar at the Eucharist is also the food board, the officiating priest represents Jesus, and all the worshippers are his invited friends. Therefore to have a woman representing Jesus is just unsuitable: not wrong or impious or iconoclastic, just unsuitable. To me, a woman minister can marry and bury and preach and preside. She can be as good as any man and often better at all these things. She can even crown herself with a mitre and still I won't worry. But if she celebrates Holy Communion, I shall not be there. A worshipping Christian will understand this, even if he cannot agree with it. But to the masses who don't go near a church, or know what on earth the Eucharist is, there can be only one reason for opposing the ordination of women: because you consider them to be inferior to the office.

We shall, I imagine, come round to women priests and probably sooner rather than later.[1] And I don't suppose the church will be split by it. All the would-be communicants like me will trundle off to a church round the corner where no woman presides.

It is sad that this service of all services should from the first have been a centre of bitter controversy. Even today there are far more worshipping Christians than complacent clergy realize who find the words of this service

---

[1] We have. The General Synod of the Church of England, by a two-thirds majority, voted for it on November 11th (Armistice Day!), 1992.

unacceptable, distressing, offensive. They may not say so, but they feel it. The words are, of course, 'eat my flesh and drink my blood.' Jesus was a mystic and a poet, as well as a realist, and I have no doubt myself that what he meant his disciples to understand at that Last Supper was: 'Just as I break this bread, so my body is going to be broken in love for mankind; just as I pour out this wine, so my blood is going to be poured out in love for mankind.'

If the author of the Fourth Gospel is reliable, how fiercely Jesus taxes the understanding of his audience by assailing them (those devout, kosher-eating Jews!) alternately with injunctions to eat his flesh and drink his blood, and then with appeals to take his words spiritually and not with crude literalism. He projected an image of incorporation, not cannibalism.

Then, like a bomb exploding in a busy, sunlit street came news that was the more destructive for being so utterly unlooked for, so pinpointed on me, so meaningless to all the people I was living and working amongst. It was the death of Nigel Day. The most enduring of all my young friends, he could not endure beyond his forties. He had been warned by his doctor that heart and blood pressure were aberrant, that he must eat and drink and smoke less, and above all drive himself less recklessly in his work. But he did none of this. He wanted to be blind to warnings. He told me all the things he could tell no one else: of his amours and infidelities, of his wife's threat to leave him, of his disenchantment with all his life's younger dreams. I believe, or at any rate I hope, that he felt his friendship with me was the one experience that had not let him down. I told him I'd always be grateful that my affection for him had never dimmed over thirty years. Or, indeed, over the years that have passed since.

6

I had been almost two years in my parish job when I became aware that I was burning myself out. I had preached 167 sermons in my time there and done a great deal of parochial visiting and paid weekly visits with Holy Communion to three nursing homes and a geriatric hospital. All this I found not only pretty exhausting but sometimes quite upsetting. So, much as I liked the vicar and congregation, I decided I must leave. To be honest, my decision to go was influenced by a discovery I should have made long before: that in all parts of England the splendid Church of England Pensions Board owned flats and houses, mostly bequeathed to them, which they let at very reasonable rents to their retired clergy. It was actually Miles who discovered this and came with me to inspect several likely properties. We found an eminently suitable bungalow in a Surrey town, and there I have lived more than contentedly ever since. Not that all was quite plain sailing, for soon after I arrived I suffered a stroke. More hospitalization ensued and once again Miles visited me almost daily. Terry came over from France to stay in the bungalow and supervise the countless chores still to be done. I was silently affected to find how we still as a family held together if any misfortune befell one of us. Even Brian helped regularly as much as he could. I say 'even' because he was much frailer than he had been.

I managed to rally surprisingly well from the stroke. Human vanity being what it is, I was extremely glad to find facial and vocal attributes were not permanently affected. I now walk with a limp, but each day I hobble to the town centre for my shopping, and I regularly drive my car. I realize that I have a great deal to be thankful for: not least that no one can now expect me to fulfil any clerical duties. It is quite sufficient for me to be a member of the congregation in my local church.

Many of the friends I made in my last parish come to see me: two elderly ladies in particular come on separate days nearly every week. They regale me with good conversation and are unbelievably helpful to me in a hundred ways. I give them lunch and often visit them and their families for excellent meals. I have pleasant neighbours and I keep all my remaining friendships in good repair. Roland now lives in Amsterdam and Basil in Tunisia (with his charming young Arab). They write and phone regularly, and are always begging me to go and stay with them. I half promise to do so, but the prospect of travel is now rather daunting. Many boys I have taught come to see me, some with wives and children, and two with grandchildren. Two or three former pupils from Harrow, laying aside their yuppiedom, come in large cars to visit me. I enjoy giving them and erstwhile colleagues extravagant meals. But I characteristically keep myself rather to myself as far as my habitat is concerned, eschewing even cups of tea in the church hall after mass. I don't fraternize easily with devout Christians.

I am a disappointment as an old, retired parson. People look in vain for a firmly held faith that I am anxious to propagate. They find in me no relish for gardening or hunger for cricket scores. Sometimes I am rather shocked to think of the universal tastes I do not share with my fellows: I have never had sexual intercourse, I have never seen a woman's body, I have never been on a dance floor, I have never watched any professional sport, or even entered a pub for pleasure. But I don't really feel cut off from other men. We have our humanity in common. We have all loved and hated, longed and lost, dreamed and harshly wakened. I can identify with the unlikeliest people, for our lives are alike in their successes and failures, their laughter and tears, and I am surprisingly glad it's so.

Moreover, the same anxious pattern endures to the end. Miles has been diagnosed HIV positive, and that is a great worry to me. I pray a cure may be found in time for him.

And Brian died recently. He did little school-mastering after Anglo-American. I think its collapse knocked the stuffing out of him, for like almost all who'd been there (except me!) he had loved the place. Just like Nigel Day, he had never looked after himself, eschewed those things that were eroding his health. At all spare moments he inhaled the dense smoke his cherished pipe emitted. Every evening he drank slowly till the time came to mount unsteadily to bed and snore resoundingly. He ate irregularly and unhealthily. His heart protested. With the greatest reluctance, and too late, he saw a doctor. I could not now look after him. He had to enter a nursing home near me, which would not allow his pipe. He ate nothing in the home (where meals were actually very good). Sometimes we took him food he could eat in his room, but most often he got in his car and visited me or old friends. We were all torn apart to find him on our doorsteps: our welcomes decimated by our fears that he would once more collapse with a minor stroke. When he could find no one at home to receive him, he dozed in his car in a layby. His memory was failing, his body getting thinner and poorer. During one visit to me, he found he could not swallow the lunch I had prepared him. Then he fell with a stroke. I called my doctor, who said he must not drive his car: he must be driven back to his nursing home and the doctor would call on him there in the morning.

He lingered for some days, eating nothing and worrying only about his car, for his 'disabled' licence was up for renewal. The doctor had sent the licensing authorities a report on him. Brian suspected he would never drive again, and quite clearly willed himself to die, which he did before a week was up. A courteous letter regretting that he could not be licensed to drive any more arrived a few days after his death. I was very glad he never saw it.

I miss him sorely, for our lives had so often and for so long run on twin tracks.

Not long before he died, he told Miles that his father was not Bob Powis but Martin Gregg, the handsome and moody young soldier who had been one of Pam's swains at that time. I don't know how much truth there was in this, or how he knew about it. Perhaps Pam told him. She was more likely to share such a confidence with Brian than with me. And certainly in temperament Miles has always seemed closer to Martin Gregg than to Bob. True or false, I am sorry he told Miles about it, for it cannot strengthen an already restless character to know such a thing.

But there: all so long ago it is hard to believe it matters any more. That, at least, was the attitude Miles adopted.

7

'Your young men shall see visions, and your old men shall dream dreams.' Well, I had a great vision when I was young, a vision I chased through most of the ensuing years, the vision of a happy, united family for myself. The years have seen only the fading of the vision, the loss of its personae. But (I say it again) for me those words refer to the earthly vision, its fleshly dress. Its eternal validity (and I laugh at myself for believing this even as I believe it) is as real to me now as was Mrs Mackenzie's painting when I was five. I do not believe, I cannot believe, that death is the end. Consciousness cannot die. Beyond death is reunion, growth, fulfilment. And any orthodox teaching, in Christianity or any other religion, that denies this is simply not for me. Last laugh: the very family about which I believe all this would dismiss it as a piece of wilful self-deception. But it abides, my intuitional hope.

When it comes to an old man's dreams, however, that's quite another matter. No fading there. I dream a great deal. And, in the manner of the ageing, it is mostly about my long-ago. I dream of the house I grew up in and of Streatham that encompassed it. I dream of domestic trivia as vivid as they were in the days when they were not trivia: of gas mantles magically lighted by wall switches and pilot lights; then of wondrously exciting electric light and of our fascinating first dial telephone. Of places, too, like Streatham library's reference room, where I endlessly browsed, watched by the skeletonic hippopotamus head mounted on its stand, and the frighteningly lifelike suit of Samurai armour in its glass case.

And I muse a good deal about what and why I have always been. I try to square what self-knowledge I have with the usual Jungian archetypes and Freudian doctored myths: a strong mother and a weak father, of course, so over-identification with the one and under-identification with the other. But that seems too easy as an explanation for all my topsy-turveydom. I never at any time repudiated all my father: only the Hyde part of him, never the Jekyll, and that for but a few years. Mother neither overdid nor underdid her care of me. There was no ever-present pampering or any starvation or remoteness. So I can't remember any maternal hang-ups. I just dwelt securely in a reasonable affection. For the same reason I have never had any religious hang-ups. Jesus was there and we liked each other. No room for guilt or dread.

Somewhere along the line I should have been afflicted with narcissism, but I think there were only the touches of it to be found in any adolescent self-consciousness.

I was always planning and writing stories, and my memory of those should provide good material for psychological investigation. But they were pretty threadbare versions of Rider Haggard or of ghost stories or war stories I had read, not, strangely, of school stories. And very little of the unconscious symbolism we find underlying the conscious imagery, the sceptical humour and the healthy realism of Forrest Reid's books. None of the moons and seas and mirroring pools, the abandoned houses and overgrown gardens, the stone statues ready to leap into life.

'Consistency,' said Emerson, 'is the virtue of a fool,' so a fool I must be. For my very earliest recollections tell me that what I loved then I love now, what I sought then I was all my life to seek. I had come into this world trailing those clouds I have been content to shelter behind. I was begotten, not made. I feel a quiet, unpretentious satisfaction in knowing this. And in knowing that I have never betrayed, never compromised, never wavered.

A few days ago Alec phoned to say that he and Philip Parrish want to come down to see me. I shall have to prepare a bumper dinner for them, for old time's sake. Miles is arriving for lunch on Tuesday. I think I'll take him out somewhere gourmetish. And on Sunday Terry descends on me for his annual month, which is a great treat for both of us. I must prepare carefully, for he is pernickety about what he eats and what he drinks. Even about the kind of sheets he has on his bed.

One way and another, I have a good deal to do. I must get on with it.

SELECT INDEX

The following index records significant references to 'public figures' mentioned in the text. It is not intended as a comprehensive guide.